Lecture Notes in Computer Science 8829

Commenced Publication in 1973
Founding and Former Series Editors:
Gerhard Goos, Juris Hartmanis, and Jan van Leeuwen

Stephan Merz   Jun Pang (Eds.)

Formal Methods and Software Engineering

16th International Conference
on Formal Engineering Methods, ICFEM 2014
Luxembourg, Luxembourg, November 3-5, 2014
Proceedings

 Springer

Volume Editors

Stephan Merz
Inria Nancy - Grand Est
615 rue du Jardin Botanique
54602 Villers-lès-Nancy, France
E-mail: stephan.merz@loria.fr

Jun Pang
Université du Luxembourg
6 rue Richard Coudenhove-Kalergi
1359 Luxembourg, Luxembourg
E-mail: jun.pang@uni.lu

ISSN 0302-9743   e-ISSN 1611-3349
ISBN 978-3-319-11736-2   e-ISBN 978-3-319-11737-9
DOI 10.1007/978-3-319-11737-9
Springer Cham Heidelberg New York Dordrecht London

Library of Congress Control Number: 2014948936

LNCS Sublibrary: SL 2 – Programming and Software Engineering

Typesetting: Camera-ready by author, data conversion by Scientific Publishing Services, Chennai, India

Printed on acid-free paper

Springer is part of Springer Science+Business Media (www.springer.com)

Preface

The International Conference on Formal Engineering Methods (ICFEM) is a premier conference for research in all areas related to formal engineering methods, such as verification and validation, software engineering, formal specification and modeling, software development, software security, and reliability. Since 1997, ICFEM has been an international forum for researchers and practitioners from academia, industry, and government. It is devoted to presentations and exchanges that advance the state of the art of applying formal methods in practice. Submissions that present combinations of conceptual and methodological aspects with their formal foundation and tool support are particularly encouraged.

In recent years, ICFEM has taken place in Queenstown, New Zealand (2013), Kyoto, Japan (2012), Durham, UK (2011), Shanghai, China (2010), and Rio de Janeiro, Brazil (2009). The 16th edition of ICFEM took place in Luxembourg during 3–5 November, 2014. The Program Committee (PC) received 73 full paper submissions, of which one was withdrawn. Each paper received at least 3 review reports from PC members or external reviewers. On the basis of these reports, each submission was extensively discussed in the virtual meeting of the PC, and the PC decided to accept 28 papers. The proceedings also include the abstracts from the 3 keynote speakers Nikolaj Bjørner, Lionel Briand, and Vincent Danos.

ICFEM 2014 was organized and sponsored by the Interdisciplinary Centre for Security, Reliability and Trust (SnT) at the University of Luxembourg. We are also grateful for the financial support received from the Fonds National de la Recherche (FNR - National Research Fund) in Luxembourg, the Computer Science and Communications Research Unit (CSC) and the Laboratory of Algorithmics, Cryptology and Security (LACS) at University of Luxembourg. We thank the Local Organizing Committee for their hard work in making ICFEM 2014 a successful and exciting event.

The main event was preceded by the seventh International Summer School on Verification Technology, Systems & Applications (VTSA 2014). The third International Workshop on Formal Techniques for Safety-Critical Systems (FTSCS 2014) and the fourth Workshop on SOFL + MSVL were co-located with ICFEM and took place immediately following the conference.

We thank all the PC members for their support, completing quality reviews on time, and being active in discussions during the review process. We thank the external reviewers for their reports that helped the PC decide on which submissions to accept. Most importantly, we thank the authors for submitting their papers to the conference, and the participants for attending it. Finally, we also thank the EasyChair team for its great conference system and Springer Verlag for the smooth cooperation in the production of this proceedings volume.

July 2014   Stephan Merz
                                                                      Jun Pang

Organization

Program Committee

Jonathan P. Bowen	Birmingham City University, UK
Michael Butler	University of Southampton, UK
Konstantinos Chatzikokolakis	CNRS & Ecole Polytechnique of Paris, France
Frank De Boer	CWI, The Netherlands
Zhenhua Duan	Xidian University, China
Colin Fidge	Queensland University of Technology, Australia
Stefania Gnesi	ISTI-CNR, Italy
Peter Gorm Larsen	Aarhus University, Denmark
Radu Grosu	Vienna University of Technology, Austria
Ian J. Hayes	University of Queensland, Australia
Michaela Huhn	Technische Universität Clausthal, Germany
Pierre Kelsen	University of Luxembourg, Luxembourg
Steve Kremer	Inria Nancy - Grand Est, France
Jean Krivine	CNRS & Paris Diderot University, France
Xuandong Li	Nanjing University, China
Shang-Wei Lin	National University of Singapore, Singapore
Shaoying Liu	Hosei University, Japan
Yang Liu	Nanyang Technological University, China
Sjouke Mauw	University of Luxembourg, Luxembourg
Dominique Mery	Université de Lorraine, LORIA, France
Stephan Merz	Inria Nancy - Grand Est, France
Mohammadreza Mousavi	Halmstad University, Sweden
Peter Müller	ETH Zürich, Switzerland
Shin Nakajima	National Institute of Informatics, Japan
Jun Pang	University of Luxembourg, Luxembourg
Ion Petre	Åbo Akademi University, Finland
Shengchao Qin	Teesside University, UK
Zongyan Qiu	Peking University, China
Jing Sun	The University of Auckland, New Zealand
Jun Sun	Singapore University of Technology and Design, Singapore
Kenji Taguchi	AIST, Japan
Viktor Vafeiadis	MPI-SWS, Germany
Jaco Van De Pol	University of Twente, The Netherlands
Hai H. Wang	University of Aston, UK
Wang Yi	Uppsala University, Sweden
Huibiao Zhu	East China Normal University, China

Additional Reviewers

Azadbakht, Keyvan
Battle, Nick
Beohar, Harsh
Bessling, Sara
Bezirgiannis, Nikolaos
Bodeveix, Jean-Paul
Boström, Pontus
Bu, Lei
Coleman, Joey
Colley, John
Craciun, Florin
Dghaym, Dana
Dima, Catalin
Dong, Naipeng
Fang, Huixing
Fantechi, Alessandro
Ferrari, Alessio
Gengler, Marc
Gheorghe, Marian
Gratie, Cristian
Gratie, Diana-Elena
Guck, Dennis
Gui, Lin
Hansen, Henri
Huang, Yanhong
Ishikawa, Fuyuki
Islam, Md. Ariful
Ivanov, Sergiu
Jongmans, Sung-Shik T.Q.
Jonker, Hugo
Kalajdzic, Kenan
Kant, Gijs
Kassios, Ioannis
Keiren, Jeroen J.A.
Khakpour, Narges
Kromodimoeljo, Sentot
Laarman, Alfons

Li, Jianwen
Lime, Didier
Lluch Lafuente, Alberto
Ma, Qin
Melnychenko, Oleksandr
Mizera, Andrzej
Mohaqeqi, Morteza
Nguyen, Truong Khanh
Noroozi, Neda
Ouchani, Samir
Petrocchi, Marinella
Petrucci, Laure
Qu, Hongyang
Rezazadeh, Abdolbaghi
Ruijters, Enno
Sanán, David
Selyunin, Konstantin
Singh, Neeraj
Solin, Kim
Song, Songzheng
Spagnolo, Giorgio Oronzo
Strejcek, Jan
Su, Wen
Sulskus, Gintautas
Trujillo, Rolando
van Dijk, Tom
Vanzetto, Hernán
Versari, Cristian
Wang, Ting
Wijs, Anton
Wildman, Luke
Winter, Kirsten
Wu, Xi
Würtz Vinther Jørgensen, Peter
Zhang, Tian
Zhao, Jianhua
Zou, Liang

Abstracts of Invited Talks

SecGuru: Azure Network Verification Using Z3

Nikolaj Bjørner[1] and Karthick Jayaraman[2]

[1] Microsoft Research
nbjorner@microsoft.com
[2] Microsoft Azure
karjay@microsoft.com

This talk describes the use of SMT solving for *Network Verification*. We take as starting point experiences using Z3 in checking network configurations in the Microsoft Azure public cloud infrastructure.

The Azure infrastructure is a prime example of a state-of-the art global and highly complex network infrastructure. It supports a wide range of usage scenarios and security is a principal concern. As a result, there is an urgent need for formal methods tools that provide diagnostic feedback when there are errors and otherwise correctness guarantees.

The Azure architecture enforces network access restrictions using ACLs that are placed on multiple routers and firewalls. Mis-configurations are a dominant source of network outages. The SecGuru tool uses the SMT solver Z3 to check contracts on firewall ACLs. ACLs are checked for containment and equivalence with contracts. SecGuru checks all routers on a continuous basis: each router is checked every 30 minutes against a data-base of contracts. SecGuru relies on checking satisfiability of bit-vector formulas. SecGuru's model extraction algorithm exploits that properties can be captured succinctly as combinations of ranges.

Each Azure data-center is built up around a hierarchy of routers that facilitate high-bandwidth traffic in and out as well as within the data-center. Traffic that leaves and enters the data-center traverses four layers of routers, while traffic within the data-center may traverse only one, two or at most three layers depending on whether the traffic is within a logical partition called a cluster. We describe a set of invariants that capture reachability properties of the Azure architecture. Data-centers are instantiations of this general architecture and we describe how SecGuru is used for checking network invariants on a continuous basis while data-centers are built out and updated.

Scalable Software Testing and Verification through Heuristic Search and Optimization

Lionel C. Briand

SnT Centre for Security, Reliability and Trust, University of Luxembourg
Email: lionel.briand@uni.lu

Testing and verification problems in the software industry come in many different forms, due to significant differences across domains and contexts. But one common challenge is scalability, the capacity to test and verify increasingly large, complex systems. Another concern relates to practicality. Can the inputs required by a given technique be realistically provided by engineers?

This talk reports on 10 years of research tackling verification and testing as a search and optimization problem, often but not always relying on abstractions and models of the system under test. Our observation is that most of the problems we faced could be re-expressed so as to make use of appropriate search and optimization techniques to automate a specific testing or verification strategy. One significant advantage of such an approach is that it often leads to solutions that scale in large problem spaces and that are less demanding in terms of the level of detail and precision required in models and abstractions. Their drawback, as heuristics, is that they are not amenable to proof and need to be thoroughly evaluated by empirical means. However, in the real world of software development, proof is usually not an option, even for smaller and critical systems. In practice, testing and verification is a means to reduce risk as much as possible given available resources and time.

Concrete examples of problems we have addressed and that I will cover in my talk include schedulability analysis, stress/load testing, CPU usage analysis, robustness testing, testing closed-loop dynamic controllers, and SQL Injection testing. Most of these projects have been performed in industrial contexts and solutions were validated on industrial software. There are, however, many other examples in the literature, a growing research trend that has given rise to a new field of study named search-based software testing.

Further information is available in the following selected references:

References

1. Ali, S., et al.: Generating test data from ocl constraints with search techniques. IEEE Transactions on Software Engineering Journal (2013)
2. Matinnejad, R., et al.: Search-based automated testing of continuous controllers: Framework, tool support, and case studies. Information and Software Technology Journal (2014)

3. Briand, L.C., et al.: Using genetic algorithms for early schedulability analysis and stress testing in real-time systems. Genetic Programming and Evolvable Machines Journal (2006)
4. Iqbal, M.Z.Z., et al.: Empirical investigation of search algorithms for environment model-based testing of real-time embedded software. In: ISSTA (2012)
5. Nejati, S., et al.: Identifying optimal trade-offs between cpu time usage and temporal constraints using search. In: ISSTA (2014)
6. Nejati, S., Di Alesio, S., Sabetzadeh, M., Briand, L.: Modeling and analysis of CPU usage in safety-critical embedded systems to support stress testing. In: France, R.B., Kazmeier, J., Breu, R., Atkinson, C. (eds.) MODELS 2012. LNCS, vol. 7590, pp. 759–775. Springer, Heidelberg (2012)

Approximations for Stochastic Graph Rewriting

Vincent Danos[1], Tobias Heindel[1], Ricardo Honorato-Zimmer[1],
and Sandro Stucki[2]

[1] School of Informatics, University of Edinburgh, Edinburgh, United Kingdom
[2] Programming Methods Laboratory, EPFL, Lausanne, Switzerland

In this note we present a method to compute approximate descriptions of a class of stochastic systems. For the method to apply, the system must be presented as a Markov chain on a state space consisting in graphs or graph-like objects, and jumps must be described by transformations which follow a finite set of local rules.

The method is a form of static analysis and uses a technique which is reminiscent of theories of critical pairs in term rewriting systems. Its output is a system of coupled ordinary differential equations (ODE) which tracks the mean evolution of the number of (typically small) subgraphs. In some cases, these ODEs form an exact and finite description of these mean numbers. But even when the ODE description is only an approximation, it can often reveal interesting properties of the original system.

The method was first conceived in relation to a special type of graphs, namely the site graphs which form the basis of the Kappa language [3]. Recently, the authors have taken again this method with the goal to extend it to a broader class of objects. In this note, the goal is rather the opposite. We narrow down the construction to consider only simple graphs and invertible rules, to not be distracted by technicalities, and give a simple account. The exposition is mostly informal.

Table of Contents

Approximations for Stochastic Graph Rewriting[*]

Vincent Danos[1], Tobias Heindel[1], Ricardo Honorato-Zimmer[1],
and Sandro Stucki[2]

[1] School of Informatics, University of Edinburgh, Edinburgh, United Kingdom
[2] Programming Methods Laboratory, EPFL, Lausanne, Switzerland

In this note we present a method to compute approximate descriptions of a class of stochastic systems. For the method to apply, the system must be presented as a Markov chain on a state space consisting in graphs or graph-like objects, and jumps must be described by transformations which follow a finite set of local rules.

The method is a form of static analysis and uses a technique which is reminiscent of theories of critical pairs in term rewriting systems. Its output is a system of coupled ordinary differential equations (ODE) which tracks the mean evolution of the number of (typically small) subgraphs. In some cases, these ODEs form an exact and finite description of these mean numbers. But even when the ODE description is only an approximation, it can often reveal interesting properties of the original system.

The method was first conceived in relation to a special type of graphs, namely the site graphs which form the basis of the Kappa language [3]. Recently, the authors have taken again this method with the goal to extend it to a broader class of objects. In this note, the goal is rather the opposite. We narrow down the construction to consider only simple graphs and invertible rules, to not be distracted by technicalities, and give a simple account. The exposition is mostly informal.

An example. Let us start with an example taken from Ref. [1] which illustrates the type of systems we are interested in. One has a graph G whose nodes can be in either of two states 0 (red) or 1 (blue). There are two possible rules to transform G which we call flips and swaps. To apply either type of transformation, we first need to locate in G a pair of neighboring nodes u, v with different states. For flips, we just flip the internal state of u or v to match its neighbor's state. For swaps, we replace the edge connecting u and v with an edge connecting u or v to another node w. In each case we obtain a new graph (on the same set of nodes). The evolution of the system consist then in repeatedly applying flips and swaps. Fig. 1 illustrates the basic transformation steps. Fig. 2 shows an example of a graph which can be transformed by both types of rules.

If we say that colors represent opinions, then we can interpret the rules as the nodes trying to not have neighbors of a different opinion. A node with a neighbor

---

[*] This research was sponsored by the European Research Council (ERC) under the grants 587327 "DOPPLER" and 320823 "RULE".

S. Merz and J. Pang (Eds.): ICFEM 2014, LNCS 8829, pp. 1–10, 2014.

of the opposite persuasion can change his (by a flip), or turn to another neighbor (by a swap). Several variants of this "voter" models are studied. For instance w, the target node of the swap, can be chosen of the same color as u the node doing the swapping, and/or can be picked within a prescribed distance of u.

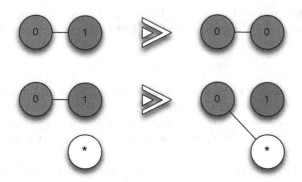

Fig. 1. Flips and Swaps - we use colors to represent the internal states of nodes: red for 0, blue for 1, and $*$ for the unknown state. The symmetric transformations are not shown. In textual notation we write the flip as $0^a, 1^a \Rightarrow 0^a, 0^a$ (flip to zero), and the swap as $0^a, 1^a, * \Rightarrow 0^a, 1, *^a$. We use common exponents to indicate edges between nodes.

At any given point, several transformation rules might be applicable to a graph, and each applicable rule can be applied in several different ways depending on where the rule left hand side is matched in the current graph. A way in which a rule can be applied is called an instance of that rule. If a graph is such that no rules can be applied to it, we call it a normal form. Normal forms are also called sometimes frozen states. In the example, normal forms are "fragmented" graphs with no edge connecting two nodes of opposing colors. The graph of Fig. 2 can be frozen in just one step. In the opinion interpretation, one is interested, among other things, in understanding how likely it is that an opinion wins over the entire graph; that is to say, how likely it is that one reaches a normal form which is monochrome. For instance, in Fig. 2, it is still possible, by a long series of steps, to propagate the red color to the entire graph. To address this type of question, one needs to define the likelihood of a given instance to apply, and equip transformations with a probabilistic structure.

Notations. Before we turn to probabilities, we fix a few notations. This example, as all the ones which we will treat in this note, has rules which preserve the underlying set of nodes and can explore only finitely many colors (those mentioned in the rules). Therefore the set of graphs reachable from a given initial graph is finite. If we write N for the set of nodes of an initial graph G_0, and $\mathscr{G}_N$ for the set of all graphs on N with reachable colors, then all graphs reachable from G_0 will be in $\mathscr{G}_N$. In our voter example, the number of edges is also preserved and this provides a further restriction on the set of reachable graphs.

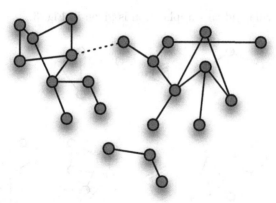

Fig. 2. An almost frozen state: it is enough to swap the dotted edge to reach a normal form where red and blue nodes no longer have any connexions; on the other hand, it also possible to reach a frozen state which is entirely red

Let us assume from now on that we are given a finite set of rules $\mathscr{R}$ and an initial graph G_0 with nodes in N. The objects which we transform are simple graphs where nodes have colors (represented by integers). In other words, we consider triples N, E, σ where N is a finite set of nodes, E a finite set of undirected edges over N, and σ maps a subset of N to integers. Partially colored graphs are only used in rules (eg the swap rule in Fig. 1).

We will use the following typographic conventions: we will write A, B, etc, for (typically small) graphs (e.g. those which appear on the left hand sides of rules in $\mathscr{R}$) which may have nodes without colors, and x, y, etc, for arbitrary graphs in $\mathscr{G}_N$ to which rules are applied and which are fully colored.

A match $f : A \rightarrow x$ is a graph morphism from A to x which 1) preserves internal states, and 2) is injective on nodes. We write $c(f)$ for the codomain x of f. The codomain of f is not to be confused with f's image, written $f(A)$, which in general is a strict subgraph of its codomain x.

Let us write $[A; x]$ for the set of matches between A and x and, $[A]$ for the map on $\mathscr{G}_N$ defined as $[A](x) = |[A; x]|$. This map $[A]$ is counting the number of instances of A in x. We call such maps graph observables. We write $\mathscr{C}$ for the set of connected graph observables, $\mathscr{B}$ for set of all graph observables, and $\mathscr{A}$ for the linear subspace spanned by $\mathscr{B}$ in the vector space $\ell(\mathscr{G}_N)$ of real-valued functions over $\mathscr{G}_N$.

Clearly:

$$\mathscr{C} \subseteq \mathscr{B} \subseteq \mathscr{A} \subseteq \ell(\mathscr{G}_N)$$

We call $\mathscr{A}$ the algebra of graph observables, because it also has a commutative algebra structure as we will see.

A rule is α is a pair of graphs α_L, α_R which are defined on the same set of nodes. To apply such a rule to a graph x, we choose a match $f \in [\alpha_L; x]$ (if any), and replace the edges and states in the image subgraph $f(\alpha_L)$ of α_L as we find them in α_R.

An example of rule and rule application is given in Fig. 3.

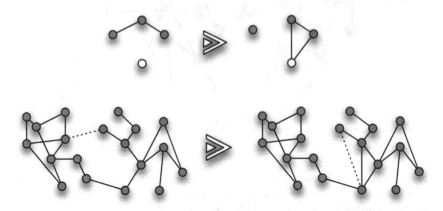

Fig. 3. Example of a rule and rule application. Note that the rule left hand side does not need to be connected. The white node stands for a node of unspecified color.

Thus, the difference between α_L and α_R, which are usually called the rule left and right hand sides, represent the modifications subsequent to the application of the rule. We write $\alpha(f)$ for the residue of the match after applying the rule (which is the same map as f on nodes).

We write $\alpha^\dagger$ for the rule inverse to α.

Stochastic dynamics. Now that we have the non-deterministic structure of the evolution of G_0 under $\mathscr{R}$ in place, we add the quantitative aspects. The set of rules $\mathscr{R}$ can be used to generate a continuous-time Markov chain (CTMC) with values in $\mathscr{G}_N$ by assigning rates to rules in $\mathscr{R}$. Thus, suppose given a rate map $k : \mathscr{R} \to \mathbb{R}^+$ which associates to each rule a positive real number.

We define the transition rates of the associated CTMC on $\mathscr{G}_N$ as follows. For α in $\mathscr{R}$, x, y in $\mathscr{G}_N$, we define a rate matrix Q_α with coefficients:

$$q_{xy}^\alpha = |\{f \in [\alpha_L; x] \mid \alpha(f) \in [\alpha_R; y]\}|$$
$$q_{xx}^\alpha = \sum_{x \neq y} -q_{xy}^\alpha$$

The coefficient q_{xy}^α counts the number of instances of the rule α which transform state x into state y.

The rate matrix Q of our system is then defined by combining the Q_α:

$$Q = \sum_{\alpha \in \mathscr{R}} k(\alpha) \cdot Q_\alpha$$

The rate matrix (also known as the infinitesimal generator of the CTMC) defines a linear operator on the vector space $\ell(\mathscr{G}_N)$. Specifically, if we write q_{xy} for Q's coefficients, and pick f a function in $\ell(\mathscr{G}_N)$, Q's action on f is given by:

$$Q(f)(x) = \sum_y q_{xy}(f(y) - f(x))$$

In words, $Q(f)(x)$ is the mean rate of change of f at x.

Suppose now we write $p(x)$ for the time-dependent probability to be at a certain state x in $\mathscr{G}_N$. We can consider p as an element of $\ell(\mathscr{G}_N)$. The rate matrix Q governs the evolution of p via the master equation [4]:

$$\frac{d}{dt}p^T = p^T Q \tag{1}$$

where p^T is the transpose of p. (The transpose comes from the convention that q_{xy} is the rate at which the chain jumps from x to y.)

For f a function in $\ell(\mathscr{G}_N)$, the (time-dependent) mean (or expected value or average) of f according to p is $E_p(f) := p^T f$, and it follows directly from the master equation that:

$$\frac{d}{dt}E_p(f) = E_p(Q(f)) \tag{2}$$

It easy to see that if we take as function $f = \delta_x$ the function which is 1 at x and zero else, $E_p(\delta_x)$ is the same as $p(x)$ and the equation we have just written is the master equation (1) for $p(x)$ (ie the projection of the master equation on the x-coordinate).

Return to the example. Suppose we pick as our f the function $[0]$ which counts the number of nodes in state 0. Clearly $Q_{swap_0}([0]) = Q_{swap_1}([0]) = 0$ as swaps do not change colors.

For the flips from 0 to 1, we compute:

$$Q_{flip_0}([0])(x) = -\sum_{y \neq x} q_{xy} = [01]$$

where 01 is short for the pattern $0^a, 1^a$, and $[01]$ is the observable which counts the number of edges between neighbors of opposite colors.

The symmetric flip is computed in the same way and by summing all contributions we get the following instance of (2):

$$\tfrac{d}{dt}E_p([0]) = -k_{01}E_p([01]) + k_{10}E_p([01]) = (k_{10} - k_{01})E_p([01])$$

with k_{01} and k_{10} the respective rates associated to *flip_0* (flip from 0 to 1), and *flip_1* (the symmetric flip).

We can already notice a few things.

First, a formal remark: the equation obtained for the evolution of $[0]$, which is in our algebra $\mathscr{A}$, introduces another function $[01]$ also in $\mathscr{A}$. In other words, $Q([0])$ is a (linear) function of $[01]$. This is a general fact. For all αs, $\mathscr{A}$ is closed under the linear map Q_α. Therefore, the same holds of Q which is a linear combination of Q_αs. In fact, this is our main result! We will derive below a concrete expression for $Q_\alpha([F])$ for any graph observable F, and any rule α. This will establish the closure of $\mathscr{A}$ under Q, and give an effective way to write (2) for all observables in $\mathscr{A}$.

Second, a concrete remark: if the flip rules are symmetric (corresponding to opinions which are equally persuasive), that is to say if $k_{01} = k_{10}$, then $\frac{d}{dt}E_p([0]) = 0$. This does not mean that the final number of 0s will be the same in all trajectories to normal form, just that, on average, this number will be exactly what it was at the start. Thus, interesting information about the dynamics can be found from ODEs such as the one we have derived above. So seeking a general method to generate them, as we do here, is a worthy pursuit.

Last, another general remark: the new observable [01] is larger than [0] in the sense that the underpinning graph is larger. This is also general. As we will see, the new observables needed to express $Q([F])$ can be larger than F. The idea is that one has to write an instance of equation (2) for them as well. Hence, the process of deriving the ODE system for a graph observable of interest can be seen as an expansion. Even if in our case the expansion is finite, as $[F] = 0$ as soon as F has more than N nodes, in practice, one needs to truncate the expansion.

Gluings. To derive an effective version of (2) in the general case, we need a additional ingredient, namely minimal gluings. A gluing μ of two graphs A, B is a pair of matches $f : A \to x$, $g : B \to x$. We write $\pi_0(\mu) = f$, $\pi_1(\mu) = g$, and $c(\mu) = x$ for the common codomain of f and g. Given μ, one can always obtain a new gluing $f_1 : A \to C$, $g_1 : B \to C$ with C the union of the images of f and g, and $f = j \circ f_1$, $g = j \circ g_1$, where j is the inclusion of C in x. We call the pair f_1, g_1 a minimal gluing of A and B.

There are finitely many minimal gluings of A and B up to isomorphism. We write $m(A, B)$ for this (finite) set of minimal gluings. In the worst case, there can be exponentially many non-isomorphic minimal gluings, as each corresponds to determining a shared subgraph of A and B in the gluing, namely the intersection of the images of f and g. There is a largest minimal gluing, corresponding to no sharing at all, which is the disjoint sum of A and B, written $A + B$.

A gluing decomposes through exactly one minimal gluing. Hence:

$$[A][B] = \sum_{\mu \in m(A,B)} [\mu]$$

It follows that $\mathscr{A}$ is closed under product, hence is a sub-algebra. Besides, we can rewrite the above as:

$$[A + B] = [A][B] - \sum_{\mu \in m(A,B) \setminus \{A+B\}} [\mu]$$

and one sees that non-connected observables can be expressed as polynomials of connected ones. In other words, $\mathscr{A}$ is the polynomial closure of $\mathscr{C}$ the set of connected observables. (The degree of the polynomial decomposition of $[F]$ in $\mathscr{C}$ is the number of connected components of F.)

Proving that $\mathscr{A}$ is closed. We can now prove that $\mathscr{A}$ is closed under the action of Q. As Q is a linear combination of Q_αs, it is enough to prove closure under Q_α, and as $\mathscr{B}$ spans $\mathscr{A}$, it is enough to examine the action of Q_α on a graph observable. So, let $[F]$ be that observable, and x a graph in $\mathscr{G}_N$. By definition of Q_α we get:

$$(Q_\alpha[F])(x) = \sum_y q^\alpha_{xy}([F](y) - [F](x))$$
$$= \sum_{f \in [\alpha_L; x]} |[F; c(\alpha(f))]| - \sum_{f \in [\alpha_L; x]} |[F; x]|$$

where $\alpha(f)$ is the post-match corresponding to f after firing α at f, and $c(\alpha(f))$ its codomain, that is the graph resulting from firing α.

We see that the action of Q_α at x decomposes naturally in two terms, $Q_\alpha = Q_\alpha^+ - Q_\alpha^-$, one which produces new instances of F and one which consumes existing ones. The consumption part is easy to evaluate:

$$Q_\alpha^-([F]) = \sum_{\mu \in m(F, \alpha_L)} [c(\mu)]$$

Indeed the right hand side is equal to $[F][\alpha_L]$ by definition of minimal gluings. For the production term, we get a similar expression:

$$Q_\alpha^+([F]) = \sum_{\mu \in m(F, \alpha_R)} [c(\alpha^\dagger(\pi_0(\mu)))]$$

Recall that $\pi_0(\mu)$ is the first match in the gluing μ. We apply the inverse rule $\alpha^\dagger$ to this post-match to obtain $c(\alpha^\dagger(\pi_0(\mu)))$. This counting is correct because there is a bijection between post-matches from $c(\pi_0(\mu))$ to $c(\alpha(f))$, and pre-matches from $c(\alpha^\dagger(\pi_0(\mu)))$ to x.

Thus we obtain that $\mathscr{B}$, and therefore evidently $\mathscr{A}$ its linear span, is closed under the action of Q_α, and therefore any linear combination of such.

Remarks. Again there are few remarks worth making.

First, even if the graph observable F which we start form is connected, the observables on the right hand side of $Q_\alpha^\pm([F])$ might not be. That is to say, the linear span of $\mathscr{C}$ is not necessarily closed under Q. However, it is not difficult to see that this will be the case if all rules in $\mathscr{R}$ have a connected left hand side. Such rules sets form an interesting subclass of "solid-state" transformations.

The second remark is a caveat. For rules more general than the ones considered here, where one can create nodes, the bijection argument which we have relied on to justify the production term fails. A more detailed analysis is needed. But the ideas are essentially the same and the formula obtained only slightly more complex.

Last, in the two terms which we have introduced above, $Q_\alpha^\pm([F])$, the summation extends to all minimal gluings of F on both sides of the rule; in practice, we can restrict these sums to gluings where F undergoes an actual modification due to the firing of α or $\alpha^\dagger$. We call these gluings relevant. The contributions of the irrelevant ones cancel out. In examples, we never consider those.

The general rate equation for graphs. From the above, using the linearity of expectations, we derive the explicit form of (2) which we seek. Specifically, for a graph observable F in $\mathscr{B}$, we get:

$$\frac{d}{dt} E_p([F]) =$$
$$\sum_{\alpha \in \mathscr{R}} k(\alpha) \left(\sum_{\mu \in m(F, \alpha_R)} E_p([c(\alpha^\dagger(\pi_0(\mu)))]) - \sum_{\mu \in m(F, \alpha_L)} E_p([c(\mu)]) \right)$$

So far there is no approximation involved. The equation is exact. But as we have seen in the example, it requires the knowledge of additional observables which leads to writing more similar equations, possibly of increasing complexity.

Example continued. To see concretely how more complex terms follow from the expansion, we can return to the example and compute the equations associated to [01] the number of opposing neighbors or the distance to normal form. As we have seen earlier, the equation for $E_p[0]$ generates [01] as a new observable (in the non symmetric case at least). So it is the natural next step.

Below we neglect irrelevant gluings. We use abbreviation similar to the ones used before, eg we write 101 instead of the correct $1^a, 0^{a,b}, 1^b$.

$$
\begin{aligned}
Q^-_{flip_0}([01]) &= -[01] - [101] \\
Q^+_{flip_0}([01]) &= [001] \\
Q^-_{flip_1}([01]) &= -[01] - [010] \\
Q^+_{flip_1}([01]) &= [011] \\
Q^-_{swap_0}([01]) &= -[01] \\
Q^+_{swap_0}([01]) &= [01 + 1] \\
Q^-_{swap_1}([01]) &= -[01] \\
Q^+_{swap_1}([01]) &= [01 + 0]
\end{aligned}
$$

Hence if we write k_0, k_1 for the swap rates we can collect all the contributions above and we obtain the following ODE:

$$
\frac{d}{dt}E_p([01]) = k_{01}(E_p[001] - E_p[01] - E_p[101]) + k_{10}(E_p[011] - E_p[01] - E_p[010])
$$
$$
+ k_0(E_p[01 + 1] - E_p[01]) + k_1(E_p[01 + 0] - E_p[01])
$$

We can simplify this general expression by supposing that flips and swaps are symmetric. If we set the following notations: $k = k_{01} = k_{10}$, $k' = k_0 = k_1$, and arrange the terms below by size, we get:

$$
\frac{d}{dt}E_p([01]) = -2(k + k')E_p[01] + k(E_p[001] + E_p[011] - E_p[101] - E_p[010])
$$
$$
+ k'(E_p[01 + 1] + E_p[01 + 0])
$$

Non-connected observables $[01 + 1]$, and $[01 + 0]$ appear as anticipated, as well as larger observables such as [001]. In Ref. [1] where this is example is developed, the authors derive a similar ODE by hand. (There is a slight difference due to the fact that their swap rules do not take into account the multiplicity of the $*$ node in the definition of an instance; but that is of no consequence for our exposition.)

At this stage, we are facing the problem of either writing an ODE for all the new terms which have appeared (which poses no conceptual problem but would be extremely tedious to do by hand), or to truncate and express the new larger observables as functions of simpler ones. Even if we were to go for the former option, we would have to find a way of truncating the expansion at some point! So let us follow the second option and see how this can be done.

To get rid of the non-connected observables, we can exploit the polynomial decomposition above. This gives us $[01+1] = [01][1] - [01]$ and hence $E_p[01+1] = E_p([01][1]) - E_p[01]$. Now, using an approximation, we can simplify the first term as:

$$E_p([01][1]) \sim E_p([01])E_p([1])$$

This type of approximation can be performed in general and consists in assuming independence of observables. To get rid of the connected terms of the form $[001]$, we need another approximation principle. We can either set them brutally to zero, or else, more subtly, apply what is known as a pair approximation which in this case takes the form:

$$E_p([001])E_p([0]) \sim E_p([00])E_p([01])$$

This second type of approximation is an assumption of conditional independence. Neither comes with a general bound on the error they introduce. But in practice, they often give interesting results.

Example concluded. Using the same machinery, one can compute higher order moments of (the distributions of) observables. Say we want to estimate the variance of $[0]$ the mean of which we have seen is a constant in the symmetric case $k = k_{01} = k_{10}$. In the extreme case where there are no swaps allowed ($k' = 0$), and assuming the initial graph G_0 is connected, normal forms can only be monochrome. This means that one opinion disappears (and it is easy to see that the probability for an opinion to win this all-or-nothing competition is equal to its initial fraction). So, intuitively, in this case $[0]$ will have a high variation, and in general, the lower the variance the more likely it is that the graph will split in two separate colors with none of the colors completely winning.

To compute this variance, it is enough to evaluate $E_p([0]^2)$ as we know that $E_p([0])$ is constant. We get

$$\tfrac{d}{dt}E_p([0]^2) = \tfrac{d}{dt}E_p([0+0]) + \tfrac{d}{dt}E_p([0]) = \tfrac{d}{dt}E_p([0+0])$$

Using the connected decomposition and, again, our general equation (2), we get after some calculations:

$$\tfrac{d}{dt}E_p([0+0]) = = 2kE_p([0+01])$$

This expression, differently to that for the mean $E_p([0])$ is not degenerate even in the symmetric case. In fact, in the symmetric case, the calculation above tell us that the right hand side is about $2kE_p([0]) \cdot E_p([01])$ and the variance will be monotonically increasing as long as there are 01-edges remaining in the graph.

Conclusion. There are many examples other than the one we have used here where the type of deterministic approximations considered in this note have been found useful. Examples abound in particular in the literature of the so-called adaptive networks [2]. The ability to define and generate them in a systematic way, as we have presented, is important on several counts. For one thing, the derivation involves combinatorics and there is a limit to the size of an expansion one can do by hand. With a proper implementation, one could go higher in the order of expansion before introducing approximations, and thus obtaining potentially more accurate approximations. For the same reason, the derivation of these approximations is quite error-prone and a mechanical derivation can be beneficial. Our careful and explicit construction carries over to several graph-like structures with little modifications. One can play with the type of objects (eg directed graphs, hypergraphs, simplicial sets), or the type of matches (eg induced subgraphs) or even the type of rules (eg considering rules which create and/or merge nodes). The general axiomatic approach leads to a more unified picture. Finally, our method to generate the differential system associated to an observable, and its subsequent expansion, could lead to interesting formalizations of the approximation principles used to cut the expansion beyond the simple pair approximation.

References

1. Durrett, R., Gleeson, J.P., Lloyd, A.L., Mucha, P.J., Shi, F., Sivakoff, D., Socolar, J.E., Varghese, C.: Graph fission in an evolving voter model. Proceedings of the National Academy of Sciences 109(10), 3682–3687 (2012)
2. Gleeson, J.P.: High-accuracy approximation of binary-state dynamics on networks. Physical Review Letters 107(6), 068701 (2011)
3. Harmer, R., Danos, V., Feret, J., Krivine, J., Fontana, W.: Intrinsic information carriers in combinatorial dynamical systems. Chaos 20(3) (2010)
4. Norris, J.R.: Markov chains. Cambridge series in statistical and probabilistic mathematics. Cambridge University Press (1998)

Computing Maximal Bisimulations

Alexandre Boulgakov, Thomas Gibson-Robinson, and A.W. Roscoe

Department of Computer Science, University of Oxford,
Wolfson Building, Parks Road, Oxford, OX1 3QD, UK
{alexandre.boulgakov,thomas.gibson-robinson,bill.roscoe}@cs.ox.ac.uk

Abstract. We present and compare several algorithms for computing the maximal strong bisimulation, the maximal divergence-respecting delay bisimulation, and the maximal divergence-respecting weak bisimulation of a generalised labelled transition system. These bisimulation relations preserve CSP semantics, as well as the operational semantics of programs in other languages with operational semantics described by such GLTSs and relying only on observational equivalence. They can therefore be used to combat the space explosion problem faced in explicit model checking for such languages.

1   Introduction

Many different variations on bisimulation have been described in the literature of process algebra, for example [1–5]. They are typically used to characterise equivalences between nodes of a labelled transition system (LTS), but they can also be used to calculated state-reduced LTSs that can represent equivalent processes. They have the latter function in the CSP-based [6–8] refinement checker FDR [9], of which the third major version FDR3 has recently been released [10]. The present paper sets out the approaches to bisimulation reduction taken in FDR and especially FDR3.

FDR typically builds the transition system of a large process as the parallel composition (closely related to Cartesian product) of those of component processes, which are often sequential. One of the approaches it takes to the state explosion problem is to supply a number of compression functions that attempt to reduce the state spaces of these components. The set of compressions introduced in [11], which included *strong* bisimulation, has been extended by several other versions of bisimulation in the most recent versions of FDR.

The main purpose of this paper is to set out the bisimulation algorithms used by FDR3 and compare them with alternatives. Our strong bisimulation algorithm is related to Paige and Tarjan's bisimulation algorithm [12, 13], and is compared with that. When more compression is needed, other tools frequently use branching bisimulation [14] due to the existence of an efficient $O(nt)$ algorithm [15]. In contrast, FDR3 uses the even coarser delay and weak bisimulations; we present innovative algorithms to compute these bisimulations based on dynamic programming. These latter algorithms were introduced because, although

S. Merz and J. Pang (Eds.): ICFEM 2014, LNCS 8829, pp. 11–26, 2014.

they typically achieve slightly poorer compression than FDR's existing compressions, bisimulations are more widely applicable. In Section 5.2 we compare these two classes of compressions.

2   Strong Bisimulation

FDR uses LTSs in which nodes sometimes have additional behaviours represented by labellings such as divergences or minimal acceptances.

Definition 1. A *generalised labelled transition system* (GLTS) is a tuple $(N, \Sigma, E, \Lambda, \lambda)$ where N is a set of nodes, Σ is a set of events, $\Sigma^\tau = \Sigma \cup \{\tau\}$, $\longrightarrow \subseteq N \times \Sigma^\tau \times N$ is a labelled transition relation (with $p \xrightarrow{a} q$ indicating a transition from p to q with action a), Λ is a set of labels, and $\lambda : N \to \Lambda$ is a total function labelling each node. The following shorthand is used:

- $initials(m) = \{e \mid \exists n \cdot m \xrightarrow{e} n\}$ denotes m's initial events;
- $afters(m) = \{(e, n) \mid m \xrightarrow{e} n\}$ denotes m's directly enabled transitions;
- $m \Uparrow \Leftrightarrow \exists m_0, m_1, \dots \cdot m_0 = m \wedge \forall i \cdot m_i \xrightarrow{\tau} m_{i+1}$ denotes *divergence*, i.e. an infinite cycle of internal τ actions corresponding to *livelock*.

Definition 2. A relation $R \subseteq N \times N$ is a *strong bisimulation* of a GLTS S if and only if it satisfies all of the following, where $n_1, n_2, m_1, m_2 \in N$ and $x \in \Sigma^\tau$:

$$\forall n_1, n_2, m_1 \cdot \forall x \cdot n_1 R n_2 \wedge n_1 \xrightarrow{x} m_1 \quad \Rightarrow \quad \exists m_2 \in N.n_2 \xrightarrow{x} m_2 \wedge m_1 R m_2$$
$$\forall n_1, n_2, m_2 \cdot \forall x \cdot n_1 R n_2 \wedge n_2 \xrightarrow{x} m_2 \quad \Rightarrow \quad \exists m_1 \in N.n_1 \xrightarrow{x} m_1 \wedge m_1 R m_2$$
$$\forall n_1, m_1 \cdot n_1 R n_2 \quad \Rightarrow \quad \lambda(n_1) = \lambda(n_2)$$

Two nodes are *strongly bisimilar* if and only if there exists a strong bisimulation that relates them. The *maximal strong bisimulation* on a GLTS S is the relation that relates two nodes if and only if they are strongly bisimilar. The FDR function `sbisim` computes the maximal strong bisimulation on its input GLTS and returns a GLTS with a single node bisimilar to each equivalence class in the input. FDR has included the `sbisim` compression function since its early days. However the algorithm has not been described in the literature in detail (a brief outline is found in [8]) until now.

2.1   Naïve Iterative Refinement

The FDR2 implementation of `sbisim` first computes the desired equivalence relation as a two-directional one-to-many map between equivalence class and node identifiers. It then generates a new GLTS based on the input and the computed equivalence relation. This final step is straightforward to implement and dependent more on the internal GLTS format than the strong bisimulation algorithm and will not be discussed in this paper. Furthermore, it is not specific to strong bisimulation and can be used to factor a GLTS by an arbitrary relation.

It is computing the desired equivalence relation that requires the most effort both on the part of the algorithm designer and on the part of the computer.

A coarse approximation of the equivalence relation is first computed by using the first-step behaviour of each node, and each class in this relation is repeatedly refined using the first-step behaviours of the nodes under the current approximation. This is related to the formulation of strong bisimulation given in [2] as a series of experiments of increasing depth.

Initial Approximation. The initial approximation can most simply be computed by identifying all nodes. However, FDR employs a finer initial approximation that saves time later on.

Unlike the *afters* of a node, whose equivalence depends on the current equivalence relation, these are fixed labels and we can save time by only comparing them once. We can compute an initial approximation by comparing the nodes' labels and *initials* and need not look at the labels again. This is equivalent to identifying all nodes and then performing one refinement using the nodes' labels and their *afters'* equivalence classes.

Iteration. Assume that we have already separated the nodes into equivalence classes, whether from the initial approximation or from a previous refinement step. We will now attempt to refine these classes further. After computing the *afters* of each node under the latest equivalence relation, we sort the *afters* for the nodes in each class in order to reclassify them. A single in-order traversal through the sorted lists allows us to reclassify the nodes in each class.

If any nodes have changed class during this pass, we must proceed to refine the classes again. Otherwise, we are done. We can determine whether any nodes have changed class during the final reclassification traversal with very little additional work.

Construction. The final step is to construct the output GLTS. To do this, we first create a node for each equivalence class. Next, we can use the already computed *afters* to create the transition system, using an arbitrary representative from each class since the *afters* for each of the nodes in an equivalence class are guaranteed to be equivalent (since the refinement phase has terminated). Any node labels can also be copied from the representative directly as they are guaranteed to be equivalent.

Complexity. The initial approximation takes up to a constant factor more time than one iterative step and construction only requires a traversal of the output of the iterative step, so the run time is dominated by the iteration.

Assume an input GLTS with n nodes and t transitions. In FDR's representation, the transition set is sorted first by source and then by event, so recomputing the *afters* is a relatively inexpensive operation requiring simply an in-order traversal of the transition set and a random lookup per transition to compute the equivalence class of its destination, taking $O(t)$ time. The following sort can take $O(n \log(n))$ time in the worst case where the nodes are spread across few classes, and the reclassification is done in $O(n)$ time. Since we refine at least one class on each iteration except the final one, there can be no more than n iterations. The worst-case time complexity is therefore in $O(nt + n^2 \log(n))$.

2.2 Change-Tracking Iterative Refinement

We will now present an improvement on Naïve Iterative Refinement that is included in FDR3. With some bookkeeping, we can determine which states' *afters* could not have changed after the previous iteration. The proposed algorithm uses this information to avoid recomputing and sorting the *afters* for these states.

It is clear that in a process such as $P(n)$ where

$$P(0) = STOP \qquad P(n) = a \rightarrow P(n-1)$$

naïve iterative refinement would first identify all the states except $P(0)$, then split off $P(1)$, then $P(2)$, and so on, recalculating the *afters* for all $n+1$ nodes, and sorting a list of $n-i$ elements and $i+1$ lists of 1 element on the ith iteration. However, we can note that only one node changes class on each iteration, so we need only to recompute the *afters* for that node.

We can also use this knowledge to reduce the number of nodes that have to be sorted. To do so, we must keep track of which nodes are affected by each node (that is, a copy of the transition system with the transitions reversed and the labels removed), and we must also keep track of which nodes change class on each iteration. As FDR represents states as consecutive integers and the transitions are stored in an array, we can easily construct a constant-time accessible map from nodes to their predecessors.

We will maintain as running state a bit vector *changed* containing the nodes whose equivalence class changed on the previous iteration, and a bit vector *affected* containing the nodes that might be affected by those changes. *affected* should be initialised with all nodes marked since we need to compute the *afters* for all of the nodes initially.

Following this initialisation, on each iteration we will perform the following sequence of actions. First, we will recompute the *afters* for each of the nodes in *affected*. All nodes that are not marked for update get to keep their *afters* from the previous iteration. Next, we compute the equivalence classes that contained the affected nodes in the previous iteration; these are the equivalence classes that might need to be refined, and this can be computed in linear time in the number of nodes by iterating over *affected*. We must also clear *changed* for the next step.

For each of the classes that we consider for refinement, we first separate the nodes that have not changed class from those that have (which are in *affected*). Next, we sort the nodes that are in *affected* and in this class in order to partition this class. At this point, we can go through the sorted nodes and assign each group a new class index. However, this does not perform well on examples like R (with the LTS shown in Figure 1) where

$$R = (\square_{i \in \{0..n\}} b \rightarrow b \rightarrow Q(i)) \,\square\, a \rightarrow R'$$

$$R' = \square_{i \in \{0..n\}} a \rightarrow Q(i)$$

$$Q(i) = a \rightarrow STOP$$

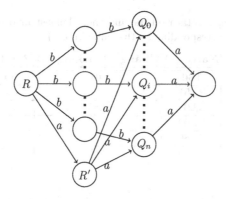

Fig. 1. R' has the same *initials* as each of the Q_i, but is in a different equivalence class from them. An initial classification based on *initials* would therefore place them in the same equivalence class, but a future refinement would reclassify either R' or all of the Q_i, which would change the *afters* of R only or all of the $b \to Q(i)$, respectively.

In particular, the initial classification places R' and each of the $Q(i)$ into the same equivalence class, but the next iteration reclassifies each of the $Q(i)$. This forces each of the $b \to Q(i)$ to be reclassified as well. However, when splitting an equivalence class we are free to assign class indices in an arbitrary way; in particular, rather than changing the indices of the $Q(i)$, we could instead have changed the index of the single node R', which has the single predecessor R. To do this algorithmically, once we have sorted the classes of all of the affected nodes in a given class, we choose the *largest* sequence of nodes with the same class to keep the original class index and assign new indices to the rest, rather than picking the *first* such sequence. We must also record the nodes that had new indices assigned in *changed*.

Once we have refined each of the classes that needed to be refined, we can iterate through *changed* and add to *affected* each of their predecessors for the next iteration. If *changed* is empty, we can conclude that we have reached a fixed point, and we can terminate the algorithm, returning the bisimulation relation we have computed implicitly in the equivalence class indices of the nodes.

2.3   Paige-Tarjan Algorithm

The algorithm outlined in [13] is an adaptation of Paige and Tarjan's solution (described in Section 3 of [12]) to the relational coarsest partition problem (which is equivalent to single-action strong bisimulation) that works with LTSs by splitting with respect to each element of the alphabet in sequence whenever the original algorithm would split a class. In summary, each time a class is split, the resulting subclasses are recorded. Refinement is then performed with respect to the initial classes (separating nodes with edges into each class from those without) and with respect to each split class (separating nodes with edges into one subclass, the other, or both) using the inverse labelled transition relation.

Table 1. sbisim timings. Total runtime and the 5 longest invocations for each algorithm (not necessarily corresponding to the same inputs).

	Naïve (s)	Change-Tracking (s)	P-T (s)
Total	**186**	**40**	**55**
1	22.51	3.38	4.32
2	22.03	2.89	3.84
3	21.99	2.84	3.68
4	21.80	2.70	3.56
5	17.10	2.69	3.07

Complexity. The worst-case time complexity for a graph with n nodes and t transitions is in $O(t \log(n))$. However, the cached in-counts (the *info maps* in [13]) necessary to achieve this bound can be unwieldy to manipulate, raising the implementation and runtime costs. In addition, as the algorithm requires frequent construction and traversal of sets, there is a time or space penalty depending on the set representation used.

2.4   Performance

We will now compare the performance of the three algorithms for sbisim on several real-world and generated examples. The test system used contains a medium-range CPU[1] and 4 GiB of memory, running 64-bit Ubuntu 12.10.

FDR3 Test Suite. To ensure proper operation of FDR3, we have developed a suite of regression and feature tests containing tests generated randomly at runtime, examples from [7] and [8], and assorted test files. Since sbisim is applied to all component processes by default, many of these tests exercise sbisim. There are about 60,000 invocations of sbisim over the test suite, and they are a good comparison of the algorithms' performance on small leaf components typical in a system that does not use sbisim explicitly. The move from naïve to change-tracking iterative refinement affords a nearly five-fold speedup, as evidenced by Table 1. The Paige-Tarjan algorithm is slightly slower than change-tracking iterative refinement, but part of this might be due to the heavy optimisation that our implementation of iterative refinement has gone through over the years.

Towers of Hanoi. The first example is a model of the classic Towers of Hanoi puzzle. The puzzle consists of three rods and N disks of varying sizes, with an invariant that the disks on any rod are arranged in ascending order. A move consists of moving the topmost disk from one rod to another, while preserving the invariant. The objective is to move all the disks from one rod to another. There are 3^N possible configurations, since each disk can be on any of the three rods at any time and its position on the rod is determined by the other disks on the rod (due to the invariant). From each configuration, either two or three

---

[1] The CPU is a quad-core Intel® Core™ i5-750 with 8 MB of cache. The number of cores is not relevant, since the strong bisimulation algorithm is single threaded.

others are reachable: if all the disks are on one rod, the two valid moves are to move the topmost disk to either of the two remaining rods, and if not all the disks are on one rod, the smallest of the topmost disks can be moved to either of the two other rods and the second smallest to one rod. In our model, if all the disks are on one rod, the system can also perform a completion event but remain in the same configuration, resulting in 3^{N+1} transitions. We have hidden (i.e., renamed to τ) all events except for one completion event (as one might do when solving the puzzle using FDR) and applied sbisim to the result.

As we can see from Table 2, there is a significant speedup due to change-tracking iterative refinement that grows even more pronounced as the problem size grows. The Paige-Tarjan algorithm is consistently faster, likely due to the small amount of branching.

Dining Philosophers. The next example is a model of the Dining Philosophers problem with N right-handed philosophers. We hide all visible events (so the states are now distinguished by how many events must occur before the inevitable deadlock) and apply sbisim to the result. We also do the same for two deadlock-free solutions (which therefore have a single state after hiding and strong bisimulation, obtained in one step of iterative refinement). The first solution involves introducing asymmetry by making one of the philosophers left-handed. The second solution introduces a butler who ensures there are never more than $N - 1$ of the philosophers seated.

As we can see in Table 2, change-tracking iterative refinement is significantly faster than naïve iterative refinement for the deadlocking problem, and increasingly so for larger numbers of philosophers, but somewhat slower for the non-deadlocking variants. This is likely due to the fact that the additional bookkeeping it must perform does not have a chance to become useful – there is no second iteration after all the nodes are identified. However, the slowdown is not significant (less than twofold). The modified Paige-Tarjan algorithm is intermediate to the two variants of iterative refinement for the deadlocking cases and slower than both for the non-deadlocking variants.

Matrix. The final example is a matrix of $N + 1$ by $N + 1$ nodes, each being able to transition to the node on its right or the node below it with an event a. This is process $Q(N)$ where

$$P(0) = STOP$$
$$P(n) = a \rightarrow P(n - 1)$$
$$Q(n) = P(n) \mathbin{|||} P(n)$$

It has $(N + 1)^2$ states and $2N * (N + 1)$ transitions, but sbisim can reduce this to $2N + 1$ states and $2N$ transitions, since each node simply performs a number of as and deadlocks, and the number is no more than $2N$, N from each of the component $P(N)$.

Summary. For most of our experiments, change-tracking iterative refinement and the modified Paige-Tarjan algorithm both outperformed naïve iterative refinement and exhibited similar performance. For problems where only a small

Table 2. sbisim statistics. Times for Naïve Iterative Refinement, Change-Tracking Iterative Refinement, and the Paige-Tarjan algorithm in seconds.

Problem	States		Transitions		Naïve	CTIR	P-T
	Output	Input	Output	Input			
Hanoi $N = 8$	1,645	6,561	4,927	19,683	1.15	0.099	0.038
Hanoi $N = 9$	4,926	19,683	14,769	59,049	9.37	0.467	0.184
Hanoi $N = 10$	14,768	59,049	44,294	177,147	79.8	2.96	0.631
Hanoi $N = 11$	44,293	177,147	132,868	531,441	702	18.2	2.91
5 Phils (deadlock)	1,558	7,774	6,825	34,241	0.283	0.034	0.087
6 Phils (deadlock)	7,825	46,656	41,054	246,613	3.06	0.399	1.13
7 Phils (deadlock)	39,994	279,934	246,549	1,726,257	29.6	2.99	11.2
7 Phils (butler)	1	218,751	2	1,266,616	0.354	0.597	0.852
7 Phils (asymm)	1	266,604	2	1,641,653	0.454	0.759	1.126
$Q(100)$	201	10,201	201	20,201	1.03	0.064	0.024
$Q(300)$	601	90,601	601	180,601	66.1	1.77	0.418
$Q(1000)$	2,001	1,002,001	2,001	2,002,001	4540	60.2	16.3

number of refinements were required, they were slightly slower due to bookkeeping overhead, but not significantly so.

3   Divergence-Respecting Delay Bisimulation

While FDR has long supported strong bisimulation, it has only recently supported variants of weak bisimulation. This was because the weak bisimulation of [2] is not compositional for most CSP models and because FDR already had compressions (e.g., diamond and normal) that successfully eliminated τ actions. However the implementation of priority, Timed CSP, and semantic models such as refusal testing in FDR created the need for further compressions, since diamond is not compositional with these and normal is problematic. The first compression introduced for this reason is dbisim (called wbisim when it was introduced in FDR 2.94), which returns the maximal divergence-respecting delay bisimulation (DRDB) of its input.

Given the transition relation $\longrightarrow$ of a GLTS S, let us define a binary relation $\Longrightarrow$ such that $p \Longrightarrow q$ if and only if there is a sequence $p_0, ..., p_n$ (with n possibly 0) such that $p = p_0$, $q = p_n$, and $\forall\, i < n.p_i \xrightarrow{\tau} p_{i+1}$. Let us further define a ternary relation $\hookrightarrow$ with $p \xrightarrow{a} q$ for $a \in \Sigma$ if and only if $\exists p'.p \Longrightarrow p' \wedge p' \xrightarrow{a} q$, and $p \xrightarrow{\tau} q$ if and only if $p \Longrightarrow q$. We will refer to this relation as the delayed transition relation, since the visible events are delayed by 0 or more τs.

Definition 3. A relation $R \subseteq N \times N$ is a *divergence-respecting delay bisimulation* of a GLTS S if and only if it satisfies all of the following requirements, where $n_1, n_2, m_1, m_2 \in N$ and $x \in \Sigma^\tau$:

$$\forall\, n_1, n_2, m_1 \cdot \forall\, x \cdot n_1 R\, n_2 \wedge n_1 \overset{x}{\hookrightarrow} m_1 \quad \Rightarrow \quad \exists m_2 \in N.n_2 \overset{x}{\hookrightarrow} m_2 \wedge m_1 R\, m_2$$

$$\forall\, n_1, n_2, m_2 \cdot \forall\, x \cdot n_1 R\, n_2 \wedge n_2 \overset{x}{\hookrightarrow} m_2 \quad \Rightarrow \quad \exists m_1 \in N.n_1 \overset{x}{\hookrightarrow} m_1 \wedge m_1 R\, m_2$$

$$\forall\, n_1, n_2 \cdot n_1 R\, n_2 \quad \Rightarrow \quad \lambda(n_1) = \lambda(n_2)$$

$$\forall\, n_1, n_2 \cdot n_1 R\, n_2 \quad \Rightarrow \quad n_1 \Uparrow \Leftrightarrow n_2 \Uparrow$$

Note that the definition is very similar to that of strong bisimulation. The differences are the use of the delayed transition relation and the added clause about divergence, which is necessary to make the compression compositional for CSP. However, if we precompute divergence information and record it in each node's label, the requirement that $n_1 \Uparrow \Leftrightarrow n_2 \Uparrow$ will be absorbed into the requirement that $\lambda(n_1) = \lambda(n_2)$.

The FDR compression function `dbisim` computes the maximal DRDB on its input GLTS and returns a GLTS with a single node DRD-bisimilar to each equivalence class in the input. It is an important compression because it preserves semantics in all CSP models, while potentially offering a significantly higher amount of compression than strong bisimulation. FDR has included this compression since version 2.94 as an effective compression for CSP models richer than the failures model [16]. However the algorithm has not been described in the literature until now.

3.1   Reduction to Strong Bisimulation

FDR2 employs an adaptation of the naïve iterative refinement discussed in 2.1 to compute a maximal DRDB. A naïve implementation can apply the algorithm directly to an input with nodes containing divergence information, but for any of the requested properties (*initials* or labels) consider the τ-closure of the node (all nodes reachable from the given node by a sequence of τs) and allow the behaviours of each of the nodes in the τ-closure for the given node.

For an input GLTS S, we can compute a GLTS $\widehat{S}$ with a transition for each delayed transition of the input and mark each node with divergence information computed from S. Care is required not to introduce divergences not present in S due to the τ self-loops introduced in $\widehat{S}$ because the original node can take an empty sequence of τs to itself. The maximal strong bisimulation of $\widehat{S}$ is the maximal DRDB of S by construction.

Complexity. A significant problem with this approach is the high worst-case space complexity. $\widehat{S}$ can have up to An^2 transitions if the input has n nodes and an alphabet of size A, even if S has $o(An^2)$ transitions. For example, a process that performs N τs before recursing exhibits this worst-case behaviour. Since all nodes are mutually τ-reachable, a transition system with N^2 transitions is constructed. Figure 2 demonstrates this quadratic explosion for $N = 4$.

Construction of $\widehat{S}$ can take a correspondingly significant amount of time. For example, using an adaptation of the Floyd-Warshall algorithm [17] requires $O(n^3)$ operations. The strong bisimulation step after this transformation takes up to $O(n^3)$ operations since the number of transitions can grow to $O(n^2)$ and dominate the $n\log(n)$ term.

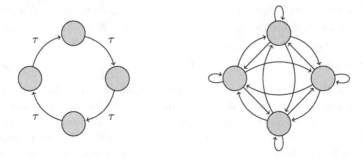

(a) The input, $P(4)$, has only four tran-   (b) The output has sixteen transitions
sitions and four nodes.   for the same four nodes. Labels
                                                 have been omitted for clarity.

Fig. 2. The constructed LTS can be quadratically larger than the input

3.2   Dynamic Programming Approach

Rather than constructing $\widehat{S}$ and keeping it in memory (which is often the limiting factor for such computations, since main memory is limited and the hard disk is prohibitively slow given the random nature of the accesses required by parts of the strong bisimulation algorithm), FDR3 instead recomputes the relevant information using the original transition system on each refinement iteration.

Algorithm. First, noting that two nodes on a τ loop are both DRD-bisimilar and divergent, we factor the input GLTS S by the relation that identifies nodes on a τ loop. FDR has a function built in that does this, `tau_loop_factor`. We will not discuss it in detail here, but it uses Tarjan's algorithm for finding strongly connected components [18] via a single depth-first search and runs in $O(n + t)$ time for a system with n nodes and t transitions. In addition to eliminating τ loops, it marks each node as divergent or stable. Now that we have ensured there are no τ loops, the τ-transition relation can be used to topologically sort the nodes with another depth-first search [19], so that there are no upstream τ-transitions.

The topological sort allows us to obtain the transitions of the $\widehat{S}$ described in Section 3.1 using a dynamic programming approach. The last node in this topological sort has no outgoing τ transitions, so its new *initials* and *afters* are precisely those in S with the addition of itself after τ. We then proceed upstream and for each node compute the union of its own *afters* (with the inclusion of a self-transition under τ) and the *afters* of each of the nodes it can reach under a single τ transition. Of course, since we are doing this in a topological order, these nodes have been processed already, so we have computed the union of the *afters* of all τ-reachable nodes from the given node.

We can apply a modified Naïve Iterative Refinement (Section 2.1) to compute the maximal strong bisimulation of $\widehat{S}$, which is itself never constructed. The faster CTIR or modified Paige-Tarjan algorithms require the inverted transition relation, and we have not found a way to do this dynamically. We compute the *initials* and labels for the initial approximation using dynamic programming on the topologically sorted nodes. For each refinement, we compute the equivalence classes of the *afters* using the dynamic programming approach described above, but keeping track of equivalence classes rather than node identifiers for each *after*. For the construction step, we compute the equivalence classes of the *afters* as above, but without inserting the τ self-transition.

Complexity. The space complexity for this algorithm is never significantly higher than that of the explicit reduction, and can be significantly lower. The only additional information we have is the transient DFS stack and bookkeeping information, and the sorted node list. The *afters* we compute for each node take no more space than the exploded transition system, and will take less if any nodes are identified – and if the user is running the algorithm there is reason to believe that they will be. In addition, since the *afters* are recomputed at each iteration, the working set for each refinement iteration can be smaller than the peak working set required by the final one. For example, for the process $P(N)$ portrayed in Figure 2, the initial classification will identify all nodes, and the first *afters* computation will have a single *after* for each node: equivalence class 0 under τ.

We still traverse the entire transition set a single time (split across nodes). But now, for each node, we have to take the union of its *afters* and the ones preceding it. Provided we keep these sorted, and use a merge sort for union, we will have in the worst case $O(Acn)$ operations for each node, where A is the size of the alphabet, c is the number of classes in this iteration, and n is the number of nodes, since Ac is the maximal number of *afters* a node could have and we could have $O(n)$ nodes following this one. This means an upper bound on the overall worst-case runtime is $O(An^4)$.

However, in practice the time complexity is much lower. Removing τ loops ensures that the graph is not fully connected and reduces the number of unions for each node significantly. The number of classes c is often much less than n. In addition, there are further optimisations that could be made to reduce the runtime, the union operation can be made faster by keeping metadata that allows us to avoid unioning duplicate *afters* sets. Section 5.2 demonstrates that the dynamic programming approach is faster on many examples with a large number of τs than the explicit reduction approach.

4 Divergence-Respecting Weak Bisimulation

FDR3 adds support for compression by an even weaker equivalence relation, divergence-respecting weak bisimulation (DRWB).

Given the transition relation $\longrightarrow$ of a GLTS S and the binary relation $\Longrightarrow \equiv \stackrel{\tau}{\longrightarrow}^*$, let us define a ternary relation $\Longrightarrow$ with $p \stackrel{a}{\Longrightarrow} q$ for $a \in \Sigma$ if and only if $\exists p', q'.p \Longrightarrow p' \land p' \xrightarrow{a} q' \land q' \Longrightarrow q$, and $p \xRightarrow{\tau} q$ if and only if $p \Longrightarrow q$. We will refer to this relation as the observed transition relation.

Definition 4. A relation $R \subseteq N \times N$ is a *divergence-respecting weak bisimulation* of a GLTS S if and only if it satisfies all of the following requirements, where $n_1, n_2, m_1, m_2 \in N$ and $x \in \Sigma^\tau$:

$$\forall n_1, n_2, m_1 \cdot \forall x \cdot n_1 R n_2 \land n_1 \xRightarrow{x} m_1 \quad \Rightarrow \quad \exists m_2 \in N.n_2 \xRightarrow{x} m_2 \land m_1 R m_2$$
$$\forall n_1, n_2, m_2 \cdot \forall x \cdot n_1 R n_2 \land n_2 \xRightarrow{x} m_2 \quad \Rightarrow \quad \exists m_1 \in N.n_1 \xRightarrow{x} m_1 \land m_1 R m_2$$
$$\forall n_1, n_2 \cdot n_1 R n_2 \quad \Rightarrow \quad \lambda(n_1) = \lambda(n_2)$$
$$\forall n_1, n_2 \cdot n_1 R n_2 \quad \Rightarrow \quad n_1 \Uparrow \Leftrightarrow n_2 \Uparrow$$

Note that the definition is very similar to that of divergence-respecting delay bisimulation. The only difference is the use of the observed transition relation in place of the delayed transition relation.

The FDR3 compression function `wbisim` computes the maximal DRWB on its input GLTS and returns a GLTS with a single node DRW-bisimilar to each equivalence class in the input. It is an important compression because, like `sbisim` and `dbisim` it preserves semantics in all CSP models, while potentially offering a higher amount of compression than `dbisim`. This compression is new in FDR3 and is the strongest implemented compression for CSP models richer than the failures model.

4.1   Algorithm

We proceed in a manner similar to that described in Section 3.2. Noting that two nodes on a τ loop are both DRW-bisimilar and divergent, we factor the input GLTS by the relation that identifies nodes on a τ loop using `tau_loop_factor`. We then topologically sort the nodes by the τ-transition relation.

The topological sort allows us to obtain the observed transitions using a two-pass dynamic programming approach. One pass as in delay bisimulation is not sufficient here since we need to determine the τ^* *afters* of the visible *afters* of each node, and these visible *afters* might not have been previously explored. In the first pass, we compute the τ^* *afters* of each node. The last node in this topological sort has no outgoing τ transitions, so its only τ^* *after* is itself. We then proceed upstream and for each node compute the union of its own τ *afters* (with the inclusion of itself) and the previously computed τ^* *afters* of each of the nodes it can reach under a single τ transition. The second pass computes the visible observed transitions. For each node, these are the union of the τ^* *afters* of its visible *afters* and the visible observed transitions of its τ *afters*. If we proceed in topological order, the visible observed transitions of each node's τ *afters* will have already been computed by the time they are needed.

We can apply a modified Naïve Iterative Refinement to compute the maximal strong bisimulation of the induced GLTS as in Section 3.2, removing the τ self-transition from each node in the construction step.

Complexity. In the typical case this algorithm will require more space to store the *afters* than the DRD-bisimulation algorithm since it must follow the

τ transitions after a visible event in addition to the ones tracked by the DRD-bisimulation algorithm. However, the worst-case space complexity for this algorithm is the same, since in the worst case all the nodes are mutually reachable under both the delayed transition relation and the observed transition relation. The time complexity is a constant factor greater since at each iteration two passes through the topologically sorted nodes must be performed.

However, in practice we have found that wbisim is nearly as fast as dbisim, and produces identical results on all example files other than ones we have contrived to prove that the two are in fact different.

5   Performance

5.1   Diamond Elimination

It is interesting to compare dbisim with alternatives available in FDR prior to its introduction. The most widely used compression was sbisim(diamond(P)), which we will call sbdia. In all the following examples sbdia is valid.

5.2   Timing

This section is primarily to compare the runtimes of sbdia and the algorithms we have presented for dbisim and wbisim. We will use the same system as for the sbisim tests, described in 2.4. Reduction to strong bisimulation has only been implemented in FDR2 and the dynamic programming approach has only been implemented in FDR3, so the timings are not directly comparable due to differences in other components such as the compiler, which is single-threaded in FDR2 and multi-threaded in FDR3. However, the examples have been designed to heavily use dbisim, and most of the runtime will be due to dbisim rather than these other components. We will use the same examples here as in the sbisim tests, so section 2.4 should be consulted for more details.

Towers of Hanoi. As in the sbisim test, we have hidden all events except for one completion event, resulting in a strongly connected network of τs, with a single visible transition. dbisim reduces this to a system with one node and two transitions in one iteration. However, FDR2 does not always reach this iteration – 4 GiB of RAM is not enough for an exploded transition system corresponding to $N \geqslant 8$, and it uses 537 MiB for the $N = 7$ problem, while FDR3 uses only 700 MiB for the 729 times larger $N = 13$ problem and 1.9 GiB for the 2187 times larger $N = 14$ problem. The situation is similar for the Dining Philosophers.

Matrix. The matrix example perhaps shows best the difference between the two algorithms using P and Q as defined in 2.4 and $R(n) = Q(n) \setminus a$.

We have tested both $Q(N)$ and $R(N)$ for various values of N. The FDR2 algorithm, which explicitly constructs an LTS representing the delay transitions performs better on Q, which doesn't contain any τs (so the exploded transition system is the same size as the original one), since the dynamic programming approach performs unnecessary work at each iteration as well as at the start.

Table 3. dbisim, wbisim, and sbdia timings in seconds

Problem	States	Transitions	Explicit dbisim	Dynamic dbisim	wbisim	sbdia
Hanoi (7)	2,187	6,561	13	0.03	0.05	0.04
Hanoi (8)	6,561	19,683	–	0.08	0.08	0.08
Hanoi (12)	531,441	1,594,323	–	2.49	2.49	2.49
Hanoi (13)	1,594,323	4,782,969	–	6.83	6.85	6.72
Hanoi (14)	4,782,969	14,348,907	–	24.1	26.21	24.1
$Q(10)$	2,601	5,101	0.01	0.01	0.01	0.01
$Q(100)$	10,201	20,201	1.29	2.05	2.18	0.10
$Q(300)$	90,601	180,601	27.5	109	109	2.28
$R(10)$	2,601	5,101	0.02	0.01	0.01	0.01
$R(100)$	10,201	20,201	69.4	0.03	0.03	0.02
$R(300)$	90,601	180,601	–	0.38	0.39	0.11
$R(1000)$	1,002,001	2,002,001	–	4.63	4.89	1.35

However, the FDR3 algorithm performs vastly better on R which has a lot of τ^*-connectivity, but relatively few τ transitions (so the FDR2 algorithm constructs an LTS with $\Theta(N^4)$ transitions, when the input only has $\Theta(N^2)$). We were unable to obtain FDR2 timings for $R(300)$ and $R(1000)$ due to insufficient memory ($R(100)$ used 2.2 GiB), while FDR3 coped with these examples very well.

Summary. For computing dbisim, the explicit reduction approach is prohibitively memory-intensive for large graphs with a high degree of τ-connectivity. The dynamic programming approach, on the other hand, is somewhat slower for problems with few τs. Little difference was observed between wbisim and dbisim, both in terms of runtime and output. The latter is not surprising given that delay bisimulation lies between weak and branching bisimulation, which are known to frequently coincide in a non divergence-respecting context.

5.3   Amount of Compression

We will examine the performance and effectiveness of dbisim and sbdia on the *bully* algorithm (the FDR implementation is outlined in Section 14.4 of [8]) with 5 processors and an implementation of Lamport's bakery algorithm (Section 18.5 of [8]) with either 3 or 4 threads and integers ranging from 0 to 7. These are typical examples composed of a variable number of parallel processes, with many τs and symmetry that can be reduced by either dbisim or sbdia. We will compress these processes *inductively*[2] (as described in Section 8.8 of [8]); that is, add them to the composition one at a time, compressing at every step. This is a common technique that allows a large portion of the system to be compressed while keeping each compression's inputs manageable. Table 5 shows that sbdia runs much faster than dbisim and Table 4 shows that it is more effective at reducing state counts, but can add transitions, whereas dbisim cannot by design.

---

[2] We used inductive compression to increase the time spent on the compressions. This is not necessarily the most efficient approach to checking these systems in FDR.

Table 4. State and transition counts with no compression, `dbisim`, and `sbdia`

Problem	States			Transitions		
	Uncompressed	dbisim	sbdia	Uncompressed	dbisim	sbdia
Bully	492,548	140,776	105,701	3,690,716	1,280,729	3,872,483
Bakery (3)	9,164,958	29,752	17,787	27,445,171	85,217	64,283
Bakery (4)	–	1,439,283	716,097	–	5,327,436	3,408,420

Table 5. Timings with no compression, `dbisim`, and `sbdia`

Problem	Compilation Time (s)			Exploration Time (s)		
	Uncompressed	dbisim	sbdia	Uncompressed	dbisim	sbdia
Bully	0.06	185.46	25.17	1.76	0.36	0.88
Bakery (3)	0.37	0.57	0.36	137.52	0.93	1.07
Bakery (4)	–	105.88	9.54	–	3.63	1.64

6   Conclusions

We have presented a number of GLTS compression algorithms, including novel algorithms as well as ones that had been implemented previously, but not characterised until now. Our change-tracking iterative refinement algorithm for `sbisim` showed comparable performance to the Paige-Tarjan algorithm (the current state of the art) and offered a significant improvement over the naïve iterative refinement used by previous versions of FDR. We have shown that explicitly constructing a τ-closed transition relation for weak bisimulations, the current state of the art, is prohibitively memory-intensive and provided an efficient alternative based on dynamic programming. Comparing `dbisim` and `wbisim`, we have noticed that they produce identical output on all the real-world examples we have tested, and exhibit a similar runtime.

Future Work. We plan to explore implementing DRD-bisimulation by reduction to strong bisimulation for FDR3 for those cases where this approach is more efficient. We can provide the alternatives to the user, but we would like to find and implement a heuristic that would allow FDR3 to automatically select of the two algorithms the one that is likely to be faster for the given problem. We would also like to find heuristics for deciding which compression to use, in particular for inductively compressing large parallel compositions.

It would be interesting to come up with versions of the dynamic DRD-bisimulation or DRW-bisimulation algorithms that use Change-Tracking Iterative Refinement or The Paige-Tarjan Algorithm.[3] This is challenging due to the difficulty of inverting the delayed and observed transition relations dynamically.

Despite the multi-threaded core of FDR3, compressions are still single threaded, though independent compressions can be run in parallel. Iterative refinement consists of massively parallel *afters* computations and parallel sorts

---

[3] Since submitting the first version of the paper, the authors have developed such an algorithm, and intend to publish results once it is implemented.

of a number of *afters* lists of arbitrary size. Both phases could be sped up by a multi-threaded implementation. The naïve parallelisation has the nice property that the transition set can be partitioned across threads and only the node to equivalence class map needs to be shared. This could allow for an efficient GPU implementation.

References

1. Park, D.: Concurrency and automata on infinite sequences. Springer, Heidelberg (1981)
2. Milner, R.: A modal characterisation of observable machine-behaviour. In: Astesiano, E., Böhm, C. (eds.) CAAP 1981. LNCS, vol. 112, pp. 25–34. Springer, Heidelberg (1981)
3. van Glabbeek, R.J., Weijland, W.P.: Branching time and abstraction in bisimulation semantics. J. ACM 43, 555–600 (1996)
4. Phillips, I., Ulidowski, I.: Ordered SOS rules and weak bisimulation. In: Theory and Formal Methods (1996)
5. Sangiorgi, D.: A theory of bisimulation for the π-calculus. Acta informatica 33(1), 69–97 (1996)
6. Hoare, C.A.R.: Communicating Sequential Processes. Prentice-Hall, Inc., Upper Saddle River (1985)
7. Roscoe, A.W.: The Theory and Practice of Concurrency (1998)
8. Roscoe, A.W.: Understanding Concurrent Systems. Springer, Heidelberg (2010)
9. Roscoe, A.W.: Model-Checking CSP. In: A Classical Mind: Essays in Honour of CAR Hoare (1994)
10. Gibson-Robinson, T., Armstrong, P., Boulgakov, A., Roscoe, A.: FDR3—A Modern Refinement Checker for CSP (2014)
11. Roscoe, A.W., Gardiner, P., Goldsmith, M., Hulance, J., Jackson, D.M., Scattergood, J.: Hierarchical compression for model-checking CSP, or How to check 10^{20} dining philosophers for deadlock. In: Brinksma, E., Steffen, B., Cleaveland, W.R., Larsen, K.G., Margaria, T. (eds.) TACAS 1995. LNCS, vol. 1019, pp. 133–152. Springer, Heidelberg (1995)
12. Paige, R., Tarjan, R.E.: Three partition refinement algorithms. SIAM Journal on Computing 16(6), 973–989 (1987)
13. Fernandez, J.-C.: An implementation of an efficient algorithm for bisimulation equivalence. Science of Computer Programming 13(2), 219–236 (1990)
14. Van Glabbeek, R., Weijland, W.: Branching time and abstraction in bisimulation semantics: extended abstract. Rep./Centrum voor wiskunde en informatica. Computer science; CS-R8911 (1989)
15. Groote, J., Vaandrager, F.: An efficient algorithm for branching bisimulation and stuttering equivalence. In: Paterson, M. (ed.) ICALP 1990. LNCS, vol. 443, pp. 626–638. Springer, Heidelberg (1990)
16. Armstrong, P., Goldsmith, M., Lowe, G., Ouaknine, J., Palikareva, H., Roscoe, A.W., Worrell, J.: Recent developments in FDR. In: Madhusudan, P., Seshia, S.A. (eds.) CAV 2012. LNCS, vol. 7358, pp. 699–704. Springer, Heidelberg (2012)
17. Floyd, R.W.: Algorithm 97: Shortest path. Commun. ACM 5, 345 (1962)
18. Tarjan, R.E.: Depth-first search and linear graph algorithms. SIAM Journal on Computing 1(2), 146–160 (1972)
19. Tarjan, R.E.: Edge-disjoint spanning trees and depth-first search. Acta Informatica 6(2), 171–185 (1976)

Improving the Model Checking of Strategies under Partial Observability and Fairness Constraints

Simon Busard[1],[*], Charles Pecheur[1], Hongyang Qu[2], and Franco Raimondi[3]

[1] ICTEAM Institute, Université catholique de Louvain, Louvain-la-Neuve, Belgium
{simon.busard,charles.pecheur}@uclouvain.be
[2] Dept. of Automatic Control and Systems Engineering, University of Sheffield,
Sheffield, United Kingdom
h.qu@sheffield.ac.uk
[3] Dept. of Computer Science, Middlesex University, London, United Kingdom
f.raimondi@mdx.ac.uk

Abstract. Reasoning about strategies has been a concern for several years, and many extensions of Alternating-time Temporal Logic have been proposed. One extension, $ATLK_{irF}$, allows the user to reason about the strategies of the agents of a system under partial observability and unconditional fairness constraints. However, the existing model-checking algorithm for $ATLK_{irF}$ is inefficient when the user is only interested in the satisfaction of a formula in a small subset of states, such as the set of initial states of the system. We propose to generate fewer strategies by only focusing on partial strategies reachable from this subset of states, reducing the time needed to perform the verification. We also describe several practical improvements to further reduce the verification time and present experiments showing the practical impact of the approach.

1 Introduction

Logics to reason about the strategies of a group of agents have been studied for years and they have a number of practical applications, from security to synthesis of plans to achieve a certain goal. Starting with Alternating-time Temporal Logic (ATL), reasoning about all strategies of the agents [1], many extensions have been developed. For example, ATL_{ir} restricts the strategies of interest to those that the players can actually play, based on their local knowledge of the system [2]. $ALTK_{irF}$ [3] is another extension that combines strategies under partial observability and unconditional fairness constraints, with branching-time and epistemic operators. This logic can be used, for example, to verify strategic properties of multi-agent programs in the presence of a fair scheduler [4]. However, the basic algorithm proposed in [3] is inefficient when the user is interested in the existence of a winning strategy in a small subset of the states of the system, such as the initial states, instead of all the states of the system.

[*] This work is supported by the European Fund for Regional Development and by the Walloon Region.

S. Merz and J. Pang (Eds.): ICFEM 2014, LNCS 8829, pp. 27–42, 2014.

The objective of this paper is to improve the practical efficiency of the algorithm presented in [3] by checking fewer strategies. Let us consider the following simple motivational example of a 3-card poker, inspired by the card game of [5]: the system is a card game played between two agents, a player and a dealer. The game is composed of three cards: the ace A, the king K and the queen Q; the ace wins over the two others and the king wins over the queen. The game is played in three steps: 1) the dealer gives a card to the player; he also takes one for himself and keeps it secret; 2) the player can abandon the game or continue; 3) the player can choose to keep his card or to swap it with the third one. If the third step is reached—the player did not abandon after the first step—the winner is the one with the winning card, and the game restarts from the beginning. The graph of the system is illustrated in Figure 1.

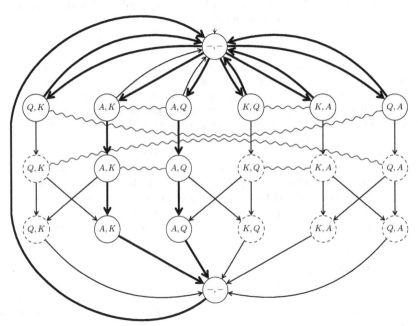

Fig. 1. The graph of the card game. Circles are states, (K, A means the player has K, the dealer has A). Arrows are transitions (actions of the agents are easily inferred). Waved edges link together the states that are indistinguishable for the player.

We are interested in whether the player has a strategy to eventually win the game before the dealer. Intuitively, to consider all strategies of the player in the initial state, we have to consider his choices at the second step—abandoning or continuing the game—and, if he chooses to continue the game, his choices at the third step—keeping or swapping his card. But if he chooses to abandon when he does not receive the ace, we do not need to consider his choice at third step when his card is the king or the queen. This amounts to considering 27 strategies. Figure 1 shows such a strategy in bold and the states in which we do not need to consider the player's choices with dashed borders.

On the other hand, the algorithm presented in [3] blindly makes a choice for all possible sets of indistinguishable states of the system. In the present case, it considers whether the player keeps or swaps his king (or queen) at the third step, even if the considered strategy is to abandon the game at step 2; that is, the algorithm enumerates the strategies in the dashed states of Figure 1, too, considering 64 strategies. The contributions of this paper are:

- an algorithm to generate only strategies that are relevant for given states;
- an new model-checking algorithm for $ATLK_{irF}$ based on these strategies;
- further practical improvements of this algorithm—for example, stopping when a winning strategy has been found instead of checking them all;
- an implementation of these algorithms (to the best of our knowledge, this is the only implementation currently available);
- experiments showing the benefits of the approach.

The paper is organized as follows: Section 2 briefly describes $ATLK_{irF}$ and the original model-checking algorithm; Section 3 proposes an algorithm to generate fewer strategies and Section 4 presents the new model-checking algorithm; Section 5 describes further improvements to the approach, and Section 6 presents experiments made on the implementation of the approach. The proof of theorems are omitted due to space constraints.

2   Background

This section presents the syntax and the semantics of $ATLK_{irF}$. This logic has been presented in [3], where it is called $ATLK_{po}^{F}$. This section also describes the original model-checking algorithm for $ATLK_{irF}$ proposed in [3] and gives an intuition of how to use partial strategies—that is, strategies that give actions for a subset of the state space—to improve the algorithm.

Syntax and Semantics. Formulas of $ATLK_{irF}$ are built from a set of atomic propositions AP, standard Boolean connectives, CTL operators [6], epistemic operators [7] and strategic operators [1]. They follow this grammar:

$$\phi ::= true \mid p \mid \neg\phi \mid \phi \vee \phi \mid E\psi \mid \langle\Gamma\rangle\psi \mid K_i\phi \mid E_\Gamma\phi \mid D_\Gamma\phi \mid C_\Gamma\phi$$
$$\psi ::= X\phi \mid \phi\, U\, \phi \mid \phi\, W\, \phi$$

where $p \in AP$, Γ is a subset of a set of agents Ag, i is an agent of Ag.

Models and Notations. $ATLK_{irF}$ formulas are interpreted over states of models $M = \langle Ag, S, Act, T, I, \{\sim_i\}_{i \in Ag}, V, FC \rangle$ where (1) Ag is a set of n agents; (2) S is a set of states; (3) $Act \subseteq Act_1 \times ... \times Act_n$ is a set of joint actions (one action for each agent); (4) $T \subseteq S \times Act \times S$ is a transition relation giving at least one successor for each state (we write $s \xrightarrow{a} s'$ for $(s, a, s') \in T$); (5) $I \subseteq S$ is the set of initial states; (6) $\{\sim_i\}_{i \in Ag}$ is a set of equivalence relations on $S \times S$, one for each agent (we write $\sim_\Gamma$ for $\bigcap_{i \in \Gamma} \sim_i$, the *distributed knowledge* relation of agents in $\Gamma \subseteq Ag$); (7) $V : S \to 2^{AP}$ is a function labeling the states of M with atomic propositions of AP; (8) $FC \subseteq 2^S$ is a set of fairness constraints.

The function $img : S \times Act \to 2^S$ returning the set of states accessible from a given state through a given action is defined as $img(s, a) = \{s' \in S | s \xrightarrow{a} s'\}$. Furthermore, the set of states that are indistinguishable for Γ from the states of Z is defined as $[Z]_\Gamma = \{s' | \exists s \in Z \text{ s.t. } s' \sim_\Gamma s\}$.

A partially joint action is an element a_Γ of $Act_\Gamma = \prod_{i \in \Gamma} Act_i$; we say that action $a \in Act$ completes a_Γ, written $a_\Gamma \sqsubseteq a$, if the actions of agents of Γ in a_Γ correspond to the actions of Γ in a. The function $enabled : S \times Ag \to 2^{Act}$ returning the actions a group of agents can perform in a state is defined as

$$enabled(s, \Gamma) = \{a_\Gamma \in Act_\Gamma | \exists s' \in S, a \in Act \text{ s.t. } a_\Gamma \sqsubseteq a \wedge s \xrightarrow{a} s'\}. \quad (1)$$

Two additional constraints are set on the models:

$$\forall s, s' \in S, s \sim_i s' \implies enabled(s, i) = enabled(s', i), \quad (2)$$

$$\forall s \in S, enabled(s, Ag) = \prod_{i \in Ag} enabled(s, i). \quad (3)$$

They ensure that an agent only needs its own information about the current state to make a choice (2), and that nobody can prevent him from choosing an enabled action (3).

A path is a sequence $\pi = s_0 \xrightarrow{a_1} s_1 \xrightarrow{a_2} ...$ such that $(s_i, a_{i+1}, s_{i+1}) \in T$ for all $i \geq 0$. We write $\pi(d)$ for s_d. A path π is fair according to FC if for each fairness constraint $fc \in FC$, there exist infinitely many d such that $\pi(d) \in fc$.

A memoryless strategy for Γ is a function $f_\Gamma : S \to Act_\Gamma$ such that $\forall s, f_\Gamma(s) \in enabled(s, \Gamma)$, specifying, for each state of the model, which action group Γ has to choose in each state. A strategy f_Γ is uniform iff $\forall s, s' \in S, s \sim_\Gamma s' \implies f_\Gamma(s) = f_\Gamma(s')$. In the sequel, we only speak about memoryless uniform strategies, and simply call them strategies. The outcomes $out(s, f_\Gamma)$ of a strategy f_Γ from state s is the set of paths reached by f_Γ from s and is defined as

$$out(s, f_\Gamma) = \left\{ \pi = s_0 \xrightarrow{a_1} s_1 ... \middle| \begin{array}{l} s_0 = s \wedge \\ \forall d \geq 0, s_{d+1} \in img(s_d, a_{d+1}) \wedge f_\Gamma(s_d) \sqsubseteq a_{d+1} \end{array} \right\}. \quad (4)$$

Finally, a move of Γ is a state/action pair, that is, an element of $S \times Act_\Gamma$. A strategy f_Γ can be represented as a set of moves as

$$\{\langle s, a_\Gamma \rangle | s \in dom(f_\Gamma) \wedge a_\Gamma = f_\Gamma(s)\}, \quad (5)$$

that is, the set of moves $\langle s, a_\Gamma \rangle$ such that s is a state for which f_Γ is defined and a_Γ is the action that f_Γ chooses.

Semantics. The semantics of $ATLK_{irF}$ is defined over states of a model M as the relation $M, s \models \phi$, where s is a state of M and ϕ is a formula of the logic. This relation is defined in the standard way for atomic propositions, Boolean connectors, branching-time and epistemic operators. The semantics of strategic operators is defined as

$$M, s \models \langle \Gamma \rangle \psi \iff \begin{array}{l} \text{there exists a strategy } f_\Gamma \text{ s.t.} \\ \forall s' \sim_\Gamma s, \forall \text{ fair paths } \pi \in out(s', f_\Gamma), M, \pi \models \psi, \end{array} \quad (6)$$

where the relation $M, \pi \models \psi$ is defined as

$$M, \pi \models X\phi \iff M, \pi(1) \models \phi; \tag{7}$$

$$M, \pi \models \phi_1 U \phi_2 \iff \exists d \geq 0 \text{ s.t. } M, \pi(d) \models \phi_2 \wedge \forall e < d, M, \pi(e) \models \phi_1; \tag{8}$$

$$M, \pi \models \phi_1 W \phi_2 \iff \forall d \geq 0, M, \pi(d) \models \phi_1 \vee \exists e \leq d \text{ s.t. } M, \pi(e) \models \phi_2. \tag{9}$$

Note that the remaining strategic operators can be expressed in terms of the previous three operators: $[\Gamma]\psi = \neg\langle\Gamma\rangle\neg\psi$, $G\phi = \phi \, W \, false$ and $F\phi = true \, U \, \phi$.

Due to space constraints, we only focus on strategic operators in this paper, but our approach can be employed for the remaining operators (our implementation has all the operators).

Standard Model-Checking Algorithm. The original algorithm consists in enumerating all the strategies of the model and accumulating, for each of them, the set of states for which the strategy is winning. Algorithm 1 is the original algorithm for evaluating the set of states satisfying a strategic operator; it uses Algorithm 2 for computing the set of strategies of the model as sets of moves and the function $eval_{IrF}(\langle\Gamma\rangle\psi, f_\Gamma)$ for computing the set of states for which strategy f_Γ is winning on ψ for Γ. The function $eval_{IrF}(\langle\Gamma\rangle\psi, f_\Gamma)$ relies on the function $Pre_{\langle\Gamma\rangle}(Z, f_\Gamma)$, defined as, given $f_\Gamma \subseteq S \times Act_\Gamma$ and $Z \subseteq S$,

$$Pre_{\langle\Gamma\rangle}(Z, f_\Gamma) = \{s | \forall a, f_\Gamma(s) \sqsubseteq a \implies img(s, a) \subseteq Z\}. \tag{10}$$

$Pre_{\langle\Gamma\rangle}(Z, f_\Gamma)$ computes the set of states for which Γ can force to reach states of Z in one step, by using the actions provided by f_Γ. $eval_{IrF}$ is defined using fix-point operations as

$$eval_{IrF}(\langle\Gamma\rangle X\phi, f_\Gamma) = Pre_{\langle\Gamma\rangle}(eval_{irF}(\phi) \cup NFair_{\langle\Gamma\rangle}(f_\Gamma), f_\Gamma) \tag{11}$$

$$eval_{IrF}(\langle\Gamma\rangle\phi_1 U \phi_2, f_\Gamma) =$$
$$\mu Z.\Phi \cap \left(\Phi_2 \cup \bigcup_{fc \in FC} Pre_{\langle\Gamma\rangle}\left(\nu Y. \frac{\Phi \cap (Z \cup \overline{fc}) \cap}{(\Phi_2 \cup Pre_{\langle\Gamma\rangle}(Y, f_\Gamma))}, f_\Gamma\right)\right) \tag{12}$$

$$eval_{IrF}(\langle\Gamma\rangle\phi_1 W \phi_2, f_\Gamma) = \nu Z.\Phi \cap \left(\Phi_2 \cup Pre_{\langle\Gamma\rangle}(Z, f_\Gamma)\right) \tag{13}$$

where

$$\overline{fc} = S \backslash fc, \tag{14}$$

$$\Phi = eval_{irF}(\phi_1) \cup eval_{irF}(\phi_2) \cup NFair_{\langle\Gamma\rangle}(f_\Gamma), \tag{15}$$

$$\Phi_2 = eval_{irF}(\phi_2), \tag{16}$$

$$NFair_{\langle\Gamma\rangle}(f_\Gamma) = \mu Z. \bigcup_{fc \in FC} Pre_{\langle\Gamma\rangle}(\nu Y.(Z \cup \overline{fc}) \cap Pre_{\langle\Gamma\rangle}(Y, f_\Gamma), f_\Gamma). \tag{17}$$

Given a set of moves SA, Algorithm 2 produces all the strategies only composed of moves of SA. When Algorithm 1 uses $Split(S \times Act_\Gamma)$ at Line 2, it gets all the strategies of the whole model.

Algorithm 1. $eval_{irF}(\langle\Gamma\rangle\psi)$

Data: Γ a set of agents of a model M, ψ an $ATLK_{irF}$ path formula.
Result: The set of states of M satisfying $\langle\Gamma\rangle\psi$.

$sat = \{\}$
2 **for** $f_\Gamma \in Split(S \times Act_\Gamma)$ **do**
$\quad\quad winning = eval_{IrF}(\langle\Gamma\rangle\psi, f_\Gamma)$
$\quad\quad sat = sat \cup \{s \in winning | \forall s' \sim_\Gamma s, s' \in winning\}$
return sat

The goal of $eval_{irF}(\langle\Gamma\rangle\psi)$ is to compute the set of states of the system that satisfy $\langle\Gamma\rangle\psi$, that is, the set of states for which there exists a winning strategy. For this, the algorithm has to produce and check all strategies of the entire model. But when we only need to know if some states satisfy the formula—for example, when we want to know if the initial states of the model satisfy $\langle\Gamma\rangle\psi$—we can improve this algorithm by only checking the partial strategies reachable from these states. We say that a strategy is partial if it provides moves for a subset of the states of the model.

Algorithm 2. $Split(SA)$

Data: Γ a given (implicit) subset of agents, $SA \subseteq S \times Act_\Gamma$.
Result: The set of all the strategies f_Γ composed only of moves of SA.

$conflicting = \{\langle s, a_\Gamma\rangle \in SA | \exists\langle s', a'_\Gamma\rangle \in SA \text{ s.t. } s' \sim_\Gamma s \wedge a_\Gamma \neq a'_\Gamma\}$
if $conflicting = \emptyset$ **then** **return** $\{SA\}$

else
$\quad\quad \langle s, a_\Gamma\rangle = $ **pick** one element in $conflicting$
$\quad\quad equivalent = \{\langle s', a'_\Gamma\rangle \in SA | s' \sim_\Gamma s\}$
$\quad\quad actions = \{a'_\Gamma \in Act_\Gamma | \exists\langle s, a'_\Gamma\rangle \in equivalent\}$
$\quad\quad substrats = Split(SA \backslash equivalent)$
$\quad\quad strats = \{\}$
$\quad\quad$ **for** $a_\Gamma \in actions$ **do**
$\quad\quad\quad\quad equivStrat = \{\langle s', a'_\Gamma\rangle \in equivalent | a'_\Gamma = a_\Gamma\}$
$\quad\quad\quad\quad strats = strats \cup \{equivStrat \cup substrat | substrat \in substrats\}$
$\quad\quad$ **return** $strats$

If a state in not reachable from the initial states through a given strategy, then it is useless to consider all the possible choices in this state, since no particular choice will modify the fact that the strategy is winning or not in the initial states. This is illustrated with the example in Figure 2. There are eight possible strategies, choosing one action per state; but if a strategy chooses action (1) in s_0, then the choice made in s_2 is irrelevant regarding the fact that the strategy is winning or not for s_0 because s_2 is not reachable from s_0 in this strategy. In fact, there are only four (partial) strategies to check to know if the initial state satisfies a given $\langle\Gamma\rangle\psi$ formula:

1. $\langle s_0, (1) \rangle, \langle s_1, (1) \rangle, \langle s_3, (1) \rangle$;   3. $\langle s_0, (2) \rangle, \langle s_2, (1) \rangle, \langle s_5, (1) \rangle$;
2. $\langle s_0, (1) \rangle, \langle s_1, (2) \rangle, \langle s_4, (1) \rangle$;   4. $\langle s_0, (2) \rangle, \langle s_2, (2) \rangle, \langle s_6, (1) \rangle$.

These partial strategies cover all the ways the agent can act from the initial state and are sufficient to know whether the initial state satisfies a strategic formula.

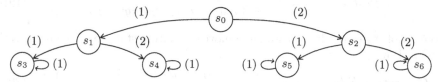

Fig. 2. A model where a strategy from the initial state s_0 makes a part of the model unreachable

3 Generating Partial Strategies

This section presents the notions of partial strategies and maximal partial strategies, and shows how to generate them. A partial strategy is a strategy that is defined for a subset of the states of the model.

Given a set of states $S' \subseteq S$, a partial strategy that contains a move for all $s \in S'$, and that contains a move for all states reachable from the moves it defines is called *maximal*. More formally, a partial strategy f_Γ is a maximal partial strategy reachable from S' iff

$$S' \subseteq dom(f_\Gamma) \wedge \forall \langle s, a_\Gamma \rangle \in f_\Gamma, \forall a \in Act, a_\Gamma \sqsubseteq a \implies img(s,a) \subseteq dom(f_\Gamma). \quad (18)$$

Such a strategy is uniform iff $\forall s, s' \in dom(f_\Gamma), s \sim_\Gamma s' \implies f_\Gamma(s) = f_\Gamma(s')$.

The main advantage of maximal partial strategies reachable from S' is that they can be used to check if there is a winning strategy for the states of S'.

Theorem 1. *Given a model $M = \langle Ag, S, Act, T, I, \{\sim_i\}_{i \in Ag}, V, FC \rangle$, a set of states $S' \subseteq S$ and a group of agents $\Gamma \subseteq Ag$, we have that for all $s \in S'$, $M, s \models \langle \Gamma \rangle \psi$ iff there exists a uniform maximal partial strategy f_Γ reachable from $[S']_\Gamma$ such that for all $s' \in [S']_\Gamma$, for all fair paths π of $out(s', f_\Gamma), M, \pi \models \psi$.*

Proof (Proof sketch). We can proof this theorem by showing that there exists a winning uniform strategy in $s' \in S'$ iff there exists a winning uniform maximal partial strategy reachable from $[S']_\Gamma$. Indeed, a strategy can be reduced to a partial one by removing unreachable moves, and a partial strategy can be augmented with moves in unreachable states, producing a complete strategy.

By Theorem 1, it is sufficient to check all maximal partial strategies reachable from $[S']_\Gamma$ to know whether there exists a winning strategy for the states of S'. Thus, if we are interested in the satisfaction of a strategic operator for only a subset of states S', it is sufficient to check the maximal partial strategies reachable from $[S']_\Gamma$. Before focusing on such a model-checking algorithm, we propose an algorithm to produce these maximal partial strategies.

Algorithm 3 can be used to generate the set of maximal partial strategies reachable from a set of states. It uses functions *Post*, *Compatible* and *Split*.

$Post(Z, f_\Gamma)$ is a version of the post-image computation modified to take actions present in f_Γ and states of Z into account. More formally, given $Z \subseteq S$ and a strategy $f_\Gamma \subseteq S \times Act_\Gamma$,

$$Post(Z, f_\Gamma) = \left\{ s \middle| \begin{array}{l} \exists \langle s', a'_\Gamma \rangle \in f_\Gamma, a' \in Act \text{ s.t.} \\ s' \in Z \wedge a'_\Gamma \sqsubseteq a' \wedge s \in img(s', a') \end{array} \right\}. \tag{19}$$

is the set of states reachable through a move of f_Γ from states of Z. *Compatible* is defined by

$$Compatible(Z, f_\Gamma) = \left\{ \langle s, a_\Gamma \rangle \middle| \begin{array}{l} s \in Z \wedge a_\Gamma \in enabled(s, \Gamma) \wedge \\ \nexists \langle s', a'_\Gamma \rangle \in f_\Gamma \text{ s.t. } s \sim_\Gamma s' \wedge a_\Gamma \neq a'_\Gamma \end{array} \right\}. \tag{20}$$

It returns the set of moves m, composed of states of Z and actions enabled in these states, such that m are not conflicting with any move of f_Γ. We say that two moves $\langle s, a_\Gamma \rangle$ and $\langle s', a'_\Gamma \rangle$ are conflicting iff $s \sim_\Gamma s'$ and $a_\Gamma \neq a'_\Gamma$, that is, if they propose different actions for states that are indistinguishable by Γ.

Given a partial strategy represented by a set of moves, Algorithm 3 returns the set of maximal partial strategies extending the given one. A partial strategy f'_Γ extends another partial strategy f_Γ if the choices made in f'_Γ match the choices in f_Γ, that is, if $f_\Gamma \subseteq f'_\Gamma$.

Algorithm 3. *ReachSplit$_\Gamma(f_\Gamma)$*

Data: Γ a subset of agents, $f_\Gamma \subseteq S \times Act_\Gamma$ a partial strategy.
Result: The set of maximal strategies extending f_Γ.

1 $new = Post(dom(f_\Gamma), strat) \backslash (dom(f_\Gamma))$
    if $new = \emptyset$ **then return** $\{f_\Gamma\}$

    else
5   $\quad$ $compatible = Compatible(new, f_\Gamma)$
    $\quad$ $newstrats = Split(compatible)$
    $\quad$ $strats = \{\}$
    $\quad$ **for** $f'_\Gamma \in newstrats$ **do** $strats = strats \cup ReachSplit_\Gamma(f_\Gamma \cup f'_\Gamma)$

    $\quad$ **return** $strats$

Algorithm 3 first gets the states reachable in one step from f_Γ that are not yet included in f_Γ (Line 1). These states are the states reachable in one step from f_Γ for which an action is not already chosen. If there are no such states, f_Γ is already maximal since a choice has already been made for each reachable state. Otherwise, we have to make some choices for *new* states. First, some uniform choices may have already been made through choices of f_Γ: if a new state s is indistinguishable from a state s' in f_Γ, the choice in s must follow the one in s'. Thus, we can remove from the choices possible in states of *new* all the choices that are conflicting with the ones in f_Γ (Line 5). After that, *compatible* can still contain conflicts, which are resolved by splitting *compatible* into strategies with *Split*. These strategies are compatible with f_Γ because all the potentially conflicting choices are removed at Line 5. Thus, any splitting f'_Γ of *compatible* combined with f_Γ is a partial strategy extending f_Γ and we can recursively call *ReachSplit* until all reachable states are encountered.

The correctness of Algorithm 3 is given by the following theorem.

Theorem 2. *Given a subset Γ of the agents of a model $M = \langle Ag, S, Act, T, I, \{\sim_i\}_{i \in Ag}, V, FC \rangle$ and a partial strategy represented by a set of moves f_Γ, the result of $ReachSplit_\Gamma(f_\Gamma)$ is the set of maximal strategies extending f_Γ.*

Finally, we can compute the set of maximal partial strategies reachable from S' by using *ReachSplit*: let *PartialStrats* be the function defined as

$$PartialStrats(S') = \bigcup \{ReachSplit_\Gamma(st) | st \in Split(Moves_\Gamma(S'))\}, \quad (21)$$

where $Moves_\Gamma(Z) = \{\langle s, a_\Gamma \rangle | s \in Z \wedge a_\Gamma \in enabled(s, \Gamma)\}$ is the set of moves that Γ can play from states of Z. $PartialStrats(S')$ computes the set of maximal partial strategies reachable from S'.

Theorem 3. *Given a model $M = \langle Ag, S, Act, T, I, \{\sim_i\}_{i \in Ag}, V, FC \rangle$, a subset Γ of the agents of M and a subset S' of states of M, $PartialStrats(S')$ is the set of maximal partial strategies reachable from S'.*

4   Model Checking $ATLK_{irF}$ with Partial Strategies

The number of partial strategies to consider to determine whether a group of agents Γ has a winning strategy in a subset of states S' can be substantially smaller than the overall number of strategies of the model (see Section 2). We can thus improve the model-checking algorithm for $ATLK_{irF}$ presented in Section 2 by using partial strategies. The idea is to only get the satisfaction of the formula in the states that matter, instead of getting it in all states of the system. For example, when checking whether a model satisfies $\langle \Gamma \rangle Fp$, we only need to know whether all the states indistinguishable from the initial states satisfy the formula, instead of knowing all states satisfying the formula. On the other hand, when checking $AG\langle \Gamma \rangle Fp$, we need to know whether all reachable states satisfy $\langle \Gamma \rangle Fp$ to say whether the formula is satisfied or not by all initial states.

Our algorithm keeps track of the set of states for which the satisfaction of the formula has to be known. Whenever an operator is evaluated, the algorithm is recursively called on the set of states in which the satisfaction of the top-level subformulas have to be known before evaluating the current operator. Given the initial states, the algorithm returns all the initial states satisfying the formula.

Given a set of states Z and a formula ϕ, Algorithm 4 returns the states of Z that satisfy ϕ. It works recursively on the structure of ϕ, and evaluates, on each step, the set of states in which it is necessary to know the satisfaction of the top-level subformulas. Due to space constraints, only the cases for strategic operators are presented. In these cases, the algorithm goes through all partial strategies reachable from Z and their indistinguishable states, and needs to know the satisfaction for the top-level subformulas in the states reachable by each partial strategy before computing the states of Z satisfying the main formula.

The goal of Algorithm 4 is to evaluate the satisfaction of the formula in as few states as possible. When dealing with strategic operators, the generation of partial strategies allows the algorithm to avoid a potentially large number of strategies. Note that, while it computes the partial strategies through a forward traversal of the model (see Section 3), it performs the evaluation of the states satisfying a given strategic operator with a backward traversal of the strategy.

Algorithm 4. $eval_{irF}^{Partial}(Z, \langle \Gamma \rangle \psi)$

Data: $Z \subseteq S$ a subset of states, $\langle \Gamma \rangle \psi$ an $ATLK_{irF}$ formula.
Result: The set of states of Z satisfying $\langle \Gamma \rangle \psi$.

$sat = \{\}$
2 **for** $f_\Gamma \in PartialStrats([Z]_\Gamma)$ **do**
3 $\quad$ **case** $\psi = X\phi'$
$\qquad$ $\Phi' = eval_{irF}^{Partial}(Post([Z]_\Gamma, f_\Gamma), \phi')$
5 $\qquad$ $win = Pre_{\langle \Gamma \rangle}(\Phi' \cup NFair_{\langle \Gamma \rangle}(f_\Gamma), f_\Gamma)$

$\quad$ **case** $\psi = \phi_1 U \phi_2$
$\qquad$ $\Phi_1 = eval_{irF}^{Partial}(dom(f_\Gamma), \phi_1); \ \Phi_2 = eval_{irF}^{Partial}(dom(f_\Gamma), \phi_2)$
8 $\qquad$ $win =$
$\qquad$ $\mu X.(\Phi_1 \cup \Phi_2 \cup NFair_{\langle \Gamma \rangle}(f_\Gamma)) \cap$
$\qquad$ $\left(\Phi_2 \cup \bigcup_{fc \in FC} Pre_{\langle \Gamma \rangle}\left(\nu Y. \frac{(\Phi_1 \cup \Phi_2 \cup NFair_{\langle \Gamma \rangle}(f_\Gamma))}{\cap (X \cup \overline{fc}) \cap (\Phi_2 \cup Pre_{\langle \Gamma \rangle}(Y, f_\Gamma))}, f_\Gamma \right) \right)$

$\quad$ **case** $\psi = \phi_1 W \phi_2$
$\qquad$ $\Phi_1 = eval_{irF}^{Partial}(dom(f_\Gamma), \phi_1); \ \Phi_2 = eval_{irF}^{Partial}(dom(f_\Gamma), \phi_2)$
11 $\qquad$ $win = \nu X.(\Phi_1 \cup \Phi_2 \cup NFair_{\langle \Gamma \rangle}(f_\Gamma)) \cap (\Phi_2 \cup Pre_{\langle \Gamma \rangle}(X, f_\Gamma))$
$\quad$ $sat = sat \cup \{s \in win \cap Z | \forall s' \sim_\Gamma s, s' \in win\}$
return sat

Finally, to get the set of initial states satisfying an $ATLK_{irF}$ formula ϕ, we can simply use Algorithm 4 on these initial states. The following theorem proves the correctness of Algorithm 4:

Theorem 4. *Given a model* $M = \langle Ag, S, Act, T, I, \{\sim_i\}_{i \in Ag}, V, FC \rangle$, *a set of states* $Z \subseteq S$ *and an* $ATLK_{irF}$ *formula* $\langle \Gamma \rangle \psi$, $eval_{irF}^{Partial}(Z, \langle \Gamma \rangle \psi)$ *is the subset of states of* Z *that satisfy* $\langle \Gamma \rangle \psi$.

The strategies considered by $ATLK_{irF}$ are slightly different from the strategies of ATL_{ir} [2]. $ATLK_{irF}$ considers the agents of Γ under supervision of a *virtual supervisor*, as in the case of ATL_{iR}^D, a variant of ATL_{ir} using distributed knowledge, perfect recall and partial observability [8]. On the other hand, ATL_{ir} considers that each agent acts independently and does not share his knowledge with the other agents of Γ. Nevertheless, the approach of this paper can be easily adapted to fit ATL_{ir} strategies: the notion of conflicting moves needs to be changed to take into account the knowledge of each agent individually instead of as a group, and the *Compatible* and *Split* algorithms must be adapted accordingly.

5   Further Optimisations

Several improvements can be added to Algorithm 4 to make it more efficient in common cases.

Checking Fewer Strategies by Early Termination. When dealing with a strategic operator $\langle \Gamma \rangle \psi$, $eval_{irF}^{Partial}$ goes through all partial strategies generated from $[Z]_\Gamma$ and accumulates in sat the subset of Z for which the current strategy is winning. The **for** loop at Line 2 could be terminated as soon as all states of Z are winning, that is, when $sat = Z$. In this case, we know that we found winning partial strategies for all states of Z and it is not necessary to check the remaining strategies. But if a state of Z does not satisfy $\langle \Gamma \rangle \psi$, all partial strategies must be checked. In the sequel, we call this improvement *full early termination*.

Following this idea, we could reconsider smaller strategies when sat grows. Indeed, when checking the strategies computed by $PartialStrats([Z]_\Gamma)$, we could recompute the smaller strategies reachable from $[Z]_\Gamma \backslash sat$ when states are added to sat, ignoring the part of these strategies taking sat states into account. This can be done by recomputing a new set of strategies whenever sat grows—we call this approach *partial early termination*.

We can also perform fewer recomputations of the strategies by recomputing them when the number of states of Z that are not in sat decreases under a certain threshold; the value given in the following is the threshold under which the part of the remaining states must be to trigger the recomputation of strategies. We call this approach *threshold-based early termination*.

The main drawback of the two last approaches is that parts of some strategies will be checked again, while we know they are not winning for the remaining states: indeed, when recomputing partial strategies for the remaining states, some of the new partial strategies will be parts of a partial strategy that has already been checked, and thus they cannot be winning for the remaining states.

Another approach to tackle this drawback would be to avoid recomputing the strategies and simply reduce the remaining ones to the moves reachable from the remaining states. In this case, we would need a mechanism to filter out the reduced strategies that are met multiple times. The current implementation (see next Section) only uses the approach of recomputing strategies.

Avoiding Recomputation of Subformulas with Caching. When the model-checking algorithm deals with a strategic operator $\langle \Gamma \rangle \psi$, it enumerates all partial strategies reachable from $[Z]_\Gamma$ and, for each of them, first computes the set of states of the strategy satisfying the top-level subformula(s) of ψ. This can perform a lot of redundant work since several strategies can share the same subpart of the model. We can improve this by accumulating, for each subformula of ψ, their satisfaction value in encountered states.

Note that there is a difference between this approach and the standard caching techniques for BDD-based CTL model checking. BDD-based CTL model checking keeps track of BDDs representing states satisfying a property; these BDDs do not change for different occurrences of a subformula since they represent *all* the states satisfying it. This mechanism can not be used here because subsets of states of interest change for different strategies, thus BDDs change, and these new BDDs must be completely recomputed. The caching mechanism we propose is to only recompute satisfaction for new states, and keep the results in two accumulated BDDs, avoiding to recompute strategies for states for which it has already been done.

Pre-filtering Out Losing Moves. A move is losing if it does not belong to a winning strategy. Experiments showed that pre-filtering out moves that are not winning under full observability can decrease the time needed to check a strategic operator [3]. We can include this improvement in $eval_{irF}^{Partial}$ by pre-filtering the state space reachable from $[Z]_\Gamma$ before building the partial strategies, and only consider the remaining submodel. This can lead to ignoring a large part of the system if this part cannot be winning, reducing the number of choices to make and the number of strategies to consider.

6 Experiments

The algorithm generating partial strategies shown in Section 3, the model-checking algorithm presented in Section 4 and the improvements discussed in Section 5 have been implemented with PyNuSMV, a Python framework for prototyping and experimenting with BDD-based model-checking algorithms based on NuSMV [9]. The implementation has been tested on two different models and several $ATLK_{irF}$ formulas.

The first model is another variant of the card game from [5]. The game is composed of two players—the player and the dealer—and n cards. The n cards $c_1, ..., c_n$ are such that c_i wins over c_j if $i > j$ or $i = 1$ and $j = n$. The game is played in four steps: 1) the dealer gives one card to himself; 2) he gives one card to the player; 3) the player can choose to keep his card or to ask for another, but cannot get back a card he discarded before; 4) the game stops when the player chooses to keep his card or when the stack of cards is empty. The winner of the game, known during the last step, is the one with the winning card. The game can then be repeated infinitely many times and the dealer is fair, that is, if the game is repeated infinitely many times, the dealer gives the cards in each possible order infinitely many times.

The second model is inspired from the ancient tale of Tian Ji. It is composed of two agents: Tian Ji and the king. Both agents have n horses $h_1, ..., h_n$ and horse h_i wins over h_j if $i > j$; if $i = j$, the winner is chosen non-deterministically. Their game is as follows: Tian Ji and the king go for n races, with n different horses. They can choose their own horses in the order they want, but do not know the horse the opponent chose. The winner is the one with the most won races. The game can then be repeated infinitely many times and the king is fair, that is, if the game is repeated infinitely many times, the king will choose his horses in each possible order infinitely many times.

Several $ATLK_{irF}$ formulas have been checked on each model to assess the impact of partial strategies and the improvements presented in Section 5. These formulas are listed in Table 1. They use different atomic propositions; for example, $playerWins$ is true when the game is done (at the fourth step) and the card of the player wins over the dealer's card; $playerHasFirst$ is true when the player has card c_1. Similarly, $tianjiWins$ is true when the game is done (all horses have been used) and Tian Ji won more races than the king; $tianjiLostUpToNow$ is true when Tian Ji has lost all races since the beginning of the game.

Table 1. Formulas checked over the models of the card game and Tian Ji's race

Card game formulas	Tian Ji's race formulas
$\langle player \rangle F\ playerWins$	$\langle tianji \rangle F\ tianjiWins$
$\langle player \rangle F\ (playerWins \wedge playerHasFirst)$	
$\langle player \rangle G\ \langle player \rangle F\ playerWins$	$\langle tianji \rangle G\ \langle tianji \rangle F\ tianjiWins$
$\langle player \rangle F \langle player \rangle [\neg dealerWins\ U\ playerWins]$	$\langle tianji \rangle F\ \langle tianji \rangle [\neg kingWins\ U\ tianjiWins]$
$AF \langle player \rangle X\ playerHasFirst$	$\langle tianji \rangle X\ tianjiLostUpToNow$
$AG(FirstStep \implies \neg \langle player \rangle X\ playerWins)$	$\langle tianji \rangle G\ \langle tianji \rangle X\ tianjiWon < 2Races$

These formulas are intended to test the proposed algorithms under different circumstances. For example, the formula $\langle tianji \rangle F\ tianjiWins$ must only be checked over the initial states. In this case, partial strategies should help since the number of strategies to check substantially decreases. On the other hand, for the formula $\langle tianji \rangle G\ \langle tianji \rangle F\ tianjiWins$, the $\langle tianji \rangle F\ tianjiWins$ subformula must be evaluated on all states, and partial strategies do not help. Other formulas, like $AF \langle player \rangle X\ playerHasFirst$, are used to test the improvements presented in Section 5. In this case, the $\langle player \rangle X\ playerHasFirst$ subformula is true in a significantly small subset of the states, thus pre-filtering out losing moves before generating partial strategies should help.

A first set of tests have been performed to assess the efficiency of the model-checking algorithm of Section 4 compared to the original algorithm presented in Section 2. For each formula of Table 1, the size of the model to check has been increased and both model-checking algorithms have been run with a limit of 15 minutes. Some of the results are shown in Table 2. They show that using partial strategies can improve the efficiency of the process: for example, for the specification $\langle player \rangle F\ playerWins$, and even more for $\langle tianji \rangle F\ tianjiWins$, the time needed for the verification is significantly decreased. This is due to the fact that in these cases, we are interested in the existence of winning strategies in the initial states, and thus the number of strategies to consider is smaller. On the other hand, for the specification $AF\ \langle player \rangle X\ playerHasFirst$, we need to know the satisfaction of the inner strategic operator in all reachable states, and thus the verification does not run faster.

A second set of tests have been performed to assess the impact of the proposed improvements. Each formula of Table 1 has been checked with partial strategies on models of increasing sizes, with all combinations of improvements of Section 5 and with the same limit of 15 minutes. This resulted in a huge set of time results that have been analyzed with box plots. More precisely, for each formula, each improvement type and each size of the model, a box plot has been drawn showing the time results for each possible value of the improvement. For example, Figure 3 shows the box plots for times to check the formula $\langle tianji \rangle F\ tianjiWins$ for 3 to 5 horses, grouped by value of early termination. The box plots show, for a given parameter, the time needed for model checking the property when the parameter takes a particular value. This means that, in a box plot, a single box

Table 2. Execution times of the original algorithm and the algorithm based on partial strategies, for some formulas checked over the card game and the problem of Tian Ji

Formula	Size	# States	Original algorithm	Partial strategies
$\langle player \rangle F\ playerWins$	3	28	$0m2.527s$	$0m2.603s$
	4	101	$0m8.035s$	$0m8.205s$
	5	326	$0m34.937s$	$0m30.885s$
	6	967	$2m14.461s$	$1m39.931s$
	7	2696	$> 15m$	$9m46.126s$
$\langle tianji \rangle F\ tianjiWins$	3	61	$0m5.388s$	$0m2.489s$
	4	409	$> 15m$	$0m25.172s$
$AF\langle player \rangle X\ playerHasFirst$	3	28	$0m1.506s$	$0m1.444s$
	6	967	$0m39.285s$	$0m38.535s$
	8	7177	$11m37.270s$	$12m9.149s$
	9	18442	$> 15m$	$> 15m$

represent the model-checking time when the other parameters vary. Thus, if a box is much lower than another, this means that whatever the other parameters are, the first parameter value gives better performances than the other.

From these box plots, we analyzed the effect of each improvement value on the time needed to model check a formula. For example, the box plots of Figure 3 show that when checking the formula $\langle tianji \rangle F\ tianjiWins$, early termination really decreases the time needed, but the kind of early termination used has no significant impact; this is expected since the formula is satisfied in all states with all strategies, and the model checking algorithm stops at the first strategy (instead of having to check all of them if early termination is deactivated).

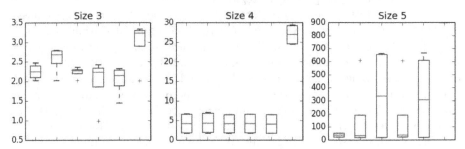

Fig. 3. Box plot of time (in seconds) needed for checking the formula $\langle tianji \rangle F\ tianjiWins$ with 3 to 5 horses. In each plot, boxes represent measures with different type of early termination (from left to right): threshold (trigger value: 0.9), partial, threshold (trigger value: 0.1), threshold (trigger value: 0.5), full, no early termination. On the third box plot, model checking exceeded the limit of 900 seconds for all checks without early termination.

The box plots of Figure 4 show that, when model checking the formula $\langle tianji \rangle G\ \langle tianji \rangle X\ tianjiWon < 2Races$, filtering can really decrease the time needed for the verification. This is expected since the $\langle tianji \rangle X\ tianjiWon < 2Races$ subformula is true in a small subset of the states, reducing the number of strategies to consider.

Finally, the box plots of Figure 5 show that, when checking the formula $\langle player \rangle G\ \langle player \rangle F\ playerWins$ without early termination, caching really helps. This is expected because without early termination, all strategies must be checked;

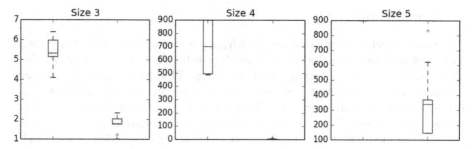

Fig. 4. Box plot of time (in seconds) needed for checking the formula $\langle tianji \rangle G \ \langle tianji \rangle X \ tianjiWon < 2Races$ with 3 to 5 horses. In each plot, boxes represent measures without filtering and with filtering (from left to right). On the third box plot, model checking exceeded the limit of 900 seconds for all checks without filtering.

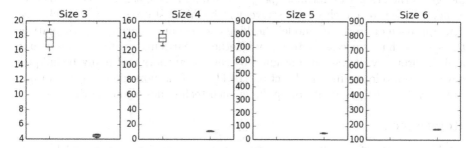

Fig. 5. Box plot of time (in seconds) needed for checking the formula $\langle player \rangle G \ \langle player \rangle F \ playerWins$ with 3 to 6 cards. In each plot, boxes represent measures without caching and with caching (from left to right), when early termination is not activated. On the last two box plots, model checking exceeded the limit of 900 seconds for all checks without caching.

thus, a lot of redundant work is performed to get the states satisfying the subformula and this redundant work is avoided with caching.

The conclusions we can make based on the test results are the following.

– Activating pre-filtering can greatly improve the process—when there is only a small part of the model that satisfies the formula under full observability—but can also generate unnecessary work when this is not the case, and this can become significant when the number of strategies is small—for example, when early termination is activated. This improvement can thus be helpful in certain cases, but decreases performances for some other cases.
– Activating early termination has, at worst, no impact. It should always be activated since it can greatly improve the verification time when most of the strategies are winning. However, the performed tests did not show a type of early termination better than the others;
– Caching increases performances in some of the tests above; for the others, it has no impact. It should thus be always activated.

7 Conclusion

The model-checking algorithm for $ATLK_{irF}$ presented in [3] is in many cases inefficient because it blindly enumerates all possible strategies to check whether there exists a winning strategy in some states. This paper has presented an approach to generate fewer strategies when we are interested in whether there exists a winning strategy in a small subset of the states of the model. More precisely, we proposed to generate partial strategies reachable from a subset of states of the model that are sufficient to determine the satisfaction of a strategic formula in these states. Based on the generation of these partial strategies, a new algorithm has been designed and the experimental results showed that in a number of cases, the new approach is more efficient than the original one.

While the presented model-checking algorithm clearly improves the efficiency of the verification, it may still be improved along different directions. For example, given the $ATLK_{irF}$ formula $\langle player \rangle F\ playerWins$, it is in theory not necessary to generate and check any strategy if the initial states satisfy $playerWins$. The approach of on-the-fly model checking consists in exploring only the part of the system that is necessary to know whether a particular state satisfies or not a given property. It has been studied by several authors and many techniques have been developed in this direction [10,11,12]. One possible extension of our work involves the possibility of applying such techniques to our setting.

References

1. Alur, R., Henzinger, T.A., Kupferman, O.: Alternating-time temporal logic. J. ACM 49(5), 672–713 (2002)
2. Schobbens, P.Y.: Alternating-time logic with imperfect recall. Electronic Notes in Theoretical Computer Science 85(2), 82–93 (2004)
3. Busard, S., Pecheur, C., Qu, H., Raimondi, F.: Reasoning about strategies under partial observability and fairness constraints. In: SR, pp. 71–79 (2013)
4. Dastani, M., Jamroga, W.: Reasoning about strategies of multi-agent programs. Proceedings of AAMAS 10, 997–1004 (2010)
5. Jamroga, W., van der Hoek, W.: Agents that know how to play. Fundamenta Informaticae 63(2), 185–219 (2004)
6. Clarke, E.M., Grumberg, O., Peled, D.: Model Checking. MIT Press (1999)
7. Fagin, R., Halpern, J.Y., Moses, Y., Vardi, M.Y.: Reasoning about Knowledge. MIT Press, Cambridge (1995)
8. Dima, C., Enea, C., Guelev, D.: Model-checking an alternating-time temporal logic with knowledge, imperfect information, perfect recall and communicating coalitions. In: GANDALF, pp. 103–117 (2010)
9. Busard, S., Pecheur, C.: PyNuSMV: NuSMV as a python library. In: Brat, G., Rungta, N., Venet, A. (eds.) NFM 2013. LNCS, vol. 7871, pp. 453–458. Springer, Heidelberg (2013)
10. Stirling, C., Walker, D.: Local model checking in the modal mu-calculus. In: Díaz, J., Orejas, F. (eds.) TAPSOFT 1989. LNCS, vol. 351, pp. 369–383. Springer, Heidelberg (1989)
11. Bhat, G., Cleaveland, R., Grumberg, O.: Efficient on-the-fly model checking for ctl. In: LICS 1995, pp. 388–397 (1995)
12. Mateescu, S.: Efficient on-the-fly model-checking for regular alternation-free mu-calculus. Science of Computer Programming 46(3), 255–281 (2003)

A Formal Model for Natural-Language Timed Requirements of Reactive Systems

Gustavo Carvalho[1,3], Ana Carvalho[2], Eduardo Rocha[1],
Ana Cavalcanti[3], and Augusto Sampaio[1]

[1] Universidade Federal de Pernambuco - Centro de Informática, 50740-560, Brazil
[2] Universidade Federal de Pernambuco - NTI, 50670-901, Brazil
[3] University of York - Department of Computer Science, YO10 5GH, UK
{ghpc,ebr,acas}@cin.ufpe.br, ana.alves@ufpe.br, ana.cavalcanti@york.ac.uk

Abstract. To analyse the behaviour of reactive systems formally, it is necessary to build a model. At the very beginning of the development, typically only natural language requirements are documented. We present a formal model, named Data-Flow Reactive Systems (DFRS), which can be automatically obtained from natural language requirements that may also describe temporal properties. We prove that a DFRS can be mapped to a timed input-output transition system, which is widely used to characterise conformance relations for timed reactive systems. To validate the proposed model as well as the mechanisation developed to support its analysis, we consider two toy examples and two examples from the aerospace and automotive industry. Test cases are independently created and we verify that they are all compatible.

Keywords: Model mapping, TIOTS, test-case generation.

1 Introduction

The need to model the behaviour of a system may become an obstacle to the use of formal methods as the requirements are commonly written in Natural Language (NL). In 2009, the Federal Aviation Administration (FAA) published a report [12] that discusses current practices concerning requirements engineering management. The report states that "*... the overwhelming majority of the survey respondents indicated that requirements are being captured as English text...*".

With this in mind, we have investigated how we can obtain formal models from NL requirements of reactive systems automatically, particularly to generate test cases. Automation is essential, since requiring knowledge of formal modelling by practitioners is often not feasible. Automation also allows an early application of formal methods within the development of reactive systems. To accomplish this goal, we have previously developed a strategy (NAT2TEST) that generates test cases from NL requirements based on different internal and hidden formalisms: SCR [14] (NAT2TEST$_{SCR}$ [8]), and IMR [18] (NAT2TEST$_{IMR}$ [6]).

Both in [8] and in [6], the input is NL requirements. The first phase of the test-generation strategy is a Syntactic Analysis to generate a syntax tree. The second

S. Merz and J. Pang (Eds.): ICFEM 2014, LNCS 8829, pp. 43–58, 2014.

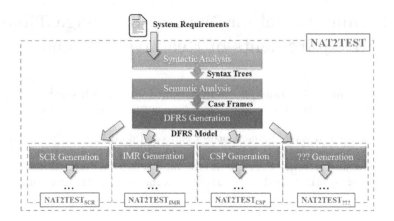

Fig. 1. The NAT2TEST Strategy

phase is a Semantic Analysis, which maps the syntax trees into an informal semantic representation based on the Case Grammar theory [13].

Based on the experience of generating test cases using two different formal representations, and with the perspective of instantiating our approach to several other target notations, translating the NL requirements to an intermediate formal notation is a more promising alternative, since the translation from a NL is a more elaborate task. Then, from an intermediate, and formal, representation, one might explore different target notations and analyse the system from several perspectives, using different languages and tools. For example, one might want to generate SCR code and then use T-VEC [2] to generate test cases, as already mentioned, but also to analyse the completeness and disjointness of system requirements [3]. As another example, it is possible to generate CSP models and use tools like FDR[1] to prove both classical and domain specific properties of the system requirements.

Therefore, a new architecture for our strategy, which is based on the generation of an intermediate notation from NL requirements, is presented in Figure 1. Our focus here is the third step of this strategy (*DFRS Generation*) and the DFRS (Data-Flow Reactive System) model that it generates.

Our claim that a DFRS is a good candidate for such an intermediate notation comes from a theoretical and an empirical perspective. First, as we detail in this paper, a DFRS can be characterised as a Timed Input-Output Transition System (TIOTS) – a labelled transition system extended with time, which is widely used to characterise conformance relations for timed reactive systems. Being more abstract than a TIOTS, a DFRS comprises a more concise representation of timed requirements. Second, we have so far derived two different formal models from NL requirements (namely, SCR [8] and IMR [6]), besides other notations that are currently being considered, and the DFRS model encompass the information required to derive models in these notations.

---

[1] https://www.cs.ox.ac.uk/projects/fdr/

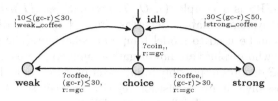

Fig. 2. The Vending Machine Specification

In [10] we briefly present our first ideas of a DFRS as it is used as a source model to derive a CSP specification, which is later used within the context of a timed conformance relation. Here, we formalise the definition and properties of a DFRS, using Z [15] with the support of Z/EVES [19]. We also prove that a DFRS can be characterised as a Timed Input-Output Transition System

To evaluate the expressiveness of DFRSs, we consider examples from four domains: a Vending Machine (VM — toy example); a control system for safety injection in a Nuclear Power Plant (NPP — toy example), a Priority Command (PC) control provided by Embraer[2]; and the Turn Indicator System (TIS) of Mercedes vehicles. Test cases are independently generated for each example, and we assess whether they are compatible with those generated using a DFRS.

The main contributions of this paper are a formalisation of DFRSs, a theoretical and a practical analysis of these models, and a strategy to generate DFRSs from NL requirements automatically.

Next section gives the formal definition of a DFRS. Section 3 defines a TIOTS and how any DFRS can be mapped to a TIOTS. Section 4 describes how a DFRS can be automatically obtained from NL requirements. Section 5 considers the test cases of our examples for an empirical analysis of DFRSs. Finally, Section 6 presents our conclusions, and addresses related and future work.

2   Definition and Properties of a DFRS

To illustrate our work, we consider a toy example — the Vending Machine (VM) presented in Figure 2 as a timed statechart — it is an adaptation of the Coffee Machine in [16]. We present this statechart just for a concise illustration of the structure of DFRSs. The input of our strategy is NL requirements.

Initially, the VM is in an *idle* state. When it receives a coin, it goes to the *choice* state and resets the *reqTimer* (r in Figure 2) clock. This assigns the current global time (gc) to this variable. After inserting a coin, when the coffee option is selected, the system goes to the *weak* or *strong* coffee state. If coffee is selected within 30 seconds after inserting the coin, the system goes to the *weak coffee* state. Otherwise, it goes to the *strong coffee* state. The time required to produce a weak coffee is also different from that of a strong coffee.

---

[2] www.embraer.com.br

Formally, a DFRS is a 7-tuple: $(I, O, T, gcvar, S, s_0, TR)$. Inputs (I) and outputs (O) are system variables, whereas timers (T) are a distinct kind of variable, which can be used to model temporal behaviour. The global clock is $gcvar$, a variable whose values are non-negative numbers representing a discrete or a dense time. S denotes a (possibly infinite) set of states, s_0 is the initial state, and TR is a (possibly infinite) transition relation between states.

Below, we describe a formal definition of a DFRS available in full in [7].

2.1   Inputs, Outpus and Timers

We use a given set $NAME$ containing the set of all valid variable names, and define gc to be the name of the system global clock $(gc : NAME)$. Also $VNAME$ is the set of all system variables except for the global clock $(NAME \setminus \{gc\})$.

Based on these definitions, we define $SVARS$ and $STIMERS$ to represent inputs and outputs (defined later as different mappings of the same type $SVARS$), and timers, respectively, as partial functions from $VNAME$ to $TYPE$. In this work, we consider as valid types boolean and numerical types (*bool, int, nat, float, p_float* – where *p_float* represents non-negative floating-point numbers). We restrict our model to these types as they are sufficient to describe the considered domain of requirements – embedded reactive systems whose inputs and outputs can be seen as signals. Despite that, one can expand the model to incorporate new types.

$$SVARS == \{f : VNAME \nrightarrow TYPE \mid f \neq \emptyset \wedge \operatorname{ran} f \subseteq \{bool, int, float\}\}$$
$$STIMERS == \{f : VNAME \nrightarrow TYPE \mid \operatorname{ran} f = \{nat\} \vee \operatorname{ran} f = \{p\_float\}\}$$

The functions f in $SVARS$ are not empty: the system needs to have at least one input and one output variable. Differently, one can have a system without timers, that is, a DFRS whose behaviour is not dependent on time elapsing.

The possible types of an element of $SVARS$ are *bool, int* and *float*. The types *nat* and *p_float* are used to restrict the possible values of timers since time is a non-negative number. Besides that, the type of all timers must be the same: you can analyse the behaviour of the system discretely or continuously, but not in both ways simultaneously.

Example. Besides the system global clock, five variables are identified in the context of the VM example: two system inputs (*coin sensor, coffee request button*), two outputs (*system mode, coffee machine output*), and one timer (*request timer*) whose types are *bool, nat*, and *p_float*, respectively.   □

2.2   States

A state is a relation between names and values $(STATE == NAME \nrightarrow VALUE)$. $VALUE$ is a free type that includes booleans and numerical values. As float numbers are not part of Standard Z, we declare them as given sets. Despite being out of the scope of this work, it is possible to represent float numbers in Z. For more details, refer, for instance, to ProofPower-Z[3].

The valuation of a variable n defined to have a type t is well typed in a state s if, and only if, n belongs to the domain of s, and the value associated with n in s belongs to the set of possible values of t. The function *values* yields all possible values of a specific type t. This property of well typedness for variables in the context of a state is captured by the following predicate.

$$well\_typed\_var : \mathbb{P}(STATE \times NAME \times TYPE)$$

$$\forall s : STATE;\ n : NAME;\ t : TYPE;\ v : VALUE \mid$$
$$n \in \operatorname{dom} s \land s(n) = v \bullet (s, n, f(n)) \in well\_typed\_var \Leftrightarrow v \in values(t)$$

Considering a set f of variables (names related to types), a state s is well typed if, and only if, it provides a value for each variable (that is, its domain is that of the function f) and those variables are well typed in s.

$$well\_typed\_state : \mathbb{P}(STATE \times (NAME \nrightarrow TYPE))$$

$$\forall s : STATE;\ f : NAME \nrightarrow TYPE \bullet$$
$$(s, f) \in well\_typed\_state \Leftrightarrow \operatorname{dom} s = \operatorname{dom} f \land$$
$$(\forall n : \operatorname{dom} f;\ t : TYPE \mid f(n) = t \bullet (s, n, t) \in well\_typed\_var)$$

The set of states is defined as a (possibly infinite) non-empty set of states ($STATE\_SET == \mathbb{P}_1\ STATE$), since it must contain at least an initial state.

Example. Considering the VM example, a possible initial state of the corresponding DFRS is the following.

$$\{(\text{coin sensor} \mapsto b(\mathit{false})), (\text{coffee request button} \mapsto b(\mathit{false}),$$
$$(\text{system mode} \mapsto n(1)), (\text{coffee machine output} \mapsto n(1)),$$
$$(\text{request timer} \mapsto p\_fl(0.0)), (\text{system global clock} \mapsto p\_fl(0.0))\}$$

where b, n, and p_fl are free type constructors associated with boolean values, natural numbers, and non-negative floating-point values, respectively. We consider that *false* is used to represent that a coin was not inserted, as well as that the coffee request button was not pressed. Regarding the variables *system mode* and *coffee machine output*, the natural numbers represent elements of an enumeration of possible values: $\{0 \mapsto choice,\ 1 \mapsto idle,\ 2 \mapsto preparing\ strong\ coffee,\ 3 \mapsto preparing\ weak\ coffee\}$, and $\{0 \mapsto strong,\ 1 \mapsto undefined,\ 2 \mapsto weak\}$.   □

2.3   Transitions

A transition relates two states by means of a label. A label represents the occurrence of a functional behaviour (*fun*) or time elapsing (*del*).

$$TRANS == (STATE \times TRANS\_LABEL \times STATE)$$
$$TRANS\_LABEL ::= fun \langle\!\langle FUNCTION\_ENTRY \rangle\!\rangle \mid$$
$$del \langle\!\langle DELAY \times STMT\_SET \rangle\!\rangle$$

---

[3] http://www.lemma-one.com/ProofPower/index/index.html

Function Transition. With the system behaviour defined as a function that describes how the system reacts in a given scenario, the occurrence of a function transition leads to the application of an entry of this function. A function entry models a scenario as a pair of static and timed guards, related to a set of statements. When both guards evaluate to true, the system reacts instantly performing the set of statements. One of the guards can be empty, but not both.

$$FUNCTION\_ENTRY ==$$
$$\{sGuard, tGuard : EXP;\ stmts : STMT\_SET\ |\ sGuard \cup tGuard \neq \emptyset\}$$

The guards are expressions whose structure adheres to a Conjunctive Normal Form: a finite set of conjunctions of disjunctions, where each disjunction is a non-empty binary expression. Above, *EXP* refers to the set of such expressions. Each binary expression is a static or a timed expression. A binary expression is said to be static if, and only if, the name it mentions is the name of a system input or output. Otherwise, it is a timed expression. Similarly, a guard is static (or timed) if all its conjunctions and disjunctions are static (or timed). A statement ($STMT == VNAME \times VALUE$) is an assignment of a value to a name, and $STMT\_SET$ a non-empty set of statements ($STMT\_SET == \mathbb{F}_1\ STMT$).

Delay Transition. Time elapsing is characterised by a delay and a set of statements, which model stimuli from the environment that happens immediately after the delay. A delay can represent a discrete or dense time elapsing. The former delay is characterised by a positive natural number ($\mathbb{N}_1$), whereas the latter by a positive float number (P_FLOAT_1), which is a subset of P_FLOAT.

$$DELAY ::= discrete\langle\!\langle \mathbb{N}_1 \rangle\!\rangle\ |\ dense\langle\!\langle P\_FLOAT_1 \rangle\!\rangle$$

Based on these definitions, we define the DFRS transition relation as a set of transitions ($TRANSREL == \mathbb{P}\ TRANS$). Each transition must be well typed. A function transition is well typed if, and only if, the statements of its label modify only values of outputs and timers. In other words, the system does not interfere with the environment stimuli, which is modelled by the input variables.

$$well\_typed\_function\_transition : \mathbb{P}(TRANS\_LABEL\times$$
$$(VNAME \nrightarrow TYPE) \times (VNAME \nrightarrow TYPE)\times$$
$$(VNAME \nrightarrow TYPE))$$

$\forall\ trans : TRANS\_LABEL;\ I, O : VNAME \nrightarrow TYPE;$
$T : VNAME \nrightarrow TYPE\ |\ trans \in \operatorname{ran} fun\ \bullet$
$\quad (trans, I, O, T) \in well\_typed\_function\_transition \Leftrightarrow$
$\quad (\forall\ stmt : (functionTransition(trans)).3\ \bullet$
$\qquad stmt.1 \in \operatorname{dom} O \cup \operatorname{dom} T)\ \wedge$
$\quad ((functionTransition(trans)).1, I, O) \in static\_exp\ \wedge$
$\quad ((functionTransition(trans)).2, T) \in timed\_exp$

Furthermore, the first guard of a function entry must be static, whereas the second must be timed. To formalise these requirements, we rely on an auxiliary

function ($functionTransition : TRANS\_LABEL \nrightarrow FUNCTION\_ENTRY$) that
extracts the corresponding function entry given a transition label. We note that
the notation $.i$ is used to refer to the projection of the i-th element of a tuple.

Similarly, a delay transition is well typed if, and only if, its statements modify
only values of inputs. Furthermore, there must be one statement concerning each
input, that is, on the occurrence of each delay transition, the system receives the
current value of all its inputs.

Moreover, the delay transitions need to be compatible with the global clock,
that is, if the delay is discrete, the type of the system global time must be
nat, whereas if the delay is dense, the type of the clock must be *p_float*. As
a consequence, all delay transitions share the same type of delay, that is, they
are all discrete or dense. This is captured by the *clock_compatible_transition*
property.

$$clock\_compatible\_transition : \mathbb{P}(TRANS\_LABEL \times (\{gc\} \rightarrow TYPE))$$

$$\forall trans : TRANS\_LABEL;\ gcvar : \{gc\} \nrightarrow TYPE \bullet$$
$$(trans, gcvar) \in clock\_compatible\_transition \Leftrightarrow trans \in \operatorname{ran} del \wedge$$
$$(((delayTransition(trans)).1 \in \operatorname{ran} discrete \wedge \operatorname{ran} gcvar = \{nat\}) \vee$$
$$((delayTransition(trans)).1 \in \operatorname{ran} dense \wedge \operatorname{ran} gcvar = \{p\_float\}))$$

From these definitions, a transition is said to be well typed (*well_typed_transition*)
if it satisfies the restrictions for function and delay transitions defined above.

Example. If s_0 is the initial state presented in Section 2.2, inserting a coin after
3.14 time units is represented by the following entry in the transition relation.
$(s_0, del(dense(3.1), \{(\text{coin sensor}, b(true)), (\text{coffee request button}, b(false))\}), s_1)$.
It leads to a new state, named s_1 □

2.4   Complete Definition

The variables of a DFRS (I, O, T, and $gcvar$) are defined by the *DFRS_Variables*
schema. It defines that the set of inputs, outputs and timers are disjoint, and
the type of the timers is equal to that of the system global clock.

$$\_\_DFRS\_Variables\_\_$$
$$I, O : SVARS;\ T : STIMERS;\ gcvar : \{gc\} \rightarrow \{nat, p\_float\}$$
$$\text{disjoint } \langle \operatorname{dom} I, \operatorname{dom} O, \operatorname{dom} T \rangle \wedge \operatorname{ran} T = \operatorname{ran} gcvar$$

The initial state and the set of states of a DFRS (s_0, S) are defined by the
following schema. The initial state of the DFRS is an element of its set of states.

$$DFRS\_States == [S : STATE\_SET;\ s_0 : STATE \mid s_0 \in S]$$

The transition relation (*TR*) is defined in *DFRS_TransitionRelation*, which establishes that for each state, it is not possible to have both function and delay

transitions; that is, or the system receives stimuli from the environment or reacts to it, but not both at the same state.

```
__ DFRS_TransitionRelation _____
 TR : TRANSREL
_____
 ∀ entry1, entry2 : TR | entry1.1 = entry2.1 •
     {entry1.2, entry2.2} ⊆ ran fun ∨ {entry1.2, entry2.2} ⊆ ran del
```

Finally, a DFRS is defined formally by the following schema that includes the three previous schemas. It establishes that each state in S is well typed with respect to the system variables. As a consequence we impose that the same name cannot be associated with values of different types in different states. We also enforce that TR relates states of S, and each transition is well typed.

```
__ DFRS _____
 DFRS_Variables
 DFRS_States
 DFRS_TransitionRelation
_____
 ∀ s : S • (s, I ∪ O ∪ T) ∈ well_typed_state
 ∀ entry : TR • {entry.1, entry.3} ⊆ S ∧
     (entry.2, I, O, T, gcvar) ∈ well_typed_transition
```

This structure is rich enough to represent requirements written using several different sentence formations in the context of a variety of application domains.

3 Theoretical Validation: Mapping DFRSs to TIOTSs

An important validation is the definition of the semantics of a DFRS. We show here that any DFRS can be mapped to a corresponding TIOTS.

3.1 Definition and Properties of a TIOTS

A TIOTS is a 6-tuple (Q, q_0, I, O, D, T), where Q is a (possibly infinite) set of states, q_0 is the initial state, I represents input actions and O output actions, D is a set of delays, and T is a (possibly infinite) transition relation relating states.

Inputs and Outputs. $TIOTS\_ACTION$ is a given set of all valid actions, that is, inputs and outputs, and $TIOTS\_ACTIONS$ the set of sets of actions.

Delays. A TIOTS delay represents a discrete or a dense time elapsing, but differently from a DFRS delay, a delay in a TIOTS can also be 0.

$$TIOTS\_DELAY ::= tiots\_discrete\langle\!\langle \mathbb{N} \rangle\!\rangle \mid tiots\_dense\langle\!\langle P\_FLOAT \rangle\!\rangle$$

$TIOTS\_DELAYS$ is defined as a set of $TIOTS\_DELAY$.

States. A state of a TIOTS is an element of the given set *TIOTS_STATE*, and *TIOTS_STATE_SET* is a non-empty set of states ($\mathbb{P}_1$ *TIOTS_STATE*).

Transition Relation. The transition relation (*TIOTS_TRANSREL*) relates two states by means of a label (*TIOTS_TRANS_LABEL*). A label may concern an input or output action, a delay, or an internal invisible action (τ – *tau*).

$$TIOTS\_TRANS\_LABEL ::= in \langle\!\langle TIOTS\_ACTION \rangle\!\rangle \mid$$
$$out \langle\!\langle TIOTS\_ACTION \rangle\!\rangle \mid tiots\_del \langle\!\langle TIOTS\_DELAY \rangle\!\rangle \mid tau$$
$$TIOTS\_TRANS == (TIOTS\_STATE \times$$
$$TIOTS\_TRANS\_LABEL \times TIOTS\_STATE)$$
$$TIOTS\_TRANSREL == \mathbb{P}\, TIOTS\_TRANS$$

Complete Definition. *TIOTS_Variables* defines input and output actions as disjoint sets, besides defining a set of delays, which needs to be time compatible (*tiots_time_compatible*): all delays must be of the same type (discrete or dense).

TIOTS_Variables

$I, O : TIOTS\_ACTIONS$; $D : TIOTS\_DELAYS$

disjoint $\langle I, O \rangle \land D \in tiots\_time\_compatible$

A TIOTS comprises a set of states and the initial state is in this set.

$$TIOTS\_States == [\, Q : TIOTS\_STATE\_SET;\ q_0 : TIOTS\_STATE \mid q_0 \in Q \,]$$

Finally, a TIOTS is defined by the schema below, which requires that each transition relates states of Q and is well-typed (*well_typed_tiots_transition*), that is, comprises elements of I, O, or D. In other words, an input transition must be labelled by an input action, and an output transition by an output action. Similarly, a delay transition must be labelled by an element of D.

TIOTS

TIOTS_Variables
TIOTS_States
$T : TIOTS\_TRANSREL$

$\forall\, entry : T \bullet \{entry.1, entry.3\} \subseteq Q \land$
$\quad (entry.2, I, O, D) \in well\_typed\_tiots\_transition$

It also makes sense to constraint a TIOTS by other properties [21]: time additivity (*time_additivity_TIOTS*), null delay (*null_delay_TIOTS*), and time determinism (*time_determinism_TIOTS*). Informally, time additivity states that if a state can be reached by two consecutive delay transitions, then it can also be reached by just one delay transition whose delay is equal to the sum of the original delays. The second property enforces that two states related by a zero delay transition are the same. Time determinism ensures that if two states can be reached by the same amount of delay, then they are the same too.

3.2 From DFRSs to TIOTSs

The function *fromDFRStoTIOTS* maps a DFRS to a TIOTS. Figure 3 presents
an informal overview of this mapping process. The states of a DFRS are mapped
to TIOTS states (for instance, $1 \mapsto A$; $2 \mapsto B$; $3 \mapsto C$), but some new states
are also introduced in the TIOTS (these are unnamed in Figure 3). The delay
of a delay transition (DFRS) is straightforwardly mapped to a delay in the
TIOTS (for example, *tiots_del*(*tiots_dense*(3.14))), whereas the statements of a
function or a delay transition (DFRS) are mapped to a chain of transitions such
that each one corresponds to an output or an input action (TIOTS), respectively
(for instance, $(coin, b(true)) \mapsto in(coin\_true)$; $(mode, n(0)) \mapsto out(mode\_0)$).

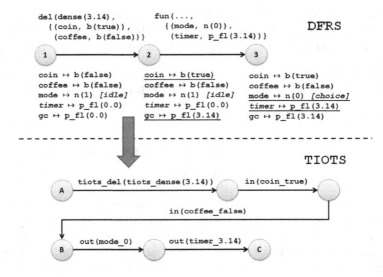

Fig. 3. From DFRS to TIOTS – Mapping Transitions

The delay transition of the DFRS is mapped to a chain of three transitions
(from states A to B) with two new intermediate states. The first transition
represents the time elapsing, whereas the next two represents the stimuli from
the environment. Similarly, the function transition of the DFRS is mapped to a
chain of two transitions (from B to C). Next, we formalise the mapping process.

TIOTS – Inputs, Outputs and Delays. The set of input actions is derived
from the statements of a delay transition as they represent stimuli provided by
the environment. This is formalised by the function *mapInputActions*. Similarly,
the output actions are derived from the statements of a function transition as it
represents a functional response of the system for a given context. The function
mapStatement maps a DFRS statement into a TIOTS action. The mapping of
delays is straightforward and its formalisation is omitted here.

$mapInputActions : TRANSREL \rightarrow TIOTS\_ACTIONS$

$\forall transRel : TRANSREL \bullet mapInputActions(transRel) =$
$\bigcup\{entry : transRel \mid entry.2 \in ran\ del \bullet$
$\{stmt : (delayTransition(entry.2)).2 \bullet (mapStatement(stmt))\}\}$

TIOTS – States. The function $mapState : STATE \rightarrowtail TIOTS\_STATE$ maps a DFRS state to a TIOTS state, represented abstractly by a name; $mapStatements :$ $STMT\_SET \rightarrow TIOTS\_ACTIONS$ maps DFRS statements to a set of TIOTS actions. Each action is a name to represent the corresponding statement.

TIOTS – Transitions. From the transition relation of a DFRS we derive that of the TIOTS using the function $mapTransitionRelation$, formalised below. Figure 3 illustrates this mapping with an example.

$mapTransitionRelation : TRANSREL \rightarrow TIOTS\_TRANSREL$

$\forall transRel : TRANSREL \bullet$
$\exists tr1, tr2 : TIOTS\_TRANSREL \mid$
$tr1 = mapFunctionTransitions(getTransitions(transRel, ran\ fun),$
$\quad ran\ mapState) \wedge$
$tr2 = mapDelayTransitions(getTransitions(transRel, ran\ del),$
$\quad ran\ mapState \cup getStates(tr1)) \bullet$
$mapTransitionRelation(transRel) = tr1 \cup tr2$

The function $getTransitions$ is used to extract the transitions of the transition relation $transRel$ of a particular type characterised by the range of the fun or del constructors. The translation functions $mapFunctionTransitions$ and $mapDelayTransitions$ for the different kinds of transitions take the sets of states already in use as an extra parameter,since, as illustrated, they create new states.

For illustration, we show the mapping of delay transitions.

$mapDelayTransitions : (TRANSREL \times TIOTS\_STATE\_SET) \rightarrowtail$
$\quad TIOTS\_TRANSREL$

$dom\ mapDelayTransitions =$
$\{tr : TRANSREL \mid \forall en : tr \bullet en.2 \in ran\ del\} \times TIOTS\_STATE\_SET$
$\forall transRel : TRANSREL;\ used : TIOTS\_STATE\_SET \bullet$
$\exists tr1, tr2 : TIOTS\_TRANSREL \bullet$
$tr1 = mapTDDelayTransitions($
$\quad \bigcup\{set : groupNTDDelayTrans(transRel) \mid \#set = 1\}, used) \wedge$
$tr2 = mapSetOfNTDDelayTransitions($
$\quad \{set : groupNTDDelayTrans(transRel) \mid \#set > 1\}, used \cup getStates(tr1)) \wedge$
$mapDelayTransitions(transRel, used) = tr1 \cup tr2$

The function mapDelayTransitions applies to sets of transitions whose entries en are of type del ($en.2 \in ran\ del$). For those, the functions $mapTDDelayTransitions$ and $mapSetOfNTDDelayTransitions$ are used to map the deterministic and nondeterministic transitions. The function $groupNTDDelayTrans$ defines a set of sets of transitions with the same delay. The sets set of size 1 contain the time deterministic transitions. The sets of size greater than one group the nondeterministic transitions. For each of these sets, a chain of transitions is defined. For the nondeterministic transitions, we ensure that the TIOTS target state obtained from the mapping of the transitions is the same. This becomes the initial state of the chain of input actions obtained from the statements of each delay transition.

Mapping a DFRS to a TIOTS. We use the functions named above to define how a DFRS is mapped to a TIOTS. The set of states of a TIOTS is defined as the union of the states obtained from its transition relation with its initial state. Our mapping function is total, that is, every data-flow reactive system can be mapped to a corresponding timed input-output system.

Theorem 1 *Totality of fromDFRStoTIOTS*

$$\forall\, d : DFRS \bullet (\exists\, t : TIOTS \bullet t = fromDFRStoTIOTS\,(d))$$

Furthermore, the obtained TIOTS preserves the time additivity and null delay properties, and it is time deterministic. The proofs of these results are in [7].

4   Formalising Natural Language Requirements

A DFRS model can automatically generated from NL requirements described by actions guarded by conditions. Here, we provide an overview of how it is done. Pseudo-code of the related algorithms can be seen in [7]. For more details about the format of the requirements we refer to [8,6,9].

First, the requirements are parsed to assess whether they are correct with respect to a Controlled Natural Language (CNL) defined in [9]. For instance, the following is an example of a valid requirement of the VM: "*When the system mode is idle, and the coin sensor changes to true, the coffee machine system shall: reset the request timer, assign choice to the system mode*" [REQ001].

Afterwards, the syntax trees obtained from the requirements are automatically mapped into an informal semantic representation based on the Case Grammar theory [13]. In this theory, a sentence is analysed in terms of the semantic roles played by each word or group of words in the sentence (e.g., Agent — who performs the action; Patient — who is affected by the action, To Value — value associated with action, and so on). Table 1 shows a concrete example obtained from REQ001. More details of this step are reported in [9].

Finally, we employ an algorithm defined to generate a DFRS from a list of case frames (Algorithm 1). First, the algorithm calls *identifyVariables* to identify

Table 1. Example of Case Frames (Vending Machine)

Condition #1 - Main Verb: *is*				
Patient:	*the system mode*	To Value:	*idle*	
Condition #1 - Main Verb: *changes*				
Patient:	*the coin sensor*	To Value:	*true*	
Action #1 - Main Verb: *reset*				
Agent:	*the coffee machine system*	To Value:	-	Patient:	*the request timer*
Action #2 - Main Verb: assign				
Agent:	*the coffee machine system*	To Value:	*choice*	Patient:	*the system mode*

Algorithm 1. Derive DFRS

```
input   : reqCFList
output  : dfrs

1  inputList, outputList, timerList = identifyVariables(reqCFList);
2  initialState = buildInitialState(inputList, outputList, timerList);
3  functionEntries = identifyFunctions(reqCFList, inputList, outputList, timerList);
4  dfrs = new DFRS();
5  dfrs.I = inputList;
6  dfrs.O = outputList;
7  dfrs.T = timerList;
8  dfrs.gcvar = setSystemGC(timerList);
9  dfrs.s₀ = initialState;
10 dfrs.TR = generateTransition(functionEntries);
```

---

the system variables (line 1). A variable is classified as an input if, and only if, it appears only in *patient* roles of conditions; otherwise it is an output. To distinguish timers, we require their names to have "timer" as a suffix.

The type of the variables is inferred from the values mentioned in the *to value* role. Then, we create an initial state for these variables (line 2) considering initial default values (like 0 for *int* and *nat*, and *false* for *bool*, for instance).

Afterwards, the algorithm calls *identifyFunctions* to identify the function transitions that describe the system behaviour (line 3). We identify one function for each different agent. Therefore, *identifyFunctions* yields a list of functions indexed by the corresponding agents. Each function is a list of action statements mapped to the respective discrete and timed guards. In the end (lines 4–9), the algorithm creates a DFRS. The complete definition can be seen in [7]. Here, we now present the algorithm for statement generation.

Algorithm 2 generates an action statement from a case frame that depicts an action. First (lines 1–3), we retrieve the verb from the Action and the name of the variable involved from the Patient. If the variable is a timer and the verb is not reset, an exception is raised since timers can only be reset (line 4–5).

The next step is the identification of the value being assigned to the variable (lines 6–10). If the verb is *"reset"* the value is the system global time (line 7). Otherwise, it is the content of the To Value (line 8). If the content of the To Value is not an integer, a float or a boolean, it is a string and the value is the index of this string within the list of possible values of the variable (lines 9–10).

If the verb being used describes a simple mathematical operation, the algorithm creates the corresponding expression considering the variable and values identified (lines 11-16). Then, a new statement is created considering the variable and values identified (lines 17–18).

5   Practical Validation: Test Cases from NL Requirements

To provide an empirical argument as to whether the DFRS model is expressive enough to represent the behaviour of a timed reactive system as defined using natural language, we consider the four examples listed in Section 1. Supported by a mechanisation of the strategy presented in Section 4, we assess whether test

---

Algorithm 2. Generate Statement

---

    input   : $action, varList$
    output : $actionStatement$

1 $verb = action.ACT$;
2 $varName = toString(action.PAT)$;
3 $var = varList.find(varName)$;
4 **if** $var.kind = timer \land \neg verb.equals(\text{"reset"})$ **then**
5    $\lfloor$ $throw\ Exception(\text{"timers can only be reset"})$;

6 $value = null$;
7 **if** $verb.equals(\text{"reset"})$ **then** $value = \text{"gc"}$;
8 **else** $value = toString(action.TOV)$;
9 **if** $\neg isInteger(value) \land \neg isFloat(value) \land \neg isBoolean(value)$ **then**
10   $\lfloor$ $value = var.possibleValuesList.getIndex(value)$;

11 $rhsExp = newExp()$;
12 **if** $verb.equals(\text{"add"})$ **then** $rhsExp = varName + \text{"+"} + value$;
13 **else if** $verb.equals(\text{"subtract"})$ **then** $rhsExp = varName + \text{"-"} + value$;
14 **else if** $verb.equals(\text{"multiply"})$ **then** $rhsExp = varName + \text{"*"} + value$;
15 **else if** $verb.equals(\text{"divide"})$ **then** $rhsExp = varName + \text{"/"} + value$;
16 **else** $rhsExp = value$;

17 $actionStatement = new\ Statement()$;
18 $actionStatement = varName + \text{":="} + rhsExp$;

---

cases, either independently written by specialists of our industrial partner or generated by a commercial tool (RT-Tester[4]) from the same set of requirements, are compatible with the corresponding DFRS models.

To analyse the compatibility with the corresponding DFRS model, we implemented a depth-first search algorithm that explores the DFRS state space guided by a test case. We provide to the DFRS the inputs described by each test vector, and check whether the outputs provided by the system are equal to those in the vector. This comparison is straightforward since we are dealing with primitive types.

The selected tests are relevant as they are able to detect a high amount of errors introduced by mutation testing as reported in [6]. The verdict of our testing experiments have been successful as all considered test vectors are compatible with the corresponding DFRS models, which gives evidence that the generated DFRSs indeed capture the NL requirements as suggested in this paper.

6 Conclusions

We have presented DFRSs, a concise formal model to represent timed reactive systems. It is part of an automatic strategy to generate test cases from natural language requirements that may also describe temporal properties. We have given a semantics for DFRSs based on TIOTSs. This mapping preserves desired properties of a TIOTS, namely, time additivity, null delay, and time determinism. We have also considered examples from four different domains, and showed that the derived DFRS models are expressive enough to represent a set of independently written and generated test cases. To support this analysis, we have

---

[4] www.verified.de/products/rt-tester/

developed a tool NAT2TEST[5] that automatically generates DFRS models from NL requirements, besides other features such as animation of DFRS models.

Previous studies have already addressed the topic of formal modelling natural languages. These works differ in two main aspects: (1) structure of NL requirements, or (2) support for timed requirements.

Some studies opt for a more free structure, whereas other impose more restrictions when writing the requirements. In general, this choice is related to the trade-off of a greater or lesser level of automation. Works such as those reported in [4,20] generate a formal model from unrestricted NL requirements. This makes the strategy more flexible than ours, but requires user interaction for the generation process, whereas our strategy is fully automated. Other studies [17] achieve a high level of automation by imposing restrictions that make the NL requirements resemble an algorithm. In our work, we reach a compromise.

Our NL imposes some restrictions, but the requirements still resemble a textual specification. Our restrictions make our approach suitable for describing actions guarded by conditions, and thus we cannot express properties like invariants; this can be accomplished by works such as [1].

A compromise similar to ours is reached, for instance, in [5], but timed requirements are not covered. In [17] timed requirements are considered, but as previously said from a not so natural textual representation. In [11] timed requirements are handled, but the strategy requires human intervention.

We intend to: (1) integrate this study with our previous works to take advantage of the generality of DFRS as indicated in Figure 1; (2) analyse the soundness of our DFRS encoding in CSP; (3) propose a conformance relation to DFRS models, and (4) compare it with typical conformance relations defined to TIOTSs, as well as with the conformance relation we define in [10].

Acknowledgments. This work was carried out with the support of the CNPq (Brazil), INES[6], and the grants: FACEPE 573964/2008-4, APQ-1037-1.03/08, CNPq 573964/2008-4 and 476821/2011-8.

References

1. Bajwa, I., Bordbar, B., Anastasakis, K., Lee, M.: On a chain of transformations for generating alloy from NL constraints. In: International Conference on Digital Information Management, pp. 93–98 (2012)
2. Blackburn, M., Busser, R., Fontaine, J.: Automatic Generation of Test Vectors for SCR-style Specifications. In: Annual Conference on Computer Assurance (1997)
3. Blackburn, M.R., Busser, R., Nauman, A.: Removing Requirement Defects and Automating Test. In: International Conference on Software Testing Analysis & Review (2001)
4. Boddu, R., Guo, L., Mukhopadhyay, S., Cukic, B.: RETNA: from Requirements to Testing in a Natural Way. In: IEEE International Requirements Engineering Conference, pp. 262–271 (2004)

---

[5] The NAT2TEST tool can be obtained by contacting the authors.
[6] www.ines.org.br

5. Brottier, E., Baudry, B., Le Traon, Y., Touzet, D., Nicolas, B.: Producing a Global Requirement Model from Multiple Requirement Specifications. In: Entreprise Distributed Object Computing Conference, pp. 390–401 (2007)

6. Carvalho, G., Barros, F., Lapschies, F., Schulze, U., Peleska, J.: Model-Based Testing from Controlled Natural Language Requirements. In: Artho, C., Ölveczky, P.C. (eds.) FTSCS 2013. CCIS, vol. 419, pp. 19–35. Springer, Heidelberg (2014)

7. Carvalho, G., Carvalho, A., Rocha, E., Cavalcanti, A., Sampaio, A.: Z Definition, Algorithms and Proofs for Data-Flow Reactive Systems. Tech. rep., UFPE (2014), http://www.cin.ufpe.br/~ghpc/

8. Carvalho, G., Falcão, D., Barros, F., Sampaio, A., Mota, A., Motta, L., Blackburn, M.: Test Case Generation from Natural Language Requirements based on SCR Specifications. In: Symposium on Applied Computing, vol. 2, pp. 1217–1222 (2013)

9. Carvalho, G., Falcão, D., Barros, F., Sampaio, A., Mota, A., Motta, L., Blackburn, M.: NAT2TEST$_{SCR}$: Test case generation from natural language requirements based on SCR specifications. Science of Computer Programming (2014)

10. Carvalho, G., Sampaio, A., Mota, A.: A CSP Timed Input-Output Relation and a Strategy for Mechanised Conformance Verification. In: Groves, L., Sun, J. (eds.) ICFEM 2013. LNCS, vol. 8144, pp. 148–164. Springer, Heidelberg (2013)

11. Cavada, R., Cimatti, A., Mariotti, A., Mattarei, C., Micheli, A., Mover, S., Pensallorto, M., Roveri, M., Susi, A., Tonetta, S.: Supporting Requirements Validation: The EuRailCheck Tool. In: International Conference on Automated Software Engineering, pp. 665–667 (2009)

12. FAA: Requirements Engineering Management Findings Report. Tech. rep., U.S. Department of Transportation - Federal Aviation Administration (2009)

13. Fillmore, C.J.: The Case for Case. In: Bach, H. (ed.) Universals in Linguistic Theory, pp. 1–88. Holt, Rinehart, and Winston, New York (1968)

14. Heninger, K., Parnas, D., Shore, J., Kallander, J.: Software Requirements for the A-7E Aircraft - TR 3876. Tech. rep., U.S. Naval Research Laboratory (1978)

15. ISO: Z formal specification notation (ISO/IEC 13568). Tech. rep., International Organization for Standardization (2002)

16. Larsen, K., Mikucionis, M., Nielsen, B.: Online Testing of Real-time Systems using Uppaal: Status and Future Work. In: Perspectives of Model-Based Testing - Dagstuhl Seminar, vol. 04371 (2004)

17. Li, J., Pu, G., Wang, Z., Chen, Y., Zhang, L., Qi, Y., Gu, B.: An Approach to Requirement Analysis for Periodic Control Systems. In: Annual IEEE Software Engineering Workshop, pp. 130–139 (2012)

18. Peleska, J., Vorobev, E., Lapschies, F., Zahlten, C.: Automated Model-Based Testing with RT-Tester. Tech. rep., Universität Bremen (2011)

19. Saaltink, M.: The Z/EVES System. In: Till, D., Bowen, J.P., Hinchey, M.G. (eds.) ZUM 1997. LNCS, vol. 1212, pp. 72–85. Springer, Heidelberg (1997)

20. Santiago Junior, V., Vijaykumar, N.L.: Generating Model-based Test Cases from Natural Language Requirements for Space Application Software. Software Quality Journal 20, 77–143 (2012)

21. Schmaltz, J., Tretmans, J.: On Conformance Testing for Timed Systems. In: Cassez, F., Jard, C. (eds.) FORMATS 2008. LNCS, vol. 5215, pp. 250–264. Springer, Heidelberg (2008)

A Hybrid Model of Connectors in Cyber-Physical Systems

Xiaohong Chen[1], Jun Sun[2], and Meng Sun[1]

[1] LMAM & Department of Informatics, School of Mathematical Sciences,
Peking University, China
[2] Singapore University of Technology and Design, Singapore
xiaohong.chen@pku.edu.cn, sunjun@sutd.edu.sg,
sunmeng@math.pku.edu.cn

Abstract. Compositional coordination models and languages play an important role in cyber-physical systems (CPSs). In this paper, we introduce a formal model for describing hybrid behaviors of connectors in CPSs. We extend the constraint automata model, which is used as the semantic model for the exogenous channel-based coordination language Reo, to capture the dynamic behavior of connectors in CPSs where the discrete and continuous dynamics co-exist and interact with each other. In addition to the formalism, we also provide a theoretical compositional approach for constructing the product automata for a Reo circuit, which is typically obtained by composing several primitive connectors in Reo.

1 Introduction

Cyber-physical systems (CPSs) are systems that integrate computing and communication with monitoring and control of physical entities. The complex interaction with the physical world through *computation, communication* and *control* leads to the dynamic behavior of CPSs. CPSs are present everywhere, such as airplanes and space vehicles, hybrid gas-electric vehicles, power grids, oil refineries, medical devices, defense systems, etc. The design of such systems requires understanding the complex interactions among software, hardware, networks and physical components. Coordination models and languages that provide a formalization of the "glue code" that interconnects the components and organizes their interactions in a distributed environment, are extremely important to the success of CPSs [9].

The use of coordination models and languages distinguishes the interaction among components from computing in single component explicitly. This can simplify the development process for complex systems and reasoning and verification of system properties. For example, Reo [2] is a powerful coordination language that offers an approach to express interaction protocols. Such coordination languages provide a proper approach that focuses on the interaction aspects in distributed applications, instead of the behavior models for individual components. However, most of existing coordination models and languages focused only on interactions among software components with discrete behavior. In CPSs, not only software components, but also physical components are coordinated together as well. This makes the integration of discrete and continuous dynamics for coordination an important issue in CPSs.

S. Merz and J. Pang (Eds.): ICFEM 2014, LNCS 8829, pp. 59–74, 2014.

In this paper, we investigated the problem of using Reo to model connectors in CPSs. As channels in CPS have often both discrete and continuous dynamics, existing semantics for Reo [2] is insufficient. Thus, we use *hybrid constraint automata* (HCA) which is an extension of constraint automata (CA), to capture the dynamic behavior of connectors in CPSs where the discrete and continuous dynamics co-exist and interact with each other. The concepts in HCA are borrowed from classical hybrid automata [1,6]. There are three types of transitions in HCA: (1) continuous flow inside one control state captured by some differential equations; (2) discrete jump between two control states representing the execution of some I/O operations; (3) discrete jump between two control states caused by violating the location invariant. Furthermore, a *compositional* approach for construction of HCA from a given Reo connector is provided, where the composition operator on HCA models the *join* operator in Reo to build complex connectors from basic channels.

This work is related to existing semantic models for connectors in CPSs. The time aspects of Reo has been investigated in [3], which uses timed constraint automata (TCA) as the operational semantics for Reo connectors and provides a variant of LTL as a specification formalism for timed Reo connectors. In [7,8] the TCA model has been translated into mCRL2 for model checking timed Reo connectors. The UTP model for timed connectors in Reo has been proposed in [12]. However, both the TCA model and UTP model lack of mechanisms to describe continuous dynamics for connectors. Lynch *et al.* proposed the Hybrid I/O Automata (HIOA) model [11,10] for the hybrid behavior in composition of components, where the input action enabling and input flow enabling axioms should be satisfied, which is not required in the constraint automata (and HCA) model.

The paper is structured as follows. We briefly summarize the coordination language Reo in Section 2. In Section 3 we introduce the hybrid constraint automata model. In Section 4 we show some examples of hybrid Reo circuits and how HCA can serve as their operational model. Finally, Section 5 concludes with further research directions.

2   A Reo Primer

Reo is a channel-based exogenous coordination model wherein complex coordinators, called *connectors*, are compositionally constructed from simpler ones. We summarize only the main concepts in Reo here. Further details about Reo and its semantics can be found in [2,4,5].

A connector provides the protocol that controls and organizes the communication, synchronization and cooperation among the components that they interconnect. Primitive connectors in Reo are channels that have two channel ends. There are two types of channel ends: *source* and *sink*. A source channel end accepts data into its channel, and a sink channel end dispenses data out of its channel. It is possible for the ends of a channel to be both sinks or both sources. Reo places no restriction on the behavior of a channel and thus allows an open-ended set of different channel types to be used simultaneously. Each channel end can be connected to at most one component instance at any given time.

Figure 1 shows the graphical representation of some simple channel types in Reo. A *FIFO1 channel* represents an asynchronous channel with one buffer cell which is empty

Fig. 1. Some basic channels in Reo

if no data item is shown in the box (this is the case in Figure 1). If a data element d is contained in the buffer of an FIFO1 channel then d is shown inside the box in its graphical representation. A *synchronous channel* has a source and a sink end and no buffer. It accepts a data item through its source end iff it can simultaneously dispense it through its sink. A *lossy synchronous channel* is similar to a synchronous channel except that it always accepts all data items through its source end. The data item is transferred if it is possible for the data item to be dispensed through the sink end, otherwise the data item is lost. For a *filter channel*, its pattern P specifies the type of data items that can be transmitted through the channel. Any value $d \in P$ is accepted through its source end iff its sink end can simultaneously dispense d; all data items $d \notin P$ are always accepted through the source end, but are immediately lost. The *synchronous drain* has two source ends and no sink end. It can accept a data item through one of its ends iff it can simultaneously accept data item through the other end, and all data accepted by the channel are lost.

Complex connectors are constructed by composing simpler ones mainly via the *join* and *hiding* operations. Channels are joined together in a node which consists of a set of channel ends. Nodes are categorized into *source*, *sink* and *mixed nodes*, depending on whether all channel ends that coincide on a node are source ends, sink ends or a combination of the two. The hiding operation is used to hide the internal topology of a component connector. The hidden nodes can no longer be accessed or observed from outside. A complex connector has a graphical representation, called a *Reo circuit*, which is a finite graph where the *nodes* are labeled with pair-wise disjoint, non-empty sets of channel ends, and the *edges* represent the connecting channels. The behavior of a Reo circuit is formalized by means of the data-flow at its sink and source nodes. Intuitively, the source nodes of a circuit are analogous to the input ports, and the sink nodes to the output ports of a component, while mixed nodes are its hidden internal details. Components cannot connect to, read from, or write to mixed nodes. Instead, data-flow through mixed nodes is totally specified by the circuits they belong to.

A component can write data items to a source node that it is connected to. The write operation succeeds only if all (source) channel ends coincident on the node accept the data item, in which case the data item is simultaneously written to every source end coincident on the node. A source node, thus, acts as a replicator. A component can obtain data items, by an input operation, from a sink node that it is connected to. A take operation succeeds only if at least one of the (sink) channel ends coincident on the node offers a suitable data item; if more than one coincident channel end offers suitable data items, one is selected nondeterministically. A sink node, thus, acts as a nondeterministic merger. A mixed node nondeterministically selects and takes a suitable data item offered by one of its coincident sink channel ends and replicates it into all of its coincident source channel ends. A component can not connect to, take from, or write to mixed nodes.

3   Hybrid Constraint Automata

In order to capture both discrete and continuous behaviors of connectors in CPSs, we extend the model of constraint automata as *hybrid constraint automata*. The formal definition of hybrid constraint automata (HCA) arises by combining the concepts of constraint automata and hybrid automata.

3.1   Syntax of HCA

Data Assignments and Data Constraints. Let *Data* be a finite and non-empty set of data items that can be transferred through channels, and $\mathcal{N}$ a finite and non-empty set of node names. A data assignment δ denotes a function $\delta : N \to Data$ where $\varnothing \neq N \subseteq \mathcal{N}$. All possible data assignments on N is denoted as $DA(N)$ or $Data^N$. For a subset $N_0 \subseteq N$, the restriction of δ over N_0 is a data assignment $\delta \restriction_{N_0} \in DA(N_0)$ defined as $\delta \restriction_{N_0}(A) = \delta(A)$ for each $A \in N_0$. We use the notation of $\delta = [A \mapsto d \mid A \in N]$ to specify a data assignment that assigns a value $d \in Data$ to every node $A \in N$. For example, if d_1 is transferred through node A and d_2 is transferred through node B, then the corresponding data assignment is $\delta = [A \mapsto d_1, B \mapsto d_2]$.

Formally, a data constraint g over N is a propositional formula built from the atoms such as "$d_A \in P$" and "$d_A = d_B$" and boolean operators $\wedge, \vee, \neg$, etc. where $A, B \in \mathcal{N}$, $P \subseteq Data$ and d_A is interpreted as $\delta(A)$. For $N \subseteq \mathcal{N}$, $DC(N)$ denotes the set of all data constraints that specify values being transferred on nodes in N. We use $\delta \models g$ to denote that the data assignment δ satisfies the data constraint g.

Example 1. Let $N = \{A, B, C\}$ and $Data = \{d_0, d_1\}$. Data assignment $\delta = [A \mapsto d_1, C \mapsto d_0]$ says that d_1 and d_0 are transferred through nodes A and C respectively, while no data item is transferred through B. Let $g_1 = (d_A = d_1)$ and $g_2 = (d_A = d_C)$ be two data constraints, then $\delta \models g_1$ and $\delta \not\models g_2$.

Dynamical Systems and Space Constraints. Dynamical systems can model systems with continuous behaviors. Consider the differential equation:

$$\dot{\xi} = f(\xi) \tag{1}$$

where the dotted variables represent the first derivatives during continuous change and $f : \mathbb{R}^n \to \mathbb{R}^n$ is an infinitely differentiable function. We also call such functions *smooth*. By a trajectory of (1) with initial condition $x \in \mathbb{R}^n$, we mean a smooth curve

$$\xi : [0, \tau) \to \mathbb{R}^n \tag{2}$$

satisfying

- $\tau > 0$;
- $\xi(0) = x$;
- $\dot{\xi}(t) = f(\xi(t))$ for each $t \in (0, \tau)$.

In this case, we say the duration of the trajectory ξ is τ.

Definition 1 (Dynamical system). *An n-dimensional dynamical system* $\Sigma = (\mathbb{R}^n, f)$ *is the real space* $\mathbb{R}^n$ *equipped with differential equation given by a smooth map* $f :$ $\mathbb{R} \to \mathbb{R}^n$. *A trajectory of a dynamical system is a trajectory of the differential equation defined by* f.

We also consider systems $(\mathcal{X}, f)$ with f defined in a subset $\mathcal{X}$ of $\mathbb{R}^n$. A trajectory ξ of the dynamical system $\Sigma = (\mathcal{X}, f)$ with a duration τ and initial condition $x \in \mathcal{X}$ is a solution to (1) satisfying

- $\tau > 0$;
- $\xi(0) = x$;
- $\dot{\xi}(t) = f(\xi(t))$ for each $t \in (0, \tau)$;
- $\xi(t) \in \mathcal{X}$ for each $t \in [0, \tau)$.

Intuitively, an n-dimensional dynamical system $\Sigma = (\mathbb{R}^n, f)$ describes how a point P evolves and flows in space $\mathbb{R}^n$ based on the rules given as differential equations. If at present time $t = t_0$, the coordination of P's location is $x_0 \in \mathbb{R}^n$, then in the near future P follows a trajectory ξ with duration τ and initial condition x_0. At time $t = t_0 + \Delta t$ where $\Delta t < \tau$, P will locate in point $\xi(\Delta t) \in \mathbb{R}^n$. This intuition makes sense in that if there are two trajectories, ξ_1 with duration τ_1 and ξ_2 with duration τ_2 sharing the same initial condition, then $\xi_1(t) = \xi_2(t)$ for each $t \in [0, \min\{\tau_1, \tau_2\})$. This is concluded in Theorem 1 which comes directly from the Peano existence theorem [13], a fundamental theorem in the study of ordinary differential equations that guarantees the existence of solutions to certain initial value problems.

Theorem 1. *Let* $\mathcal{X} \subseteq \mathbb{R}^n$ *be a nonempty subset,* $f : \mathcal{X} \to \mathbb{R}^n$ *a continuously differentiable function, and* $x_0 \in \mathcal{X}$ *an interior point. Then there exists some* $\tau > 0$ *and a unique solution* $\xi : [0, \tau) \to \mathcal{X}$ *of the differential equation* $\dot{\xi} = f(\xi)$ *satisfying* $\xi(0) = x_0$.

A space constraint φ to an n-dimensional dynamical system Σ is defined as a predicate over free variables $\{\#_1, \#_2, \cdots, \#_n\}$ where $\#_i$ is interpreted as the i-th coordinate of a point $x \in \mathbb{R}^n$ for each $i \in \{1, 2, \cdots, n\}$. If the dimension $n = 1$, then we abbreviate $\#_1$ as $\#$. The set of all n-dimensional space constraints is denoted as $SC(n)$ or SC. We use $x \vDash \varphi$ to denote that the point x in space $\mathbb{R}^n$ satisfies the space constraint φ.

Example 2. Let x_1, x_2, x_3 be three points in space $\mathbb{R}^3$ with their coordinations:

$$x_1 = (1, 2, 3) \,,\; x_2 = (1, 0, -1) \,,\; x_3 = (0, 0, 0) \tag{3}$$

and φ_1 and φ_2 two space constraints defined as

$$\varphi_1 = (\#_1 = \#_2) \wedge (\#_2 \le \#_3) \,,\; \varphi_2 = (\#_1 + \#_2 + \#_3 = 0) \,. \tag{4}$$

Then we have

$$
\begin{aligned}
x_1 \nvDash \varphi_1 \,,\; x_1 \nvDash \varphi_2 \,, \\
x_2 \nvDash \varphi_1 \,,\; x_2 \vDash \varphi_2 \,, \\
x_3 \vDash \varphi_1 \,,\; x_3 \vDash \varphi_2 \,.
\end{aligned}
\tag{5}
$$

Hybrid Constraint Automata. We now give the formal definition of HCA and some intuitive interpretation on how it operates.

Definition 2 (Hybrid constraint automata). *A hybrid constraint automata (HCA) $\mathcal{T}$ is a tuple $(S, \mathbb{R}^n, \mathcal{N}, \mathcal{E}, IS, \{In_s\}_{s\in S}, \{f_s\}_{s\in S}, \{re_t\}_{t\in\mathcal{E}})$ consisting of*

- *a finite set of control states S and a set of initial control states $IS \subseteq S$;*
- *the dynamical system space $\mathbb{R}^n$;*
- *a finite set of nodes $\mathcal{N}$;*
- *an n-dimensional dynamical system $\Sigma_s = (In_s, f_s)$ for each $s \in S$;*
- *an edge relation $\mathcal{E}$ which is a subset of $S \times 2^{\mathcal{N}} \times DC \times SC \times S$;*
- *a reset function $re_{(s,N,g,\varphi,\bar{s})} : Data^N \times In_s \to In_{\bar{s}}$.*

Instead of writing $(s, N, g, \varphi, \bar{s}) \in \mathcal{E}$, we use $s \xrightarrow{N,g,\varphi} \bar{s}$. If $re_{(s,N,g,\varphi,\bar{s})} = r$ then we say $s \xrightarrow[r]{N,g,\varphi} \bar{s}$.

The intuitive interpretation of how an HCA $\mathcal{T}$ operates is as follows. In the beginning, $\mathcal{T}$ stays in one of the initial control states $s_0 \in IS$ and behaves exactly as the dynamical system Σ_{s_0}, that is, it starts with a point $x_0 \in In_{s_0}$ and then flows based on the differential equation given by f_{s_0}. If $\mathcal{T}$ stays in control state $s \in S$ and locates at point $x \in In_s$, it

- must choose an edge $t = (s, N, g, \varphi, \bar{s})$ from $\mathcal{E}$ such that the data assignment $\delta \models g$ and $x \models \varphi$, if some I/O operations specified by δ happen on exact those nodes in N. If more than one edges are available, $\mathcal{T}$ chooses one of them nondeterministically. If $\mathcal{T}$ chooses $t = (s, N, g, \varphi, \bar{s})$, it successfully accepts I/O operations and jumps to control state $\bar{s}$ and then behaves exactly as the dynamical system $\Sigma_{\bar{s}}$ with initial condition $re_t(\delta, x) \in In_{\bar{s}}$. If no such edge is available, $\mathcal{T}$ halts;
- must choose an edge $t = (s, N, g, \varphi, \bar{s})$ from $\mathcal{E}$ where $N = \varnothing$ and $g = []$ such that $x \models \varphi$, if $\mathcal{T}$ is about to violate the invariant In_s and no I/O operation happens at the time. If more than one edges are available, $\mathcal{T}$ chooses one of them nondeterministically. If $\mathcal{T}$ chooses $t = (s, \varnothing, [], \varphi, \bar{s})$, it jumps to control state $\bar{s}$ and then behaves exactly as the dynamical system $\Sigma_{\bar{s}}$ with initial condition $re_t([], x) \in In_{\bar{s}}$. If no such edge is available, $\mathcal{T}$ halts;
- may stay in the control state s and behaves exactly as the dynamical system Σ_s as long as it is not forced to make a jump to a new control state.

3.2   The State-Transition Graph of an HCA

So far we described the syntax of HCA and gave some intuitive explanations for their meaning. The following definition formalizes this intuitive behavior by means of a state-transition graph.

Definition 3 (State-transition graph). *Given an HCA $\mathcal{T} = (S, \mathbb{R}^n, \mathcal{N}, \mathcal{E}, IS, \{In_s\}_{s\in S}, \{f_s\}_{s\in S}, \{re_t\}_{t\in\mathcal{E}})$ as above, $\mathcal{T}$ induces a state-transition graph $\mathcal{A}_{\mathcal{T}} = (Q, \longrightarrow, IQ)$ consisting of*

- *a set of states* $Q = \{\langle s, x \rangle \mid s \in S \wedge x \in In_s\};$
- *a set of initial states* $IQ = \{\langle s, x \rangle \mid s \in IS \wedge x \in In_s\};$
- *a transition relation* $\longrightarrow\ \subseteq Q \times 2^N \times DA \times \mathbb{R}_{\geq 0} \times Q;$

where $\langle s, x \rangle \xrightarrow{N, \delta, \tau} \langle \bar{s}, \bar{x} \rangle$ *if and only if one of the following conditions holds:*

- *(Flows)* $s = \bar{s}$, $N = \varnothing$, $\delta = []$, $\tau > 0$ *and there exists a trajectory* ξ *with duration* τ *and initial condition* x *in the dynamical system* $\Sigma_s = (In_s, f_s)$. *The trajectory heads for the point* $\bar{x}$, *that is*

$$\lim_{t \to \tau^-} \xi(t) = \bar{x}; \tag{6}$$

- *(External interactions)* $s \xrightarrow[re]{N, g, \varphi} \bar{s}$, $N \neq \varnothing$, $\delta \in DA(N)$, $\delta \vDash g$, $x \vDash \varphi$, $\tau = 0$ *and* $\bar{x} = re(\delta, x);$
- *(Internal jumps)* $s \xrightarrow[re]{N, g, \varphi} \bar{s}$, $N = \varnothing$, $\delta = []$, $g = true$, $x \vDash \varphi$, $\tau = 0$ *and* $\bar{x} = re([], x)$.

According to Definition 3, transitions in a state-transition graph $\mathcal{A}_{\mathcal{T}}$ are disjointly divided into three categories: flows, external interactions (or briefly interactions) and internal jumps (or briefly jumps). Both interactions and jumps are discrete behavior while flows are continuous. Given a state $q \in Q$, a successor of q is a state $p \in Q$ such that there exists a transition $q \xrightarrow{N, \delta, \tau} p$ in $\mathcal{A}_{\mathcal{T}}$. If this transition is a flow, then p is called a *flow-successor* of q with duration τ. Similarly, we can define *interaction-successor* and *jump-successor*. A state $q = \langle s, x \rangle$ is called *terminal* if and only if it has no outgoing transition.

Given an HCA $\mathcal{T}$ and a state $q = \langle s, x \rangle$ in $\mathcal{A}_{\mathcal{T}}$, a q-*run* (or briefly run) in $\mathcal{T}$ denotes any finite or infinite sequence of successive transitions in $\mathcal{A}_{\mathcal{T}}$ starting in state q. Formally, a q-run has the form

$$\varrho = q_0 \xrightarrow{N_0, \delta_0, \tau_0} q_1 \xrightarrow{N_1, \delta_1, \tau_1} \cdots \tag{7}$$

where $q_0 = q$. It is required that for any sequence segment

$$q_i \xrightarrow{N_i, \delta_i, \tau_i} q_{i+1} \xrightarrow{N_{i+1}, \delta_{i+1}, \tau_{i+1}} q_{i+2} \tag{8}$$

in ϱ, exactly one of the two transitions is flow for the following reasons. If a run ϱ contains two consecutive flow-transitions, say, $q_i \xrightarrow{\varnothing, [], \tau_i} q_{i+1} \xrightarrow{\varnothing, [], \tau_{i+1}} q_{i+2}$, then it can be replaced by one flow-transition $q_i \xrightarrow{\varnothing, [], \tau_i + \tau_{i+1}} q_{i+2}$ without any change of its behavior. On the other hand, if ϱ contains two consecutive discrete actions (interaction- or jump-transition), then these actions occur at the same time point, which violates the general idea of constraint automata where all observable activities that occur simultaneously are collapsed into a single transition. Therefore, a run ϱ in HCA actually consists of an alternating sequence of continuous transitions (flows) and discrete actions (interactions or jumps).

Let $t = q \xrightarrow{N, \delta, \tau} \bar{q}$ be a transition in $\mathcal{A}_{\mathcal{T}}$, we introduce some abbreviate notations as follows:

- instead of writing $q \xrightarrow{\varnothing, [], \tau} \bar{q}$, we say $q \xrightarrow{\tau} \bar{q}$ if t is a flow-transition. Under this circumstances, $\tau > 0$;
- instead of writing $q \xrightarrow{N, \delta, 0} \bar{q}$, we say $q \xrightarrow{N, \delta} \bar{q}$ if t is an interaction-transition. Under this circumstances, $N \neq \varnothing$;
- instead of writing $q \xrightarrow{\varnothing, [], 0} \bar{q}$, we say $q \xrightarrow{0} \bar{q}$ if t is a jump-transition.

The q-run ϱ is called initial if $q \in IQ$ and the first transition of ϱ is a flow. The q-run ϱ is called *time divergent* if ϱ is infinite and

$$\lim_{n \to +\infty} \sum_{i=0}^{n} \tau_i = +\infty .\tag{9}$$

For an initial run ϱ, instead of using general notation as in (7), we use the following simplified notation:

$$\varrho = q_0 \xrightarrow{\tau_0} q_1 \xrightarrow{N_1, \delta_1} q_2 \xrightarrow{\tau_2} q_3 \xrightarrow{N_3, \delta_3} \cdots \tag{10}$$

where the notation $q_1 \xrightarrow{N_1, \delta_1} q_2$ should be regarded as an interaction-transition if $N_1 \neq \varnothing$ or a jump-transition if $N_1 = \varnothing$ and $\delta_1 = []$. Maximality of a run means that it is either time divergent or finite and ends in a terminal state.

Intuitively, N_i is the set of nodes in state q_i that are scheduled to synchronously perform the next set of I/O operations, while δ_i represents the concrete values that are exchanged through those operations at the nodes $A \in N_i$. The value τ_i stands for the duration time when the system evolves based on differential equations.

We now define the notion of *timed data stream* (TDS) which serves to formalize the observable data flows of the runs in an HCA and thus formally define the behavior of an HCA. A TDS is a sequence of triples (N, δ, t) where N is a non-empty set of nodes, δ is a data assignment over N and t is a time point. The intuitive meaning of (N, δ, t) is that at time t the nodes in N simultaneously perform some I/O-operations specified by the pair (N, δ).

Definition 4 (Timed data stream). *A timed data stream for a node-set N denotes any finite or infinite sequence*

$$\Theta = (N_0, \delta_0, t_0) , (N_1, \delta_1, t_1) , \cdots \in (2^N \times DA \times \mathbb{R}_{\geq 0})^* \tag{11}$$

such that $N_i \neq \varnothing$, $\delta_i \in DA(N_i)$, $0 < t_0 < t_1 < \cdots$. The empty timed data stream is denoted by the symbol ε. The length $\|\Theta\| \in \mathbb{N} \cup \{\infty\}$ is defined as the number of triples (N, δ, t) in Θ. The execution time

$$\tau(\Theta) = \begin{cases} t_k & \|\Theta\| = k + 1 \\ \lim_{i \to +\infty} t_i & \|\Theta\| = \infty \\ 0 & \Theta = \varepsilon \end{cases}$$

Θ is called time divergent if it is infinite and $\tau(\Theta) = +\infty$.

Definition 5 (Timed data stream language). *If ϱ is a run of HCA $\mathcal{T}$ as above then the induced TDS $\Theta(\varrho) = (N_{i_0}, \delta_{i_0}, t_{i_0}) , (N_{i_1}, \delta_{i_1}, t_{i_1}) , \cdots$ is obtained by*

1. *removing all flow- and jump-transitions in ϱ;*
2. *building the projection on the transition labels;*
3. *replacing the duration time τ_i by the absolute time points $t_i = \sum_{j=0}^{i} \tau_i$.*

The generated TDS language of a state q in $\mathcal{A}_\mathcal{T}$ is

$$\mathcal{L}(\mathcal{T}, q) = \{\Theta(\varrho) : \varrho \text{ is a maximal } q\text{-run}\} . \tag{12}$$

The language $\mathcal{L}(\mathcal{T})$ consists of all timed data streams $\Theta(\varrho)$ where ϱ is a maximal and initial run.

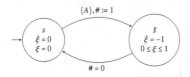

Fig. 2. HCA for a delay channel

Example 3. Let *Data* $= \{d\}$ and $\mathcal{N} = \{A\}$. Fig. 2 shows an HCA $\mathcal{T}$ with the set of control states $S = \{s, \bar{s}\}$ and the initial control state $s \in S$ [1]. $\mathcal{T}$ has two edges: $s \xrightarrow[\#:=1]{\{A\},true,true} \bar{s}$ and $\bar{s} \xrightarrow[\sigma_x]{\varnothing,true,\#=0} s$. Here, $\# := 1$ is an abbreviation of the function $re : [A \mapsto d] \times \{0\} \mapsto \{1\}$ and $\sigma_x : Data^\mathcal{N} \to \mathbb{R}$ is the projection function satisfying $\sigma_x(\delta, x) = x$ for any $\delta \in DA(\mathcal{N})$ and $x \in \mathbb{R}$. According to Definition 3, we can give the corresponding state-transition graph $\mathcal{A}_\mathcal{T} = (Q, \longrightarrow, IQ)$ of the HCA $\mathcal{T}$, where $Q = \{\langle s, 0 \rangle\} \cup \{\langle \bar{s}, x \rangle \mid 0 \le x \le 1\}$, $IQ = \{\langle s, 0 \rangle\}$ and $\longrightarrow$ consists of

- flow-transitions in control state s, that is $\langle s, 0 \rangle \xrightarrow{\varnothing,[],\tau} \langle s, 0 \rangle$ for each $\tau > 0$;
- flow-transitions in control state $\bar{s}$, that is $\langle \bar{s}, x \rangle \xrightarrow{\varnothing,[],\tau} \langle \bar{s}, x - \tau \rangle$ for each $x \in (0, 1]$ and $0 < \tau \le x$;
- an interaction-transition $\langle s, 0 \rangle \xrightarrow{\{A\},[A \mapsto d],0} \langle \bar{s}, 1 \rangle$;
- a jump-transition $\langle \bar{s}, 0 \rangle \xrightarrow{\varnothing,[],0} \langle s, 0 \rangle$.

The intuitive interpretation of how $\mathcal{A}_\mathcal{T}$ works is as follows. At the beginning, $\mathcal{A}_\mathcal{T}$ stays in state $\langle s, 0 \rangle$, where there are two outgoing transitions: one is an interaction-transition to state $\langle \bar{s}, 1 \rangle$ and the other is a self-loop flow-transition to state $\langle s, 0 \rangle$ itself. Therefore if no I/O-transition is performed, then $\mathcal{A}_\mathcal{T}$ must stay in state $\langle s, 0 \rangle$, until some I/O-operations happen. Because $\mathcal{T}$ has only one node A and the data set *Data* contains only one data item d, the only I/O-operation that can happen here is the one specified by the data assignment $\delta = [A \mapsto d]$, which triggers $\mathcal{A}_\mathcal{T}$ moving to state $\langle \bar{s}, 1 \rangle$ through the only interaction-transition $\langle s, 0 \rangle \xrightarrow{\{A\},[A \mapsto d],0} \langle \bar{s}, 1 \rangle$. From then on, $\mathcal{A}_\mathcal{T}$ will flow based

---

[1] To make the graph simple and clear, here we omit all the trivial conditions and labels such as the projection function σ_x, the *true* predicate and empty node-set $\varnothing$.

on the differential equation $\dot{\xi} = -1$. Notice that in any state $\langle \bar{s}, x \rangle$ where $x \in (0, 1]$, the only outgoing transitions for $\mathcal{A}_T$ is flow-transitions, which implies that $\mathcal{A}_T$ will stay in control state $\bar{s}$ and keep flowing until it reaches the state $\langle \bar{s}, 0 \rangle$. As soon as it reaches $\langle \bar{s}, 0 \rangle$, it will choose the only outgoing transition $\langle \bar{s}, 0 \rangle \xrightarrow{\varnothing, [], 0} \langle s, 0 \rangle$ and finally come back to the initial state $\langle s, 0 \rangle$.

A typical maximal and initial run ϱ of the HCA $\mathcal{T}$ has the form

$$\varrho = \langle s, 0 \rangle \xrightarrow{\tau_1} \langle s, 0 \rangle \xrightarrow{\{A\}, [A \mapsto d]} \langle \bar{s}, 1 \rangle \xrightarrow{1} \langle \bar{s}, 0 \rangle \xrightarrow{0} \langle s, 0 \rangle \xrightarrow{\tau_2} \cdots \qquad (13)$$

where $\tau_1, \tau_2, \ldots$ are positive real numbers and $\tau(\varrho) = \tau_1 + 1 + \tau_2 + 1 + \cdots = +\infty$, which means ϱ is time divergent. The corresponding TDS $\Theta(\varrho)$ induced by $\mathbf{q}$ is

$$\Theta(\varrho) = (\{A\}, [A \mapsto d], \tau_1), (\{A\}, [A \mapsto d], \tau_1 + 1 + \tau_2), \cdots \qquad (14)$$

and the TDS-language $\mathcal{L}(\mathcal{T})$ of $\mathcal{T}$ is set of sequences $(\{A\}, [A \mapsto d], t_1), (\{A\}, [A \mapsto d], t_2), \cdots$ where $t_{i+1} - t_i > 1$ for each $i \geq 1$.

4   Hybrid Reo Circuits

This section explains how HCA is able to formalize connectors with hybrid behaviors in Reo in a compositional way.

4.1   Hybrid Primitive Channels

Reo defines what a channel is and how channels can be composed into more complex connectors. Reo places no restrictions on the behavior of channels. This allows an open-ended set of user-defined channel types as primitives for constructing complex connectors (also called circuits in Reo). In the sequel, we introduce a number of common channel types when considering the hybrid behavior of CPSs.

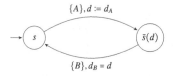

Fig. 3. HCA for FIFO1 channel

FIFO channels. FIFO channels are the most common form of asynchronous channels. The word "asynchronous" here means that there exists some delay after a data item is written into the input port for the data item to be available on the output port. The simplest FIFO channel with discrete behavior only is the FIFO1 channel. A FIFO1 channel is a FIFO channel with one buffer cell, which has a source end and a sink end. The corresponding HCA for the FIFO1 channel is shown in Fig. 3, where all the trivial conditions and labels are omitted intentionally.

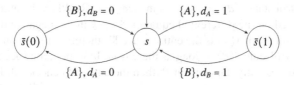

Fig. 4. Non-parametric HCA for FIFO1 channel

Note that in Fig. 3 we use a parametric notation for HCA which can be easily un-folded to a standard HCA as in Definition 2. For example, let $Data = \{0, 1\}$ be the set of data items, the unfolded non-parametric HCA is given in Fig. 4.

There are FIFO channels with some time properties such as the expiring FIFO1 channel, where a data item is lost if it is not taken out from the buffer through the sink end within τ time units after it enters the source end. The HCA for an expiring FIFO1 channel is shown in Fig. 5. The edge from s to $\bar{s}(d)$ models a write action on the source end A, which triggers the HCA moving to control state $\bar{s}(d)$, where the differential equation $\dot{\xi} = -1$ forces the automata to flow from the point $\tau \in \mathbb{R}$ towards $0 \in \mathbb{R}$. If no interaction-transition is available, i.e., the sink end B is not ready for a take operation, then the automata will reach the point $0 \in \mathbb{R}$ finally and immediately jump to the control state s trough $\bar{s}(d) \xrightarrow{\# = t} s$ in order to avoid violating the invariant predicate $\xi \geq 0$. Under this circumstance, the channel loses the data item in its buffer, which is exactly the behavior as we supposed. It is also possible that when the automaton is in the control state $\bar{s}(d)$ a take operation happens on the sink end B. This will force the automata to accept the I/O-operation and move back to the initial state s through $\bar{s}(d) \xrightarrow[\# := 0]{\{B\}, d_B = d, \# \geq 0} s$.

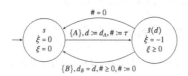

Fig. 5. HCA for expiring FIFO1 channel

A more interesting example is the data-sensitive FIFO1 channel where the behavior is determined by not only the external environment (i.e., the I/O-operations on its channel ends) but also the data items which are transferred through the channel. A typical example is a variant of a standard FIFO1 channel where after a write operation happens on the source end A, the times it takes to "transfer" the data item from A to the sink end B depends on the size of the data item being transferred. Let $size : Data \rightarrow \mathbb{R}_{>0}$ be a primitive function where $size(d)$ gives the size of data item $d \in Data$ and a constant data transferring speed $k \in \mathbb{R}_{>0}$. The HCA for such a channel is shown in Fig. 6. The edge $s \xrightarrow[\# := size(d)]{\{A\}, d := d_A} \bar{s}(d)$ models a write operation on A which forces the automata to move to the control state $\bar{s}(d)$ and locates in $size(d) \in \mathbb{R}$. When the automata stays in $\bar{s}(d)$, it flows based on the differential equation $\dot{\xi} = -k$ in the negative direction in $\mathbb{R}$. Notice the invariant set of $\bar{s}(d)$ is the entire space $\mathbb{R}$, therefore the automata is allowed to stay in the control state $\bar{s}(d)$ as long as there is no I/O-operation succeeds on B. If a take operation successfully happens on B, then the automata checks all legal outgoing transitions from $\bar{s}(d)$. Since the only outgoing transition is $\bar{s}(d) \xrightarrow[\# := 0]{\{B\}, d_B = d, \# \leq 0} s$ where the space constraint is $\# \leq 0$, the automata is able to make the transition only when it reaches the non-positive part in $\mathbb{R}$, that is at least $size(d)/k$ time units after the write operation happened on A.

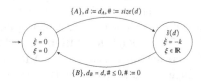

{A}, $d := d_A$, # := $size(d)$

s
$\dot{\xi} = 0$
$\xi = 0$

$\bar{s}(d)$
$\dot{\xi} = -k$
$\xi \in \mathbb{R}$

{B}, $d_B = d$, # ≤ 0, # := 0

Fig. 6. HCA for constant speed transferring FIFO1 channel

4.2   Join on HCA

In Reo, complex circuits can be composed by primitive channels. We now define the composition operator on HCA that serves to formalize Reo circuits in a compositional way.

Definition 6 (HCA product). *Let $\mathcal{T}_1$ and $\mathcal{T}_2$ be two HCA*

$$\mathcal{T}_i = (S_i, \mathbb{R}^{n_i}, \mathcal{N}_i, \mathcal{E}_i, IS_i, \{In_s\}_{s \in S_i}, \{f_s\}_{s \in S_i}, \{re_t\}_{t \in \mathcal{E}_i}) \tag{15}$$

where $i \in \{1, 2\}$ such that the set of all shared nodes $\mathcal{N}_0 = \mathcal{N}_1 \cap \mathcal{N}_2$. The product $\mathcal{T}_1 \bowtie \mathcal{T}_2$ is defined as an HCA

$$\mathcal{T} = (S, \mathbb{R}^n, \mathcal{N}, \mathcal{E}, IS, \{In_s\}_{s \in S}, \{f_s\}_{s \in S}, \{re_t\}_{t \in \mathcal{E}}) \tag{16}$$

consisting of

- *a set of control states $S = S_1 \times S_2$ and a set of initial control states $IS = IS_1 \times IS_2$;*
- *the dynamical system space $\mathbb{R}^n$ where $n = n_1 + n_2$;*
- *a finite set of nodes $\mathcal{N} = \mathcal{N}_1 \cup \mathcal{N}_2$;*
- *an n-dimensional dynamical system $\Sigma_s = (In_s, f_s)$ for each $s = \langle s_1, s_2 \rangle \in S$, where $In_s = In_{s_1} \times In_{s_2}$, and $f_s : In_s \rightarrow \mathbb{R}^n$ is a function defined as $f_s(x_1, x_2) = (f_{s_1}(x_1), f_{s_2}(x_2))$ for each $x_1 \in In_{s_1}$ and $x_2 \in In_{s_2}$;*
- *an edge relation $\mathcal{E}$ which is a subset of $S \times 2^{\mathcal{N}} \times DC \times SC \times S$;*
- *a reset function $re_t : Data^N \times In_s \rightarrow In_{\bar{s}}$ for each $t = (s, N, g, \varphi, \bar{s}) \in \mathcal{E}$.*

Intuitively, the compositional product HCA $\mathcal{T}$ behaves exactly as the parallel of $\mathcal{T}_1$ and $\mathcal{T}_2$, with the only constraint that all I/O-operations happen on the shared ports in N should coincide with each other. Therefore, $\langle s_1, s_2 \rangle \xrightarrow[re]{N, g, \varphi} \langle \bar{s}_1, \bar{s}_2 \rangle \in \mathcal{E}$ is defined by the following rules.

- *The first rule deals with the situation when $\mathcal{T}_1$ and $\mathcal{T}_2$ are about to do some I/O-operations on the nodes in N_1 and N_2 respectively at the same time. This is allowed only when they coincide on the shared nodes, that is*

$$
\frac{
\begin{array}{c}
s_1 \xrightarrow[re_1]{N_1, g_1, \varphi_1} \bar{s}_1 \in \mathcal{E}_1 \\
s_2 \xrightarrow[re_2]{N_2, g_2, \varphi_2} \bar{s}_2 \in \mathcal{E}_2 \\
N_1 \cap \mathcal{N}_0 = N_2 \cap \mathcal{N}_0 \\
g_1 \wedge g_2 \not\equiv false \\
\varphi_1 \wedge \varphi_2 \not\equiv false
\end{array}
}{
\langle s_1, s_2 \rangle \xrightarrow[re]{N_1 \cup N_2, g_1 \wedge g_2, \varphi_1 \wedge \varphi_2} \langle \bar{s}_1, \bar{s}_2 \rangle \in \mathcal{E}
} \tag{17}
$$

where $re : Data^N \times In_{\langle s_1, s_2 \rangle} \rightarrow \langle \bar{s}_1, \bar{s}_2 \rangle$ is a function defined as follows. For each $\delta \in Data^N$ and $i \in \{1, 2\}$, let $\delta_i \in Data^{N_i}$ satisfy $\delta_i(A) = \delta(A)$ for each $A \in N_i$. For each $\delta \in Data^N$ and $\langle x_1, x_2 \rangle \in \langle In_{s_1}, In_{s_2} \rangle$,

$$
re(\delta, \langle x_1, x_2 \rangle) = \langle re_1(\delta_1, x_1), re_2(\delta_2, x_2) \rangle.
$$

- *The second rule deals with the situation when $\mathcal{T}_1$ is about to make a discrete transition while $\mathcal{T}_2$ continues in flowing. This is allowed if $\mathcal{T}_1$'s transition does not ask $\mathcal{T}_2$ to coordinate with it, that is*

$$
\frac{
\begin{array}{c}
s_1 \xrightarrow[re_1]{N_1, g_1, \varphi_1} \bar{s}_1 \in \mathcal{T}_1 \\
s_2 \in S_2 \\
N_1 \cap \mathcal{N}_0 = \emptyset
\end{array}
}{
\langle s_1, s_2 \rangle \xrightarrow[re]{N_1, g_1, \varphi_1} \langle \bar{s}_1, s_2 \rangle
} \tag{18}
$$

where $re : Data^N \times In_{\langle s_1, s_2 \rangle} \rightarrow \langle \bar{s}_1, \bar{s}_2 \rangle$ is a function defined as $re(\delta, \langle x_1, x_2 \rangle) = re_1(\delta, x_1)$ which is well defined since $N = N_1$. There is a symmetric rule which deals with the situation when $\mathcal{T}_2$ is about to make a discrete transition while $\mathcal{T}_1$ continues in flowing:

$$
\frac{
\begin{array}{c}
s_2 \xrightarrow[re_2]{N_2, g_2, \varphi_2} \bar{s}_2 \in \mathcal{T}_2 \\
s_1 \in S_1 \\
N_2 \cap \mathcal{N}_0 = \emptyset
\end{array}
}{
\langle s_1, s_2 \rangle \xrightarrow[re]{N_2, g_2, \varphi_2} \langle s_1, \bar{s}_2 \rangle
} \tag{19}
$$

Roughly speaking, the product HCA $\mathcal{T}$ needs to deal with three situations:

- both HCA choose to make discrete transitions. This is captured by (17);
- one of the HCA chooses to make a discrete transition while the other chooses to stay in current control state and continues in flowing. This is captured by (18) and (19).
- both HCA choose to stay in their current control states respectively and continue in flowing. This is captured by the composed dynamical systems $\Sigma_{\langle s_1, s_2\rangle}$.

Here we introduce some convenient notations for the join operation. For $s = \langle s_1, s_2\rangle$, we use $s.first$, $s.second$ to denote s_1, s_2 respectively. Similarly, for $x = \langle x_1, x_2\rangle$, we use $x.first$, $x.second$ to denote x_1, x_2 respectively.

The join operator introduced in Definition 6 captures the replicator semantics of source nodes in Reo. Therefore it can serve as the semantic operator for the join of two nodes where at least one of them is a source node. To mimic the merge semantics of sink nodes, we introduce the HCA $\mathcal{T}_{Merger}$ shown in Fig. 7. To join two sink nodes A and B, we first choose a new node named C and then return $\mathcal{T}_{Merger}(A, B, C) \bowtie \mathcal{T}_A \bowtie \mathcal{T}_B$ where $\mathcal{T}_A$ and $\mathcal{T}_B$ are the HCA that model the sub-circuits containing A and B respectively.

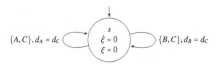

Fig. 7. HCA for merger

The correctness of the join operator on HCA is guaranteed by means of TDS-languages. For this purpose, we define the join operator on TDS-languages and establish a compositionality result in Theorem 2.

Definition 7 (Join on timed data streams and TDS languages). *Let* $\Theta = ((N_i, \delta_i, t_i))_i$ *and* $\Phi = ((M_j, \gamma_j, s_j))_j$ *be two TDS over* $\mathcal{N}$ *and* $\mathcal{M}$ *respectively. The common node-set is denoted as* $\mathcal{N}_0 = \mathcal{N} \cap \mathcal{M}$. *We say that* Θ *and* Φ *are inconsistent if there exist* $i \in \mathbb{N}$ *and* $j \in \mathbb{N}$ *such that* $t_i = s_j$, $(N_i \cup M_j) \cap \mathcal{N}_0 \neq \emptyset$ *and* $\delta_i \upharpoonright_{\mathcal{N}_0} \neq \gamma_j \upharpoonright_{\mathcal{N}_0}$. *We say that* Θ *and* Φ *are consistent if they are not inconsistent. The join* $\Theta \bowtie \Phi$ *of two consistent TDS can be inductively defined as a sequence generated by*

- *appending* (N_1, δ_1, t_1) *to* $\Theta' \bowtie \Phi$, *if* $t_1 < s_1$;
- *appending* (M_1, γ_1, s_1) *to* $\Theta \bowtie \Phi'$, *if* $s_1 < t_1$;
- *appending* $(N_1 \cup M_1, \delta_1 \cup \gamma_1, t_1)$ *to* $\Theta' \bowtie \Phi'$, *if* $s_1 = t_1$. $\delta_1 \cup \gamma_1$ *is well defined since* Θ *and* Φ *are consistent.*

Let L_1 *and* L_2 *be two TDS-languages over* $\mathcal{N}_1$ *and* $\mathcal{N}_2$ *respectively. The join* $L_1 \bowtie L_2$ *is a TDS-language over* $\mathcal{N}_1 \cup \mathcal{N}_2$ *consists of all timed data streams* Θ *that can be obtained by joining two consistent timed data streams* $\Theta_1 \in L_1$ *and* $\Theta_2 \in L_2$.

Lemma 1. *Let* $\mathcal{T}_1$ *and* $\mathcal{T}_2$ *be HCA, then*

$$\mathcal{L}(\mathcal{T}_1 \bowtie \mathcal{T}_2) = \mathcal{L}(\mathcal{T}_1) \bowtie \mathcal{L}(\mathcal{T}_2) . \tag{20}$$

Lemma 1 directly leads to the following compositional theorem, which implies the correctness of the product operator on HCA.

Theorem 2. *Let $\mathcal{T}_1$, $\mathcal{T}_2$ and $\mathcal{T}_3$ be HCA, then*

$$\mathcal{L}((\mathcal{T}_1 \bowtie \mathcal{T}_2) \bowtie \mathcal{T}_3) = \mathcal{L}(\mathcal{T}_1 \bowtie (\mathcal{T}_2 \bowtie \mathcal{T}_3)) \tag{21}$$

Example 4. Figure 8 shows a Reo circuit consisting of two expiring FIFO1 channels, with expiring limit τ and ω respectively. The HCA for the two channels and the whole circuit obtained by their join are shown in Fig. 9.

Fig. 8. The Reo circuit obtained by joining two expiring FIFO1 channels

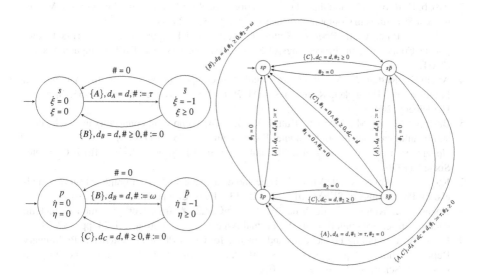

Fig. 9. HCA for two expiring FIFO1 channels and the Reo circuit consisting of them

5   Conclusion

In this paper we introduced hybrid constraint automata (HCA) as a formal model to define hybrid behavior for Reo component connectors. We presented a compositional product operator that can serves as a basis for the automated construction of a hybrid constraint automaton model from a given Reo circuit, and as a starting point for its formal verification.

In terms of future work, what we would like to do in the next step is to develop proper logics for specifying hybrid properties of Reo connectors. Development of suitable algorithms and model checking tools to verify hybrid properties of connectors in Reo based on the HCA model will also be studied.

Acknowledgement. The work was partially supported by the National Natural Science Foundation of China under grant no. 61202069 and 61272160, project IGDSi1305012 from SUTD, and Research Fund for the Doctoral Program of Higher Education of China under grant no. 20120001120103.

References

1. Alur, R., Courcoubetis, C., Henzinger, T.A., Ho, P.-H.: Hybrid Automata: An Algorithmic Approach to the Specification and Verification of Hybrid Systems. In: Grossman, R.L., Ravn, A.P., Rischel, H., Nerode, A. (eds.) HS 1991 and HS 1992. LNCS, vol. 736, pp. 209–229. Springer, Heidelberg (1993)
2. Arbab, F.: Reo: A Channel-based Coordination Model for Component Composition. Mathematical Structures in Computer Science 14(3), 329–366 (2004)
3. Arbab, F., Baier, C., de Boer, F., Rutten, J.: Models and Temporal Logics for Timed Component Connectors. In: Proceedings of SEFM2004, pp. 198–207. IEEE Computer Society (2004)
4. Arbab, F., Rutten, J.: A coinductive calculus of component connectors. In: Wirsing, M., Pattinson, D., Hennicker, R. (eds.) WADT 2003. LNCS, vol. 2755, pp. 34–55. Springer, Heidelberg (2003)
5. Baier, C., Sirjani, M., Arbab, F., Rutten, J.: Modeling component connectors in Reo by constraint automata. Science of Computer Programming 61, 75–113 (2006)
6. Henzinger, T.A.: The theory of hybrid automata. In: LICS, pp. 278–292. IEEE Computer Society (1996)
7. Kokash, N., Krause, C., de Vink, E.: Time and data aware analysis of graphical service models. In: Proceedings of SEFM 2010, pp. 125–134. IEEE Computer Society (2010)
8. Kokash, N., Krause, C., de Vink, E.: Reo+mCRL2: A framework for model-checking dataflow in service compositions. In: Formal Aspects of Computing, vol. 24, pp. 187–216.
9. Lee, E.A.: Computing Foundations and Practice for Cyber Physical Systems: A Preliminary Report. Technical Report UCB/EECS-2007-72, Department of Electrical Engineering and Computer Sciences, UC Berkeley (2007)
10. Lynch, N.A., Segala, R., Vaandrager, F.W.: Hybrid I/O Automata Revisited. In: Di Benedetto, M.D., Sangiovanni-Vincentelli, A.L. (eds.) HSCC 2001. LNCS, vol. 2034, pp. 403–417. Springer, Heidelberg (2001)
11. Lynch, N., Segala, R., Vaandrager, F., Weinberg, H.: Hybrid I/O Automata. In: Alur, R., Sontag, E.D., Henzinger, T.A. (eds.) HS 1995. LNCS, vol. 1066, pp. 496–510. Springer, Heidelberg (1996)
12. Meng, S.: Connectors as designs: The time dimension. In: Proceedings of TASE 2012, pp. 201–208. IEEE Computer Society (2012)
13. Peano, G.: Demonstration de l'intégrabilité des équations defférentielles ordinaires. Mathematische Annalen 37, 182–228 (1890)

A Language-Independent Proof System for Mutual Program Equivalence*

Ştefan Ciobâcă[1], Dorel Lucanu[1], Vlad Rusu[2], and Grigore Roşu[1,3]

[1] "Alexandru Ioan Cuza" University, Romania
[2] Inria Lille, France
[3] University of Illinois at Urbana-Champaign, USA

Abstract. Two programs are mutually equivalent if they both diverge or they both terminate with the same result. In this paper we introduce a language-independent proof system for mutual equivalence, which is parametric in the operational semantics of two languages and in a state-similarity relation. We illustrate it on two programs in two different languages (an imperative one and a functional one), that both compute the Collatz sequence.

1 Introduction

Two terminating programs are equivalent if the final states that they reach are similar (they have the same result). Nontermination can be incorporated in equivalence in several ways. In this article, we explore *mutual equivalence*, an equivalence relation that is also known in the literature as full equivalence [6]. Two programs are said to be *mutually equivalent* iff they either both diverge or they both terminate and then the final states that they reach are similar. Mutual equivalence is thus an adequate notion of equivalence for programs written in deterministic sequential languages and is useful, e.g., in compiler verification.

In this paper we formalize the notion of mutual equivalence and propose a logic with a deductive system for stating and proving mutual equivalence of two programs that are written in two possibly different languages. The deductive system is language-independent, in the sense that it is parametric in the semantics of the two-languages. We prove that the proposed system is sound: when it succeeds it proves the mutual equivalence of the programs given to it as input. The key idea is to use the proof system to build a relation on configurations that is closed under the transition relations given by the corresponding operational semantics. This involves constructing a single language that is capable of executing pairs of programs written in the two languages. The challenge is how to achieve that generically, where the two languages are given by their formal semantics, without relying on the specifics of any particular language. The aggregated language must be capable of independently "executing" pairs of

---

* This paper is supported by the Sectorial Operational Programme Human Resource Development (SOP HRD), financed from the European Social Fund and by the Romanian Government under the contract number POSDRU/159/1.5/S/137750.

S. Merz and J. Pang (Eds.): ICFEM 2014, LNCS 8829, pp. 75–90, 2014.

programs in the original languages. Once the aggregated language constructed, the most important rule in our proof system for mutual equivalence is the Circularity rule, which incrementally postulates synchronization points in the two programs. We illustrate the proof system on two programs (Fig. 5 on page 88) that both compute the Collatz sequence, but in different ways: one is written in an imperative language and the other one in a functional language. We prove with our system that they are mutually equivalent without, of course, knowing whether they terminate.

Section 2 introduces preliminaries needed in the rest of the paper. Section 3 presents matching logic, a specialization of first-order logic, and shows how it can be used to give operational semantics to programming languages. Section 4 then shows how to aggregate matching logic semantics. Section 5 shows how our formalism can be used to specify equivalent programs and Section 6 presents our proof system for mutual equivalence and applies it to two programs computing the Collatz sequence. Section 7 discusses related work and concludes. Proofs not included due to space constraints can be found in the technical report [2].

2   Preliminaries

We present the syntax and semantics of **many-sorted first-order logic**, used to define matching logic. We state the amalgamation theorem for first-order logic, a known result that allows us to construct a model for the pushout construction of two signatures, from the the models of the two signatures, even when the two signature share function symbols. We use the amalgamation result to construct the aggregated semantics of two languages from their individual semantics.

2.1   Many-Sorted First Order Logic

Let S be a set of **sorts**, Σ an S-sorted algebraic signature (i.e., an indexed set $\Sigma = \cup_{w \in S^*, s \in S} \Sigma_{w,s}$, where $\Sigma_{w,s}$ is the set of function symbols of arity w with a result of sort s) and Π an indexed set $\Pi = \cup_{w \in S^*} \Pi_w$ of predicate symbols. Then $\Phi = (S, \Sigma, \Pi)$ is called a **many-sorted FOL signature**. We write $x \in \Phi$ instead of $x \in S \cup \Sigma \cup \Pi$. By $T_{\Sigma,s}(Var)$ we denote the set of terms of sort s built over the variables Var with function symbols in Σ. We sometimes omit Σ if it is clear from the context and we write $T_s(Var)$ instead of $T_{\Sigma,s}(Var)$.

Example 1. The signatures $\Phi_I = (S_I, \Sigma_I, \Pi_I)$ and $\Phi_F = (S_F, \Sigma_F, \Pi_F)$ in Figure 1 model the syntax of an imperative and a functional programming language, with sorts $S_I = \{\text{Int}, \text{Var}, \text{ExpI}, \text{Stmt}, \text{Code}, \text{CfgI}\}$ in IMP and sorts $S_F = \{\text{Var}, \text{Int}, \text{ExpF}, \text{Val}, \text{CfgF}\}$ in FUN, and function symbols

$$\Sigma_I = \{\_+\_, \_*\_, \_-\_, \_+_{Int}, \_-_{Int}, \_*_{Int}, \_:=\_, \text{skip}, \_;\_, \text{i\_t\_e\_}, \text{while\_do\_}, \langle\_,\_\rangle\},$$
$$\Sigma_F = \{\_+\_, \_*\_, \_-\_, \_+_{Int}, \_-_{Int}, \_*_{Int}, \_\_, \text{letrec\_=\_in\_}, \text{i\_t\_e\_}, \mu\_.\_, \lambda\_.\_, \langle\_\rangle\}.$$

The functions above are written in Maude-like notation, the underscore (_) denoting the position of an argument. The symbol i_t_e_ stands for if_then_else_. Although not written explicitly above, the signatures also include the one-argument injections needed to inject sorts like Int and Var into ExpI.

```
ExpI ::= Var | Int | ExpI + ExpI        ExpF ::= Var | Val | ExpF + ExpF
Stmt ::= Var := ExpI                           | ExpF ExpF
         | skip | Stmt ; Stmt                   | letrec Var Var = ExpF in ExpF
         | if ExpI then Stmt else Stmt          | if ExpF then ExpF else ExpF
         | while ExpI do Stmt                   | μ Var . ExpF
Code ::= ExpI | Stmt                     Val  ::= Int | λ Var . ExpF
CfgI ::= ⟨Code, Map{Var,Int}⟩            CfgF ::= ⟨ExpF⟩
```

Fig. 1. $\Phi_I = (S_I, \Sigma_I, \Pi_I)$ and $\Phi_F = (S_F, \Sigma_F, \Pi_F)$, the signatures of IMP and FUN, detailed in Example 1. Only the function symbols are detailed in the figure; the predicates consist of the arithmetic comparison operators: $\Pi_I = \Pi_F = \{=_{Int}, <_{Int}, \leq_{Int}\}$. The difference between the operators $\_+\_$, $\_*\_$, etc. and their correspondants $\_+\_{Int}$, $\_*\_{Int}$, etc. is that the former are the syntactic language constructs for addition, etc., while the later are the actual function symbols denoting integer addition, etc.

Definition 1. *We say that $\mathcal{T} = (\llbracket\cdot\rrbracket_\mathcal{T}^S, \llbracket\cdot\rrbracket_\mathcal{T}^F, \llbracket\cdot\rrbracket_\mathcal{T}^P)$ is a **model** of a many-sorted signature $\Phi = (S, \Sigma, \Pi)$ if:*

1. *$\llbracket s \rrbracket_\mathcal{T}^S$, the interpretation of the sort s in the model $\mathcal{T}$, is a set for each $s \in S$*
2. *$\llbracket f \rrbracket_\mathcal{T}^F$, read as the interpretation of the function symbol f in the model $\mathcal{T}$, is a function defined on $\llbracket s_1 \rrbracket_\mathcal{T} \times \ldots \times \llbracket s_n \rrbracket_\mathcal{T}$ with values in $\llbracket s \rrbracket_\mathcal{T}$, for every function symbol $f \in \Sigma_{s_1,\ldots,s_n,s}$.*
3. *$\llbracket p \rrbracket_\mathcal{T}^P$, read as the interpretation of the predicate symbol p in the model $\mathcal{T}$, is a subset of $\llbracket s_1 \rrbracket_\mathcal{T} \times \ldots \times \llbracket s_n \rrbracket_\mathcal{T}$ for every predicate symbol $p \in \Pi_{s_1,\ldots,s_n}$.*

From now on, we write $\llbracket\cdot\rrbracket_\mathcal{T}$ instead of $\llbracket\cdot\rrbracket_\mathcal{T}^S$, $\llbracket\cdot\rrbracket_\mathcal{T}^F$ and $\llbracket\cdot\rrbracket_\mathcal{T}^P$ when the type of the argument (sort, function symbol or predicate symbol), is clear from context.

Example 2. We consider $\mathcal{T}_I$ to be a model of $\Phi_I = (S_I, \Sigma_I, \Pi_I)$ where the interpretation $\llbracket\mathtt{Var}\rrbracket_{\mathcal{T}_I}$ of the sort $\mathtt{Var}$ is the set of strings, the interpretation $\llbracket\mathtt{Int}\rrbracket_{\mathcal{T}_I}$ of the sort $\mathtt{Int}$ is the set of integers and the function symbols are interpreted syntactically (as terms). The predicates $=_{Int}, <_{Int}, \leq_{Int}$ are interpreted as the respective comparison relations between integers.

Definition 2. *Let $\Phi = (S, \Sigma, \Pi)$ and $\Phi' = (S', \Sigma', \Pi')$ be two many-sorted FOL signatures and let h be a function from $S \cup \Sigma \cup \Pi$ to $S' \cup \Sigma' \cup \Pi'$. The function h is a **morphism** between Φ and Φ' if it preserves sort compatibility.*

Definition 3. *Let h be a morphism from $\Phi = (S, \Sigma, \Pi)$ to $\Phi' = (S', \Sigma', \Pi')$ and $\mathcal{T}'$ be a model of $\Phi' = (S', \Sigma', \Pi')$. We define $\mathcal{T}'|_h$ (the **reduct** of $\mathcal{T}'$ through h) to be the model of Φ such that:*

1. *$\llbracket s \rrbracket_{\mathcal{T}'|_h} = \llbracket h(s) \rrbracket_{\mathcal{T}'}$ for all $s \in S$.*
2. *$\llbracket f \rrbracket_{\mathcal{T}'|_h}(e_1, \ldots, e_n) = \llbracket h(f) \rrbracket_{\mathcal{T}'}(e_1, \ldots, e_n)$ for all $f \in \Sigma_{s_1,\ldots,s_n,s}$ and for all $e_1 \in \llbracket s_1 \rrbracket_{\mathcal{T}'|_h}, \ldots, e_n \in \llbracket s_n \rrbracket_{\mathcal{T}'|_h}$.*
3. *$(e_1, \ldots, e_n) \in \llbracket p \rrbracket_{\mathcal{T}'|_h}$ iff $(e_1, \ldots, e_n) \in \llbracket h(p) \rrbracket_{\mathcal{T}'}$ for all $p \in \Pi_{s_1,\ldots,s_n}$ and for all $e_1 \in \llbracket h(s_1) \rrbracket_{\mathcal{T}'}, \ldots, e_n \in \llbracket h(s_n) \rrbracket_{\mathcal{T}'}$.*

$$(S_0, \Sigma_0, \Pi_0) \xrightarrow{\ h_R\ } (S_R, \Sigma_R, \Pi_R)$$
$$h_L \downarrow \qquad \xrightarrow{\ h'_L\ } \qquad \downarrow h'_R$$
$$(S_L, \Sigma_L, \Pi_L) \xrightarrow{\ h'_L\ } (S', \Sigma', \Pi')$$

Fig. 2. Push-out diagram assumed throughout the paper

Example 3. Let $\Phi = (\{\text{Int}\}, \{op_{Int} \mid op \in \{\_+\_, \_-\_, \_*\_\}\}, \{op_{Int} \mid op \in \{=, <, \le\})$ be a signature and let h (with $h(\text{Int}) = \text{Int}$ and $h(op_{Int}) = op_{Int}$ for $op \in \{\_+\_, \_-\_, \_*\_\}$) be a morphism from Φ to Φ_I (defined above in Example 1). Let $\mathcal{T}_I$ be the model of Φ_I considered above in Example 2. We have that $\llbracket \text{Int} \rrbracket_{\mathcal{T}' \restriction_h}$ is the set of integers, $\llbracket \_+\_{Int} \rrbracket_{\mathcal{T}' \restriction_h}$ is the addition of integers, etc.

2.2   The Amalgamation Theorem

Theorem 1 (Pushout). *Let Φ_R, Φ_L and Φ_0 be three FOL signatures, h_R a morphism from Φ_0 to Φ_R and h_L a morphism from Φ_0 to Φ_L. There exists a tuple (h'_L, Φ', h'_R), called the **pushout** of $\Phi_L \xleftarrow{h_L} \Phi_0 \xrightarrow{h_R} \Phi_R$, where h'_L is a morphism from Φ_L to Φ' and h'_R a morphism from Φ_R to Φ' such that:*

1. *(commutativity) $h'_L(h_L(x)) = h'_R(h_R(x))$ for all $x \in \Phi_0$ and*
2. *(minimality) if there exist Φ'' and morphisms h''_L (from Φ_L to Φ'') and h''_R (from Φ_R to Φ'') such that $h''_L(h_L(x)) = h''_R(h_R(x))$ for all $x \in \Phi_0$ then there exists a morphism h from Φ' to Φ''.*

Furthermore, the pushout is unique (up to renaming). See, e.g., [7], for a proof. The push-out is summarised in Figure 2, which is used throughout the paper.

Proposition 1. *In the push-out in Figure 2, if $x' \in \Phi' = (S', \Sigma', \Pi')$ such that there exist $x_L \in \Phi_L$ and $x_R \in \Phi_R$ with $h'_R(x_R) = x' = h'_L(x_L)$, then there exists $x \in \Phi$ such that $h_L(x) = x_L$ and $h_R(x) = x_R$.*

Theorem 2 (Amalgamation). *If $\mathcal{T}_R$, $\mathcal{T}_L$ and $\mathcal{T}_0$ are models of Φ_R, Φ_L and respectively Φ_0 such that $\mathcal{T}_R \restriction_{h_R} = \mathcal{T}_L \restriction_{h_L} = \mathcal{T}_0$, there exists a unique model $\mathcal{T}'$ of Φ' such that $\mathcal{T}' \restriction_{h'_L} = \mathcal{T}_L$ and $\mathcal{T}' \restriction_{h'_R} = \mathcal{T}_R$.*

3   Matching Logic Syntax and Semantics

We introduce notation used throughout the paper and the recently introduced *matching logic* [16,17], a language-parametric logic for reasoning about program configurations, and its use in language semantics. We choose matching logic as it allows to faithfully represent all of the usual operational semantics styles such as small-step, big-step, etc [16]. Matching logic extends FOL with *basic patterns*, which are open terms (i.e., terms with variables) that can be used as basic formulae in the logic. We first introduce **matching logic signatures** (ML signatures), which extend FOL signatures by fixing a sort of program **configurations**.

Definition 4. *A matching logic signature is a tuple (Cfg, S, Σ, Π), where the tuple (S, Σ, Π) is a FOL signature and $Cfg \in S$.*

Example 4. Recall the first-order signature $\Phi_I = (S_I, \Sigma_I, \Pi_I)$ in Example 1. We have that $(\texttt{CfgI}, S_I, \Sigma_I, \Pi_I)$ is a matching logic signature. Note that ground instances of sort $\texttt{CfgI}$ represent actual configurations of $\texttt{IMP}$ programs.

Matching logic formulae extend FOL formulae with terms of sort Cfg as atomic formulae called **basic patterns**:

Definition 5. *Given a matching logic signature (Cfg, S, Σ, Π), the following are* **matching logic formulae** *(ML formulae) over (Cfg, S, Σ, Π) and the set of sorted variables Var: $\varphi ::= \neg\varphi, \varphi \wedge \varphi, \exists x.\varphi, \pi$ where $\pi \in T_{Cfg}(Var), x \in Var$.*

Example 5. Continuing Example 4, $\varphi = \langle \texttt{skip}, \texttt{x} \mapsto x, \texttt{y} \mapsto y \rangle \wedge x >_{Int} 10$ is a matching logic formula over the matching logic signature $(\texttt{CfgI}, S_I, \Sigma_I, \Pi_I)$. Note that $\texttt{x}$ and $\texttt{y}$ (written in $\texttt{teletype}$ font) are program variables (therefore constant symbols in Σ_I, while x and y (written in *italics*) are variables. Intuitively, and as we will see later on, the formula above denotes $\texttt{IMP}$ configurations that have terminated (only the instruction $\texttt{skip}$ is left in the code to execute) and in which the program variable $\texttt{x}$ is mapped to an integer strictly greater than 10 and the program variable $\texttt{y}$ is mapped to an integer y that is unconstrained.

Definition 6. *We say that $\mathcal{T}$ is a* **matching logic model** *of (Cfg, S, Σ, Π) if $\mathcal{T}$ is a first order model of (S, Σ, Π).*

Example 6. The model $\mathcal{T}$ defined in Example 2 is also a model of the matching logic signature $(\texttt{CfgI}, S_I, \Sigma_I, \Pi_I)$.

In what follows, we fix a model $\mathcal{T}$ of (Cfg, S, Σ, Π). Elements of $[\![Cfg]\!]_{\mathcal{T}}$ are called concrete **configurations**. We represent concrete configurations by $\gamma, \gamma', \gamma_1$ and variations thereof. Valuations $\rho : Var \to \mathcal{T}$ of matching logic are simply valuations of the corresponding first order logic. The satisfaction relation of matching logic is defined between pairs (γ, ρ) of configurations and valuations and ML formulae φ as follows:

Definition 7. *The* **matching logic satisfaction** *relation $\models$ (written as $(\gamma, \rho) \models \varphi$ and read as (γ, ρ) is a* **model** *of φ) is defined inductively as follows:*

1. *$(\gamma, \rho) \models \neg\varphi'$ if it is not true that $(\gamma, \rho) \models \varphi'$*
2. *$(\gamma, \rho) \models \varphi_1 \wedge \varphi_2$ if $(\gamma, \rho) \models \varphi_1$ and $(\gamma, \rho) \models \varphi_2$*
3. *$(\gamma, \rho) \models \exists x.\varphi'$, where x is of sort s, if there exists $e \in [\![s]\!]_{\mathcal{T}}$ such that $(\gamma, \rho[e/x]) \models \varphi'$ (where $\rho[e/x]$ is the valuation obtained from ρ by updating the value of x to be e).*
4. *$(\gamma, \rho) \models \pi$, where π is a basic pattern if $\rho(\pi) = \gamma$.*

Example 7. We continue Example 5, where we defined $\varphi = \langle \texttt{skip}, \texttt{x} \mapsto x, \texttt{y} \mapsto y \rangle \wedge x >_{Int} 10$. Let ρ be a valuation where $\rho(x) = 12$ and $\rho(y) = 3$. Let $\gamma = \langle \texttt{skip}, \texttt{x} \mapsto 12, \texttt{y} \mapsto 3 \rangle$. We have that $(\gamma, \rho) \models \varphi$. Considering $\gamma' = \langle \texttt{skip}, \texttt{x} \mapsto$

$3, \mathtt{y} \mapsto 13\rangle$ and a valuation ρ' with $\rho'(x) = 3$ and $\rho'(y) = 13$, we have that $(\gamma', \rho') \not\models \varphi$ because the condition $x >_{Int} 10$ is not satisfied. Furthermore, if $\gamma'' = \langle\mathtt{skip}, \mathtt{x} \mapsto 3, \mathtt{y} \mapsto 13\rangle$ and ρ'' is a valuation with $\rho''(x) = 7$ and $\rho''(y) = 13$, we have that $(\gamma'', \rho'') \not\models \varphi$ because γ'' will not match against the basic pattern $\langle\mathtt{skip}, \mathtt{x} \mapsto x, \mathtt{y} \mapsto y\rangle$ with the valuation ρ'' (the valuation ρ'' assigns 7 to the variable x, while x should be 3 due to matching).

Definition 8. *A **matching logic semantic domain** for a language is a tuple* $(Cfg, S, \Sigma, \Pi, \mathcal{T})$, *where* (Cfg, S, Σ, Π) *is a matching logic signature and* $\mathcal{T}$ *a matching logic model of* (Cfg, S, Σ, Π).

Example 8. For $\mathcal{T}_I$ defined in Example 6, we have that $(\mathtt{CfgI}, S_I, \Sigma_I, \Pi_I, \mathcal{T}_I)$ is a matching logic semantic domain for the IMP language.

Note that the matching logic semantic domain fixes the abstract syntax of the language (programs are first-order terms of sort Cfg) and the configuration space (given by the model $\mathcal{T}$). However, the matching logic semantic domain does not say anything about the dynamic behavior of configurations. This is the role of the matching logic semantics. A matching logic semantics for a programming language extends the matching logic semantic domain by the addition of several reachability rules:

Definition 9. *A **reachability rule** is a pair* $\varphi \Rightarrow \varphi'$ *of matching logic formulae.*

Example 9. Let us consider the rule $\langle\mathtt{skip}; s, m\rangle \Rightarrow \langle s, m\rangle$. In the rule above, s is a variable of sort $\mathtt{Stmt}$ and m is a variable of sort $\mathtt{Map\{Var, Int\}}$. It describes what happens in the IMP language when the code to execute is a sequence composed of the $\mathtt{skip}$ instruction and another statement s. The $\mathtt{skip}$ instruction is simply dissolved and the sequence is simply replaced by s. The environment (captured in the variable m) is not changed during this step.

Definition 10. *The **matching logic semantics** for a language is a tuple* $(Cfg, S, \Sigma, \Pi, \mathcal{T}, \mathcal{A}, \rightarrow_{\mathcal{T}})$, *where* $(Cfg, S, \Sigma, \Pi, \mathcal{T})$ *is matching logic semantic domain,* $\mathcal{A}$ *a set of reachability rules and* $\rightarrow_{\mathcal{T}}$ *is the transition system generated by* $\mathcal{A}$ *on* $\mathcal{T}$, *that is,* $\rightarrow_{\mathcal{T}} \subseteq \mathcal{T}_{Cfg} \times \mathcal{T}_{Cfg}$ *with* $\gamma \rightarrow_{\mathcal{T}} \gamma'$ *iff there exist* $\varphi \Rightarrow \varphi' \in \mathcal{A}$ *and* ρ *such that* $(\gamma, \rho) \models \varphi$ *and* $(\gamma', \rho) \models \varphi'$.

Example 10. Figure 3 presents the set of reachability rules $\mathcal{A}_I$ of IMP. Due to space constraints, the rules $\mathcal{A}_F$ for FUN can be found in the technical report [2].

As discussed in [16], conventional operational semantics of programming languages can be regarded as matching logic semantics: Σ includes the abstract syntax of the language as well as the syntax of the various operations in the needed mathematical domains; $\mathcal{A}$ is the (possibly infinite) set of operational semantics rules of the language; $\mathcal{T}$ is the model of configurations of the language merged together with needed mathematical domains, and the relation $\rightarrow_{\mathcal{T}}$ is precisely the transition relation defined by the operational semantics. Fig. 3 shows the matching logic semantics of the IMP, obtained by mechanically

$\langle x,\ env \rangle \Rightarrow \langle env(x),\ env \rangle \in \mathcal{A}_I$
$\langle i_1\ \mathtt{op}\ i_2,\ env \rangle \Rightarrow \langle i_1\ \mathtt{op}_{Int}\ i_2,\ env \rangle \in \mathcal{A}_I$
$\langle x\ \mathtt{:=}\ i,\ env \rangle \Rightarrow \langle \mathtt{skip},\ env[x \mapsto i] \rangle \in \mathcal{A}_I$
$\langle \mathtt{skip;} s,\ env \rangle \Rightarrow \langle s,\ env \rangle \in \mathcal{A}_I$
$\langle \mathtt{if}\ i\ \mathtt{then}\ s_1\ \mathtt{else}\ s_2,\ env \rangle \wedge i \neq 0 \Rightarrow \langle s_1,\ env \rangle \in \mathcal{A}_I$
$\langle \mathtt{if}\ 0\ \mathtt{then}\ s_1\ \mathtt{else}\ s_2,\ env \rangle \Rightarrow \langle s_2,\ env \rangle \in \mathcal{A}_I$
$\langle \mathtt{while}\ e\ \mathtt{do}\ s,\ env \rangle \Rightarrow \langle \mathtt{if}\ e\ \mathtt{then}\ s\ \mathtt{while}\ e\ \mathtt{do}\ s\ \mathtt{else}\ \mathtt{skip},\ env \rangle \in \mathcal{A}_I$
$\langle C[code],\ env \rangle \Rightarrow \langle C[code'],\ env' \rangle \in \mathcal{A}_I \qquad \text{if}\ \langle code,\ env \rangle \Rightarrow \langle code',\ env' \rangle \in \mathcal{A}_I$

where $C\ \mathtt{::=}\ \_\ |\ C\ \mathtt{op}\ e\ |\ i\ \mathtt{op}\ C\ |\ \mathtt{if}\ C\ \mathtt{then}\ s_1\ \mathtt{else}\ s_2\ |\ v\ \mathtt{:=}\ C\ |\ C\ s$

Fig. 3. Matching logic semantics of IMP as a set $\mathcal{A}_I$ of reachability rules (schemata). op ranges over the binary function symbols and op_{Int} is their denotation in $\mathcal{T}_I$.

representing the conventional operational semantics of this language based on reduction semantics with evaluation contexts into matching logic. The only observable difference between the original semantics of these languages and their matching logic semantics is that the side conditions have been conjuncted with the left-hand-side patterns in the positive case of the conditionals. Note that $\mathcal{A}_{\mathrm{IMP}}$ and $\mathcal{A}_{\mathrm{FUN}}$ are infinite, as the rules in Fig. 3 are schemata in meta-variable C (the evaluation context).

Given a matching logic language semantics as a set of reachability rules, it is possible to derive other reachability rules that "hold" as consequences of the initial set of rules. This is captured by the following definition.

Definition 11. *Given a matching logic semantics* $(Cfg, \Sigma, \Pi, \mathcal{T}, \mathcal{A}, \rightarrow_{\mathcal{T}})$, *we say that* $\varphi \rightarrow^* \varphi'$ *(resp.* $\varphi \rightarrow^+ \varphi'$) *is a **semantic consequence** of* $\mathcal{A}$, *and we write* $\mathcal{A} \models \varphi \rightarrow^* \varphi'$ *(resp.* $\mathcal{A} \models \varphi \rightarrow^+ \varphi'$), *if for any* $\gamma \in [\![Cfg]\!]_{\mathcal{T}}$, *for any valuation* ρ *such that* $(\gamma, \rho) \models \varphi$, *there exists* $\gamma' \in [\![Cfg]\!]_{\mathcal{T}}$ *such that* $(\gamma', \rho) \models \varphi'$ *and* $\gamma \rightarrow^*_{\mathcal{T}} \gamma'$ *(resp.* $\gamma \rightarrow^+_{\mathcal{T}} \gamma'$).

Example 11. In the set of reachability rules $\mathcal{A}_I$ for the IMP languages (given in Figure 3), if we let $\mathtt{SUM} \equiv \mathtt{while\ i\ <=\ n\ do\ (s\ :=\ s\ +\ i;\ i\ :=\ i\ +\ 1)}$ be the program that computes the sum of all numbers between i and n, then we have

$$\mathcal{A}_I \models \langle \mathtt{SUM},\ \mathtt{n} \mapsto n, \mathtt{i} \mapsto 0; \mathtt{s} \mapsto 0 \rangle \wedge n \geq_{Int} 0 \rightarrow^+$$
$$\langle \mathtt{skip},\ [\mathtt{n} \mapsto n; \mathtt{i} \mapsto n + 1; \mathtt{s} \mapsto n(n +_{Int} 1)/_{Int} 2] \rangle.$$

Intuitively the above reachability rule that is a semantic consequence of the IMP set of leachability rules claims that the program SUM indeed computes the sum of the numbers 1 upto n.

We have previously shown (see [16] and subsequent papers) that there exists a sound and (relatively) complete proof system for establishing semantic consequences such as the above. In this article, we assume that such a system is available as an oracle to our proof system for program equivalence.

4   Aggregation of Matching Logic Semantic Domains

In this section we show how, given the matching logic semantic domains for two languages, we can construct a matching logic semantic domain for the **aggregation** of the two languages. The aggregation of two languages is a new language in which programs consists of pairs of programs in the two languages. The challenge is how to construct the domain such that sorts that are common in the two languages (i.e. the sort of integers) has a common interpretation in the aggregated domain. Note that it is always possible to aggregate two languages, because the common part Σ_0 can be chosen to be empty. We rely on pushout construction in Section 2 (Theorem 1) and the amalgamation theorem (Theorem 2) in order to perform the aggregation as expected. This construction involves significant technical and conceptual difficulties and, to our knowledge, it has not been described before.

Let $\mathcal{S}_i = (Cfg_i, S_i, \Sigma_i, \Pi_i, \mathcal{T}_i)$, $i \in \{L, R\}$ be the matching logic semantic domains of two languages, (S_0, Σ_0, Π_0) a matching logic signature, h_L and h_R morphisms from (S_0, Σ_0, Π_0) to (S_L, Σ_L, Π_L) and from (S_0, Σ_0, Π_0) to (S_R, Σ_R, Π_R). Let $\mathcal{T}_L, \mathcal{T}_R, \mathcal{T}_0$ be models of $(S_L, \Sigma_L, \Pi_L), (S_R, \Sigma_R, \Pi_R)$ and resp. (S_0, Σ_0, Π_0) such that $\mathcal{T}_L\restriction_{h_L} = \mathcal{T}_0 = \mathcal{T}_R\restriction_{h_R}$. Let $(h'_L, (S', \Sigma', \Pi'), h'_R)$ be the pushout of $(S_L, \Sigma_L, \Pi_L) \xleftarrow{h_L} (S_0, \Sigma_0, \Pi_0) \xrightarrow{h_R} (S_R, \Sigma_R, \Pi_R)$.

By Theorem 2, there exists a unique (S', Σ', Π')-model $\mathcal{T}'$ such that $\mathcal{T}'\restriction_{h'_L} = \mathcal{T}_L$ and $\mathcal{T}'\restriction_{h'_R} = \mathcal{T}_R$. We define now the **aggregation** of the two matching logic semantic domains. We let $\mathcal{S} = (Cfg, S, \Sigma, \Pi, \mathcal{T})$, where

- Cfg is a new distinguished sort;
- $S = S' \cup \{Cfg\}$
- $\Sigma = \Sigma' \cup \{\langle\_,\_\rangle : h_L(Cfg_L) \times h_R(Cfg_R) \to Cfg, pr_i : Cfg \to Cfg_i, i \in \{L, R\}\}$;
- $\Pi = \Pi'$;
- $\mathcal{T}_{Cfg} = \mathcal{T}'_{h'_L(Cfg_L)} \times \mathcal{T}'_{h'_R(Cfg_R)}$
- $\mathcal{T}_{\langle\_,\_\rangle}(\gamma_L, \gamma_R) = (\gamma_L, \gamma_R)$, $\mathcal{T}_{pr_L}((\gamma_L, \gamma_R)) = \gamma_L$, $\mathcal{T}_{pr_R}((\gamma_L, \gamma_R)) = \gamma_R$.
- $\mathcal{T}_o = \mathcal{T}'_o$ for any other object $o \in S \cup \Sigma \cup \Pi$.

We define a new matching logic semantic domain $\mathcal{S}'_i = (h'_i(Cfg_i), S', \Sigma', \Pi', \mathcal{T}')$ for each $i \in \{L, R\}$. The matching logic semantic domain $\mathcal{S}'_i$ is the embedding of $\mathcal{S}_i$ into S. The difference between $\mathcal{S}_i$ and $\mathcal{S}'_i$ is that $\mathcal{S}'_i$ works in a slightly larger algebra that contains symbols from the other language. However, since the matching logic semantics rules do no mention these additional symbols, executions of programs in $\mathcal{S}_i$ coincide with executions of programs in $\mathcal{S}'_i$. In the rest of this section we show that this is indeed the case and we establish relations between executions of the aggregate language and the individual languages.

Remark 1. Let $i \in \{L, R\}$. For every valuation $\rho : Var \to \mathcal{T}_i$, we define $h(\rho)$ to be the valuation $h(\rho) : h(Var) \to \mathcal{T}_i$, with $h(\rho)(x) = \rho(x)$ for all $x \in Var$.

We first show that applying the morphism h'_i on both the matching logic formula and valuation does not change the matching logic satisfaction relation.

Proposition 2. *For any pattern π and any valuation ρ, $\rho(\pi) = h(\rho)(\pi)$.*

Let $\gamma_i \in \llbracket h_i'(Cfg_i) \rrbracket_{\mathcal{T}'}$ be a configuration and φ_i a matching logic formula over (S_i, Σ_i, Π_i) and the set of variables Var, for each $i \in \{L, R\}$. Note that the same set of variables Var is used for both semantic domains S_L and S_R.

Lemma 1. *For all valuations $\rho : Var \to \mathcal{T}_i$, $(\gamma_i, h_i'(\rho)) \models h_i'(\varphi_i)$ iff $(\gamma_i, \rho) \models \varphi_i$ (where $i \in \{L, R\}$).*

The above lemma allow us to conclude that executions in $\mathcal{S}_i$ and $\mathcal{S}_i'$ coincide:

Proposition 3. *If $\gamma_i, \gamma_i' \in \llbracket h_i'(Cfg_i) \rrbracket_{\mathcal{T}'}$, then $\gamma_i \to_{\mathcal{S}_i'} \gamma_i'$ iff $\gamma_i \to_{\mathcal{S}_i} \gamma_i'$.*

We now establish the connection between matching logic formulae over the aggregate language and the two individual languages. We first define the **left-** and **right-projection** of matching logic formulae.

Definition 12. *Let φ be a (S, Σ, Π)-matching logic formula. For $i \in \{L, R\}$, we define the $(S'^i, \Sigma'^i, \Pi'^i)$-matching logic formula $pr_i(\varphi)$ (for $i = L$, the **left-projection** and for $i = R$, the **right-projection**) to be φ where every term $\langle t_L, t_R \rangle$ of sort Cfg is replaced by t_i.*

We now distinguish a class of matching logic formulae which behave well with respect to the aggregate semantics.

Definition 13. *A (S, Σ, Π)-matching logic formula is **pure** if no term of sort Cfg in the formula appears under a negation.*

For such pure formulae, we establish the following proposition, which connects satisfaction of matching logic formulae over the aggregate language with satisfaction of matching logic formulae over the individuals languages:

Proposition 4. *Let $(\gamma_L, \gamma_R) \in \llbracket Cfg \rrbracket_{\mathcal{T}}$ be a configuration. Let φ be a pure matching logic formula with no variables of sort Cfg. For any $\rho : Var \to \mathcal{T}$, we have that $((\gamma_L, \gamma_R), \rho) \models_{\mathcal{S}} \varphi$ iff $(\gamma_L, \rho) \models_{\mathcal{S}_L'} pr_L(\varphi)$ and $(\gamma_R, \rho) \models_{\mathcal{S}_R'} pr_R(\varphi)$.*

In order to define programming language semantics, which have been shown to be written as sets of rewrite rules of the form $a \Rightarrow b \ if \ c$ [16], only pure matching logic formulae are needed. In the rest of this article, we will assume that we only deal with such formulae.

5   Specifying Equivalent Programs

Aggregate matching logic patterns can be used to specify pairs of configurations of the two involved languages:

Definition 14. *The denotation of an aggregated matching logic pattern φ, written $\llbracket \varphi \rrbracket$, is the set of all pairs of configurations that satisfy it:*

$$\llbracket \varphi \rrbracket = \{(\langle \gamma_L, \gamma_R \rangle \mid \text{there exists a valuation } \rho \text{ such that } ((\gamma_L, \gamma_R), \rho) \models \varphi\}.$$

This notation extends to sets E of patterns, written $\llbracket E \rrbracket$, as expected:

$$\llbracket E \rrbracket = \cup_{\varphi \in E} \llbracket \varphi \rrbracket.$$

Example 12. The following set

$$E = \{\exists i. \langle\langle \texttt{skip}, (\texttt{x} \mapsto i, \_)\rangle, \langle j \rangle\rangle \wedge i =_{Int} j\} \tag{1}$$

containing one matching logic formula, captures in its denotation all pairs of IMP and respectively FUN configurations that have terminated (since there is no more code to execute) and where the IMP variable x holds the same integer as the result of the FUN program. Note that in the above pattern, $\_$ is an anonymous variable meant to capture all of the variable bindings other than x.

Suppose we have an IMP program that computes its result in a variable x and suppose we want to show it computes the same integer result as a FUN program. Then the denotation $[\![E]\!]$ of set E above holds exactly the set of pairs of terminal configurations in which the two programs should end in order for them to compute the same result.

When trying to prove that two programs compute the same result, it is tempting to say that the two programs should reach the same configuration at the end. However, this is not feasible since the configuration might contain additional information (such as temporary variables) that was used in the computation but is not part of the result. When testing if the final configurations are the same in the two programs, it is important to ignore such additional information. In the example above, only the variable x is inspected (the values of all other variables are ignored) when comparing final configurations. Another aspect is that, when working in a general setting where we are comparing programs from two arbitrary programming languages, the configurations of the two languages might be significantly different. This is the case above, with the configuration for IMP holding code and an environment and the configuration for FUN holding only (extended) lambda expressions. Therefore, in general, to show that two programs end up with the same result there is a need to design such a set $[\![E]\!]$ of "base" pairs which are known to be equivalent.

6   Proving Mutual Program Equivalence

Here we provide a language-parametric foundation for showing equivalence of programs written in possibly different languages. Like in the previous section, we generically assume that the two languages are given as matching logic semantics $\mathcal{S}_L = (Cfg_L, \Sigma_L, \Pi_L, \mathcal{A}_L, \mathcal{T}_L, \rightarrow_{\mathcal{T}_L})$ and $\mathcal{S}_R = (Cfg_R, \Sigma_R, \Pi_R, \mathcal{A}_R, \mathcal{T}_R, \rightarrow_{\mathcal{T}_R})$ with aggregation $\mathcal{S} = (Cfg, \Sigma, \Pi, \mathcal{A}, \mathcal{T}, \rightarrow_{\mathcal{T}})$, but when we discuss examples we assume them to be the semantics $\mathcal{S}_{\texttt{IMP}}$ and $\mathcal{S}_{\texttt{FUN}}$ of, respectively, IMP and FUN.

Two programs are then considered *mutually equivalent* when, for all inputs, they both diverge or they both reach a pair in the base equivalence $[\![E]\!]$. This intuition is captured by the following definition:

Definition 15. *We write* $\models \varphi \Downarrow^\infty E$, *and say that* φ ***reaches*** E, *iff for all configurations* γ_L, γ_R *and for all valuations* ρ *such that* $(\langle \gamma_L, \gamma_R \rangle, \rho) \models \varphi$ *we have that at least one of the following conditions holds:*

1. both γ_L and γ_R diverge (i.e. $\gamma_C \to_T \gamma_C^1 \to_T \ldots \to_T \gamma_C^i \to_T$ for any natural number i and any $C \in \{L, R\}$);
2. there are configurations γ'_L, γ'_R with $\gamma_L \to_T^* \gamma'_L$, $\gamma_R \to_T^* \gamma'_R$ and $(\gamma'_L, \gamma'_R) \in \llbracket E \rrbracket$.

Example 13. Let $E = \{\exists i.\langle\langle \text{skip}, (n \mapsto i, \_)\rangle, \langle i \rangle\rangle\}$ and let

$$\varphi_1 = \exists n.\langle\langle\text{code}_1, \ n \mapsto n\rangle, \langle\exp_1(n)\rangle\rangle$$
$$\varphi_2 = \langle\langle\text{while 1 do skip}, \ \emptyset\rangle, \langle\text{letrec f x = f(x + 1) in f(1)}\rangle\rangle$$
$$\varphi_3 = \exists n.\langle\langle\text{code}_3, \ n \mapsto n\rangle, \langle\exp_3(n)\rangle\rangle.$$

where $\text{code}_1 \equiv$ i:=1; n:=0; while i<=n do (n:=n+i; i:=i+1) is the IMP program that computes the sum of the numbers from 1 to n, where $\exp_1(n) \equiv$ letrec f x = if x=1 then 1 else x+f(x-1) in f(n) is the FUN program computing the same sum, and where $\text{code}_3 \equiv \text{PGM}_L$ and, resp., $\exp_3(n) \equiv \text{PGM}_R(n)$ are the IMP and FUN programs in Fig. 5 that compute the Collatz function.

We have that $\models \varphi_1 \Downarrow^\infty E$ since both programs end up in a pair from $\llbracket E \rrbracket$: $\langle\text{code}_1, \ n \mapsto n\rangle \to_T^* \langle\text{skip}, \ n \mapsto 1+2+\ldots+n\rangle$ and $\langle\exp_1(n)\rangle \to_T^* \langle 1+2+\ldots+n\rangle$. We also have that $\models \varphi_2 \Downarrow^\infty E$, since both configurations in φ_2 clearly diverge. We also have that $\models \varphi_3 \Downarrow^\infty E$, but this is more difficult to establish. In fact, it is currently only conjectured (not proven) that the programs terminate no matter what the input value n is. But it can be proven that if one does not terminate, the other does not terminate either and therefore $\models \varphi_3 \Downarrow^\infty E$ holds independently of the Collatz conjecture. However, $\models \varphi_3 \Downarrow^\infty E$ is more difficult to show than the previous examples since it is not clear if both programs terminate or diverge. We next propose a proof system that allows us to derive such properties.

6.1   Proof System

In this section, we introduce a proof system that is able to derive sequents of the form $\vdash \varphi \Downarrow^\infty E$ denoting mutual equivalences that are sound in the sense that $\vdash \varphi \Downarrow^\infty E$ implies $\models \varphi \Downarrow^\infty E$. Fig. 4 contains the 5-rule proof system for proving mutual equivalence of programs. The first rule is AXIOM. There is nothing suprizing about this rule; it simply states that if an equivalence is known to be true, then it can be derived.

The second rule is STEP. It allows to take an arbitrary finite number of steps (zero, one or more steps) in each of the two programs. If by taking such steps from φ to φ', we reach an equivalence φ' that is derivable, then we conclude that φ must also be derivable. The STEP rule requires an oracle to reason about reachability in operational semantics. This oracle can be, for example, the reachability proof system in [16], but any other valid reasoning will also work.

The third rule is CONSEQ(uence). This rule states that if an equivalence formula φ implies another equivalence formula φ' (which means that φ' is more general than φ) and the formula φ' is derivable, then φ must also be derivable. The required implication might seem surprizing at first (we might expect it in reverse), but the intuition is that φ' is more general than φ. Therefore if we are able to prove the equivalence φ', then φ must also hold. This rule is used

$$\text{AXIOM} \ \frac{\varphi \in E}{\vdash \varphi \Downarrow^{\infty} E} \qquad \text{STEP} \ \frac{\varphi \Rightarrow^{*} \varphi' \quad \vdash \varphi' \Downarrow^{\infty} E}{\vdash \varphi \Downarrow^{\infty} E} \qquad \text{CONSEQ} \ \frac{\models \varphi \rightarrow \varphi' \quad \vdash \varphi' \Downarrow^{\infty} E}{\vdash \varphi \Downarrow^{\infty} E}$$

$$\text{CASE ANALYSIS} \ \frac{\vdash \varphi \Downarrow^{\infty} E \quad \vdash \varphi' \Downarrow^{\infty} E}{\vdash \varphi \vee \varphi' \Downarrow^{\infty} E} \qquad \text{CIRCULARITY} \ \frac{\vdash \varphi' \Downarrow^{\infty} E \cup \{\varphi\} \quad \varphi \Rightarrow^{+} \varphi'}{\vdash \varphi \Downarrow^{\infty} E}$$

Fig. 4. Mutual Equivalence Proof System. We use $\varphi \Rightarrow^{*} \varphi'$ as syntactic sugar for $\mathcal{A}_L \models pr_L(\varphi) \rightarrow^{*} pr_L(\varphi')$ and $\mathcal{A}_R \models pr_R(\varphi) \rightarrow^{*} pr_R(\varphi')$ and $\varphi \Rightarrow^{+} \varphi'$ as syntactic sugar for $\mathcal{A}_L \models pr_L(\varphi) \rightarrow^{+} pr_L(\varphi')$ and $\mathcal{A}_L \models pr_R(\varphi) \rightarrow^{+} pr_R(\varphi')$.

in the example proof tree below (in Fig. 5) to rearrange a formula of the form $(n > 0 \vee n = 0) \wedge \dots$ into $n \geq 0 \wedge \dots$. Another possible use of CONSEQ would be, for example, to transform a more particular case, like "$n = 20$", into a more general case "n is even" in order to be able to apply other rules.

The fourth case is CASE ANALYSIS. This allows to branch the proof depending on the different cases to consinder. Typically, CASE ANALYSIS is used to branch the proof when the two programs also branch. In the proof tree below (in Fig. 5), this rule is used to perform a case analysis between the case where both programs end (because of reaching the termination condition $n = 0$) and where the programs continue ($n > 0$).

The fifth rule is CIRCULARITY. This rule is used to handle repetitive program structures such as loops or recursive functions. CIRCULARITY allows to *postulate* that the equivalence being proven (φ) holds, make progress ($\varphi \Rightarrow^{+} \varphi'$) in both programs that we want to show equivalent, and then derive φ' possibly using φ as an axiom, i.e., $\vdash \varphi' \Downarrow^{\infty} E \cup \{\varphi\}$. We use this rule in the proof tree below to assume that at the start of the repetitive behavior (the loop for the program on the left and the recursive call for the program on the right) the two programs are equivalent; we make progress by executing the body of the loop on the left and the body of the recursive call on the right and end up with the equivalence that we assumed to hold. The rule is sound because we require both programs to make progress. Therefore, intuitively, when $\vdash \varphi' \Downarrow^{\infty} E \cup \{\varphi\}$ is derivable, either both programs diverge because φ is applied as an axiom in the proof tree or the programs end up in E. As for the first rule, an oracle to reason about reachability in operational semantics is also needed here.

Theorem 3 (Soundness). *For any set of aggregated matching logic patterns E and for any aggregated matching logic pattern φ, if the sequent $\vdash \varphi \Downarrow^{\infty} E$ is derivable using the proof system given in Fig. 4 then $\models \varphi \Downarrow^{\infty} E$.*

In order to prove the above theorem, we need several intermediate steps that follow. In the following, we let $c \in \{L, R\}$ denote either left or right. By $\bar{c}$ we denote the single element of the set $\{L, R\} \setminus \{c\}$.

Let E be a set of mutual matching logic formulae. Let $\mathcal{A}_L$ and $\mathcal{A}_R$ be a set of reachability formulae which describe the semantics of two languages: $\mathcal{A}_L$

the "left" language and $\mathcal{A}_R$ the "right" language. We extend the definition of $\models \varphi \Downarrow^\infty E$ to sets of mutual matching logic formulae as expected:

Definition 16. *If F is a set of mutual matching logic formulae, then we write*

$$\models F \Downarrow^\infty E \text{ if } \models \varphi \Downarrow^\infty E \text{ for all } \varphi \in F.$$

The following definitions will be useful in the proof of soundness. Let G denote a set of pairs of configurations.

Definition 17. *We say that a pair (γ_L, γ_R) reaches G, written $(\gamma_L, \gamma_R) \to^* G$, if there exist configurations γ'_L and γ'_R such that $\gamma_L \to^*_{\mathcal{A}_L} \gamma'_L$, $\gamma_R \to^*_{\mathcal{A}_R} \gamma'_R$ and $(\gamma'_L, \gamma'_R) \in G$.*

Definition 18. *We say that a pair (γ_L, γ_R) diverges, written $(\gamma_L, \gamma_R)\uparrow^\infty$, if both γ_L and γ_R diverge (in $\mathcal{A}_L$ and respectively $\mathcal{A}_R$).*

Definition 19. *We say that a pair (γ_L, γ_R) co-reaches G, written $(\gamma_L, \gamma_R) \to^{*,\infty} G$, if at least one of the following conditions holds:*

1. *(γ_L, γ_R) diverges (i.e. $(\gamma_L, \gamma_R)\uparrow^\infty$),*
2. *(γ_L, γ_R) reaches G (i.e. $(\gamma_L, \gamma_R) \to^* G$).*

The following utility lemma establishes the link between models of mutual matching logic formulae and the notion of co-reachability introduced above. Its proof following trivially by unrolling the above definitions.

Lemma 2. *For all sets of mutual matching logic formulae E and for any mutual matching logic formula φ, we have that:*

$$\models \varphi \Downarrow^\infty E \text{ iff for all } \gamma_L, \gamma_R \text{ such that } (\gamma_L, \gamma_R) \in \llbracket \varphi \rrbracket, (\gamma_L, \gamma_R) \to^{*,\infty} \llbracket E \rrbracket.$$

The next lemma is the core of our soundness proof.

Lemma 3 (Circularity Principle).
   Let F be a set of mutual matching formulae. If for each $(\gamma_L, \gamma_R) \in \llbracket F \rrbracket$ there exist γ'_L, γ'_R such that $\gamma_L \to^+_{\mathcal{A}_L} \gamma'_L$, $\gamma_R \to^+_{\mathcal{A}_R} \gamma'_R$, and $(\gamma'_L, \gamma'_R) \to^{*,\infty} \llbracket E \cup F \rrbracket$, then $\models F \Downarrow^\infty E$.

It lies at the core of the proof for Theorem 3, which can be found in our accompanying technical report [2].

6.2 Example

We next show the proof tree for the equivalence of the two Collatz programs in Fig. 5. As we have already discussed, in order to talk about mutual equivalence, we have to establish a "base" equivalence that contains programs that are clearly equivalent. For this case study, for the "base" equivalence, we choose to equate FUN programs that terminate by returning an integer i with IMP

```
PGM_L := c := 1; LOOP_L          | PGM_R(n) := letrec f n i = LOOP_R in f n 0
LOOP_L := while (n != 1)         |   LOOP_R := if (n != 1)
        c := c + 1;              |              then if (n % 2 != 0)
        if (n % 2 != 0)          |                   then f (3 * n + 1) (i + 1)
          then n := 3 * n + 1    |                   else f (n / 2) (i + 1)
          else n := n / 2        |              else i
```

$$\varphi := \exists i, n.(n > 0 \land \langle \text{LOOP}_L, \ n \mapsto n, c \mapsto i \rangle, \langle i + \text{LOOP}_R \rangle)$$

1. $\vdash (\langle \text{skip}, \ c \mapsto i, \_ \rangle, \langle i \rangle)$ $\Downarrow^\infty E$ AXIOM
2. $\vdash (\langle \text{skip}, \ c \mapsto i, \_ \rangle, \langle i \rangle)$ $\Downarrow^\infty E \cup \{\varphi\}$ AXIOM
3. $\vdash (\langle \text{skip}, \ n \mapsto n, c \mapsto i \rangle, \langle i \rangle)$ $\Downarrow^\infty E$ CONSEQ(1)
4. $\vdash (\langle \text{skip}, \ n \mapsto n, c \mapsto i \rangle, \langle i \rangle)$ $\Downarrow^\infty E \cup \{\varphi\}$ CONSEQ(2)
5. $\vdash (n = 0 \land \langle \text{LOOP}_L, \ n \mapsto n, c \mapsto i \rangle, \langle \text{LOOP}_R \rangle)$ $\Downarrow^\infty E$ STEP(3)
6. $\vdash \exists i, n.(n = 0 \land \langle \text{LOOP}_L, \ n \mapsto n, c \mapsto i \rangle, \langle \text{LOOP}_R \rangle) \Downarrow^\infty E \cup \{\varphi\}$ STEP(4)
7. $\vdash \exists i, n.(n > 0 \land \langle \text{LOOP}_L, \ n \mapsto n, c \mapsto i \rangle, \langle \text{LOOP}_R \rangle) \Downarrow^\infty E \cup \{\varphi\}$ AXIOM
8. $\vdash \exists i, n.(n \geq 0 \land \langle \text{LOOP}_L, \ n \mapsto n, c \mapsto i \rangle, \langle \text{LOOP}_R \rangle) \Downarrow^\infty E \cup \{\varphi\}$ CONSEQ(CA(6,7))
9. $\vdash \exists i, n.(n > 0 \land \langle \text{LOOP}_L, \ n \mapsto n, c \mapsto i \rangle, \langle \text{LOOP}_R \rangle) \Downarrow^\infty E$ CIRCULARITY (8)
10. $\vdash \exists i, n.(n \geq 0 \land \langle \text{LOOP}_L, \ n \mapsto n, c \mapsto i \rangle, \langle \text{LOOP}_R \rangle) \Downarrow^\infty E$ CONSEQ(CA(5,9))
11. $\vdash \exists i, n.(n \geq 0 \land \langle \text{PGM}_L, \ n \mapsto n \rangle, \langle \text{PGM}_R(n) \rangle) \Downarrow^\infty E$ STEP (10)

Fig. 5. Formal proof showing that the two Collatz programs are mutually equivalent. CA stands for CASE ANALYSIS. CONSEQ is used in the proof tree above to show that $n > 0 \lor n = 0$ implies $n \geq 0$.

programs that terminate with the same integer i in the variable c. The set $E = \{\exists i.\langle \langle \text{skip}, \ (c \mapsto i, \_) \rangle, \langle i \rangle \rangle\}$ defined in Equation 1 captures the intuition above. It says that an IMP configuration $\langle \text{skip}, \ (c \mapsto i, \_) \rangle$ (describing programs that stopped (because the code cell contains skip) and that have the integer i in the c memory cell) is equivalent to a FUN configuration that contains exactly the integer i. The proof tree in Fig. 5 shows that the two programs are equivalent.

7 Discussion, Related Work and Conclusion

We have introduced mutual matching logic, a 5-rule proof system for proving mutual equivalence of programs. Mutual equivalence is a natural equivalence between programs: two programs are mutually equivalent if either they both diverge or if they eventually reach the same state. Mutual equivalence can be used, for example, to prove that compiler transformations preserve behavior.

Our approach is language independent. The proof system takes as input two language semantics (in the form of reachability rules) that share certain domains such as integers (the model of the shared domain is also an input to the aggregation operation) and produces sequents of the form $\vdash \varphi \Downarrow^\infty E$ whose semantics is that for any pair of programs that matches φ, both programs diverge or they reach a state in E. Note that in our running example (the two Collatz programs), both programs have a parameter n that is left unspecified. This shows that our approach allows parameterized programs.

Symbolic programs are considered in [12] but for a different notion of bisimulation-based program equivalence.

Related Work. It was first remarked by Hoare in [8] that program equivalence might be easier than program correctness. Among the recent works on equivalence we mention [6,5,3]. The first one targets programs that include recursive procedures, the second one exploits similarities between single-threaded programs in order to prove their equivalence, and the third one extends the equivalence-verification to multi-threaded programs. They use operational semantics (of a specific language they designed, called LPL) and proof systems, and formally prove their proof system's soundness. In [6] a classification of equivalence relations used in program-equivalence research is given, one of which is mutual equivalence (called *full equivalence* there). The main difference with our approach is that our proof system is language-independent, i.e., it is parametric in the semantics of the two languages in which candidate equivalent programs are written; whereas the deductive system of [6] proves equivalence for LPL programs. On the other hand, [6] propose deductive systems for several kinds of equivalences, whereas we focus on mutual (a.k.a. full) equivalence only. In [9], an implementation of a parametrized equivalence prover is presented.

A lot of work on program equivalence arise from the verification of compilation in a broad sense. One approach is full compiler verification (e.g. CompCert [11]), which is incomparable to our work since it produces computer-checked proofs of equivalence for a particular language, while our own work produces proofs (not computer-checked) of equivalence for any language. Another approach is the individual verification of each compilation [14] (we only cite two of the most relevant recent works). Other work targets specific classes of languages: functional [15], microcode [1], CLP [4]. In order to be less language-specific some approaches advocate the use of intermediate languages, such as [10], which works on the Boogie intermediate language. However, our approach is better, since our proof system works directly with the language semantics; therefore there is no need to trust the compiler from the original language to Boogie. Finally, our own related work [13] gives a proof system for another equivalence relation between programs that is based on bisimulation and an observation relation and that uses other technical mechanisms. We believe that the equivalence relation that we consider in this article in more natural for certain classes of applications such as proving compilers.

Further Work. Our definition (Definition 15) of mutual equivalence is *existential* in the sense that two programs are equivalent when there exists execution paths in each of the programs such that the paths diverge or end in configurations that are known to be equivalent. Although for deterministic languages this cannot constitute a problem (there exists exactly one execution path for each program), for non-deterministic languages stronger equivalences might be desirable. We leave such stronger equivalences as object of further study. Another issue is completeness. Although relative completeness results have been shown for matching logic based proof systems for showing partial correctness [16], it is less clear how a relevant relative-completeness result can be obtained for equivalence, since the problem is known to be Π_2^0-complete. Another issue that we leave for further study is compositionality. Our goal here was just to obtain a sound and useful language independent proof system for reasoning about equivalence. We also plan to implement a semi-automated version of the proof system.

References

1. Arons, T., Elster, E., Fix, L., Mador-Haim, S., Mishaeli, M., Shalev, J., Singerman, E., Tiemeyer, A., Vardi, M.Y., Zuck, L.D.: Formal verification of backward compatibility of microcode. In: Etessami, K., Rajamani, S.K. (eds.) CAV 2005. LNCS, vol. 3576, pp. 185–198. Springer, Heidelberg (2005)
2. Çiobâcă, S., Lucanu, D., Rusu, V., Roşu, G.: A language independent proof system for mutual program equivalence. Technical Report 14-01, Al. I. Cuza Univ.
3. Chaki, S., Gurfinkel, A., Strichman, O.: Regression verification for multi-threaded programs. In: Kuncak, V., Rybalchenko, A. (eds.) VMCAI 2012. LNCS, vol. 7148, pp. 119–135. Springer, Heidelberg (2012)
4. Craciunescu, S.: Proving the equivalence of CLP programs. In: Stuckey, P.J. (ed.) ICLP 2002. LNCS, vol. 2401, pp. 287–301. Springer, Heidelberg (2002)
5. Godlin, B., Strichman, O.: Regression verification: proving the equivalence of similar programs. Software Testing, Verification and Reliability (To appear)
6. Godlin, B., Strichman, O.: Inference rules for proving the equivalence of recursive procedures. Acta Informatica 45(6), 403–439 (2008)
7. Haxthausen, A.E., Nickl, F.: Pushouts of order-sorted algebraic specifications. In: Nivat, M., Wirsing, M. (eds.) AMAST 1996. LNCS, vol. 1101, pp. 132–147. Springer, Heidelberg (1996)
8. Hoare, C.A.R.: An axiomatic basis for computer programming. Communications of the ACM 12(10), 576–580 (1969)
9. Kundu, S., Tatlock, Z., Lerner, S.: Proving optimizations correct using parameterized program equivalence. In: PLDI, pp. 327–337. ACM (2009)
10. Lahiri, S., Hawblitzel, C., Kawaguchi, M., Rebêlo, H.: Symdiff: A language-agnostic semantic diff tool for imperative programs. In: Madhusudan, P., Seshia, S.A. (eds.) CAV 2012. LNCS, vol. 7358, pp. 712–717. Springer, Heidelberg (2012)
11. Leroy, X.: Formal verification of a realistic compiler. Communications of the ACM 52(7), 107–115 (2009)
12. Lucanu, D., Rusu, V.: Program equivalence by circular reasoning. Technical Report RR-8116, INRIA (2012)
13. Lucanu, D., Rusu, V.: Program equivalence by circular reasoning. In: Johnsen, E.B., Petre, L. (eds.) IFM 2013. LNCS, vol. 7940, pp. 362–377. Springer, Heidelberg (2013)
14. Necula, G.: Translation validation for an optimizing compiler. In: PLDI, pp. 83–94. ACM (2000)
15. Pitts, A.: Operational semantics and program equivalence. In: Barthe, G., Dybjer, P., Pinto, L., Saraiva, J. (eds.) APPSEM 2000. LNCS, vol. 2395, pp. 378–412. Springer, Heidelberg (2002)
16. Roşu, G., Ştefănescu, A.: Checking reachability using matching logic. In: OOPSLA, pp. 555–574. ACM (2012)
17. Roşu, G., Ellison, C., Schulte, W.: Matching logic: An alternative to hoare/Floyd logic. In: Johnson, M., Pavlovic, D. (eds.) AMAST 2010. LNCS, vol. 6486, pp. 142–162. Springer, Heidelberg (2011)

PHASE: A Stochastic Formalism for Phase-Type Distributions

Gabriel Ciobanu and Armand Stefan Rotaru

Romanian Academy, Institute of Computer Science,
Blvd. Carol I no. 8, 700505, Iaşi, Romania
gabriel@info.uaic.ro, armand@iit.tuiasi.ro

Abstract. Models of non-Markovian systems expressed using stochastic formalisms often employ phase-type distributions in order to approximate the duration of transitions. We introduce a stochastic process calculus named PHASE which operates with phase-type distributions, and provide a step-by-step description of how PHASE processes can be translated into models supported by the probabilistic model checker PRISM. We then illustrate our approach by analysing the behaviour of a simple system involving both non-Markovian and Markovian transitions.

1 Introduction

In general, stochastic systems are divided into Markovian systems and non-Markovian systems, based on the temporal properties of their transitions: in the former, the time after which the system leaves any particular state (i.e., performs a transition) does not depend on the time already spent in that state, while in the latter, there is at least one transition between two states which does not satisfy the aforementioned property. A potential shortcoming of current stochastic process calculi refers to the fact that almost all of these formalisms were designed for Markovian systems, which can be expressed in terms of continuous-time Markov chains (CTMCs), and for which a solid mathematical theory exists [20]. This body of theory greatly facilitates performance analysis and allows one to easily derive the exact numerical value of transient, passage time, and steady-state performance measures. However, a sometimes severe downside of this approach lies in having to use only exponential distributions for stochastic variables. This restriction limits the possibility of accurately modelling certain performance variables, such as job service times or process execution times in software/hardware systems, which follow heavy tailed distributions [6], or the durations of pointing gestures in human-computer interaction systems, which follow log-normal distributions [9], to name but a few (for additional examples, see [17]). More specifically, the theory underlying non-Markovian systems is far less developed than that for Markovian systems, which means that performance measures typically cannot be derived analytically (but only approximated). The derivation of these measures is usually performed either by employing non-Markovian formalisms, which rely on discrete event simulation techniques, or by constructing

S. Merz and J. Pang (Eds.): ICFEM 2014, LNCS 8829, pp. 91–106, 2014.

a Markovian system which approximates the behaviour of a non-Markovian system, and then analysing the Markovian system.

At the current stage in the evolution of stochastic process calculi, effectively using non-Markovian process calculi is a real challenge. The main impediment that arises is the almost complete lack of dedicated software tools. Several theoretical approaches to representing non-Markovian systems have been put forward [5,17], and a number of non-Markovian process calculi have been created (e.g., SPADES [12]; ♠ [8,7]; SM-PEPA [4]), but tool support for these process calculi is either absent, or limited to prototype implementations. Two notable exception are the tools Ymer [25] and MODEST [11], which employ statistical model checking. However, both tools are still in development and have not yet attracted a substantial community of users.

An alternative to employing non-Markovian process calculi is that of relying on phase-type approximations for transition durations, in the context of Markovian process calculi. Phase-type distributions are adequate for such an enterprise given their strong closure properties (i.e., their are closed under convolution, maximum, minimum and convex mixture, unlike exponential distributions, which are closed only under minimum) and the fact that they can approximate any positive-valued distribution to an arbitrary degree of accuracy [18]. A number of Markovian process calculi which support phase-type distributions do exist (e.g., [10,24,21,26]), but they too suffer from a lack of tool support. Furthermore, some of these calculi ([10]) are compatible only with certain subclasses of non-Markovian systems, while others ([24,21,26]) do not support certain complex patterns of interaction between processes, such as those generated by processes synchronizing over user-defined sets of shared actions.

As a possible solution to the aforementioned problems, we develop a new Markovian process calculus, called PHASE, for modelling non-Markovian systems through the use of phase-type distributions. Our formalism is parsimonious in terms of syntax and semantics, it includes action-based synchronisation, and it can be faithfully translated into the stochastic language of PRISM. The structure of our paper is as follows. In Section 2, we introduce the new calculus, describe its syntax and semantics, and give a detailed account of how it can be implemented in PRISM. We present a small example of a non-Markovian system in Section 3, and illustrate our approach by approximating its behaviour in PHASE and analysing the resulting model in PRISM. We end the paper with conclusions and references.

2   Phase-Type Distributions and Process Calculi

In order to allow a better integration of phase-type distributions within stochastic process calculi, we propose a very simple process calculus, inspired by PEPA [15], $PEPA_{ph}^{\infty}$ [10] and IMC [13], and describe an algorithm for its implementation in the model checker PRISM. The new calculus employs transitions whose durations are phase-type distributed [19]. For ease of modelling, we restrict our calculus to phase-type representations whose probability of starting in state 1 is equal to 1 (i.e., there is a single initial state), which can therefore be fully specified in terms of their infinitesimal generator matrix. We denote by $PH(A)$ the phase-type distribution whose generator is A. The distribution $PH(A)$ describes the time until absorption for a CTMC of size $ord(A)$ (i.e., the order of A), which we denote by $CTMC(A)$, where state $ord(A)$ is absorbing, and all the other states are transient. The element $A(i,j)$, for $1 \leq i,j \leq ord(A)$ and $i \neq j$, represents the rate of a transition from state i to state j. Furthermore, the element $A(i,i)$, for $1 \leq i \leq ord(A)$, is the negative sum of the rates of all the transitions originating in state i.

Our calculus includes only three operators, namely the *sequential operator*, the *choice operator*, and the *parallel operator*. The full syntax of PHASE can be given as follows, where P_{seq} is a sequential process, P_{par} is a parallel process, α is an action, $(\alpha, PH(A))$ is a phase-type transition, $\{L\}$ is a set of actions, and $n \geq 2$ is a natural number:

$$P_{seq} ::= (\alpha, PH(A)).P_{seq} \mid (\alpha_1, PH(A_1)).P_{seq}^1 + \ldots + (\alpha_n, PH(A_n)).P_{seq}^n$$
$$P_{par} ::= P_{seq} \mid P_{par}^1 \underset{\{L\}}{\bowtie} P_{par}^2$$

The sequential expression $(\alpha, PH(A)).P_{seq}$ indicates that the process performs the action α, after a delay distributed according to $PH(A)$, and then behaves like P_{seq}. The choice expression $(\alpha_1, PH(A_1)).P_{seq}^1 + \ldots + (\alpha_n, PH(A_n)).P_{seq}^n$ indicates a race for execution between the transitions $(\alpha_1, PH(A_1))$, with $1 \leq i \leq n$, such that the first transition to complete (i.e., the transition with the shortest duration) is selected and performed, while all the other transitions are halted and discarded. In other words, the choice operator denotes a competition between processes, via their current transitions, in which the fastest process wins. The parallel expression $P_{par}^1 \underset{\{L\}}{\bowtie} P_{par}^2$ indicates that the processes P_{par}^1 and P_{par}^2 must synchronize whenever performing an action from the *cooperation set* $\{L\}$. This means that, for any action $\alpha \in \{L\}$, if P_{par}^1 finishes a transition $(\alpha, PH(A_1))$, then P_{par}^1 is afterwards blocked and cannot make any further transitions until P_{par}^2 completes a corresponding transition $(\alpha, PH(A_2))$, and vice-versa. The interpretation of this operator is that it forces processes to cooperate on certain transitions (whose actions are included in $\{L\}$), by waiting for each other to complete, therefore generating a shared transition. However, the transitions whose actions are not in $\{L\}$ can proceed unaffected by cooperation. In addition, no associativity rules are defined for the parallel composition of more than two processes: the order in which the processes are composed must be made explicit through the use of parentheses.

In order to define the formal operational semantics of PHASE, we first separate transition durations from the occurrence of actions, and then we express phase-type distributions in terms of their associated CTMC. More specifically, we make the distinction between *Markovian transitions* and *action transitions*: Markovian transitions, denoted by $\langle r \rangle$ (or $\overset{r}{\Rightarrow}$), indicate a temporal delay drawn from an exponential distribution with a rate of r, while action transitions, denoted by α (or $\overset{\alpha}{\rightarrow}$), indicate the (immediate) occurrence of action α. Next, we translate any sequential expression $(\alpha, PH(A)).P_{seq}^{fin}$ into the following equivalent form, where $o = ord(A)$ and $\oplus$ denotes an internal choice between Markovian transitions (as in classical process calculi, such as PEPA):

$$Int_1 = \langle A(1,1) \rangle.Int_1 \oplus \langle A(1,2) \rangle.Int_2 \oplus \ldots \oplus \langle A(1,o) \rangle.Int_o$$
$$Int_2 = \langle A(2,1) \rangle.Int_1 \oplus \langle A(2,2) \rangle.Int_2 \oplus \ldots \oplus \langle A(2,o) \rangle.Int_o$$
$$\vdots$$
$$Int_{o-1} = \langle A(o-1,1) \rangle.Int_1 \oplus \langle A(o-1,2) \rangle.Int_2 \oplus \ldots \oplus \langle A(o-1,o) \rangle.Int_o$$
$$Int_o = \alpha.P_{seq}^{fin}$$

As a result, $P_{seq}^{init} = (\alpha, PH(A)).P_{seq}^{fin}$ becomes $P_{seq}^{init} = Int_1$, while $P_{seq} = (\alpha_1, PH(A_1)).P_{seq}^1 + \ldots + (\alpha_n, PH(A_n)).P_{seq}^n$ becomes $P_{seq} = Int_1^1 + \cdots + Int_1^n$. The states $Int_1, \ldots, Int_o$ correspond to the states of $CTMC(A)$, while the values $A(i,j)$, with $1 \leq i,j \leq o$, correspond to the rates of the transitions from $CTMC(A)$, as described at the beginning of this section. The operational semantics of PHASE, which makes use of both Markovian and action transitions, is given in Table 1, where the transitions above the line form the necessary conditions for the transitions bellow the line to take place. Since the operators $\oplus$, $+$ and $\underset{\{L\}}{\bowtie}$ are commutative, rules $CH1$ through $PAR5$ remain valid when replacing $P1$ with $P2$, and vice-versa.

Rules $SEQ1$ and $SEQ2$ make explicit the (immediate) occurrence of actions, in the case of action transitions, and the passage of time, for Markovian transitions. Rule $CH1$ describes the usual race between the Markovian transitions

Table 1. PHASE Operational Semantics

$$(SEQ1) \quad \frac{}{\alpha.P \xrightarrow{\alpha} P} \qquad (SEQ2) \quad \frac{}{\langle r \rangle.P \xRightarrow{r} P} \qquad (CH1) \quad \frac{P_1 \xRightarrow{r_1} Q_1}{P_1 \oplus P_2 \xRightarrow{r_1} Q_1}$$

$$(CH2) \quad \frac{P_1 \xRightarrow{r_1} Q_1 \quad P_2 \xRightarrow{r_2} Q_2}{P_1 + P_2 \xRightarrow{r_1} Q_1 + P_2} \qquad (CH3) \quad \frac{P_1 \xrightarrow{\alpha_1} Q_1 \quad P_2 \xRightarrow{r_2} Q_2}{P_1 + P_2 \xrightarrow{\alpha_1} Q_1}$$

$$(PAR1) \quad \frac{P_1 \xRightarrow{r_1} Q_1 \quad P_2 \xRightarrow{r_2} Q_2}{P_1 \underset{\{L\}}{\bowtie} P_2 \xRightarrow{r_1} Q_1 \underset{\{L\}}{\bowtie} P_2}$$

$$(PAR2) \quad \frac{P_1 \xrightarrow{\alpha_1} Q_1 \quad P_2 \xRightarrow{r_2} Q_2}{P_1 \underset{\{L\}}{\bowtie} P_2 \xrightarrow{\alpha_1} Q_1 \underset{\{L\}}{\bowtie} P_2} \quad (\alpha_1 \notin \{L\})$$

$$(PAR3) \quad \frac{P_1 \xrightarrow{\alpha_1} Q_1 \quad P_2 \xRightarrow{r_2} Q_2}{P_1 \underset{\{L\}}{\bowtie} P_2 \xRightarrow{r_2} P_1 \underset{\{L\}}{\bowtie} Q_2} \quad (\alpha_1 \in \{L\})$$

$$(PAR4) \quad \frac{P_1 \xrightarrow{\alpha_1} Q_1 \quad P_2 \xrightarrow{\alpha_2} Q_2}{P_1 \underset{\{L\}}{\bowtie} P_2 \xrightarrow{\alpha_1} Q_1 \underset{\{L\}}{\bowtie} P_2} \quad (\alpha_1 \notin \{L\})$$

$$(PAR5) \quad \frac{P_1 \xrightarrow{\alpha} Q_1 \quad P_2 \xrightarrow{\alpha} Q_2}{P_1 \underset{\{L\}}{\bowtie} P_2 \xrightarrow{\alpha} Q_1 \underset{\{L\}}{\bowtie} Q_2} \quad (\alpha \in \{L\})$$

that produce the phase-type distributions in PHASE. Rule $CH2$ is similar to $CH1$, except that now the race takes place not within a phase-type distribution, but between two (or more) such distributions, as required by the choice operator in PHASE. Next, rule $CH3$ specifies the race policy through which the action associated with the fastest phase-type transition is selected for execution, while the rest of the phase-type transitions (and their corresponding actions) are discarded. The remaining rules refer to the parallel composition of PHASE processes. Firstly, rule $PAR1$ treats the case in which two processes are engaged in Markovian transitions, which means that they do not interact with each other. Secondly, rule $PAR2$ deals with the parallel composition of an action transition and a Markovian transition: given that the action in question does not belong to the cooperation set $\{L\}$, its associated action transition gains precedence over the Markovian transition, due to the immediacy of actions. In contrast, whenever the action is included in $\{L\}$, as in rule $PAR3$, the process that contains the action transition needs to wait for the other process to enable a matching action transition. Finally, rules $PAR4$ and $PAR5$ handle the synchronization between action transitions: those transitions which are not part of the cooperation set proceed independently, while matching transitions with actions in $\{L\}$ are performed simultaneously.

Given that the semantics of PHASE employs both Markovian and action transitions, it is possible to have instances of action non-determinism during the evolution of certain PHASE processes. Somewhat surprisingly, this form of non-determinism is caused by the parallel operator, and not by the choice operator. As an example of action non-determinism, let us consider the following processes:

$$P_1 = (\alpha, PH(A_1)).P_1 \qquad P_2 = (\alpha, PH(A_2)).P_2 \qquad P_3 = (\alpha, PH(A_3)).P_3$$

$$P = (P_1 \bowtie_{\emptyset} P_2) \bowtie_{\{\alpha\}} P_3$$

Within P, if the duration of transitions $tr_1 = (\alpha, PH(A_1))$ and $tr_2 = (\alpha, PH(A_2))$ is shorter than that of transition $tr_3 = (\alpha, PH(A_3))$, then tr_3 can synchronize with either tr_1 or tr_2, since both transitions are available for cooperation once the delay associated with tr_3 has elapsed. In order to be able to derive performance measures over PHASE processes such as P, we need to resolve all instances of action non-determinism. Our option in this matter is to assume that the competing alternatives are all equally likely to be chosen (i.e., the winning shared action transition is drawn from a uniform distribution defined over all the competitors) [1]. In the case of P, this results in tr_1 and tr_2 each having a probability of 0.5 to be selected for synchronization.

The intermediate states and transitions, introduced when defining the meaning of PHASE transitions and operators, are useful in making explicit the relationship between PHASE, which deals with phase-type distributions, and classical Markovian process calculi, such as PEPA, which employ exponential

---

[1] If necessary, there are plenty of other solutions for dealing with non-determinism, which employ priority levels and weights, or more advanced schedulers [3].

distributions. However, when reasoning about the behaviour of PHASE processes, it is natural to ignore these internal states and transitions, given that their utility is solely technical. Therefore, unless otherwise noted, when we refer to the states and transitions of a sequential PHASE process P, we have in mind only transitions of the form $(\alpha, PH(A))$ and the states that these transitions connect, with respect to P. The set of states that can be reached by P is denoted by $ds(P)$, while the multiset of transitions that can occur between the states in $ds(P)$ is denoted by $trm(P)$.

A model P specified in PHASE can be translated into the stochastic subset of the PRISM language, by going through the following steps:

1. Express P in a form compatible with the structure of PRISM models;
2. Generate the states and transitions of P, while ignoring the duration of the transitions and internal parallelism;
3. Implement the sequential and choice operators;
4. Implement the parallel operator, to finalize the description of P in PRISM.

We now dedicate a separate subsection for the detailed description of each step.

2.1   Step 1: Bringing the Model to a Simpler Form

Since PRISM models are limited to sets of sequential components, composed in parallel, we express P in an equivalent form, denoted by P_B, which consists only of sequential processes, parallel operators, and parentheses. However, the presence of the parallel operator and that of parentheses is not compulsory, being dictated by the structure of the model. The form P_B is generated by replacing any parallel process P_{par} with its explicit decomposition, in terms of its subcomponents. The decomposition is performed in a recursive manner, until all the resulting subcomponents are sequential. Finally, let $SP = \{P_1, \ldots, P_m\}$ denote the multiset of sequential PHASE processes that form the definition of P_B, and let $TR(P_B) = \biguplus_{1 \leq i \leq m} trm(P_i)$ denote the multiset of the transitions that can (eventually) be performed by the sequential processes in SP.

2.2   Step 2: Representing the States and the Transitions of the Model

At this stage, we are not yet interested in the stochastic elements that make up the behaviour of P_B, namely the phase-type distributions which determine the duration of its transitions. These stochastic elements, as well as the internal parallelism of P_B, are treated in Steps 3 and 4. More specifically, we focus only on the states that can be reached by P_B during its evolution, as well as on the transitions that exist between these states. Also, for tractability, we do not model P_B in a global manner, but instead deal with each P_i individually, for $1 \leq i \leq m$, leaving the final, complete description of P_B to be discussed in Step 4.

Within PRISM, the states of a process are described by associating one or more local variables with that process, such that each state is mapped to a different valuation over the set of said variables. Moreover, the local variables must be part of a module, to indicate that they belong to a particular process. To begin with, we assign a valid PRISM name to each process P_i, by defining an injective function $f : SP \to ID_{PRISM}$. We find it intuitive and convenient to represent each P_i through a single variable. Having just one variable per process makes the behaviour of P_i easier to examine, and it allows us to use the notions of "module" and "variable" interchangeably, for the purposes of our paper. This is where the function f comes in handy, as it gives us the name of both the variable corresponding to P_i, and that of the module in which this variable is placed. Next, we encode the possible states of P_i as numerical values for the previously mentioned variable, by defining an injective function $g_i : ds(P_i) \to \mathbb{N}$. So far, we obtain the following module, whose initial state is exactly P_i:

module $f(P_i)$

$$f(P_i) : \left[0.. \max_{S \in ds(P_i)} (g_i(S)) \right] \text{ init } g_i(P_i);$$

endmodule .

Thus, we map sequential PHASE processes to PRISM modules, in terms of their possible states, such that if process P_i is in state S, then module $f(P_i)$ (represented by the variable $f(P_i)$) is in state $g_i(S)$. Then, we need to turn our attention to the transitions that can be performed by P_i during its evolution. Similar to the case for states, we assign a valid PRISM name for each transition in $TR(P_B)$, by defining an injective function $h : TR(P_B) \to ID_{PRISM}$. We encode any transition tr of the form $(\alpha, PH(A))$, leading P_i from state S_0 to S_1, in the following manner:

$[\alpha]\ (f(P_i) = g_i(S_0))\ \&\ (h(tr)\_won{=}true) \mathrel{-\!>} 1 : (f(P_i)' = g_i(S_1));$

The interpretation is that whenever P_i is in state S_0 (i.e., $f(P_i) = g_i(S_0)$) and the transition tr won the race for execution (i.e., $h(tr)\_won{=}true$), then the transition becomes enabled and action α is performed, which results in P_i entering state S_1 (i.e., $f(P_i)' = g_i(S_1)$). The meaning of the variable $h(tr)\_won$, and the fact that the rate of the transition is equal to 1, are properly explained in Steps 3 and 4, respectively. Finally, the transition tr is added to module $f(P_i)$.

At the end of this step, the states and the transitions of the sequential PHASE processes P_i, for $1 \leq i \leq m$, have been translated into PRISM. However, any PHASE transition $tr = (\alpha, PH(A))$, whose duration is phase-type distributed according to $PH(A)$, is represented in PRISM by a transition $tr' = (\alpha, 1)$, the duration of which is exponentially distributed, with a rate of 1. In Step 3, we present our solution to this problem.

2.3   Step 3: Implementing the Sequential and Choice Operators

Before we can tackle the sequential and choice operators, we must first clarify how to accommodate the phase-type duration of transitions, since PRISM only handles exponentially distributed transitions. To deal with this issue, we begin by separating transition durations from the occurrence of actions, which are assumed to be (nearly) instantaneous. If we consider a transition tr of the form $(\alpha, PH(A))$, originating in state S_0 of process P_i, the action α is performed immediately after a delay has elapsed, and the delay is sampled from the distribution $PH(A)$.

One elegant (but tentative) solution for implementing this separation is to create a module for tr, which becomes active whenever P_i enters state S_0 and whose stochastic behaviour matches that of $CTMC(A)$, state by state and transition by transition. Given that PRISM does not allow the dynamic creation of new modules (i.e., all modules must be specified explicitly when describing the initial system), we cannot create a new module each time tr is encountered, and then discard it after serving its purpose. Instead, we define a single module for tr, and reuse it whenever necessary. In addition, we need to make sure that P_i can execute the action α only after the module for tr has entered the absorbing state of $CTMC(A)$ (i.e., after the delay associated with tr has expired). The resulting module is the following:

module $h(tr)$

$h(tr)$_won : bool init false;
$h(tr)$: $[0..ord(A)]$ init 1;
...
$[]$ $(f(P_i) = g_i(S_0))$ & $(h(tr) = j)$ $->$ $A(j,1) : (h(tr)' = 1) + \ldots +$
$+ A(j, j-1) : (h(tr)' = j-1) + A(j, j+1) : (h(tr)' = j+1) + \ldots +$
$+ A(j, ord(A) - 1) : (h(tr)' = ord(A) - 1) + A(j, ord(A)) : (h(tr)' = ord(A))$ &
$(h(tr)$_won$'$=true);
...
endmodule .

where $1 \leq j \leq ord(A) - 1$, and the $+$ operator denotes a choice between exponentially distributed PRISM transitions, based on the usual race condition. The states of the module $h(tr)$, given by the values of the variable $h(tr)$ (with the exception of 0), correspond exactly to the states of $CTMC(A)^2$. This correspondence also holds for the transitions of the module $h(tr)$ and those of $CTMC(A)$ (except for self loops, which are redundant). We also add a Boolean variable $h(tr)$_won, which was mentioned in Step 2 and has the role of signalling the current status of transition tr: if $h(tr)$_won=false, then the delay for tr is in still in progress (or, alternatively, process P_i is not in state S_0, and the module $h(tr)$ is inactive); on the other hand, if $h(tr)$_won=true, then the delay has elapsed and the process P_i must perform the action α. Unfortunately, the

---

[2] State 0 is included, but never used, simply because PRISM cannot handle intervals of the form $[1..1]$, which arise when $ord(A) = 1$.

straightforward translation we have just described is incomplete, because it fails to consider two aspects. Firstly, after process P_i leaves state S_0, the module $h(tr)$ becomes inactive[3], as expected, but if P_i re-enters state S_0 at a later time, then the module $h(tr)$ does not reset itself to its initial state, leading to incorrect behaviour. Secondly, phase-type transitions in sequential PHASE processes usually occur within choice expressions, in which case the module $h(tr)$ must take into account the context in which the transition tr is situated.

We can now proceed to translate the sequential and choice operators into PRISM. Let us note that the sequential operator is equivalent to a choice over a single possible transition, which means that it is sufficient to discuss only the choice operator. In order to correctly implement the functionality of the choice operator, and also make sure that phase-type transitions are reset properly, we must operate certain changes to the modules which capture the duration of phase-type transitions. Let us assume that the state S_0 of P_i is defined in terms of the choice operator, such that:

$$S_0 = (\alpha_1, PH(A_1)).S_1 + \ldots + (\alpha_n, PH(A_n)).S_n \ .$$

Also, let $tr_k = (\alpha_k, PH(A_k))$, for $1 \le k \le n$. We begin by enforcing the rule that the module $h(tr_k)$ is active only as long as none of the transitions from S_0 have yet won the race for execution, as imposed by the race condition of the choice operator. To do so, we create a Boolean property $f(P_i)\_g_i(S_0)\_race\_on$, defined by the following PRISM formula:

formula $f(P_i)\_g_i(S_0)\_race\_on = (h(tr_1)\_won=false)$ & $\ldots$ & $(h(tr_n)\_won=false)$;

The property is true if the race between the PHASE transitions tr_k, for $1 \le k \le n$, is currently in progress, and is false otherwise. We add this property to the guards for all the transitions in the module $h(tr_k)$, such that any PRISM guard of the form

$$(f(P_i) = g_i(S_0)) \ \& \ (h(tr_k) = j)$$

is now replaced by the guard

$$(f(P_i) = g_i(S_0)) \ \& \ (h(tr_k) = j) \ \& \ f(P_i)\_g_i(S_0)\_race\_on \ .$$

As a result, once the outcome of the choice is decided, the modules for the PHASE transitions that were involved in the choice are inactivated. Next, we ensure that these modules are reset once the race for execution is over. The reset can be performed at any moment between that at which the race is over, and that at which P_i returns to state S_0. We apply the reset as soon as the choice is

---

[3] An inactive module is one in which no transition is currently enabled. Such a module can reactivate itself at a later time, if the guards for (at least) one of its transitions are satisfied. Otherwise, the module retains its current state (i.e., the values of its local variables) indefinitely.

settled, since this seems the most natural choice in the context of our approach, and it is also easy to implement. More specifically, within the module $h(tr_k)$ we replace all updates $h(tr_k)' = ord(A_k)$ with the following update:

$$(h(tr_1)' = 1) \; \& \; \ldots \; \& \; (h(tr_n)' = 1) \, .$$

The update $h(tr_k)' = ord(A_k)$ can be safely eliminated since its functionality is redundant, as the expressions $h(tr_k)' = ord(A_k)$ and $h(tr_k)\_won'=$true both serve the same purpose, which is to indicate that transition tr_k won the race. However, the new update does not yet work as intended, given that PRISM does not allow modules to change the values of local variables defined in other modules (i.e., local variables can be read globally, but modified only locally). Thus, it is also necessary to turn the local variable $h(tr_k)$ into a global one, so that it can be updated by the competitors of tr_k, if they happen to win the race. This is the reason why, unlike the functions $g_1, \ldots, g_m$, which are defined locally, the function h is defined globally: if local functions $h_1, \ldots, h_m$ would have been used instead of h, then naming conflicts could have occurred at this stage. Practically, we have to remove the declaration

$h(tr_k) : [0..ord(A_k)]$ init 1;

from the module $h(tr_k)$, and instead declare the variable $h(tr_k)$ globally, outside any module, as follows:

global $h(tr_k) : [0..ord(A_k)]$ init 1;

At this stage, if the transition tr_k wins the race for execution, then the modules corresponding to the losing transitions are blocked and reset, as expected. Nevertheless, whenever the process P_i re-enters the state S_0, the modules $h(tr_1), \ldots, h(tr_n)$ remain inactive, given that $f(P_i)\_g_i(S_0)\_race\_on$ is (still) false, since $h(tr)\_won$ is (still) true. Therefore, to avoid such incorrect behaviour, once the transition tr_k is performed we also reset the variable $h(tr_k)\_won$ to false, thus guaranteeing that $f(P_i)\_g_i(S_0)\_race\_on$ is true. In order to implement this final part of the reset, we include the following transition in the module $h(tr_k)$:

$[\alpha_k] \; (f(P_i) = g_i(S_0)) \; \& \; (h(tr_k)\_won=$true$) \; -> \; 1 : (h(tr_k)\_won'=$false$);$

By synchronizing the module $h(tr_k)$ with the module $f(P_i)$ over the action α_k, as will be shown in Step 4, we know that $h(tr)\_won$ is set to false as soon as P_i finishes transition tr_k.

After completing this step, all that is left to do is to translate the interactions between the sequential PHASE processes from SP, and to make sure that actions are indeed immediate (i.e., at this point, actions are still represented by exponentially distributed PRISM transitions, with rates equal to 1).

2.4   Step 4: Implementing the Parallel Operator and Generating the Final Model

Unlike the sequential and choice operators, which are relatively difficult to implement in PRISM, the parallel operator can be translated into PRISM in a simpler manner. This is a direct consequence of the separation between transition durations and the occurrence of actions, combined with the fact that actions are performed instantaneously. Since PRISM does not support immediate transitions, we approximate this functionality by creating a module named inst_sync, such that for any action α which can (eventually) be performed by one of the processes P_i, with $1 \leq i \leq m$, the module inst_sync contains a transition of the form

$$[\alpha] \text{ true } -> infty : \text{true};$$

where $infty$ is a very large number [4]. When the module inst_sync is synchronized with the rest of the modules, the multiplicative law used by PRISM in computing synchronization rates forces the immediacy of actions: all transitions of the form $[\alpha] \ldots -> \ldots$, executed by any single module $f(P_i)$ (or by any cooperation between the modules for SP), have a rate of $1 \cdot \ldots \cdot 1 \cdot infty = infty$, which means that their average duration is equal to $1/infty \approx 0$.

We are now ready to put all the modules together and obtain the full translation of P in PRISM, starting from P_B. All we have to do is to use the parallel operators offered by PRISM, which follow the same waiting condition as the parallel operator in PHASE. Firstly, we replace any process P_i from P_B with the following parallel composition of modules:

$$f(P_i) \ || \ \left(\underset{tr \in trm(P_i)}{|||} h(tr) \right) .$$

The operator $|||$ denotes parallel composition without any synchronization over actions, and it is used to indicate that the modules $h(tr)$ interact with one another by means of shared variables, and not actions. The operator $||$ denotes parallel composition over all the actions common to both participants, and it is employed in both separating transition durations from the occurrence of actions, and assuring the correct reset of the modules $h(tr)$. Secondly, we replace all instances of the $\underset{\{L\}}{\bowtie}$ operator with its analogue in PRISM, namely $|[L]|$, and we denote the resulting PRISM expression by P'_B. Just like the PHASE operator $\underset{\{L\}}{\bowtie}$, the parallel operator $|[L]|$ forces the participants to synchronize only on the actions in $\{L\}$. Thirdly, we link P'_B to the module inst_sync, resulting in the model $P' = P'_B \ || \ $ inst_sync. Thanks to the module inst_sync, the actions in the model P' are (almost) immediate. However, a caveat is in order here: given that

---

[4] The exact definition of a "very large number" depends on the structure of the PHASE process P, and especially on the rates of the transitions that produce the phase-type distributions employed by the process. Our recommendation is to select a value for $infty$ that is at least a few orders of magnitude larger than any value found in the generator matrices associated with the transitions from $TR(P_B)$.

immediate actions are not allowed by PRISM, in our translation the duration of the PHASE transition $tr = (\alpha, PH(A))$ is distributed according not to $PH(A)$, but instead to the convolution of $PH(A)$ (i.e., the delay associated with tr) and $Exp(infty)$ (i.e., the duration for generating the "immediate" action α). Nevertheless, selecting an appropriately large value for $infty$ can reduce the error introduced by $Exp(infty)$ to a negligible level. Finally, we inform PRISM that the model we wish to work with is indeed P', by using the construct system P' endsystem, and that our model ultimately describes a CTMC, by inserting the keyword ctmc at the very beginning of the specification for P'. Thus, the PRISM implementation of the PHASE model P is complete, in the form of the corresponding model P'.

3   PHASE Example of a Non-Markovian System

In order to illustrate our approach to modelling non-Markovian systems by using PHASE and PRISM, we present and analyse the behaviour of a very simple system, which employs both non-exponential and exponential transitions. The structure of the system is shown in Figure 1, in terms of states and transitions.

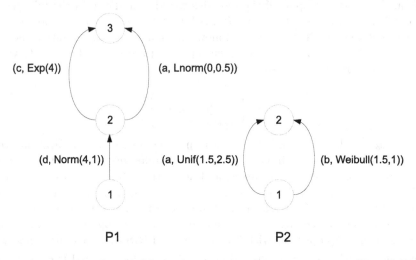

Fig. 1. An example of a non-Markovian system, where two processes $P1$ and $P2$ co-operate over the shared action a

The system consists of two processes, $P1$ and $P2$, which operate in parallel and synchronize over the action a. The delay associated with each transition is given by a different distribution, where $Norm(4,1)$ is a normal distribution with a mean of 4 and a standard deviation of 1, $Exp(4)$ is an exponential distribution with a rate of 4, $Lnorm(0,0.5)$ is a log-normal distribution with a mean of 0 and a standard deviation of 0.5, on the log scale, $Unif(1.5,2.5)$ is a uniform distribution with a lower bound of 1.5 and an upper bound of 2.5, and finally, $Weibull(1.5, 1)$ is a Weibull distribution with a shape of 1.5 and a scale of 1.

This system can be represented in PHASE by approximating all transitions with PH transitions, as follows:

$$P1_1 = (d, PH(A_1)).P1_2$$
$$P1_2 = (c, PH(A_2)).P1_3 + (a, PH(A_3)).P1_3$$
$$P2_1 = (a, PH(A_4)).P2_2 + (b, PH(A_5)).P2_2$$

$$Sys = P1_1 \bowtie_{\{a\}} P2_1 \ .$$

The complete PHASE system is denoted by Sys, where $PH(A_1) \approx Norm(4, 1)$, $PH(A_2) \approx Exp(4)$, $PH(A_3) \approx Lnorm(0, 0.5)$, $PH(A_4) \approx Unif(1.5, 2.5)$, and $PH(A_5) \approx Weibull(1.5, 1)$. There are several options for generating the distributions $PH(A_1)$ through $PH(A_5)$, given the existence of multiple, general purpose tools for fitting phase-type distributions, such as EMpht [1], jPhase [23], Hyper-Star [22] and PhFit [16]. Our decision is to use the tool EMpht, for two main reasons: it allows us to impose structural constraints on the resulting PH representations (i.e., in our case, the requirement that there must be a single initial state for each representation), and also, its pre-specified input distributions already include all the distributions that appear in our example, which means that the input to the fitting algorithm can be provided in an effortless manner. Since we wish to obtain accurate approximations, we employ moderately large PH representations, having either 1 phase $(PH(A_2))$, 10 phases $(PH(A_3), PH(A_5))$, 15 phases $(PH(A_1))$, or 20 phases $(PH(A_4))$. The match between the PH distributions produced by EMpht and the initial distributions is excellent, with the exception of the uniform distribution, which is approximated by a (normal-like) Erlang distribution. We now have everything we need to implement the full PHASE model in PRISM.

In order to test how well the behaviour of the PRISM model for Sys matches that of the non-Markovian model depicted in Figure 1, which we refer to as Sys_{NM}, we simulated the dynamics of Sys_{NM} using an R script. The simulation involved generating 1 million traces for Sys_{NM} and recording the moment at which any event of interest took place, for each trace. Then, we compared the results of the simulation with those produced by PRISM's numerical engine, for the model corresponding to Sys. Firstly, we looked at the time it took $P1$ and $P2$ to reach their final states, in the cases where there was no deadlock due to a failed synchronization over a. The distributions for Sys and Sys_{NM}, shown in Figure 2, are very similar, and we believe that the existing differences between the two distributions are caused not by faults in the translation of Sys into PRISM, but rather by the imperfect approximation for the duration of transition $tr4$. Secondly, we computed the percentage of deadlocks that were caused by the synchronization between $P1$ and $P2$ (i.e., in situations where $tr3$ became enabled, but $tr4$ did not, or vice-versa), yielding a value of 0.118744 for Sys, and 0.105986 for Sys_{NM}. Furthermore, we also calculated the probability of successful synchronization over a, finding a value of 0.003618 for Sys, and

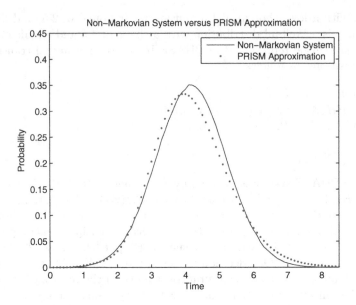

Fig. 2. The distributions of the time elapsed until Sys_{NM} and Sys terminate

0.003007 for Sys_{NM}. Taken together, the comparable results obtained for the performance measures involving Sys and Sys_{NM} support the correctness of our PHASE-to-PRISM translation.

4   Conclusion

In our study, we introduce a new stochastic process calculus, named PHASE, which allows phase-type distributions for transition durations. The new formalism has a very simple syntax, involving only the sequential, choice, and parallel operators. This parsimony is motivated by the practical purpose for which PHASE was created: we did not wish to design a comprehensive, theoretically oriented calculus, such as those developed by Hermanns and his colleagues [13,24,21,26], but rather to propose a formalism whose specifications can be easily implemented and analysed in an existing model checker. As a result, we provide a step-by-step description of how PHASE processes can be translated into PRISM models, in a relatively straightforward manner. The guiding idea for our translation is that of separating the structural and the stochastic aspects of PHASE, inspired by the definition of the elapse operator in IMC [14].

Our option for expressing PHASE processes in PRISM is based on two important reasons: firstly, due to its advanced language elements (i.e., action guards, local and global variables, complex effects for single transitions), PRISM is ideally suited for implementing the PH distributions and operators in PHASE; secondly, PRISM is arguably one of the most powerful stochastic model checkers currently available. More specifically, PRISM allows the specification and verification of steady-state, transient and passage-time measures, by employing an extended version of Continuous Stochastic Logic (CSL) [2]. In addition to CSL, the model checker also supports reward properties: instead of reasoning about the probabilities of certain behaviours, as is usually done when employing stochastic process calculi, it is possible to assign numerical values (i.e., rewards) to the states and the transitions which form a particular behaviour, in order to compute the expected values of the rewards associated with that behaviour. Furthermore, PRISM includes features such as statistical model checking (i.e., a type of statistically informed, discrete event simulation, in which a number of model executions are generated, in order to perform an approximate verification of CSL formulas), interactive simulation (i.e., a user-guided, step-by-step simulation of model behaviour), as well as the possibility of exporting models in the MATLAB and Markov Reward Model Checker (MRMC) formats.

To illustrate our approach, we give an example of a non-Markovian system Sys_{NM} and approximate its stochastic behaviour in PHASE, using the software tool EMpht for producing the required phase-type representations. We then translate the PHASE model into PRISM, and analyse some of its quantitative properties. We also construct an R implementation for Sys_{NM}, based on discrete event simulation, and show that the PHASE/PRISM and R models produce closely matching results, with respect to the performance measures in question.

Acknowledgement. The work was supported by a grant of the Romanian National Authority for Scientific Research CNCS-UEFISCDI, project number PN-II-ID-PCE-2011-3-0919.

References

1. Asmussen, S., Nerman, O., Olsson, M.: Fitting Phase-type Distributions via the EM Algorithm. Scandinavian Journal of Statistics 23(4), 419–441 (1996)
2. Baier, C., Katoen, J.-P., Hermanns, H.: Approximate Symbolic Model Checking of Continuous-Time Markov Chains (Extended Abstract). In: Baeten, J.C.M., Mauw, S. (eds.) CONCUR 1999. LNCS, vol. 1664, pp. 146–161. Springer, Heidelberg (1999)
3. Bernardo, M., Gorrieri, R.: Extended Markovian Process Algebra. In: Sassone, V., Montanari, U. (eds.) CONCUR 1996. LNCS, vol. 1119, pp. 315–330. Springer, Heidelberg (1996)
4. Bradley, J.T.: Semi-Markov PEPA: Modelling with generally distributed actions. International Journal of Simulation 6(3-4), 43–51 (2005)
5. Bravetti, M., D'Argenio, P.R.: Tutte le algebre insieme: Concepts, discussions and relations of stochastic process algebras with general distributions. In: Baier, C., Haverkort, B.R., Hermanns, H., Katoen, J.-P., Siegle, M. (eds.) Validation of Stochastic Systems. LNCS, vol. 2925, pp. 44–88. Springer, Heidelberg (2004)
6. Crovella, M.E.: Performance Evaluation with Heavy Tailed Distributions. In: Feitelson, D.G., Rudolph, L. (eds.) JSSPP 2001. LNCS, vol. 2221, pp. 1–10. Springer, Heidelberg (2001)
7. D'Argenio, P.: Algebras and Automata for Timed and Stochastic Systems. PhD thesis, University of Twente (1999)

8. D'Argenio, P., Katoen, J.-P., Brinksma, E.: A compositional approach to generalised semi-Markov processes. In: Guia, A., Spathopoulos, M., Smedinga, R. (eds.) Proceedings of WODES 1998, pp. 391–397. IEEE Press, New York (1998)

9. Doherty, G., Massink, M., Faconti, G.: Reasoning about interactive systems with stochastic models. In: Johnson, C. (ed.) DSV-IS 2001. LNCS, vol. 2220, pp. 144–163. Springer, Heidelberg (2001)

10. El-Rayes, A., Kwiatkowska, M., Norman, G.: Solving infinite stochastic process algebra models through matrix-geometric methods. In: Hillston, J., Silva, M. (eds.) Proceedings of PAPM 1999, Zaragoza, Spain, pp. 41–62. Prensas Universitarias de Zaragoza (1999)

11. Hahn, E.M., Hartmanns, A., Hermanns, H., Katoen, J.-P.: A compositional modelling and analysis framework for stochastic hybrid systems. In: Formal Methods in System Design (2012)

12. Harrison, P.G., Strulo, B.: Stochastic process algebra for discrete event simulation. In: Baccelli, F., Jean-Marie, A., Mitrani, I. (eds.) Quantitative Methods in Parallel Systems, pp. 18–37. Springer, Berlin (1995)

13. Hermanns, H.: Interactive Markov Chains - The Quest for Quantified Quality. Springer, Berlin (2002)

14. Hermanns, H., Katoen, J.-P.: Automated compositional Markov chain generation for a plain-old telephone system. Science of Computer Programming 36(1), 97–127 (2000)

15. Hillston, J.: A Compositional Approach to Performance Modelling. Cambridge University Press, Cambridge (1996)

16. Horváth, A., Telek, M.: PhFit: A General Phase-Type Fitting Tool. In: Computer Performance Evaluation: Modelling Techniques and Tools, pp. 82–91. Springer, Heidelberg (2002)

17. Katoen, J.-P., D'Argenio, P.R.: General distributions in process algebra. In: Brinksma, E., Hermanns, H., Katoen, J.-P. (eds.) EEF School 2000 and FMPA 2000. LNCS, vol. 2090, pp. 375–429. Springer, Heidelberg (2001)

18. Nelson, R.: Probability, Stochastic Processes, and Queueing Theory. Springer, New York (1995)

19. Neuts, M.F.: Matrix-geometric solutions in stochastic models: an algorithmic approach. Dover Publications (1981)

20. Norris, J.R.: Markov chains. Cambridge University Press, Cambridge (1998)

21. Pulungan, M.R.: Reduction of Acyclic Phase-Type Representations. PhD thesis, Saarland University, Germany (2009)

22. Reinecke, P., Krauss, T., Wolter, K.: HyperStar: Phase-type Fitting Made Easy. In: Proceedings of QEST 2012, pp. 201–202. IEEE Computer Society, Washington, DC (2012)

23. Riaño, G., Pérez, J.F.: jPhase: an Object-Oriented Tool for Modeling Phase-Type Distributions. In: Meini, B., van Houdt, B. (eds.) Proceeding of SMCTools 2006, vol. 5, ACM, New York (2006)

24. Wolf, V.: Equivalences on phase type processes. PhD thesis, University of Mannheim, Germany (2008)

25. Younes, H.L.S.: Ymer: A statistical model checker. In: Etessami, K., Rajamani, S.K. (eds.) CAV 2005. LNCS, vol. 3576, pp. 429–433. Springer, Heidelberg (2005)

26. Zeng, K.: Logics and Models for Stochastic Analysis Beyond Markov Chains. PhD thesis, Technical University of Denmark, Denmark (2012)

CASSANDRA: An Online Failure Prediction Strategy for Dynamically Evolving Systems[*]

Francesco De Angelis[1], Maria Rita Di Berardini[1], Henry Muccini[2], and Andrea Polini[1]

[1] Computer Science Division, University of Camerino, Italy
[2] Dipartimento di Informatica, University of L'Aquila, Italy

Abstract. Dynamically evolving systems are characterized by components that can be inserted or removed while the system is being operated leading to unsafe run-time changes that may compromise a correct execution. To mitigate the effects of such a failure we propose an online analysis technique that admit an integration "a-priori" and a monitoring of the run-time behaviour to provide information about possible errors *when* these can happen. Our CASSANDRA technique proposes a novel run-time monitoring and verification algorithm with the ability to predict potential failures that can happens in future states of the systems. CASSANDRA combines design-time and run-time information. Both are used to identify the current execution state, and to drive the construction of predictions that look to a number k of steps ahead of the current execution state. This paper provides a detailed formalization of the technique then it introduces a formal definition of the CASSANDRA algorithms and reports some complexity measures. Finally the paper closes with a description of a first concrete implementation of the approach, and its evaluation.

1 Introduction

Software is not anymore an artifact that can be (always) potentially fully designed and understood at design-time. It emerges instead at run-time, with behaviors and configurations that can be modified while the system is being operated. This is for instance the case of SOA-based and Future Internet-oriented applications [1], where dynamically integrated components or services[1] may come from partially unknown third parties, thus further limiting the trust on their correct and unmalicious behavior.

The very late integration of software elements limits the possibility of carrying on software quality related activities in advance. Therefore, preventing failures on those dynamically evolving systems is far from simple, and requires the

---

[*] This work has been partially supported by the project "Open City Platform - SCN 00467" in the "Smart Cities and Communities" initiative sponsored by the Italian Ministry of Education, University and Research.
[1] Hereafter, we will use the term component(s), to refer to both concepts.

S. Merz and J. Pang (Eds.): ICFEM 2014, LNCS 8829, pp. 107–122, 2014.

introduction and reinforcement of software quality verification activities during the run-time phase.

Nevertheless, when we consider a running context in which many components are involved in a composition, and they can discover each other at run-time, immediately trying to start to interact, it becomes really difficult to check the correctness of the resulting composition before to permit the integration and communication among the components. Moreover, with the emergence of short living compositions, we think that it could be more fruitful to permit the integration "a-priori", and then to monitor components behaviour in order to detect possible failures, and (if possible) to avoid them. In such a context, traditional testing and static analysis strategies may not be enough and they should be complemented with run-time validation and verification activities. Moreover the off-line analysis of some configurations, when feasible, may be also inefficient since the lifetime of a certain configuration can be limited with a small fragment of the provided behavior exercised before the system evolves. In this scenario, new verification techniques need to be devised, that may take advantage of both (classical) design-time and (more recent) run-time verification techniques, that can efficiently and effectively manage frequent run-time updates, and may enable actions to predict and prevent potential failures allowing the implementation of recovery strategies if failures are detected. This will lead to systems in which dependability and resilience are managed even in the presence of frequent configuration updates.

The goal of this research paper is to propose and formalize an online failure prediction strategy for dynamically evolving systems[2]. Towards this research goal, we here propose CASSANDRA, a novel approach to predict potential failures by looking ahead the current execution state. To this end, CASSANDRA *combines design-time and run-time information* for *proactive run-time verification of dynamic component-based systems*.

This paper contributes to the state-of-the-art in failure prediction of dynamically evolving systems in this respect: i) it introduces a new approach for predicting integration failures in systems subject to dynamic evolution, ii) it provides and formalizes new failure prediction algorithms enabling the discovery of potential run-time integration problems, iii) it provides reasoning on the algorithms complexity, applicability, and implementation issues, derived from a real experience on a concrete implementation of the approach.

Section 2 provides some introductory material on Interface Automata. The approach is introduced in Section 3 and fully elaborated in Section 4. General remarks in terms of the CASSANDRA complexity, ideas and issues related to a concrete implementation of the proposed approach are introduced in Section 5. Related work are discussed in Section 6 while Section 7 concludes the paper and provides a list of future research directions.

---

[2] Fault prevention [2] strategies are not the focus of this paper. Nevertheless the approach can certainly foster novel prevention and avoidance strategies.

2   Background

Interface automata have been introduced in [3] as a light-weight formalism for modeling temporal aspects of software components interfaces. Interface automata interact through the synchronization of input and output actions, and asynchronously interleave all the other (i.e. internal) actions. Below we provide some basic definition mostly taken from [3].

Definition 1. *An interface automaton is a tuple* $P = \langle V_P, V_P^{init}, \mathcal{A}_P^I, \mathcal{A}_P^O, \mathcal{A}_P^H, \mathcal{T}_P \rangle$ *where:*

- V_P *is a set of* states *and* V_P^{init} *is a set of* initial states *that contains at most one state.*
- $\mathcal{A}_P^I, \mathcal{A}_P^O$ *and* $\mathcal{A}_P^H$ *are mutually disjoint sets of* input, output *and* internal *actions. We define* $\mathcal{A}_P = \mathcal{A}_P^I \cup \mathcal{A}_P^O \cup \mathcal{A}_P^H$.
- $\mathcal{T}_P \subseteq V_P \times \mathcal{A}_P \times V_P$ *is a set of* steps.

We say that an action $a \in \mathcal{A}_P$ is enabled at a state $v \in V_P$ if there is a step $(v, a, v') \in \mathcal{T}_P$. $\mathcal{A}_P^I(v)$, $\mathcal{A}_P^O(v)$ and $\mathcal{A}_P^H(v)$ are the subsets of input, output and internal actions that are enabled at v and $\mathcal{A}_P(v) = \mathcal{A}_P^I(v) \cup \mathcal{A}_P^O(v) \cup \mathcal{A}_P^H(v)$ is the set of action enabled at v. A key feature is that interface automata are *not* required to be input-enabled, i.e. we do not assume that $\mathcal{A}_P^I(v) = \mathcal{A}_P^I$ for each $v \in V_P$. The inputs in $\mathcal{A}_P^I \backslash \mathcal{A}_P^I(v)$ are called illegal inputs at v. The set of *input steps* is the subset of steps $\mathcal{T}_P^I = \{(v, a, u) \in \mathcal{T}_P \mid a \in \mathcal{A}_P^I\} \subseteq \mathcal{T}_P$. Similarly we define the sets $\mathcal{T}_P^O$ and $\mathcal{T}_P^H$ of *output* and *internal steps*. Moreover, a state u is reachable from v if there is an *execution sequence*, namely an alternating sequence of states and actions of the form $v = v_0, a_0, v_1, a_1, \ldots, v_n = u$ where each (v_i, a_i, v_{i+1}) is a step.

Two interface automata are *mutually composable* if their set of actions are disjoint, except that some input actions of one automaton can be output actions of the other one [3].

Definition 2. *Two interface automata* P *and* Q *are* mutually composable *(composable, for short) if* $\mathcal{A}_P^H \cap \mathcal{A}_Q = \mathcal{A}_Q^H \cap \mathcal{A}_P = \emptyset$ *and* $\mathcal{A}_P^I \cap \mathcal{A}_Q^I = \mathcal{A}_P^O \cap \mathcal{A}_Q^O = \emptyset$. *Essentially,* P *and* Q *are composable whenever they only share some input and output actions and, hence,* $\mathsf{shared}(P, Q) = \mathcal{A}_P \cap \mathcal{A}_Q = (\mathcal{A}_P^I \cap \mathcal{A}_Q^O) \cup (\mathcal{A}_Q^I \cap \mathcal{A}_P^O)$.

If two interface autoamata P and Q are composable, their product $P \otimes Q$ is an interface automaton whose set of states is $V_P \times V_Q$ and that will synchronize on shared actions, while asynchronously interleave all other (i.e. internal) actions. Since P and Q are not required to be input-enabled, their product $P \otimes Q$ may have one or more states where one component produces an output that the other one is not able to accept. The states where this happens, i.e. all pairs $(v, u) \in V_P \times V_Q$ where there is an action $a \in \mathsf{shared}(P, Q)$ such that either $a \in \mathcal{A}_P^O(v) \backslash \mathcal{A}_Q^I(u)$ or $a \in \mathcal{A}_Q^O(u) \backslash \mathcal{A}_P^I(v)$, are called *illegal* in [3]. They represent error states that the composed system should not be able to reach. Indeed, in [3], two interface automata P and Q can be used together if there is at least a legal environment, i.e. an environment that can prevent (by generating appropriate inputs) $P \otimes Q$ from entering its illegal states.

3   Approach Overview

CASSANDRA defines an approach to forecast possible failures in the dynamic integration of software components. It explores design-time system models together with events observed at run-time. The exploration strategy, starting from the current system state (monitored at run-time), builds a global design-time model looking k steps ahead (with respect to the current system state) to check if a possible illegal state is reachable. Different strategies can be defined to choose the value of k in order to improve performace or prediction capability. Also dynamic strategies could be conceived to adapt to increasing/reducing load. Nevertheless in this paper we do not further investigate such problem and we assume that the value of k is defined by the user.

The online failure prediction algorithm we have implemented (described in Section 4.2) relies on a specification of the component behaviour based on the interface automata formalism. The algorithm suitably composes the specifications of those components under execution. Nevertheless instead of using the classical composition operator defined in [3], we base our algorithm on a slightly different composition operator (defined in Section 4.1, Def. 4) that, according to us, is more suitable for the online prediction of failures in a dynamic environment (see Section 4.1). According to our composition operator, any pair of components sharing a set o I/O actions can be integrated. Then, the composed automata is navigated by looking ahead to the current execution state. It is the task of our failure prediction approach to check whether the system is approaching an *illegal state*, and so to inform a possible failure avoidance mechanism that will possibly take care of repair actions. In our approach an illegal state corresponds to an integration failure, by any path shorter than k steps and originating in the current state. In a sense, we assume that an illegal state can be reached as consequence of a wrong invocation/message done by one component on a component that either is not willing to accept it in the current state or does not exist at all.

Figure 1 sketches the general idea of our algorithm in case of two simple components P and Q. The component Q models a simple resource which can be accessed (read) and modified (write) after it has been correctly opened (open). The automaton P represents a process that wants to use the resource made available by Q. The two components cannot always correctly cooperate since they make different assumptions on their respective behaviour. P assumes that after a successful opening the resource can be used without receiving any failure, and till its usage is interrupted (closed). Q (which may work through a not completely realiable medium) can return a failure also on correspondence of a read or write action. It can be noticed that the system resulting from the composition of P and Q is closed (the communication medium is embedded in Q) therefore according to the standard Interface Automata theory the two automata cannot be composed since no environment exist permitting a correct integration.

On the right side of Figure 1 we provide some additional details about the CASSANDRA strategy. Here, we consider the system whose components are P and Q and we assume that the number k of lookahead steps is equal to 2 (i.e. we look 2 steps in the future). CASSANDRA will start its execution deriving the composed

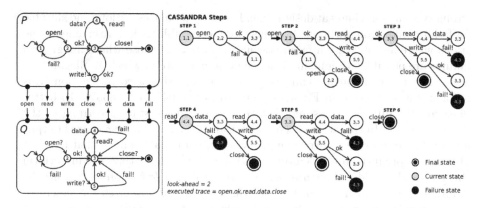

Fig. 1. Composition and CASSANDRA model exploration for two simple components

model (that we call *exploration tree*) shown in step 1. This tree describes how the system can evolve in the next k steps. Now, assuming that the *open* action is performed by the two components, CASSANDRA will bring the exploration one step ahead as shown in step 2; the reader can notice the new states outgoing from the states (1,1) and (3,3). At step 3, after that the action *ok* has been observed, CASSANDRA will encounter two possible failure states (represented in black). This two failure states are those which will be reached in case a *fail* action is raised by Q after a *read* or a *write* action. CASSANDRA will report the traces bringing to the failure states; nevertheless, the execution can continue. In case a *read* action is requested by P the exploration tree will be the one shown at step 4. Here it is still possible to reach a failure within two steps, and the failure trace will be reported. In case Q correctly replies with a *data* action, the tree will be modified as shown in step 5. Also in this case the possibility of reaching failure states is reported by CASSANDRA. Finally P decides to stop the usage of Q and closes the interaction.

4   Cassandra – Approach Details

4.1   A Model for Dynamic Composition and Compatibility

In this section we formally define the new product operator on which our algorithm is based on. Before providing all the technical details, we illustrate the main differences w.r.t. the original product operator introduced by De Alfaro and Henzinger in [3]. The changes we introduce are mainly concerned with the notion of illegal or error states. As already said, in [3] an *illegal state* of $P \otimes Q$ is a state where one component can produce an output that the other one is not able to accept. More formally, a state $(v, u) \in V_P \times V_Q$ is illegal if there is a shared action such that either $a \in \mathcal{A}_P^O(v) \backslash \mathcal{A}_Q^I(u)$ or $a \in \mathcal{A}_Q^O(u) \backslash \mathcal{A}_P^I(v)$.

This notion of error states essentially considers as erroneous the states where integration failures are possible and clearly reflects the intention of preventing wrong system behaviours at design time. In our opinion, this notion is no suitable for failure prediction purposes. It seems more reasonable to declare erroneous the states where an integration failure occurred, instead of those where integration failures are possible, as done in [3], since even in a state in which an illegal state is possible the components can decide to interact using a correct action (this is for instance the case in Figure 1 going from "Step4" to "Step5"). To better illustrate the difference, assume that (v, u) is an illegal state according to the definition in [3]. In this state, P (symmetrically Q) can produce a shared output a (and, hence, there is a corresponding step (v, a, w) enabled at v) that Q is not able to accept. Instead of declaring (v, u) illegal, we admit that P can perform this step and consider the state (w, u) so reached as a *failure state*. Essentially, failure states are witnesses of the fact that a protocol mismatch has emerged. Below we refer to the actions leading to a failure state as *failure actions*.

Another main difference w.r.t. the approach in [3] is that we are considering dynamically evolving systems, i.e. systems whose components may vary at run-time. In these contexts, it may happen that one component tries to communicate (via output actions) with another component that does not exist any more because removed at some previous stage of the system evolution. To be able to monitor also this kind of erroneous behaviour, we collect in a set W all the actions that represent an attempt to synchronize with some removed component. We call actions in W *warning actions* and the states reached by means of their execution *warning states*. All the states which are neither a failure nor a warning state are called *ordinary states*. Below we write $P \otimes_W Q$ to denote the interface automaton resulting from the composition of P and Q when W is the set of warning actions. Moreover, since actions in W are actions that either P and Q (but *not both*) has shared with some other component, we assume that $W \cap \mathsf{shared}(P, Q) = W \cap \mathcal{A}_P^H = W \cap \mathcal{A}_Q^H = \emptyset$.

In a nutshell, $P \otimes_W Q$ is an interface automaton whose set of states is still $V_P \times V_Q$, that still synchronizes on shared actions and asynchronously interleaves any other action (exactly as in the original definition in [3]), but now we distinguish two different kinds of illegal or error states (failure and warning states) and we want to prevent any step from the failure ones.

Finally we are ready to provide the definition of the product automaton.

Definition 3. *The product automaton $\bigotimes_W \{P_i\}_{i \in [1,n]}$ of $n \geq 2$ mutually composable automata $P_1, \ldots, P_n$ defined as $\mathcal{T}_P = I \bigcup S$ where:*

$$I = \bigcup_{i \in [1,n]} \{ (v, a, v[u_i/v_i]) \mid v \notin \mathcal{A}_P^F \wedge (v_i, a, u_i) \in \mathcal{T}_i \wedge$$
$$(a \notin \bigcup_{j \in [1,n]} \mathsf{shared}(P_i, P_j) \vee a \in \mathcal{A}_i^F(v)) \}$$

$$S = \bigcup_{i,j \in [1,n]} \{ (v, a, (v[u_i/v_i, u_j/v_j]) \mid v \notin \mathcal{A}_P^F \wedge (v_i, a, u_i) \in \mathcal{T}_i \wedge$$
$$(v_j, a, u_j) \in \mathcal{T}_j \wedge a \in \mathsf{shared}(P_i, P_j) \}$$

Definition 4. *Let $\{P_i\}_{i \in [1,n]}$ be a set of $n \geq 2$ mutually composable interface automata and W a set of actions such that $W \cap \mathsf{shared}(P_i, P_j) = W \cap A_i^H = \emptyset$*

for each i, j. We define $P = \bigotimes_W \{P_i\}_{i \in [1,n]}$ to be the interface automaton such that:

- $V_P = V_1 \times V_2 \times \cdots \times V_n$,
- $V_P = V_1^{init} \times V_2^{init} \times \cdots \times V_n^{init}$,
- $\mathcal{A}_P^I = \left(\bigcup_{i \in [1,n]} \mathcal{A}_i^I \right) \backslash \left(\bigcup_{i,j \in [1,n]} \text{shared}(P_i, P_j) \right)$,
- $\mathcal{A}_P^O = \left(\bigcup_{i \in [1,n]} \mathcal{A}_i^O \right) \backslash \left(\bigcup_{i,j \in [1,n]} \text{shared}(P_i, P_j) \right)$,
- $\mathcal{A}_P^H = \left(\bigcup_{i \in [1,n]} \mathcal{A}_i^H \right) \cup \left(\bigcup_{i,j \in [1,n]} \text{shared}(P_i, P_j) \right)$

and whose set of steps is provided in Def. 3.

In Def. 4. we use the following notation: given two states $v = (v_1, \ldots, v_n) \in V_P$ and $u_i \in V_i$, $v[u_i/v_i]$ is the state we obtain from v by replacing the state component v_i by u_i; i.e. $v[u_i/v_i] = (v_1, \ldots, v_{i-1}, u_i, v_{i+1} \ldots, v_n) \in V_P$. Finally, $v[u_i/v_i, u_j/v_j]$ denotes the state $(v[u_i/v_i])[u_j/v_j]$.

The set of failure actions enabled at $v \in V_P$ is

$$\mathcal{A}_P^F(v) \bigcup_{i \in [1,n]} \mathcal{A}_i^F(v)$$

where, for each $i \in [1,n]$, the set

$$\mathcal{A}_i^F(v) = A_i^O(v_i) \cap \bigcup_{j \in [1,n]} (\mathcal{A}_j^I \backslash \mathcal{A}_j^I(v_j))$$

contains all the actions of the automaton P_i that can lead v to a failure state. Due to the mutual composability, each action is shared by at most one pair of interface automata. So, for each $i \in [1,n]$, there is at most one $j \neq i$ such that $\mathcal{A}_i^O(v_i) \cap (\mathcal{A}_j^I \backslash \mathcal{A}_j^I(v_j)) \neq \emptyset$.

If $v \in V_P$, $a \in A_i^F(v)$ ($a \in W$) and there is a step $(v_i, a, u_i) \in \mathcal{T}_i$ for some $i \in [1,n]$, then $v[u_i/v_i]$ is a failure (respectively, a warning) state. The sets of failure and warning states are denoted by $\mathcal{A}_P^F$ and $\mathcal{A}_P^W$.

The following proposition, the proof is not shown given the page limit, shows that our product operator is still associative. This is a key result because it allows components to be composed on-the-fly depending on the dynamical evolution of the system

Proposition 1. *Let P_1, P_2 and P_3 be three mutually composable interface automata and W be a set of warning actions such that, for each $i, j \in [1,3]$, $W \cap \text{shared}(P_i, P_j) = W \cap A_i^H = \emptyset$. Then: $(P_1 \otimes_W P_2) \otimes_W P_3 = P_1 \otimes_W (P_2 \otimes_W P_3)$.*

4.2   The Online Failure Prediction Algorithm

From now on we assume that at any time an arbitrary number (let say n) of components are running on our platform; each component is provided with an interface automaton $P_i = \langle V_i, V_i^{init}, \mathcal{A}_i^I, \mathcal{A}_i^O, \mathcal{A}_i^H, \mathcal{T}_i \rangle$ ($i \in [1,n]$) that describes its interface. We also assume that these automata are *deterministic* and *mutually composable.* Below W denotes the set of warning actions, while the global variable k represents the number of lookahead steps.

To keep track of how $P = \bigotimes_W \{P_i\}_{i \in [1,n]}$ evolves over time, we use an *exploration tree* $T = (V_T, E_T)$ whose nodes and edges basically correspond to states and steps of P. The underlying assumption is that the sub-tree of T whose nodes are those reachable from ρ (the current node, see below) by means of a depth-first search describes how the system will evolve in the next k steps. Each node in V_T stores a state together with some additional information; more precisely, a node is tuple $\alpha = (v, d, t, p)$ where $v \in V_P$ is a state and:

- d is a non-negative integer that represents the *distance* (in terms of number of steps) of v from the initial state $v^{init} = (v_1^{init}, \ldots, v_n^{init})$.
- t is the *type* of the node; t can assume values 0, 1 or 2 to denote that v is an ordinary, a warning or a failure state, respectively.
- p is the parent of the node α in the exploration tree.

Nodes of the exploration tree are ranged over by $\alpha, \beta, \ldots$; a special symbol ρ represents the *current node*, i.e. the node containing the current system state. If α is a node, we often write α.distance, α.type and α.parent to denote the distance, the type and the parent of α. Finally, an edge (α, a, β) belongs to E_T if $\alpha, \beta \in V_T$ such that $\alpha = (v, d, t, p)$, $t \neq 2$ (i.e. α is not a failure node), $\beta = (u, d+1, t', \alpha)$ and there is a step $(v, a, u) \in \mathcal{T}_P$. Below we use the following notation.

- $\mathsf{shared}(P_i) = \bigcup_{j \in [1,n]: j \neq i} \mathsf{shared}(P_i, P_j)$ is the set of actions that each P_i shares with the other components.
- If Q is the interface automaton associated with a new component, $v = (v_1, \ldots, v_n) \in V_P$ and $v_q \in V_Q$, we write $v \bullet v_q$ to denote the state $(v_1, \ldots, v_n, v_q) \in V_P \times V_Q$. Finally, if $\alpha = (v, d, s) \in V_G$, we often write $\alpha \bullet v_q$ to denote the node $(v \bullet v_q, d, t)$.

Our algorithm for failure prediction is described by Algorithm 1. It first sets W to be empty and then builds the initial exploration tree (see Algorithm INIT). Once the exploration tree has been initialized, this algorithm repeatedly waits for an event e. This event can be either the occurrence of a monitored action a or a request of adding/removing a component from the system; as expected, for each event there is a corresponding algorithm able to manage it.

Procedure INIT() calls – at most k times – NEXTFROM(X) (Algorithm 3) which takes in input a set X of nodes in V_T and, by using information provided by each automaton P_i, adds to the tree T all the nodes (and the corresponding edges) that are obtained from those in X in exactly one step. At first, X only contains the initial node $\rho = (v^{init}, 0, 0, \mathsf{null})$; afterwards, each iteration of a while cycle uses as X the set of nodes produced by the previous one.

Algorithm NEXTFROM considers each node $\alpha = (v, d, t, p)$ in X that does not contain a failure state (recall that no steps are possible from a failure state). Then, for each action a enabled at v, the algorithm distinguishes two possible sub-cases: a is either a non-shared[3] or a failure action (line 6), and a is a shared

---

[3] By Definition 4 this also includes the case where a is a warning action.

```
1  Input: A set {P_i}_{i∈[1,n]} of mutually composable interface automata
2  W := ∅; INIT();
3  while true do
4  |    wait until en event e occurs
5  |    switch e do
6  |    |    case  e = a ∈ ⋃_{i∈[1,n]} 𝒜_i
7  |    |    |    EXPLORE(a);
8  |    |    case e = remove(i)
9  |    |    |    REMOVE(i);
10 |    |    case e = add(Q)
11 |    |    |    ADD(Q);
12 |    endsw
13 end
```

Algorithm 1. The online failure prediction algorithm.

```
1  Output: The initial exploration tree T = ⟨V_T, E_T⟩
2  ρ ← newNode(v^{init}, 0, 0, null);
3  V_T ← {ρ}; E_T ← ∅;
4  X ← {ρ};
5  i ← 1;
6  while i ≤ k and X ≠ ∅ do
7  |    X ← NEXTFROM(X);
8  |    i ← i + 1;
9  end
```

Algorithm 2. INIT()

but not a failure action (line 18). In the former case, there is an index $i \in [1, n]$ and a corresponding step (v_i, a, u_i) in $\mathcal{T}_i$ that either does not require synchronization or leads to a failure state. In this case, we create a new node β whose state is $v[u_i/v_i]$, whose distance from ρ is $d+1$, whose parent is α and whose type is initially set to 0 (see line 8). The type of β can be changed in the next two lines according to the type of the action a. Finally the node β and the edge (α, a, β) are added to T; β is also added to Y. In case a is a shared but not a failure action we proceed similarly. The only difference is that now, in the construction of β, we consider that the execution of a is the result of a synchronization between two components P_i and P_j.

Algorithm EXPLORE(a) inspects the exploration tree T to check if there are nodes containing failure or warning states along the next k steps from the node α such that $(\rho, a, \alpha) \in E_T$. This algorithm is a breath-first search with α as starting node. Moreover, to be able to produce the proper warnings, we collect in the set *Illegal* all the nodes with a warning or failure state we meet during this search. Note that, during each iteration of the while cycle of line 6, X is the set of all nodes reachable from α in $i-1$ steps. The next for-each cycle (line 8) stores in Y all nodes reachable from those in X in one step. So, at the end of the while cycle of line 6, X contains all nodes that are reachable from α in exactly $k-1$

```
1  Input: A set of nodes X ⊆ V_T
2  Output: The set Y of nodes reachable from X in one step.
3  Y ← ∅;
4  foreach α ∈ X with α.type ≠ 2 do
5  |   foreach a ∈ ⋃_{i∈[1,n]} A_i do
6  |   |   if ∃i ∈ [1,n] s.t. a ∈ (A_i(v_i)\shared(P_i)) ∪ A_i^F(v) and (v_i, a, u_i) ∈ T_i
   |   |   then
7  |   |   |   u ← v[u_i/v_i];
8  |   |   |   β ← newNode(u, α.distance + 1, 0, α);
9  |   |   |   if a ∈ W then
10 |   |   |   |   β.type ← 1;
11 |   |   |   end
12 |   |   |   if a ∈ A_i^F(v) then
13 |   |   |   |   β.type ← 2;
14 |   |   |   end
15 |   |   |   V_T ← V_T ∪ {β};    E_T ← E_T ∪ {(α, a, β)};
16 |   |   |   Y ← Y ∪ {β}
17 |   |   end
18 |   |   if ∃i, j ∈ [1,n] such that a ∈ shared(P_i, P_j), (v_i, a, u_i) ∈ T_i and
   |   |   (v_j, a, u_j) ∈ T_j then
19 |   |   |   u ← v[u_i/v_i, u_j/v_j];
20 |   |   |   β ← newNode(u, α.distance + 1, 0, α);
21 |   |   |   V_T ← V_T ∪ {β};    E_T ← E_T ∪ {(α, a, β)};
22 |   |   |   Y ← Y ∪ {β}
23 |   |   end
24 |   end
25 end
26 return Y
```

Algorithm 3. NextFrom(X)

steps. If this set is not empty, we update the tree T by using NextFrom(X) (line 15). This keeps the exploration tree coherent with the assumption that it describes the evolution of the system k steps ahead the current node, i.e. α. Finally, we provide information about the error states we have met. In particular, the procedure PrintTrace(β) provides the trace bringing to the error node β by going up the tree T from the node β to ρ by using the information stored by the parent component of each node.

Now we briefly describe the behaviour of our algorithm when the component of index i is removed or added from the system. Pseudo-code for these two algorithms is not provided given the page limit. Algorithm Remove(i) is essentially a breadth-first search of the exploration tree T that starts from ρ and aims at replacing each state $v = (v_1, \ldots, v_n)$ of each node α we meet during this search with a state $u = (v_1, \ldots, v_{i-1}, v_{i+1}, \ldots, v_n)$. It also has to remove all the edges that correspond to steps to which only component P_i can contribute because they are no longer possible. Let instead Q be the interface automaton describing the interface of a newly added component. As already mentioned, we assume that

Q is mutually composable with any other automaton we are already monitoring and that no internal action of Q belongs to the set warning actions W. The basic idea of procedure $\text{ADD}(Q)$ is quite easy: it combines nodes of the exploration tree before the insertion with states of Q. To keep track of how these nodes and states are combined, this algorithm uses a set X that contains tuples of the form (α, v, γ) where: $\alpha \in V$ is a node before the insertion, $v \in V_Q$ and γ is the node of T (after the insertion) we get by merging the state in α with v. All nodes that can be reached from γ are then obtained by properly combining those reachable from α with steps from the state v. At first, $X = \{(\rho, v_Q^{init}, \rho_{new})\}$ where $\rho_{new} = \rho \bullet v_Q^{init}$.

1 **Input:** An action $a \in \bigcup_{i \in [1,n]} \mathcal{A}_i$

2 Let $\alpha \in V_T$ such that $(\rho, a, \alpha) \in E_T$;

3 $X \leftarrow \{\alpha\}$; $Illegal \leftarrow \emptyset$;

4 **If** $\alpha.\text{type} \neq 0$ **then** $Illegal \leftarrow Illegal \cup \{\alpha\}$;

5 $i \leftarrow 1$;

6 **while** $X \neq \emptyset$ *and* $i \leq k - 1$ **do**

7     $Y \leftarrow \emptyset$;

8   **foreach** $\beta \in X$ *and* $(\beta, b, \gamma) \in E_T$ **do**

9        $Y \leftarrow Y \cup \{\gamma\}$;

10   **If** $\gamma.\text{type} \neq 0$ **then** $Illegal \leftarrow Illegal \cup \{\gamma\}$;

11   **end**

12    $X \leftarrow Y$; $i \leftarrow i + 1$;

13 **end**

14 $\alpha.\text{distance} \leftarrow 0$; $\alpha.\text{parent} \leftarrow \text{null}$; $\rho \leftarrow \alpha$;

15 **If** $X \neq \emptyset$ **then** $X \leftarrow \text{NEXTFROM}(X)$;

16 **foreach** $\beta \in X$ **do**

17   **If** $\beta.\text{type} \neq 0$ **then** $Illegal \leftarrow Illegal \cup \{\beta\}$;

18 **end**

19 **foreach** $\beta \in Illegal$ **do**

20   **if** $\beta.\text{type} = 1$ **then** $\text{WARNING}(\text{"Warning state"})$;

21   **else** $\text{WARNING}(\text{"Failure state"})$;

22    $\text{PRINTTRACE}(\beta)$;

23 **end**

Algorithm 4. $\text{EXPLORE}(a)$

5   General Remarks

This section wants to provide further details on the CASSANDRA approach, in particular it reports some complexity measures for the algorithms illustrated in the previous section, and successively we report ideas and issues in order to derive a possible concrete implementation of the proposed approach.

5.1   Time Complexity

The complexity of our online failure prediction algorithm mainly depends on the size (in terms of number of nodes and edges) of the exploration tree T. So, we first determine the size of T as a function of the number of lookahead steps k and the sizes of the interface automata in $\{P_i\}_{i\in[1,n]}$, where the size of each automaton P_i is defined by $|P_i| = (|\mathcal{A}_i| + |\mathcal{T}_i|)$.

Among the presented algorithms, NEXTFROM(X) is particularly important since it is used to proceed with each exploration step. Assume $X = \{\alpha_1, \ldots, \alpha_m\}$ where each node α_ℓ ($\ell \in [1,m]$) is of the form $\alpha_\ell = (v^\ell, d_\ell, t_\ell, p_\ell)$ and contains a composed state $v^\ell = (v_1^\ell, \ldots, v_n^\ell)$. NEXTFROM($X$) generates a new node (and its outgoing edges) for each node $\alpha_\ell \in X$ with $t_\ell \neq 2$ and for each action a enabled at v^ℓ. For the sake of simplicity, we can assume that N is the upper bound to the number of actions enabled at each state of the composed automaton $P = \bigotimes_W \{P_i\}_{i\in[1,n]}$. In other terms we assume that, for each $v = (v_1, \ldots, v_n) \in V_P$, it is $\left|\bigcup_{i\in[1,n]} \mathcal{A}_i(v_i)\backslash\text{shared}(P_i)\right| + \left|\bigcup_{i\in[1,n]} (\mathcal{A}_I^O(v_i) \cap \bigcup_{j\in[1,n]} \mathcal{A}_j^I\backslash\mathcal{A}_j^I(v_j))\right| + \left|\bigcup_{i,j\in[1,n]:\, i\neq j} \mathcal{A}_i(v_i) \cap \mathcal{A}_j(v_j)\right| \leq N$.

On the basis of this assumption, each node without a failure state generates (visits) at most N nodes and, hence, NEXTFROM(X) produces at most $|X| \cdot N$ nodes and edges.

Now, observe that INIT() consists of (at most) k calls of NEXTFROM, where the i-th call ($1 \leq i \leq k$) of NEXTFROM(X_i) inside the body of INIT produces at most $|X_i| \cdot N = N^{i-1} \cdot N = N^i$ new nodes and edges. As a result NEXTFROM will have a complexity in $O(N^k)$.

Both EXPLORE(a) and REMOVE(i) are essentially breadth-first searches of T and, as well-known, their time complexity is $O(|V_T| + |E_T|) = O(N^k)$.

Finally the ADD procedures has a complexity in $O((2N - S)^k)$ edges where S is an upper bound to the actions that the inserted component share with the already integrated one.

In conclusion the complexity analysis not surprisingly says that the cost of the CASSANDRA strategy increases the more we try to forecast in the future (which relates to the value of k).

5.2   Implementing Cassandra

The CASSANDRA approach has been tested on the simple scenario of Figure 1 implemented using the actor programming model. Actor model appears to be a scalable solution for distributed system design and implementations. It takes advantage of entities - called actors - that have an internal behavior and are able to send and receive messages concurrently with other actors in the system. An actor system provides a dynamic context for actor execution: actors can generate other actors, actors can be started, stopped, managed in case of fault, etc.

The actor model implementation we use is Akka (http://www.akka.io) and our demo system is made by 2 Java actors that behave as P and Q and one actor that behave as a *bridge* to CASSANDRA. This system allows the message exchange between P and Q through an observable *event bus* that is responsible to call CASSANDRA to add/remove components and to initialize the exploration.

The design of this demo and of other applications that use CASSANDRA are based on a set of following assumptions.

Run-time models. Each component/service to be integrated at run-time must be augmented with model definitions describing how the provided functionality should be used, and how the components interacts with the environment. In some real context this assumption can be judged a bit strong, nevertheless we think that in a multi-parties and dynamic environment the availability of models at run-time will become frequent so to enable run-time analysis activities. We use the State Chart XML (SCXML) specification (State Machine Notation for Control Abstraction) to describe the behavior of an actor. SCXML provide a general-purpose event-based state machine language that is suitable to describe an interface automata.

Centralized control. CASSANDRA algorithms are currently relying on a centralized analysis, i.e. all the interactions happening between the various components should be reported to the CASSANDRA *bridge*. This logical component should have an up-to-date view over the current system configuration since the exploration of the model depends on the actual components and then on the run-time synchronization. In turn this means that "add" and "remove" actions must be notified to the CASSANDRA component. In our actor system, each actor is able to send its SCXML description to CASSANDRA using a special message that is sent to the event bus and recognized by the CASSANDRA bridge. Cassandra is able to react to these messages during the system execution altering the exploration tree to reflect the available components at runtime. In the future, an extension of CASSANDRA to a decentralized scenario is certainly an interesting challenge.

Events Monitoring and Prediction notification. CASSANDRA should receive information about the run-time events that are included in the interface automata models declared by the components. Our implementation rely on a shared bus used by Akka to convey messages among actors. While actors exchange messages each other to synchronize, CASSANDRA should be notified to explore the tree of possible future states. We can do this in two ways:

- Asynchronous monitoring: The actors are not coupled with CASSANDRA, the bridge intercepts the messages exchanged by P and Q and send them to the CASSANDRA algorithm. The algorithm establish a possible future, i.e. a *prediction*, that is returned to the bridge to implement fault handling strategies that impact on the entire system asynchronously. The execution of P and Q is not directly affected nor modified by the prediction that is reported to the bridge.
- Synchronous notifications: The actors are coupled with CASSANDRA and call the algorithm implementation without the bridge intermediation. Each actor asks CASSANDRA for a prediction *before* sending a message on the bus and change its internal state. The prediction is returned to the actor

synchronously to the system execution and the management of the possible futures is left to the programmer of the actor. This strategy allow the programmer to implementation a fault tolerant component that *ask* the environment to check if an action can be performed safely.

In both ways the characterization of the states in the explored trees will result from the observed events and the actual configuration of the system to make prediction that can be coupled with the system behavior and used into a strategy for fault management or used for logging and analysis purpose without altering the component implementation. The monitoring implemented in our demo is *explicit* in the sense that we intercept messages already sent to the bus or ask CASSANDRA if a specific message can be sent to the bus. Other *implicit* approaches can rely on different styles of monitoring performing more complex inferences to observing the system, infer a message/action and send it to CASSANDRA.

Evaluation. We evaluate the impact of CASSANDRA on the test scenario using a system that will perform 10, 100 and 200 read cycles stated by traces of P containing *read!.data?* actions and traces of Q containing *read?.data!*. These traces allow Q to respond correctly for almost all the cycles but in last interaction the synchronization is broken by a *fail!* action bringing the state of the system to a failure reported by CASSANDRA (if used for synchronous monitoring) or prevented by CASSANDRA (if used for synchronous notifications).

We evaluate the running time of the system with and without CASSANDRA. The system performs real actions to a file at each *read* action synchronization. When CASSANDRA is involved we evaluate the duration of each portion of the algorithm. We run these experiments using a machine with a Core2 duo processor, 4 Gb of ram, Java SE Runtime Environment (build 1.6.0). We use the tool *btrace* to measure the CASSANDRA time and the *java.lang.System* utilities to track the running time.

Table 1. Running time for the composition of Figure 1

trace length	time w/o c.	time w/ c.	time of c.				num. of calls
			init	*explore*	*nextFrom*	total	
10	13351	15513	21,82	70,59	57,85	150,51	46
100	121720	204508	22,88	526,14	424,79	973,82	203
200	242205	764202	20,28	716,36	444,74	1181,39	403

Table 1 shows the result of our evaluation. The footprint of our algorithm is acceptable for short traces while for long traces the execution time is altered by the garbage collection time However the running time of CASSANDRA is acceptable for us in this first evaluation considering the type of scenarios in which CASSANDRA will be used, distributed systems, dominated by latency due to networking. We are working now to improve the implementation performance and to apply the strategy on a more complex scenario.

6   Related Work

This section provides related work on failure prediction, and run-time verification of dynamically evolving systems.

Failure Prediction. The most significant paper on online failure prediction can be most probably considered the survey conducted by Salfner et al. in [4]. This survey analyzes and compares a number of existing online failure prediction methods. First, a taxonomy is proposed in order to structure and classify the existing online failure prediction methods. Then, forty seven online prediction methods are considered and mapped into the taxonomy. Most of them use heuristics, statistics or probabilistic models to predict failures that may potentially happen in the near future. Metrics are also defined to be able to compare the failure prediction accuracy of the surveyed approaches. Although CASSANDRA belongs to the online failure prediction research branch, differently from the surveyed approaches we specialize on component-based, dynamically evolving systems. In [5] the authors discuss how to use model checking techniques for discovering defects before they happen. While in general related to our approach, this work does not focus on failure prediction of dynamically evolving systems. CASSANDRA could also be used in service-based modeling. In this respect the SOFL [6] engineering approach could be an interesting notation to use to model services in combination/substitution of the IA modeling notation.

Run-Time Verification of Dynamically Evolving Systems. A considerable number of approaches have been developed for run-time monitoring of dynamically evolving systems (e.g., [7,8])The authors in [7] show how it is possible to generate a snapshot of the structure of a running application, and how this can be combined with behavioral specifications for components to check compatibility against system properties. Barringer et al. [8] describe mechanisms for combining programs from separate components and an operational semantics for programmed evolvable systems. Goldsby et al. [9] propose a run-time monitoring and verification technique that can check whether dynamically adaptive software satisfies its requirements. Baresi et al. [10] propose Dynamo, a simple architecture that, through specific and simple annotations, enables the automatic creation of instrumented WS-BPEL processes that can be monitored. The level of monitoring can be dynamically set through a web-based interface. Filieri et al. [11], propose the KAMI holistic approach to support the continuous verification of non functional properties (and specifically, reliability and performance). KAMI, while supporting fault detection, may possibly lead to failure prediction. In this line, it shares similar goals with CASSANDRA, even if we focus on functional failures. The work in [12] shares with CASSANDRA the need to monitor the system execution for inferring a run-time model of it. The approach is used for monitoring functional properties in dynamically evolving systems, but not for failure prediction.

7   Conclusions and Future Work

This paper has proposed a novel theoretical framework and algorithms for run-time failure prediction of dynamically evolving systems. The approach, named

CASSANDRA, captures the current state of a component/service based system through monitoring its execution, and uses observed interactions to explore on-the-fly design-time system models to check if in the near future possible protocol mismatches can emerge. Proposed algorithms have a time complexity in $O(N^k)$ We think that the approach embedded in CASSANDRA is quite promising and it can open different research paths, both of technical and more theoretical nature. On the "theoretical list" two items seem particularly interesting and we consider to investigate in the near future. The first one concerns investigations on a decentralized version of CASSANDRA. The second item refers to a possible extension of CASSANDRA to check safety and bounded liveness properties. On the "technical list" the first item refers to a running example able to scale in a large context. Successively we intend to investigate on possible strategies to optimize the choice of the k parameter respect to the number of potential interactions made by the components. Finally, we aim to investigate the application of the strategy in the service-oriented architecture setting.

References

1. Baresi, L., Nitto, E.D., Ghezzi, C.: Towards open-world software: Issue and challenges. In: SEW-30 2006, Columbia, MD, USA, April 25-28, pp. 249–252 (2006)
2. Mariani, L., Pastore, F., Pezzè, M.: Dynamic analysis for diagnosing integration faults. IEEE Trans. Software Eng. 37(4), 486–508 (2011)
3. de Alfaro, L., Henzinger, T.A.: Interface automata. In: ESEC/SIGSOFT FSE, pp. 109–120 (2001)
4. Salfner, F., Lenk, M., Malek, M.: A survey of online failure prediction methods. ACM Comput. Surv. 42(3) (2010)
5. de Alfaro, L., Henzinger, T.A., Mang, F.Y.C.: Detecting errors before reaching them. In: Emerson, E.A., Sistla, A.P. (eds.) CAV 2000. LNCS, vol. 1855, pp. 186–201. Springer, Heidelberg (2000)
6. Liu, S., Offutt, A., Ho-Stuart, C., Sun, Y., Ohba, M.: Sofl: a formal engineering methodology for industrial applications. IEEE Transactions on Software Engineering 24(1), 24–45 (1998)
7. Chatley, R., Savani, R., Kramer, J., Magee, J., Uchitel, S.: Predictable dynamic plugin systems. In: Wermelinger, M., Margaria-Steffen, T. (eds.) FASE 2004. LNCS, vol. 2984, pp. 129–143. Springer, Heidelberg (2004)
8. Barringer, H., Gabbay, D.M., Rydeheard, D.E.: From runtime verification to evolvable systems. In: Sokolsky, O., Taşıran, S. (eds.) RV 2007. LNCS, vol. 4839, pp. 97–110. Springer, Heidelberg (2007)
9. Goldsby, H., Cheng, B.H.C., Zhang, J.: Amoeba-rt: Run-time verification of adaptive software. In: MoDELS Workshops, pp. 212–224 (2007)
10. Baresi, L., Guinea, S.: Towards dynamic monitoring of WS-BPEL processes. In: Benatallah, B., Casati, F., Traverso, P. (eds.) ICSOC 2005. LNCS, vol. 3826, pp. 269–282. Springer, Heidelberg (2005)
11. Filieri, A., Ghezzi, C., Tamburrelli, G.: A formal approach to adaptive software: continuous assurance of non-functional requirements. Formal Aspects of Computing 24, 163–186 (2012)
12. Ghezzi, C., Mocci, A., Sangiorgio, M.: Runtime monitoring of component changes with spy@runtime. In: ICSE 2012, pp. 1403–1406 (June 2012)

Modal Characterisations of Probabilistic and Fuzzy Bisimulations

Yuxin Deng[1],[*] and Hengyang Wu[2],[**]

[1] Department of Computer Science and Engineering, Shanghai Jiao Tong University, China
[2] Information Engineer College, Hangzhou Dianzi University, China

Abstract. This paper aims to investigate bisimulation on fuzzy systems. For that purpose we revisit bisimulation in the model of reactive probabilistic processes with countable state spaces and obtain two findings: (1) bisimilarity coincides with simulation equivalence, which generalises a result on finite-state processes originally established by Baier; (2) the modal characterisation of bisimilarity by Desharnais et al. admits a much simpler completeness proof. Furthermore, inspired by the work of Hermanns et al. on probabilistic systems, we provide a sound and complete modal characterisation of fuzzy bisimilarity.

1 Introduction

The analysis of fuzzy systems has been the subject of active research during the last sixty years, and many formalisms have been proposed to model them: fuzzy automata (see, for example, [3,4,8,24,26,30,37]), fuzzy Petri nets [31,33], fuzzy Markov processes [5] and fuzzy discrete event systems [25,32].

Recently, a new formal model for fuzzy systems, fuzzy labelled transition systems (fLTSs, for short), has been proposed [15,7,21]. fLTSs are a natual generalization of the classical labelled transition systems in computer science in that after performing some action a system evolves from one state to a fuzzy set of successor states instead of a unique state. Many formal description tools for fuzzy systems, such as fuzzy Petri nets and fuzzy discrete event systems, are not fLTSs. However, it is possible to translate a system's description in one of these formalisms into an fLTS to represent its behaviour.

Bisimulation [28] has been investigated in depth in process algebras because it offers a convenient co-inductive proof technique to establish behavioural equivalence [27]. It has been mostly used for verifying formal systems and is the foundation of state-aggregation algorithms that compress models by merging bisimilar states. State aggregation is routinely used as a preprocessing step before model checking [1,17].

Errico and Loreti [15] proposed a notion of fuzzy bisimulation and applied it to fuzzy reasoning; Kupferman and Lusting [22] defined a latticed simulation between two lattice-valued Kripke structures, and applied it to latticed games; Cao et al. [7]

---

[*] Partially supported by the National Natural Science Foundation of China (61173033, 61033002, 61261130589) and ANR 12IS02001 "PACE".
[**] Supported by the Zhejiang Provincial Natural Science Foundation of China under Grant No. LY13F020046 and Zhejiang Provincial Education Department Fund of China under Grant No. Y201223001.

defined a fuzzy bisimulation relation between two different fLTSs by a correlational pair based on some relation; Ćirić et al. [9] introduced four types of bisimulations (forward, backward, forward-backward, and backward-forward) for fuzzy automata.

All these approaches can be divided into two classes. In the first class, bisimulations are based on a crisp relation on the state space, so one state is either bisimilar to another state or not. As in [7,15], the current paper falls into this class. In the second class, simulations or bisimulations are based on a fuzzy relation (or a lattice-valued relation) on the state space, which shows the degree of one state being bisimilar to another. This approach was adapted in [9,22]. In addition, in [15] a bisimulation is necessarily an equivalence relation, which is not the case for [7] and the current work.

Following the seminal paper on exploring the connection between bisimulation and modal logic [19], a great amount of work has appeared that characterizes various kinds of bisimulations by appropriate logics. A logical characterizations of fuzzy bisimulation appeared in [15], which uses recursive formulas, and interprets a formula as a fuzzy set that gives the measure, respectively, of satisfaction and unsatisfaction of the formula.

In this paper we seek a variant of the Hennessy-Milner Logic (HML) to characterise fuzzy bisimulation. Since fuzzy systems are close to probabilistic systems, we revisit probabilistic bisimulations and their logical characterisations e.g. [13,14,20,23]. We find that two results in probabilistic concurrency theory can be generalised or simplified.

- For finite-state reactive probabilistic labelled transition systems (rpLTSs) it is known that bisimilarity coincides with simulation equivalence. The result was originally proved by Baier [2], using techniques from domain theory. That proof is sophisticated and later on simplified by Zhang [39]. In the current work we generalise the above coincidence result to rpLTSs with *countable* state space. Our proof is surprisingly elementary and employs only some basic concepts of set theory.
- Desharnais et al. [14] proposed a probabilistic version of the HML to capture bisimilarity on rpLTSs. Their logic has neither negation nor infinite conjunctions, but is expressive enough to work for general rpLTSs that may have continuous state spaces. Their proof of this fact uses the machinery of analytic spaces. For rpLTSs with countable state spaces, we find that the completeness proof of their modal characterisation can be greatly simplified.

By adding negation and infinite conjunctions to the logic of Desharnais et al. we obtain a fuzzy variant of the HML to characterise bisimulation on general fLTSs. Unlike [15], there is no need of recursive formulas in our logic. For fLTSs with countable state spaces and finite-support possibility distributions, infinite conjunctions can be replaced by binary conjunctions. The completeness proofs of our logical characterisations are inspired by Hermanns et al. [20]. Since the differences between the two models, fLTSs and rpLTSs, seem to be small, one is tempted to think that the current work might be a straightforward generalization of the above mentioned works for rpLTSs. However, this is not the case. For rpLTSs, negation is unnecessary to characterize bisimulation and binary conjunction is already sufficient, whereas for fLTSs both negation and infinite conjunction are necessary to characterize bisimulation for general fLTSs that may be infinitely branching. Therefore, fLTSs resemble more to nondeterministic systems rather than to deterministic systems in this aspect. Moreover, different techniques are needed for proving characterization theorems for fLTSs and rpLTSs. For example, in the case of rpLTSs the famous π-λ theorem [6] holds, which greatly simplifies the completeness proof of the logical characterization. However, the π-λ theorem is invalid for fLTSs, so we adopt a different approach to proving completeness: the basic idea is to construct a characteristic formula for each equivalence class, i.e. the formula is satisfied only by the states in that equivalence class. See Section 6 for more details.

The rest of this paper is structured as follows. We briefly review some basic concepts used in this paper in Section 2. Section 3 is devoted to showing the coincidence of bisimilarity with simulation equivalence in countable rpLTSs. Section 4 gives a modal characterization of probabilistic bisimulation for rpLTSs. Fuzzy bisimulation is introduced in Section 5 and a modal characterisation is provided in Section 6. Finally, this paper is concluded in Section 7.

2   Preliminaries

Let S be a set and $\Delta : S \to [0,1]$ a fuzzy set. The *support* of Δ is the set $supp(\Delta) = \{s \in S \mid \Delta(s) > 0\}$. We denote by $\mathcal{F}(S)$ the set of all fuzzy sets in S, and $\mathcal{F}_f(S)$ the set of all fuzzy sets with finite supports, i.e. $\mathcal{F}_f(S) = \{\Delta \in \mathcal{F}(S) \mid supp(\Delta) \text{ is finite}\}$. With a slight abuse of notations, we sometimes write a possibility distribution to mean a fuzzy set[1].

A probability distribution on S is a fuzzy set Δ with $\sum_{s \in S} \Delta(s) = 1$. We write $\mathcal{D}(S)$ for the set of all probability distributions on S. We use $\bar{s}$ to denote the point distribution, satisfying $\bar{s}(t) = 1$ if $t = s$, and 0 otherwise. If $p_i \geq 0$ and Δ_i is a distribution for each i in some index set I, then $\sum_{i \in I} p_i \cdot \Delta_i$ is given by

$$\left(\sum_{i \in I} p_i \cdot \Delta_i\right)(s) = \sum_{i \in I} p_i \cdot \Delta_i(s)$$

If $\sum_{i \in I} p_i = 1$ then this is easily seen to be a distribution in $\mathcal{D}(S)$.

Let S be a set. For a binary relation $R \subseteq S \times S$ we write $s \, R \, t$ if $(s,t) \in R$. A *preorder* relation R is a reflexive and transitive relation; an *equivalence* relation is a reflexive, symmetric and transitive relation. An equivalence relation R partitions a set S into equivalence classes. For $s \in S$ we use $[s]_R$ to denote the unique equivalence class containing s. We drop the subscript R if the relation considered is clear from the context. Let $R(s)$ denote the set $\{s' \mid (s,s') \in R\}$. A set U is said to be R-closed if $R(s) \subseteq U$ for all $s \in U$, i.e. the image of U under R, written $R(U)$, is contained in U. We let R^* be the reflexive transitive closure of R. Note that if R is a preorder then R^* coincides with R. For any $s \in S$, the set $R^*(s)$ is clearly a R-closed set.

Definition 1. *A fuzzy labelled transition system (fLTS) is a triple* $(S, A, \to)$ *where* S *is a countable set of states[2], A is a set of actions, and the transition relation $\to$ is a*

---

[1] Strictly speaking a possibility distribution is different from a fuzzy set, though the former can be viewed as the generalized characteristic function of the latter. See [38] for more detailed discussion.

[2] The constraint that S is countable will be important for later development, especially for the validity of the proof of Theorem 5.

partial function from $S \times A$ to $\mathcal{F}(S)$. If the transition relation $\rightarrow$ is a partial function from $S \times A$ to $\mathcal{D}(S)$, we say the fLTS is a reactive probabilistic labelled transition system (rpLTS).

We sometimes write $s \xrightarrow{a} \Delta$ and $s \xrightarrow{a[\lambda]} s'$ for $\rightarrow (s, a) = \Delta$ and $\rightarrow (s, a)(s') = \lambda$, respectively. An fLTS $(S, A, \rightarrow)$ is said to be *image-finite* if for each state s and label a, we have $\rightarrow (s, a) \in \mathcal{F}_f(S)$.

The fLTSs defined above are deterministic in the sense that for each state s and label a, there is at most one possibility distribution Δ with $s \xrightarrow{a} \Delta$. The rpLTSs defined above are usually called reactive probabilistic systems [18] or labelled Markov chains [13] in probabilistic concurrency theory. Similar to simple probabilistic automata [36], one could also define nondeterministic fuzzy transition systems by allowing for more than one transitions labelled with a same action leaving from a state.

3   Probabilistic Bisimulation and Simulation Equivalence

Let s and t be two states in a probabilistic labelled transition system, we say t can simulate the behaviour of s if whenever the latter can exhibit action a and lead to distribution Δ then the former can also perform a and lead to a distribution, say Θ, which can mimic Δ in successor states. We are interested in a relation between two states, but it is expressed by invoking a relation between two distributions. To formalise the mimicking of one distribution by the other, we make use of a lifting operation by following [11].

Definition 2. *Given a set S and a relation $R \subseteq S \times S$, we define $R^\dagger \subseteq \mathcal{D}(S) \times \mathcal{D}(S)$ as the smallest relation that satisfies:*

1. *$s \, R \, t$ implies $\overline{s} \, R^\dagger \, \overline{t}$*
2. *$\Delta_i \, R^\dagger \, \Theta_i$ implies $(\sum_{i \in I} p_i \cdot \Delta_i) \, R^\dagger \, (\sum_{i \in I} p_i \cdot \Theta_i)$, where I is an index set and $\sum_{i \in I} p_i = 1$.*

The proposition below is immediate.

Proposition 1. *Let Δ and Θ be two distributions over S, and $R \subseteq S \times S$. Then $\Delta \, R^\dagger \, \Theta$ if and only if there are two collections of states, $\{s_i\}_{i \in I}$ and $\{t_i\}_{i \in I}$, and a collection of probabilities $\{p_i\}_{i \in I}$, for some index set I, such that $\sum_{i \in I} p_i = 1$ and Δ, Θ can be decomposed as follows:*

1. *$\Delta = \sum_{i \in I} p_i \cdot \overline{s_i}$*
2. *$\Theta = \sum_{i \in I} p_i \cdot \overline{t_i}$*
3. *For each $i \in I$ we have $s_i \, R \, t_i$.*

An important point here is that in the decomposition of Δ into $\sum_{i \in I} p_i \cdot \overline{s_i}$, the states s_i are not necessarily distinct: that is, the decomposition is not in general unique. Thus when establishing the relationship between Δ and Θ a given state s in Δ may play a number of different roles.

If R is an equivalence relation, the lifted relation $R^\dagger$ can be defined alternatively as given in the orginal work by Larsen and Skou [23].

Proposition 2. *Let* Δ, Θ *be two distributions over* S *and* $R \subseteq S \times S$ *be an equivalence relation. Then* $\Delta\ R^\dagger\ \Theta$ *if and only if* $\Delta(C) = \Theta(C)$ *for each equivalence class* $C \in S/R$, *where* $\Delta(C)$ *stands for the accumulation probability* $\sum_{s \in C} \Delta(s)$.

Proof. See Theorem 2.4 (2) in [10]. □

Lemma 1. *Let* $\Delta, \Theta \in \mathcal{D}(S)$ *and* R *be a binary relation on* S. *If* $\Delta\ R^\dagger\ \Theta$ *then we have* $\Delta(A) \leq \Theta(R(A))$ *for each set* $A \subseteq S$.

Proof. Since $\Delta\ R^\dagger\ \Theta$, by Proposition 1 we can decompose Δ and Θ as follows.

$$\Delta = \sum_{i \in I} p_i \cdot \overline{s_i} \qquad s_i\ R\ t_i \qquad \Theta = \sum_{i \in I} p_i \cdot \overline{t_i}$$

Note that $\{s_i\}_{i \in I} = supp(\Delta)$. We define an index set $J \subseteq I$ in the following way: $J = \{i \in I \mid s_i \in A\}$. Then $\Delta(A) = \sum_{j \in J} p_j$. For each $j \in J$ we have $s_j\ R\ t_j$, i.e. $t_j \in R(s_j)$. It follows that $\{t_j\}_{j \in J} \subseteq R(A)$. Therefore, we can infer that

$$\Delta(A) = \Delta(\{s_j\}_{j \in J}) = \sum_{j \in J} p_j = \Theta(\{t_j\}_{j \in J}) \leq \Theta(R(A)).$$

□

Remark 1. The converse of Lemma 1 also holds [34], though it is not used in this paper. So an alternative way of lifting relations [12] is to say that Δ is related to Θ by lifting R if $\Delta(A) \leq \Theta(R(A))$ for each set $A \subseteq S$.

Corollary 1. *Let* $\Delta, \Theta \in \mathcal{D}(S)$ *and* R *be a binary relation on* S. *If* $\Delta\ R^\dagger\ \Theta$ *then* $\Delta(A) \leq \Theta(A)$ *for each* R-*closed set* $A \subseteq S$.

Proof. Let $A \subseteq S$ be R-closed. Then we have $R(A) \subseteq A$, and thus $\Theta(R(A)) \leq \Theta(A)$. By Lemma 1, if $\Delta\ R^\dagger\ \Theta$ then $\Delta(A) \leq \Theta(R(A))$. It follows that $\Delta(A) \leq \Theta(A)$. □

Remark 2. Let $\Delta, \Theta \in \mathcal{D}(S)$ and R be a binary relation on S. A curious reader may ask if the follwoing two conditions are equivalent:

1. $\Delta(A) \leq \Theta(R(A))$ for each set $A \subseteq S$;
2. $\Delta(A) \leq \Theta(A)$ for each R-closed set $A \subseteq S$.

Obviously, item 1 implies item 2. The converse, however, is not valid in general. For example, let $S = \{s, t\}$, $R = \{(s, t)\}$, $\Delta = \frac{1}{2}\overline{s} + \frac{1}{2}\overline{t}$ and $\Theta = \frac{1}{3}\overline{s} + \frac{2}{3}\overline{t}$. There are only two non-empty R-closed sets: $\{t\}$ and S. We have both $\Delta(\{t\}) \leq \Theta(\{t\})$ and $\Delta(S) \leq \Theta(S)$. However, $\Delta(\{t\}) = \frac{1}{2} \nleq 0 = \Theta(\emptyset) = \Theta(R(\{t\}))$.

Nevertheless, if R is a preorder, then item 2 does imply item 1. For any set $A \subseteq S$, the transitivity of R implies that $R(A)$ is R-closed and the reflexivity of R tells us that $A \subseteq R(A)$, from which, together with item 2, we have $\Delta(A) \leq \Delta(R(A)) \leq \Theta(R(A))$.

Lemma 2. *Let* R *be a preorder on a set* S *and* $\Delta, \Theta \in \mathcal{D}(S)$. *If* $\Delta\ R^\dagger\ \Theta$ *and* $\Theta\ R^\dagger\ \Delta$ *then* $\Delta(C) = \Theta(C)$ *for all equivalence classes* C *with respect to the kernel* $R \cap R^{-1}$ *of* R.

Proof. Let us write $\equiv$ for $R \cap R^{-1}$. For any $s \in S$, let $[s]_\equiv$ be the equivalence class that contains s. Let A_s be the set $\{t \in S \mid s \mathrel{R} t \wedge t \mathrel{\not{R}} s\}$. It holds that

$$
\begin{aligned}
R(s) &= \{t \in S \mid s \mathrel{R} t\} \\
&= \{t \in S \mid s \mathrel{R} t \wedge t \mathrel{R} s\} \uplus \{t \in S \mid s \mathrel{R} t \wedge t \mathrel{\not{R}} s\} \\
&= [s]_\equiv \uplus A_s
\end{aligned}
$$

where $\uplus$ stands for a disjoint union. Therefore, we have

$$
\Delta(R(s)) = \Delta([s]_\equiv) + \Delta(A_s) \qquad \text{and} \qquad \Theta(R(s)) = \Theta([s]_\equiv) + \Theta(A_s) \quad (1)
$$

We now check that both $R(s)$ and A_s are R-closed sets, that is $R(R(s)) \subseteq R(s)$ and $R(A_s) \subseteq A_s$. Suppose $u \in R(R(s))$. Then there exists some $t \in R(s)$ such that $t \mathrel{R} u$, which means that $s \mathrel{R} t$ and $t \mathrel{R} u$. As a preorder R is a transitive relation. So we have $s \mathrel{R} u$ which implies $u \in R(s)$. Therefore we can conclude that $R(R(s)) \subseteq R(s)$.

Suppose $u \in R(A_s)$. Then there exists some $t \in A_s$ such that $t \mathrel{R} u$, which means that $s \mathrel{R} t$, $t \mathrel{\not{R}} s$ and $t \mathrel{R} u$. As a preorder R is a transitive relation. So we have $s \mathrel{R} u$. Note that we also have $u \mathrel{\not{R}} s$. Otherwise we would have $u \mathrel{R} s$, which means, together with $t \mathrel{R} u$ and the transitivity of R, that $t \mathrel{R} s$, a contradiction to the hypothesis $t \mathrel{\not{R}} s$. It then follows that $u \in A_s$ and then we conclude that $R(A_s) \subseteq A_s$.

We have verified that $R(s)$ and A_s are R-closed sets. Since $\Delta \mathrel{R^\dagger} \Theta$ and $\Theta \mathrel{R^\dagger} \Delta$, we apply Corollary 1 and obtain that $\Delta(R(s)) \le \Theta(R(s))$ and $\Theta(R(s)) \le \Delta(R(s))$, that is

$$
\Delta(R(s)) = \Theta(R(s)) \tag{2}
$$

Similarly, using the fact that A_s is R-closed we obtain that

$$
\Delta(A_s) = \Theta(A_s) \tag{3}
$$

It follows from (1)-(3) that

$$
\Delta([s]_\equiv) = \Theta([s]_\equiv)
$$

as we have desired. $\qquad\qquad\square$

Remark 3. Note that in the above proof the equivalence classes $[s]_\equiv$ are not necessarily R-closed. For example, let $S = \{s, t\}$, $Id_S = \{(s, s), (t, t)\}$ and $R = Id_S \cup \{(s, t)\}$. Then $\equiv\ =\ R \cap R^{-1} = Id_S$ and $[s]_\equiv = \{s\}$. We have $R(s) = S \nsubseteq [s]_\equiv$. So a more direct attempt to apply Corollary 1 to those equivalence classes would not work.

A restricted version of Lemma 2 (by requiring the state set S to be finite) has appeared as Lemma 5.3.5 in [2], but the proof given there is much more complicated as it relies on some properties of DCPOs, which is then simplified in [39]. In this paper, we allow the state set of a rpLTS to be a countably *infinite* set. With this key technical lemma at hand, we are ready to prove the coincidence of simulation equivalence and bisimilarity, which was originally given as Theorem 5.3.6 in [2].

Definition 3. *A relation $R \subseteq S \times S$ is a* probabilistic simulation *if $s \mathrel{R} t$ and $s \xrightarrow{a} \Delta$ implies that some Θ exists such that $t \xrightarrow{a} \Theta$ and $\Delta \mathrel{R^\dagger} \Theta$. If both R and R^{-1} are probabilistic simulations, then R is a* probabilistic bisimulation. *The largest probabilistic bisimulation, denoted by $\sim_p$, is called* probabilistic bisimilarity. *The largest probabilistic simulation, denoted by $\precsim_p$, is called* probabilistic similarity. *The kernel of probabilistic similarity, i.e $\precsim_p \cap \precsim_p^{-1}$, is called* simulation equivalence, *denoted by $\simeq_p$.*

In general, simulation equivalence is coarser than bisimilarity. However, for rpLTSs, the two relations do coincide.

Theorem 1. *For rpLTSs, simulation equivalence coincides with bisimilarity.*

Proof. It is obvious that $\sim_p$ is included in $\asymp_p$. For the other direction, we show that $\asymp_p$ is a bisimulation. Let $s, t \in S$ and $s \asymp t$. Suppose that $s \xrightarrow{a} \Delta$. There exists a transition $t \xrightarrow{a} \Theta$ with $\Delta\ (\prec_p)^\dagger\ \Theta$. Since we are considering reactive probabilistic systems, the transition $t \xrightarrow{a} \Theta$ from t must be matched by the transition $s \xrightarrow{a} \Delta$ from s, with $\Theta\ (\prec_p)^\dagger\ \Delta$. Note that $\prec_p$ is obviously a preorder on S. It follows from Lemma 2 that $\Delta(C) = \Theta(C)$ for any $C \in S/\asymp_p$. Since $\asymp_p$ is clearly an equivalence relation, by Proposition 2 we see that $\Delta\ (\asymp_p)^\dagger\ \Theta$. Therefore, $\asymp_p$ is indeed a bisimulation relation.
□

4   Modal Characterisation of Probabilistic Bisimulation

Let A be a set of *actions* ranged over by $a, b, \cdots$, and let $\top$ be a propositional constant. The language $\mathcal{L}_p$ of formulas is the least set generated by the following BNF grammar:

$$\varphi ::= \top \mid \varphi_1 \wedge \varphi_2 \mid \langle a \rangle_p \varphi.$$

where a is an action and p is a rational number in the unit interval $[0, 1]$. This is the basic logic with which we establish the logical characterization of bisimulation.

Let us fix a rpLTS $(S, A, \rightarrow)$. The semantic interpretation of formulas in $\mathcal{L}_p$ is given by:

- $s \models_p \top$, for any state s;
- $s \models_p \varphi_1 \wedge \varphi_2$, if $s \models_p \varphi_1$ and $s \models_p \varphi_2$;
- $s \models_p \langle a \rangle_p \varphi$, if $s \xrightarrow{a} \Delta$ and $\exists A \subseteq S. (\forall s' \in A.\ s' \models_p \varphi) \wedge (\Delta(A) \geq p)$.

We write $[\![\varphi]\!]$ for the set $\{s \in S \mid s \models_p \varphi\}$. Then it is immediate that $s \models_p \langle a \rangle_p \varphi$ iff $s \xrightarrow{a} \Delta$ and $\Delta([\![\varphi]\!]) \geq p$, i.e. $\sum_{s' \in [\![\varphi]\!]} \Delta(s') \geq p$. Thus $s \models_p \langle a \rangle_p \varphi$ says that the state s can make an a-move to a distribution that evolves into a state satisfying φ with probability at least p. In the sequel we always use this fact as the semantic interpretation of the formula $\langle a \rangle_p \varphi$ in $\mathcal{L}_p$.

The logic above induces a logical equivalence relation between states.

Definition 4. *Let s and t be two states in a rpLTS. We write $s =_p t$ if $s \models_p \varphi \Leftrightarrow t \models_p \varphi$ for all $\varphi \in \mathcal{L}_p$.*

The following lemma says that the transition probabilities to sets of the form $[\![\psi]\!]$ are completely determined by the formulas. It has appeared as Lemma 7.7.6 in [35].

Lemma 3. *Let s and t be two states in a rpLTS. If $s =_p t$ and $s \xrightarrow{a} \Delta$, then some Θ exists with $t \xrightarrow{a} \Theta$, and for any formula $\psi \in \mathcal{L}_p$ we have $\Delta([\![\psi]\!]) = \Theta([\![\psi]\!])$.*

Proof. First of all, the existence of Θ is obvious because otherwise the formula $\langle a \rangle_1 \top$ would be satisfied by s but not by t.

Let us assume, without loss of generality, that there exists a formula ψ such that $\Delta(\llbracket \psi \rrbracket) < \Theta(\llbracket \psi \rrbracket)$. Then we can squeeze in a rational number p with $\Delta(\llbracket \psi \rrbracket) < p \leq \Theta(\llbracket \psi \rrbracket)$. It follows that $t \models_p \langle a \rangle_p \psi$ but $s \not\models_p \langle a \rangle_p \psi$, which contradicts the hypothesis that $s =_p t$. $\qquad\square$

We will show that the logic $\mathcal{L}_p$ can characterise bisimulation. The completeness proof of the characterisation crucially relies on the π-λ theorem [6]. Let $\mathcal{P}$ be a family of subsets of a set X. We say $\mathcal{P}$ is a π-class if it is closed under finite intersections; $\mathcal{P}$ is a λ-class if it is closed under complementations and countable disjoint unions.

Theorem 2 (The π-λ theorem). *If $\mathcal{P}$ is a π-class, then $\sigma(\mathcal{P})$ is the smallest λ-class containing $\mathcal{P}$, where $\sigma(\mathcal{P})$ is a σ-algebra containing $\mathcal{P}$.*

The next proposition is a typical application of the π-λ theorem [16], which tells us that when two probability distributions agree on a π-class they also agree on the generated σ-algebra.

Proposition 3. *Let S be a state space, $\mathcal{A}_0 = \{\llbracket \varphi \rrbracket \mid \varphi \in \mathcal{L}_p\}$, and $\mathcal{A} = \sigma(\mathcal{A}_0)$. For any $\Delta, \Theta \in \mathcal{D}(S)$, if $\Delta(A) = \Theta(A)$ for any $A \in \mathcal{A}_0$, then $\Delta(B) = \Theta(B)$ for any $B \in \mathcal{A}$.*

Proof. Let $\mathcal{P} = \{A \in \mathcal{A} \mid \Delta(A) = \Theta(A)\}$. Then $\mathcal{P}$ is closed under countable disjoint unions because probability distributions are σ-additive. Furthermore, $\Delta(S) = \Theta(S) = 1$ implies that if $A \in \mathcal{P}$ then $\Delta(S \backslash A) = \Delta(S) - \Delta(A) = \Theta(S) - \Theta(A) = \Theta(S \backslash A)$, i.e. $S \backslash A \in \mathcal{P}$. Thus $\mathcal{P}$ is closed under complementation as well. It follows that $\mathcal{P}$ is a λ-class. Note that $\mathcal{A}_0$ is a π-class in view of the equation $\llbracket \varphi_1 \wedge \varphi_2 \rrbracket = \llbracket \varphi_1 \rrbracket \cap \llbracket \varphi_2 \rrbracket$. Since $\mathcal{A}_0 \subseteq \mathcal{P}$, we can apply the π-λ Theorem to obtain that $\mathcal{A} = \sigma(\mathcal{A}_0) \subseteq \mathcal{P} \subseteq \mathcal{A}$, i.e. $\mathcal{A} = \mathcal{P}$. Therefore, $\Delta(B) = \Theta(B)$ for any $B \in \mathcal{A}$. $\qquad\square$

Theorem 3. *Let s and t be two states in a rpLTS. Then $s \sim_p t$ iff $s =_p t$.*

Proof. The proof of soundness is carried out by a routine induction on the structure of formulas. Below we focus on the completeness. It suffices to show that $=_p$ is a bisimulation. Note that $=_p$ is clearly an equivalence relation. For any $u \in S$ the equivalence class in $S/_{=_p}$ that contains u is

$$[u] = \bigcap \{\llbracket \varphi \rrbracket \mid u \models_p \varphi\} \cap \bigcap \{S \backslash \llbracket \varphi \rrbracket \mid u \not\models_p \varphi\}. \tag{4}$$

In (4) only countable intersections are used because the set of all the formulas in the logic $\mathcal{L}_p$ is countable. Let $\mathcal{A}_0$ be defined as in Proposition 3. Then each equivalence class of $S/_{=_p}$ is a member of $\sigma(\mathcal{A}_0)$.

On the other hand, $s =_p t$ and $s \xrightarrow{a} \Delta$ implies that some distribution Θ exists with $t \xrightarrow{a} \Theta$ and for any $\varphi \in \mathcal{L}_p$, $\Delta(\llbracket \varphi \rrbracket) = \Theta(\llbracket \varphi \rrbracket)$ by Lemma 3. Thus by Proposition 3 we have

$$\Delta([u]) = \Theta([u]) \tag{5}$$

where $[u]$ is any equivalence class of $S/_{=_p}$. Then it follows from Proposition 2 that $\Delta \, (=_p)^\dagger \, \Theta$. Symmetrically, any transition of t can be mimicked by a transition from s. Therefore, the relation $=_p$ is a bisimulation. $\qquad\square$

Theorem 3 tells us that $\mathcal{L}_p$ can characterize bisimulation for rpLTSs, and this logic has neither negation nor infinite conjunction. Moreover, the above result holds for general rpLTSs which are not necessarily finitely branching.

Remark 4. The proof of Theorem 3 does not carry over to fLTSs. For possibility distributions the family of sets $\mathcal{P}$ in the proof of Proposition 3 is closed under neither complementations nor countable intersections. So we cannot show that all equivalence classes are in $\mathcal{P}$ (i.e. $\sigma(\mathcal{A}_0)$). It follows that (5) cannot be established for fLTSs.

5 Fuzzy Simulation and Bisimulation

In this section we introduce our notions of simulation and bisimulation for fLTSs and discuss their properties.

In line with probabilistic simulation and bisimulation (Definition 3), we require that if (s,t) is a pair of states in a fuzzy simulation then t can mimic all stepwise behavior of s with respect to R that is lifted to compare possibility distributions. For probability distributions, we use $\Delta(U)$ to mean accumulation probabilities $\sum_{s \in U} \Delta(s)$, which no longer makes sense for possibility distributions. Now we replace the summation by a supremum. That is, for any $\Delta \in \mathcal{F}(S)$ and $U \subseteq S$, the notation $\Delta(U)$ stands for $\sup_{s \in U} \Delta(s)$, the supremum of all the possibilities in U. Possibility distributions are then compared by using R-closed sets.

Definition 5. *A relation* $R \subseteq S \times S$ *is a* fuzzy simulation *relation if* $(s,t) \in R$ *implies that, for any action* $a \in A$, *if* $s \xrightarrow{a} \Delta$ *then there exists some* Θ *such that* $t \xrightarrow{a} \Theta$ *and* $\Delta(U) \leq \Theta(U)$ *for any* R-*closed set* $U \subseteq S$. *If both* R *and* R^{-1} *are fuzzy simulations, then* R *is a* fuzzy bisimulation. *The largest fuzzy simulation, denoted by* $\prec_f$, *is called* fuzzy similarity; *the largest fuzzy bisimulation, written* $\sim_f$, *is called* fuzzy bisimilarity.

The following proposition follows easily from the above definition.

Proposition 4. *1.* $\sim_f$ *is an equivalence relation and* $\prec_f$ *is a preorder.*
2. If R *is a bisimulation and* $t \in R^*(s)$, *then for any action* $a \in A$ *we have* $s \xrightarrow{a} \Delta$
implies $t \xrightarrow{a} \Theta$ *for some* Θ *with* $\Delta(U) = \Theta(U)$ *for any* R-*closed set* U.

The kernel of fuzzy similarity, $\prec_f \cap \prec_f^{-1}$, is called fuzzy simulation equivalence. Different from rpLTSs, in fLTSs bisimilarity is strictly finer than simulation equivalence.

Fig. 1. Fuzzy bisimilarity is strictly finer than fuzzy simulation equivalence

Example 1. Consider the fLTS depicted in Figure 1. We let $S = \{s, t, s_1, s_2, s_3, t_1, t_2\}$ and $R = \{(s,t), (s_1, t_1), (s_2, t_2), (s_3, t_1)\}$. It is easy to check that R is a simulation, thus $s \prec_f t$. Now let $R' = \{(t,s), (t_1, s_1), (t_2, s_2)\}$. Obviously R' is also a simulation, and hence we have $t \prec_f s$. It follows that s and t are simulation equivalent.

Now assume by contradiction that s and t are bisimilar. Then there exists a bisimulation R with $(s,t) \in R$. Let $s \xrightarrow{a} \Delta$ and $t \xrightarrow{a} \Theta$. Then we have $\Delta(R^*(s_3)) = \Theta(R^*(s_3))$. Since $\Delta(R^*(s_3)) \neq 0$ and Θ takes a non-zero value only at t_1, we infer that $t_1 \in R^*(s_3)$. By Proposition 4 (2), s_3 and t_1 can mimic the behaviour of each other, which contradicts the fact that t_1 can perform the action b to a nonempty distribution while s_3 cannot. Hence s and t are not bisimilar.

The following property is a counterpart of Proposition 2, by replacing accumulation probabilities by suprema of possibilities.

Proposition 5. *Let $R \subseteq S \times S$ be an equivalence relation. It is a fuzzy bisimulation iff for all $(s,t) \in R$ and $a \in A$, $s \xrightarrow{a} \Delta$ implies $t \xrightarrow{a} \Theta$ with $\Delta(U) = \Theta(U)$ for any equivalence class $U \in S/R$.*

6   Modal Characterisation of Fuzzy Bisimulation

Since the differences between the models fLTSs and rpLTSs do not seem to be big, one is tempted to think that a logic more or less the same as $\mathcal{L}_p$ might characterise fuzzy bisimulation. However, as we have hinted in Remark 4, the modal characterisation of bisimulation for rpLTSs cannot be simply transplanted to fLTSs. In this section, we introduce another variant of the Hennessy-Milner Logic by adding negation to $\mathcal{L}_p$, and by allowing infinite conjunctions.

The language $\mathcal{L}_f$ of formulas is the least set generated by the following BNF grammar:

$$\varphi ::= \top \mid \bigwedge_{i \in I} \varphi_i \mid \neg\varphi \mid \langle a \rangle_p \varphi.$$

where I is a countable index set and p is a rational number in the unit interval $[0, 1]$.

Let us fix an fLTS $(S, A, \rightarrow)$. The semantic interpretation of formulas in $\mathcal{L}_f$ is similar to that of $\mathcal{L}_p$ (cf. Section 4). We have $s \models_f \langle a \rangle_p \varphi$ iff $s \xrightarrow{a} \Delta$ and $\Delta(\llbracket\varphi\rrbracket) \geq p$, i.e. $\sup_{s' \in \llbracket\varphi\rrbracket} \Delta(s') \geq p$. Thus $s \models_f \langle a \rangle_p \varphi$ says that the state s can make an a-move to a state that satisfies φ with possibility greater than p. The interpretation of negation is standard. We denote by $=_f$ the logical equivalence induced by $\mathcal{L}_f$. That is, $s =_f t$ iff $s \models_f \varphi \Longleftrightarrow t \models_f \varphi$ for any $\varphi \in \mathcal{L}_f$.

Consider again the fLTS depicted in Figure 1, we see that s satisfies, among others, the formula $\langle a \rangle_{\frac{1}{2}} \neg \langle b \rangle_{\frac{3}{4}} \top$ because s can make an a-move to state s_3 which is a deadlock state and thus cannot perform action b with possibility at least $\frac{3}{4}$.

Example 2. We give an example to show the importance of negation in $\mathcal{L}_f$ but not in $\mathcal{L}_p$.

Consider the rpLTSs in Figure 2, where $m \neq 0$. It is easy to see that $t \models_p \langle a \rangle_1 \langle b \rangle_1 \top$ but $s \not\models_p \langle a \rangle_1 \langle b \rangle_1 \top$. Hence s and t can be distinguished without negation in this rpLTS.

However, the case is different for fLTSs. In Example 1 we have shown that the two states s and t in Figure 1 are not bisimilar. But they cannot be distinguished by the

Fig. 2. Two states can be distinguished without negation in rpLTSs

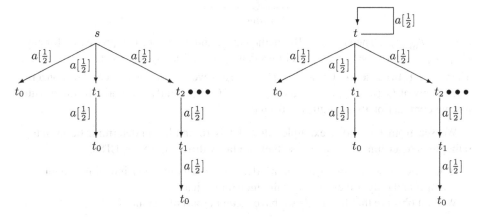

Fig. 3. Two states cannot be distinguished without infinite conjunction in fLTSs

logic $\mathcal{L}_f$ if negation is removed. The reason is as follows. Since $s \models_f \langle a \rangle_p \varphi$ iff $s \xrightarrow{a} \Delta$ for some Δ with $\sup_{s' \in \llbracket \varphi \rrbracket} \Delta(s') \geq p$, the non-trivial formulas that both s and t satisfy are $\langle a \rangle_p \top$ $(p \leq \frac{2}{3})$, $\langle a \rangle_q \langle b \rangle_r \top$ $(q \leq \frac{2}{3}$ and $r \leq \frac{3}{4})$ and binary conjunction of these formulas. Moreover the non-trivial formulas that both s and t do not satisfy are $\langle a \rangle_p \top$ $(p > \frac{2}{3})$ and $\langle a \rangle_q \langle b \rangle_r \top$ $(q > \frac{2}{3}$ or $r > \frac{3}{4})$. Hence the logic $\mathcal{L}_f$ without negation cannot differentiate s from t. However, we can easily tell apart these two states if negation is allowed. For instance, we have $s \models_f \langle a \rangle_{\frac{1}{2}} \neg \langle b \rangle_{\frac{3}{4}} \top$ but $t \not\models_f \langle a \rangle_{\frac{1}{2}} \neg \langle b \rangle_{\frac{3}{4}} \top$.

Example 3. This example shows that finite conjunctions are insufficient to characterize bisimulations for fLTSs. It is adapted from Example 5.1 in [20].

The only difference between the two fLTSs in Figure 3 is that t has a transition to itself. We first show that s and t are not bisimilar. Let $S = \{s, t, t_0, t_1, t_2, \cdots\}$, $t \xrightarrow{a} \Delta$, $t_n \xrightarrow{a} \Delta_n (n = 1, 2, \cdots)$, and $s \xrightarrow{a} \Theta$. Now suppose that s and t are bisimilar. Then there exists a bisimulation R with $(s, t) \in R$. It follows that $\Theta(R^*(t)) = \Delta(R^*(t)) \geq \frac{1}{2}$. Since Θ takes value 0 at s and t, $R^*(t)$ includes at least a $t_n (n = 0, 1, 2, \cdots)$ besides s and t. Thus it follows from Proposition 4 that $\Delta_n(R^*(t)) = \Theta(R^*(t))$. Since Δ_n takes value $\frac{1}{2}$ only at t_{n-1} and 0 otherwise, $t_{n-1} \in R^*(t)$ and $\Delta_{n-1}(R^*(t)) = \Delta(R^*(t)) = \frac{1}{2}$. Continue this way and we obtain $t_0 \in R^*(t)$ in the end, which leads to a contradiction because t can perform an a-action to a nonempty distribution while t_0 cannot. Hence s and t are not bisimilar.

However, if only finite conjunctions are used in the logic $\mathcal{L}_f$ then we cannot find a formula which can differentiate s from t. The reason is as follows. For each formula φ, the maximum number of nested diamond connectives in the formula is finite, thus the satisfiability of φ is determined by some state t_n for a finite number n. Such a state t_n can also be reached from s immediately after one step of transition.

The situation is different if infinite conjunction is allowed. Consider the formula φ_i defined as follows: $\varphi_0 = \top$, and $\varphi_i = (\langle a \rangle_{\frac{1}{2}})^{(i)} \top$ for $i > 0$, which means

$$\underbrace{\langle a \rangle_{\frac{1}{2}} \langle a \rangle_{\frac{1}{2}} \cdots \langle a \rangle_{\frac{1}{2}}}_{i \text{ times}} \top.$$

Let $\varphi = \bigwedge_{i \in \mathbb{N}} \varphi_i$. Then $t \models_f \varphi$. By mathematical induction one can prove that for any n, $t_n \models_f \varphi_n$ but $t_n \not\models_f \varphi_{n+1}$. It follows that $t_n \not\models_f \varphi$ for any n. Now let $\psi = \langle a \rangle_{\frac{1}{2}} \varphi$. Then $t \models_f \psi$ because $t \in [\![\varphi]\!]$ and $\Delta(t) = \frac{1}{2}$. However, $s \not\models_f \psi$ since Θ takes nonzero values only at t_n ($n = 0, 1, \cdots$) and $t_n \notin [\![\varphi]\!]$. Consequently, we find a formula with infinite conjunction to distinguish s from t.

We see from the above examples that fLTSs resemble nondeterministic systems rather than deterministic systems, so they are fairly different from rpLTSs.

Below we show that two states in an fLTS are observationally indistinguishable or bisimilar if and only if they are logically indistinguishable.

We first observe that for fLTSs we have a counterpart of Lemma 3.

Lemma 4. *Let s and t be two states in an fLTS. If $s =_f t$ and $s \xrightarrow{a} \Delta$, then there is some Θ such that $t \xrightarrow{a} \Theta$ and $\Delta([\![\varphi]\!]) = \Theta([\![\varphi]\!])$ for any $\varphi \in \mathcal{L}_f$.*

Proof. Similar to the arguments for proving Lemma 3.   □

Theorem 4. *Let s and t be two states in an fLTS. Then $s \sim_f t$ iff $s =_f t$.*

Proof. First we show soundness. Suppose that $s \sim_f t$. For any $\psi \in \mathcal{L}_f$, we show $s \models_f \psi \Longleftrightarrow t \models_f \psi$ (meaning that $[\![\psi]\!]$ is $\sim_f$-closed) by structural induction on ψ. The cases of $\top$ and conjunction are trivial. Now consider other cases:

- $\psi \equiv \neg \varphi$. In this case $s \models_f \psi \Longleftrightarrow s \not\models_f \varphi$. By structural induction we have $s \not\models_f \varphi \Longleftrightarrow t \not\models_f \varphi$. Notice that we also have $t \not\models_f \varphi \Longleftrightarrow t \models_f \psi$.
- $\psi \equiv \langle a \rangle_p \varphi$. If $s \models_f \psi$ then $s \xrightarrow{a} \Delta$ for some Δ with $\Delta([\![\varphi]\!]) \geq p$. By induction, $[\![\varphi]\!]$ is $\sim_f$-closed. It follows from $s \sim_f t$ that $t \xrightarrow{a} \Theta$ for some Θ such that $\Theta([\![\varphi]\!]) = \Delta([\![\varphi]\!])$. Then it is immediate that $t \models_f \psi$. By symmetry, if $t \models_f \psi$ then we have $s \models_f \psi$.

For completeness, it suffices to prove that $=_f$ is a bisimulation. Obviously $=_f$ is an equivalence relation. Let $E = \{U_i \mid i \in I\}$ be the set of all equivalence classes of $=_f$. Then by Proposition 5 it remains to show that, for any s, t with $s =_f t$, if $s \xrightarrow{a} \Delta$ then $t \xrightarrow{a} \Theta$ for some Θ with

$$\Delta(U_i) = \Theta(U_i) \text{ for any } i \in I. \tag{6}$$

We first claim that, for any equivalence class U_i, there exists a characteristic formula φ_i in the sense that $[\![\varphi_i]\!] = U_i$. This can be proved as follows:

- If E contains only one equivalence class U_1, then $U_1 = S$. So we can take the characteristic formula to be $\top$ because $[\![\top]\!] = S$.
- If E contains more than one equivalence class, then for any $i, j \in I$ with $i \neq j$, there exists a formula φ_{ij} such that $s_i \models_f \varphi_{ij}$ and $s_j \not\models_f \varphi_{ij}$ for any $s_i \in U_i$ and $s_j \in U_j$. Otherwise, for any formula φ, $s_i \models_f \varphi$ implies $s_j \models_f \varphi$. Since the negation connective exists in the logic $\mathcal{L}_f$, we also have $s_i \models_f \neg\varphi$ implies $s_j \models_f \neg\varphi$, which means $s_j \models_f \varphi$ implies $s_i \models_f \varphi$. Then $s_i \models_f \varphi \Leftrightarrow s_j \models_f \varphi$ for any $\varphi \in \mathcal{L}_f$, which contradicts the fact that s_i and s_j are taken from different equivalence classes. For each $i \in I$, define $\varphi_i = \bigwedge_{j \neq i} \varphi_{ij}$, then by construction $[\![\varphi_i]\!] = U_i$. Let us check the last equality. On one hand, if $s' \in [\![\varphi_i]\!]$, then $s' \models_f \varphi_i$ which means that $s' \models_f \varphi_{ij}$ for all $j \neq i$. That is, $s' \notin U_j$ for all $j \neq i$, and this in turn implies that $s' \in U_i$. On the other hand, if $s' \in U_i$ then $s' \models_f \varphi_i$ as $s_i \models_f \varphi_i$, which means that $s' \in [\![\varphi_i]\!]$.

This completes the proof of the claim that each equivalence U_i has a characteristic formula φ_i.

Now suppose $s =_f t$. By Lemma 4, if $s \xrightarrow{a} \Delta$ then there exists some Θ such that $t \xrightarrow{a} \Theta$ and $\Delta([\![\varphi_i]\!]) = \Theta([\![\varphi_i]\!])$ for all $i \in I$. Using the above claim, we can infer that

$$\Delta(U_i) = \Delta([\![\varphi_i]\!]) = \Theta([\![\varphi_i]\!]) = \Theta(U_i)$$

for each $i \in I$. Hence the equation in (6) holds. $\square$

In the above proof, the idea of using characteristic formulas is inspired by [20]. We can see that the logic $\mathcal{L}_f$ is very expressive, since it characterizes not only bisimulation but also equivalence classes in the sense that there does necessarily exist a formula for each equivalence class which is satisfied only by the states in that class.

Moreover, from the construction of formula φ_i above we can see that infinite conjunctions are indeed necessary. The advantage of infinite conjunctions lie in the fact that they allow for a universal description of a class of states of interest. However, infinity is difficult to process in real applications. Fortunately, in most practical applications the supports of fuzzy sets are finite and then the logic $\mathcal{L}_f$ restricted to binary conjunctions is already sufficient to characterize fuzzy bisimulation. Let us write $=_{f'}$ for the logical equivalence induced by $\mathcal{L}_f$ restricted to binary conjunctions.

Theorem 5. *Let $(S, A, \rightarrow)$ be an image-finite fLTS. Then for any two states $s, t \in S$, $s \sim_f t$ iff $s =_{f'} t$.*

Proof. Theorem 4 implies the soundness. For the completeness, let E and $\{\varphi_{ij}\}_{i,j \in I}$ be defined as in the proof of that theorem. Note that E is countable because the state space S is countable. We fix an arbitrary index k. For each $i \in I$, define $\Phi_i^k = \bigwedge_{j \leq k} \varphi_{ij}$. It is then easy to see that for each $i \in I$, the formula Φ_i^k only has finite conjunctions, and

$$U_i \subseteq [\![\Phi_i^k]\!] \subseteq U_i \cup \bigcup_{m \in I \wedge m > k} U_m.$$

Hence for any $\Gamma \in \mathcal{F}_f(S)$, $\Gamma(U_i) \leq \Gamma([\![\Phi_i^k]\!]) \leq \Gamma(U_i \cup \bigcup_{m \in I \wedge m > k} U_m)$. Recall that for any $U \subseteq S$, the notation $\Gamma(U)$ means the maximal possibility assigned by Γ to a state in U. Therefore, we have

$$\Gamma(U_i) \le \Gamma([\![\Phi_i^k]\!]) \le \Gamma(U_i) \sqcup \Gamma(\bigcup_{m \in I \wedge m > k} U_m) \tag{7}$$

for any $\Gamma \in \mathcal{F}_f(S)$, where we use the notation $p_1 \sqcup p_2$ to mean $\max(p_1, p_2)$. Fix an arbitrary index i and then take the infimum for $k \in I$, we can get

$$\Gamma(U_i) \le \inf_{k \in I} \Gamma([\![\Phi_i^k]\!]) \le \inf_{k \in I} [\Gamma(U_i) \sqcup \Gamma(\bigcup_{m \in I \wedge m > k} U_m)],$$

i.e.

$$\Gamma(U_i) \le \inf_{k \in I} \Gamma([\![\Phi_i^k]\!]) \le \Gamma(U_i) \sqcup \inf_{k \in I} \Gamma(\bigcup_{m \in I \wedge m > k} U_m). \tag{8}$$

We argue that

$$\inf_{k \in I} \Gamma(\bigcup_{m \in I \wedge m > k} U_m) = 0. \tag{9}$$

As a matter of fact, since $supp(\Gamma)$ is finite, there exists a sufficiently large number $N \in I$ such that for any $s \in supp(\Gamma)$, there exists some $m_s \in I$ with $m_s < N$ and $s \in U_{m_s}$. Thus we always have $\Gamma(\bigcup_{m \in I \wedge m > k} U_m) = 0$ when $k \ge N$. Hence the equation in (9) holds.

By combining (8) and (9), for any $i \in I$ and any $\Gamma \in \mathcal{F}_f(S)$, we have

$$\Gamma(U_i) = \inf_{k \in I} \Gamma([\![\Phi_i^k]\!]). \tag{10}$$

Now assume that $s =_{\mathbf{f}'} t$ and $s \xrightarrow{a} \Delta$. Then s satisfies the formula $\langle a \rangle_1 \top$. In order for t to satisfy that formula, there must exist a transition $t \xrightarrow{a} \Theta$ for some Θ. It remains to show that $\Delta(U_i) = \Theta(U_i)$ for any $i \in I$. By the left part of (7) applied to Δ we have $\Delta([\![\Phi_i^k]\!]) \ge \Delta(U_i)$ for each $i \in I$, implying $s \models_{\mathbf{f}} \langle a \rangle_{p_i} \Phi_i^k$ for each $i, k \in I$ where $p_i = \Delta(U_i)$. Then $t \models_{\mathbf{f}} \langle a \rangle_{p_i} \Phi_i^k$ for each $i, k \in I$. Hence $\Theta([\![\Phi_i^k]\!]) \ge p_i$ for each $i \in I$. By the right part of (7) applied to Θ, for an arbitrary index i and any $k \in I$ we can get

$$p_i \le \Theta([\![\Phi_i^k]\!]) \le \Theta(U_i) \sqcup \Theta(\bigcup_{m \in I \wedge m > k} U_m).$$

It follows that $p_i \le \Theta(U_i) \sqcup \inf_{k \in I} \Theta(\bigcup_{m \in I \wedge m > k} U_m)$. Thus, by (9) we have $p_i \le \Theta(U_i)$. That is, $\Delta(U_i) \le \Theta(U_i)$ for each $i \in I$. Now suppose that there exists an $i_0 \in I$ such that $\Delta(U_{i_0}) < \Theta(U_{i_0})$. Then we can take $\epsilon_0 > 0$ such that $\Delta(U_{i_0}) < \Delta(U_{i_0}) + \epsilon_0 < \Theta(U_{i_0})$. For this ϵ_0, by (10) applied to U_{i_0} we can see that there exists some $k_0 \in I$ such that $\Delta([\![\Phi_{i_0}^{k_0}]\!]) < \Delta(U_{i_0}) + \epsilon_0$. Thus $s \not\models_{\mathbf{f}} \langle a \rangle_{\Delta(U_{i_0}) + \epsilon_0} \Phi_{i_0}^{k_0}$ but $t \models_{\mathbf{f}} \langle a \rangle_{\Delta(U_{i_0}) + \epsilon_0} \Phi_{i_0}^{k_0}$ since $\Theta([\![\Phi_{i_0}^{k_0}]\!]) \ge \Theta(U_{i_0}) > \Delta(U_{i_0}) + \epsilon_0$, which contradicts the assumption that $s =_{\mathbf{f}'} t$. Hence for each $i \in I$, $\Delta(U_i) = \Theta(U_i)$ as desired. $\square$

7   Conclusions and Future Work

We have shown that on reactive probabilistic processes with countable state-space bisimilarity coincides with simulation equivalence, and the proof is very elementary. We have also simplified the modal characterisation of bisimilarity proposed by Desharnais et al.; our completeness proof does not invole advanced machinery on analytic spaces. For fuzzy labelled transition systems, we have presented a variant of the Hennessy-Milner Logic to capture bisimilarity. If the systems are image-finite, it is possible to use binary conjunctions instead of infinite conjunctions in the fuzzy logic, but negation has to be kept.

As future work, it would be interesting to investigate logical characterizations for nondeterministic fuzzy transition systems [8]. We believe that the logic for nondeterministic systems may need distribution semantics [29], i.e. semantic interpretation of the logic is given in terms of distributions.

Acknowledgement We thank the anonymous referees for their helpful comments on a preliminary version of the paper.

References

1. Abdulla, P.A., Legay, A., d'Orso, J., Rezine, A.: Tree regular model checking: A simulation-based approach. J. Logic. Algebr. Progr. 69(1/2), 93–121 (2006)
2. Baier, C.: On Algorithmic Verification Methods for Probabilistic Systems. Habilitationsschrift zur Erlangung der venia legendi der Fakultät für Mathematik und Informatik, Universität Mannheim (1998)
3. Bailador, G., Triviño, G.: Pattern recognition using temporal fuzzy automata. Fuzzy Sets Syst. 161(1), 37–55 (2010)
4. Bělohlávek, R.: Determinism and fuzzy automata. Inform. Sci. 142(1-4), 205–209 (2002)
5. Bhattacharyya, M.: Fuzzy Markovian decision process. Fuzzy Sets Syst. 99(3), 273–282 (1998)
6. Billingsley, P.: Probability and Measure. Wiley-Interscience, New York (1995)
7. Cao, Y., Chen, G., Kerre, E.E.: Bisimulations for fuzzy transition systems. IEEE Trans. Fuzzy Syst. 19(3), 540–552 (2010)
8. Cao, Y., Ezawa, Y.: Nondeterministic fuzzy automata. Inform. Sci. 191(1), 86–97 (2012)
9. Ćirić, M., Ignjatović, J., Damljanović, N., Bašić, M.: Bisimulations for fuzzy automata. Fuzzy Sets Syst. 186(1), 100–139 (2012)
10. Deng, Y., Du, W.: Logical, Metric, and Algorithmic Characterisations of Probabilistic Bisimulation., Technical Report CMU-CS-11-145, Carnegie Mellon University (2011)
11. Deng, Y., van Glabbeek, R.J., Hennessy, M., Morgan, C.C.: Testing finitary probabilistic processes. In: Bravetti, M., Zavattaro, G. (eds.) CONCUR 2009. LNCS, vol. 5710, pp. 274–288. Springer, Heidelberg (2009)
12. Desharnais, J.: Labelled Markov Processes. Ph.D. thesis, McGill University (1999)
13. Desharnais, J., Edalat, A., Panangaden, P.: Bisimulation for labelled Markov processes. Inf. Comput. 179(2), 163–193 (2002)
14. Desharnais, J., Gupta, V., Jagadeesan, R., Panangaden, P.: Approximating labelled Markov processes. Inf. Comput. 184(1), 160–200 (2003)
15. D'Errico, L., Loreti, M.: A process algebra approach to fuzzy reasoning. In: Proceedings of the Joint 2009 International Fuzzy Systems Association World Congress and 2009 European Society of Fuzzy Logic and Technology Conference, pp. 1136–1141 (2009)
16. Doberkat, E.-E.: Stochastic Coalgebraic Logic. Springer, Heidelberg (2010)
17. Fisler, K., Vardi, M.Y.: Bisimulation minimization and symbolic model checking. Form. Method. Syst. Des. 21(1), 39–78 (2002)

18. van Glabbeek, R.J., Smolka, S.A., Steffen, B., Tofts, C.M.N.: Reactive, generative, and stratified models of probabilistic processes. In: Proc. 5th Annu. IEEE Symp. Logic in Computer Science, pp. 130–141 (1990)
19. Hennessy, M., Milner, R.: Algebraic laws for nondeterminism and concurrency. J. ACM. 32(1), 137–161 (1985)
20. Hermanns, H., Parma, A., et al.: Probabilistic logical characterization. Inf. Comput. 209(2), 154–172 (2011)
21. Ignjatović, J., Ćirić, M., Simović, V.: Fuzzy relation equations and subsystems of fuzzy transition systems. Knowl-Based Syst. 38(1), 48–61 (2013)
22. Kupferman, O., Lustig, Y.: Latticed simulation relations and games. Int. J. Found. Comput. S. 21(2), 167–189 (2010)
23. Larsen, K.G., Skou, A.: Bisimulation through probabilistic testing. Inf. Comput. 94(1), 1–28 (1991)
24. Li, Y.M., Pedrycz, W.: Fuzzy finite automata and fuzzy regular expressions with membership values in lattice-ordered monoids. Fuzzy Sets Syst. 156(1), 68–92 (2005)
25. Lin, F., Ying, H.: Modeling and control of fuzzy discrete event systems. IEEE Trans. Syst., Man, Cybern., B, Cybern. 32(4), 408–415 (2002)
26. Mordeson, J.N., Malik, D.S.: Fuzzy Automata and Languages:Theory and Applications. Chapman & Hall/CRC, Boca Raton (2002)
27. Milner, R.: A Calculus of Communication Systems. LNCS, vol. 92. Springer, Heidelberg (1980)
28. Park, D.: Concurrency and automata on infinite sequences. In: Deussen, P. (ed.) GI-TCS 1981. LNCS, vol. 104, pp. 167–183. Springer, Heidelberg (1981)
29. Parma, A., Segala, R.: Logical characterizations of bisimulations for discrete probabilistic systems. In: Seidl, H. (ed.) FOSSACS 2007. LNCS, vol. 4423, pp. 287–301. Springer, Heidelberg (2007)
30. Pedrycz, W., Gacek, A.: Learning of fuzzy automata. Int. J. Comput. Intell. Appl. 1(1), 19–33 (2001)
31. Pedrycz, W., Gomide, F.: A generalized fuzzy Petri net model. IEEE Trans. Fuzzy Syst. 2(4), 295–301 (1994)
32. Qiu, D.W.: Supervisory control of fuzzy discrete event systems: a formal approach. IEEE Trans. Syst., Man, Cybern., B, Cybern. 35(1), 72–88 (2005)
33. Shen, V.R.L.: Knowledge representation using high-level fuzzy Petri nets. IEEE Trans. Syst., Man, Cybern. A, Syst., Humans 36(6), 1220–1227 (2006)
34. Sack, J., Zhang, L.: A General Framework for Probabilistic Characterizing Formulae. In: Kuncak, V., Rybalchenko, A. (eds.) VMCAI 2012. LNCS, vol. 7148, pp. 396–411. Springer, Heidelberg (2012)
35. Sangiorgi, D., Rutten, J. (eds.): Advanced Topics in Bisimulation and Coinduction. Cambridge University Press (2011)
36. Segala, R., Lynch, N.A.: Probabilistic simulations for probabilistic process. Nord. J. Comput. 2(2), 250–273 (1995)
37. Wee, W.G., Fu, K.S.: A formulation of fuzzy automata and its application as a model of learning systems. IEEE Trans. Syst. Sci. Cybern. SSC-5(3), 215–223 (1969)
38. Zadeh, L.A.: Fuzzy sets as a basis for a theory of possibility. Fuzzy Sets Syst. 1, 3–28 (1978)
39. Zhang, L.: Decision Algorithms for Probabilistic Simulations. Ph.D. thesis, Saarland University (2008)

Pointer Program Derivation Using Coq: Graphs and Schorr-Waite Algorithm

Jean-François Dufourd*

University of Strasbourg - CNRS, ICUBE Laboratory,
Pôle API, Boulevard S. Brant, CS 10413, 67412 Illkirch, France
jfd@unistra.fr

Abstract. We present a specification, a derivation and total correctness proofs of operations for bi-functional graphs implemented with pointers, including the Schorr-Waite algorithm. This one marks such a graph with an economical depth-first strategy. Our approach is purely algebraic and functional, from a simple graph specification to the simulation of a tail-recursive imperative program, then to a true C pointer program by elementary classical transformations. We stay in the unique higher-order formalism of the Calculus of Inductive Constructions for specifications, programs and proofs. All the development is supported by Coq.

1 Introduction

The Schorr-Waite (in short SW) algorithm [31] traverses iteratively a bi-functional graph coded by pointers in depth-first order from an initial vertex and marks all the visited vertices. The problem is classical, but the solution of Schorr and Waite is inexpensive because it avoids any auxiliary storage by a clever use of temporarily unemployed graph pointers. Such an algorithm is useful in the cell marking step of a garbage collector, when the available memory is scarce. Many researchers used this algorithm as a *benchmark* to test manual (or little automated) methods of program transformation and verification [32,33,8,20,19,17,9,4,28,34]. Since 2000, studies have addressed the proofs with automatic tools, for partial or total correctness [3,1,27,22,26,15,29]. Indeed, the proof of total correctness is considered as the first montain to climb in the verification of pointer programs [3].

Here, we report a new experiment of formal specification, derivation and total correctness proof of a bi-functional graph datatype with its concrete operations, including the SW algorithm whose study is particularly difficult. We highlight the following *novelties* of the derivation process:

• **Formalism.** We stay in the general higher-order *Calculus of Inductive Constructions* (in short CiC) formalism for specifications, programs and proofs, and use the *Coq proof assistant* as single software tool [2]. The only added axioms are *proof-irrelevance*, *extensionality*, and an axiom of *choice* for a fresh address during an allocation. We thus intentionally avoid *assertions method* and *Hoare logic* underlying most works in verification of programs.

---

* This work was supported in part by the French ANR white project Galapagos.

S. Merz and J. Pang (Eds.): ICFEM 2014, LNCS 8829, pp. 139–154, 2014.

- **Abstract level.** We first focus on the algebraic specification in Coq of abstract datatypes. We define by structural or Noetherian induction the results as abstract functions and prove required properties.
- **Concrete level.** We specify a memory algebraic type with pointers in which we implement the abstract specification. We seek *morphisms* carrying properties from abstract to concrete levels.
- **Programming.** Coq does an extraction in OCaml, while forgetting proof-parameters. Memory parameters are removed to go into an imperative program.
- **Orbits.** At the abstract and concrete levels, the *orbit* notion helps to manage the track of function iterations, e.g. to concisely write type invariants and to manage linkage traversals as in *shape analysis* [21]. Orbits were approached in [6,30,3,27,21] and deeply studied in [13]. They allow to deal with *separation* problems [30] without extending the CiC. To specify *combinatorial hypermaps* [18,10], and to derive imperative pointer *geometric* datatypes and programs, *orbits* are particularly efficient [14]. So, our correctness proof of the SW algorithm can be considered as another case study for orbits.
- **SW algorithm.** Finally, this process provides a version of the SW algorithm acting on any marked bi-functional graph, for which there is a proof that the corresponding operation is *idempotent*, i.e. it has the same effect whatever applied once or several times.

Sect. 2 specifies marked bi-functional graphs and Sect. 3 a depth-first graph marking. Sect. 4 defines internal stacks and Sect. 5 constructs a depth-first marking with them. Sect. 6 specifies memories and Sect. 7 defines a graph-memory isomorphism. Sect. 8 carries the marking with internal stack from graph to memory. Sect. 9 extracts it into an OCaml function, which is transformed "by hand" into an iterative C-program. Sect. 10 proves that the initial specification fits well with reachability. Sect. 11 presents work related to the SW algorithm, and Sect. 12 concludes. The complete Coq development (with proofs) is available on-line [12], including [13]. A preliminary French version, with another specification, is in [11]. A basic knowledge of Coq makes the reading of this article easier.

2   Bi-functional Graphs

Basic definitions. As in Coq [2], we write `nat` for the type of natural numbers. We assume that `undef` and `null`, not necessarily distinct, code particular natural values. In this work, a *(marked bi-functional) graph* g = (E,mark,son0,son1) is a finite subset E of *vertices* (or *nodes*) in `nat` - {undef,null}, so-called *support* of g, equipped with three functions: `mark` returning a number inside {0,1,2}, `son0` and `son1` returning natural numbers named *left* and *right* sons, which do not necessarily belong to E. An example is given in Fig. 1(Left), with E = {1,...,8}, marks in the vertex circles (filled with blank, light or dark grey depending on the mark value: 0, 1 or 2), `son0` and `son1` represented by arcs with labels 0 or 1.

In the specification, the functions are extended at the whole `nat`: outside E, `mark` returns 0, and `son0`, `son1` return `undef`. To avoid tedious elementary tests, we first inductively (here just enumeratively) define in Coq the mark type `nat2`

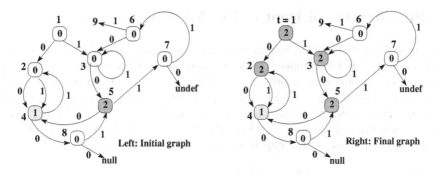

Fig. 1. Graph before (Left) and after (Right) depth-first marking from $t = 1$

(**Type** is viewed as the "type of types"). Then, it is convenient to inductively define the type **graph** by two *constructors*: **vg**, returning the *empty* (or *void*) graph, and **iv g x m x0 x1**, *inserting* in the graph **g** a new vertex, **x**, with its mark, **m**, and its two sons, **x0** and **x1**:

```
Inductive nat2 : Type:= zero : nat2 | one : nat2 | two : nat2.
Inductive graph : Type:= vg : graph | iv : graph -> nat -> nat2 -> nat -> nat -> graph.
```

Observers and graph invariant. A predicate, **exv g z**, for testing the existence of any **z:nat** in a graph **g** is recursively defined in Coq by a pattern matching on **graph** (**Prop** is the type of *propositions* and _ is a placeholder). Then, functions **mark** and **son** are also recursively written in functional style (**son0**, **son1** are compacted into a unique **son** parameterized by a label **k = 0** or 1). However, to construct only *well-formed* graphs, the calls of **iv** must respect the precondition **prec_iv**. So, if necessary, **graph** may be constrained by the *invariant* **inv_graph** (~ is written for *not* and <> for $\neq$):

```
Fixpoint exv(g:graph)(z:nat): Prop:=
  match g with vg => False | iv g0 x _ _ _ => x = z \/ exv g0 z end.
Definition prec_iv(g:graph)(x:nat): Prop := ~ exv g x /\ x <> null /\ x <> undef.
Fixpoint inv_graph(g:graph): Prop :=
  match g with vg => True | iv g0 x m _ _ => inv_graph g0 /\ prec_iv g0 x end.
```

Other graph *observers* are similarly defined: **nv** is the number of vertices and **marksum** is the sum of the mark values of the existing vertices. Numerous results on them are proved, often by structural induction on **graph**, e.g. the lemma:

```
Lemma marksum_bound: forall g, marksum g <= 2 * nv g.
```

Mutators. Functions to update graphs are also written: **chm g z m** changes the mark of **z** into **m**, and **cha g k z zs** the k-th son (or *arc*, for **k = 0** or 1) of **z** into **zs**. They *preserve* the graph invariant and enjoy properties of *idempotence*, *permutativity* and *absorption* which are essential in the following, e.g. (**eq_nat_dec** tests the equality in **nat**):

```
Lemma chm_chm: forall g z1 m1 z2 m2,
  chm (chm g z1 m1) z2 m2 = if eq_nat_dec z1 z2 then chm g z2 m2 else chm (chm g z2 m2) z1 m1.
Lemma chm_idem: forall g z, chm g z (mark g z) = g.
Lemma cha_chm: forall g x y z k m, k <= 1 -> cha (chm g z m) k x y = chm (cha g k x y) z m.
```

3   Specification of Depth-First Marking

Preliminaries. We slightly enlarge the traditional *marking* problem: (*i*) we deal with any graph g, i.e. equipped *with any marking* (between 0 and 2) and *any sons* (in the support of g or not); (*ii*) starting from any natural number t, the problem consists in traversing in depth-first order the *subgraph* of g of all the 0-marked vertices reachable from t and in marking them by 2. Fig. 1(Right) gives the final marking of the graph in Fig. 1(Left) when t = 1. With this setting, the *stopping condition* of the depth-first traversal from any t is:

```
Definition stop g t := ~ exv g t \/ mark g t <> 0.
```

Then, naming `stop_dec` the function which tests if `stop g t` is satisfied or not (`stop` is easily proved *decidable*), the entire problem is solved by the function which we name `df` and define in Coq syntax as follows (surrounded by quotes because this non-primitive recursive definition is not accepted as such by the Coq system):

```
"Definition df(g:graph)(t:nat): graph :=
  if stop_dec g t then g
  else let g0 := df (chm g t two) (son g 0 t) in df g0 (son g 1 t)."
```

As other authors [19,33,9], we consider that `df` explicitly states the problem as simply as possible, as if g was a binary tree. From now on we consider it as our *specification*. Unfortunately, such a recursive definition cannot be directly written in Coq without dealing with *termination*. Moreover, the *nested (double)* recursion adds a difficulty. But such problems of general recursion can be overcome in Coq [2] (p. 419-420, for numerical problems).

True Coq specification. First, we define a graph *measure*, `mes`, which will decrease at each recursive call. Then, we consider two binary relations on `graph`:

```
Definition mes g := 2 * nv g - marksum g.
Definition ltg g' g := mes g' < mes g.
Definition leg g' g := mes g' <= mes g.
```

They are a *strict* and a *large preorder*, `ltg` is *Noetherian* (or *well-founded*), and the use of `chm` inside `df`'s body decreases `mes`. In fact, the termination of `df` needs `ltg (chm g t two) g`, which is immediate, and `ltg g0 g`, which is satisfied if `leg g0 (chm g t two)`. This requires as result a graph, and also the fact that this graph is less than or equal to g. In Coq, such a result has the *existential* type *depending on* g denoted by {g':graph | leg g' g}, as for usual mathematical subsets. Then, an auxiliary function of `df`, named `df_aux`, with a result of this type, has itself a *functional type* which is defined by:

```
Definition df_aux_type := fun g:graph => nat -> {g':graph | leg g' g}.
```

So, `df_aux` must be a function which transforms a graph, g:graph, into a function which in turn transforms t:nat into a *pair*, (g', H'), where g' is the marked graph and H' a proof of `leg g' g`. The building of `df_aux` corresponds with the proof of a theorem. Indeed, Coq implements the *Curry-Howard correspondence*, stating that proofs and functions are isomorphic. The proof, which has roughly the skeleton of df's informal specification, uses our results on the decreasing of mes in the recursive calls of df. We do not give the exact definition of df_aux which is rather technical, but the interested reader may consult [11]. Finally, remembering that exist is the Coq constructor of {g':graph | leg g' g}, the "true" df is obtained by extracting the *witness* of the result, i.e. the marked graph g':

```
Definition df(g:graph)(t:nat): graph := match df_aux g t with exist g' _ => g' end.
```

Of course, the *termination* of df_aux, and of df, is *automatically ensured* by these constructions. The definition of df is rather mysterious for non-specialists, but the following properties are illuminating.

Properties of the Coq specification. Most properties of df are obtained by Noetherian induction on df_aux using built-in recursors. First of all, df preserves inv_graph, the initial graph *vertices* and *sons*, and the marking is always *increasing*. An important result — absent from all studies considering an initial marking with 0 only —, is that df is *idempotent*, i.e. reapplying it does not change the result. Finally, we exactly obtain the expected original definition of df by proving the *fixpoint equation* df_eqpf. So, since it possesses all the properties we want to prove, df is a solid reference for transformations towards a real program:

```
Lemma inv_graph_df: forall g t, inv_graph g -> inv_graph (df g t).
Lemma exv_df: forall g t z, exv (df g t) z <-> exv g z.
Lemma son_df: forall g t z k, son (df g t) k z = son g k z.
Lemma mark_le_mark_df: forall g t z, mark g z <= mark (df g t) z.
Lemma df_idem: forall g t, df (df g t) t = df g t.
Theorem df_eqpf: forall g t,
  df g t = if stop_dec g t then g
           else let g0 := df (chm g t two) (son g 0 t) in df g0 (son g 1 t).
```

4   Succession Function, Orbits, Internal Stack

Orbits. Now, we simulate an *(internal) stack* inside a graph g , thanks to a *total function* succ:

```
Definition succ g z :=
  if eq_nat_dec z null then null
  else if eq_nat_dec (mark g z) 0 then null else son g ((mark g z) - 1) z.
```

This function can be *iterated*: for any integer k, the k-th iterate of succ g from z is zk := Iter (succ g) k z, where Iter is the classical iteration functional (with z0 = z). The iterates form in g's support a list that we call the *orbit* of z. We studied this notion in a general way [13]. Here, it is used to express that such a list always ends on null, outside g's support.

Internal stack. For us, the orbit of z in g's support — the orbit length is written lenorb g z — is an *internal stack* if it satisfies the following *invariant*:

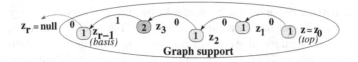

Fig. 2. Shape of a (non-empty) internal stack, with r = 5

```
Definition inv_istack g z : Prop :=
  let r := lenorb g z in let zr := Iter (succ g) r z in let zr_1 := Iter (succ g) (r-1) z in
  zr = null /\ (0 < r -> 1 <= mark g zr_1 <= 2).
```

In Fig. 2, r (= 5) gives the internal stack *height*, whereas z (= $z0$) and zr_1 can be viewed as its *top* and *basis* when the orbit is non-empty. Consequently, all the internal stack elements are (genuine) non-**zero** marked vertices of g. Internal stacks are affected by mark or son updates. For general orbits, the different updating cases are thoroughly analyzed [13] as in *shape analysis* [21]. However, the SW algorithm only uses some particular configurations which are related to three basic operations, which we present now.

Internal stack operations. They are defined as follows:

```
Definition ipush g t p := cha (chm g t one) 0 t p.
Definition iswing g t p := cha (cha (chm g p two) 0 p t) 1 p (succ g p).
Definition ipop g t p := cha g 1 p t.
```

• ipush g t p pushes a vertex t on an internal stack whose top is p, after a change of t's mark into **one** (Fig. 3(a1)). Its precondition requires that t is a true **zero**-marked vertex. After ipush g t p, p remains the top of an internal stack, but t is also the top of another one including the former. The left son of t is now used to access to t's successor, i.e. p, in the new stack.
• iswing g t p is a *rotation* at the top p of an internal stack to change its sons after change of its mark from **one** into **two**. This "stack" operation is emblematic of the SW algorithm (Fig. 3(b1)): iswing g t p replaces the left son which led to the successor in the internal stack by the right son, reestablishing the initial left son of p into t, p being no more father of its true right son.
• ipop g t p pops from an internal stack p its top (i.e. p), and reestablishes its right son. The precondition requires that p's mark is **two** (so exv g p is verified) (Fig. 3(c1)): after ipop g t p, succ g p is the top of the remaining stack, whose height decreases by 1 and which might become empty.

It is proved that these operations preserve the graph and internal stack invariants, the graph vertices, and that ipush and iswing add 1 to the mark sum, whereas ipop leaves it unchanged.

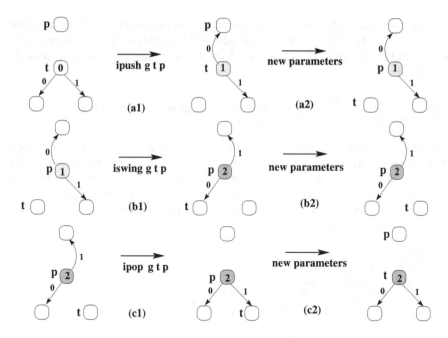

Fig. 3. Operations on internal stacks

5   Depth-First Marking Using an Internal Stack

Cartesian product. To simulate the SW algorithm, we have to deal with the type, named `graphistack`, of the pairs `(g,p)` composed of a graph g and an internal stack top p (In Coq, `*` is the Cartesian type product, used with `%type` to remove ambiguities). We equip it with the invariant `inv_graphistack` (`fst` and `snd` are the classical projections). This invariant is satisfied with the empty internal stack and is preserved by each of the three operations defined in Sect. 4:

```
Definition graphistack := (graph * nat)%type.
Definition inv_graphistack(gp:graphistack) := inv_graph (fst gp) /\ inv_istack (fst gp) (snd gp).
```

Designing the algorithm. The algorithm we look for is *simply tail-recursive*. For the parameter `gp = (g,p)`, its termination will be warranted by the strict decreasing of the *measure* `2 * mes g + lenorb g p` at each recursive call involving one of the operations `ipush`, `iswing` or `ipop`. Our previous results entail this decreasing. So, a suitable binary relation on `graphistack` is `ltgip`, which is quickly proved to be a *Noetherian strict preorder*:

```
Definition ltgip (gp' gp:graphistack) := let (g',p') := gp' in let (g,p) := gp in
    2 * mes g' + lenorb g' p' < 2 * mes g + lenorb g p.
```

The same method as for `df` allows us to define `dfi`, our new recursive marking function *with internal stack*. A large preorder is useless since the algorithm is simply recursive. However, the proofs of measure decreasing need `inv_graphistack` at each recursive call. So, for the result of our auxiliary function dfi_aux, whose type is dfi_aux_type, we introduce the subtype {gp:graphistack | inv_graphistack gp}. We then complete the stopping predicate stop of df into stopi:

```
Definition dfi_aux_type :=
  fun gp:graphistack => inv_graphistack gp -> nat -> {gp':graphistack | inv_graphistack gp'}.
Definition stopi p g t := p = null /\ stop g t.
```

The algorithm stops when p is null, and t is not in g or has a non-zero mark, the corresponding testing function being stopi_dec. To construct dfi_aux, the method is similar to that of df_aux (Sect. 3), following the subsequent informal specification written in Coq *pseudo-code*. The new parameters g, p, t for the three recursive internal calls to dfi_aux corresponding to ipop, iswing and ipush are given in Fig. 3(a2,b2,c2):

```
"Definition dfi_aux (g, p) t :=
  if stopi_dec p g t then (g, p)
  else if stop_dec g t
      then if eq_nat_dec (mark g p) 2
          then dfi_aux (ipop g t p, son g 1 p) p
          else dfi_aux (iswing g t p, p) (son g 1 p)
      else dfi_aux (ipush g t p, t) (son g 0 t)"
```

Finally, dfi is obtained by the projection of dfi_aux on the graph component when starting with an empty stack (inv_graphistack_null g hg is a proof that inv_graphistack is satisfied for the genuine graph g with the empty stack):

```
Definition dfi (g:graph)(hg:inv_graph g)(t:nat) : graph:=
  match dfi_aux (g,null) (inv_graphistack_null g hg) t with exist (g',s) _ => g' end.
```

Note that dfi keeps a proof argument, hg:inv_graph g. Besides, a fixpoint equation similar to the above informal specification is proved for dfi_aux in the same way as for df (Sect. 3).

Total correctness of the algorithm. The *termination* of dfi being automatically ensured, the great question is the *partial correctness* of dfi with respect to df. In fact, our *fundamental result* is the *identity* between dfi and df: for the same g and t, they return the same graph *regardless of what the actual proof argument* hg *for* dfi *is*:

```
Theorem df_dfi : forall g hg t, dfi g hg t = df g t.
```

The proof uses a new iteration function on an argument gp:graphistack [11] and the general properties of *orbit* update operations, particularly the *mutation* [13]. The consequences are numerous, since all the nice properties of df are immediately transposed to dfi, e.g. *preservation of the graph invariant, preservation of the initial vertices and sons, mark growing, idempotence* (Sect. 3). As far as the SW algorithm, we could stop the study at this point, considering that the path is well traced towards an imperative iterative C-program for an experienced programmer, especially since df is simply tail-recursive. But a lot of implementation problems are still to be solved, particularly regarding pointers, because the graph which we use for convenience is a "ghost", i.e. it does not explicitly appear in the final program. Indeed, in imperative programming, a function like dfi should only be parameterized by an *address* t. So, we now model memories to translate our graph specification into a C-program.

6   Memory Model

Cells and memory. Advanced memory models allow to capture allocator subtleties which are useful to prove the correctness of compilers or intricate programs with composite data [25]. Our present goal being to derive only one structured program on a unique datatype, our memory model is directly specialized towards a graph pointer representation. Memory *cells* are of the following type, cell, where mkcell is the constructor, and val, s0, s1 are field selectors, for mark, left and right sons. An *exception* cell, initcell, is defined. Rather than giving a complex − dangerous in sense of consistency − axiom system, we found it safe to algebraically define the memory type Mem as follows:

```
Record cell:Type:= mkcell {val : nat2; s0 : nat; s1 : nat}.
Definition initcell := mkcell zero undef undef.
Inductive Mem:Type:= init : Mem | alloc : Mem -> nat -> cell -> Mem.
```

The *addresses* are simulated by natural numbers, init returns the empty memory, and alloc inserts in a memory a cell value at a (new) address, during an *allocation*. Our memories are finite, unbounded, and allocations never fail.

Memory operations. Now, a predicate exm tests if an address is *valid* in a memory, i.e. corresponds to an allocated cell. Then, the usual functions, load, free and mut, respectively to *get* from an address a cell contents, to *free* a cell (and its address), and to *change* a cell contents giving its address, are easily defined by pattern matching [11]. However, allocations must satisfy the following precondition, which leads to an *invariant* inv_Mem for Mem:

```
Definition prec_alloc M a := ~exm M a /\ a <> undef /\ a <> null.
Fixpoint inv_Mem(M:Mem): Prop :=
  match M with init => True | alloc M0 a c => inv_Mem M0 /\ prec_alloc M0 a end.
```

A lot of lemmas about the behavior of the operations are proved by induction on Mem. We have mimicked more realistic programming primitives, particularly a C-like malloc returning from a memory a fresh address, thanks to an *address generator*, whose behavior is governed by a *dedicated axiom* [11].

7   Memory to Graph, Graph to Memory

Abstraction and representation. We define two operations: Abs, to *abstract* a memory into a graph, and Rep to *represent* a graph as a memory, the *reversibility* of which is confirmed by the following theorems:

```
Fixpoint Abs(M:Mem): graph :=
    match M with init => vg | alloc M0 a c => iv (Abs M0) a (val c) (s0 c) (s1 c) end.
Fixpoint Rep (g:graph) : Mem :=
    match g with vg => init | iv g0 x m x0 x1 => alloc (Rep g0) x (mkcell m x0 x1) end.
Theorem Rep_Abs : forall M, Rep (Abs M) = M.
Theorem Abs_Rep : forall g, Abs (Rep g) = g.
Theorem inv_graph_Abs : forall M, inv_Mem M -> inv_graph (Abs M).
Theorem inv_Mem_Rep : forall g, inv_graph g -> inv_Mem (Rep g).
```

Transposition of operations and properties. Graph operations are implemented by load and mut into memory ones, here with the same name preceded by "R", e.g. Rcha and Rchm. In fact, Abs and Rep make graph and Mem *isomorphic*. So, the behavioral proofs of graph operations are simply carried on Mem:

```
Lemma Rchm_chm : forall M x m, Rchm M x m = Rep (chm (Abs M) x m).
Lemma chm_Rchm : forall g x m, chm g x m = Abs (Rchm (Rep g) x m).
Lemma Rcha_cha : forall M k x y, Rcha M k x y = Rep (cha (Abs M) k x y).
Lemma cha_Rcha : forall g k x y, cha g k x y = Abs (Rcha (Rep g) k x y).
```

8 Depth-First Marking in Memory

Specification of marking in a memory. The predicates stop and ltg become Rstop and Rltg for memories. The lemmas we had for df are transposed to specify the (nested) recursive depth-first marking Rdf in memories, with exchange theorems. Consequently, all the properties of df in graph are transposed to Rdf in Mem, e.g. we have a *fixpoint equation*, Rdf_eqpf, similar to df_eqpf:

```
Theorem df_Rdf : forall g t, df g t = Abs (Rdf (Rep g) t).
Theorem Rdf_df : forall M t, Rdf M t = Rep (df (Abs M) t).
```

Depth-first memory marking with internal stack. Operations ipush, iswing and ipop are easily transposed for Mem into Ripush, Riswing and Ripop with the same properties. Then, the counterpart of graphistack is Memistack, with the invariant inv_Memistack:

```
Definition Memistack := (Mem * nat) %type.
Definition inv_Memistack(Mp:Memistack) := inv_Mem (fst Mp) /\ inv_Ristack (fst Mp) (snd Mp).
```

At stopi and ltgip correspond Rstopi and Rltgip. The definition of the *marking in memory with internal address stack*, i.e. Rdfi (with Rdfi_aux), follows.

Total correctness. Of course, Rdfi is *terminating*. Then, by our isomorphism graph - Mem, we transpose in Mem our proof of correctness of dfi w.r.t. df into a proof of correctness of Rdfi w.r.t. dfi. Better, we have for free the *correctness* of Rdfi w.r.t. our specification df in graphs:

```
Theorem Rdfi_dfi : forall (M : Mem) (hM : inv_Mem M) (t : nat),
    Rdfi M hM t = Rep (dfi (Abs M) (inv_graph_Abs M hM) t).
Theorem Rdfi_df : forall (M : Mem) (hM : inv_Mem M) (t : nat),
    Rdfi M hM t = Rep (df (Abs M) t).
```

9   Towards Concrete Programming

Extraction in OCaml. The *extraction-of-functional-program* Coq tool [2] leads to an OCaml version of our development. Hence, after an elementary substitution, we get the following program for Rdfi_aux and Rdfi (in OCaml, "R" and "M" are in lower case, the Coq decision functions, Rstopi_dec and Rstop_dec, become Boolean functions, and the natural numbers are in Peano notation). As usual, the extraction removes all the proof-terms and retains the common data only. A *functional form* of the SW algorithm follows. Since rdfi_aux is *tail-recursive*, it will be easy to write it *iteratively* without a stack:

```
let rec rdfi_aux m p t =
  if rstopi_dec p m t then (m, p)
  else if rstop_dec m t
        then if eq_nat_dec (rmark m p) (S (S 0))
             then rdfi_aux (ripop m t p) (rson m (S 0) p) p
             else rdfi_aux (riswing m t p) p (rson m (S 0) p)
        else rdfi_aux (ripush m t p) x (rson m 0 t)
let rdfi m t = fst (rdfi_aux m null t)
```

Derivation of a C-program. From the OCaml version, we derive graph imperative operations. We first define in C the types of cells and addresses, which were integers (**nat2** is suppressed for simplicity):

```
typedef struct strcell {nat val; struct strcell * s0; struct strcell * s1;} cell, * address;
```

As usual in C, **null** is written NULL, the memory is *implicit* and modified by *side-effects*. As far as the SW algorithm, Fig. 3(a2,b2,c2) explains how the parameter pair (p, t) mutates by ripush, riswing and ripop, like in the functional version. An *auxiliary variable*, q, is used to serialize C assignments. We can as usual replace exm t by t != NULL, and the way undef is translated is not important. Finally, we transform the tail-recursion into an iteration, unfold all internal functions, and the imperative iterative (ingenious) SW procedure looks like a variant of the C version in [22], where each mark is coded by two bits. The procedure works correctly *regardless of what the initial marking is*, the standard situation − all marks are 0 − being just a particular case:

```
void rdfi(address t){
   address p = NULL, q;
   while (!(p == NULL && (t == NULL || t->val != 0)))){
     if(t == NULL || t->val != 0){
        if(p->val==2) {q = p->s1; p->s1 = t; t = p; p = q;}
        else {p->val = 2; q = p->s0; p->s0 = t; t = p->s1; p->s1 = q;}
     }
     else {t->val = 1; q = t->s0; t->s0 = p; p = t; t = q;}
   }
}
```

10   Back to the Specification

Although the starting point of numerous studies, **df** can be considered as *too constructive* w.r.t. the *reachability* (Sect. 3) [19,27,22,26,24]. If reachable g t z means that, in g, z can be reached from t only via zero-marked vertices, its definition can be (nat2_to_nat maps nat2 into nat):

```
Fixpoint reachable(g:graph)(t z:nat): Prop : match g with
    vg => False
  | iv g0 x m x0 x1 => reachable g0 t z \/ nat2_to_nat m = 0 /\
    (x = t /\ x = z \/ (x = t \/ reachable g0 t x)
    /\ (x0 = z \/ reachable g0 x0 z \/ x1 = z \/ reachable g0 x1 z))
end.
```

Under some simple conditions, **reachable** g is proved *decidable* (with decision function **reachable_dec**), *reflexive* and *transitive*. The specifications **reachable** and **df** should be compared. We did it through a simply recursive marking, named **dfs**, using a classical *external vertex stack* and enjoying the same behavior as **dfi**. So **df** = **dfs**, and since **df** = **dfi** (Sect. 5), then **df** = **dfs** = **dfi**. Finally, the following theorem *fully characterizes* the effect of **dfs**, and **df**, on all g's vertices. It also entails the *correctness* of **dfi**, and **Rdfi**, *with respect to reachability*:

```
Theorem reachable_dfs : forall g hg t z, mark (dfs g t hg) z =
    if reachable_dec g t z then if stop_dec g z then mark g z else two else mark g z.
```

In summary, the whole derivation process is synthesized in Fig. 4 where all functions, relations, equalities, isomorphisms and equivalences appear.

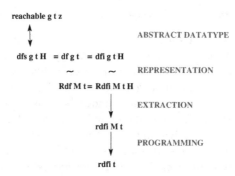

Fig. 4. Derivation levels, functions and relations

11   Work Related to Schorr-Waite Algorithm

Pioneering work. The SW algorithm, discovered independently by Deutsch ([23], p. 417) was published as a routine for garbage collection [31]. Many *program constructions by derivation*, e.g. by Griffiths [20], start with a doubly recursive imperative procedure, introduce progressively (internal) stack elements, and show that transformations preserve good properties.

Topor and Suzuki give the first formal proofs "by hand" [33,32]. Topor introduces predicates and procedures comparable to **df**, **dfs** and **dfi**, but acting on sets and lists with side-effects. The proof applies the *intermittent assertions* method, with an induction on the data structure size that our graph inductions sometimes remind. Suzuki develops an automatic program verifier able to deal with pointers, but his attempt on the SW algorithm remains incomplete.

Gries publishes a correctness proof of the SW program using the *assertions method* with *weakest preconditions* [19]. In a vertex array simulating the memory, the graph is represented by a set of paths. Morris writes a proof in the same spirit using Hoare logic [28]. Gerhart [17] proposes a proof *by derivation* from an abstract problem of transitive closure to Gries's program using sets, sequences and arrays. The proof using the *assertions method* is partially verified by Affirm. Following Topor's proof, de Roever [8] illustrates the *greatest fixpoint theory* by the total correctness of a SW algorithm which is far enough a way from the C program. Dershowitz revisits in rather informal style the SW algorithm *derivation* and proof for vertices with d sons [9]. He starts with a recursive procedure having an internal loop, progressively introduces counters, then an internal stack, and ends with a version including two *goto*'s. Ward uses a *transformational model-based method* to set the problem then to derive in WSL and prove the SW algorithm [34]. It uses transformation rules which are proved correct, thus avoiding to prove the correctness of the derivation itself.

Broy and Pepper use *algebraic specifications* to derive and prove the total correctness of the algorithm [4]. They specify marked vertex sets, then 2-graphs as sets with 2 functions. An axiom of *permutativity* forces to use an *equality modulo* for graphs. The same in Coq would alter *Leibniz equality* and prevent proofs of equality for functions returning graphs. This explains our focus on the `graph` specification. The starting point is a doubly recursive procedure acting on a set and a graph. They algebraically specify generic arrays to simulate memories. Several imperative procedures are obtained thanks to a generic transformation rule eliminating double recursions. The last version mentions a set and a path and is still far from the C program. Our study can be viewed as a logical continuation of this work.

Work using automated tools. Following Burstall [6], Bornat [3] gives a rationale to prove pointer programs in *Hoare logic* with semantic models of *stack* and *heap*. In a memory (heap) viewed as an array, he follows iterated addresses by an f function, defines *f-linked sequences*, and studies their dynamic behavior. The SW algorithm is partially verified in the proof editor Jape [3].

Abrial uses the model-based *Event B method* to refine and merge (in 8 steps) specifications given by separate elementary assignments into a final pointer program [1]. Invariants, with pre-postconditions on sets and relations are progressively built with proof *obligations*. The Atelier B is used to prove the partial correctness, 70% automatically.

Mehta and Nipkow propose an Isabelle framework to prove pointer programs in *higher-order logic* [27]. They implement a small language for annotated programs and tools to reason in *Hoare logic* with a semantic model of *heap* and *stack*. A special attention is paid to capture *separation* properties [3,30] with list and path abstractions. They prove the *partial correctness* of two versions of the SW algorithm from Bornat's work [3].

Loginov et al. elaborate a completely automated proof of total correctness using *three-valued logic*, with deep analysis of reachability in pointer structures, but only for binary trees or dags [26]. Hubert and Marché use the *assertion method* in the Caduceus system for a direct proof of a C source version of the SW algorithm [22]. A big invariant concerns the evolution of reachability, marking, stack, sons, paths, etc. They automatically prove about 60% of the correctness, the rest, e.g. termination, being left to Coq (about 3000 lines). Bubel relates a proof part of a Java implementation. The specification in Java Card DL is based on reachability, the proofs use the KeY system but do not mention termination [5].

Leino describes in Dafny a very performing implementation. Big pre-, postconditions and loop invariant group four kinds of properties. The total correctness verification is automatic (in a few sec.) thanks to SMT solvers [24]. However, the author says he finally prefers a method by refinement, like [1]. Yang uses the relational separation logic to show that the SW algorithm is equivalent to a depth-first traversing, but he mentions no automation [35].

Giorgino et al. study a *method by refinement*, first based on spanning trees then enriched to graphs, for the total correctness of the SW algorithm, using Isabelle/HOL [15]. Finally, they use state-transformers and monads (in Isabelle) to deal with imperative programs. Proteasa and Back present the *invariant based programming*, a refinement approach by *predicate transformers* supported by *invariant diagrams* [29]. A diagram contains the information necessary to verify that each derivation towards the SW algorithm is totally correct. The process has been verified by Isabelle.

12   Conclusion

Coq development. We derived a graph library and the SW algorithm, and proved their *total correctness* with Coq. The development *from scratch* represents about 8,400 lines, with 480 definitions, lemmas or theorems. That is the price for such a complete study with a general proof assistant.

Advantages of our approach. We deal with a *single* powerful logical framework, i.e. CiC and Coq, at abstract and concrete levels. Coq allows us to simulate algebraic datatypes with *inductive types* equipped with preconditions and invariants. It offers good facilities for *general recursive functions* if proof parameters are added to address nested recursions [2]. This is facilitated by the mechanism of *dependent type*.

Our approach is *global* because, at the two levels, graph types and operations have to be specified, implemented and proved correct all together. Constraints are distributed among invariants, preconditions and proof-parameters. So, big complex invariants, as in monolithic proofs of the SW algorithm, are broken in several pieces easier to manage.

Besides, *orbit* features allow to express predicates about data separation or collision at high and low levels in a synthetical way [13,14].

Abstraction and representation *morphisms* carry on operations and properties, which are *proved once*, and, with *extensionality*, help to prove the *equality* of functions. The final step towards programming uses the *extraction-from-proof* mechanism and classical elementary program transformations.

Limitations and future work. Complex algebraic data must be studied to see how equalities of objects and functions will behave. For instance, dependent constructors force to *congruences*, which are difficult to deal with in Coq, even with *setoids*, and we could sometimes be happy with *observational equalities*.

The transformation of a functional recursive version with memory into an iterative imperative program is classical and has good solutions in well-defined cases. However, it should be computer-aided, even automated in a *compiler*.

Our approach prevents the help of program verification tools based on Hoare logic, e.g. Why3 [16] or Bedrock [7], which also use Coq. However, the introduction of our orbits in such frameworks must be considered to write predicates about separation and collision, as in [13,14].

Finally, as our predecessors, we found the total correctness proof of the SW algorithm to be hard work. But the memory management is still simple in this algorithm, since it *does not include allocation nor deallocation*. In fact, the most delicate was not to do proofs, but to find how the problem should be posed.

References

1. Abrial, J.-R.: Event Based Sequential Program Development: Application to Constructing a Pointer Program. In: Araki, K., Gnesi, S., Mandrioli, D. (eds.) FME 2003. LNCS, vol. 2805, pp. 51–74. Springer, Heidelberg (2003)
2. Bertot, Y., Casteran, P.: Interactive Theorem Proving and Program Development - Coq'Art: The Calculus of Inductive Constructions. Springer-Verlag (2004)
3. Bornat, R.: Proving Pointer Programs in Hoare Logic. In: Backhouse, R., Oliveira, J.N. (eds.) MPC 2000. LNCS, vol. 1837, pp. 102–126. Springer, Heidelberg (2000)
4. Broy, M., Pepper, P.: Combining Algebraic and Algorithmic Reasoning: An Approach to the Schorr-Waite Algorithm. ACM-TOPLAS 4(3), 362–381 (1982)
5. Bubel, R.: The schorr-waite-algorithm. In: Beckert, B., Hähnle, R., Schmitt, P.H. (eds.) Verification of Object-Oriented Software. LNCS (LNAI), vol. 4334, pp. 569–587. Springer, Heidelberg (2007)
6. Burstall, R.M.: Some techniques for proving correctness of programs which alters data structures. Machine Intelligence 7, 23–50 (1972)
7. Chlipala, A.: Mostly-automated verification of low-level programs in computational separation logic. In: PLDI, pp. 234–245 (2011)
8. de Roever, W.-P.: On Backtracking and Greatest Fixpoints. In: Salomaa, A., Steinby, M. (eds.) ICALP 1977. LNCS, vol. 52, pp. 412–429. Springer, Heidelberg (1977)
9. Dershowitz, N.: The Schorr-Waite Marking Algorithm Revisited. Inf. Proc. Lett. 11(3), 141–143 (1980)
10. Dufourd, J.-F.: Polyhedra genus theorem and Euler formula: A hypermap-formalized intuitionistic proof. Theor. Comp. Sci. 403(2-3), 133–159 (2008)
11. Dufourd, J.-F.: Dérivation de l'algorithme de Schorr-Waite en Coq par une méthode algébrique. In: JFLA 2012, INRIA (2012),
    http://hal.inria.fr/hal-00665909
12. Dufourd, J.-F.: Schorr-Waite Coq Development On-line Documentation (2013),
    http://dpt-info.u-strasbg.fr/~jfd/SW-LIB-PUBLI.tar.gz

13. Dufourd, J.-F.: Formal Study of Functional Orbits in Finite Domains, 35 pages (2013) (submitted)
14. Dufourd, J.-F.: Hypermap specification and certified linked implementation using orbits. In: Klein, G., Gamboa, R. (eds.) ITP 2014. LNCS, vol. 8558, pp. 242–257. Springer, Heidelberg (2014)
15. Giorgino, M., Strecker, M., Matthes, R., Pantel, M.: Verification of the schorr-waite algorithm – from trees to graphs. In: Alpuente, M. (ed.) LOPSTR 2010. LNCS, vol. 6564, pp. 67–83. Springer, Heidelberg (2011)
16. Filliâtre, J.-C.: Verifying two lines of C with why3: An exercise in program verification. In: Joshi, R., Müller, P., Podelski, A. (eds.) VSTTE 2012. LNCS, vol. 7152, pp. 83–97. Springer, Heidelberg (2012)
17. Gerhardt, S.L.: A derivation-oriented proof of the Schorr-Waite algorithm. In: Gerhart, S.L., et al. (eds.) Program Construction. LNCS, vol. 69, pp. 472–492. Springer, Heidelberg (1979)
18. Gonthier, G.: Formal Proof - The Four-Color Theorem. Notices of the AMS 55(11), 1382–1393 (2008)
19. Gries, D.: The Schorr-Waite Graph Marking Algorithm. Acta Informatica 11, 223–232 (1979)
20. Griffiths, M.: Development of the Schorr-Waite algorithm. In: Gerhart, S.L., Pair, C., Pepper, P.A., Wössner, H., Dijkstra, E.W., Guttag, J.V., Owicki, S.S., Partsch, H., Bauer, F.L., Gries, D., Griffiths, M., Horning, J.J., Wirsing, M. (eds.) Program Construction. LNCS, vol. 69, pp. 464–471. Springer, Heidelberg (1979)
21. Hackett, B., Rugina, R.: Region-Based Shape Analysis with Tracked Locations. In: 32nd ACM POPL 2005, pp. 310–323 (2005)
22. Hubert, T., Marché, C.: A case study of C source code verification; the Schorr-Waite algorithm. In: 3rd IEEE SEFM 2005, pp. 190–199 (2005)
23. Knuth, D.E.: The Art of Computer Programming: Fundamental Algorithms, vol. I. Add. -Wesley (1968)
24. Leino, K.R.M.: Dafny: An automatic program verifier for functional correctness. In: Clarke, E.M., Voronkov, A. (eds.) LPAR-16 2010. LNCS, vol. 6355, pp. 348–370. Springer, Heidelberg (2010)
25. Leroy, X., Blazy, S.: Formal Verification of a C-like Memory Model and Its Uses for Verifying Program Transformations. JAR 41(1), 1–31 (2008)
26. Loginov, A., Reps, T., Sagiv, M.: Automated verification of the deutsch-schorr-waite tree-traversal algorithm. In: Yi, K. (ed.) SAS 2006. LNCS, vol. 4134, pp. 261–279. Springer, Heidelberg (2006)
27. Mehta, F., Nipkow, T.: Proving pointer programs in higher-order logic. Info. and Comp. 199(1-2), 200–227 (2005)
28. Morris, J.M.: A Proof of the Schorr-Waite Algorithm. In: TFPM, vol. 91, pp. 43–51. NATO, D. Reidel (1982)
29. Preoteasa, V., Back, R.-J.: Invariant diagrams with data refinement. FAC 24(1), 67–95 (2012)
30. Reynolds, J.C.: Separation Logic: A Logic for Shared Mutable Data Structures. In: LICS 2002, pp. 55–74 (2002)
31. Schorr, H., Waite, W.R.: An Efficient Machine-Independent Procedure for Garbage Collection in Various List Structures. CACM 10(8), 501–506 (1967)
32. Suzuki, N.: Automatic Verification of Programs with Complex Data Structures. PhD Th., Dept. of CS, Stanford (1976)
33. Topor, R.W.: The Correctness of the Schorr-Waite List Marking Algorithm. Acta Inf. 11, 211–221 (1979)
34. Ward, M.: Derivation of Data Intensive Algorithms by Formal Transformation. IEEE-TOSE 22(9), 665–686 (1996)
35. Yang, H.: Relational separation logic. TCS 375(1-3), 308–334 (2007)

An LTL Model Checking Approach for Biological Parameter Inference

Emmanuelle Gallet[1], Matthieu Manceny[2],
Pascale Le Gall[1], and Paolo Ballarini[1]

[1] Laboratoire MAS, Ecole Centrale Paris, 92195 Châtenay-Malabry, France
{emmanuelle.gallet,pascale.legall,paolo.ballarini}@ecp.fr
[2] Laboratoire LISITE, ISEP, 28 Rue Notre-Dame-des-Champs 75006 Paris, France
matthieu.manceny@isep.fr

Abstract. The identification of biological parameters governing dynamics of Genetic Regulatory Networks (GRN) poses a problem of combinatorial explosion, since the possibilities of parameter instantiation
are numerous even for small networks. In this paper, we propose to
adapt LTL model checking algorithms to infer biological parameters
from biological properties given as LTL formulas. In order to reduce
the combinatorial explosion, we represent all the dynamics with one
parametric model, so that all GRN dynamics simply result from all
eligible parameter instantiations. LTL model checking algorithms are
adapted by postponing the parameter instantiation as far as possible.
Our approach is implemented within the SPuTNIk tool.

Keywords: LTL Model Checking, Parameter Identification, Symbolic
Execution, Genetic Regulatory Network, Thomas Discrete Modeling.

1 Introduction

Gene expression is a biological process where proteins are synthesized from
genes. These proteins can regulate the synthesis of other proteins provided that
their concentrations are sufficient. A collection of regulatory inter-dependencies
between genes/proteins is called a *Genetic Regulatory Network* (GRN). In this
paper we consider a discrete-state formalism, the René Thomas' formalism [2,
3, 6, 18, 19], according to which the amounts of proteins in a GRN are discrete
abstractions of continuous concentrations. Hence the overall evolution of protein
concentration along time, called the *dynamics* of the network, is captured by a
discrete-state transition system. Given a René Thomas GRN model, the main
interest is in analyzing the possible dynamics that may be associated to it.
However, from the dynamics point of view, a GRN on its own is an underspecified
type of representation: it represents the dependencies between a set of genes,
but it does not describe what effect the combination of all such dependencies
has on a given state of the network, hence on its evolution. The mapping of
a GRN model to a specific dynamic (i.e. a transition system) is achieved by
considering an instantiation of so-called *biological parameters*, i.e., a specification

S. Merz and J. Pang (Eds.): ICFEM 2014, LNCS 8829, pp. 155–170, 2014.

of the combined effect that all *activated regulators* have on a given state of the network. Since the number of possible instantiations of biological parameters is a double exponential function of the GRN *size* (in terms of number of genes and of interactions), the analysis of the possible dynamics associated to a GRN model is a complex task. In this paper we consider the application of formal methods, namely model checking [1], as a means to reason about the possible dynamics associated to a GRN specification. In particular we tackle the following problem: given a relevant behavior of interest, formally expressed in terms of a temporal logic property, say φ, we want to be able to automatically identify the biological parameters instances which give rise to dynamics complying with φ.

Related work. Model checking techniques have been widely advocated in several works to verify whether a given discrete Thomas model fulfills some relevant biological temporal properties. In [3] Bernot *et al.* expressed biological knowledge with *Computation Tree Logic* (CTL) formulas [1]. To exhaustively search the parameters' space, the set of all possible dynamics is generated and a CTL model checking procedure is iterated, one dynamics after the other. This approach is implemented in the SMBioNet tool [16] and has been illustrated in [8]. In [12], the approach has been extended to cope with the formation of complexes from proteins which allows modelers to express relationships between biological parameters leading to a reduced set of dynamics to be investigated. This work prefigures the interest of using constraints on the parameters. [2, 13] define an approach based on an encoding technique to share computations between different dynamics. Sets of dynamics are encoded by a binary vector, one bit (or color) per dynamics, and LTL model checking algorithms [1] are extended with Boolean operations on vectors. In [5, 6], the tool GNBox uses Constraint Logic Programming (CLP) techniques to identify parameters. GRN dynamics and biological knowledge are described by declarative rules and constraints on parameters, then target behaviors are expressed as some kind of finite paths that models have to verify. [9] also uses CLP techniques to adapt CTL model checking, but the encoding introduces a lot of fresh logical variables that hamper to scale up the method.

Our contribution. We propose a new approach that is based on a *parametric model*, called Parametric GRN (PGRN). This allows us to encompass all the dynamics of a GRN in a unique representation, biological parameters being processed as symbols, and to implement an efficient (on-the-fly) searching of (a symbolic representation of) the parameter's space. Similarly to [13], our approach is based on LTL model checking. While in, [13], LTL model checking algorithms are optimized for the particular case of *time series*, that are sequences of states made of one expression level per gene, observed one by one, we follow the same creed as the one advocated in [5, 6]: model sets are handled through some logical language both to avoid combinatorial explosion and to take benefit of constraint solving techniques. A preliminary version of our approach has been described in [14]. In the present version, algorithms combining symbolic execution and constraint solving techniques have been reengineered and tuned to be more efficient and cope with GRN features. Thereby, we consider the full

LTL language while [13] essentially focuses on time series and [5, 6] focuses on properties carrying on finite paths.

Paper organization. We reformulate the logical description of Thomas' modeling framework in section 2, and explain how we encode the set of dynamics of a GRN with Parametric GRN in section 3. Section 4 presents our adaptation of LTL model checking algorithms with symbolic execution techniques. In section 5, we briefly discuss the validity of our approach with our dedicated tool SPuTNIk. Finally, section 6 contains some concluding remarks.

2 Genetic Regulatory Networks

A Genetic Regulatory Network (GRN) is a collection of regulatory inter-dependencies between genes to represent the mechanism of gene expression, i.e. the biological process by means of which proteins are synthesized. Two kinds of interactions exist: activation or inhibition depending on whether the protein expressed from the source gene can enhance or reduce the expression of the target gene. Moreover, an interaction is effective only if the concentration of the source protein is sufficient, in other words if its *level of expression* is above a given threshold. From the modeling point of view, a gene g is assimilated to the protein it synthesizes. In particular, it inherits the protein's level of expression, denoted x_g, which, in this context, is abstractly represented by a non-negative integer ranging from 0 (absence of protein or very low concentration level) to a maximal value m_g. A GRN is classically represented by an *interaction graph*.

Definition 1 (Interaction graph). *An n-order interaction graph (IG) is a labeled directed graph $\Gamma = (G, I)$ where G is a finite set of gene nodes, $n = |G|$ and $I \subseteq G \times \{+, -\} \times \mathbb{N}^+ \times G$ is the set of interactions. Given $(g_1, s, t, g_2) \in I$, s indicates the effect of g_1 over g_2 (sign "+" for activation and "−" for inhibition) and t denotes the threshold of the interaction. Moreover, the following properties hold: i) $\forall (g_1, g_2) \in G^2$, there exists at most one interaction $(g_1, s, t, g_2) \in I$; ii) $\forall (g_1, s, t, g_2) \in I, t > 1 \Rightarrow \exists (g_1, s', t', g_3) \in I, t' = t - 1$.*

The threshold t of an interaction $(g_1, s, t, g_2) \in I$ indicates the minimal level that g_1 needs to be at in order to affect the expression of g_2. The condition on thresholds states that for any gene g_1 every intermediate threshold level must appear on at least an interaction arc originating in g_1. Since an interaction graph may contain at most one interaction between two genes, then for an interaction $(g_1, s, t, g_2) \in I$, we denote $s(g_1, g_2)$ its sign, and $t(g_1, g_2)$ its threshold. $m_g = max\{t \mid \exists (g, s, t, g') \in I\}$ is[1] the maximal level of expression of gene g, and $G^-(g) \subseteq G$ is the set of *regulators* of g (i.e. $G^-(g) = \{g'' \mid \exists (g'', s, t, g) \in I\}$).

A dynamics of a GRN corresponds to an evolution over time of the levels of expression of all genes, The *state space* describes the states that may be observed during such a possible evolution.

---

[1] m_g is equal to 1 if there does not exist edges outgoing from g.

Definition 2 (State space of an interaction graph). *For $\Gamma = (G, I)$ an interaction graph we define $\mathbb{X} = \prod_{g \in G} \mathbb{X}_g$ the state space underlying Γ, where $\mathbb{X}_g = \{0, ..., m_g\}$ is the set of possible levels of expression for gene g.*

Example 1 (Interaction graph and state space). Figure 1 presents a two-genes interaction graph Γ_0 where gene α is both an activator of β and of itself (self-activator) while β is an inhibitor of α. In particular α activates the expression of β whenever its level of expression is at least 1, while when its level of expression is at least 2 it activates both itself and β. The thresholds of Γ_0 induce the following sets of levels for the two genes, $\mathbb{X}_\alpha = \{0, 1, 2\}$ and $\mathbb{X}_\beta = \{0, 1\}$, hence the state space $\mathbb{X} = \{(0, 0), (0, 1), (1, 0), (1, 1), (2, 0), (2, 1)\}$.

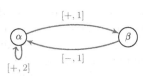

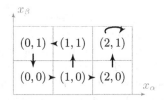

Fig. 1. Γ_0: an example of a two-genes interaction graph.

Fig. 2. *Dynamics $\mathcal{D}_K$ induced by the parameters mapping K*

For Γ an interaction graph with state space $\mathbb{X}$, we denote $\mathcal{D} = (\mathbb{X}, \rightarrow)$ a generic transition system[2] called *dymanics* of Γ. With respect to $\mathcal{D}$, Γ can be regarded as an underspecified formalism: from Γ, on its own, one cannot devise any concrete dynamics $\mathcal{D}$. To obtain a dynamics for Γ we need to describe for each gene g the effect that any subset of its regulators $\omega \subseteq G^-(g)$ would have on g. This is achieved by associating *biological parameters* with Γ.

Definition 3 (Biological parameters). *For g a gene of $\Gamma = (G, I)$, the set of biological parameters of g is $\mathbb{K}_g = \{K_g(\omega) \mid \omega \subseteq 2^{G^-(g)}\}$ and the set of all biological parameters of Γ is $\mathbb{K} = \cup_{g \in G} \mathbb{K}_g$.*

An instantiation of biological parameters is defined by any mapping $K : \mathbb{K} \rightarrow \cup_{g \in G} \mathbb{X}_g$ associating to any parameter $K_g(\omega)$ a value in $\mathbb{X}_g$. Any instantiation $K : \mathbb{K} \rightarrow \cup_{g \in G} \mathbb{X}_g$ defines a mapping $\mathcal{K} : \otimes_{g \in G} 2^{G^-(g)} \rightarrow \mathbb{X}$ verifying $\forall (\omega_{g_1}, ..., \omega_{g_n}) \in \otimes_{g \in G} 2^{G^-(g)}, \mathcal{K}((\omega_{g_1}, ..., \omega_{g_n})) = (K(K_{g_1}(\omega_{g_1})), ..., K(K_{g_n}(\omega_{g_n})))$ (with $G = \{g_1, ..., g_n\}$).

In the sequel, for simplicity purpose, an instantiation K associating the value x to the parameter $K_g(\omega)$ will be simply given by the equality $K_g(\omega) = x$.

The *biological parameters* of an IG indicate the values the genes of the GRN tend towards when a certain n-tuple of regulators is activated. Thus to obtain the *dynamics $\mathcal{D}_K$* corresponding to parameters K we need to know what regulators

---

[2] A transition system (E, R) verifies that R is a binary relation on $E \times E$.

are activated in a state $x \in \mathbb{X}$. We say that a set of regulators $\omega \subseteq G^-(g)$ of gene g is activated in state $x = (x_1, \ldots, x_n) \in \mathbb{X}$, denoted $(x_1, \ldots, x_n) \models \omega$, iff $\left(\bigwedge_{g' \in \omega} x_{g'} \geq t(g', g) \wedge \bigwedge_{g' \in G^-(g) \setminus \omega} x_{g'} < t(g', g) \right)$, that is: if and only for every regulator $g' \in \omega$ the corresponding component $x_{g'}$ of state x is above the corresponding activation threshold (i.e., $x_{g'} \geq t(g', g)$) while no other regulator of g does. In the remainder we denote $ActR : \mathbb{X} \to \otimes_{g \in G} 2^{G^-(g)}$ the function that maps each state x into the corresponding n-tuples of activated regulators for the n genes of a GRN. In the remainder, for $x \in \mathbb{X}$, we denote $x[x_g \uparrow]$ (resp. $x[x_g \downarrow]$) the state resulting from x by increasing (resp. decreasing) the x_g component of one unit.

Definition 4 (dynamics induced by an instantiation of parameters).
For $\Gamma = (G, I)$ an n-order IG, $K : \mathbb{K} \to \cup_{g \in G} \mathbb{X}_g$ a set of biological parameters of Γ, we define $\mathcal{D}_K = (\mathbb{X}, \to_K)$ the dynamics (transition system) of Γ induced by K. The transition relation $\to_K \subseteq \mathbb{X} \times \mathbb{X}$ is minimally defined as follows: $\forall x = (x_1, \ldots x_n) \in \mathbb{X}$ let $x^* = (x_1^*, \ldots, x_n^*) = \mathcal{K} \circ ActR((x_1, \ldots, x_n))$:

- *if $x \neq x^*$ then $\forall i, 1 \leq i \leq n$*
  - *if $x_i < x_i^*$, then $x \to_K x[x_i \uparrow]$ (increment gene i)*
  - *if $x_i > x_i^*$, then $x \to_K x[x_i \downarrow]$ (decrement gene i)*
- *else if $x = x^*$ then $x \to_K x$ (self-loop)*

Then for each state $x \in \mathbb{X}$ we determine the corresponding attractor state x^* (by application of the parameters mapping $\mathcal{K}$ to the regulators activated in x i.e., $x^* = \mathcal{K} \circ ActR(x)$). If the attractor state x^* is different from x then for each different component $x_i \neq x_i^*$ we add either an increment or a decrement transition in $\to_K$. Conversely if $x^* = x$ we add a self-loop in $\to_K$.

Example 2 (Biological parameters and Dynamics). The subsets of regulators for the two genes of Γ_0 (Figure 1) are $2^{G^-(\alpha)} = \{\{\}, \{\alpha\}, \{\beta\}, \{\alpha, \beta\}\}$, resp. $2^{G^-(\beta)} = \{\{\}, \{\alpha\}\}$ hence the biological parameters of Γ_0 are: $\mathbb{K} = \{K_\alpha(\{\}), K_\alpha(\{\alpha\}), K_\alpha(\{\beta\}), K_\alpha(\{\alpha, \beta\}), K_\beta(\{\}), K_\beta(\{\alpha\})\}$. According to $\models$ the association between states of $\mathbb{X}$ and n-tuples of activated regulators is: $(0, 0) \models (\{\}, \{\}), (0, 1) \models (\{\beta\}, \{\}), (1, 0) \models (\{\}, \{\alpha\}), (1, 1) \models (\{\beta\}, \{\alpha\}), (2, 0) \models (\{\alpha\}, \{\alpha\}), (2, 1) \models (\{\alpha, \beta\}, \{\alpha\})$. As an example we consider the following mapping (instantiation) of the parameters for gene α and β into corresponding target levels: $K_\alpha(\{\}) = 2$, $K_\alpha(\{\alpha\}) = 2$, $K_\alpha(\{\beta\}) = 0$, $K_\alpha(\{\alpha, \beta\}) = 2$, $K_\beta(\{\}) = 0$ and $K_\beta(\{\alpha\}) = 1$ yielding the combined mapping $K = K_\alpha \times K_\beta = \{(\{\}, \{\}) \to (2, 0), (\{\{\}, \{\alpha\}) \to (2, 1), \ldots, (\{\alpha, \beta\}, \{\alpha\}) \to (2, 1)\}$ Figure 2 shows the *dynamics* $\mathcal{D}_K$ yielded by the parameters mapping K.

A parameters mapping K for an IG Γ yields a dynamics $\mathcal{D}_K$. However some mappings K may result into inconsistent dynamics. To rule out inconsistent dynamics, mapping must comply with the following constraints.

Definition 5 (Constraints for parameters mapping). *Let $\Gamma = (G, I)$ be an IG. Definition constraint: $\forall g \in G, \forall g' \in G^-(g), \forall \omega \subseteq G^-(g) \setminus \{g'\}$: if $s(g', g) = +$*

then $K_g(\omega) \le K_g(\omega \cup \{g'\})$, if $s(g',g) = -$ then $K_g(\omega) \ge K_g(\omega \cup \{g'\})$. Observation constraint: $\forall g \in G$, $\forall g' \in G^-(g)$, there exists $\omega \subseteq G^-(g) \setminus \{g'\}$: if $S(g',g) = +$ then $K_g(\omega) < K_g(\omega \cup \{g'\})$, if $s(g',g) = -$ then $K_g(\omega) > K_g(\omega \cup \{g'\})$. Min/Max constraint: $\forall g \in G$, $K_g(\{g'|g' \in G^-(g), s(g',g) = -\}) = 0$ and $K_g(\{g'|g' \in G^-(g), s(g',g) = +\}) = m_g$.

The *Definition constraint* (or Snoussi constraint [17]) states that if the level of expression of a gene g' which activates (resp. inhibits) a gene g becomes greater than its threshold, then the expression level of g cannot decrease (resp. increase). The *Observation constraint* expresses how we identify regulators. If g' is an activator (resp. inhibitor) of g, then there exists at least one dynamic state where the increase of the level of expression of g' leads to an increase (resp. decrease) of the expression level of g. Finally, the *Min/Max constraint* states that in a dynamic state where all the activators (resp. inhibitors) of a gene are above the threshold and simultaneously none of the inhibitors (resp. activators) is, then the level of expression of the attractor of the gene is maximum (resp. minimum).

Example 3. The *Constraints* for IG Γ_0 (Figure 1) correspond to the following conditions: $K_\alpha(\{\alpha\}) = 2$, $K_\alpha(\{\beta\}) = 0$, $K_\beta(\{\}) = 0$, $K_\beta(\{\alpha\}) = 1$, $(K_\alpha(\{\}) < 2 \lor 0 < K_\alpha(\alpha,\beta))$ and $(K_\alpha(\{\}) > 0 \lor 2 > K_\alpha(\alpha,\beta))$. Notice that amongst the 324 possible parameter mappings[3] for Γ_0, only 7 are consistent with the *Constraints* for Γ_0.

Even if these constraints are well-founded, there are not always considered by biologists. In the sequel, by default, they will be considered and generically denoted as C_I, but they can be relaxed on demand.

3   Modeling Dynamics with Parametric GRN

In order to study all the dynamics simultaneously, we represent them all through a single (meta)model, called *Parametric GRN* (PGRN), i.e. a facility of transition systems parameterized by the biological parameters.

Parametric GRN. A PGRN is a transition system associated with an interaction graph $\Gamma = (G, I)$. It involves two families of symbols: the biological parameters $\mathbb{K} = \{K_g(\omega) \mid g \in G, \omega \subseteq 2^{G^-(g)}\}$ and the state variables $\mathbb{G} = \{x_g | g \in G\}$. Note that, according to the context, x_g will denote either a state variable or a value representing a concentration level.

The main idea is to encode state evolution with transitions parameterized by parameters of $\mathbb{K}$. A PGRN is composed of two states: T (transient) corresponding to configurations such that at least one gene can change its current level, and S (stable) corresponding to situations where no change is possible for any gene. A transition of a PGRN is characterized by a guard (a condition

---

[3] The number of possible parameters instantiation is equal to $\prod_{g \in G} (m_g + 1)^{2^{|G^-(g)|}}$.

over parameters $\mathbb{K}$ and state variables of $\mathbb{G}$) and an assignment (an application $\mathbb{X} \to \mathbb{X}$ expressing how states of a dynamics evolve). For example, transition $T \xrightarrow{(x_\alpha<2 \wedge x_\beta=0 \wedge x_\alpha<K_\alpha(\{\}))[x_\alpha\uparrow]} T$ (see Fig. 3) indicates that for any (transient) state $x \in \mathbb{X}$ such that $x_\beta=0$, $x_\alpha<2$ and $x_\alpha<K_\alpha(\{\})$ then a transition corresponding to an increase of the level of α exists.

More precisely, for each gene g, there is a transition from T to T for each kind of variation (increase or decrease) of x_g. For $\omega \subseteq G^-(g)$ a subset of regulators of g, let us introduce the predicate $P_g(\omega) : \mathbb{X} \to \{\top, \bot\}$ defined by: $(\bigwedge_{g'\in\omega} x_{g'} \geq t(g',g)) \wedge (\bigwedge_{g'\in G^-(g)\setminus\omega} x_{g'} < t(g',g))$. $P_g(\omega)$ characterises the set of states in which regulators ω are the only effective ones on g. The transition associated to the increase of x_g is conditioned by the guard $Increase(g) = \bigvee_{\omega\subseteq G^-(g)}(P_g(\omega) \wedge x_g < K_g(\omega))$. Similarly, the transition associated to the decrease of x_g is conditioned by the guard $Decrease(g) = \bigvee_{\omega\subseteq G^-(g)}(P_g(\omega) \wedge x_g > K_g(\omega))$. Finally there is one transition from T to S when the expression level of all genes remains stable, *i.e.* if any gene g satisfies the condition $Stable(g) = \bigwedge_{\omega\subseteq G^-(g)} (P_g(\omega) \wedge x_g = K_g(\omega))$, and one last transition from S to S where the guard is always true.

Definition 6 (PGRN). *A PGRN associated to an interaction graph $\Gamma = (G, I)$ is a pair $P = (Q_P, \delta_P)$ with $Q_P = \{T, S\}$ the set of states and δ_P a set of transitions. A transition of δ_P is of the form (q_P, g_P, a_P, q'_P), also denoted $q_P \xrightarrow{(g_P)[a_P]} q'_P$, with q_P and q'_P states of Q_P, g_P a guard, i.e. a formula over $\mathbb{K}\cup\mathbb{G}$ and a_P an assignment, i.e. an application $\mathbb{X} \to \mathbb{X}$. More precisely, δ_P is the set of all following transitions:*

- $(T, Increase(g), x_g\uparrow, T)$ *with g in G,*
- $(T, Decrease(g), x_g\downarrow, T)$ *with g in G,*
- $(T, \bigwedge_{g\in G}Stable(g), id, S)$ *where id is the identity assignment,*
- $(S, \top, id, S)$ *where $\top$ indicates the guard always true.*

Let us remark that unfolded versions of guards can be rather long and complex, but in the best cases they can be simplified by application of the initial constraints C_I. Nevertheless, generally, the most complex guard is the one labelling the transition $T \to S$ since it corresponds to the conjunction of all $Stable(g)$ conditions. On the other hand, once in S, the guard of the only possible transition $(S \to S)$ is simply true ($\top$). Moreover, transitions involving disjunctions in their guard can be split. Indeed, transition $(T, g_P \vee g'_P, a_P, T)$ can be equivalently split in (T, g_P, a_P, T) and (T, g'_P, a_P, T).

Example 4 (PGRN). Fig. 3 represents the PGRN associated with the interaction graph of Fig. 1. In relation with the different possible subsets ω, one can explicit the different guards: e.g. $Increase(\beta) \equiv (x_\alpha < 1 \wedge x_\beta < K_\beta(\{\})) \vee (x_\alpha \geq 1 \wedge x_\beta < K_\beta(\{\alpha\})))$. The Initial constraints C_I (cf. Def 5) can be used to simplify the guards: e.g. C_I implies $K_\beta(\{\}) = 0$ and $K_\beta(\{\}) = 1$ and then $Increase(\beta) \equiv (x_\alpha > 0 \wedge x_\beta = 0)$.

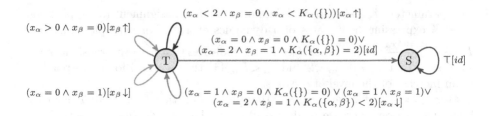

Fig. 3. PGRN associated to the interaction graph in Figure 1

Annotated dynamics. A PGRN characterizes a set of dynamics, one for each possible instantiation of biological parameters, that is, for any parameter mapping $K : \mathbb{K} \to \cup_{g \in G} \mathbb{X}_g$. For g_P a transition guard of a PGRN, $x \in \mathbb{X}$ a state of the corresponding GRN, and K an instance of biological parameters, we denotes $[\![g_P]\!]_{x,K}$ the instance of g_P obtained by substituting g_P's state variables and g_P's biological parameters with the corresponding state value of x, and parameter values of K. Similarly, we denote $[\![g_P]\!]_x$ the resulting substitution only of g_P's state variables (parameters in $\mathbb{K}$ remain symbolic).

Definition 7 (Annotated Dynamics). *Let $P = (Q_P, \delta_P)$ be a PGRN associated with an interaction graph $\Gamma = (G, I)$, and let $K : \mathbb{K} \to \cup_{g \in G} \mathbb{X}_g$. The annotated dynamics associated to P and K is a pair $D_K = (Q_D, \delta_D)$ where the set of states $Q_D \subset Q_P \times \mathbb{X}$ and the set of transitions $\delta_D \subset Q_D \times Q_D$ are mutually defined by: $\forall x \in \mathbb{X}, (T, x) \in Q_D$ and for all $(q_P, x) \in Q_D$ and $(q_P, g_P, a_P, q_P') \in \delta_P$ s.t. $[\![g_P]\!]_{x,K}$ is evaluated to True, then $(q_P', a_P(x)) \in Q_D$ and $((q_P, x), (q_P', a_P(x))) \in \delta_D$.*

Example 5 (Annotated Dynamics). Figure 4 presents one possible annotated dynamics for the PGRN represented in Figure 3, with the following instantiation of parameters: $K_\alpha(\{\}) = 2$, $K_\alpha(\{\alpha\}) = 2$, $K_\alpha(\{\beta\}) = 0$, $K_\alpha(\{\alpha, \beta\}) = 2$, $K_\beta(\{\}) = 0$ and $K_\beta(\{\alpha\}) = 1$.

$$(T, (0,1)) \leftarrow (T, (1,1)) \qquad (T, (2,1)) \rightarrow (S, (2,1))$$
$$\downarrow \qquad\qquad \uparrow \qquad\qquad\qquad \uparrow$$
$$(T, (0,0)) \rightarrow (T, (1,0)) \rightarrow (T, (2,0))$$

Fig. 4. A possible annotated dynamics for the PGRN in Figure 3

By construction, for a given instantiation $K : \mathbb{K} \to \cup_{g \in G} \mathbb{X}_g$, the associated annotated dynamics D_K corresponds to the dynamics $\mathcal{D}_K$ of the underlying IG Γ induced by the instantiation K (cf Def 4). For a transition $((q_P, x), (q_P', a_P(x)))$ in δ_D, it suffices to give up the first component and keep the second one, $x \mapsto a_P(x)$, to retrieve a dynamics of Γ. Thus, the dynamics represented in Fig. 2

can be obtained from the annotated dynamics of Fig. 4. The first component (T or S) is somehow a technical artifact annotating the presence of a stable state when building sequences of consecutive states. Depending on the context, we will assimilate $\mathcal{D}_K$ and D_K or will work with the most appropriate of the two forms. Motivated by efficiency considerations, we will apply a specific treatment for states x already recognized as stable, that is, annotated by S.

4   Adapting LTL Model-Checking to PGRN

The classical approach of LTL model-checking [15] consists in confronting a model (e.g. a dynamics) against an LTL formula. To do so, the negation of the LTL formula is transformed into a Büchi automaton and the product between the automaton and the dynamics is computed. We then look for accepting paths in the product by checking the existence of reachable cycles containing at least an accepting state. Model checking is usually time consuming, and since the number of dynamics is large, this method is not applicable in our case. To avoid the combinatorial explosion, we want to check all the dynamics simultaneously, i.e. we check directly the PGRN. To do so, we first build the Parametric Product between the PGRN and the Büchi Automaton associated to the LTL formula φ. We then use symbolic execution technics in order to search for accepting cycles. As a result, we obtain a set of constraints C that a parameter instantiation K must fulfill such that the associated dynamics $\mathcal{D}_K$ verifies φ.

Büchi Automaton and Parametric Product. Biological properties on a sequence of states can be expressed using LTL formulas built from a set of atomic propositions using the usual logical operators in $\{\top, \bot, \neg, \wedge, \vee\}$ and the temporal operators **X** (for neXt time), **G** (Globally), **F** (Finally) and **U** (Until) [1]. Since we need to express biological knowledge on levels of expression of genes, atomic propositions are of the form $x_g \bowtie c$ where x_g denotes the level of expression of a gene g, $\bowtie \in \{=, \neq, <, >, \leq, \geq\}$ and $c \in \mathbb{N}$. Any LTL formula φ can be translated into a Büchi automaton $B(\varphi)$.

Definition 8 (Büchi Automaton associated to an LTL formula). *Let Γ be a GRN and φ an LTL formula over the levels of expression of genes of Γ. A Büchi Automaton associated to φ is a tuple $B(\varphi) = (Q_B, q_B^0, A_B, \delta_B)$ where Q_B is the set of states, $q_B^0 \in Q_B$ is the initial state, $A_B \subseteq Q_B$ is the set of accepting states and δ_B is the set of transitions. A transition of δ_B is of the form (q_B, g_B, q_B') with q_B and q_B' states of Q_B and g_B a non temporal formula over the levels of expressions of genes in Γ. Moreover, $B(\varphi)$ is such that an infinite sequence of states provided with truth values for all atomic propositions (a path) verifies φ iff this path is accepted by $B(\varphi)$, i.e. iff this path contains at least a so-called accepting state infinitely often.*

Example 6 (LTL formula and associated Büchi automaton). The existence of a steady state (*i.e.* a state which is itself its only own successor) in $(x_\alpha, x_\beta) = (2, 1)$ corresponds to the LTL formula $\mathbf{G}((x_\alpha = 2 \wedge x_\beta = 1) \rightarrow \mathbf{X}(x_\alpha = 2 \wedge x_\beta = 1))$. Fig. 5 presents a Büchi Automaton associated to the negation of this formula.

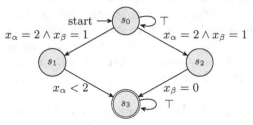

Fig. 5. $B(\neg\varphi)$ with $\varphi \equiv \mathbf{G}\big((x_\alpha = 2 \wedge x_\beta = 1) \Rightarrow \mathbf{X}(x_\alpha = 2 \wedge x_\beta = 1)\big)$

Definition 9 (Parametric Product). *Let* $P = (Q_P, \delta_P)$ *be a PGRN and* $B(\neg\varphi) = (Q_B, q_B^0, A_B, \delta_B)$ *a Büchi Automaton associated to the LTL formula* $\neg\varphi$. *The product* $\Pi = P \otimes B(\neg\varphi)$ *is the tuple* $(Q_\Pi, q_\Pi^0, A_\Pi, \delta_\Pi)$ *with* $Q_\Pi = Q_P \times Q_B$ *the set of vertices,* $q_\Pi^0 = (T, q_B^0)$ *the initial vertex,* $A_\Pi = Q_P \times A_B$ *the set of accepting vertices, and* δ_Π *the set of transitions. A transition of* δ_Π *is of the form* $(q_\Pi, g_\Pi, a_P, q_\Pi')$ *with* $q_\Pi = (q_P, q_B)$, $q_\Pi' = (q_P', q_B')$, $g_\Pi = g_P \wedge g_B$ *such that* $(q_P, g_P, a_P, q_P') \in \delta_P$, $(q_B, g_B, q_B') \in \delta_B$ *and* g_Π *is satisfiable.*

Example 7. The product of the PGRN in Fig. 3 and the Büchi Automaton in Fig. 5 is represented in Fig. 6. The product has been simplified by removing output transitions whose guard on expression levels is not satisfiable according to the guards and assignments of the input transitions of the same vertex; we also remove the transitions whose guard is not satisfiable according to the guards on parameters necessarily crossed (ϕ_{2_1} and ϕ_{2_2} here). Finally, we remove vertices which can not be reached and those belonging to a terminal cycle without accepting vertex.

Search for Parametric Accepting Cycles. The search for accepting cycles is based on symbolic execution techniques which are program analysis techniques. The key point is the substitution of actual values by symbolic variables in order to symbolically perform computations. Each execution (or path) of the program associates to each variable a symbolic computation together with a *path condition* that expresses what are the conditions on input values to execute the given path. Symbolic execution techniques has been extended to symbolic transition systems [11] by unfolding transition systems as symbolic trees. As symbolic execution is only applicable for finite paths, selection criteria are used to cut infinite paths when considering testing. In the sequel, we will take particular care to cut infinite paths in identifying situations of return on a node already encountered. Indeed such situations reveal the presence of cycles.

In the symbolic execution of the parametric product Π, the parameters $K_g(\omega)$ are handled as symbolic variables (i.e. not evaluated), and Π is unfolded leading to the construction of several *Symbolic Execution Trees* (SET), one for any $x \in \mathbb{X}$.

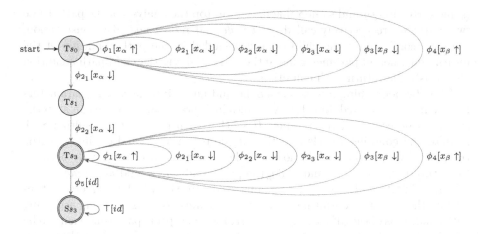

Fig. 6. Parametric product $P \otimes B(\neg\varphi)$ associated to the *Parametric GRN* in Figure 3 and the Büchi Automaton in Figure 5 (after simplification), with:

$\phi_1 \equiv x_\alpha < 2 \wedge x_\beta = 0 \wedge x_\alpha < K_\alpha(\{\})$ $\phi_3 \equiv x_\alpha = 0 \wedge x_\beta = 1$

$\phi_{2_1} \equiv x_\alpha = 2 \wedge x_\beta = 1 \wedge K_\alpha(\{\alpha, \beta\}) < 2$ $\phi_4 \equiv x_\alpha > 0 \wedge x_\beta = 0$

$\phi_{2_2} \equiv x_\alpha = 1 \wedge x_\beta = 1$ $\phi_5 \equiv x_\alpha = 0 \wedge x_\beta = 0 \wedge K_\alpha(\{\}) = 0.$

$\phi_{2_3} \equiv x_\alpha = 1 \wedge x_\beta = 0 \wedge K_\alpha(\{\}) = 0$

Definition 10 (Symbolic Execution Tree). *Let* $\Pi = (Q_\Pi, q_\Pi^0, A_\Pi, \delta_\Pi)$ *be a parametric product. The Symbolic Execution Tree associated to* Π *and* $x \in \mathbb{X}$ *is a transition system* (Q_T, δ_T) *where the set of* nodes Q_T *and the set of transitions* $\delta_T \subset Q_T \times Q_T$ *are mutually defined by:* $(q_\Pi^0, x, \top) \in Q_T$ *and for all* $q_T = (q_\Pi, x, pc) \in Q_T$, *for all* $(q_\Pi, g_\Pi, a_P, q'_\Pi) \in \delta_\Pi$ *such that* $pc' = pc \wedge [\![g_\Pi]\!]_x \neq \bot$, *then* $q'_T = (q'_\Pi, a_P(x), pc') \in Q_T$ *and* $(q_T, q'_T) \in \delta_T$. *If* $q_\Pi \in A_\Pi$, *then the node is said to be* accepting.

For any node $(q_\Pi, x, pc) \in Q_T$ with $q_\Pi = (q_P, q_B) \in Q_P \times Q_B$, pc is the *path condition* in the form of a constraint over parameters in $\mathbb{K}$. It defines the set of annotated dynamics D that can reach the state (q_P, x) from the state in $Q_P \times \mathbb{X}$ associated to the ancestor of (q_Π, x, pc). With the process described in the section 3, D itself allows the definition of the set of dynamics of the corresponding GRN which can reach all the states associated to nodes of the node path along the same sequence of traversed states. By construction, path conditions expressed over parameters increase along paths of SET and reduce the number of dynamics compatible with the path under construction.

Biological properties are expressed along infinite sequences, and thus, paths of the product and paths of SET are also infinite. But, by disregarding path conditions, the number of possible nodes in a SET is finite[4]. So, when we are building a new node (q_Π, x, pc') whereas it is descendant of a node (q_Π, x, pc)

---

[4] it is bounded by the product of all combinations of levels of expression, the number of vertices of the Büchi automaton and the number of vertices (2) of the PGRN.

(same vertex in Q_Π and same value in $\mathbb{X}$), we stop the analysis of the path; these two nodes are respectively called *child node* and *return node*. By construction, the path condition of the child node is included in the path condition of the return node, i.e. all parameter instantiations satisfying the child path condition also satisfy the return path condition.

Thus, by performing a mixed symbolic and numerical execution (parameters in $\mathbb{K}$ remain unchanged and state variables in $\mathbb{X}$ are evaluated), we can stop the execution procedure of the product Π so that each path of the resulting SET is finite and contains a cycle (starting at the return node and ending with the transition leading to the child node). If there exists an accepting node between the return node and the child node, the path condition is said *accepting*.

Once all finite SET are built, it remains to compute for which parameter instantiations there exist accepting paths. For that, it suffices to consider every accepting path conditions of the SET associated to Π. Each accepting path condition can be satisfied by (at least) one instantiation of parameters in $\mathbb{K}$, it means that there exists a path in Π going infinitely often through the associated cycle, and thus passing infinitely often by an accepting state. And so there exists a path in the dynamics corresponding to this accepting path condition verifying $\neg\varphi$.

Thus, instantiations of parameters verifying the conjunction of the negation of every accepting path condition of the SET associated to Π correspond to the dynamics such that there is no path verifying $\neg\varphi$, in other words, all paths verify φ. Note that the obtained dynamics verify φ along *all* paths; if the model must verify φ only on *at least one* path, our approach remains adequate with a small adaptation: to do this, we have to get the disjunction of all accepting path conditions of the SET associated to the product $P \otimes B(\varphi)$.

Example 8. For the Product in Figure 6, there are two solutions after computation; the corresponding values of parameters are: $K_\alpha(\{\}) = 1$ or 2, $K_\alpha(\{\alpha\}) = 2$, $K_\alpha(\{\beta\}) = 0$, $K_\alpha(\{\alpha, \beta\}) = 2$, $K_\beta(\{\}) = 0$ and $K_\beta(\{\alpha\}) = 1$. One of the corresponding dynamics (with $K_\alpha(\{\}) = 2$) is represented in Figure 2.

Algorithm of Traversal of SET. Algorithm 1, based on a *Depth First Search* schema, gives an overview of how we practically compute the accepting path conditions. We use three global variables: the parametric product Π, the list of accepting path conditions $acceptingPC$, and the list $nodesList$ of SET nodes which have already been analyzed.

Starting with a SET node, line 2 to line 4 test and compute its successors, as explained in the "Symbolic Execution Trees" part of section 4. Three tests are then performed successively. Firstly, if the path condition of the successor node is already known, it cannot provide additional information (the pc becomes more specific every depth call), and we stop the study of this successor (line 5). Secondly, line 7 tests if one of the ancestors of the successor is a return node (ancestor with the same vertex and state). If it is the case, then there is an infinite cycle between them and, if there is an accepting node in that cycle, then the successor node is an accepting return node, and its path condition is added to the list *accepting_PCs* (lines 8 to 9). Thirdly, if the successor is not a return

Algorithm 1. Overview of DFS((q_Π, x, pc), $ancestorsList$)

Data: global $\Pi = (Q_\Pi, q^0{}_\Pi, A_\Pi, \delta_\Pi)$, global $acceptingPC$, global $nodesList$

1 $ancestorsList$.add((q_Π, x, pc));

2 **forall the** $(q_\Pi, g_\Pi, a_P, q'_\Pi) \in \delta_\Pi$ **do**   // calculation of all successors

3      $pc' \leftarrow pc \wedge [\![g_\Pi]\!]_x$;   // pc of the new node

4   **if** $pc' \neq \bot$ **then**   // the transition can be crossed

5   **if** $pc' \not\subseteq acceptingPC$ **then**   // pc not included in the analyzed
            $accepting\ pc$

6              $x' \leftarrow a_P(x)$;   // state of the new node

7   **if** $\exists(q'_\Pi, x', pc'') \in ancestorsList$ **then** // an ancestor of the new
                node is a return node

8   **if** $\exists(q'''_\Pi \in A_\Pi, x''', pc''') \in [(q'_\Pi, x', pc''), \ldots, (q_\Pi, x', pc')] \subset$
                    $ancestorsList$ **then** // a descendant of the return node is
                    accepting

9                      $acceptingPC$.add(pc')

10   **else if** $\nexists(q'_\Pi, x', pc'''') \in nodesList$ with $pc' \subset pc''''$ **then**   // no
                copy node: recall of DFS()

11   DFS((q'_Π, x', pc'), $ancestorsList$);

12                 $nodesList$.add((q'_Π, x', pc'));

---

node, we check (line 10) if the node corresponds to a node in *nodesList* with the same vertex, the same state and the same or a more general path condition. If it is not the case (no *copy node*), then the DFS function is recalled with the successor node in argument (line 11), which is then added to *nodesList* (line 12).

Transient and Stable. Nodes of the tree are of the form (q_Π, x, pc) with $q_\Pi = (q_P, q_B) \in Q_P \times Q_B$. According to the value of q_P (either T or S, from the PGRN), we say that the node is either *transient* or *stable*. By construction of the PGRN, the target vertices of all transitions outgoing from a stable vertex are vertices of the same type, hence the appellation *stable*. Furthermore, the guards of the transitions between the stable vertices are always of the form $g_\Pi = g_P \wedge g_B$ with $g_P = \top$, and the assignment of the transitions is $a_P = id$ (identity assignment). Thus a specific treatment can be provided for the stable nodes, briefly described in the sequel.

In the algorithm 1, the line 11 can be split in two calls, one for the current function and another for the specific treatment of stable nodes (called if the successor node is stable, called *stable root* in the sequel). In this case, the second argument of the function, the list of ancestors, is an empty list since none of the previous ancestors (all transient) can be a return node of a stable node. According to the characteristics of the transitions between stable vertices mentioned above, for the treatment of stable nodes there is no need to test if the path condition is already known (line 5, already tested with the corresponding stable root), there is no guard on parameters to symbolically verify and no

substitution of levels of expression (lines 3 to 4), and there is no update of the
state to do (line 6). Furthermore, if a node is accepting then all the explorations
of the SET from the stable root can be stopped; indeed, its path condition is
identical to all path conditions of the nodes which can be built from it.

5   Assessment

The methodology described above has been implemented in a prototype software
tool called SPuTNIk. SPuTNIk is written in Java and relies on the Z3 constraint
solver [7] to check the satisfiability of path conditions during the traversal of SET
and on the ltl2ba and LTL2BA4J libraries [4,10] to generate a Büchi Automaton
of minimal size from an LTL formula. To validate our approach with SPuTNIk,
we have considered a common biological case study: the analysis of the genetic
network that controls the life cycle of the λ phage virus [19]. The λ phage can
infect the *E. coli* bacterium with two different outcomes: either it integrates the
genome of the host through a process called *lysogeny* or it enters a *lytic* phase
where it kills the residing cell to reproduce itself. We based our approach on
the λ phage model studied in [13] by Klarner *et al.* and composed of four genes,
denoted cI, cII, cro and N, and ten interactions described Fig. 7.

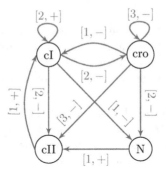

Fig. 7. The interaction graph G_λ for the λ phage

Klarner *et al.* describe biological properties as *time series*: a sequence of
specific states given in the form $\theta \equiv s_1, *, s_2, *, \ldots, *, s_n$ where s_i is the ith
observed state while $*$ denotes a possibly empty sequence of unspecified states.
Times series are equivalent to LTL formulas of the form $\phi \equiv s_1 \wedge \mathbf{F}(s_2 \wedge \mathbf{F}(\cdots \wedge \mathbf{F}(s_n)\ldots))$ (i.e. only composed of $\wedge$ and $\mathbf{F}$ operators). Moreover, the states
of time series are fully determined, each level of expression corresponds to a
single value. For example for G_λ, each state is a quadruple $(x_{cI}, x_{cII}, x_{cro}, x_N) \in \{0, 1, 2\} \times \{0, 1\} \times \{0, 1, 2, 3\} \times \{0, 1\}$). Given a time series θ and an interaction
graph, the goal of Klarner *et al.* is to find out all models which contain at least
one path matching θ (i.e. passing through the states of θ in the correct order).
Klarner *et al.* distinguish the following states: $init \equiv [0000]$, $lyt_1 \equiv [0021]$,

$lyt_2 \equiv [0020]$, $lyt_3 \equiv [0030]$, $lys_1 \equiv [2101]$ and $lys_2 \equiv [2000]$, belonging to time series $\theta_1 \equiv init, *, lyt_1, *, lyt_2, *, lyt_3$ and $\theta_2 \equiv init, *, lys_1, *, lys_2$, which correspond to evolution towards lytic and lysogenic phases. The equivalent LTL counterparts for θ_1 and θ_2 are respectively $\phi_1 \equiv init \wedge \mathbf{F}(lyt_1 \wedge \mathbf{F}(lyt_2 \wedge \mathbf{F}(lyt_3 \wedge \mathbf{F}(lyt_2))))$ and $\phi_2 \equiv init \wedge \mathbf{F}(lys_1 \wedge \mathbf{F}(lys_2))$.

In order to reproduce the same experiment than Klarner *et al.*, we discard the Min/Max constraint for all genes (as it is not supported in [13]), and we relax the Observation constraint for the specific case where cI is activator of itself (as done in [13]). We then use SPuTNIk to find out the parameter instantiations corresponding to dynamics which are guaranteed to exhibit either a lytic or a lysogenic phenotype in compliance with series θ_1 and θ_2 (i.e. all models that contain at least one path that satisfies ϕ_1 and at least one that satisfies ϕ_2).

The obtained results are in accordance: amongst the 7 billions possible models, we obtain the same number (8759) of valid ones as in [13]. But unlike Klarner *et al.* our method is not restricted to time series: we can consider any form of LTL formulas and there is no need to fully specify all the levels of expression. For example, it is known that a lytic λ phage can not become lysogenic in the future (and conversely). This knowledge cannot be expressed with time series, but it corresponds to the following LTL formulas: $\phi_3 \equiv \mathbf{G}(lys_2 \Rightarrow \neg\mathbf{F}(lyt_3))$ and $\phi_4 \equiv \mathbf{G}(lyt_3 \Rightarrow \neg\mathbf{F}(lys_2))$. By adding these formulas to the previous, we reduce the number of solutions to 2390.

6   Conclusion

In this paper we introduced a new methodology for reverse-engineering of genetic network models, based on adaptation of classical LTL model-checking with symbolic execution. In order to find dynamics consistent with biological knowledge, we use the whole extent of LTL to express biological knowledge in terms of constraints over time. Instead of checking each dynamics of the GRN, we propose a method which performs checking with a novel formalism, the Parametric GRN, a compact (symbolic) representation of all the dynamics associated to an interaction graph within a single structure. From the Parametric GRN and LTL formulas, our algorithm processes parameters, defining the dynamics, as symbols in order to avoid combinatorial explosion. The solutions are in the form of a set of constraints that the parameters must fulfill. Such analysis has been carried out through the SPuTNIk tool, a prototype software of the proposed method. We are working on a parallel version of SPuTNIk, based on the splitting of the Parametric Product into strongly connected components in order to detect the accepting cycles in each component.

References

1. Baier, C., Katoen, J.-P.: Principles of Model Checking. The MIT Press (2008)
2. Barnat, J., Brim, L., Krejci, A., Streck, A., Safránek, D., Vejnar, M., Vejpustek, T.: On parameter synthesis by parallel model checking. IEEE/ACM Trans. Comput. Biology Bioinform. 9(3), 693–705 (2012)

3. Bernot, G., Comet, J.-P., Richard, A., Guespin, J.: Application of formal methods to biological regulatory networks: extending Thomas' asynchronous logical approach with temporal logic. Journal of Theoretical Biology 229(3), 339–347 (2004)
4. Bodden, E.: LTL2BA4J Software. RWTH Aachen University (2011), http://www.sable.mcgill.ca/~ebodde/rv/ltl2ba4j/
5. Corblin, F., Fanchon, E., Trilling, L.: Applications of a formal approach to decipher discrete genetic networks. BMC Bioinformatics 11, 385 (2010)
6. Corblin, F., Tripodi, S., Fanchon, E., Ropers, D., Trilling, L.: A declarative constraint-based method for analyzing discrete genetic regulatory networks. BioSystems 98, 91–104 (2009)
7. de Moura, L., Bjørner, N.S.: Z3: An Efficient SMT Solver. In: Ramakrishnan, C.R., Rehof, J. (eds.) TACAS 2008. LNCS, vol. 4963, pp. 337–340. Springer, Heidelberg (2008)
8. Filopon, D., Mérieau, A., Bernot, G., Comet, J.-P., Leberre, R., Guery, B., Polack, B., Guespin, J.: Epigenetic acquisition of inducibility of type III cytotoxicity in P. aeruginosa. BMC Bioinformatics 7, 272–282 (2006)
9. Fromentin, J., Comet, J.-P., Le Gall, P., Roux, O.: Analysing gene regulatory networks by both constraint programming and model-checking. In: 29th IEEE Engineering in Medicine and Biology Society, EMBC 2007, pp. 4595–4598 (2007)
10. Gastin, P., Oddoux, D.: Fast LTL to büchi automata translation. In: Berry, G., Comon, H., Finkel, A. (eds.) CAV 2001. LNCS, vol. 2102, pp. 53–65. Springer, Heidelberg (2001)
11. Gaston, C., Le Gall, P., Rapin, N., Touil, A.: Symbolic execution techniques for test purpose definition. In: Uyar, M.Ü., Duale, A.Y., Fecko, M.A. (eds.) TestCom 2006. LNCS, vol. 3964, pp. 1–18. Springer, Heidelberg (2006)
12. Khalis, Z., Comet, J.-P., Richard, A., Bernot, G.: The SMBioNet method for discovering models of gene regulatory networks. Genes, Genomes and Genomics 3(special issue 1), 15–22 (2009)
13. Klarner, H., Streck, A., Šafránek, D., Kolčák, J., Siebert, H.: Parameter identification and model ranking of thomas networks. In: Gilbert, D., Heiner, M. (eds.) CMSB 2012. LNCS, vol. 7605, pp. 207–226. Springer, Heidelberg (2012)
14. Mateus, D., Gallois, J.-P., Comet, J.-P., Le Gall, P.: Symbolic modeling of genetic regulatory networks. Journal of Bioinformatics and Computational Biology 5(2B), 627–640 (2007)
15. Pnueli, A.: The temporal logic of programs. In: Proceedings of the 18th Annual Symposium on Foundations of Computer Science, SFCS 1977, pp. 46–57. IEEE Computer Society, Washington, DC (1977)
16. Richard, A.: SMBioNet User manual (2010), http://www.i3s.unice.fr/~richard/smbionet/
17. Snoussi, E., Thomas, R.: Logical identification of all steady states: the concept of feedback loop characteristic states. Bull. Math. Biol. 55(5), 973–991 (1993)
18. Thieffry, D., Colet, M., Thomas, R.: Formalisation of regulatory networks: a logical method and its automation. Math. Modelling and Sci. Computing 2, 144–151 (1993)
19. Thieffry, D., Thomas, R.: Dynamical behaviour of biological regulatory networks - II. immunity control in bacteriophage lambda. Bull. Math. Biol. 57(2), 277–297 (1995)

SCC-Based Improved Reachability Analysis for Markov Decision Processes[*]

Lin Gui[1], Jun Sun[2], Songzheng Song[3], Yang Liu[3], and Jin Song Dong[1]

[1] National University of Singapore, Singapore
[2] Singapore University of Technology and Design, Singapore
[3] Nanyang Technological University, Singapore

Abstract. Markov decision processes (MDPs) are extensively used to model systems with both probabilistic and nondeterministic behavior. The problem of calculating the probability of reaching certain system states (hereafter reachability analysis) is central to the MDP-based system analysis. It is known that existing approaches on reachability analysis for MDPs are often inefficient when a given MDP contains a large number of states and loops, especially with the existence of multiple probability distributions. In this work, we propose a method to eliminate strongly connected components (SCCs) in an MDP using a divide-and-conquer algorithm, and actively remove redundant probability distributions in the MDP based on the convex property. With the removal of loops and parts of probability distributions, the probabilistic reachability analysis can be accelerated, as evidenced by our experiment results.

1 Introduction

Markov decision processes (MDPs) are extensively used to model a system with both non-determinism and probabilistic behavior. One fundamental task in probabilistic model checking is to decide the probability of reaching a set of target states in an MDP. We refer to this as the *reachability analysis* problem. A discrete time Markov chain (DTMC) can be considered as a special form of MDPs with unique reachability probability since it has only one probability distribution at each state. For general MDPs, there are multiple probability distributions in a state, and thus the practical interests for the reachability analysis focus on the maximum and minimum reachability probabilities.

Given an MDP and a set of target states, a variable can be created for each state to present the probability of that state reaching the target states. There are two main methods to calculate or approximate the values of these variables [4]. One method encodes the probabilistic reachability problem into a linear optimization problem where each probability distribution is encoded into an inequality. Thus, the goal is to maximize or minimize the sum of the variables. It should be noted that the state-of-the-art linear solvers are limited to small systems. However, a practical MDP model is often resulted from parallel composition of several MDPs/DTMCs, which would have an even larger number of states.

---

[*] This project is partially supported by project IDD11100102A/IDG31100105A from SUTD.

S. Merz and J. Pang (Eds.): ICFEM 2014, LNCS 8829, pp. 171–186, 2014.

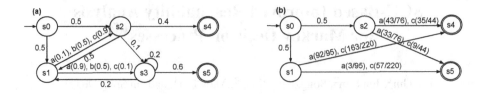

Fig. 1. Running examples of (a) an MDP and (b) an acyclic MDP

The other method is based on value iteration by finding a better approximation itera-tively until the result satisfies a certain stopping criterion, and performs generally better in system with a large number of states [4]. The approximation of the variable of a state needs to be updated whenever any of its successive states are changed. When there are loops in an MDP, this approach tends to require many iterations before converging to a value, and thus lead to *slow convergence*. Fig. 1(a) shows an example of a simple MDP with loops among states s_1, s_2 and s_3. Suppose the task is to calculate the probability of reaching state s_4 from state s_0. If the approximation in s_2 is updated during the kth iteration, the approximation in s_1 will be updated during the $(k + 1)^{th}$ iteration as s_2 is successive to s_1. The update of s_1 will trigger s_3 to update its value subsequently, which requires s_2 to be updated again. This iteration can only be stopped by enforcing a stopping criterion, thus one major issue associated with such an approach is that the difference between the approximated and 'actual' probabilities remains unknown even after the iteration is stopped [9]. On the other hand, in an acyclic MDP in Fig. 1(b), each state will be visited only a few rounds for backward calculation without iterations. In this case, the exact maximum and minimum probabilities can be calculated without the necessity of approximation. Therefore, we are motivated to improve reachability analysis by removing loops in an MDP.

Some foundation has been established by recent works on the elimination of strongly connected components (SCCs) in DTMC [3,2,13]. To remove the loops, SCCs are first identified, and the transition probabilities from every input to output states of each SCC are calculated. The loops can then be removed by connecting the inputs to the outputs with the computed probability transitions (i.e., *abstraction* of SCC). After all the SCCs are abstracted, the whole model becomes acyclic. With such an acyclic set of states, value iteration can be used to calculate the probability from initial states to the target states. Although this approach works for DTMCs, eliminating loops in an MDP is par-ticularly challenging due to the existence of multiple probability distributions. In an MDP, the number of memoryless schedulers increases exponentially with the number of the states that have multiple probability distributions. During the abstraction of a group of states, a probability distribution must be calculated under different memory-less scheduler in the group. As a result, the total number of probability distributions can increase exponentially after abstraction. Therefore, directly applying the existing approaches [3,2,13] to MDPs is often infeasible.

To overcome this challenge, we propose a divide-and-conquer algorithm to remove loops in an MDP. For each SCC in the MDP, we first construct *partitions*, i.e., each state in the SCC forms a partition. By solving sets of linear equations, new probability dis-tributions can be calculated from each partition to replace the loops without varying the overall reachability probabilities. With the new equivalent probability distributions, the new partition will be free of loops, and have the same reachability probabilities with the original model. We repeatedly merge a few partitions into one partition, and eliminate loops in this new partition by performing the above abstraction until only one partition is left in the SCC. After the reduction for all the SCCs, the remaining acyclic MDP can be solved efficiently via the value iteration approach. After this reduction, the maximum and minimum reachability probabilities of the reduced MDP remain unchanged as compared with those of the original MDP. As introduced earlier, reducing states in SCCs of an MDP may result in exponentially many probability distributions, and our algorithm is thus designed to eliminate redundant or infeasible probability distributions on-the-fly to achieve better performance. The underlying observation is that, a probability distribution will not affect the maximum or the minimum reachability probability, if it is not a vertex of the convex hull of a set of probability distributions. Our contributions are three-fold and are summarized as follows.

1. To tackle the problem of slow convergence, we propose a divide-and-conquer approach to eliminate SCCs in an MDP. Our approach works on the partitions and can effectively avoid generating large number of schedulers.
2. To reduce the cost of loop eliminations within each partition of an MDP, we remove redundant nondeterministic choices/probability distributions based on convex hull theory.
3. The new approach has been implemented in our model checking framework PAT [15], and two practical case studies (i.e., software reliability assessment and tennis tournament prediction) have been conducted to show its effectiveness.

2 Preliminaries

2.1 Markov Decision Processes

Markov Decision Processes. (MDPs) are popular choices to model a system exhibiting both probabilistic and nondeterministic behavior [4]. Given a set of states S, a probability distribution (PD) is a function $u : S \to [0,1]$ such that $\Sigma_{s \in S} u(s) = 1$. The PD can also be expressed in the vector form as $\mathbf{u}$, and $Distr(S)$ denotes the set of all discrete probability distributions over S. The formal definition of MDP is introduced as follows.

Definition 1 (Markov Decision Process). *A Markov decision process is a tuple $\mathcal{M} = (S, init, Act, Pr)$ where S is a set of states; $init \in S$ is the initial state; Act is an alphabet; and $Pr : S \times Act \to Distr(S)$ is a labeled transition relation.* □

Without loss of generality, in this work, we assume that MDP has an unique initial state and is always deadlock free. It is known that we can add a self-looping transition with a probability of 1 to a deadlock state without affecting the calculation result [4]. A state without any outgoing transitions to other states is called an *absorbing* state, which has only a self-loop with a probability of 1. An example of MDP is shown in Fig. 1(a), where states s_4 and s_5 are both absorbing states, denoted by circles with double lines, and state s_0 is the initial state. Given a state s, we denote the set of probability distributions of s as $\mathbf{U}_s$, s.t., $\mathbf{U}_s = \{Pr(s,a)|a \in Act\}$. An infinite or a finite path in $\mathcal{M}$ is defined as a sequence of states $\pi = s_0, s_1, \cdots$ or $\pi = s_0, s_1, \cdots, s_n$, respectively, such that $\forall i \geq 0$ (for finite paths, $i \in [0, n-1]$), $\exists a \in Act, Pr(s_i, a)(s_{i+1}) > 0$. An MDP is nondeterministic if any state has more than one probability distribution. As a special MDP, a discrete time Markov chain (DTMC) has only one event (and one probability distribution) at each state, and thus is deterministic.

Similar to [3,2,13], in an MDP $\mathcal{M} = (S, init, Act, Pr)$, we define inputs and outputs of a group of states $\mathcal{K} \subseteq S$ as follows.

$$Inp(\mathcal{K}) = \{s' \in \mathcal{K} \mid \exists s \in S \backslash \mathcal{K}, \exists a \in Act \cdot Pr(s, a)(s') > 0\},$$
$$Out(\mathcal{K}) = \{s' \in S \backslash \mathcal{K} \mid \exists s \in \mathcal{K}, \exists a \in Act \cdot Pr(s, a)(s') > 0\}.$$

Here, the set of input states of $\mathcal{K}$, $Inp(\mathcal{K})$, contains the states in $\mathcal{K}$ that have incoming transitions from states outside $\mathcal{K}$; and the set of output states of $\mathcal{K}$, $Out(\mathcal{K})$, contains all the states outside $\mathcal{K}$ that have direct incoming transitions from states in $\mathcal{K}$. In addition, without loss of generality, if a group contains the initial state $init$, we include $init$ to its input states (with an imaginary transition leading to $init$ from outside). Furthermore, given a set $\mathcal{K}$, if a state is not an input state, we call it as an inner state. We can eliminate all the inner states by calculating the direct transition probabilities from $Inp(\mathcal{K})$ to $Out(\mathcal{K})$. This process is called *abstraction*. It eliminates all loops in $\mathcal{K}$, and meanwhile, *preserves* the maximum and minimum reachability probabilities from inputs to the outputs of $\mathcal{K}$. There are known algorithms in [2,13] to perform the abstraction. However, they are only applicable to DTMCs. In this work, we extend the abstraction to MDPs.

Schedulers. A scheduler is used to resolve the non-determinism in each state. Intuitively, given a state s, an action is first selected by a scheduler. Once an action is selected, the respective PD is also determined; and then one of the successive states is reached according to the probability distribution. Formally, a *memoryless scheduler* for an MDP $\mathcal{M}$ is a function $\sigma : S \to Act$. At each state, a memoryless scheduler always selects the same action in a given state. This choice is independent of the path that leads to the current state. In the following, unless otherwise specified, the terms 'schedulers' and 'memoryless schedulers' are used interchangeably. An induced MDP, $\mathcal{M}_\sigma$, is a DTMC defined by an MDP $\mathcal{M}$ and a scheduler σ. A non-memoryless scheduler is the scheduler that can select different action in a given state according to the execution history.

Strongly Connected Components. A set of states $C \subseteq S$ is called *strongly connected* in $\mathcal{M}$ iff $\forall s, s' \in C$, there exists a finite path $\pi = \langle s_0, s_1, \cdots, s_n \rangle$ satisfying $s_0 = s \wedge s_n = s' \wedge \forall i \in [0, n], s_i \in C$. *Strongly connected components* (SCCs) are the maximal sets of the strongly connected states. All SCCs can be automatically identified by Tarjan's approach [16], with a complexity of $\mathcal{O}(n+l)$, where n and l are the numbers of states and transitions, respectively. In Fig. 1(a), $\{s_0\}$, $\{s_4\}$, $\{s_5\}$ and $\{s_1, s_2, s_3\}$ are the SCCs in the model. We define SCCs as trivial if they do not have any outgoing transitions (e.g., $\{s_4\}$, $\{s_5\}$) or are not involved in loops (e.g., $\{s_0\}$, an SCC of one single state without any loop). As a result, $\{s_1, s_2, s_3\}$ is the only nontrivial SCC in Fig. 1(a). An MDP is considered *acyclic* if it contains only trivial SCCs. An example of an acyclic MDP is shown in Fig. 1(b). Note that an acyclic MDP may still have absorbing states, but it does not affect the computation of reachability probabilities.

2.2 Probability Reachability Analysis in MDPs

One fundamental question in quantitative analysis of MDPs is to compute the probability of reaching target states G from the initial state. Noted that with different schedulers, the result may be different. The measurement of interest is thus the maximum and minimum reachability probabilities. The maximum probability of reaching any state in G is denoted as $P^{max}(\mathcal{M} \models \Diamond G)$, which is defined as: $P^{max}(\mathcal{M} \models \Diamond G) = \sup_\sigma P(\mathcal{M}_\sigma \models \Diamond G)$. Similarly, the minimum is defined as: $P^{min}(\mathcal{M} \models \Diamond G) = \inf_\sigma P(\mathcal{M}_\sigma \models \Diamond G)$, which yields the lower bound of the probability of reaching G. The supremum/infimum ranges over all and potentially infinitely many schedulers. Rather than considering all schedulers, it suffices to consider only memoryless schedulers, in order to obtain maximum and minimum reachability probabilities [4].

In the following, with the MDP in Fig. 1(a), we demonstrate how to numerically calculate the maximum probability of reaching any state in G from the initial state. The minimum probability can be obtained similarly. Here, state s_0 is the initial state, and G contains a single target state s_4. Let V be a vector such that, given a state s, $V(s)$ is the maximum probability of reaching G from a state s. For instance, $V(s_0)$ is the maximum probability of reaching G from the initial state. First of all, $V(s) = 1$, for all $s \in G$. Using backward reachability analysis, we can identify the set of states $X = \{s_0, s_1, s_2, s_3, s_4\}$ such that G is reachable from any state in X; and a set of states $Y = \{s_5\}$ from where G is unreachable, i.e., $V(s) = 0$ for $\forall s \in Y$. Therefore, $V(s_4) = 1$ and $V(s_5) = 0$. There are two main approaches on calculating the reachability probabilities for states $X \setminus G$, i.e., $\{s_0, s_1, s_2, s_3\}$.

Linear Programming. The method encodes each probability distribution (PD) for a state in $X \setminus G$ into a linear inequality. This is defined as

$$V(s) \geqslant \sum_{t \in S} P(s, \alpha)(t) \cdot V(t), \quad \text{for } s \in X \setminus G \tag{1}$$

with an additional constraint $V(s) \in [0, 1]$, and the goal is to minimize the sum of V. Taking state s_2 for example, there is a unique PD $\{0.5 \mapsto s_1, 0.1 \mapsto s_3, 0.4 \mapsto s_4\}$, which can be encoded as: $V(s_2) \geqslant 0.5V(s_1) + 0.1V(s_3) + 0.4V(s_4)$. Noted that state s_1 has three PDs, thus three inequalities are required. $V(s_0)$ is then obtained by solving such linear programming using standard algorithms.

Value Iteration. This method iteratively builds an approximation of V based on the previous approximation. Let V^i be the i-th approximation. For $\forall s \in X \setminus G$, we have $V^0(s) = 0; V^{i+1}(s) = \max\{\sum_{t \in S} Pr(s, a)(t) \cdot V^i(t) \mid a \in Act(s)\}$. For example, at the 1st iteration, $V^1(s_2) = 0.5V^0(s_1) + 0.4 + 0.1V^0(s_3) = 0.4$ and the others remains unchanged; at the 2nd iteration, $V^2(s_1) = \max\{0.1V^1(s_2) + 0.9V^1(s_3), 0.5V^1(s_2) + 0.5V^1(s_3), 0.9V^1(s_2) + 0.1V^1(s_3)\} = 0.36$, $V^2(s_0) = 0.2$; at the 3rd iteration, $V^3(s_0) = 0.38$ and $V^3(s_3) = 0.2V^2(s_1) = 0.072$; at the 4th iteration, since the value of state s_3 has been updated in the previous round, $V^4(s_1)$ and $V^4(s_2)$ shall be computed again and the similar iterations repeat. Notice that states s_1, s_2 and s_3 form a loop, within which an update of any state will trigger the updates of other states in the next few iterations. After 39 iterations, $V^{39}(s_0)$ is calculated to be 0.74627.

It can be shown that for every state s, $V^{i+1}(s) \geqslant V^i(s)$ and we can obtain V in the limit, $\lim_{i \to \infty} V^i = V$. In reality, it may take many iterations before V^i converges and thus value iteration is often stopped when the absolute/relative difference between two successive iterations falls below a certain threshold ϵ. The number of iterations required is related to the subdominant eigenvalue of the transition matrix [14]. Each iteration involves a series of matrix-vector multiplications, with a complexity of $\mathcal{O}(n^2 \cdot m)$ in the worst case, where n is the number of states in S and m is the maximum number of actions/distributions from a state. However, as stressed in [9], value iteration does not guarantee the resulting values to be within ϵ of the true answer. Although theoretically guaranteed precisions are base on the denominators of the (rational) numbers, it is still unclear if these are practically applicable.

3   SCC Reductions on Markov Decision Processes

As both approaches based on solving linear programming and value iteration have their own limitations, we propose a new approach to abstract away the loops in each strongly connected component (SCC) of an MDP based on a divide-and-conquer algorithm, and then apply value iteration to the resulting acyclic MDP. Without loops, the calculation of reachability probabilities will be faster, and also will be more accurate than the pure value iteration case with an unspecified amount of errors.

Reducing SCCs in an MDP while preserving the results of reachability analysis is highly nontrivial, and may lead to extra schedulers and an exponential increase in the number of probability distributions (PDs) if not handled properly. In this work, the proposed divide-and-conquer algorithm works on partitions; hence effectively avoids the generation of extra PDs. Moreover, we can further reduce the redundant PDs based on the convex property.

In the following, we will use a running example to illustrate the main idea of the divide-and-conquer approach, and then present the overall algorithm and detailed methodologies on performing state abstraction in an MDP, followed by its optimization on the reductions of probability distributions.

3.1   A Running Example

To reduce an SCC, our reduction approach starts from adding each state in the SCC into a new partition. It then divides these partitions into groups. For each group, it eliminates loops within the group and merges its components into a new partition. We call this process abstraction. This step repeats until the whole SCC becomes one partition, which is guaranteed to be free of loops. In this part, we demonstrate our main idea with a running example that transfers the MDP in Fig. 1(a) to the acyclic MDP in Fig. 1(b). The execution of each step is demonstrated in Fig. 2.

First, the states $\{s_1, s_2, s_3\}$ are identified as the only nontrivial SCC in the MDP, and there are three partitions, i.e., $\{s_1\}, \{s_2\}, \{s_3\}$, labeled using different grayscale in Fig. 2(a). Let Λ be the set of all current partitions in the SCC, i.e., $\Lambda = \{\{s_1\}, \{s_2\}, \{s_3\}\}$. We then divide Λ into two groups, as enclosed by dashed lines, such that the partitions $\{s_1\}$ and $\{s_2\}$ form one group, and $\{s_3\}$ alone forms the other.

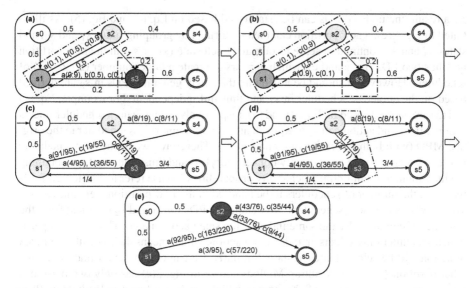

Fig. 2. A running example of transforming the MDP in Fig. 1(a) to the acyclic MDP in Fig. 1(b)

Subsequently, abstraction is performed on both groups. The main idea of the abstraction is to eliminate loops in the group by connecting the inputs and outputs using equivalent non-redundant probability distributions (PDs). In the first step, we need to remove the redundant probability distributions in each partition of the group. Recall that each PD can form a linear constraint according to Eq. (1) in Section 2.2. According to the PDs in Fig. 2(a), it can be proved that the constraint from PD b of state s_1 is redundant as it can be represented by a linear combination of the constraints from PDs a and c. As a result, PD b can be removed. The updated MDP is shown in Fig. 2(b).

The second step of the abstraction is to calculate the equivalent PDs. In the present case, partition $\{s_1\}$ has two actions and partition $\{s_2\}$ has only one action, thus there are two $(2 \cdot 1)$ schedulers in total. We define σ_1 as the scheduler selecting PD a at partition $\{s_1\}$, based on which a set of linear equations can be formed as

$$V(s_1) = 0.1V(s_2) + 0.9V(s_3); \quad V(s_2) = 0.5V(s_1) + 0.1V(s_3) + 0.4V(s_4) \quad (2)$$

Similar definition applies to scheduler σ_2 for PD c, we have

$$V(s_1) = 0.9V(s_2) + 0.1V(s_3); \quad V(s_2) = 0.5V(s_1) + 0.1V(s_3) + 0.4V(s_4) \quad (3)$$

To eliminate the transitions between s_1 and s_2, we need to first select a particular scheduler, and then perform Gauss Jordan elimination. Under the selection of scheduler σ_1, we can have the following new transitions based on Eq. (2),

$$V(s_1) = \frac{4}{95}V(s_3) + \frac{91}{95}V(s_4); \quad V(s_2) = \frac{11}{19}V(s_3) + \frac{8}{19}V(s_4) \quad (4)$$

Similarly, with the selection of σ_2, we have the following based on Eq. (3),

$$V(s_1) = \frac{36}{55}V(s_3) + \frac{19}{55}V(s_4); \quad V(s_2) = \frac{3}{11}V(s_3) + \frac{8}{11}V(s_4) \quad (5)$$

As a result, the updated PDs can be established based on Eq. (4) and Eq. (5). As illustrated in Fig. 2(c), a new partition can then be formed by grouping states s_1 and s_2, and states s_3 and s_4 continue to serve as outputs. Each state (s_1 or s_2) in the new partition now has two PDs (i.e. a and c), which appears to create a larger number ($2 \cdot 2 = 4$) of schedulers. However, it should be noted that the newly generated PDs in s_2 are derived based on the choice of scheduler in s_1 and thus **not** independent. For example, Eq. (4) and (5) are derived based on Eq. (2) and (3), respectively. That means a scheduler selects action a in s_1 and action c in s_2 is equivalent to a non-memoryless scheduler in the original MPD (with both selections of a and c at s_1). Therefore, two of the four schedulers in the new partition are equivalently non-memoryless and thus redundant for obtaining the maximum and minimum reachability probabilities (please refer to Section 2.2). Effectively, the number of schedulers to be handled in the new partitions remains as two. To easily allocate these schedulers, we denote the PDs for s_1 and s_2 obtained from the same set of equations by the same index or the same action name. Thus, given a partition, a scheduler only selects an index or an action, which means the PD with that index or action will be selected at each state. Similarly, we can obtain the abstraction on the other partition $\{s_3\}$. The resulting MDP as shown in Fig. 2(c) has only two partitions ($\Lambda = \{\{s_1, s_2\}, \{s_3\}\}$) in the SCC, both of which are free of loops and redundant PDs.

To finally achieve a single partition, another round of grouping and abstraction needs to be performed. There are now two partitions, and we combine them into one group as shown in Fig. 2(d). As explained above, during the calculation of the maximum and minimum reachability probabilities, partition $\{s_1, s_2\}$ can be described using two schedulers, and the other partition $\{s_3\}$ has only one scheduler. Therefore, the total number of schedulers within the group is two (i.e., $2 \cdot 1$). Let σ_3 be a scheduler selecting the PD of action a, i.e., $\sigma_3(\{s_1, s_2\}) = a$, and σ_4 be the other scheduler selecting the PD with action c, i.e., $\sigma_4(\{s_1, s_2\}) = c$. A set of linear equations can be formed similarly as Eq. (2) and (3), and the solutions connect the input states s_1 and s_2 directly to the output states s_4 and s_5. With such a new partition, the inner state s_3 can be removed from the MDP. Up to this point, there is only one partition left and our reduction finishes. The final acyclic MDP is shown in Fig. 2(e).

3.2 Overall Algorithm

The overall algorithm for SCCs reduction is presented in Algorithm 1. It is based on a divide-and-conquer approach that works on *partitions* of an MDP. Given a set of states S, a partition $\mathcal{E}$ is a subset of S such that $\bigcup_i \mathcal{E}_i = S$; and $\forall \mathcal{E}_i, \mathcal{E}_j, \mathcal{E}_i \neq \mathcal{E}_j, \mathcal{E}_i \cap \mathcal{E}_j = \emptyset$. Given an MDP $\mathcal{M} = (S, S_{init}, Act, Pr)$ and target states $G \subset S$, Algorithm 1 removes all loops in $\mathcal{M}$ (i.e., resulting an acyclic MDP $\mathcal{M}'$) and computes reachability probabilities in $\mathcal{M}'$. We remove loops according to the following steps.

- Line 1 finds all SCCs by Tarjan's approach [16], and adds all nontrivial SCCs to $\mathcal{C}$. Lines 2–12 present the divide-and-conquer procedure for each SCC in $\mathcal{C}$. Let Λ be a set of partitions of an SCC. Initially, each state of SCC forms a partition in Λ, as shown in lines 3–4.
- Lines 5–12 perform the divide-and-conquer in the partitions of Λ until there is only one partition left. Within each round, line 6 first divides all the partitions Λ into several groups, denoted by $\mathcal{A}$. Here, the groups are formed dynamically that each

---

Algorithm 1. SCC Reduction in an MDP via Divide-and-Conquer

---

input : An MDP $\mathcal{M} = (S, s_{init}, Act, Pr)$, target states $G \subseteq S$
output: $\mathcal{P}(\mathcal{M} \models \Diamond G)$

1 $\mathcal{M}' = \mathcal{M}$; $\mathcal{C} :=$ the set of all nontrivial SCCs in $\mathcal{M}'$;
2 **for** *each* $\mathcal{D} \in \mathcal{C}$ **do**
3     $\Lambda := \emptyset$;   //to record a set of partitions
4     $\forall s \in \mathcal{D}, \Lambda := \Lambda \cup \{\{s\}\}$; //each state is a partition initially
5   **repeat**
6   Divide Λ into a set of groups of partitions denoted as $\mathcal{A}$;
7        $\Lambda' = \emptyset$;
8   **for** *each* $\mathcal{J} \in \mathcal{A}$ **do**
9           $\mathcal{E}' = Abstraction(\mathcal{J})$;   //$\mathcal{J}$ is a set of partitions
10          $\Lambda' = \Lambda' \cup \mathcal{E}'$;
11        $\Lambda = \Lambda'$;
12   **until** $|\Lambda| == 1$;
13 **return** $ValueIteration(\mathcal{M}', G)$;

---

has relatively small number of output states. Each element $\mathcal{J}$ in $\mathcal{A}$ is a group of partitions. There is always a group containing more than one partitions unless there is only one partition in $\mathcal{A}$. Next, lines 8–10 remove loops and the inner states in each $\mathcal{J}$ through $Abstraction()$ method, which takes a group of partitions as the input and returns a new acyclic partition that can represent the previous group. As a result, after each round, the number of partitions decreases and loops inside each partition are eliminated. Details for the abstraction process will be presented in Section 3.3.

– After the iteration terminates, the resulting MDP becomes acyclic. The standard value iteration method, detailed in Section 2.2, can then be applied to calculate the probability from the initial state to the target states efficiently.

As we can see, in order to support the divide-and-conquer algorithm for MDPs, the overall algorithm incorporates methods like abstraction and PD reduction. In the following parts, we will introduce details of these two methods.

3.3 States Abstraction

Given a set of partitions, denoted by $\mathcal{J}$, the *abstraction* process removes the inner states in each partition, and merges all partitions into a new partition, denoted by $\mathcal{E}'$. The detailed algorithm of abstraction is presented in Algorithm 2. It takes $\mathcal{J}$ as the input and returns a new acyclic partition $\mathcal{E}'$. The procedure works as follows.

– The first step, as shown in lines 1–7, is to reduce redundant PDs in each partition. As demonstrated in Section 3.1, within a partition, the PDs of the same index are originated from the same scheduler in the original model. Thus, they are not independent and can only be removed if they are all redundant. The detailed operations are as follows. For each partition, we use a Boolean set $\mathcal{I}$ to record whether a PD is redundant. Initially, line 2 sets all elements in $\mathcal{I}$ to $false$. For each state of the partition, line 4 gets all indices of the non-redundant PDs, and line 5 sets the respective elements in

---

Algorithm 2. Abstraction

---

 input : A set of partitions of states $\mathcal{J}$ in an MDP
 output: A new partition $\mathcal{E}'$

   //step 1: remove redundant PDs in each partition
1 **for** *each* $\mathcal{E} \in \mathcal{J}$ **do**
    //$\mathcal{I}$ is to record whether a PD is non-redundant
2 | Let $\mathcal{I}$ be a set of Boolean variables initialized with *false*;
3 | **for** *each* $s \in \mathcal{E}$ **do**
4 | | *Indices* := indices non-redundant PDs of s;
5 | | **for** *each index* $\in$ *Indices* **do** $\mathcal{I}'[index] =: true;$;
6 | | $\mathcal{I} = \mathcal{I}'$;
7 | **for** *each* $s \in \mathcal{E}$ **do** Update PDs according to $\mathcal{I}$;;

   //step 2: calculate new PDs from inputs to outputs
8 $\mathcal{K} = \bigcup_{\mathcal{E} \in \mathcal{J}} \mathcal{E}$;
9 $\forall s \in Inp(\mathcal{K}) \cdot \mathbf{U}'_s := \emptyset$;
10 $\Sigma :=$ all the schedulers in $\mathcal{J}$ based on partitions;
11 **for** *each* $\sigma \in \Sigma$ **do**
12 | calculate PDs from $Inp(\mathcal{K})$ to $Out(\mathcal{K})$ according to σ;
13 | Let u_s be the calculated PD of a input state s;
14 | $\forall s \in Inp(\mathcal{K}) \cdot \mathbf{U}'_s := \mathbf{U}'_s \cup \{u_s\}$;

   //step 3: form a new partition
15 $\mathcal{E}' = Inp(\mathcal{K})$;
16 $\forall s \in \mathcal{E}'$, replace PDs of s by $\mathbf{U}'_s$; //re-connect $Inp(\mathcal{E}')$ to $Out(\mathcal{E}')$
17 **return** $\mathcal{E}'$;

$\mathcal{I}$ to *true*. Here, the non-redundant PDs can be identified by finding the vertices of the convex hull, detailed in Section 3.4. After the **for** loop in lines 3 - 6, a *false* in $\mathcal{I}$ means the corresponding PD in each state is redundant. As a result, line 7 removes the respective PDs at the indices for all states.

– Line 8 combines states in all partitions of $\mathcal{J}$ into one group $\mathcal{K}$. The second step is to calculate new PDs from $Inp(\mathcal{K})$ to $Out(\mathcal{K})$ for all schedulers. Line 9 creates an empty set for each state in $Inp(\mathcal{K})$, which is used to store new PDs. Line 10 finds all the schedulers in $\mathcal{J}$ and assigns them to Σ. As reviewed in Section 2.1, for any given state, a scheduler is used to select a PD, and the total number of the schedulers is exponential to the number of states. As mentioned, within a partition, the PDs with the same index are not independent, we thereby create a scheduler in such a way that it can only select PDs with the same index at all states in the partition. This can avoid the generation of extra schedulers by including all the combinations of PDs. Lines 11 –14 calculate the new equivalent PDs by calculating the transition probabilities, from $Inp(\mathcal{K})$ to $Out(\mathcal{K})$. For each scheduler σ, we calculate the probabilities from any input to output states in the DTMC $\mathcal{K}^\sigma$, which can be done by the standard algorithm, e.g., Gaussian Jordan elimination. Line 14 adds the new PDs to each state.

– Since the sets of PDs from $Inp(\mathcal{K})$ to $Out(\mathcal{K})$ have been obtained, the inner states of $\mathcal{K}$ are then redundant for the calculation of reachability probabilities. As a result, line 15 creates a new partition $\mathcal{E}'$ by adding only the inputs states of $\mathcal{K}$, and updates the PDs of each state in $\mathcal{E}'$ by $\mathbf{U}'_s$. The new partition $\mathcal{E}'$ is free of loops.

3.4   Reduction of Probability Distributions Based on Convex Hull

Within a set of probability distributions (PDs), if a PD can be represented by a convex combination of the other PDs, we call it a *redundant* PD. As demonstrated, PD b in Fig. 1(a) is redundant as it can be represented by a combination of 50% of PD a and 50% of PD b. It can be proved that the redundant PDs are irrelevant to the maximum and minimum reachability probabilities [6].

There are two scenarios that might introduce redundant PDs. One is during system modeling. For instance, PDs could be originated from a set of working profiles (modeling complex system environment) and some of working profiles are indeed redundant for calculating the maximum or minimum probability. The other is during the removal of the inner states within a group of states $\mathcal{K}$. The equivalent PDs are created to connect inputs to outputs of $\mathcal{K}$, the number of those is equal to the total number of schedulers in $\mathcal{K}$. As a result, there could be redundant PDs, especially when obtained PDs of a state have only a few successive states. In fact, the number of PDs of a state can be minimized and replaced by a *unique* and *minimal* set of PDs. If we consider PDs as a set of points in a Euclidean space and each successive state in a PD provides a dimension in the Euclidean space, finding the set of non-redundant PDs is equivalent to the problem of identifying all the vertices of the convex hull of all the PDs. This has been already proved in [6]. In the following, we have a brief review on the convex hull property.

The *convex hull* of a set Q of points, denoted by $CH(Q)$, is the smallest convex polygon or polytope in the Euclidean plane or Euclidean space that contains Q [8]. Mathematically, the convex hull of a finite point set, e.g., $Q = \{\mathbf{q}_1, \cdots, \mathbf{q}_n\}$, is a set of all *convex combinations* of each point $\mathbf{q}_i$ assigned with a coefficient r_i, in such a way that the coefficients are all non-negative with a summation of one; i.e., $CH(Q) = \{\sum_{i=1}^{n} r_i \cdot \mathbf{q}_i | (\forall i : r_i \geqslant 0) \wedge \sum_{i=1}^{n} r_i = 1\}$. We denote the set of *vertices of a convex hull* as $V_{CH}(Q)$. Each $\mathbf{q}_i \in V_{CH}(Q)$ is also in Q, but it is not in the convex hull of the other points (i.e., $\mathbf{q}_i \notin CH(Q \setminus \{\mathbf{q}_i\})$). In other word, the points $V_{CH}(Q)$ are the essential points that generate all the other points in $CH(Q)$ via a convex combination. Given a set of n points (Q) in d-dimension, the algorithms to determine the vertices of the convex hull are also known as the redundancy removal for a point set Q in $\mathbb{R}^d$. This problem can be reduced to solving $\mathcal{O}(n)$ linear programming problems with many polynomial time algorithms available [6].

To further accelerate the calculation, we adopt an approximation algorithm proposed by Bentley et al. [5], who use the convex hull of some *subset* of given points as an approximation to the convex hull of all the points. Here, a user-defined parameter β controls degree of approximation. For instance, in xy-plane, we first divide the area between the minimum and maximum (i.e., extreme) values in x-dimension into 'strips', with a width of β. We then select the points with the extreme values in y-dimension within each strip, and the points with x-dimension extreme. Last, we construct the convex hull based on these selected points (in the worst case, there are only $2(1/\beta + 2)$ points). Here, β specifies the relative approximation error; i.e., any point outside the approximate hull is within β distance of the 'true' hull, as proved in [5]. Hence, a larger

β implies a faster calculation but a coarser approximation. In terms of reachability analysis, the schedulers, after approximation, are only a subset of original ones. Ignoring some of the PDs means the maximum or minimum reachability probability will be a safe approximation; i.e., the maximum probability is smaller than the 'true' maximum, and the minimum probability is larger than the 'true' minimum.

3.5 Termination and Correctness

In this section, we discuss the termination and the correctness of our approach.

Theorem 1. *Given a finite states MDP, Algorithm 1 always terminates.*

Proof: Given a finite number of states, the **for** loop in Algorithm 1 always terminates as the number of SCCs is finite. The theorem can then be proved by showing (1) the **repeat** loop can terminate and (2) *Abstraction*() can also terminate.

For (1), the proof for the one state SCC is trivial. For an SCC having more than one states, there are at least one group in $\mathcal{A}$ that has more than one partition, which can be merged into one new partition through *Abstraction*(). The total number of partitions is guaranteed to decrease after each round of the **repeat** loop. Thus the termination condition $|A| == 1$ can always be fulfilled. For (2), the abstraction, as in Algorithm 2, always terminates because all **for** loops work on a finite set of elements. As both conditions are fulfilled, the theorem holds.   □

Theorem 2. *Given a finite states MDP, Algorithm 1 always produces an acyclic MDP.*

Proof: To prove the theorem, it is equal to show that Algorithm 1 can remove all loops in each SCC. As proved above, Algorithm 1 always transfers each SCC into one partition, the theorem can be proved by showing that the abstraction process always returns a loop-free partition. Assuming a set of partitions $\mathcal{J}$ are the input, Algorithm 2 always creates a new partition by recalculating the probability distributions from $Inp(\mathcal{J})$ to $Out(\mathcal{J})$. As $Inp(\mathcal{J}) \cap Out(\mathcal{J}) = \emptyset$, the new partition is guaranteed to be acyclic. Therefore, the theorem holds.   □

As Algorithm 1 always terminates with an acyclic MDP, our approach can always provide an accurate result. Recall that loops in each SCC of the MDP are resolved by solving sets of equations, which is based on an accurate method. Further, we could trade off a certain level of accuracy for better performance with approximate convex hull.

4   Implementation and Evaluation

We implement the algorithm in our model checking framework PAT [15]. As the only difference between the ordinary and our proposed value iteration methods is the algorithm of reachability analysis, it is fair to check the effectiveness of the new method through direct comparison of their performance. Hereafter, we refer the implementations with and without our approach as PAT(w) and PAT(w/o), respectively. For the value iteration method, we use the default stopping criterion in PAT, i.e., the maximum ratio of difference is $1E$-6. For the new approach, we set the maximum number of partitions in a group to 3, and the parameter for convex hull approximation to 0.001. The

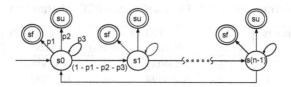

Fig. 3. A reliability model, the states s_u and s_f are copied for a clear demonstration

testbed is an Intel Xeon® CPU at 2.67 GHz with 12 GB RAM. All related materials, including the tools, models, and evaluation results, are available at [1]. We perform an analysis on two case studies: one is software reliability assessment model and the other is tennis tournament prediction model. Both systems have many probability transitions and loops, thus may encounter slow convergence issue especially when the systems become large. Thus, we evaluate how our new approach can benefit those cases.

4.1 Case Study on Software Reliability Assessment

Reliability and fault tolerance are central concerns to many software systems. The reliability problem can be transferred into a reachability problem in an MDP [10,12]. In this case study, we model a system that undergoes n tasks and then standbys at the initial state. Each task is exposed to a certain probability of failure or self-recovering situation, before successfully transferring to the next task or service. A highly abstracted reliability model is shown in Fig. 3, which consists of $n + 2$ states, i.e., $\{s_f, s_u, s_0, s_1, \cdots, s_{n-1}\}$, representing different system status. The failure state s_f is the state that the system fails, and the success state s_u is the state that the system finishes a requirement successfully. Each state s_i transits to s_f with a probability of p_1; to s_u with a probability of p_2; to itself with a probability of p_3; and otherwise, to the next state $s_{(i+1)\%n}$. Multiple sets of values for $\{p_1, p_2, p_3\}$ are considered. We then perform reachability analysis, e.g., computing the maximum probability of reaching state s_u, under different scale by varying the parameters n and m, where n controls the number of states and m is the number of probability distributions of each state.

The experiments are summarized in Table 1. The number of states being generated is approximately equal to n; $Trans.$ represents the total number of transitions in the model; P_{max} represents the maximum reachability probability; and $Time$ represents the total time spent on the verification. We have the following observations.

– The overall verification time of the new approach (PAT(w)) is much less than that of the previous approach (PAT(w/o)). Three factors here can affect the rate of value iteration in this model: (1) the self-loops at each state s_i; (2) the large SCC formed by $\{s_0, s_1, \cdots, s_{n-1}\}$; and (3) the various probability distributions in the model. Our approach reduces loops prior to value iteration, as detailed in Section 3. With PAT(w), the resulting acyclic MDP consists of only three states, s_0 (the only input of the SCC), and s_f and s_u (the outputs of the SCC). Thus, time spent on value iteration can almost be negligible (less than 0.001s). In addition, due to the PD reductions based on the convex hull, our reduction approach can work under many probability distributions without much overhead, as evidenced by the cases with $m = 10$.

Table 1. Comparison between PAT with and without SCC reduction for reliability model

Parameters			PAT (w/o)		PAT (w)	
m	n	#Trans.	Pmax	Time(s)	Pmax	Time(s)
4	40	0.6K	0.499985	0.03	0.500000	0.01
	400	6K	0.499999	0.22	0.500000	0.13
	20K	320K	0.499999	547.52	0.500000	55.97
	40K	640K	0.499999	1389.55	0.500000	314.73
10	40	2K	0.499985	0.04	0.500000	0.11
	400	16K	0.499999	0.41	0.500000	0.20
	20K	800K	0.499999	894.34	0.500000	111.62
	40K	1600K	0.499999	2168.04	0.500000	597.44

States $\approx n$

- The result obtained from the new approach is closer to the true value. Through manual analysis, we know that 0.5 is the accurate result. In fact, our reduction approach removes loops by solving a set of linear equations, which yields accurate results. As mentioned above, the resulting model is an acyclic MDP of only three states, on which value iteration stops naturally without using any stopping criterion. On the other hand, the ordinary value iteration approach keeps iterating over loops until a stopping criterion is met, thus the result is an approximation.

The experiment above considers only one SCC in the reliability model. However, often, a system may have a large number of SCCs in its reliability model. Our preliminary result shows that, with the increase of SCCs, the total time increases exponentially for the ordinary value iteration approach, while remains at a low level with our approach [1]. This is because our approach resolves each SCC independently while the ordinary approach has to iterate over all SCCs until converging to a stable result.

4.2 Case Study on Tennis Tournament Prediction

A tennis match is won when a player wins the majority of prescribed sets. At a score of 6 - 6 of a set, an additional 'tiebreaker' game is played to determine the winner of the set. In this case study, we model a 7 point tiebreaker. Our model encodes the outcomes of individual player's actions (e.g., serve and baseline) according to the past scoring profiles available at http://www.tennisabstract.com, and predicts the winning probability for one player against the other. In particular, we predict the game between two tennis giants Federer and Nadal. A play wins the set if he wins one tiebreaker, or best of 3 (or 5) tiebreakers. Thus, we analyze all the three situations. For each situation, we calculate four probabilities: (a) Federer scores the first point in any tiebreaker; (b) Nadal scores the first point in any tiebreaker; (c) Federer wins the set; and (d) Nadal wins the set.

The verification results are shown in Table 2. $\#$ represents the numbers of tiebreakers; $Pro.$ represents the properties to be verified; $\#States$ and $\#Trans.$ represent the total numbers of states and transitions in the system, respectively; P_{min}/P_{max} records the minimum/maximum reachability probability; and B and V record the time costs on building the MDP model (for PAT(w), it includes the additional time spent on SCC

Table 2. Comparison between PAT with and without SCC reduction for tennis prediction model

#	Pro.	#States	#Trans.	PAT (w/o)				PAT (w)			
				Pmin	Pmax	B (s)	V (s)	Pmin	Pmax	B (s)	V (s)
1	a	15K	26K	0.4585	0.5077	0.16	0.01	0.4585	0.5077	0.22	0.00
	b	15K	26K	0.4923	0.5415	0.14	0.01	0.4923	0.5415	0.24	0.00
	c	17K	30K	0.4678	0.4786	0.19	13.44	0.4678	0.4786	0.58	0.33
	d	17K	30K	0.5214	0.5322	0.16	13.34	0.5214	0.5322	0.50	0.32
3	a	62K	108K	0.7877	0.8075	0.66	64.72	0.7877	0.8075	1.55	2.94
	b	62K	108K	0.8116	0.8303	0.64	65.54	0.8116	0.8303	1.48	2.96
	c	71K	123K	0.4576	0.4649	0.74	133.89	0.4576	0.4649	1.95	9.32
	d	71K	123K	0.5351	0.5424	0.72	133.03	0.5351	0.5424	1.98	8.45
5	a	141K	278K	0.9194	0.9271	1.42	266.26	0.9194	0.9271	3.66	23.25
	b	141K	245K	0.9332	0.9401	1.43	265.80	0.9332	0.9401	3.65	23.35
	c	160K	279K	0.4486	0.4554	1.58	434.29	0.4486	0.4554	4.37	41.65
	d	160K	278K	0.5446	0.5514	1.53	428.62	0.5446	0.5514	4.32	36.93

reduction) and on value iteration, respectively. Notice that the summation of these two time costs is the total time spent on the verification. We have the following observations.

Comparing the time costs in B and V columns, for the ordinary approach, though the time for building an MDP model is very short, the verification time increases quickly when the size of system becomes large. On the other hand, with slightly longer time spent on model building, our new approach reduces the value iteration time significantly. This is because the new approach removes all SCCs prior to value iteration and the probability computation is thereby accelerated. In this case study, both approaches generate the same results up to four decimal points.

5   Related Work and Conclusion

In recent years, some approaches [11,7,3,2,13] have been proposed to improve probability reachability calculation. The key idea is to reduce iterations on the state space. [11,7] improve value iteration in MDPs by backward iterating over each SCC in topological order, i.e., an SCC will not be visited until the reachability probabilities of all its successive SCCs converge. However, since it requires iterating over each SCC (i.e., SCC-based value iteration), this approach only alleviates the slow convergence problem to a certain degree without completely solving the problem. Compared to their SCC based value iteration approach, our approach eliminates SCCs and produces an acyclic MDP where the standard value iteration is applied. Moreover, our reduction on each SCC is independent to others, so that multi-cores or distributed computers can be directly applied, which can make the verification even faster.

The approaches [3,2,13] are on SCCs elimination by connecting inputs to outputs of an SCC with equivalent probability transitions. But they are only applicable to DTMCs. In particular, the algorithms proposed in [2] and [13] can both work with large SCCs. [2] iteratively searches for and solves the smallest loops within an SCC. [13] uses a divide-and-conquer algorithm that iteratively divides an SCC into several smaller parts and resolves loops in each part. However, eliminating loops in an MDP is particularly challenging due to the existence of many probability distributions. To the best of our knowledge, there has been no previous work on SCC reductions for MDP. Instead of a simple extension of the divide-and-conquer for DTMC in [13], our divide-and-conquer algorithm for MDP is carefully designed to avoid generation of extra schedulers. To further accelerate the elimination of loops, we actively detect and remove redundant probability distributions of each state based on the convex hull property.

Conclusion. In this work, we have proposed a divide-and-conquer algorithm to eliminate SCCs in MDPs, for achieving an efficient reachability analysis. To cope with the non-determinism in MDPs, our divide-and-conquer algorithm is designed to work on partitions. Initially, each state in an SCC is considered as a partition. The partitions are repeatedly merged together until there is only one left. During the abstraction, loops within a partition are replaced by equivalent probability distributions between inputs and outputs. The convex hull property is applied to further reduce the redundant probability distributions. We have implemented this algorithm in a model checker PAT. The evaluation results on two practical case studies show that our method can improve reachability analysis.

References

1. http://www.comp.nus.edu.sg/~pat/rel/mdpcut
2. Abrahám, E., Jansen, N., Wimmer, R., Katoen, J., Becker, B.: DTMC model checking by SCC reduction. In: QEST, pp. 37–46. IEEE (2010)
3. Andrés, M.E., D'Argenio, P.R., Rossum, P.V.: Significant diagnostic counterexamples in probabilistic model checking. In: HCV, pp. 129–148 (2008)
4. Baier, C., Katoen, J.: Principles of model checking. The MIT Press (2008)
5. Bentley, J.L., Preparata, F.P., Faust, M.G.: Approximation algorithms for convex hulls. Communications of the ACM 25(1), 64–68 (1982)
6. Cattani, S., Segala, R.: Decision algorithms for probabilistic bisimulation. In: Brim, L., Jančar, P., Křetínský, M., Kučera, A. (eds.) CONCUR 2002. LNCS, vol. 2421, pp. 371–386. Springer, Heidelberg (2002)
7. Ciesinski, F., Baier, C., Grosser, M., Klein, J.: Reduction techniques for model checking Markov decision processes. In: QEST, pp. 45–54. IEEE (2008)
8. De Berg, M., Van Kreveld, M., Overmars, M., Schwarzkopf, O.C.: Computational geometry. Springer, Heidelberg (2000)
9. Forejt, V., Kwiatkowska, M., Norman, G., Parker, D.: Automated verification techniques for probabilistic systems. In: FMENSS, pp. 53–113. Springer, Heidelberg (2011)
10. Gui, L., Sun, J., Liu, Y., Si, Y.J., Dong, J.S., Wang, X.Y.: Combining model checking and testing with an application to reliability prediction and distribution. In: ISSTA, pp. 101–111. ACM (2013)
11. Kwiatkowska, M., Parker, D., Qu, H.: Incremental quantitative verification for Markov decision processes. In: DSN, pp. 359–370. IEEE (2011)
12. Liu, Y., Gui, L., Liu, Y.: MDP-based reliability analysis of an ambient assisted living system. In: FM Industry Track, Singapore (May 2014)
13. Song, S., Gui, L., Sun, J., Liu, Y., Dong, J.S.: Improved reachability analysis in DTMC via divide and conquer. In: Johnsen, E.B., Petre, L. (eds.) IFM 2013. LNCS, vol. 7940, pp. 162–176. Springer, Heidelberg (2013)
14. Stewart, W.J.: Introduction to the numerical solution of Markov chains. Princeton University Press (1994)
15. Sun, J., Liu, Y., Dong, J.S., Pang, J.: PAT: Towards flexible verification under fairness. In: Bouajjani, A., Maler, O. (eds.) CAV 2009. LNCS, vol. 5643, pp. 709–714. Springer, Heidelberg (2009)
16. Tarjan, R.E.: Depth-first search and linear graph algorithms. SIAM J. Comput. 1(2), 146–160 (1972)

Comprehension of Spacecraft Telemetry Using Hierarchical Specifications of Behavior*

Klaus Havelund and Rajeev Joshi

Jet Propulsion Laboratory,
California Institute of Technology,
California, USA

Abstract. A key challenge in operating remote spacecraft is that ground operators must rely on the limited visibility available through spacecraft telemetry in order to assess spacecraft health and operational status. We describe a tool for processing spacecraft telemetry that allows ground operators to impose structure on received telemetry in order to achieve a better comprehension of system state. A key element of our approach is the design of a domain-specific language that allows operators to express models of expected system behavior using partial specifications. The language allows behavior specifications with data fields, similar to other recent runtime verification systems. What is notable about our approach is the ability to develop hierarchical specifications of behavior. The language is implemented as an internal DSL in the SCALA programming language that synthesizes rules from patterns of specification behavior. The rules are automatically applied to received telemetry and the inferred behaviors are available to ground operators using a visualization interface that makes it easier to understand and track spacecraft state. We describe initial results from applying our tool to telemetry received from the Curiosity rover currently roving the surface of Mars, where the visualizations are being used to trend subsystem behaviors, in order to identify potential problems before they happen. However, the technology is completely general and can be applied to any system that generates telemetry such as event logs.

1 Introduction

One of the key challenges in operating remote spacecraft is that ground operators must rely on limited telemetry visible on the ground in order to assess the health and operational status of the spacecraft. Such telemetry typically consists of a log of system events and sensor measurements (such as battery voltage or probe temperature) which, for the purposes of this paper, may be viewed as a sequence of timestamped records with named fields. Because this telemetry comprises essentially *all* the knowledge that ground operators have about a given

---

* The work described in this publication was carried out at Jet Propulsion Laboratory, California Institute of Technology, under a contract with the National Aeronautics and Space Administration.

S. Merz and J. Pang (Eds.): ICFEM 2014, LNCS 8829, pp. 187–202, 2014.

spacecraft, processing this telemetry in a timely manner is of utmost importance to any mission. However, as spacecraft have become more autonomous and capable, and improvements in radio performance have resulted in greater downlink bandwidth, the resulting volume and complexity of the telemetry requires more automated processing tools so that any potential problems are diagnosed quickly and accurately. Unfortunately, currently such tools are developed by ground operators in an ad-hoc manner, typically using libraries developed by various subsystem teams that mine the telemetry to infer summaries that are of interest to that subsystem. These summaries are typically presented to ground operators using various visualization interfaces. While these tools have been overall quite effective, and the domain knowledge encoded in these libraries has led to many problems being identified early, the current approach of relying on ad-hoc scripts also makes the resulting tools fragile, hard for new team members to understand, and difficult to maintain. The maintainability issue is especially important for long-running missions that are expected to last many years.

To address this problem, this paper presents a declarative notation for expressing domain-specific knowledge about telemetry structure. In our formalism, the behavior of spacecraft subsystems may be expressed in terms of *behaviors*, in a language that resembles regular expressions, but with support for conjunction and data arguments to nonterminals. A key feature of our notation is that behaviors may be nested, since in our experience, most subsystems are usually viewed as a set of (possibly interrelated) hierarchical behaviors, and often viewed using visualization interfaces that allow behaviors of interest to be explored interactively. We demonstrate our approach in practice by showing how it is being applied to telemetry received from the Curiosity rover [3] currently on Mars. However, although applied to spacecraft operation, the techniques are fully general, and can be used for analysis of any form of event logs produced by a software system.

There has been much previous work in processing telemetry event logs in the field of *runtime verification* (RV), typically checking logs against user provided specifications, often expressed in some form of temporal logic. Such analysis may take place pre-deployment, as the system is being developed, or post-deployment, during operation. Orthogonally, the monitoring may be done online, processing telemetry on-board during execution, or offline by analyzing logs. We are concerned with post-deployment offline trace analysis. Most previous work, however, focuses on checking if a given event log satisfies a given specification or not (sometimes extending the Boolean domain with extra values to 3 or 4-valued logics, indicating grade of satisfaction). In our experience, coming up with formally verifiable properties is difficult in practice, especially for complex missions where design requirements were not in a formal notation to begin with. Thus our focus is more on providing a framework for performing *log comprehension*. This form of log comprehension can often be useful in identifying problems not easily formalized, but can also serve as a stepping stone to eventually writing (traditional) formal properties that may be checked for satisfaction.

To provide flexibility in expressing varied subsystem models, we have implemented our notation as an internal DSL (Domain-Specific Language), essentially an API, in the SCALA programming language. SCALA offers language constructs that makes definition of such APIs have the appearance of DSLs. Specifically we use SCALA's implicit functions to define concrete syntax, and case classes to define abstract syntax. The resulting DSL is largely a so-called *deep embedding*, in contrast to a *shallow* embedding. In a deep embedding a particular program in the DSL is completely defined by an abstract syntax tree, which can be processed as an internal data structure. In contrast, in a shallow embedding host language constructs are made part of the DSL. A deep embedding makes it easier to analyze DSL programs. As we shall see, however, we do allow the DSL to contain arbitrary SCALA code in limited positions, hence our approach is a mix of deep and shallow embedding.

We implement our DSL using the rule-based LOGFIRE system [17], which is itself an internal SCALA DSL. Rule-based systems, which have been extensively studied within the artificial intelligence (AI) community, allow formulation of rules of the form:

$$condition_1, \ldots, condition_n \Rightarrow action$$

The state of a rule-system can abstractly be considered as consisting of a set of *facts*, referred to as the *fact memory*, where a fact is a mapping from field names to values. A condition in a rule's left-hand side can check for the presence or absence of a particular fact. A left-hand side matching against the fact memory usually requires unification of variables occurring in conditions. In case all conditions on a rule's left-hand side match (become true), the right-hand side action is executed, which can be any SCALA code, including adding and deleting facts, or generating error messages. LOGFIRE is an implementation of the RETE algorithm [13] used in many AI rule systems.

The rule formalism, although very natural and expressive, turns out to be slightly verbose for writing log properties. The core problem can be illustrated by an example. Assume that one wants to monitor that the events E_1 and E_2 occur in that order. A rule system would have to explicitly create an intermediate fact E_1Seen representing the fact that E_1 has occurred. The issue is similar to that of state machines where all states must be explicitly defined. Regular expressions and temporal logics provide a solution to this problem. We here show a regular expression-like formalism which (i) makes this more convenient, and (ii) which allows for abstraction as discussed above. The DSL we present is defined as patterns that are translated to rules, in a similar manner as discussed in [17].

The paper is organized as follows. Section 2 outlines related work. Section 3 introduces briefly the rule-based system LOGFIRE, and outlines the inconveniences in using this solution for this problem. Section 4 introduces the new DSL and its translation to rules. Section 5 presents the application to a spacecraft scenario, illustrating visualization of event abstractions. Finally, Section 6 concludes the paper.

2   Related Work

Several systems have been developed over the last decade for supporting monitoring of parameterized events. These systems support various formalisms, such as state machines [14,19,11,7,5], regular expressions [4,19], variations over the μ-calculus [6], temporal logics [6,19,7,15,9,10,12], grammars [19], and rule-based systems [8,17]. Some of these systems focus on being efficient. However, this efficiency is typically achieved at the price of some lack of expressiveness, as discussed in [5]. Our previous research has focused on more expressive formalisms, including rule-based systems, such as RULER [8] and more recently LOGFIRE [17]. Rule-based systems in general provide a rich formalism, which can be used to encode the kind of abstraction needed for our behavior definitions. LOGFIRE is based on the RETE algorithm [13], which is the basis for many rule-based systems developed over time, including for example DROOLS [2]. Standard rule systems usually enable processing of facts, which have a life time. In contrast, LOGFIRE in addition implements events, which are instantaneous, and which are needed for the kind of application presented in this paper. DROOLS supports a notion of events, which are facts with a limited life time. These events, however, are not as short-lived as possibly desirable in runtime verification. The event concept in DROOLS is inspired by the concept of *Complex Event Processing* (CEP), described by David Luckham in [18]. This concept is related to our approach using hierarchical behaviors. CEP is concerned with processing streams of events in (near) real time, where the main focus is on the correlation and composition of atomic events into complex (compound) events. TRACECONTRACT [7] and DAUT [16] are internal SCALA DSLs for trace analysis based on state machines. They allow for multi-transitions without explicitly naming the intermediate states, which corresponds to sequential composition of events. MOPBOX [11], and its more efficient successor PRM4J, are JAVA APIs for a set of algorithms implementing MOP's [19] functionality.

3   The LOGFIRE Rule Engine

As already mentioned, LOGFIRE is a SCALA API for writing rule-based programs in a manner that has the appearance of a DSL. It was originally created as a study of how the RETE algorithm could be used for runtime verification purposes, where the main goal is to check event traces against formalized specifications, and emit verdicts in a Boolean domain, stating whether the event stream satisfies the specification or not. In the following, we shall first illustrate the originally intended application, and in the subsequent sub-section we shall illustrate its use for abstraction, which is the topic of this paper. We then suggest that a more convenient solution is desirable for this objective.

3.1   LOGFIRE used for Verification

Consider a system that emits two kinds of events: $E_1(clk \rightarrow t_1)$ and $E_2(clk \rightarrow t_2)$, each being a named record (names are E_1 and E_2) with a field clk that is

```
class  Verifier  extends Monitor {
   "v1"  ---  'E1('clk → 't1) ⟼ insert('E1Seen('t1))

   "v2"  ---  'E2('clk → 't2) & not('E1Seen('t1)) ⟼ fail()

   "v3"  ---  'E2('clk → 't2) & 'E1Seen('t1) ⟼ {
      if ('t2-'t1 > 5000) fail ()
   }
}
```

Fig. 1. A LogFire verifier

mapped to a time stamp t_i indicating the time when these events were generated. Suppose we want to enforce that E_2 can only occur after E_1, and furthermore, if E_2 occurs, it has to occur within 5 seconds of the occurrence of E_1. This property is shown in Figure 1. The main component of LogFire is the **trait**[1] *Monitor*, which any user-defined monitor must extend to get access to the constants and methods provided by the rule DSL. The *events* E_1 and E_2 are short-lived instantaneous observations about the system being monitored, those submitted to the monitor. In contrast, *facts*, in this case E_1Seen, are long-lived pieces of information stored in the fact memory of the rule system, generated and deleted explicitly by the rules. In the monitor above the fact $E_1Seen(t_1)$ is used to represent the fact that the event $E_1(clk \rightarrow t_1)$ has been seen. The monitor contains three rules, named v_1, v_2 and v_3. Each rule has the form:

$$name \; \texttt{--} \; condition_1 \; \& \ldots \& \; condition_n \; \longmapsto \; action$$

Event and fact names, as well as parameter names are values of the SCALA type *Symbol*, which contains quoted identifiers. The need for representing user-defined names as symbols is a consequence of the fact that LogFire is a deep embedding (we don't use SCALA's names). Events and facts can have arguments specified in one of two ways: using *positional notation* or *using map notation*. Positional notation means just listing arguments as a list of patterns (identifiers or literals). In our example facts are represented using positional notation. The positional notation is convenient if events/facts carry few arguments. Map notation means considering the events/facts as being maps from field names to values. In our example event patterns are shown using map notation, assuming each event has a time stamp named *'clk*. When using map notation only fields relevant for the rule need be mentioned. An action is any SCALA statement, that specifically for example can add or delete facts, or call failure methods.

The rules are to be read as follows. Rule v_1 states that when an E_1 event is observed, a fact, E_1Seen is created to record this. Rule v_2 states that an error is

---

[1] A **trait** in SCALA is a module concept closely related to the notion of an *abstract class*, as for example found in JAVA.

generated if an E_2 event is observed, but no E_1 event has been observed before that. Finally, rule v_3 states that in the case an E_1 event and subsequently an E_2 event is observed, the time difference must be within 5 seconds. A monitor can be applied as shown in Figure 2, which also shows an example of an error trace produced. Each entry in the error trace shows the number of the event, the event, the fact that it causes to be generated, and the rule that triggers. In this case the 5 second requirement is violated.

```
object ApplyMonitor {
  def main(args: Array[String]) {
    val m = new Verifier
    m.addMapEvent('E1)('clk → 1023)
    m.addMapEvent('E3)('clk → 3239)
    m.addMapEvent('E2)('clk → 7008)
  }
}
  ...


*** error :

[1]  'E1('clk → 1023) ⟹ 'E1Seen(1023)
       rule : "v1" −− 'E1('clk → 't1) ⟼ {...}

[3]  'E2('clk → 7008) ⟹ 'Fail("ERROR")
       rule : "v3" −− 'E2('clk → 't2) & 'E1Seen('t1) ⟼ {...}
```

Fig. 2. Applying a LOGFIRE verifier

3.2   LOGFIRE **Used for Abstraction**

In this sub-section we shall illustrate how LOGFIRE may be used to model the hierarchical behaviors of interest in our application. We consider a scenario with a top-level behavior (denoted *alpha*) that consists of an inner behavior (denoted *beta*) in parallel with a single event E_3. The behavior *beta* in turn consists of two events E_1 and E_2 that must occur in that order. Denoting the three atomic events as $E_1(clk \rightarrow t_1)$, $E_2(clk \rightarrow t_2)$, and $E_3(clk \rightarrow t_3)$, we want to record two facts: that E_2 occurs after E_1 is to be recorded as an occurrence of $beta(t_1, t_2)$, and that E_3 occurs either before or after (that is: in parallel with) $beta(t_1, t_2)$ is to be recorded as an occurrence of $alpha(t_1, t_2, t_3)$. The resulting monitor is shown in Figure 3.

The monitor contains four rules. The first rule, a_1, records when an $E_1(clk \rightarrow t_1)$ event is seen. Rule r_2 records a $beta(t_1, t_2)$ fact when an $E_2(clk \rightarrow t_2)$ event

```
class Abstracter extends Monitor {
  "a1" —— 'E1('clk → 't1) ⟼ insert('E1Seen('t1))

  "a2" —— 'E1Seen('t1) & 'E2('clk → 't2) ⟼ {
    remove('E1Seen);
    insert ('beta('t1, 't2))
  }

  "a3" —— 'E3('clk → 't3) ⟼ insert('E3Seen('t3))

  "a4" —— 'beta('t1, 't2) & 'E3Seen('t3) ⟼ {
    remove('E3Seen);
    insert ('alpha('t1, 't2, 't3))
  }
}
```

Fig. 3. A LOGFIRE abstracter

is seen after an $E_1(clk \rightarrow t_1)$ event. It also removes the intermediate event recording that E_1 was seen, in order to not clutter the set of facts generated. Rule a_3 records when an $E_3(clk \rightarrow t_3)$ event is seen, and finally rule a_4 creates the $alpha(t_1, t_2, t_3)$ fact. When applying the abstracter to the same event sequence as shown in Figure 2, instead of an error trace, we obtain a set of generated facts, as shown in Figure 4.

The main observation to be made, about this specification, as well as the verifier in Figure 1, is that it is inconvenient that we have to add (and delete) intermediate facts such as $E_1 Seen$ and $E_3 Seen$ explicitly, which makes these rules cumbersome to write and maintain. To avoid this problem, in the next section, we introduce notation that allows hierarchical events to be described more directly, in a form similar to the way one writes regular expressions, but with support for conjunctive composition and event parameters.

4   A DSL for Log Abstraction

We start by presenting our notation first in an idealized form, showing how the LOGFIRE abstracter presented in the previous section can be written, as well as an idealized grammar. Subsequently we show how our notation is embedded as an internal SCALA DSL, and we briefly sketch how our DSL implementation automatically generates LOGFIRE rules from such descriptions.

```
object ApplyMonitor {
  def main(args: Array[String]) {
    val m = new Abstracter
    m.addMapEvent('E1)('clk → 1023)
    m.addMapEvent('E3)('clk → 3239)
    m.addMapEvent('E2)('clk → 7008)
  }
}
  ...


––– facts: –––––––
'beta(1023,7008)
'alpha(1023,7008,3239)
–––––––––––––––
```

Fig. 4. Applying a LOGFIRE abstracter

4.1   A More Convenient Notation for Abstraction

Our proposed idealized syntax for the example shown in Figure 3 is shown in Figure 5. The model contains two so-called *behaviors*, one generating $beta(t_1, t_2)$ facts, and one generating $alpha(t_1, t_2, t_3)$ facts. The first rule shows an example of sequential composition, and reads as follows: when an $E_1(clk \rightarrow t_1)$ event is observed *followed by* an $E_2(clk \rightarrow t_2)$ event, a $beta(t_1, t_2)$ fact is generated. The second behavior shows an example of *parallel composition*, and reads: when a $beta(t_1, t_2)$ facts has been generated at some point, and a $E_3(clk \rightarrow t_3)$ event has been observed at some point, an $alpha(t_1, t_2, t_3)$ is generated, the ordering is unimportant. The fact generated, occurring to the left of the symbol |==, is referred to as the *behavior head*. The expression occurring on the right of the symbol |== is referred to as the *behavior expression*. Such behavior definitions have some resemblance to PROLOG, but differ by being focused on events, and by supporting sequential composition as well as choice.

```
beta(t1, t2)  |==  E1(clk -> t1)  >>  E2(clk -> t2)

alpha(t1, t2, t3)  |==  beta(t1, t2)  &&  E3(clk -> t3)
```

Fig. 5. Abstracter using idealized syntax

The idealized grammar for our language is shown in Figure 6, using a form of extended BNF, where $\langle N \rangle$ denotes a non-terminal, $\langle N \rangle ::= \ldots$ defines the non-terminal $\langle N \rangle$, S^* denotes zero or more occurrences of S, $S^{*,*}$ denotes zero or more occurrences of S separated by commas (','), $S \mid T$ denotes the choice between S and T, and finally an expression in single quotes (such as '$\gg$') denotes a terminal symbol. A $\langle behaviorModel \rangle$ is a sequence of definitions, each being either a $\langle variableDef \rangle$ or a $\langle behaviorDef \rangle$. We already saw examples of behavior definitions in Figure 5. Variable definitions allow us to define convenient abbreviations for expressions which simplify the definition of a behavior expression and make it more readable. A $\langle behaviorExp \rangle$ can have one of six forms. We have already seen examples of sequential ($\gg$) and parallel (&&) composition. In addition behavior expressions can be composed with choice (++), meaning: one of the two sub-behaviors are observed. Behavior expressions can be grouped with parentheses. At the atomic level we distinguish between events observed and facts generated. They differ in two ways: event names are in all capital, and the arguments are given using map notation (see page 191), mapping field identifiers to identifiers representing their value. Fact names cannot be all capital, and arguments are provided in positional style.

$\langle behaviorModel \rangle ::= (\langle variableDef \rangle \mid \langle behaviorDef \rangle)^*$

$\langle variableDef \rangle ::= \langle id \rangle \text{ ':='} \langle expr \rangle$

$\langle behaviorDef \rangle ::= \langle name \rangle \text{ '('} \langle id \rangle^{*,*} \text{ ')'} \text{ '}\models\text{'} \langle behaviorExp \rangle$

$\langle behaviorExp \rangle ::= \langle behaviorExp \rangle \text{ '}\gg\text{'} \langle behaviorExp \rangle$
$\qquad \mid \langle behaviorExp \rangle \text{ '\&\&'} \langle behaviorExp \rangle$
$\qquad \mid \langle behaviorExp \rangle \text{ '++'} \langle behaviorExp \rangle$
$\qquad \mid \text{ '('} \langle behaviorExp \rangle \text{ ')'}$
$\qquad \mid \langle event \rangle$
$\qquad \mid \langle fact \rangle$

$\langle fact \rangle ::= \langle identifier \rangle \text{ '('} \langle id \rangle^{*,*} \text{ ')'}$

$\langle event \rangle ::= \langle identifier \rangle \text{ '('} \langle binding \rangle^{*,*} \text{ ')'}$

$\langle binding \rangle ::= \langle id \rangle \text{ '}\rightarrow\text{'} \langle id \rangle$

Fig. 6. Idealized grammar for abstracter DSL

4.2   Embedding as an Internal DSL in SCALA

A variant of the idealized example shown in Figure 5, formalized in our internal SCALA DSL, is shown in Figure 7. We have augmented the example with two variable definitions, one defining the variable $'min$ as the minimal value to the two time stamps t_1 and t_3, and one defining the variable $'max$ as the maximal value to the two time stamps t_2 and t_3. These variables will be computed for each *alpha* fact generated, representing the time interval within which all important events occurred.

```scala
trait Example extends Abstracter {
  'tmin := { Math.min('t1.toDouble, 't3.toDouble) }
  'tmax := { Math.max('t2.toDouble, 't3.toDouble) }

  'beta('t1, 't2) |= 'E1('clk → 't1)  ≫  'E2('clk → 't2)

  'alpha('tmin, 'tmax) |= 'beta('t1, 't2)  &&  'E3('clk → 't3)
}
```

Fig. 7. Abstracter in SCALA DSL

As can be observed, the syntax has the same look and feel as the idealized syntax presented earlier. This is achieved by using some of SCALA's features for defining domain-specific languages, including implicit functions, possibility to define methods using non-alphanumeric symbols, and the possibility of leaving out dots and parentheses in calls of methods on objects. Generally, implicit functions automatically convert values of the argument type into values of the result type as follows. Whenever a SCALA expression fails to type check, the SCALA compiler will consult the implicit functions in scope and determine whether the application of a such will make the expression type check, and in this case the compiler will insert an application of the function (there can be no more than one such implicit conversion function, otherwise the SCALA compiler will complain).

This is illustrated with the *Abstracter* **trait** in Figure 8, shown in part, that behavior models extend. Consider the rule for generating $'beta('t_1, 't_2)$ in Figure 7. The SCALA compiler fails to make meaning out of this definition for a number of reasons. First of all, symbols like $'beta$ are being applied as if they were functions, and methods $\models$ and $\gg$ are being applied to objects on which they are not defined. The compiler searches the implicit functions, and finds that S will lift a symbol to an object that defines an *apply* method, which when applied generates a *Fact* object. Furthermore, the compiler finds that the implicit function F lifts such a *Fact* object to an object that defines a $\models$ method, which as argument takes a behavior expression. The behavior expression itself likewise is composed by calling the method $\gg$ on the firstly created behavior expression, without dot notation. When all implicit function calls and dots and parentheses have been inserted, the definition is equivalent to the following.

```scala
F(S('beta).apply('t1, 't2)).|=(
  (S('E1).apply('clk → 't1)).≫(S('E2).apply('clk → 't2)))
```

```
trait Abstracter {
  ...
  implicit def S(s: Symbol) = new {
    def apply(args: Any*): Fact = Fact(s, args.toList)
  }

  implicit def F(lhs: Fact) = new {
    def ⊨(rhs: BehExp) = ruleGen.generate(rhs, lhs)
  }
  ...
  trait BehExp {
    def ≫(n: BehExp): BehExp = SeqBehExp(this, n)
    def &&(n: BehExp): BehExp = ParBehExp(this, n)
    def ++(n: BehExp): BehExp = ChoBehExp(this, n)
    ...
  }
  ...
}
```

Fig. 8. Definition of a DSL

4.3 Rule Generation with SCALA

The synthesized method call creates an abstract syntax tree, upon which a method is finally called, which generates LOGFIRE rules. We shall not illustrate this in detail, but only outline the general idea. Figure 9 illustrates the method, $mkParRule$, that generates rules from a parallel composition of behavior expressions. The method takes four parameters: pre, which is a pre-condition, a fact that has to occur before the sub-behaviors of the parallel composition will be observed. The two sub-behaviors a and b, being arguments to the $\gg$ operator, and finally a post condition: a fact that is generated when the two sub-behaviors have been observed. Two intermediate facts P_1 and P_2 are first generated. Note how the parameters coming from the pre-condition are carried over such that generated facts accumulate all parameters seen so far. Rules for the two subexpressions a and b are subsequently generated, inheriting the pre-condition, and with respectively P_1 and P_2 as post-conditions: these facts are generated once the sub-behaviors have been observed. Finally, the main rule for parallel composition is generated, using the LOGFIRE DSL. It gets an internal name generated by $newRuleId()$, and triggers once P_1 and P_2 have occurred, with the proper parameters. As a result the post-condition fact of the parallel composition is generated and the intermediate facts are removed. The rules generated are very similar to the rules shown in Figure 3.

```
trait BehaviorMonitor extends Monitor {
  ...
  def mkParRule(pre: Fact, a: BehExp, b: BehExp, post: Fact) = {
    val P1 = new Fact(mkSym("par"), params(pre) ⊕ params(a))
    val P2 = new Fact(mkSym("par"), params(pre) ⊕ params(b))

    generate(pre, a, P1)
    generate(pre, b, P2)

    newRuleId() −− P1.s(params(P1): _*) & P2.s(params(P2): _*) ⟼ {
      insert (post.s(params(post): _*))
      remove(P1.s)
      remove(P2.s)
    }
  }
  ...
}
```

Fig. 9. Synthesis of LOGFIRE rules from a parallel behavior expression

5 Application: Mars-Earth Communication Sessions

In this section, we briefly describe how our notation is applied to analyze telemetry received from the Curiosity rover on Mars. In particular, we describe how we
process telemetry related to the rover's direct communication sessions with Earth.
A communication session with Earth consists of two behaviors that happen in parallel: a *tracking* behavior that moves the high-gain antenna to point towards the
Earth and starts tracking to compensate for Mars's rotation, and a *configuration*
behavior that turns on and configures the radios to communicate with the deep
space network back on Earth. Since the Mars-Earth distance varies over time, this
requires compensating for variable one-way light time, to ensure that the rover antenna is pointed and the radio ready when the signal from Earth arrives at Mars.
Because communication is a critical behavior for the spacecraft, the operations
team carefully monitors telemetry received from the rover to ensure adequate mar-
gins are being maintained for the signal arrival at Mars.

Figure 10 shows a sample event log from a typical communication session[2].
Each window has an assigned unique identifier and a configuration parameter.
As shown in the figure, our sample log consists of two back-to-back communica-
tion sessions performed on the rover. The first session (with identifier W25211)

---

[2] In the interests of readability, and to comply with guidelines about sharing telemetry
details, we have omitted various technical details about radio configurations, and
modified times and arguments from the original values.

```
09:23:10  WINDOW_BEGINS("W25211", "HGA")
09:23:16  HGA_START_TRACK
09:23:18  XBAND_CONFIG("RECEIVE_ONLY")
09:23:30  HGA_EARTH_ACQUIRE
09:29:59  START_COMM
09:59:11  STOP_COMM
09:59:12  HGA_STOP_TRACK
09:59:27  WINDOW_CLEANUP

10:04:59  WINDOW_BEGINS("W60002", "HGA")
10:05:05  HGA_START_TRACK
10:05:06  XBAND_CONFIG("CARRIER_ONLY_2")
10:05:21  HGA_EARTH_ACQUIRE
10:07:03  START_COMM
10:16:46  STOP_COMM
10:16:48  HGA_STOP_TRACK
10:17:04  WINDOW_CLEANUP
```

Fig. 10. Sample event log from a communication session

is configured as a RECEIVE_ONLY window and is used to uplink commands to the rover. One of the commands uplinked adds a second comm session (with identifier W60002) that is configured as CARRIER_ONLY and is used to send a 'beep' to Earth indicating successful receipt of commands from the first session. As shown in the figure, each session is bracketed by two events (named WINDOW_BEGINS and WINDOW_CLEANUP), and internally consists of two parallel behaviors: a *configuration* behavior that turns on the telecommunication hardware and configures it for communication, and a *tracking* behavior that points and tracks the high-gain antenna. The configuration behavior consists of three events: XBAND_CONFIG, indicating the start of radio configuration, START_COMM, indicating that the radio is ready to communicate, and STOP_COMM, indicating that the radio is being turned off. The tracking behavior also consists of three events: the HGA_START_TRACK event, indicating that pointing has commenced, the HGA_EARTH_ACQUIRE event, indicating that the antenna is pointed towards Earth, and the HGA_STOP_TRACK event, indicating that the antenna is terminating the tracking operation. As shown, each log event has an associated timestamp, along with optional arguments that provide additional information (such as the exact configuration used for the radio).

Figure 11 shows the behavior model for such a communication session in our notation. As shown in the figure, we define a SCALA **trait** called *CommSession* that extends the *Abstracter* **trait** defined in the previous Section 4, Figure 8. Nested within a *CommSession* is a parallel composition of the *config* and *track* behaviors, each of which is a sequential composition of the three log events described above. To extract event times, we rely on a SCALA library that processes spacecraft event logs and generates primitive LOGFIRE events (named *EVR*) that contain a map with a timestamp (denoted by key *lmst*) and optional event arguments (denoted by key *args*), which can be recovered using the *getArg* library function.

```
trait CommSession extends Abstracter {
  'wid   := { getArg('wargs, 0) }
  'wtype := { getArg('wargs, 1) }
  'session ('wid, 'wtype, 'tws, 'twe, 'tts) |=
    (  'EVR('id → "WINDOW_BEGINS", 'lmst → 'tws, 'args → 'wargs)
    ≫ ('config ('ckind, 'tcs, 'tas, 'tce)  && 'track ('tts, 'tte))
    ≫ 'EVR('id → "WINDOW_CLEANUP", 'lmst → 'twe)
    )

  'kind := { getArg('cargs, 0) }
  'config ('kind, 'tcs, 'tas, 'tce) |=
    (  'EVR('id → "XBAND_CONFIG", 'lmst → 'tcs, 'args → 'cargs)
    ≫ 'EVR('id → "START_COMM", 'lmst → 'tas)
    ≫ 'EVR('id → "STOP_COMM", 'lmst → 'tce)
    )

  'track ('tts, 'tacq, 'tte) |=
    (  'EVR('id → "HGA_START_TRACK", 'lmst → 'tts)
    ≫ 'EVR('id → "HGA_EARTH_ACQUIRE", 'lmst → 'tacq)
    ≫ 'EVR('id → "HGA_STOP_TRACK", 'lmst → 'tte)
    )
}
```

Fig. 11. The model for a communication session in our notation

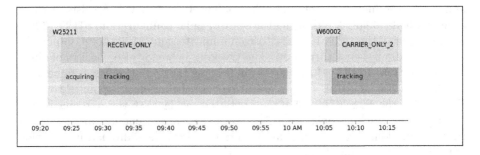

Fig. 12. Visualization of the two communication sessions from Figure 10

After the model has been interpreted, the resulting LOGFIRE rules generated may be used to process the event log shown above. The resulting nested structure is then saved in a web-readable format and processed by visualization tools, developed with D3 [1], resulting in the display shown in figure 12, which is integrated into an online *dashboard* used by the operations team. The figure shows the two *sessions* captured, composed sequentially, identified by $W25211$ and $W60002$. Each session in turn contains a *configuration* behavior and a *tracking* behavior, shown on top of each other, and each divided into two sections corresponding to the three events that define them. The visualization capability is crucial for presenting the hierarchical abstractions extracted by the tool from the telemetry. In addition to communication sessions, we have also applied our notation for writing models for other rover subsystems, including behaviors describing the boot timeline, and certain behaviors involving on-board data management.

6   Conclusion and Future Work

We have described a notation for expressing domain-specific knowledge about subsystem behaviors that can be used for writing hierarchical models of telemetry streams (logs). These models are written using a SCALA API that provides a great deal of flexibility. The formalism supports the following concepts: events, hierarchical abstraction, sequential, conjunctive and disjunctive composition, and allows users to write partial specifications that ignore events not of interest. The result of an analysis is a set of facts, rather than a boolean verdict. This allows existing models written in ad-hoc scripting languages to be easily expressed in our notation. The models are translated into a set of rules that can be used by the LOGFIRE rule-based engine to automatically process telemetry received on the ground, allowing higher-level patterns to be matched and presented to ground operators. We have described how our method is applied to telemetry being received from the Curiosity rover, as part of an ongoing effort to build a system-wide dashboard for monitoring and analyzing spacecraft state. We are currently working on applying our methods to generate behavior models automatically from the hierarchical plans that are used to schedule rover activities every day. These models will then be applied to highlight discrepancies between predicted and actual rover activities. An interesting direction of research is to identify events that do not match any of the planned behaviors, since such events are often indicative of anomalous or unexpected behavior.

References

1. D3 website, http://d3js.org
2. Drools website, http://www.jboss.org/drools
3. Mars Science Laboratory (MSL) mission website, http://mars.jpl.nasa.gov/msl
4. Allan, C., Avgustinov, P., Christensen, A.S., Hendren, L., Kuzins, S., Lhoták, O., de Moor, O., Sereni, D., Sittamplan, G., Tibble, J.: Adding trace matching with free variables to AspectJ. In: OOPSLA 2005, ACM Press (2005)
5. Barringer, H., Falcone, Y., Havelund, K., Reger, G., Rydeheard, D.: Quantified event automata: Towards expressive and efficient runtime monitors. In: Giannakopoulou, D., Méry, D. (eds.) FM 2012. LNCS, vol. 7436, pp. 68–84. Springer, Heidelberg (2012)
6. Barringer, H., Goldberg, A., Havelund, K., Sen, K.: Rule-based runtime verification. In: Steffen, B., Levi, G. (eds.) VMCAI 2004. LNCS, vol. 2937, pp. 44–57. Springer, Heidelberg (2004)

7. Barringer, H., Havelund, K.: TRACECONTRACT: A scala DSL for trace analysis. In: Butler, M., Schulte, W. (eds.) FM 2011. LNCS, vol. 6664, pp. 57–72. Springer, Heidelberg (2011)

8. Barringer, H., Rydeheard, D.E., Havelund, K.: Rule systems for run-time monitoring: from Eagle to RuleR. J. Log. Comput. 20(3), 675–706 (2010)

9. Basin, D.A., Klaedtke, F., Müller, S.: Policy monitoring in first-order temporal logic. In: Touili, T., Cook, B., Jackson, P. (eds.) CAV 2010. LNCS, vol. 6174, pp. 1–18. Springer, Heidelberg (2010)

10. Bauer, A., Küster, J.-C., Vegliach, G.: From propositional to first-order monitoring. In: Legay, A., Bensalem, S. (eds.) RV 2013. LNCS, vol. 8174, pp. 59–75. Springer, Heidelberg (2013)

11. Bodden, E.: MOPBox: A library approach to runtime verification. In: Khurshid, S., Sen, K. (eds.) RV 2011. LNCS, vol. 7186, pp. 365–369. Springer, Heidelberg (2012)

12. Decker, N., Leucker, M., Thoma, D.: Monitoring modulo theories. In: Ábrahám, E., Havelund, K. (eds.) TACAS 2014 (ETAPS). LNCS, vol. 8413, pp. 341–356. Springer, Heidelberg (2014)

13. Forgy, C.: Rete: A fast algorithm for the many pattern/many object pattern match problem. Artificial Intelligence 19, 17–37 (1982)

14. Goubault-Larrecq, J., Olivain, J.: A smell of ORCHIDS. In: Leucker, M. (ed.) RV 2008. LNCS, vol. 5289, pp. 1–20. Springer, Heidelberg (2008)

15. Hallé, S., Villemaire, R.: Runtime enforcement of web service message contracts with data. IEEE Transactions on Services Computing 5(2), 192–206 (2012)

16. Havelund, K.: Data automata in Scala. In: Leucker, M., Wang, J. (eds.) 8th International Symposium on Theoretical Aspects of Software Engineering, TASE 2014, Changsha, China, September 1-3. IEEE Computer Society Press, Los Alamitos (2014)

17. Havelund, K.: Rule-based runtime verification revisited. Software Tools for Technology Transfer (STTT) (April 2014); Published online

18. Luckham, D. (ed.): The Power of Events: An Introduction to Complex Event Processing in Distributed Enterprise Systems. Addison-Wesley (2002)

19. Meredith, P., Jin, D., Griffith, D., Chen, F., Roşu, G.: An overview of the MOP runtime verification framework. Software Tools for Technology Transfer (STTT) 14(3), 249–289 (2012)

Timed Automata Verification via IC3 with Zones

Tobias Isenberg and Heike Wehrheim

Universität Paderborn,
Institut für Informatik,
33098 Paderborn, Germany
isenberg@mail.upb.de,wehrheim@upb.de

Abstract. Timed automata are a formal method for the modelling of real-time systems. With a large number of sophisticated tools, ample support for not only specification but also verification is available today. However, although all these tools are highly optimized, verification of timed automata, in particular *networks* of timed automata, remains challenging. This is due to the large amount of memory needed for storing automata states.

In this paper, we present a new approach to timed automata verification based on the SAT-based induction method IC3. Unlike previous work on extending IC3 to timed systems, we employ *zones*, not regions, for the symbolic representation of timed automata states. While this complicates a timed IC3 procedure, specifically, necessitates the computation of a zone from possibly infinitely many counterexamples to induction, it pays off with respect to memory consumption. Experimental results show that our approach can outperform Uppaal for networks with large numbers of timed automata.

Keywords: Verification, timed automata, zone abstraction, IC3, SMT.

1 Introduction

The verification of hard- and software systems often addresses the question whether or not the system of interest (or its model) adheres to a particular property.

With many of today's systems relying on real-time behavior, the verification of timed systems is of special interest. For modelling and verification of timed systems specified by timed automata, a number of tools (Uppaal [6], Kronos [10], Red [24], PAT [22]) are available today. They address the specific difficulty in the verification of timed systems – infinitely many states – by digitization [20] or appropriate symbolic representations of sets of states, either by regions or by zones. The latter come with efficient data structures for storage and manipulation in the form of Difference Bound Matrices (DBMs) [14], as well as specialized data structures for unions of zones, e.g., Clock Difference Diagrams [5] or Clock-Restriction Diagrams [23]. Despite such optimizations, verification of timed automata remains challenging due to the need for examining and storing all reachable states, which is costly even with these data structures.

S. Merz and J. Pang (Eds.): ICFEM 2014, LNCS 8829, pp. 203–218, 2014.

Recently, a new approach for the verification of timed systems based on the induction-based method IC3 was proposed by Kindermann et al. [18]. IC3 [11], originally developed for hardware verification, is a technique for incrementally computing inductive invariants of finite transitions systems and makes heavy use of SAT solvers for queries about inductiveness. The technique proposed in [18] extended this to timed systems by (1) using SMT solvers for modelling and checking constraints on clock or integer variables, and (2) using region abstraction to cope with the inherent infinity of timed systems. This combination seemed promising, in particular due to the fact that IC3 constructs over-approximations of i-step reachability and is rather efficient in this due to several improvements and extensions, e.g., [16,21,12,3]. However, the experimental results given in [18] showed that this new approach could not bring improvements over state-of-the-art timed automata verification as done by Uppaal. The results show once more a general problem of region abstraction: Larger constants in the model result in a larger number of regions, which then annihilates the desired effect of IC3 with respect to memory consumption.

Here, we propose a new approach to the application of IC3-type induction methods for the verification of timed automata. Instead of using region abstraction, we employ *zones* as our technique for representing infinitely many timed automaton states. With respect to the combination with IC3, this poses two challenges: (1) we need a technique for computing a zone from a counterexample to induction as returned from the IC3 algorithm, and (2) this zone has to be constructed in such a way that it rules out possibly infinitely many counterexamples to induction which can occur in a timed system. A third challenge results from the fact that we allow for integer variables in the timed automata, and their constraints need to be incorporated into the general algorithm as well.

For the evaluation of our technique, we wrote a verification tool checking safety properties for given networks of timed automata using our new approach. The results show our combination of IC3 with zone abstraction to be superior to the approach of Kindermann et al. Moreover, a comparison with Uppaal reveals a number of instances in which our approach outperforms Uppaal. Specifically, for the often employed benchmark of Fischer's mutual exclusion protocol, our new approach can handle instances with up to 30 processes whereas Uppaal already runs out of memory for 14 processes.

2   Background

In the following, we will briefly present some basics about timed automata and IC3 which are required in order to follow the presentation of our approach.

2.1   Timed Automata

In the early 90's, timed automata [1] were proposed as a formalism for the specification of timed systems, i.e., systems with a time-dependent behavior. A finite state automaton is enriched with real valued variables, called *clocks*, to model the elapse of time since their last reset. Clock constraints can be used to restrict the allowed behavior of the automaton depending on time. Furthermore, more recent formalisms allow integer variables which are not subject to time elapse. Several timed automata can be composed into a network in order to model a distributed system.

In the following, we formally define timed automata as used in the successive sections. We start with clocks and their valuations plus two operations on clocks, namely time elapse (the passing of time) and clock reset.

Definition 1. *A* clock *is a non-negative, real valued variable. The set of clocks is denoted by C. Mapping each clock $x \in C$ to a value $v^c(x) \in \mathbb{R}_{\geq 0}$ is called a* clock valuation v^c *(over C).*

For a clock valuation v^c and some $\delta \in \mathbb{R}_{\geq 0}$, the elapse *of δ time units, $v^c + \delta$, is defined as follows: $\forall x \in C : (v^c + \delta)(x) = v^c(x) + \delta$.*
Resetting *of a set $R \subseteq C$ of clocks in v^c is defined by*

$$\forall x \in C : v^c[R](x) = \begin{cases} 0 & \text{if } x \in R \\ v^c(x) & \text{else.} \end{cases}$$

We let v_0^c be the special *initial clock valuation* assigning value 0 to all clocks.

Clocks are used to control time-dependent behavior. To this end, clock constraints can be used to restrict the allowed actions.

Definition 2. *Let C be the set of clocks. $\Phi(C)$ is the set of* clock constraints *ϕ defined by $\phi := x \bowtie n \mid \phi_1 \wedge \phi_2 \mid true$ with $x \in C$, $n \in \mathbb{N}^1$ and $\bowtie \in \{<, \leq, =, \geq, >\}$. If a clock valuation v^c satisfies a clock constraint $\phi \in \Phi(C)$, we write $v^c \models \phi$.*

In addition to real valued clocks modelling the timed behavior, some classes of timed automata allow for non-related integer variables. Similar to clocks, we can however constrain the allowed integer valuations.

Definition 3. *Let $\mathcal{IV}$ be a set of integer variables. Mapping each integer variable $iv \in \mathcal{IV}$ to a value $v^i(iv) \in \mathbb{Z}$ is called an* integer valuation v^i.
$\Psi(\mathcal{IV})$ is the set of integer constraints *ψ defined by $\psi := iv \bowtie n \mid \psi_1 \wedge \psi_2 \mid true$ with $iv \in \mathcal{IV}, n \in \mathbb{Z}$ and $\bowtie \in \{<, \leq, =, \geq, >\}$. If an integer valuation v^i satisfies an integer constraint $\psi \in \Psi(\mathcal{IV})$, we write $v^i \models \psi$.*

The initial integer valuation v_0^i maps each integer variable $iv \in \mathcal{IV}$ to its initial value $v_0^i(iv) \in \mathbb{Z}$. In contrast to clocks, which can only be reset to zero, we allow more complex assignments for integer variables.

Definition 4. *Let $\mathcal{IV}$ be the set of integer variables. $\Omega(\mathcal{IV})$ is the set of* integer assignments *ω defined by*

$$iv := n \mid iv := iv + n \mid \omega_1 \wedge \omega_2 \mid true$$

---

[1] As usual, we restrict these bounds to be integers. This is due to the fact, that otherwise we could upscale the whole timed automaton in order to obtain clock constraints that are solely bound by integers.

with $iv \in \mathcal{IV}$ and $n \in \mathbb{Z}$ and the limitation that an integer variable iv must not occur in more than one of the conjuncts to prevent ambiguity due to undefined order. The resulting integer valuation $v^i[\omega]$ after applying integer assignment ω is defined as:

$$\forall iv \in \mathcal{IV} : v^i[\omega](iv) = \begin{cases} n & \text{if } \omega = iv := n \\ v^i(iv) + n & \text{if } \omega = iv := iv + n \\ v^i[\omega_1](iv) & \text{if } \omega = \omega_1 \wedge \omega_2 \text{ and } iv \text{ is defined in } \omega_1 \\ v^i[\omega_2](iv) & \text{if } \omega = \omega_1 \wedge \omega_2 \text{ and } iv \text{ is defined in } \omega_2 \\ v^i(iv) & else \end{cases}$$

Additionally, we need to define synchronization labels including an empty label (ϵ) as to allow for communication between automata in a network.

Definition 5. Let Σ be an alphabet. We define the set of synchronization labels $\Sigma_{sync} = \{\epsilon\} \cup (\Sigma \times \{!, ?\})$.

Timed automata communicate in a CCS-like fashion, where senders of messages $(m!)$ synchronize with receivers $(m?)$. Given these definitions, we can next formalize timed automata.

Definition 6 (Timed automaton). A timed automaton $\mathcal{A}$ is a tuple $A = (L, l_0, C, \mathcal{IV}, \Sigma, Inv^c, Inv^i, E)$:

- L is a finite set of locations,
- $l_0 \in L$ is the initial location,
- C is a finite set of clocks with initial valuation v_0^c,
- $\mathcal{IV}$ is a finite set of integer variables with initial valuation v_0^i,
- $Inv^c : L \to \Phi(C)$ is a total function of clock-invariants, s.t. $v_0^c \models Inv^c(l_0)$,
- $Inv^i : L \to \Psi(\mathcal{IV})$ is a total function of integer-invariants, s.t. $v_0^i \models Inv^i(l_0)$, and
- $E \subseteq L \times \Sigma_{sync} \times \Phi(C) \times \Psi(\mathcal{IV}) \times \Omega(\mathcal{IV}) \times 2^C \times L$ is the set of edges.

Example 1. Consider the timed automaton depicted in Fig. 1. It has 4 locations (l_0 to l_3) with initial location l_0, clock c and two integer variables id and $count$ (both with initial value 0). Furthermore, it includes clock constraints ($c \leq 1024$), integer constraints ($id == 0$), integer assignments ($id := 0 \wedge count := count - 1$), clock resets ($c := 0$) and one clock invariant at location l_1 ($c \leq 1024$). All edges are labeled with the empty synchronization label and labels are thus simply elided. Serveral of these automata are used to model the Fischer mutual exclusion algorithm, where each timed automaton models a process trying to enter its critical section, represented as location l_3. The mutual exclusion is ensured by the processes waiting for some time and setting and checking a shared variable id. Time constants (e.g. 1024) are key to some of the models and can be large.

Ultimately, we will be interested in proving properties on timed automata, or on networks of timed automata. To this end, we first need to define the semantics of timed automata. Informally, this works as follows. The current state of the timed

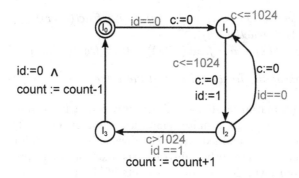

Fig. 1. Timed automaton A

automaton consists of a location l, a clock valuation v^c with $v^c \models Inv^c(l)$ and an integer valuation v^i with $v^i \models Inv^i(l)$. To allow an edge $(l \xrightarrow{\sigma, \phi, \psi, \omega, R} l') \in E$ to be taken, clock and integer valuations have to satisfy the constraints ϕ and ψ, i.e., $v^c \models \phi$ and $v^i \models \psi$, and after applying reset R and assignment ω satisfy the invariants of the target location l', i.e., $v^c[R] \models Inv^c(l')$ and $v^i[\omega] \models Inv^i(l')$. An edge is taken instantaneously (without time elapse), whilst time can pass arbitrarily in a location (as long as the location invariant is satisfied). The synchronization labels are only taken into account when combining several timed automata into a network, which we define later. This concrete semantics can be formalized as a transition system, e.g., as was done by Behrmann [4].

Definition 7. *Let $A = (L, l_0, C, \mathcal{IV}, \Sigma, Inv^c, Inv^i, E)$ be given. The transition system $TS = (S, s_0, \rightarrow)$ defines the concrete semantics:*

- $S = L \times \mathbb{R}_{\geq 0}^C \times \mathbb{Z}^{\mathcal{IV}}$ *is the set of states,*
- $s_0 = (l_0, v_0^c, v_0^i) \in S$ *is the initial state,*
- $\rightarrow \subseteq S \times S$ *contains delay transitions $\rightarrow_d$ and edge transition $\rightarrow_e$:*
  - $(l, v^c, v^i) \rightarrow_d (l, v^c + \delta, v^i)$ *iff* $\forall 0 \leq \delta' \leq \delta : (v^c + \delta') \models Inv^c(l)$
  - $(l, v^c, v^i) \rightarrow_e (l', v^{c'}, v^{i'})$ *iff* $\exists (l \xrightarrow{\epsilon, \phi, \psi, \omega, R} l') \in E$ *s.t.* $v^c \models \phi$, $v^{c'} = v^c[R]$, $v^{c'} \models Inv^c(l')$, $v^i \models \psi$, $v^{i'} = v^i[\omega]$, $v^{i'} \models Inv^i(l')$.

The transition system as described by the concrete semantics is infinite and thus, several finite abstractions have been developed, e.g., the region abstraction of Alur and Dill [1]. Based on the fact that some clock valuations are indistinguishable for any clock constraint, equivalence classes (regions) of clock valuations are built. This is possible because clock constraints use integer bounds only.

Definition 8. *Let $A = (L, l_0, C, \mathcal{IV}, \Sigma, Inv^c, Inv^i, E)$ be a given timed automaton. For every clock $x \in C$ let n_x be the largest constant with which x is compared to. Two clock valuations v^c and $v^{c'}$ are in the same region, iff:*

- $\forall x \in C : \lfloor v^c(x) \rfloor = \lfloor v^{c'}(x) \rfloor$ *or* $v^c(x) > n_x \wedge v^{c'}(x) > n_x$,

- $\forall x, y \in C$ with $v^c(x) \leq n_x$ and $v^c(y) \leq n_y$: $fract(v^c(x)) \leq fract(v^c(y))$ iff $fract(v^{c'}(x)) \leq fract(v^{c'}(y))$,
- $\forall x \in C$ with $v^c(x) \leq n_x$: $fract(v^c(x)) = 0$ iff $fract(v^{c'}(x)) = 0$.

with fract meaning the fractional part of the value.

Every timed automaton as defined above only has a finite number of regions [2]. Furthermore, to ensure a finite semantics, we allow only a finite number of integer valuations, as explained later. The downside of the region abstraction is its huge size and therefore other abstractions, like zones, are preferred by most tools and also our own. Zones are convex sets of clock valuations.

Definition 9. *A zone Z is a convex set of clock valuations, specified as a conjunction of clock difference constraints $x_i - x_j \bowtie n$ with $x_i, x_j \in C \cup \{x_0 = 0\}, \bowtie \in \{<, \leq\}$ and $n \in \mathbb{Z}$.*

Note that bounds on single clocks are expressed using a special clock x_0. Zones can efficiently be stored using Difference Bound Matrices (DBMs) [14]. Furthermore, DBMs allow for an efficient backwards reachability analysis [7] using the following operations [9] which we also need for our own approach. Let Z, Z' be two zones:

- **Past:** $\overleftarrow{Z} = \{v^c - t | v^c \in Z$ and $t \in \mathbb{R}_{\geq 0}\}$
- **Intersection:** $Z \cap Z' = \{v^c | v^c \in Z$ and $v^c \in Z'\}$
- **Inverse reset of clocks in R:** $Z[R]^{-1} = \{v^c | v^c[R] \in Z\}$
- **Predecessor:**
$$Pre_e(Z) = (\overleftarrow{Z} \cap \{v^c | v^c \models Inv^c(l')\})[R]^{-1} \cap \phi \cap \{v^c | v^c \models Inv^c(l)\}$$
$$\text{for } e = (l \xrightarrow{\epsilon, \phi, \psi, \omega, R} l') \text{ an edge}$$

A zone is bounded solely by integers and thus, whenever the bounds are constants obeying the maximal bound as in the definition of regions, it can be seen as a *finite union of regions*. The following properties of operations on zones are important for our own approach and cited from [9]:

Lemma 1. *If Z is a zone, $Pre_e(Z)$ is a zone. Additionally, if it is a finite union of regions, $Pre_e(Z)$ is a finite union of regions, too.*

Lemma 2. *If Z is a zone, the predecessor computation $Pre_e(Z)$ is exact, i.e. $Pre_e(Z)$ contains all clock valuations that enable e with target valuation $v^c \in Z$.*

Using the zone abstraction, a finite abstract *symbolic* transition system with states (l, Z, v^i) using zones of valuations can be defined for every timed automata. The same can be done using the region abstraction. We refer to [4,9] for a more precise overview.

As stated earlier, several timed automata can be composed with each other describing a parallel execution of timed systems. This composition of timed automata $A_1, ..., A_n$ is called a network of timed automata.

Definition 10. *Let the timed automata A_1 to A_n be given with $A_j = (L^j, l_0^j, C^j,$ $\mathcal{IV}, \Sigma, Inv^{cj}, Inv^{ij}, E^j)$ with Σ and $\mathcal{IV}$ being equal in all n automata. Furthermore, we require the sets C^j of clocks to be distinct for all timed automata. The product automaton defining the network $NTA = \langle A_1, ..., A_n \rangle$ is defined as $A = (L, l_0, C, \mathcal{IV}, \Sigma, Inv^c, Inv^i, E)$ with*

- $L = L^1 \times ... \times L^n$
- $l_0 = (l_0^1, ..., l_0^n)$
- $C = C^1 \cup ... \cup C^n$
- $Inv^c(l^1, ..., l^n) = Inv^{c1}(l^1) \wedge ... \wedge Inv^{cn}(l^n)$
- $Inv^i(l^1, ..., l^n) = Inv^{i1}(l^1) \wedge ... \wedge Inv^{in}(l^n)$
- E *is defined as*
  - $\forall i \in \{1, ..., n\} : (..., l^i, ...) \xrightarrow{\sigma, \phi, \psi, \omega, R} (..., l^{i'}, ...) \ if \ l^i \xrightarrow{\sigma, \phi, \psi, \omega, R} l^{i'} \in E^i$
  - $\forall i \neq j \in \{1, ..., n\} : (..., l^i, ..., l^j, ...) \xrightarrow{\epsilon, \phi, \psi, \omega, R} (..., l^{i'}, ..., l^{j'}, ...)$
    if $l^i \xrightarrow{a!, \phi_1, \psi_1, \omega_1, R_1} l^{i'} \in E^i$ *and* $l^j \xrightarrow{a?, \phi_2, \psi_2, \omega_2, R_2} l^{j'} \in E^j$
    with $\phi = \phi_1 \wedge \phi_2$, $\psi = \psi_1 \wedge \psi_2$, $\omega = \omega_1 \wedge \omega_2$, $R = R_1 \cup R_2$.

This composition of several timed automata is also reflected within the definition of the safety property.

Definition 11 (Safety Property). *Let $NTA = \langle A_1, ..., A_n \rangle$ be a given network of timed automata. The safety property is defined as $P = \neg(l^i \wedge ... \wedge l^j \wedge Z \wedge \psi) | P_1 \wedge P_2$ for some mutually distinct timed automata $A_i, ..., A_j \in NTA$, their locations $l^i \in L^i, ..., l^j \in L^j$ and Z being a Zone over C and $\psi \in \Psi(\mathcal{IV})$.*

In the definition, arbitrary combinations of locations of the single timed automata with several clock and integer valuations can be described as $l^i \wedge ... \wedge l^j \wedge Z \wedge \psi$. These combinations are used to describe error-states that are excluded from the safety property, expressed by the negation.

Example 2. As running example of this paper, we consider a model describing the Fischer mutual exclusion algorithm. This network of timed automata consists of an arbitrary, but finite, number of timed automata, all similiar to the one in Fig. 1. Every automaton has its own identifier i and its own clock c (now called c_i). The identifier i replaces the "1" in the integer assignment $id := 1$, as well as in the integer constraint $id == 1$. We are interested in a safety property stating that no more than one timed automaton can be in its location l_3. Using the integer variable *count* this can easily be expressed as $P = \neg(\bigwedge_{A_j \in NTA} c_j \geq 0 \wedge count > 1)$. The formula states that any valid clock valuation ($\bigwedge_{A_j \in NTA} c_j \geq 0$) with *count* > 1 and any combination of locations (since no locations are specified), is an error-state and thus, does not satisfy the safety property.

2.2   IC3

In the following, we present a brief overview of IC3 [11], the algorithm we intend to adapt for checking safety properties of timed automata. IC3 is a technique for incrementally constructing inductive invariants. It assumes the system to be specified by two propositional formulae, a formula $Init$ describing the set of initial states, and a formula $Trans$ describing transitions of the system. Both range over a set of variables used to define states, where T uses both unprimed and primed versions of the variables as to refer to a current state and its successor. We write F' to denote the formula F with all variables in primed form. The objective of the technique is to show that a property P is invariant, i.e., none of the reachable states invalidates P. Most often, P is not inductive itself. To prove P to be invariant we thus need a strengthening of P which is inductive. This is what IC3 is computing.

The basic principle of the algorithm is to incrementally build sets F_i over-approximating the states reachable in $i \in \{0, ..., k\}$-steps. These sets are represented as propositional formulae. The sequence of sets $F_0, F_1, \ldots, F_k$ satisfies the following conditions:

$$
\begin{align}
(1) &\quad Init \Rightarrow F_0 \\
(2) &\quad F_i \Rightarrow F_{i+1} \\
(3) &\quad F_i \Rightarrow P \\
(4) &\quad F_i \wedge Trans \Rightarrow F'_{i+1}
\end{align}
$$

The algorithm terminates once we find some i for which $F_i = F_{i+1}$. In this case, the set F_i is an inductive invariant and a strengthening of P.

The incremental construction of the sequence works as follows. IC3 searches the currently largest set F_k, called *frontier*, for predecessors s of states violating the safety property, i.e., checks whether $F_k \wedge Trans \wedge \neg P'$ is satisfiable. It then tries to exclude s, called the *counterexample to induction (CTI)*, from the frontier. For this, the largest set F_n to which the negation of the CTI s is inductive relative to is found. A negation of a state s is inductive relative to a set F_n if $F_n \wedge \neg s \wedge Trans \Rightarrow \neg s'$ holds. Then s is *generalized* meaning that literals in the formula denoting s are dropped from the formula while maintaining relative inductiveness to F_n. This generalization is key to IC3. Afterwards, the negation of the generalized CTI (which is a clause) is conjoined with F_1 to F_{n+1} to exclude s from each of these sets.

The CTI s has successfully been excluded from the frontier if $n + 1 \geq k$. Otherwise, as $\neg s$ is not inductive relative to F_{n+1} the query $F_{n+1} \wedge \neg s \wedge Trans \wedge s'$ is satisfiable, i.e. there exists the state $t \neq s$ in F_{n+1} that hinders the inductive relativeness of $\neg s$ to F_{n+1}. Thus, this CTI t must itself be excluded. If this recursive procedure reaches a state in F_0, a counterexample trace has been found which proves the safety property not to hold. Otherwise, eventually all CTIs are excluded and a new frontier will be created. The whole process is repeated until an error-trace is found or two consecutive sets F_i and F_{i+1} are equal which means that the safety property actually is invariant. IC3 gains additional efficiency by propagating relative inductive clauses of a set F_i to its successor set F_{i+1}, resulting in an additional refinement and possibly faster termination.

For more details, we refer to the original paper from Aaron Bradley [11].

3   IC3 for Timed Automata Verification

For using the basic procedure of IC3 for checking safety of timed automata, we essentially need to solve two tasks: (1) we need a way of representing networks of timed automata and their safety properties in terms of logical formulas $Init, Trans$ and P, and (2) we need a way of extracting counterexamples to induction when we find the negation of the property to still be reachable from F_k or the relative inductiveness to be violated. For task (1) we follow [18] in that we now use first order logic (and consequently SMT solvers for satisfiability queries) to encode constraints on clocks and integer variables. We do not give the full encoding here, just an example, as it is rather straightforward.

Example 3. For the single timed automaton in Figure 1 we would for instance get the following. We use two boolean variables b_0^1 and b_1^1 for encoding the four locations, and use the names of clocks and integer variables as given in the automaton. Then the formula for $Init$ is $\neg b_0^1 \wedge \neg b_1^1 \wedge c = 0 \wedge id = 0 \wedge count = 0$ and $Trans = \bigvee_{e \in E} enc(e)$ where the encoding of the edge e from l_1 to l_2 is

$$enc(e) = \neg b_0^1 \wedge b_1^1 \wedge c \leq 1024 \wedge c' = 0 \wedge id' = 1 \wedge {b_0^1}' \wedge \neg {b_1^1}' \wedge count' = count$$

In addition, the encoding takes into account invariants and synchronization in a network of timed automata.

With respect to task (2), we deviate from Kindermann et al's approach. To see why a solution to task (2) cannot simply be taken from IC3, we look at the procedure again. In the original algorithm, the CTIs are extracted using the satisfying models of the following queries (1) and (2):

$$F_k \wedge Trans \wedge \neg P' \tag{1}$$

$$F_n \wedge \neg s \wedge Trans \wedge s' \tag{2}$$

This poses a problem when verifying timed systems using IC3 as there are infinitely many models. Thus, within this domain the original IC3 algorithm can no longer guarantee termination. However, by making the algorithm aware of the used domain during the computation of CTIs the termination problem can be conquered. In contrast to previous approaches utilizing region abstraction for the CTI computation [18], we use zone abstraction. This decision in favor of the zone abstraction promises better performance since zones are insusceptible to large constants, but is also more challenging. In general, the satisfying models of queries (1) and (2) are encoding pairs of predecessor (p) and successor (s) state:

$$((l_p^1, l_p^2, \ldots, l_p^n), v_p^c, v_p^i) \;,\; ((l_s^1, l_s^2, \ldots, l_s^n), v_s^c, v_s^i)$$

This refers to networks of n timed automata. Note that this model describes a pair of states such that there is (at least) one edge e in the network taking us from the predecessor to the successor state. One such edge e can (and needs to) be computed from the model.

We now cannot simply compute the CTI from such a model and abstract its concrete clock valuation v_p^c into a zone like done for regions in [18]. The difficulty for zones is that there is no uniquely defined zone surrounding a concrete clock valuation. In general, there are several surrounding zones Z satisfying $v_p^c \in Z$, and the one we are interested in is the maximal zone Z that enables the edge e as represented by the satisfying model plus leads to a target valuation as stated by the issued query (1) or (2), i.e., either $\neg P'$ or s'. We compute this zone Z using backwards reachability computation $Z = Pre_e(Z_2)$ from a zone Z_2. The question is what Z_2 to use for this. A closer look at the involved queries gives us two cases.

Query (1): The successor state described by the satisfying model is (l_s, v_s^c, v_s^i) with $l_s = (l_s^1, l_s^2, \ldots, l_s^n)$, and thus, what is known about the successors' clock valuation is v_s^c. Since we need a zone Z_2 for the computation of Z, the trivial choice would be to compute the region surrounding v_s^c and use it as Z_2. However, this would be a waste since the safety property often contains more than this one region reachable via edge e. Thus, we utilize the structure of our safety property to gain further information about a good candidate zone Z_2. All states violating the safety property P are defined (Def. 11) as $\neg P = (l^i \wedge \ldots \wedge l^j \wedge Z_e \wedge \psi) \vee \ldots$ for some mutually distinct timed automata $A_i, \ldots, A_j \in NTA$, their locations $l^i \in L^i, \ldots, l^j \in L^j$ and Z_e being a Zone over C and $\psi \in \Psi(\mathcal{IV})$. At least one of the combinations $(l^i \wedge \ldots \wedge l^j \wedge Z_e \wedge \psi)$ within the safety property must include the found successor (l_s, v_s^c, v_s^i). We find this combination by issuing cheap queries $(l^i \wedge \ldots \wedge l^j \wedge Z_e \wedge \psi \wedge l_s \wedge v_s^c \wedge v_s^i)$ to the solver, obtaining Z_2 as some such Z_e.

Query (2): The successor state (l_s, v_s^c, v_s^i) is a concrete state enclosed in the CTI s. Since we must have computed s previously in the IC3 algorithm, we know its zone Z_2 and can easily reuse it to compute the predecessors' zone $Z = Pre_e(Z_2)$.

In order to make this approach work efficiently, we store all zones computed for the CTIs as DBMs for later use.

Example 4. Consider the example of Fischer's algorithm as stated before. A satisfiable SMT-query $F_k \wedge Trans \wedge \neg P'$ might return the following model (written informally): $l_p^1 = l_2$, $l_s^1 = l_3$ and $c_1 = c_1' = 1025$ and $count = 1$, $count' = 2$ and others. As the successor violates the safety property P, we search through P as described above. Finding $Z_2 = \bigwedge_{A_j \in NTA} c_j \geq 0$, we compute the predecessors' zone $Z = Pre_e(Z_2)$ according to the taken transition e from $l_p^1 = l_2$ to $l_s^1 = l_3$. The result is $Z = \bigwedge_{A_j \in NTA, j \neq 1} c_j \geq 0 \wedge c_1 > 1024$. This is the zone of the CTI, which can now be generalized and is used for refinement of the sets F_i.

Using the search within the safety property and the backwards reachability analysis, we can lift any concrete CTI (l_p, v_p^c, v_p^i) to a symbolic one (l_p, Z, v_p^i). The concrete clock valuation v_p^c, which was described in the model is discarded, as it is within zone Z due to the exact backwards reachability computation (see Lemma 2). This computation of zones is where the change from concrete to symbolic CTIs requires the main modification – besides moving to first order logic – to IC3.

In the description so far, the integer valuations have just been left as they are. In order to improve performance, we however do not store the single integer valuation v_p^i extracted from the satisfying model within each CTI, but store a set of such valuations using integer constraints. To do so, we use the same methodology as for zones. We obtain the integer constraint ψ_2 from the successor CTI (Query (2)) or find it within the safety property (see above). For the taken edge $e = (l_p \xrightarrow{\epsilon, \phi, \psi, \omega, R} l_s)$ we compute $wp_\omega(\psi_2 \wedge Inv^i(l_s)) \wedge \psi \wedge Inv^i(l_p)$ using the weakest precondition [13] operator wp_ω regarding the integer assignment ω. The result includes all integer constraints that have to hold in the predecessor CTI in order to be able to take the edge and reach one of the successor valuations. These constraints are stored as part of the CTI alongside its zone and location.

In the following, we discuss the termination of our approach.

Lemma 3 (Termination without integer variables). *Given a network of timed automata $NTA = \langle A_1, ..., A_n \rangle$ with $\mathcal{IV} = \emptyset$, our algorithm terminates.*

Proof sketch: The number of computable zones using backwards reachability computation is finite, as all zones used in the safety property and, thus, all zones computed via backwards reachability analysis are finite unions of regions (Lemma 1). With only a finite number of zones and locations, the number of distinct CTIs is finite. Thus, the sets can only be refined a finite number of times, and eventually two sets have to be equal or a counterexample is found.   □

However, ensuring termination requires additional effort when dealing with integer variables, e.g., by using a widening operator. Thus, our approach then only terminates under special assumptions.

Lemma 4 (Termination with integer variables). *Given the network of timed automata $NTA = \langle A_1, ..., A_n \rangle$, our algorithm terminates, whenever the network contains no cycle, that increases or decreases the value of an integer variable as a function of its previous value ($iv := iv \pm c$ with $c \neq 0$).*

Proof sketch: Taking into account lemma 3, termination with integer variables is guaranteed, if there exist only a finite number of sets of integer valuations for the CTIs. Thus, termination holds, since there are only finitely many integer constraints and invariants within NTA and no cycles to increase or decrease their integer valuations infinitely many times.   □

4   Implementation and Evaluation

We have implemented our approach and have carried out a number of experiments. Our experiments show very promising results. The combination of IC3 with the zone abstraction exhibits the known advantage over the region approach, namely being insusceptible to large constants, resulting in a better runtime. Furthermore, a comparison of our tool to the state of the art tool Uppaal [6], Version 4.0.13, indicates that none is completely superior over the other.

Some instances were solved faster using Uppaal and others were solved faster using our tool.

Our tool is implemented in Java using the SMT-solver Z3 [19]. The implementation of the IC3-algorithm is done following the reference implementation of IC3 [11] by Aaron Bradley, including the optimizations PDR [15] and better Generalization [16]. The experiments were done on an Intel i5, M540 @ 2.53GHz with Windows 7 Professional.

Our experiments employ models of the Fischer Mutual Exclusion algorithm (Fig. 1), the CSMA/CD protocol and the FDDI token ring protocol and their respective safety properties as can be found as benchmarks on the Uppaal website. These three models can easily be scaled to include an arbitrary number of timed automata and, thus, are suitable to examine the scalability of our tool.

Table 1. Using different constants in the Fischer model with 10 processes

used	IC3&Regions		IC3&Zones		Uppaal	
Constant	Runtime (s)	Memory (MB)	Runtime (s)	Memory (MB)	Runtime (s)	Memory (MB)
1	237,16	262,5	109,90	137,0	13,65	30,7
4	378,30	281,7	109,48	136,6	13,48	30,7
16	557,19	285,8	108,70	136,8	13,68	30,7

We compare our zone-based approach and the zone-based tool Uppaal with the region-based technique of Kindermann et al. [18] regarding the scalability of constants within the model. Due to Kindermann's tool using a different SMT-solver (Yices), we reimplemented his approach in our tool for a comparison without the influence of different solvers. Table 1 shows the effect of larger constants used in the Fischer model to all three examined tools. Both zone-based approaches show no significant change, whereas the runtime and memory consumption of Kindermann's approach grows when using larger constants. This growth is due to the number of regions depending on the largest used constant and, thus, resulting in heavily increased amounts of CTIs. This fundamentally different behavior of our tool compared to Kindermann's was anticipated and has been explained in several papers before.

Table 2. Scalability experiments using the token ring FDDI protocol

# of	IC3&Regions		IC3&Zones		Uppaal	
stations	Runtime (s)	Memory (MB)	Runtime (s)	Memory (MB)	Runtime (s)	Memory (MB)
2	62,00	227,2	2,75	62,6	0,02	6,7
3	964,84	1217,9	10,07	71,7	0,02	6,7
4	-	OOM	14,56	75,2	0,03	6,8
5	-	OOM	58,57	101,9	0,03	6,8
10	-	OOM	1527,15	292,9	0,17	7,1
14	-	OOM	6030,13	580,6	0,59	7,4
15	-	OOM	-	OOM	0,93	7,4
20	-	OOM	-	OOM	5,68	7,9

In addition to the scalability experiments regarding the size of constants, we performed several experiments regarding the number of automata in a network comparing our tool to the state of the art tool Uppaal using the three models stated above. The results of these experiments were very diverse, as our tool performed less well in some instances (Table 2) while being superior in others (Table 4). In these experiments, we limited the runtime of a single instance to 12 hours. Uppaal threw an OutOfMemory-Exception when reaching a memory consumption of approximately 2 GB, whereas our tool threw it at approximately 1,5 GB due to Z3 being unable to allocate more memory.

Table 2 presents the experiments for the FDDI token ring protocol. Uppaal scales much better for these instances than our tool. This tremendous advantage of Uppaal originates from its exploration algorithm that searches all reachable states in a depth- or breadth-first search, saving already visited states in a clever data structure. Naturally, if the fraction of reachable state is small, then Uppaal is finished fast, which is the case here (only 8061 explored states for 20 stations). Our tool, on the other hand, does not benefit from a small set of reachable states, as every additional station increases the number of variables and makes the SMT-formulae more complex. Thus, our experiments using the FDDI protocol show a definite advantage of Uppaal. However, this is not generally the case.

Table 3. Scalability experiments using the CSMA/CD protocol

# of senders	IC3&Regions		IC3&Zones		Uppaal	
	Runtime (s)	Memory (MB)	Runtime (s)	Memory (MB)	Runtime (s)	Memory (MB)
2	1,71	82,7	0,68	52,9	0,02	6,7
3	27,85	171,7	1,62	59,9	0,02	6,7
4	260,38	408,5	3,25	69,8	0,02	6,8
5	-	OOM	6,18	78,4	0,02	6,9
10	-	OOM	80,23	114,3	2,84	19,1
14	-	OOM	278,24	205,1	139,65	519,2
15	-	OOM	490,14	223,9	365,39	1268,7
16	-	OOM	509,17	277,7	-	OOM
25	-	OOM	5044,73	641,9	-	OOM
26	-	OOM	-	OOM	-	OOM

The next experiments were run using models of the CSMA/CD protocol (Table 3) and the Fischer Mutual Exclusion algorithm (Table 4). For the smaller instances, i.e., small numbers of timed automata in the network, Uppaal is faster. It, however, loses this advance with growing number of automata until running out of memory when exploring the model with 16 senders (CSMA/CD) or 14 processes (Fischer), respectively. Although Uppaal has compact datastructures for storing already explored states, the need for storing all previously seen states makes Uppaal easily run out of memory. In each of the instances on which Uppaal runs out of memory, it has to explore and store more than ten million states. Our technique, on the contrary, does not rely on storing each found state, but uses generalized states for the refinement of overapproximations. Thus, it can be more efficient regarding memory. This can for instance be seen in the experiments with more than 16 CSMA/CD senders that can be verified by our tool, but not by Uppaal. Likewise, for the Fischer model our tool is able to check instances (of up to 30 Fischer processes), which Uppaal cannot verify with a reasonable amount of memory. But in addition, our tool is also competitive regarding runtime (see Table 4, 13 processes). Thus, within these experiments our tool was capable to successfully compete with Uppaal both regarding runtime and memory.

Table 4. Scalability experiments using the Fischer algorithm

# of processes	IC3&Regions		IC3&Zones		Uppaal	
	Runtime (s)	Memory (MB)	Runtime (s)	Memory (MB)	Runtime (s)	Memory (MB)
3	4,16	81,8	1,42	61,9	0,02	6,6
5	16,93	111,8	7,20	80,9	0,02	6,7
10	567,00	286,5	107,42	136,7	13,38	30,8
12	1078,81	344,2	246,45	173,7	216,56	273,1
13	1584,50	380,5	395,13	179,6	845,11	875,9
14	6826,73	614,3	495,93	200,7	-	OOM
17	32368,94	1010,6	1763,82	320,8	-	OOM
18	OOT	-	2015,09	344,9	-	OOM
20	OOT	-	4084,05	466,8	-	OOM
25	OOT	-	14268,46	858,7	-	OOM
30	OOT	-	36812,32	1468,9	-	OOM

Taking all these experiments into account, we have presented evidence that neither Uppaal nor our tool is superior to the other in general. In conclusion, both tools could be used complementary, where Uppaal works best for instances with a small or medium sized set of reachable states and our tool is efficient for instances with large state spaces. In addition, we can say that our approach is a definite improvement over the technique of Kindermann et al., providing a huge improvement in runtime and also insusceptibility against large constants.

5 Related Work

The verification of timed automata started in the early 90's, when the region abstraction [1] laid the foundation for the decidability results. However, the practical value of that abstraction is small due to its exponential blowup in terms of clocks and size of the used constants.

In contrast, the zone abstraction is widely used for the verification of timed systems, e.g., in tools like Uppaal [6], Kronos [10] or Red [24]. Most of these tools verify a safety property by doing explicit reachability analysis in a DFS- or BFS-manner. They differ in the data-structures used to store already examined states, e.g., CDDs [5] or CRDs [23], as well as in their used optimizations.

Other tools use a discretized semantics of timed automata in order to employ BDDs, e.g., Rabbit [8] or PAT [22], which also offers zone-based analysis.

Furthermore, several SAT-based approaches have been proposed, e.g., [17]. These transfer successful ideas from untimed domains, but even so have to cope with the specific problems present in a timed domain. To the best of our knowledge, there exists only one approach utilizing IC3 for the verification of timed systems: Kindermann et al. [18] combine IC3 with the region abstraction. We pick up their idea, as the use of IC3 is very promising with its clever combination of over-approximation and refinement. Our technique combines IC3 with the zone abstraction, resulting in coarser symbolic CTIs and a faster refinement.

6 Conclusion

In this paper, we presented an approach for the verification of safety properties for timed systems utilizing a combination of IC3 with the zone abstraction. Concrete clock valuations found by IC3 are abstracted into a zone, s.t. termination of our approach is guaranteed. This technique provides for a fast refinement process in IC3 due to the coarse abstraction of time.

We compared our approach with the technique of Kindermann et al. [18] that combines IC3 with the region abstraction. Our experiments with a prototype implementation showed promising results. Our zone-based approach seems to be a definite improvement over the region-based technique of Kindermann, both regarding runtime and memory consumption. Furthermore, a comparison of our technique with the state of the art tool Uppaal [6] reveals a number of instances in which our approach outperforms Uppaal. Specifically, for the often employed benchmark of Fischer's mutual exclusion protocol, our new approach can handle instances with twice as much processes as Uppaal before running out of memory.

As future work, we plan to investigate, how a found inductive strengthening for a network of timed automata can be reused, if the network changes in different ways. This reuse could save a lot of time for frequently changing networks of timed automata.

References

1. Alur, R., Dill, D.: Automata for modeling real-time systems. In: Paterson, M. (ed.) ICALP 1990. LNCS, vol. 443, pp. 322–335. Springer, Heidelberg (1990)
2. Alur, R., Dill, D.L.: A theory of timed automata. Theoretical Computer Science 126(2), 183–235 (1994)
3. Baumgartner, J., Ivrii, A., Matsliah, A., Mony, H.: IC3-guided abstraction. In: Cabodi, G., Singh, S. (eds.) FMCAD, pp. 182–185. IEEE (2012)
4. Behrmann, G., Bouyer, P., Larsen, K.G., Pelánek, R.: Lower and upper bounds in zone-based abstractions of timed automata. Int. J. Softw. Tools Technol. Transf. 8(3), 204–215 (2006)
5. Behrmann, G., Larsen, K.G., Pearson, J., Weise, C., Yi, W.: Efficient timed reachability analysis using clock difference diagrams. In: Halbwachs, N., Peled, D.A. (eds.) CAV 1999. LNCS, vol. 1633, pp. 341–353. Springer, Heidelberg (1999)
6. Bengtsson, J., Larsen, K.G., Larsson, F., Pettersson, P., Yi, W.: Uppaal — a Tool Suite for Automatic Verification of Real–Time Systems. In: Alur, R., Sontag, E.D., Henzinger, T.A. (eds.) HS 1995. LNCS, vol. 1066, pp. 232–243. Springer, Heidelberg (1996)
7. Bengtsson, J., Yi, W.: Timed automata: Semantics, algorithms and tools. In: Desel, J., Reisig, W., Rozenberg, G. (eds.) Lectures on Concurrency and Petri Nets. LNCS, vol. 3098, pp. 87–124. Springer, Heidelberg (2004)

8. Beyer, D., Lewerentz, C., Noack, A.: Rabbit: A tool for BDD-based verification of real-time systems. In: Hunt Jr., W.A., Somenzi, F. (eds.) CAV 2003. LNCS, vol. 2725, pp. 122–125. Springer, Heidelberg (2003)

9. Bouyer, P.: From Qualitative to Quantitative Analysis of Timed Systems. Mémoire d'habilitation, Université Paris 7, Paris, France (January 2009)

10. Bozga, M., Daws, C., Maler, O., Olivero, A., Tripakis, S., Yovine, S.: Kronos: A model-checking tool for real-time systems. In: Vardi, M.Y. (ed.) CAV 1998. LNCS, vol. 1427, pp. 546–550. Springer, Heidelberg (1998)

11. Bradley, A.R.: SAT-based model checking without unrolling. In: Jhala, R., Schmidt, D. (eds.) VMCAI 2011. LNCS, vol. 6538, pp. 70–87. Springer, Heidelberg (2011)

12. Cimatti, A., Griggio, A.: Software model checking via IC3. In: Madhusudan, P., Seshia, S.A. (eds.) CAV 2012. LNCS, vol. 7358, pp. 277–293. Springer, Heidelberg (2012)

13. Dijkstra, E.: Guarded commands, nondeterminacy, and formal derivation of programs. In: Gries, D. (ed.) Programming Methodology, pp. 166–175. Springer, New York (1978)

14. Dill, D.L.: Timing assumptions and verification of finite-state concurrent systems. In: Sifakis, J. (ed.) CAV 1989. LNCS, vol. 407, pp. 197–212. Springer, Heidelberg (1990)

15. Een, N., Mishchenko, A., Brayton, R.: Efficient implementation of property directed reachability. In: Proceedings of the International Conference on Formal Methods in Computer-Aided Design, FMCAD 2011, pp. 125–134. FMCAD Inc., Austin (2011)

16. Hassan, Z., Bradley, A., Somenzi, F.: Better generalization in IC3. In: Formal Methods in Computer-Aided Design (FMCAD), pp. 157–164 (October 2013)

17. Kindermann, R., Junttila, T., Niemelä, I.: Beyond Lassos: Complete SMT-Based Bounded Model Checking for Timed Automata. In: Giese, H., Rosu, G. (eds.) FORTE 2012 and FMOODS 2012. LNCS, vol. 7273, pp. 84–100. Springer, Heidelberg (2012)

18. Kindermann, R., Junttila, T., Niemelä, I.: SMT-Based Induction Methods for Timed Systems. In: Jurdziński, M., Ničković, D. (eds.) FORMATS 2012. LNCS, vol. 7595, pp. 171–187. Springer, Heidelberg (2012)

19. de Moura, L., Bjørner, N.S.: Z3: An efficient SMT solver. In: Ramakrishnan, C.R., Rehof, J. (eds.) TACAS 2008. LNCS, vol. 4963, pp. 337–340. Springer, Heidelberg (2008)

20. Nguyen, T.K., Sun, J., Liu, Y., Dong, J.S., Liu, Y.: Improved BDD-based discrete analysis of timed systems. In: Giannakopoulou, D., Méry, D. (eds.) FM 2012. LNCS, vol. 7436, pp. 326–340. Springer, Heidelberg (2012)

21. Suda, M.: Triggered Clause Pushing for IC3. ArXiv e-prints (July 2013)

22. Sun, J., Liu, Y., Dong, J.S., Pang, J.: Pat: Towards flexible verification under fairness. In: Bouajjani, A., Maler, O. (eds.) CAV 2009. LNCS, vol. 5643, pp. 709–714. Springer, Heidelberg (2009)

23. Wang, F.: Symbolic verification of complex real-time systems with clock-restriction diagram. In: Kim, M., Chin, B., Kang, S., Lee, D. (eds.) FORTE. IFIP Conference Proceedings, vol. 197, pp. 235–250. Kluwer (2001)

24. Wang, F., Wu, R.S., Huang, G.D.: Verifying timed and linear hybrid rule-systems with RED. In: Chu, W.C., Juzgado, N.J., Wong, W.E. (eds.) SEKE, pp. 448–454 (2005)

GRL: A Specification Language for Globally Asynchronous Locally Synchronous Systems*

Fatma Jebali, Frédéric Lang, and Radu Mateescu

Inria,
Univ. Grenoble Alpes, LIG, F-38000 Grenoble, France
CNRS, LIG, F-38000 Grenoble, France

Abstract. A GALS (*Globally Asynchronous, Locally Synchronous*) system consists of several synchronous subsystems that evolve concurrently and interact with each other asynchronously. Most formalisms and design tools support either the synchronous paradigm or the asynchronous paradigm but rarely combine both, which requires an intricate modeling of GALS systems. In this paper, we present a new language, called GRL (*GALS Representation Language*) designed to model GALS systems in an abstract and versatile manner for the purpose of formal verification. GRL has formal semantics combining the synchronous reactive model underlying dataflow languages and the asynchronous concurrent model underlying process algebras. We present the basic concepts and the main constructs of the language, together with an illustrative example.

1 Introduction

Computer science has led to new generations of heterogeneous systems called GALS (*Globally Asynchronous, Locally Synchronous*). A GALS system is composed of several synchronous subsystems, executing and interacting in asynchronous concurrency: no assumption is made, neither on the relative frequency of each subsystem, nor on the communication delays between subsystems. Each subsystem is composed of several components running together synchronously, all governed by a single clock and encompassing the zero-delay assumption: computations and communications between components are instantaneous (these are called the synchronous assumptions). As such, GALS systems involve a high degree of synchronous and asynchronous concurrency (introducing nondeterminism), which requires tedious effort to design and debug. Formal modeling and verification is then a crucial part in the design process of such usually safety-critical systems.

Many different approaches have been proposed for GALS modeling and verification. Some propose to model GALS systems in synchronous frameworks (such as Signal [26]) directly or to extend synchronous languages with an asynchronous layer (Multiclock Esterel [4], CRSM [29]). Such representations are well-suited

---

* This work was partly funded by the French *Fonds unique interministériel* (FUI), Pôle Minalogic (project "Bluesky for I-Automation").

S. Merz and J. Pang (Eds.): ICFEM 2014, LNCS 8829, pp. 219–234, 2014.

to hardware-based subsystems distributed on one single hardware platform, each with its own clock.

Other approaches, conversely, extend asynchronous languages to incorporate synchronous features. The most common approach is to surround each locally synchronous subsystem by an asynchronous wrapper, which provides an asynchronous interface to other subsystems. This way, GALS systems can be modeled and verified in asynchronous frameworks. In [9], Signal modules are translated to Promela, the input language of the SPIN model checker [20]. In [13], Sam synchronous programs are represented by Mealy functions without internal state and are encapsulated into wrappers modeled in LNT [7], a language of asynchronous concurrent processes inheriting process algebraic concepts and extended with data and the control structures of classical algorithmic programming. LNT is equipped with the CADP verification toolbox [11], which comprises tools for visual checking, model checking, and equivalence checking. Previously, LNT had been used successfully for the analysis of other GALS systems [8,12,22].

All the aforementioned approaches adopt specific techniques of a specific paradigm (synchronous or asynchronous) to accommodate GALS systems. On the one hand, synchronous frameworks are deterministic by nature, and not appropriate to model asynchrony. On the other hand, asynchrony and nondeterminism are granted for free in asynchronous frameworks, but those lack built-in constructs dedicated to synchronous components, which guarantee that system models fulfill the synchronous assumptions.

Moreover, most existing approaches depend strongly on the considered application field (e.g., distributed control systems [31], FPGA and ASIC digital designs [6,28], or networks on chip), the target platform (e.g., software [24], hardware [9], or heterogeneous), and the preferred specification methods (e.g., based on Petri nets [27], automata [16], process algebras [13]). This narrows down the range of systems that can be addressed. On the other hand, the surge in complexity of GALS systems forces designers to tackle (among others) design concepts, synchronous and asynchronous computations, deterministic and nondeterministic behaviour, and verification approaches, which makes the design of such systems increasingly challenging.

To circumvent this complexity, an appealing trend has been to design new languages dedicated to GALS system modeling [3,24,5], which enforce the assumptions of the GALS paradigm. In this paper, we propose GRL (*GALS Representation Language*), a new specification language with textual syntax and formal semantics, targeting systems consisting of a network of distributed synchronous systems (called blocks) that interact with their environments and exchange data asynchronously via communication mediums. The design of GRL has originally been driven by the need of general-purpose, designer-friendly, and formal representation of GALS systems suitable for efficient verification.

Our approach draws mainly from two semantic foundations. As regards synchrony, GRL holds a dataflow-oriented model based on the block-diagram model, widely used in industry: synchronous components are modeled by blocks connected together hierarchically to build higher-level blocks. Therefore, the GRL synchronous model inherits from the simplicity and modularity of the block-diagram model. As regards asynchrony, GRL was inspired by process algebras, and more particularly by LNT: blocks exchange data by (implicit) rendezvous synchronization with communication mediums connected to other blocks, and the interactions between blocks and their environments work similarly. Thereby, GRL leverages process algebra expressiveness, versatility, and verification efficiency, with a specialization to the GALS paradigm.

GRL was designed with several concerns in mind. First, it provides a sufficiently high abstraction level to fit a wide range of applications, independently from both the target platform (hardware, software, or heterogeneous), the architecture (single or distributed platforms), and the application domain.

Second, GRL is aimed at being a pivot language between industrial design tools (in particular those based on function block diagrams for the synchronous part) and verification tools for both synchronous and asynchronous systems, which guarantee system reliability and correctness. This way, we hope that formal verification methods – claimed traditionally to require high level expertise in theoretical issues – are easier to learn by industrial users, without requiring companies to shift from their actual tools and languages to entirely new production approaches. Indeed, although some approaches seem efficient [15], the high cost of such a shift makes it unlikely to happen in the near future.

Last but not least, GRL is intended to have a user-friendly syntax as it does not require users to have solid background in neither synchronous programming (e.g., clocks are not modeled explicitly), asynchronous concurrent programming (e.g., parallel composition and synchronization), nor formal verification methods. All features are smoothly and tightly integrated to form a language with homogeneous syntax and semantics.

In this paper, we introduce GRL as a first step towards fully-automated verification of GALS systems. It is organized as follows. Section 2 presents some related work. Section 3 presents the language, its formal semantics, and the current status of software tools. Section 4 gives an illustrative GRL model of an aircraft flight control system used in the avionics industry. Finally, Section 5 summarizes the paper and indicates directions for future work.

2 Related Work

In this section, we review the languages combining synchronous and asynchronous features. CRP [3] combines the Esterel [2] synchronous language and the CSP [19] asynchronous language. Despite its mathematical elegance, CRP is still rarely used in industry since it requires the user to have expertise in both Esterel and CSP. Such expertise is not required for GRL, which was designed to facilitate industrial GALS design. A language close to CRP is SystemJ [24], which extends Java with Esterel-like synchronous model and CSP-like asynchronous model. SystemJ allows efficient code to be generated automatically. However, it lacks rigorous support for fully-automated formal verification and is not suitable for systems with limited resources because of its reliance on Java virtual machine as target. To the contrary, GRL is intended to be general-purpose and verification-oriented. Action Language [5] is a state-based approach, which aims at bridging the gap between high specification languages (Statecharts [17], SCR [18], and RSML [23]) and the SPIN model checker. A key difference between this approach and ours is that Action Language adopts a low-level condition/action model whereas GRL is equipped with high-level control structures making GRL models clearer and more structured.

3   The GRL Language

The syntax and semantics of GRL are formally described in a research report [21] (76 pages). In this section, we present them briefly and informally. Figure 1 is a simplified presentation[1] described in EBNF (*Extended Backus-Naur Form*), where square brackets denote optional syntactic parts and vertical bars denote alternatives. The symbols K, X, and E denote respectively literal constants, variables, and expressions (built upon constants, variables, and function applications). The symbols S, B, N, M, T, and f denote respectively system, block, environment, medium, type, and record field identifiers.

3.1   Overview

GRL specifications are structured in modules, called *programs*. Each program can import other programs, which promotes code organization and reuse. A GRL program contains the following constructs:

1. *types*, ranging from predefined types (such as Booleans and naturals) to user-defined types (such as arrays and record types),
2. *named constants*, visible by all other constructs,
3. *blocks*, representing the synchronous components,
4. *mediums* and *environments*, representing respectively communication mediums and physical or logical constraints on block inputs, and
5. *systems*, representing the composition and interactions of blocks, environments, and mediums.

In the sequel, these five constructs are called *entities*, and blocks, environments, and mediums are called *actors*.

As regards synchronous behaviours, blocks are the synchronous composition of one or several subblocks, all governed by the clock of the highest level block. A block performs a sequence of discrete deterministic steps and preserves an internal state, hereafter called *memory*. At each step (each cycle of the clock), it consumes a set of inputs, computes a reaction instantaneously, produces a set of outputs, and updates its memory. Within one block (i.e., at *actor level*), connections between subblocks are carried out using parameters in modes "**in**" (input) and "**out**" (output). Every output parameter can be connected to several

---

[1] 70 EBNF productions were necessary to present the full language in [21].

$$
\begin{aligned}
system ::=\ & \textbf{system } S\ [(X_0:T_0,\dots,X_m:T_m)]\ \textbf{is} \\
& \textbf{allocate } actor_0,\dots,actor_n\ [\textbf{temp } X_0':T_0',\dots,X_l':T_l'] \\
& \textbf{network } block\_call_0,\dots,block\_call_p \\
& [\textbf{constrainedby } env\_call_0,\dots,env\_call_q] \\
& [\textbf{connectedby } med\_call_0,\dots,med\_call_r] \\
& \textbf{end system}
\end{aligned}
$$

$$
\begin{aligned}
block ::=\ & \textbf{block } B\ [[const\_param]]|(inout\_param_0;\dots;inout\_param_m)] \\
& \qquad\qquad\qquad\qquad [\{com\_param_0;\ \dots;\ com\_param_m\}]\ \textbf{is} \\
& [\textbf{allocate } sub\_block_0,\dots,sub\_block_p]\ [local\_var_0,\dots,local\_var_l] \\
& I \\
& \textbf{end block} \\
|\ & \textbf{block } B\ [[const\_param]]|(inout\_param_0;\dots;inout\_param_m)]\ \textbf{is} \\
& \textbf{!c } string\ |\ \textbf{!Int } string \\
& \textbf{end block}
\end{aligned}
$$

$$
\begin{aligned}
env ::=\ & \textbf{environment } N\ [[const\_param]]|(inout\_param_0\ |\dots|\ inout\_param_m)]\ \textbf{is} \\
& [\textbf{allocate } sub\_block_0,\dots,sub\_block_n]\ [local\_var_0,\dots,local\_var_l] \\
& I \\
& \textbf{end environment}
\end{aligned}
$$

$$
\begin{aligned}
med ::=\ & \textbf{medium } M\ [[const\_param]]|\{com\_param_0\ |\dots|\ com\_param_m\}]\ \textbf{is} \\
& [\textbf{allocate } sub\_block_0,\dots,sub\_block_n]\ [local\_var_0,\dots,local\_var_l] \\
& I \\
& \textbf{end medium}
\end{aligned}
$$

$$
\begin{aligned}
const\_param ::=\ & \textbf{const } X_0:T_0\ [:= E_0],\dots,X_n:T_n\ [:= E_n] \\
inout\_param ::=\ & (\textbf{in}\ |\ \textbf{out})\ X_0:T_0\ [:= E_0],\dots,X_n:T_n\ [:= E_n] \\
com\_param ::=\ & (\textbf{send}\ |\ \textbf{receive})\ X_0:T_0,\dots,X_n:T_n \\
local\_var ::=\ & (\textbf{perm}\ |\ \textbf{temp})\ X_0:T_0\ [:= E_0],\dots,X_n:T_n\ [:= E_n] \\
sub\_block ::=\ & B\ [[arg_0,\dots,arg_n]]\ \textbf{as } Bi \\
actor ::=\ & B[[arg_0,\dots,arg_n]]\ \textbf{as } Bi\ |\ N[[arg_0,\dots,arg_n]]\ \textbf{as } Ni \\
|\ & M[[arg_0,\dots,arg_n]]\ \textbf{as } Mi \\
block\_call ::=\ & Bi\ [(arg_{(0,0)},\dots,arg_{(0,m_0)};\dots;arg_{(n,0)},\dots,arg_{(n,m_n)})] \\
|\ & Bi\ [(arg_{(0,0)},\dots,arg_{(0,m_0)};\dots;arg_{(n,0)},\dots,arg_{(n,m_n)})] \\
& [\{arg_{(0,0)}',\dots,arg_{(0,p_0)}';\dots;arg_{(q,0)}',\dots,arg_{(p,p_q)}'\}] \\
env\_call ::=\ & Ni\ (arg_{(0,0)},\dots,arg_{(0,m_0)}\ |\dots|\ arg_{(n,0)},\dots,arg_{(n,m_n)}) \\
med\_call ::=\ & Mi\ \{arg_{(0,0)},\dots,arg_{(0,m_0)}\ |\dots|\ arg_{(n,0)},\dots,arg_{(n,m_n)}\} \\
signal ::=\ & \textbf{on } [?]X_0,\dots,[?]X_n \texttt{ -> } I \\
I ::=\ & \textbf{null}\ |\ X:=E\ |\ X[E_0]:=E_1\ |\ X.f:=E\ |\ I_0;I_1\ |\ Bi(arg_0,\dots,arg_n) \\
|\ & \textbf{if } E_0 \textbf{ then } I_0 \textbf{ elsif } E_1 \textbf{ then } I_1\ \dots\ \textbf{elsif } E_n \textbf{ then } I_n \textbf{ else } I_{n+1} \textbf{ end if} \\
|\ & \textbf{while } E \textbf{ loop } I_0 \textbf{ end loop}\ |\ \textbf{for } I_0 \textbf{ while } E \textbf{ by } I_1 \textbf{ loop } I_2 \textbf{ end loop} \\
|\ & \textbf{case } E \textbf{ is } K_0 \texttt{ -> } I_0\ |\ \dots\ |\ K_n \texttt{ -> } I_n\ |\ [\textbf{any} \texttt{ -> } I_{n+1}]\ \textbf{end case} \\
|\ & X := \textbf{any } T\ [\textbf{where } E]\ |\ \textbf{select } I_0\ []\ \dots\ []\ I_n \textbf{ end select}\ |\ signal
\end{aligned}
$$

Fig. 1. The syntax of GRL (excerpts)

input parameters of different blocks; however, an input parameter can be connected to only one output parameter of another block. Such connections describe synchronous communication by instantaneous broadcasting.

As regards asynchronous behaviours, blocks are composed, together with environments and mediums, within systems to form networks of distributed connected synchronous subsystems. Within a GRL system (i.e., at *system level*), the separate blocks execute asynchronously, i.e., each block evolves cyclically at its own frequency (blocks have independent clocks). Blocks interact with each other across mediums, which allows separate blocks to be loosely coupled so that communication is performed asynchronously (i.e., takes an arbitrary amount of time). Connections between blocks and mediums are carried out using parameters in modes "**receive**" and "**send**". Receive parameters of mediums can be connected to send parameters of blocks, and conversely. Such connections describe synchronisation and communication by message-passing rendezvous between blocks and mediums. Mediums may exhibit nondeterministic behaviour,

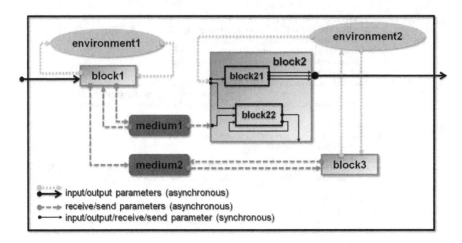

Fig. 2. Schematic representation of a GRL system

a key feature for asynchronous systems modeling and compositional specification; this provides descriptions with accuracy and high abstraction capability.

Blocks behaviour can also be constraint-driven by a collection of user-defined environments. In essence, environments exhibit a similar behaviour as mediums, except that their connections to blocks are carried out using modes "**in**" and "**out**". They have been introduced in GRL to explicitly separate the specification of communication mediums from external constraints imposed by the environment; this contributes to provide more comfort and insight about the system composition. With such a composition, we seek enhanced user-convenience to smoothly and tightly tailor complex network topologies, environment requirements and constraints, as well as communication protocols.

As an example, GRL can be used to model the network topology depicted in Figure 2: *block1* is constrained by *env1* and communicates with *block2* and *block3* respectively across *med1* and *med2*; *block2* and *block3* are both constrained by *env2*; *block2* is the synchronous composition of two subblocks.

3.2   Block

Blocks, defined by the non-terminal *block* in Figure 1, are the central building unit of the language. At actor level, a block is defined by the following elements:

- a list "*const_param*" of typed constant parameters (read-only variables).
- a list "*inout_param$_0$*, . . . , *inout_param$_m$*" of typed input and output parameters preceded by their mode ("**in**" or "**out**").
- a list "*local_var$_0$*, . . . , *local_var$_l$*" of local variables. Temporary variables are declared using the keyword "**temp**"; their values are lost when the current block execution terminates. Permanent variables are declared using the keyword "**perm**"; their values are kept until the next execution cycle. The *memory* of the block is the list of values assigned to its permanent variables.

- a list "sub_block_0, ..., sub_block_p" of subblock *allocations*, which enables subblock instances to be created, each maintaining its own memory. This concept is inherited from the block-diagram model, which is similar to, but simpler than, the class-instance paradigm in object-oriented languages.

- a body "I" expressed as a deterministic statement defined by combination of high-level control structures (bounded loops, if-then-else, sequential composition, etc.) and synchronous subblock invocations. The scheduling of subblock executions is inherently specified by the order in which the subblocks are invoked, using the sequential composition operator ";". Nondeterministic statements such as "X := **any** T **where** E" and "**select**" (arbitrary choice of one statement among a set) are forbidden within block bodies.

Alternatively, blocks can be specified in an external language. Their body consists of a pragma denoting the language in which the external function implementing the block is written, followed by the name of the function in the external code. So far, the supported external languages are C and LNT: an external function identifier in C (resp. LNT) is preceded by the pragma "**!c**" (resp. "**!lnt**"). Although C external blocks provide more flexibility for the user, they should be defined to comply with the GRL block semantics (in particular, side effects in external C code are prohibited to enable model checking). LNT external blocks, however, have formal semantics and can thus be used safely.

In a block invocation, actual parameters have different forms according to their modes. A question mark precedes both output and send actual parameters, meaning that the parameter will have a value assigned when returning from the block. An underscore ("_") is used for unconnected parameters (i.e., unused inputs or outputs). An output parameter X_i declared in "**out** $X_0 : T_0$, ..., $X_n : T_n$" of a block Bi and an input parameter Y_j declared in "**in** $Y_0 : T_0$, ..., $Y_m : T_m$" of a block Bi' can thus be connected synchronously using a variable "$Z : T_i$" by passing "$?Z$" to Bi and "Z" to Bi' in a subsequent invocation.

Additional elements can be used to define a block that can only be invoked at system level, namely lists "com_param_0, ..., com_param_n" of typed receive and send parameters preceded by their mode "**receive**" or "**send**". They enable blocks to interact asynchronously within a network of blocks via mediums. Such a block cannot be allocated nor invoked inside another actor since communication between blocks within actors is necessarily synchronous. At system level, actual input parameters of blocks can have the additional form "**any** T", meaning that an arbitrary value of type T is passed as input to the block.

The behaviour of a block is the following. In each cycle of its clock, (1) the block consumes data received over input and receive parameters, (2) the block computes by executing its body, then (3) the block produces data sent over output and send parameters. During computation, its memory is assigned the updated values of permanent variables so as to keep them stored up to the next cycle. As usual in the synchronous paradigm, all these steps are performed in zero-delay, i.e., instantaneously and atomically.

3.3 Medium

Mediums, defined by the non-terminal *med* in Figure 1, are dedicated to the modeling of communications and asynchronous interactions within a network of synchronous blocks. A medium is defined by the following elements:

- a list "*const_param*" of constant parameters.
- a list "*com_param$_0$* , . . . , *com_param$_m$*" of send and receive parameters.
- a list "*sub_block$_0$* , . . . , *sub_block$_p$*" of subblock allocations enabling blocks to be used in mediums in the same way as functions in programming languages.
- a list "*local_var$_0$* , . . . , *local_var$_l$*" of local (temporary and permanent) variable declarations.
- a body "*I*" expressed as a statement (not necessarily deterministic) defined as a combination of high-level control structures, subblock compositions, and nondeterministic statements.

A medium sends and receives messages to and from several blocks. When a block wants to send a message to or receive a message from a medium, it triggers the execution of the medium, which we call medium *activation*. Therefore, the invocation of mediums is demand-driven by different blocks at unpredictable instants. In this respect, mediums are *passive actors*, whereas blocks are *active actors*. Each medium is activated during a block execution cycle at most once to send messages to the block, then at most once to receive messages from the block. Since several messages may have to transit via one medium, those messages are grouped in tuples, called *channels*, all messages of a channel being exchanged within a single block-medium interaction. The channel under consideration is then called *activated*. The activations of a given medium are thus guided by the separate activations of its channels, as is suggested by the pipe symbol ("|") used to delimit formal and actual channel parameters, each channel activation leading to a separate execution of the medium.

To control medium activations, we introduce *signal statements*, whose syntax is defined by the non-terminal *signal* in Figure 1. A signal guards the part of the medium code that needs to be executed upon the activation of a particular channel. When a channel of the form "**receive** X_0 , . . . , X_n" is activated, the signal statement "**on** X_0 , . . . , X_n -> *I*" can be executed and the values of variables X_0 , . . . , X_n passed to the channel can be read within the statement *I*. When a channel of the form "**send** Y_0 , . . . , Y_m" is activated, the signal statement "**on** ?Y_0 , . . . , ?Y_m -> *I*" can be executed and the statement *I* must assign values to the variables Y_0, . . . , Y_m. Static semantics prohibit sequential composition of signals, loop statements containing signals, and nested signals, so that at most one signal is present on each execution path.

Mediums introduce flexibility in system models since they provide an accurate design of complex network topologies (e.g., bus, star, ring, mesh), connection modes (e.g., point-to-point, multi-point), as well as communication protocols. This way, we address a lack identified in existing languages confined to rigid topologies and point-to-point communications between separate synchronous subsystems, such as those based on CSP rendezvous [24,3,9]. Limitations of adopting point-to-point communications in GALS models are considered as drastically restrictive to design complex networks of arbitrary topologies [30].

3.4   Environment

Since synchronous systems are often recognized to be outside-aware, GRL allows the user to model explicitly, yet abstractly, the behaviour of the environment. There are two major roles the environment can play: impose outside physical and logical requirements that block inputs may undergo, and put constraints on the scheduling of blocks executing in parallel. Additionally, an environment may be local, i.e., connected only to one block, or global, i.e., connected to several blocks at the same time. Environments, defined by the non-terminal *env* in Figure 1, are syntactically and semantically very similar to mediums, except that send and receive parameters are replaced by input and output parameters.

3.5   System

Systems, defined by the non-terminal *system* in Figure 1, are the top level entities in GRL programs, within which actors are invoked and connected to each other. A system is defined by the following elements:

- a list "$X_0 : T_0, \ldots, X_m : T_m$" of parameters, which can be used in actual channels to connect blocks to environments and mediums. They are the visible parameters of the system, observable from the outside world.
- a list "$actor_0, \ldots, actor_n$" of actor instance declarations.
- a list "$X'_0 : T'_0, \ldots, X'_l : T'_l$" of temporary variables, which can be used in actual channels to connect blocks to environments and mediums. They are the invisible parameters of the system, not observable from the outside world.
- a list "$block\_call_0, \ldots, block\_call_p$" of block invocations.
- a list "$env\_call_0, \ldots, env\_call_q$" of environment invocations that constrain the blocks.
- a list "$med\_call_0, \ldots, med\_call_r$" of medium invocations that ensure the traffic inside the network of blocks.

All interactions between actors within a system are built on message-passing synchronisations (rendezvous). Since blocks are the active actors of systems, the scheduling of the whole system is focused around their executions. Blocks execute cyclically, each at its own frequency, and force environments and mediums to perform some operations by sending messages (requesting or providing data) through channels. Environments and mediums, consequently, are passive actors responding to arisen demands from different blocks. At system level; GRL prohibits blocks to be connected directly to each other in order to preserve an independent behaviour of each block and an asynchronous behaviour of the network. Thus, blocks communicate only indirectly across mediums.

Each interaction between two actors is performed through exactly one channel. Namely, an output channel of the form "**out** $X_0 : T_0, \ldots, X_n : T_n$" of an actor Ai

and an input channel of the form "**in** $Y_0 : T_0 , \ldots , Y_n : T_n$" of another actor Ai' can thus be connected using a set of variables "$Z_0 : T_0 , \ldots , Z_n : T_n$" by passing $?Z_0, \ldots, ?Z_n$ to Ai and $Z_0, \ldots, Z_n$ to Ai', in their respective invocations within a system. Send and receive channels can be connected similarly.

The semantics of a system are the following. Blocks execute arbitrarily often and cyclically. Each time a block begins its execution cycle, all environments and mediums connected respectively to input and receive channels of the block are activated to provide the needed input and receive values. Unconnected input and receive channels are assigned arbitrary values. Then, the block executes its body, and thus updates its output and send channels as well as its memory. Finally, all environments and mediums connected to respectively output or send channels of the block are activated.

The combined execution cycle of a block, and its related environments and mediums is performed instantaneously according to the synchronous assumptions. As a consequence, a block is executed only if all its connected environments and mediums are able to respond to all input, output, receive, and send signals of the block.

3.6   Formal Semantics

The semantics of GRL are formally defined in [21]. They consist in 145 rules of static semantics and 24 rules of Plotkin-style structural operational semantics for the dynamic part. In this paper, we only sketch briefly the principles of the dynamic semantics, defined in terms of LTSs (*Labelled Transition Systems*). An LTS is a quadruple $(S, L, \rightarrow, s_0)$ where S is a set of states, $s_0 \in S$ is the initial state, L is a set of labels, and $\rightarrow \subseteq S \times L \times S$ is the labelled transition relation.

The memory of an actor, denoted by μ, is a partial function mapping all permanent variables of the actor and its subblocks to their current values. A state S of the system is the union of memories μ_i of all actors composing the system, and the initial state s_0 maps all permanent variables to their initialization values. Each label has the form $Bi(a_0, \ldots, a_n)\{a'_0, \ldots, a'_m\}$ with Bi a block identifier, $a_0, \ldots, a_n$ the visible actual parameters of input and output channels, and $a'_0, \ldots, a'_m$ the visible actual parameters of receive and send channels. A transition $\mu \xrightarrow{Bi(a_0,\ldots,a_n)\{a'_0,\ldots,a'_m\}} \mu'$ expresses the combined execution of one cycle of the block instance Bi, together with its connected environments and mediums. The semantics of the system are obtained by interleaving all possible block executions. Verification (e.g., visual checking, equivalence checking, model checking) can be done by inspection of the LTS.

3.7   Tools for GRL

There are currently two software tools for handling GRL models. The first one is a parser for GRL (2000 lines), developed using the SYNTAX and Lotos NT compiler construction technology [10], which performs lexical and syntax analysis, type checking, binding analysis, and variable initialisation analysis of GRL programs.

The second one, named GRL2LNT (8000 lines), is an automated translator from GRL to LNT. Each block is mapped to an LNT function that takes inputs and produces outputs. Its permanent variables are mapped to *inout* parameters, i.e., parameters whose values are updated during function invocation. Synchronous block composition is mapped to sequential composition. Additionally, each actor invoked within a system is also mapped to a *wrapper* process, which contains communication actions to exchange data with its connected actors. The whole system is mapped to the LNT parallel composition of the wrapper processes with appropriate synchronizations of the communication actions.

GRL and GRL2LNT play the role of an intermediate and appropriate layer of abstraction and compositionality to provide generated LNT code with accuracy and conciseness, since scalability of automated model checking is limited. We can take advantage from the CADP toolbox available for LNT to build state spaces and apply visual, equivalence, and model checking techniques.

4 Example: Flight Control System

Our aim here is not to present a full case study, but rather to illustrate the main concepts of GRL via a feature rich example: the aircraft Flight Control System (FCS)[2], whose role is to control the aircraft turning and which is one of the most critical systems inside new generations of Airbus aircraft designs. Subsets of FCS have been studied at different levels of abstraction. In [25], the Flight Guidance System component of the FCS has been studied as a composition of synchronous systems following a single-platform GALS architecture. In [1], control systems have been studied as synchronous systems following a distributed-platforms PALS (*Physically Asynchronous, Locally synchronous*) architecture. For the sake of simplicity, we model the global behaviour, at a very high level of abstraction, of an FCS containing the following subsystems:

- Flight Control Surfaces adjust and control the aircraft's flight turning. We consider only one aileron (a flap attached to the end of a wing) controller.
- Fly-By-Wire Computers command the movement of the Flight Control Surfaces. We consider only two Fly-By-Wire Computers commanding the position of the aileron, one being used as a backup in case the other fails.
- A Flight Control Data Concentrator schedules the execution of Fly-By-Wire Computers and allows interaction with pilot displays.

The GRL model. The FCS system depicted in Figure 3 (see the GRL code below) consists of four block instances, whose cyclic behaviour is as follows:

- The *Ail* (for *aileron*) block instance receives movement requirements from the network, computes the next position of the aileron depending on its current position, then sends it to the network.

___
[2] http://www.skybrary.aero/index.php/Flight_Control_Laws

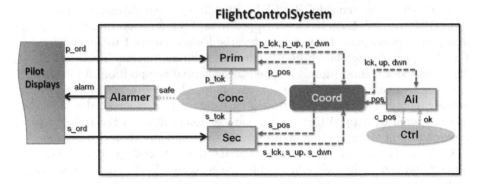

Fig. 3. Architecture of the Flight Control System

- The *Prim* (for *primary*) and *Sec* (for *secondary*) instances of block *FBW-Comp* (for *fly-by-wire computer*) receive: tokens from the environment indicating whether *Prim* or *Sec* should control *Ail*; an order from the pilot displays; and the current position of the aileron from the network. They compare the two latter values, and then send to the network the decision about whether the aileron should move up, move down, or not move (if the order matches the position).
- The *Alarmer* block instance checks whether the system is evolving safely by receiving from the environment a message indicating whether *Ail* is still controlled by either *Prim* or *Sec*, then informs the pilot about the safety state of the system.

Communications within the network of blocks are modeled by the medium *Coord* (for *coordinator*) as follows. *Prim* provides *Ail* with move requirements, then *Ail* achieves the required computations and sends its new position to *Prim*. *Sec* and *Ail* communicate similarly.

The environment constraints are modeled by two environments. The first environment *Conc* (for *concentrator*) ensures that either *Prim* or *Sec*, but not both, can control *Ail*, the priority being given to *Prim* by activating its token. *Conc* determines whether *Prim* is in a safety state (i.e., able to control *Ail*). Once *Prim* is not in safety state, it is considered out of order (not alive). Then, *Conc* blocks the execution of *Prim* by inactivating its token and gives the control of *Ail* to *Sec* by activating its token. Once *Sec* is not in safety state anymore, which means that neither *Prim* nor *Sec* is in safety state, then *Ail* is considered out of control and *Alarmer* warns the pilot.

The second environment *Ctrl* (for *controller*) constrains the execution of *Ail* as follows. *Ail* sends cyclically its new position to *Ctrl*. *Ctrl* verifies whether the position is still within a predefined interval, which means that *Ail* moves smoothly; if not, the execution of *Ail* is blocked. The GRL specification of the system follows.

```
system FlightControlSystem (p_ord:nat, s_ord:nat, alarm:bool) is
    allocate FBWComp as Prim, FBWComp as Sec, Ail as Ail, Alarmer as Alarmer,
            Conc as Conc, Ctrl[3] as Ctrl, Coord as Coord
    temp p_tok:bool, p_pos:nat, p_lck, p_up, p_dwn:bool, s_tok:bool, s_pos:nat,
            s_lck, s_up, s_dwn:bool, c_pos, pos:nat, lck, up, dwn:bool, safe, ok:bool
    network
        Prim (p_tok;p_ord){p_pos;?p_lck,?p_up,?p_dwn},
        Sec (s_tok;s_ord){s_pos;?s_lck,?s_up,?s_dwn},
        Ail (ok;?c_pos){lck,up,dwn;?pos}, Alarmer(safe;?alarm)
    constrainedby
        Conc (?p_tok | ?s_tok | ?safe), Ctrl (c_pos | ?ok)
    connectedby
        Coord {pos | ?lck, ?up, ?dwn | p_lck, p_up, p_dwn | ?p_pos | s_lck, s_up, s_dwn | ?s_pos}
end system

block FBWComp (in tok:bool; in ord:nat){receive pos:nat; send lck, up, dwn:bool} is
    if tok then
        if ord > pos then lck := false; up := true; dwn := false
        elsif ord < pos then lck := false; up := false; dwn := true
        else lck := true; up := false; dwn := false
        end if
    else lck := false; up := false; dwn := false
    end if
end block

block Ail (in ok:bool; out c_pos:nat){receive lck:bool, up, dwn:bool; send pos:nat} is
    perm pos_buf:nat := 0
    if not(lck) and ok then
        if up then pos_buf := pos_buf + 1
        elsif dwn then pos_buf := pos_buf - 1
        end if
    end if;
    c_pos := pos_buf; pos := pos_buf
end block

block Alarmer (in safe:bool; out alarm:bool) is
    if safe then alarm := false else alarm := true end if
end block

environment Ctrl [const threshold:nat] (in pos:nat | out ok:bool) is
    perm lastPos:nat := 0
    select
        on pos -> lastPos := pos
    [] on ?ok -> if (((lastPos > threshold) and ((lastPos - threshold) < 5))
                    or ((lastPos <= threshold) and ((threshold - lastPos) < 5))) then
                    ok := true
                 else ok := false
                 end if
    end select
end environment

environment Conc (out p_tok:bool | out s_tok:bool | out safe:bool) is
    perm p_alive, s_alive:bool := true
    if p_alive then
        select
            on ?p_tok -> p_tok := true -- primary responds
        [] p_alive := false -- primary fails
        end select
    elsif s_alive then
        select
            on ?s_tok -> s_tok := true -- secondary responds
        [] s_alive := false -- secondary fails
        end select
    else on ?safe -> safe := false
    end if
end environment

medium Coord {receive pos:nat | send lck, up, dwn:bool |
                receive p_lck, p_up, p_dwn:bool | send p_pos:nat |
                receive s_lck, s_up, s_dwn:bool | send s_pos:nat} is
```

```
perm lckBuff:bool := true, upBuff, dwnBuff:bool := false, posBuff:nat := 0
select
    on p_lck, p_up, p_dwn -> lckBuff := p_lck; upBuff := p_up; dwnBuff := p_dwn
[] on s_lck, s_up, s_dwn -> lckBuff := s_lck; upBuff := s_up; dwnBuff := s_dwn
[] on pos -> posBuff := pos
[] on ?p_pos -> p_pos := posBuff
[] on ?s_pos -> s_pos := posBuff
[] on ?lck, ?up, ?dwn -> lck := lckBuff; up := upBuff; dwn := dwnBuff
end select
end medium
```

LTS generation. The GRL model has been translated into an LNT specification using the GRL2LNT tool, yielding a code that is 2.5 times larger than the input GRL model. Using CADP [11], the LTS of the model has been generated (2, 653 states, 7, 406 transitions) then reduced modulo branching bisimulation (5 states, 1, 287 transitions), naturals being represented on 8 bits. This apparently small LTS size can be explained by the following facts. Different states represent different values of permanent variables whereas inputs and outputs only appear on transitions (temporary variables are not stored but only used in intermediate computations). Only variables *p_ord*, *s_ord*, and *alarm* are visible on the LTS. Other variables (17 inputs and outputs) are hidden and thus do not occur in transition labels. Environment *Ctrl* constraints the range of possible positions to which *Ail* can move, thus drastically reducing the LTS. Reduction modulo branching bisimulation also helps in keeping the LTS small.

5   Conclusion and Future Work

We gave an overview of GRL, a new language with user-friendly syntax and formal semantics for modeling GALS systems, intended to enhance their design process. GRL combines synchronous features of dataflow languages and asynchronous features of process algebras, and makes possible a versatile, modular description of synchronous subsystems, environment constraints, and asynchronous communications. We designed GRL initially as a pivot language intended to facilitate the connection of industrial environments for designing PLCs (*Programmable Logic Controllers*) to formal verification tools. However, the language appears to be sufficiently expressive and general-purpose to model a wide range of GALS architectures (possibly nondeterministic), implemented on single or distributed platforms, and involving point-to-point or multi-point communications. Moreover, its user-friendly syntax and abstraction level, which is close to the dataflow model used in industry, makes GRL easier to learn and employ than a full-fledged process algebraic language like LNT.

GRL can independently be connected to verification frameworks based on either the synchronous or the asynchronous paradigms. The language is currently equipped with an automated translator to LNT, which makes possible the analysis of GRL descriptions using the rich functionalities of the CADP toolbox (e.g., simulation, verification, performance evaluation), focusing on the asynchronous behaviour of the GALS. GRL and the GRL2LNT translator start to be used in the Bluesky industrial project[3], which addresses the validation of

---

[3] www.minalogic.com

PLC networks. After a positive feedback received from our industrial partners, we are investigating an automated connection between their PLC design software (based on function block diagrams) and GRL, which would provide a complete analysis chain having CADP as verification back-end. We also develop reusable GRL programs describing basic function blocks and mediums corresponding to communication protocols used in PLC networks.

We plan to continue our work by applying equivalence checking and model checking techniques to industrial GALS systems described in GRL. Hardware/-software co-simulation is also possible using the EXEC/CAESAR framework [14] of CADP, which enables the C code generated from a GRL description to be integrated with a physical platform. We also plan to investigate the connection of GRL to verification frameworks based on the synchronous paradigm to analyse the behaviour of individual blocks corresponding to synchronous subsystems.

References

1. Bae, K., Ölveczky, P.C., Meseguer, J.: Definition, semantics, and analysis of multirate synchronous aadl. In: Proc. of FM. Springer (2014)
2. Berry, G., Gonthier, G.: The ESTEREL synchronous programming language: design, semantics, implementation. Science of Computer Programming 19(2), 87–152 (1992)
3. Berry, G., Ramesh, S., Shyamasundar, R.K.: Communicating reactive processes. In: Proc. of POPL, pp. 85–98. ACM Press (1993)
4. Berry, G., Sentovich, E.: Multiclock Esterel. In: Margaria, T., Melham, T.F. (eds.) CHARME 2001. LNCS, vol. 2144, pp. 110–125. Springer, Heidelberg (2001)
5. Bultan, T.: Action language: A specification language for model checking reactive systems. In: Proc. of ICSE. ACM (2000)
6. Carlsson, J., Palmkvist, K., Wanhammar, L.: Synchronous design flow for Globally Asynchronous Locally Synchronous systems. In: Proc. of ICC, WSEAS (2006)
7. Champelovier, D., Clerc, X., Garavel, H., Guerte, Y., McKinty, C., Powazny, V., Lang, F., Serwe, W., Smeding, G.: Reference manual of the LOTOS NT to LOTOS translator (version 5.4). INRIA/VASY (September 2011)
8. Coste, N., Hermanns, H., Lantreibecq, E., Serwe, W.: Towards Performance Prediction of Compositional Models in Industrial GALS Designs. In: Bouajjani, A., Maler, O. (eds.) CAV 2009. LNCS, vol. 5643, pp. 204–218. Springer, Heidelberg (2009)
9. Doucet, F., Menarini, M., Krüger, I.H., Gupta, R.K., Talpin, J.-P.: A verification approach for GALS integration of synchronous components. Electr. Notes Theor. Comput. Sci. 146(2), 105–131 (2006)
10. Garavel, H., Lang, F., Mateescu, R.: Compiler Construction Using LOTOS NT. In: Nigel Horspool, R. (ed.) CC 2002. LNCS, vol. 2304, p. 9. Springer, Heidelberg (2002)
11. Garavel, H., Lang, F., Mateescu, R., Serwe, W.: CADP 2011: A Toolbox for the Construction and Analysis of Distributed Processes. STTT 15(2), 89–107 (2013)
12. Garavel, H., Salaun, G., Serwe, W.: On the Semantics of Communicating Hardware Processes and their Translation into LOTOS for the Verification of Asynchronous Circuits with CADP. In: Science of Computer Programming (2009)

13. Garavel, H., Thivolle, D.: Verification of GALS Systems by Combining Synchronous Languages and Process Calculi. In: Păsăreanu, C.S. (ed.) Model Checking Software. LNCS, vol. 5578, pp. 241–260. Springer, Heidelberg (2009)
14. Garavel, H., Viho, C., Zendri, M.: System design of a CC-NUMA multiprocessor architecture using formal specification, model-checking, co-simulation, and test generation. STTT 3(3), 314–331 (2001)
15. Girault, A., Ménier, C.: Automatic Production of Globally Asynchronous Locally Synchronous Systems. In: Sangiovanni-Vincentelli, A.L., Sifakis, J. (eds.) EMSOFT 2002. LNCS, vol. 2491, pp. 266–281. Springer, Heidelberg (2002)
16. Günther, H., Milius, S., Möller, O.: On the Formal Verification of Systems of Synchronous Software Components. In: Ortmeier, F., Lipaczewski, M. (eds.) SAFECOMP 2012. LNCS, vol. 7612, pp. 291–304. Springer, Heidelberg (2012)
17. Harel, D.: Statecharts: A visual formalism for complex systems. Science of Computer Programming 8(3), 231–274 (1987)
18. Heitmeyer, C.L., Jeffords, R.D., Labaw, B.G.: Automated consistency checking of requirements specifications. ACM Trans. on Software Engineering and Methodology 5(3), 231–261 (1996)
19. Hoare, C.A.R.: Communicating Sequential Processes. Communications of the ACM 21(8), 666–677 (1978)
20. Holzmann, G.J.: The model checker SPIN. IEEE Transactions on Software Engineering 23(5) (1997)
21. Jebali, F., Lang, F., Mateescu, R.: GRL: A Specification Language for Globally Asynchronous Locally Synchronous Systems. Research Report 8527, Inria (April 2014), http://hal.inria.fr/hal-00983711
22. Lantreibecq, E., Serwe, W.: Model Checking and Co-simulation of a Dynamic Task Dispatcher Circuit Using CADP. In: Salaün, G., Schätz, B. (eds.) FMICS 2011. LNCS, vol. 6959, pp. 180–195. Springer, Heidelberg (2011)
23. Leveson, N.G., Heimdahl, M.P.E., Hildreth, H., Reese, J.D.: Requirements specification for process-control systems. IEEE Trans. on Software Engineering 20(9), 684–707 (1994)
24. Malik, A., Salcic, Z., Roop, P.S., Girault, A.: SystemJ: A GALS language for system level design. Comput. Lang. Syst. Struct. 36(4), 317–344 (2010)
25. Miller, S., Anderson, E., Wagner, L., Whalen, M., Heimdahl, M.: Formal verification of flight critical software. In: Proc. of the AIAA Guidance, Navigation and Control Conference and Exhibit (2005)
26. Mousavi, M.R., Le Guernic, P., Talpin, J.-P., Shukla, S.K., Basten, T.: Modeling and Validating Globally Asynchronous Design in Synchronous Frameworks. In: Proc. of DATE. IEEE Computer Society (2004)
27. Moutinho, F., Gomes, L.: State space generation for Petri nets-based GALS systems. In: Proc. of ICIT (2012)
28. Muttersbach, J., Villiger, T., Fichtner, W.: Practical design of globally-asynchronous locally-synchronous systems. In: Proc. of the International Symposium on Advanced Research in Asynchronous Circuits and Systems (2000)
29. Ramesh, S.: Communicating reactive state machines: Design, model and implementation. In: IFAC Workshop on Distributed Computer Control Systems (1998)
30. Singh, M., Theobald, M.: Generalized latency-insensitive systems for single-clock and multi-clock architectures. In: Proc. of DATE, vol. 2. IEEE (2004)
31. Yoong, L.H., Shaw, G., Roop, P.S., Salcic, Z.: Synthesizing Globally Asynchronous Locally Synchronous Systems With IEC 61499. IEEE Transactions on Systems, Man, and Cybernetics, Part C 42(6), 1465–1477 (2012)

A Formal Framework to Prove
the Correctness of Model Driven Engineering
Composition Operators

Mounira Kezadri Hamiaz[1], Marc Pantel[1], Benoit Combemale[2],
and Xavier Thirioux[1]

[1] Université de Toulouse, IRIT, France
[2] Université de Rennes 1, IRISA, France

Abstract. Current trends in system engineering combine modeling, composition and verification technologies in order to harness their ever growing complexity. Each composition operator dedicated to a different modeling concern should be proven to be property preserving at assembly time. These proofs are usually burdensome with repetitive aspects. Our work[1] targets the factorisation of these aspects relying on primitive generic composition operators used to express more sophisticated language specific ones. These operators are defined for languages expressed with `OMG MOF` metamodeling technologies. The proofs are done with the Coq proof assistant relying on the Coq4MDE framework defined previously. These basic operators, `Union` and `Substitution`, are illustrated using the `MOF` Package Merge as a composition operator and the preservation of model conformance as a verified property.

1 Introduction and Motivation

Safety critical systems are getting more and more complex and software intensive while the safety rules are more and more stringent (e.g. DO-178 in aeronautics [41]). Several technologies are playing a key role to tackle these issues.

First, Model-Based Systems Engineering (MBSE) relying on Model Driven Engineering (MDE) [7] promotes the use of models at the various development phases, composition operators and model transformations to automate parts of the development. Models are abstract specifications of the various system concerns/aspects that are usually purpose oriented and allow early Validation and Verification (V & V) (e.g. the new DO-331 standard [40]).

Then, formal methods allow the assessment of the completeness and consistency of specification models, and of the correctness of design models and implementations with respect to specification models. Their mathematical nature provides high level of confidence in their result (e.g. the new DO-333 standard [39]).

---

[1] This work was partly funded by the French ministry of research through the ANR-12-INSE-0011 grant for the GEMOC project.

S. Merz and J. Pang (Eds.): ICFEM 2014, LNCS 8829, pp. 235–250, 2014.

In order to benefit from these technologies and avoid doing all the V & V activities on the final system, safety standards require the associated process, methods and tools to be qualified (e.g. the new DO-330 standard: Software Tool Qualification Considerations that adapts the DO-178C to the development and the verification tools [42]). These qualification activities are very costly and can benefit from the use of formal methods relying on the DO-333 standard [39].

To ease the integration of formal specification and verification technologies, some of the authors proposed in [44] a formal embedding of some key aspects of MDE in Set Theory. This embedding was then implemented using the Calculus of Inductive Construction [15] and the CoQ[2] proof-assistant. This framework called CoQ4MDE[3] provides sound mathematical foundations for the study and the validation of MDE technologies. The choice of constructive logic with type theory as formal specification language allows to extract prototype tools from the executable specification that can be used to validate the specification itself with respect to external tools implementing the MDE principles (for example, in the Eclipse[4] Modeling Project).

We proposed in [25] an extension of CoQ4MDE to support the Invasive Software Composition (ISC) [1] style. We then experimented the design of formalized primitive operators and their use to ease the implementation, and especially the proof of correctness of the ISC operators and other high level ones. This contribution specifies and assesses the properties of the primitive composition operators Union and Substitution that can be used to specify higher level composition operators sharing parts of their implementation and associated properties. The assessed property is the conformance of models to metamodels which is mandatory for all model composition operators. Our proposal is illustrated by the use of these primitive operators to specify and prove the MOF (Meta Object Facility) [32] Package Merge. Other sophisticated composition operators like ISC (adaptation and glueing) [1] [20] and aspect weaving [29] can also be built from these primitive ones, and their proofs of conformance preservation are also built from the ones of primitive operators. One key point is the use of property specific contracts (pre and post conditions) for the composition operators in order to ensure compositional verification.

This contribution is structured as follows. First, the concepts and an example for a targeted high level operator and the expected properties are given in Section 2. Then, Section 3 presents the formal support for the CoQ4MDE framework that is extended to handle the definition of the primitive composition operators associated with the proofs of property preservation. Then, some use cases are provided in Section 4. Related work are given in Section 5. Finally, conclusion and perspectives are provided in Section 6.

---

[2] http://coq.inria.fr

[3] http://coq4mde.enseeiht.fr/FormalMDE/

[4] https://www.eclipse.org/

2   Use Case : MOF Package Merge

This section introduces our verification proposal applied to the MOF Package Merge operator.

2.1   Model Driven Engineering

The core principle of MDE is *"everything is a model"* [7]. Models are defined using modeling languages. Metamodels are models of modeling languages defined using metamodeling languages. A model M is conforming to a metamodel MM if MM models the language used to define M. Metamodels, like data types, define the structure common to all its conforming models, but can also give semantics properties like dependent types. Derived from [23], Coq4MDE separates the model level (value or object) from the metamodel level (type or class), and describes them in Coq with different types.

2.2   Meta-Object Facility

The OMG has standardized the MOF, that provides a reflexive metamodeling language (i.e. MOF is defined as a model in the MOF language). MOF is used for the specification of the OMG modeling language standards like MOF itself, UML [33], OCL [46], SysML [21] and many others. The relation between MOF and the metamodels is the same as the one between a metamodel and its conforming models. Based on these principles, the OMG introduced the MDA (Model Driven Architecture) [6] view of software modeling illustrated by the pyramid given in Figure 2. Since the MOF version released in 2006 [31], a kernel named EMOF was extracted from the complete version of MOF (CMOF). EMOF provides a minimal set of elements required to model languages. Figure 1 gives the key concepts of EMOF specified as an UML class diagram. The principal concept is Class to define classes (usually called metaclasses) that represent concepts in a modeling language. Classes allow to create objects in models. The type of an object is the class that was used to create it. Classes are composed of an arbitrary number of Property (we will call them reference and attribute in order to avoid ambiguities with the model property we want to assess) and Operation (not detailled here). References allow to create the relations between the objects in the models. Classes can inherit references and attributes from other classes. Inheritance is expressed using the superClass reference from Class. Inheritance introduces a subtyping relation between the types associated to classes. Classes can be abstract (isAbstract): no object can have the type associated to an abstract class as smallest type according to the subtyping relation. Property has a lower and upper attributes that bound the number of objects contained in a given reference. Two references can be opposite to build a bidirectional relation between objects in a model.

In MBSE, many models are used to represent the various system's concerns. They must be composed to build the global system. We present in the following subsection the MOF composition operator that is used in the OMG UML specification [33] to define and assemble metamodel parts.

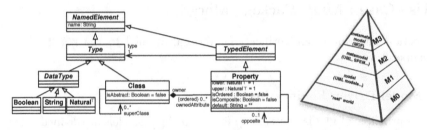

Fig. 1. The basic concepts of EMOF   **Fig. 2.** The OMG Pyramid

2.3   MOF Package Merge

Package Merge is a directed relation from a package (**merged**) to another package (**receiving**) as mentioned in Figure 3. It can be seen as an operation that takes the content of both packages and produces a new package (**resulting**) that merges the contents of the initial packages. In the case where some elements in these packages represent the same entity, theirs contents must be combined according to the rules given in [33].

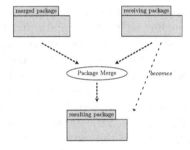

Fig. 3. Conceptual view of the Package Merge [33]

When there are no conflicts between the two packages, Package Merge is equivalent to an union for all the packages elements (in fact, a special union that preserves the references and attributes for classes).

When conflicts occur, two major kinds are considered: a) when the same class has different attributes and references in the two packages, this conflict is resolved by keeping all the attributes and references from both classes in the **merged** and **receiving** models (this is obviously an application of the previous special union operator), b) when two corresponding attributes or references have different values (for example different multiplicity values); the conflicts are resolved by combining the values according to the semantics of the conflicting attribute or reference.

2.4   Expected Property

The expected property in this use case is the preservation of the metamodel conformance during composition. For a model M and a metamodel MM, this property checks that: 1) every object o in M was created from a class C in MM. 2) every relation between two objects in M is such that there exists, in MM, a reference between the two classes used for creating the two objects. 3) every semantics property defined in MM is satisfied in M. The semantics properties from EMOF (see Figure 1) are: Inheritance (subClass), Abstract classes (isAbstract), Multiplicities (lower, upper), Opposite (isOpposite) and Composite (areComposite) references.

As verifying these properties directly for the MOF Package Merge operator is complex and contains many common aspects with other high level composition operators, we target a divide and conquer approach to capture these commonalities.

2.5   Verification Strategy

We advocate the use of generic primitive composition operators that are then used to specify and prove more sophisticated ones like MOF Package Merge or ISC. We target pragmatic compositional verification: minimize the residual verification that must be conducted on the result of the composition of correct models. We rely on a simple methodology to design the contract (pre and post conditions) for the composition operators in that purpose. If Φ is the expected property for a model built using composition operators, then Φ must be, on the one hand, the postcondition on the model resulting from the application of each operator; and, on the other hand, the weakest precondition on each parameter of each operator. These preconditions are eventually consolidated with an additional glueing property Ψ depending on the value of all the parameters of the operator. Ψ is the residual property that must be checked at each composition.

Definition 1 (Correct composition operator). *For a set of models $m_1, \ldots, m_n$ and an n-ary composition operator f over models, we say f is correct (or property preserving) with respect to a property Φ and a glueing condition Ψ if:*

$$\bigwedge_{1 \leq i \leq n} \Phi(m_i) \wedge \Psi(m_1, \ldots, m_n) \Rightarrow \Phi(f(m_1, \ldots, m_n))$$

The verification that the composition operators are correct will be conducted using the CoQ proof assistant, the details are presented in the next Section.

3   Formalization Using Coq4MDE

The concepts of Model and Metamodel are formally defined in CoQ4MDE in the following way. Let us consider two sets of labels: Classes, respectively References, represents the set of all possible classes, respectively reference, labels. Then, let us consider instances of such classes, the set Objects of object labels. References includes a specific *inh* label used to specify the direct inheritance relation.

Definition 2 (Model).
Let $\mathscr{C} \subseteq$ Classes be a set of class labels. Let $\mathscr{R} \subseteq \{\langle c_1, r, c_2 \rangle \mid c_1, c_2 \in \mathscr{C}, r \in$ References$\}$[5] be a set of references between classes.

A Model over $\mathscr{C}$ and $\mathscr{R}$, written $\langle MV, ME \rangle \in Model(\mathscr{C}, \mathscr{R})$ is a multigraph built over a finite set MV of typed object vertices and a finite set ME[6] of reference edges. such that:

$$MV \subseteq \{\langle o, c \rangle \mid o \in \text{Objects}, c \in \mathscr{C}\}$$
$$ME \subseteq \left\{ \langle \langle o_1, c_1 \rangle, r, \langle o_2, c_2 \rangle \rangle \mid \langle o_1, c_1 \rangle, \langle o_2, c_2 \rangle \in MV, \langle c_1, r, c_2 \rangle \in \mathscr{R} \right\}$$

In case of inheritance, the same object label will be used several times in the same model graph. It will be associated to the different classes in the inheritance hierarchy going from a root down to the class used to create the object. This label reuse encodes subtyping. Direct inheritance is represented in the metamodel with a special reference called inh. The following property states that c_2 is a direct subclass of c_1.

$$subClass(c_1, c_2 \in \text{Classes}, \langle MV, ME \rangle) \triangleq \forall o \in \text{Objects},$$
$$\langle o, c_2 \rangle \in MV \Rightarrow \langle \langle o, c_2 \rangle, inh, \langle o, c_1 \rangle \rangle \in ME$$

Abstract Classes that are specified in a metamodel using the *isAbstract* attribute are not suitable for instantiation. They are often used to represent abstract concepts that gather common attributes and references.

$$isAbstract(c_1 \in \text{Classes}, \langle MV, ME \rangle) \triangleq \forall o \in \text{Objects},$$
$$\langle o, c_1 \rangle \in MV \Rightarrow \exists c_2 \in \text{Classes}, \langle \langle o, c_2 \rangle, inh, \langle o, c_1 \rangle \rangle \in ME$$

Definition 3 (Metamodel). *A MetaModel is a multigraph representing classes as vertices and references as edges as well as semantics properties over instantiation of classes and references. It is represented as a pair composed of a multigraph (MMV, MME) built over a finite set MMV of vertices and a finite set MME of edges, and as a predicate (conformsTo) over models representing the semantics properties.*

A MetaModel is a pair $\langle (MMV, MME), conformsTo \rangle$ such that:

$$MMV \subseteq Classes$$
$$MME \subseteq \{\langle c_1, r, c_2 \rangle \mid c_1, c_2 \in MMV, r \in References\}$$
$$conformsTo : Model(MMV, MME) \rightarrow Bool$$

A minimum and maximum number of values that can be associated to an attribute or reference can be defined using the *lower* and *upper* attributes. This pair is usually named *multiplicity*. In order to ease the manipulation of this datatype, we introduce the type $Natural^{\top} = \mathbb{N} \cup \{\top\}$. Using both attributes, it is used to represent a range of possible numbers of values. Unbounded ranges can be modelled using the $\top$ value for the *upper* attribute.

$$lower(\mathtt{c_1} \in \text{MMV}, \mathtt{r_1} \in \text{MME}, \mathtt{n} \in Natural^{\top}, \langle \text{MV}, \text{ME} \rangle) \triangleq$$
$$\forall o \in \text{Objects}, \langle \mathtt{o}, \mathtt{c_1} \rangle \in \text{MV} \Rightarrow |\{\mathtt{m_2} \in \text{MV} \mid \langle \langle \mathtt{o}, \mathtt{c_1} \rangle, \mathtt{r_1}, \mathtt{m_2} \rangle \in \text{ME}\}| \geq \mathtt{n}$$

---

[5] $\langle c_1, c_2, r \rangle$ in the CoQ code is denoted here for simplification as: $\langle c_1, r, c_2 \rangle$.

[6] $\langle \langle o_1, c_1 \rangle, r, \langle o_2, c_2 \rangle \rangle$ is denoted in the CoQ code as: $\langle \langle o_1, c_1 \rangle, \langle o_2, c_2 \rangle, r \rangle$.

An analogous formalization is defined for the **upper** property replacing $\geq$ by $\leq$.

A reference can be associated to an *opposite* reference. It means that, in a model conforming to its metamodel, for each link instance of this reference between two objects, there must exists a link in the opposite direction between these two objects.

$$isOpposite(\mathbf{r_1}, \mathbf{r_2} \in \mathsf{MME}, \langle \mathsf{MV}, \mathsf{ME} \rangle) \triangleq$$
$$\forall\ \mathbf{m_1}, \mathbf{m_2} \in \mathsf{MV}, \langle \mathbf{m_1}, \mathbf{r_1}, \mathbf{m_2} \rangle \in \mathsf{ME} \Leftrightarrow \langle \mathbf{m_2}, \mathbf{r_2}, \mathbf{m_1} \rangle \in \mathsf{ME}$$

A reference can be *composite*. In this case, instances of the target concept belong to a single instance of source concepts.

$$areComposite(\mathbf{c_1} \in \mathsf{MMV}, R \subseteq \mathsf{MME}, \langle \mathsf{MV}, \mathsf{ME} \rangle) \triangleq$$
$$\forall\ o \in \mathsf{Objects} \Rightarrow\ |\{\mathbf{m_1} \in \mathsf{MV} \mid \langle \mathbf{m_1}, \mathbf{r}, \langle o, \mathbf{c_1} \rangle \rangle \in \mathsf{ME}, \mathbf{r} \in R\}| \leq 1$$

Figure 4 shows a simple example of metamodel on the left and his CoQ4MDE representation on the right.

$$
\begin{aligned}
MMV &= \{Component, Port\}, \\
MME &= \{(Component, hasA, Port)\}, \\
conformsTo &= lower(Component, hasA, 2) \\
&\quad \wedge\ upper(Component, hasA, 2))
\end{aligned}
$$

Fig. 4. A metamodel in the CoQ4MDE notation

Given one **Model** M and one **MetaModel** MM, we can check conformance using the *conformsTo* predicate embedded in MM. This predicate identifies the set of models conforming to a metamodel.

Figure 5 shows an example of a model that conforms to the metamodel given in Figure 4. At the right of this figure is the CoQ4MDE representation associated to this model. All the structural (well typedness) and semantics properties of the metamodel in Figure 4 are respected in this model. Namely, C is an object of the class *Component*, *In* and *Out* are objects of the class *Port*, the component C is linked with the relation *hasA* to exactly 2 ports (the *lower* and *upper* attributes specified in the metamodel are respected).

$$
\begin{aligned}
MV &= \{(C, Component), (In, Port), (Out, Port)\}, \\
ME &= \{((C, Component), hasA, (In, Port)), \\
&\quad ((C, Component), hasA, (Out, Port))\}
\end{aligned}
$$

Fig. 5. A model in the CoQ4MDE notation

For the implementation, a model in CoQ4MDE is a multigraph defined as finite sets of vertices and edges satisfying some properties. Based on this model's definition, every new operator in the CoQ4MDE framework needs to be addressed at the three hierarchically related levels (the sets level, the graph level and the MDE level). The following **Union** and **Substitution** operators definitions follow this three levels schema.

3.1   The Union Primitive Operator

For the set level, we use the union encoded in the CoQ library `Uniset`[7] that we note $\cup$. The same notation or symbolic abbreviation $\cup$ is used in our CoQ code.

For the graph's level, the result is defined with a proof[8] by induction that the union of two graphs is also a graph. The vertices/edges set for the resulting graph is the union of vertices/edges sets of the two initial graphs.

The union of two models $\langle vs_1, es_1 \rangle$ and $\langle vs_2, es_2 \rangle$ is the union of their vertices and edges sets in addition to the proof that the two sets constitute a graph. For simplification, this can be denoted as follows: $\langle vs_1 \cup vs_2, es_1 \cup es_2 \rangle$.

3.2   The Substitution Primitive Operator

As explained in Definition 1, the models are graphs having as nodes typed objects. For example, (o, c) is a model's object whose type is c and whose name is o. The `Substitution` operator aims to replace the name of an object of a model by another name. This operator is also defined using the three hierarchical levels.

Substituting a model's object whose name is src by a model's object whose name is dst inside the sets of vertices and edges is implemented using a generic map operator encoded in CoQ using three basic functions: $mapv$, $mapa$ and $mape$ that are applied respectively on: the model's objects, the references and the edges. The function $mapv$ is defined as follows: $mapv\,(o, c) = \begin{cases} (dst, c) \; if \; o = src \\ (o, c) \; otherwise. \end{cases}$
The function $mape$ replaces the names of the model's objects in the edges such as: $mape\,(v_1, a, v_2) = (mapv\,v_1, mapa\,a, mapv\,v_2)$.

The graph's image[9] is then constructed from the initial graph using the images of the vertices and the edges by $mapv$, $mapa$ and $mape$.

The sets and the graph obtained from the previous levels and the associated proofs constitute the substituted model.

3.3   Proofs of Primitive Operators

We consider the well typedness $(instanceOf)$ and the semantics properties discussed in Section 2.4. For every property (Φ), we prove the preservation by the primitive operators. Some properties are fully compositional: no residual verification activity (Ψ) needs to be conducted at the composition time. Others will require additional verification activities (Ψ) that can be modeled as preconditions.

For space reason, we only give the example of the hierarchy property $(\Phi$: subClass$)$ for the `Union` operator. Theorem 1 states[10] that the hierarchy property is preserved by `Union`. So, for any classes c_1 and c_2, if c_1 is a $subClass$ of c_2 in the models M_1 and M_2, then c_1 is also a $subClass$ of c_2 in the model resulting from the `Union` of M_1 and M_2.

---

[7] http://coq.inria.fr/stdlib/Coq.Sets.Uniset.html

[8] http://coq4mde.enseeiht.fr/FormalMDE/Graph.html#MG.EG

[9] http://coq4mde.enseeiht.fr/FormalMDE/Subst_Verif.html#elements

[10] http://coq4mde.enseeiht.fr/FormalMDE/Union.html#SCUP

Theorem 1. (subClassUnionPreserved) $\forall$ M_1 M_2 $\in$ *Model*, c_1 c_2 $\in$ *Classes*, $subClass(c_1\ c_2\ \mathrm{M}_1)$ $\wedge$ $subClass(c_1\ c_2\ \mathrm{M}_2)$ $\Rightarrow$ $subClass(c_1\ c_2\ (Union\ \mathrm{M}_1\ \mathrm{M}_2))$.

Table 1 summarizes the pre and postconditions for the verification of the meta-model conformance for the Union and Substitution operators. The proofs for the Union, respectively Substitution, operator are accessible at: http://coq4mde.enseeiht.fr/FormalMDE/Union_Verif.html, respectively http://coq4mde.enseeiht.fr/FormalMDE/Subst_Verif.html.

Table 1. pre and postconditions for the Union and Substitution operators

Φ	M_r=Substitution $((o_1, c_1), (o_2, c_2), M)$	M_r=Union (M_1, M_2)
instanceOf	$\Psi(M)$=True	$\Psi(M_{i\in\{1,2\}})$=True
subClass	$\Psi(M)$=True	$\Psi(M_{i\in\{1,2\}})$=True
	$\Phi(M_r) = subClass(c_1, c_2, M)$	$\Phi(M_r) = subClass(c_1, c_2, M_r)$
isAbstract	$\Psi(M)$=True	$\Psi(M_{i\in\{1,2\}})$=True
lower	$\Psi(M) = (c_1 = c_2) \wedge ((o_2, c) \notin MV)$	$\Psi(M)$=$lowerCond(c, r, nM_1, M_2)$
upper	$\Psi(M) = (c_1 = c_2) \wedge ((o_2, c) \notin MV)$	$upperCond(c, r, n, M_1, M_2)$
isOpposite	$\Psi(M)$=True	$\Psi(M_{i\in\{1,2\}})$=True
areComposite	$\Psi(M) = (c_1 = c_2) \wedge ((o_2, c) \notin MV)$	$\Psi(M) = 1 >$
		$\|\{o_2 \in MV_1\ \|\ \langle\langle o, c\rangle, r, o_2\rangle \in ME_1\}\|$
		$+\|\{o_2 \in MV_2\ \|\ \langle\langle o, c\rangle, r, o_2\rangle \in ME_2\}\|$
		$-\|\{o_2 \in (MV_1 \cap MV_2)\ \|$
		$\langle\langle o, c\rangle, r, o_2\rangle \in (ME_1 \cap ME_2)\}\|$

The basic CoQ4MDE framework is about 1107 lines, the actual version containing the primitive composition operators and also the proved implementation of the Package Merge described in the next section is about 18000 lines with about 300 Lemmas and Theorems and 200 Definitions. The proofs for the elementary operators are about 3300 lines. The implementation and proofs of the Package Merge using the elementary operators is about 7200, this implementation take advantage from reusing the proofs previously done for the primitive operators. The alternative is the implementation without elementary operators and that would require multiple repetitions of the elementary proofs and would be about 20400 lines. So, our approach enables a reduction with more then 180% in this case.

4   Validation

The primitive operators have been used for the implementation of higher level composition operators including MOF Package Merge, ISC (considering the adaptation and glueing of components) and aspect weaving. These operators share parts of their implementation and conformance preservation proof that can be captured by the use of the primitive operators. For their implementations, other model operations are required (e.g. extraction of matching between models, verification of some conditions, ...) but the only modifications of the models are primitive substitutions and unions. The verifications of the fully compositional properties reuse directly the proofs of the primitive operators without any additional parts. The verification of the properties requiring additional preconditions needs to ensure that the preconditions are satisfied.

We show mainly in this section that our minimal set of primitive operators is sufficient to formalize a high level operator like the MOF Package Merge. A mature formalization for the ISC operators based on the elementary ones is also available, for the details see [24].

The Package Merge implementation as summarized hereafter is accessible at: http://coq4mde.enseeiht.fr/PackageMergeCoq/.

To illustrate our methodology, we give an example derived from [48].

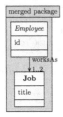

Fig. 6. BasicEmployee

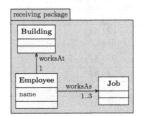

Fig. 7. EmployeeLocation

The source package (in this case the package BasicEmployee mentioned in Figure 6) is the package receiving. The package EmployeeLocation shown in Figure 7 is the package merged. This package contains the additional elements that must be merged with the package receiving. Two conflicts occur between the models merged and receiving. The first one is related to the attribute *upper* of *worksAs* (the maximal bound is equal to 2 in the model BasicEmployee (Figure 6) and is equal to 3 in the model EmployeeLocation (Figure 7)). The second conflict is related to the class *Employee* that is abstract (name in italic) in the merged package and concrete in the receiving package.

The resolution of this kind of conflicts is done according the the UML specification [33]. The rule to resolve the conflict for the **upper** attribute is: $upper_{Resulting} = max(upper_{Merged}, upper_{Receiving})$. The rule for the **isAbstract** attribute is: $isAbstract_{Resulting} = isAbstract_{Merged} \land isAbstract_{Receiving}$. The list of all the possible transformations is available on page 166 of the specification [33].

Concretely in our abstract syntax, we manipulate the metamodels as models conforming to MOF, so the abstraction property for classes is represented with attributes *isAbstract* suffixed with the name of the class (this attribute is equal to True in the model BasicEmployee (Figure 6) and equal to False in the model EmployeeLocation (Figure 7)). The same principle is used to represent all the properties linked to MOF such as **lower** and **upper**. We show in Figure 8 the representation of the package BasicEmployee as a model conforming to MOF. The EmployeeLocation package is represented using the same principle, we don't show it here for space reason. The first step is to resolve all the conflicts. For this, the **Substitution** operator is applied twice. The first application replaces 2 by 3 for the $upper_{Job}$ attribute in the merged model. The second application of

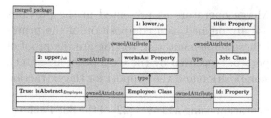
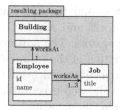

Fig. 8. An excerpt from the `BasicEmployee` model   **Fig. 9.** The resulting metamodel

the `Substitution` operator replaces $True$ by $False$ for the $isAbstract_{Employee}$ attribute in the `merged` model.

Once the conflicts are resolved, the final step is the `Union` of the obtained models `merged` and `receiving` (the constraints of the `Union` operator are satisfied in this case). The result is exactly the merge of the two packages `merged` and `receiving` shown in Figure 9.

In the previous example, the `Package Merge` is expressed using the primitive composition operators `Union` and `Substitution`. Defining the `Package Merge` in this manner ensures that the resulting model is well typed in relation with the packages `merged` and `receiving` and also that it satisfies the semantics properties of the metamodel when the preconditions are satisfied.

We have also experimented the use of our primitive operators to define: the aspect weaving [29], the merge of statecharts specifications [30], the weave of State and Sequence Diagrams, the attributes composition [43] and also to reimplement the operators of the Invasive Software Composition (`ISC`) [1].

5   Related Work

This work targets a formal certified model composition framework. Our notion of model follows the MDE vision and we are interested in the problems of composition and compositional verification. This work is related to several issues highlighted in this Section. First, we take a look at some composition approaches and we rely on a MOF Package Merge formalization to explain our contribution. Then, we discuss some formalizations of the MDE to position our proposal. Finally, we present some work on compositional verification to situate our work.

5.1   Composition Approaches

We previously proposed in [25] [19] the formalization and verification of some REUSEWARE [20] operators. Several composition methods have focused on the implementation of the merge operators using mappings between models like Rational Software Architect[11], Bernstein et al. data model [6], Atlas Model Weaver[12] [16], Epsilon[13], Theme/UML [13] and EMF Facet[14]. The REUSEWARE

---

[11] http://www-306.ibm.com/software/awdtools/architect/swarchitect/
[12] http://www.eclipse.org/gmt/amw/
[13] http://www.eclipse.org/gmt/epsilon/
[14] www.eclipse.org/proposals/emf-facet/

operators and the MOF Package Merge operators as presented in the previous frameworks and also in [11] and [4] are defined as a composition of the primitive operators. The advantages of these implementation relying are the proof of termination of the composition operators (ensured by the COQ proof-assistant), the properties verification for the composition and the support for the extraction of the validated executable code.

Zito in [48] presented an implementation using Alloy[15] [22] of the MOF Package Merge. As Alloy has a poor performance when analysing models with many signatures (e.g. 20 signatures or higher), the analysis is currently limited to an interval between 5 and 10. The UML metamodel contains more than 30 classes which are all modelled with a signature. The authors applies several strategies to reduce the size of the Alloy model: reduce the depth of inheritance, merge similar classes, do not model classes that do not contain any information and do not change by applying the fusion (e.g. PackageImport, PackageMerge, ElementImport, Comment and Constraint), merge multiple inheritance, eliminate recursion, and finally do not model derived attributes and associations.

Elaborating a proved development allows specifying generically the properties and verifying these properties a priori for all the instances. This universal quantification used in the proofs enables to avoid all the constraints and the limitation in relation with the models' size.

5.2   Formalization of MDE

A lot of work was conducted aiming to formalize the concepts of MDE.

First, MoMENT (MOdel manageMENT) [8] is an algebraic model management framework that provides a set of generic operators to manipulate models. The metamodels are represented as algebraic specifications and the operators are defined independently of the metamodel using the MAUDE language [14].

Also, A. Vallecillo et al. have designed and implemented a different embedding of metamodels, models ([38]) and model transformations ([45]) using MAUDE. This embedding is shallow, it relies strongly on the object structure proposed by MAUDE in order to define model elements as objects, and relies on the object rewriting semantics in order to implement model transformations.

Furthermore, I. Poernomo has proposed an encoding of metamodels and models using type theory ([35]) in order to allow correct by construction development of model transformation using proof-assistants like COQ ([36]). Some simple experiments have been conducted using COQ mainly on tree-shaped models ([37]) using inductive types. General graph model structure can be encoded using co-inductive types. However, as shown in [34] by C. Picard and R. Matthes, the encoding is quite complex as COQ enforces structural constraints when combining inductive and co-inductive types that forbid the use of the most natural encodings proposed by Poernomo et al. M. Giorgino et al. rely in [18] on a spanning tree of the graph combined with additional links to overcome that constraint using the ISABELLE proof-assistant. This allows to develop a model transformation

---

[15] http://alloy.mit.edu/alloy/

relying on slightly adapted inductive proofs and then extract classical imperative implementations. Also, another implementation of the MDE is the HOL-OCL system [9] [10] that constitutes an environment for interactive modelling with UML and OCL and can be used for example to proof class invariants.

These embeddings are all shallow: they rely on sophisticated similar data structure to represent model elements and metamodels (e.g. COQ (co-)inductive data types for model elements and object and (co-)inductive types for metamodel elements). The work described in this paper is a deep embedding, each concept from models and metamodels was encoded in [44] using primitive constructs instead of relying on similar elements in MAUDE, COQ or ISABELLE. The purpose of this contribution is not only to implement model transformation using correct-by-construction tools but also to give a kind of denotational semantics for the MDE concepts that should provide a deeper understanding and allow the formal validation of the various implemented technologies. Another formalisation in COQ of the MDE concepts by F.Barbier et al is accessible[16] [2], this representation is attached to the proof of the properties shown in [26] (instantiation relations and model transformations). Other work aiming to define a semantics for a modelling language by explicitly and denotationally defining the kind of systems the language describes and to focus on the variations and variability in the semantics [12] [28]. Compared to the last work, we are interested in a generic, complete and unique formalisation of the conformity to metamodels and we are focused mainly in the proof of the preservation of this conformity relation by the composition operators.

5.3 Compositional Verification

The compositional verification, in other words to break up the verification of a system into the verification of its components, is a very old dream. Several work were conduced in this direction using the model checking technique.

For instance, Nguyen, T.H. proposed in [5] a compositional verification approach to check safety properties of component-based systems described in the BIP (Behavior - Interaction - Priority) language [3].

Also, another approach allowing to verify systems by composition from verified components was proposed in [47] where the temporal properties of a software component are specified, verified, and packaged with the component.

In this paper, regarding the previous cited methods, we adopted a generic composition technology that takes into account the EMOF metamodel properties making it usable with any language that can be described with a metamodel.

6 Conclusions

We have tackled in this paper the problem of model composition formalization and verification. In this purpose, starting from our formal framework for model

---

[16] http://web.univ-pau.fr/~barbier/Coq/

and metamodel formal specification CoQ4MDE, we propose to rely on primitive composition operators that can then be used to build more sophisticated operators. We prove the correctness of the expected properties for these primitive ones introducing mandatory preconditions to reach compositional verification for the targeted properties. The proofs of property preservation for the high level operators combine the proofs of the primitive ones. Our proposal is validated in this contribution with the MOF model conformance property and the MOF package merge operator. All these notions are also currently reflected in the CoQ proof-assistant, following the line of thought of our previous work around model and metamodel formalization. This embedding provides correct-by-construction pieces of executable code for the different model operations related to composition. As we target a general purpose MDE-oriented framework, our work applies to any model, modelling language, application and is not restricted to some more-or-less implicit language context.

This proposal is a preliminary mandatory step in the formalization of compositional formal verification technologies. We have tackled the formal composition of models independently of the properties satisfied by the model and the expected properties for the composite model. The next step in our work is to improve the notion of model compositional verification relying on several use cases from simple static constraints such as verification of OCL constraints satisfaction, to more dynamic properties such as deadlock freedom as proposed in the BIP framework [3].

In this last purpose, we need to model the behavioural part of each language. We propose to rely on the generic behaviours applicable to several meta-models sharing some features presented in [27]. This can be applied to families of unrelated meta-models. We plan to experiment the behavioural aspect by considering the merging of Statecharts Specifications [30]. In the long run, we plan to integrate the work of Garnacho et al. [17] that provide an embedding in CoQ of timed transition systems in order to model the behavioral aspect of languages.

References

1. Aßmann, U.: Invasive software composition. Springer-Verlag New York Inc. (2003)
2. Barbier, F., Castéran, P., Cariou, E., Le Goaer, O., et al.: Adaptive software based on correct-by-construction metamodels. In: Progressions and Innovations in Model-Driven Software Engineering, pp. 308–325 (2013)
3. Basu, A., Bozga, M., Sifakis, J.: Modeling heterogeneous real-time components in BIP. In: Fourth IEEE International Conference on Software Engineering and Formal Methods, SEFM 2006, pp. 3–12. IEEE (2006)
4. Baya, A., Asri, B.E.: Composing specific domains for large scale systems. Journal of Communication and Computer 10, 844–856 (2013)
5. Bensalem, S., Bozga, M., Nguyen, T., Sifakis, J.: Compositional verification for component-based systems and application. Software, IET 4(3), 181–193 (2010)
6. Bernstein, P., Halevy, A., Pottinger, R.: A vision for management of complex models. ACM Sigmod Record 29(4), 55–63 (2000)
7. Bézivin, J.: In search of a basic principle for model driven engineering. Novatica Journal, Special Issue 5(2), 21–24 (2004)

8. Boronat, A., Meseguer, J.: An algebraic semantics for MOF. Formal Aspects of Computing 22(3-4), 269–296 (2010)

9. Brucker, A.D., Wolff, B.: A proposal for a formal OCL semantics in isabelle/HOL. In: Carreño, V.A., Muñoz, C.A., Tahar, S. (eds.) TPHOLs 2002. LNCS, vol. 2410, pp. 99–114. Springer, Heidelberg (2002)

10. Brucker, A.D., Wolff, B.: HOL-OCL: A formal proof environment for UML/OCL. In: Fiadeiro, J.L., Inverardi, P. (eds.) FASE 2008. LNCS, vol. 4961, pp. 97–100. Springer, Heidelberg (2008)

11. Brunet, G., Chechik, M., Easterbrook, S., Nejati, S., Niu, N., Sabetzadeh, M.: A manifesto for model merging. In: Proceedings of the 2006 International Workshop on Global Integrated Model Management, pp. 5–12. ACM (2006)

12. Cengarle, M.V., Grönniger, H., Rumpe, B., Schindler, M.: System model semantics of class diagrams. Technische Universitat Braunschweig (2008)

13. Clarke, S.: Extending standard UML with model composition semantics. Science of Computer Programming 44(1), 71–100 (2002)

14. Clavel, M., Durán, F., Eker, S., Lincoln, P., Martí-Oliet, N., Meseguer, J., Quesada, J.: Maude: specification and programming in rewriting logic. Theoretical Computer Science 285(2), 187–243 (2002)

15. Coquand, T., Huet, G., et al.: The calculus of constructions (1986)

16. Del Fabro, M.D., Valduriez, P.: Towards the efficient development of model transformations using model weaving and matching transformations. Software and System Modeling 8(3), 305–324 (2009)

17. Garnacho, M., Bodeveix, J.-P., Filali-Amine, M.: A mechanized semantic framework for real-time systems. In: Braberman, V., Fribourg, L. (eds.) FORMATS 2013. LNCS, vol. 8053, pp. 106–120. Springer, Heidelberg (2013)

18. Giorgino, M., Strecker, M., Matthes, R., Pantel, M.: Verification of the schorr-waite algorithm – from trees to graphs. In: Alpuente, M. (ed.) LOPSTR 2010. LNCS, vol. 6564, pp. 67–83. Springer, Heidelberg (2011)

19. Hamiaz, M.K., Pantel, M., Combemale, B., Thirioux, X.: Correct-by-construction model composition: Application to the invasive software composition method. In: FESCA, pp. 108–122 (2014)

20. Henriksson, J., Heidenreich, F., Johannes, J., Zschaler, S., Aßmann, U.: Extending grammars and metamodels for reuse: the Reuseware approach. Software, IET 2(3), 165–184 (2008)

21. Holt, J., Perry, S.: SysML for systems engineering, vol. 7. IET (2008)

22. Jackson, D.: Software abstractions-logic, language, and analysis, revised edition (2012)

23. Jouault, F., Bézivin, J.: Km3: A dsl for metamodel specification. In: Gorrieri, R., Wehrheim, H. (eds.) FMOODS 2006. LNCS, vol. 4037, pp. 171–185. Springer, Heidelberg (2006)

24. Kezadri, M.: Assistance à la validation et vérification de systèmes critiques: ontologies et intégration de composants. PhD thesis (2013)

25. Kezadri, M., Combemale, B., Pantel, M., Thirioux, X.: A proof assistant based formalization of MDE components. In: Arbab, F., Ölveczky, P.C. (eds.) FACS 2011. LNCS, vol. 7253, pp. 223–240. Springer, Heidelberg (2012)

26. Kühne, T.: Matters of (meta-) modeling. Software & Systems Modeling 5(4), 369–385 (2006)

27. Lara, J., Guerra, E.: From types to type requirements: genericity for model-driven engineering. Software and Systems Modeling 12(3), 453–474 (2013)

28. Maoz, S., Ringert, J.O., Rumpe, B.: Semantically configurable consistency analysis for class and object diagrams. In: Whittle, J., Clark, T., Kühne, T. (eds.) MODELS 2011. LNCS, vol. 6981, pp. 153–167. Springer, Heidelberg (2011)

29. Morin, B., Klein, J., Barais, O., Jézéquel, J.-M.: A generic weaver for supporting product lines. In: Proceedings of the 13th International Workshop on Early Aspects, pp. 11–18. ACM (2008)
30. Nejati, S., Sabetzadeh, M., Chechik, M., Easterbrook, S., Zave, P.: Matching and merging of statecharts specifications. In: Proceedings of the 29th international conference on Software Engineering, pp. 54–64. IEEE Computer Society (2007)
31. Object Management Group, Inc. Meta Object Facility (MOF) 2.0 Core Specification (January 2006); Final Adopted Specification.
32. Object Management Group, Inc. Meta Object Facility (MOF) 2.4.2 Core Specification (January 2014)
33. O. OMG. Unified modeling language (omg uml)-infrastructure(v2.4.1) (2011), http://www.omg.org/spec/UML/2.4.1
34. Picard, C., Matthes, R.: Coinductive graph representation: the problem of embedded lists. In: Electronic Communications of the EASST, Special issue Graph Computation Models, GCM 2010 (2011)
35. Poernomo, I.: The meta-object facility typed. In: Haddad, H. (ed.) SAC, pp. 1845–1849. ACM (2006)
36. Poernomo, I.: Proofs-as-model-transformations. In: Vallecillo, A., Gray, J., Pierantonio, A. (eds.) ICMT 2008. LNCS, vol. 5063, pp. 214–228. Springer, Heidelberg (2008)
37. Poernomo, I., Terrell, J.: Correct-by-construction model transformations from partially ordered specifications in coq. In: Dong, J.S., Zhu, H. (eds.) ICFEM 2010. LNCS, vol. 6447, pp. 56–73. Springer, Heidelberg (2010)
38. Romero, J.R., Rivera, J.E., Durán, F., Vallecillo, A.: Formal and tool support for Model Driven Engineering with Maude. Journal of Object Technology 6(9), 187–207 (2007)
39. RTCA / EUROCAE. "Formal Methods Supplement to DO-178C [ED-12C]", DO-333/ED-218 (2011)
40. RTCA / EUROCAE. "Model-Based Development and Verification Supplement to DO-178C [ED-12C]", DO-331/ED-216 (2011)
41. RTCA / EUROCAE. "Software Considerations in Airborne Systems and Equipment Certification", DO-178C/ED-12C (2011)
42. RTCA / EUROCAE. "DO-330/ED-215: Software Tool Qualification Considerations" - clarifying software tools and avionics tool qualification (2012)
43. Sentilles, S., Štěpán, P., Carlson, J., Crnković, I.: Integration of extra-functional properties in component models. In: Lewis, G.A., Poernomo, I., Hofmeister, C. (eds.) CBSE 2009. LNCS, vol. 5582, pp. 173–190. Springer, Heidelberg (2009)
44. Thirioux, X., Combemale, B., Crégut, X., Garoche, P.-L.: A Framework to Formalise the MDE Foundations. In: Paige, R., Bézivin, J. (eds.) International Workshop on Towers of Models (TOWERS), Zurich, pp. 14–30 (June 2007)
45. Troya, J., Vallecillo, A.: Towards a rewriting logic semantics for ATL. In: Tratt, L., Gogolla, M. (eds.) ICMT 2010. LNCS, vol. 6142, pp. 230–244. Springer, Heidelberg (2010)
46. Warmer, J.B., Kleppe, A.G.: The object constraint language: getting your models ready for MDA. Addison-Wesley Professional (2003)
47. Xie, F., Browne, J.: Verified systems by composition from verified components. ACM SIGSOFT Software Engineering Notes 28(5), 277–286 (2003)
48. Zito, A.: UML's Package Extension Mechanism: Taking a Closer Look at Package Merge. Queen's University (2006)

A Formula-Based Approach for Automatic Fault Localization of Imperative Programs

Si-Mohamed Lamraoui[1,2] and Shin Nakajima[1,2]

[1] The Graduate University for Advanced Studies (SOKENDAI), Japan
[2] National Institute of Informatics, Tokyo, Japan

Abstract. Among various automatic fault localization methods, two of them are specifically noticed, coverage-based and formula-based. While the coverage-based method relies on statistical measures, the formula-based approach is an algorithmic method being able to provide fine-grained information account for identified root causes. The method combines the SAT-based formal verification techniques with the Reiter's model-based diagnosis theory. This paper adapts the formula-based fault localization method, and improves the efficiency of computing the potential root causes by using the push & pop mechanism of the Yices solver. The technique is particularly useful for programs with multiple faults. We implemented the method in a tool, SNIPER, which was applied to the TCAS benchmark. All single and multiple faults were successfully identified and discriminated by using the original test cases of the TCAS.

Keywords: Model-based Diagnosis Theory, Multiple faults, Partial Maximum Satisfiability, LLVM, Yices.

1 Introduction

Debugging is one of the most expensive tasks of software development. A challenging activity in debugging is fault localization, which consists of identifying root cause locations of a program that shows faulty behavior. Automatic fault localization was introduced to help software engineers tackle this task. Automatic fault localization of imperative programs is a well-known problem, and has been studied from various approaches (cf. [6][7][18][21]). Among these, coverage-based or spectrum-based debugging [8] is considered a promising method. It is an empirical method that calculates ranking orders between the program statements or spectrums to show that a particular fragment of code is more suspicious than the others. The method, however, needs a lot of both successful and failing executions to calculate the statistical measures. Generating an unbiased input test data set is a major challenge. In addition, the causal explanation of results is not clear in regard to program semantics.

The formula-based fault localization method uses only failing executions, and is more systematic than the coverage-based approach. This is because it has a logical foundation developed in the model-based diagnosis (MBD) theory [16].

S. Merz and J. Pang (Eds.): ICFEM 2014, LNCS 8829, pp. 251–266, 2014.

However, existing tools following the formula-based method, such as BugAssist [9] or Wotawa's tool [20], do not guarantee to cover all the root causes. It is partly because the complete enumeration of root causes requires a high computational effort. Its complexity grows exponentially with the size of the program, the number of test cases used and the number of faults in the program.

Furthermore, most of the methods mainly consider single-fault programs. However, in practice it is common to have more than one fault in a program. Automatic fault localization of multi-fault programs is not an easy task. DiGiuseppe et al [4] empirically studied the coverage-based fault localization on multi-fault programs and concluded that at least one of the faults could be effectively localized. However, the method is not efficient for localizing simultaneously all the faults. Contrarily, the MBD theory considers the case of artifacts with multiple faults, but it needs more work for imperative programs.

This paper reports a new formula-based automatic fault localization approach, which follows the MaxSAT approach as in [9][17]. Our method, as in [2], uses a full flow-sensitive trace formula in order to consider control-oriented faults. It is equivalent to the SSA form of the LLVM [11] program intermediate representation. We adapt a new enumeration algorithm [14] to ensure obtaining all the root causes efficiently by using the Yices SMT solver [5] in an incremental fashion with its push & pop mechanism. Furthermore, our approach uses a fault localization algorithm that can work on a set of failing test cases in order to deal with multi-fault programs. It is not enough to use a single failing program path to identify such multiple faults.

This paper makes two contributions. First, we reformulate systematically the problem of automatic fault localization for imperative programs from a view point of formula-based approach. Second, we present an efficient method to calculate and combine diagnosis obtained from different failing test cases. This method is mandatory for the fault localization of multi-fault programs.

We implemented our method in a tool, called SNIPER (SNIPER is Not an Imperative Program Errors Repairer). SNIPER was applied to the TCAS benchmark. In addition to identifying all single and multiple faults with the given test cases, the Code Size Reduction (CSR) obtained is almost the same as BugAssist [9] and Wotawa's tool [20]. Furthermore, the efficiency could be improved by using an incremental solving method.

This paper is organized as follows. Section 2 presents the background of the work. Section 3 provides basic definitions. Section 4 presents our approach for localizing faults automatically. Section 5 reports experiments made on the TCAS benchmark. Section 6 compares our approach with related work, which is followed by Section 7 for the conclusions.

2   Background

This section introduces technical backgrounds of the formula-based automatic fault localization method. It essentially combines the SAT-based formal verification techniques [15] with the model-based diagnosis (MBD) theory.

The MBD theory establishes a logical formalism of the fault localization problem [16]. The *model* is presented as a formula expressed in *suitable* logic. The formula is unsatisfiable as it represents an artifact containing faults. The MBD theory distinguishes conflicts and diagnoses. Conflicts are the erroneous situations represented by minimal unsatisfiable subsets (MUSes) of the unsatisfiable formula. Diagnoses are the fault locations to be identified and are minimal correction subsets (MCSes). The MBD theory states that MUSes and MCSes are connected by the hitting set relationship. Therefore, the problem is to enumerate either all MUSes or all MCSes. Such sets can be calculated automatically if the formula is represented in decidable fragments of first-order theory.

The MBD methods, including the model-based debugging [20], first calculate MUSes and then obtain MCSes. An early work used graph-based algorithms to compute a static slice of programs in order to obtain MUSes [19]. Later, MUSes were obtained by calculating irreducible infeasible subsets of constraints [20]. Both methods resulted in rather large MUSes for the TCAS benchmark.

An alternative approach to obtain MCSes was employed in the fault localization of VLSI circuits [17]. The method reduces the fault localization problem to maximum satisfiability of the unsatisfiable formula in propositional logic and calculates maximal satisfiable subsets (MSSes). MCS is the complement of MSS [12]. This idea was applied to the fault localization problem of imperative programs [9]. The algorithm of BugAssist, however, does not guarantee the enumeration of all the MSSes. It may miss some faults, especially in programs with multiple-faults.

Dealing with programs with multiple faults is one of the important issues in automated fault localization methods. The MBD theory [16] generally considers the multiple fault cases. For simplicity, consider a case where MUSes are extracted from an unsatisfiable formula and each MUS in MUSes refers to a particular error, a single fault. Then, MUSes may contain, in principle, multiple faults because many MUS are included. MCSes, calculated using the minimal hitting set of MUSes, contain MCS elements with multiple faults.

Further consideration is required for the case of programs with multiple faults. In the formula-based approach, the unsatisfiable formula is φ^{AL}, which encodes failing program paths under a given input data EI; we write $\varphi^{AL}(EI)$ to show that the formula is dependent on EI. Usually, one test case may identify an erroneous situation caused by a single fault. Lots of test cases are needed to show the existence of many faults. It implies that we check the unsatisfiability of $\varphi^{AL}(EI)$ with many different EI. A single counterexample approach does not work well for a general case of programs with multiple faults.

Example. We illustrate the problem of multi-fault program with an example shown in Listing 1.1. This program contains two faults. In line 4 the variable y should be set to 42 and in line 6 it should be set to 0. We can find two failing paths, one that goes through the line 4 with the value 1 as argument, and the other that goes through the line 6 with the value 0 as argument. We face two problems with this kind of program. First, we need to take into account both failing paths to localize all the faults. Considering only one path is not sufficient. Second, the quantity of faults in the program creates noise that may affect the precise localization of faults. An accurate localization implies an high complexity of analysis.

```
1 void foo(int x) {
2     int y;
3     if (x>0) {
4         y = 1;
5     } else {
6         y = 42;
7     }
8     assert((x<=0 && y==0) || (x>0 && y==42));
9 }
```

Listing 1.1. A multi-fault program

3   Preliminaries

This section provides basic definitions on formula-based automatic localization method. Definitions of the basic concepts such as MUS, MCS, MSS, and hitting set, are found in the literature (cf. [12]).

Failing Program Paths. Let φ^{AL} be a formula $EI \wedge TF \wedge AS$ in conjunctive normal form (CNF) where EI is a formula that encodes the error-inducing inputs, TF is a trace formula that encodes all the possible program paths, and AS is a formula that encodes the assertion the program must satisfy. AS can be the post-condition or the test oracle. EI represents the input arguments, which take some particular values that make TF violate AS. The detailed representation of TF is irrelevant here, and will be introduced in Section 4.2.

Fault Localization Problem. Since φ^{AL} encodes failing program paths with EI, the formula is unsatisfiable; $\not\models \varphi^{AL}$. By definition, EI and AS are supposed to be satisfied. The trace formula TF is responsible for the unsatisfiability. It is exactly the situation that the program contains faults. The fault localization problem is to find a set of clauses in TF that are responsible for the unsatisfiability. Such clauses are found in minimal unsatisfiable subsets (MUS) of φ^{AL}. Note that it requires some post-processing to extract the root causes in the MUS since MUS shows an erroneous situation, namely, the conflicts.

In the following definitions C is a set of clauses, which constitutes a CNF formula.

Definition 1 (Minimal Unsatisfiable Subset). *$M \subseteq C$ is a Minimal Unsatisfiable Subset (MUS) iff M is unsatisfiable and $\forall c \in M : M \setminus \{c\}$ is satisfiable.*

Definition 2 (Minimal Correction Subset). $M \subseteq C$ *is a Minimal Correction Subset (MCS) iff* $C \backslash M$ *is satisfiable and* $\forall c \in M : (C \backslash M) \cup \{c\}$ *is unsatisfiable.*

MCS is a set of clauses such that C can be corrected by removing MCS from C. Therefore, MCS is considered to contain the root causes.

Definition 3 (Hitting Set). H *is a hitting set of* Ω *iff* $H \subseteq D$ *and* $\forall S \in \Omega :$ $H \cap S \neq \emptyset$

Let Ω be a collection of sets from some finite domain D, a hitting set of Ω is a set of elements from D that covers (*hits*) every set in Ω by having at least one element in common with it. A minimal hitting set is a hitting set from which no element can be removed without losing the hitting set property.

Definition 4 (Maximal Satisfiable Subset). $M \subseteq C$ *is a Maximal Satisfiable Subset (MSS) iff* M *is satisfiable and* $\forall c \in C \backslash M : M \cup \{c\}$ *is unsatisfiable.*

By definition, MCS is the complement of MSS (MSS^C) [12].

Fault Localization Problem Revisited. The fault localization problem is to find MCSes of φ^{AL}. Two approaches are possible. A classical model-based debugging method first calculates MUSes of φ^{AL} and then obtains MCSes using the hitting set of MUSes. The formula-based method adapted in this paper first calculates MSS of φ^{AL} and then obtain MCSes by taking the complement of MSS. In both approaches, enumerating all the MUSes or MCSes is mandatory to cover all the root causes.

Example. Using the example in Listing 1.2, we explain the above concepts. In line 6, there is an error in the computation of the absolute value. The absolute value of x is equal to x*1 (with x negative), which violates the assertion at line 8 which expects abs to be greater or equal to zero.

```
 1 int absValue(int x) {
 2      int abs;
 3      if(x>=0) {
 4          abs = x;
 5      } else {
 6          abs = x * 1;     // should be: abs=x*-1;
 7      }
 8      assert(abs>=0);
 9      return abs;
10 }
```

Listing 1.2. A function that computes an absolute value

A failing trace can be obtained with an input value equal to -1. The error-inducing input extracted from the failing trace is encoded in EI and takes the following form: $EI = (x_0 = -1)$. The Static Single Assignment (SSA) form of the function body (lines 2 to 7) is encoded in TF, as shown below. For recall, SSA form is a property of an intermediate representation (IR), which requires that each variable is assigned exactly once, and every variable is defined before it is used.

$$TF = (guard_0 = (x_0 \geq 0)) \land (abs_1 = x_0) \land (abs_2 = x_0 \times 1) \land$$
$$((guard_0 \land (abs_3 = abs_1)) \lor (\neg guard_0 \land (abs_3 = abs_2)))$$

The assertion in line 8 is encoded in AS as follows: $AS = (abs_3 \geq 0)$.

We obtain two MSS and two MCS below. The set elements represent the line numbers of the program in Listing 1.2. The minimal hitting set of the union of the MCSes give us the two MUSes, which are the conflicts:

$$MSS_0 = \{6\} \qquad MCS_0 = MSS_0^{\mathsf{C}} = \{3,4\}$$
$$MSS_1 = \{3,4\} \qquad MCS_1 = MSS_1^{\mathsf{C}} = \{6\}$$
$$MCSes = \{MCS_0\} \cup \{MCS_1\} = \{\{3,4\},\{6\}\}$$
$$MUSes = MCSes^{\mathsf{MHS}} = \{\{4,6\},\{3,6\}\}$$

We here obtained two conflicts; one with the line numbers 4 and 6, another with 3 and 6. If we only need a set of potential root causes, we may extract the line numbers from either MCSes or MUSes to have a set, for example, $\{3,4,6\}$. The results are the same regardless of using MCSes or MUSes since only the line numbers are significant. It is what BugAssist [9] does to calculate the CSR. Note that with such a combination method, relations between root cause candidates are lost.

Partial Maximum Satisfiability. The maximum satisfiability (MaxSAT) problem for a CNF formula is to find an assignment that maximizes the number of satisfied clauses (MSS). In the partial MaxSAT (pMaxSAT) problem for a CNF formula, some clauses are declared to be *soft*, or relaxable, and the rest are declared to be *hard*, or non-relaxable. The problem is to find an assignment that satisfies all the hard clauses and the maximum number of soft clauses.

4   Our Approach

4.1   Program Pre-processing

Before the program is encoded into a Trace Formula, it must be pre-processed. We assume the program to be sequential and deterministic. Pre-processing a program starts by translating it to an Intermediate Representation (IR) with LLVM [11]. The resulting IR is then transformed into a loop-free IR that contains a single function. Most of these operations are standard in the Bounded Model-Checking (BMC) of imperative programs (cf. [3][13]). First, all function calls are inline-expanded, meaning that the call instructions are replaced by the callee function bodies. The second step consists of unrolling all loops to a specified bound. Finally, the IR is put in Static Single Assignment (SSA) form. At this point the IR contains a single local function with arithmetic, comparison, ϕ (join), and branching instructions only.

4.2   SSA-Based Trace Formula

We describe how we translate a pre-processed LLVM IR to a partial SMT formula. The representation has an important impact on the accuracy of the fault localization [2]. Our encoding takes into account both the control- and data-flow of programs. We can produce flow-sensitive trace formulas[1].

Data-Flow. The arithmetic and comparison instructions in LLVM take two arguments and return one result. We restrict the type of variables to integers and booleans. Let OP be a set of operators. The arithmetic and comparison instructions are encoded in equality constraints as follows:

$$r = (x \; \Delta \; y) \quad \Delta \in OP$$

where r is the result of the computation of the variables x and y. In the case of comparison operators, the result r is a boolean variable, called a guard, that will be used in the representation of the control-flow.

Control-Flow. A function definition contains a list of basic blocks, forming the Control Flow Graph (CFG) of the function body. Each basic block consists of a labeled entry point, a series of ϕ nodes, a list of instructions, and ends with a terminator instruction such as a branch or function return.

Let BB be the set of all basic blocks. Let $T \subseteq BB \times BB$ be a subset of all transitions between the basic blocks. For each transition $(bb_i, bb_j) \in T$ with $bb_i, bb_j \in BB$, we have a boolean variable t_{ij} that is *true* iff the control-flow goes from bb_i to bb_j. The set of predecessors of a basic block bb_j is equal to:

$$\text{pred}(bb_j) = \{bb_i \in BB \mid (bb_i, bb_j) \in T\}$$

Let $\text{on}(bb_i)$ with $bb_i \in BB$ be the *enabling condition* that is *true* iff the basic block bb_i is executed. The value of $\text{on}(bb_i)$ is computed as:

$$\text{on}(bb_i) = \bigvee_{bb_j \in \text{pred}(bb_i)} \text{on}(bb_j) \wedge t_{ji}$$

Unconditional branches between basic blocks are encoded by setting the transition variable to the value of the *enabling condition* of the basic block where the branch occurs:

$$\text{on}(bb_i) = t_{ij}$$

Conditional branches make the control-flow jump from a basic block bb_i to either a basic block bb_j if the guard g is *true*, or to a basic block bb_k otherwise:

$$(t_{ij} = g) \wedge (t_{ik} = \neg g)$$

---

[1] For sake of simplicity we omit some details about the IR [11].

As is usual in SSA representation, ϕ nodes join together values from a list of its predecessor basic blocks. Each ϕ node takes a list of (value, label) pairs to indicate the value chosen when the control flow transfers from a predecessor basic block with the associated label. Below, the encoding of a ϕ node, where the new symbol x_i refers to the variable x in bb_i.

$$\bigvee_{x_j \in \text{pred}(bb_i)} (x_i = x_j) \wedge t_{ji}$$

The CFG takes the formula below. The *entry* basic block in a function is immediately executed on entrance to the function and has no predecessor basic blocks. Its enabling condition on($entry$) is always *true*. Φ_{on} is the formula that encodes the *enabling conditions* for all basic blocks, Φ_{uncond} is the conjunction of all constraints on unconditional branches, Φ_{cond} is the conjunction of all constraints on conditional branches, and Φ_{phi} is the conjunction of the constraints encoding the ϕ nodes.

$$\Phi_{\text{CFG}} \equiv \text{on}(entry) \wedge \Phi_{\text{on}} \wedge \Phi_{\text{uncond}} \wedge \Phi_{\text{cond}} \wedge \Phi_{\text{phi}}$$

The whole Trace Formula for the IR (*TF*) takes the form below. Φ_{CFG} is the formula that encodes the control-flow of the program and $\Phi_{\text{arith/comp}}$ is the conjunction of the constraints encoding the arithmetic and comparison instructions.

$$TF = \underbrace{\Phi_{\text{CFG}}}_{\text{hard}} \wedge \underbrace{\Phi_{\text{arith/comp}}}_{\text{soft}}$$

The clauses that encode the CFG of the program are put as *hard* because they represent the skeleton of the program and we do not want the solver to retract these clauses. The rest of the clauses are set as *soft* (retractable) because they contribute to the computations of the program, and are then susceptible to be root cause candidates. Note that with our encoding we can still identify root causes related to the CFG. Since a branch occurs depending on the result of a comparison instruction, which is marked as soft, the solver can still retract this associated comparison instruction.

4.3   Computing Diagnoses

Algorithm 1 implements by using pMaxSMT the AllMinMCS function, which finds all the minimum size MCSes (diagnoses) of *TF*. This algorithm makes use of the *push & pop* mechanism of Yices [5]. The push operation saves the current logical context on the stack. The pop operation restores the context from the top of the stack, and pops it off the stack. Any changes to the logical context (adding or retracting predicates) between the matching push and pop operators are flushed, and the context is completely restored to what it was right before the push. This mechanism is very useful in our method because we apply many small modifications (lines 19 and 30) to the context C. It does not need to create a completely new context between the calls to the solver. We can just flush the modifications and reuse the same context basis many times.

Algorithm 1. AllDiagnoses

Input: a set of error-inducing inputs E, a trace formula φ_{TF} and a formula φ_{AS} that encodes the assertions the program must satisfy.
Output: D a set of diagnoses (MCSes)

```
 1: φ_W ← φ_TF                                          ▷ φ_W is the working formula
 2: AV ← ∅
 3: φ_soft ← ∅
 4: ▷ Create a set of unit soft clauses
 5: for each w ∈ φ_W, w tagged as soft do
 6:     AV ← AV ∪ {a_i}                                 ▷ a_i is a new auxiliary var. created
 7:     φ_soft ← φ_soft ∪ {(¬a_i)}
 8:     w_A ← (w ∨ a_i)
 9:     ▷ Remove w and add w_A as hard
10:     φ_W ← φ_W \ {w} ∪ {(w_A)^HARD}
11: end for
12: if AV = ∅ then
13:     return ∅                                        ▷ No MaxSMT solution
14: end if
15: D ← ∅
16: C ← φ_W ∪ φ_soft ∪ φ_AS                             ▷ Add the formulas in the context
17: for each e_i ∈ E do
18:     push(C)                                          ▷ Save the context
19:     C ← C ∪ e_i                                      ▷ Add the error-inducing input in the context
20:     M ← ∅
21:     while true do
22:         (st, φ_MSS, A) ← pMaxSMT(C)                  ▷ Solve the context
23:         ▷ "φ_MSS" is a MSS if st is true
24:         ▷ "A" is a maximal satisfying assignment if st is true
25:         if st = true then
26:             ▷ The complement of MSS is a MCS
27:             φ_MCS ← CoMSS(φ_MSS)
28:             M ← M ∪ {φ_MCS}
29:             ▷ Add the blocking constraint
30:             C ← C ∪ {(⋁_{A(a_i)=true} ¬a_i)}
31:         else
32:             break
33:         end if
34:     end while
35:     if M ≠ ∅ then
36:         D ← D ∪ {M}
37:     end if
38:     pop(C)                                           ▷ Restore the context (pushed in line 18)
39: end for
40: return D
```

The MCSes are enumerated for all *error-inducing inputs*. A set of minimal MCS (MCSes) can be computed using MaxSAT. Algorithm 1 uses a technique for blocking MCSes introduced by [14]. This technique has the advantage of not using *relaxation variables* to block MCSes. This is particularly suited when using a MaxSMT solver because the MCSes will remain "blocked" regardless of how the solver manipulates the relaxation variables. The method consists of initially transforming each soft clause into a hard clause after adding a new boolean variable called an auxiliary variable. Additionally, a set of unit soft clauses is added that corresponds to the negation of each auxiliary variable (line 30).

Algorithm 2. DiagCombine

Input: D a set of diagnoses (MCSes)
Output: C a set of combined diagnoses (MCSes)
 1: $n \leftarrow |D|$
 2: $a_i \leftarrow 0 \;\; \forall i \in \{0, 1, ..., n - 1\}$
 3: **repeat**
 4:     $S \leftarrow \{\emptyset\}$
 5:     **for** $i \leftarrow 0$ to $i < n$ **do**   ▷ Union for the current indexes in a
 6:         $j \leftarrow a_i$
 7:         $A \leftarrow D_i$ ▷ A is a set of MCSes
 8:         $B \leftarrow A_j$ ▷ B is a MCS
 9:         $S \leftarrow S \cup B$
10:     **end for**
11:     $C \leftarrow C \cup \{S\}$
12:     $a_0 \leftarrow a_0 + 1$
13:     **for** $i \leftarrow 0$ to $i < n - 1$ **do**   ▷ Update indexes in a
14:         **if** $a_i \geq |D_i|$ **then**
15:             $a_i \leftarrow 0$
16:             $a_{i+1} \leftarrow a_{i+1} + 1$
17:         **end if**
18:     **end for**
19: **until** $a_{n-1} \geq |D_{n-1}|$
20: **return** C

4.4 Combination of MCSes

Algorithm 1 provides a function that returns MCSes for each error-inducing inputs given as arguments. Each of these sets are root cause candidates for one failing execution, which are triggered by the error-inducing inputs associated to the set. The problem of combining MCSes is to generate sets of root cause locations that potentially fix all the failing executions induced by the provided error-inducing inputs. We call such gathering of sets a *complete diagnosis*.

Definition 5 (Complete Diagnosis). *Given a formal representation TF of a program P, a formula AS that encodes the assertion the program P must satisfy, and a set of error-inducing inputs E, a complete diagnosis Δ is a set of clauses of TF such that $\forall e \in E \mid (\{e\} \cup (TF \setminus \Delta) \cup AS)$ is satisfiable. A minimal complete diagnosis is a complete diagnosis from which no clauses can be removed without losing the property of being a complete diagnosis.*

In this definition, we assume that we have a set of error-inducing inputs that trigger all the faults in the program. Algorithm 2 shows how a set of minimal *complete diagnoses* is calculated from the MCSes obtained with (D) in Algorithm 1. The algorithm implements a *n-ary pair-wise union* for combining the MCSes. It takes as argument a set of set of MCSes (D) and returns a set of MCSes (C). Each MCS of C is a set of candidate root causes. Below, we have the following properties of Definition 5 and Algorithm 2.

Property 1. *Given a program P, a set of minimal complete diagnoses Δ for P, no faults are missed in P after combining the MCSes obtained with Algorithm 1.*

Property 2. *Given a program P and a set of error-inducing inputs E, we miss faults in P if the failing executions triggered by E do not cover the faults.*

Property 1 is important for our method to be conservative. It assumes that an appropriate set of test suites to trigger all faults is used. This property holds because the faults are present in the MCSes obtained with Algorithm 1, and still present after the combination because Algorithm 2 covers all elements in D for constructing the resulting set C. Equivalently, as shown in Property 2, if some faults are missing in the output of Algorithm 1, they will still not be present after the combination.

Example. When running Algorithm 1 on the program in Listing 1.1 with the following error-inducing inputs: x=0 and x=1, we obtain a set of MCSes and D below.

$$MCSes_a = \{\{3,4\},\{6\}\}, \quad MCSes_b = \{\{3\},\{4\}\}, \quad D = \{MCSes_a, MCSes_b\}$$

The root cause locations in $MCSes_a$ are related to the failing path triggered by x=0, and those in $MCSes_b$ are related to the failing path triggered by x=1. The combination of MCSes of D gives us the following minimal *complete diagnoses*:

$$\begin{aligned}\texttt{DiagCombine}(D) &= \{\{3,4\}\cup\{3\},\{3,4\}\cup\{4\},\{6\}\cup\{3\},\{6\}\cup\{4\}\}\\ &= \{\{3,4\},\{3,6\},\{4,6\}\}\end{aligned}$$

A set of fault locations to check is needed to fix all faults in the program. For example, the set $\{4,6\}$ provides information to fix the program since it combines root cause from both failing paths.

In some cases, multiple faults can lie in one program path. In such situation, a single error-inducing input is enough to localize all the faults. In other cases, if two faults are in different paths or triggered by different error-inducing inputs it requires more than one error-inducing inputs that trigger different failing paths. For the program in Listing 1.1, we need at least two error-inducing inputs to trigger both failing paths. In summary, a basic MCS enumeration method that only uses a single failing test case is not sufficient when dealing with multi-fault program whose faults are spread in different program paths or execution paths. The association of Algorithm 1 and the combination method of Definition 5 of this paper allow the efficient combination of MCSes, each obtained from different failing paths.

5 Experiments

5.1 SNIPER

We implemented our approach in a tool called SNIPER (SNIPER is Not an Imperative Program Errors Repairer). Since SNIPER includes in itself the LLVM and Yices libraries, the tool can be considered as standalone.

SNIPER takes as input a source program with some specifications (cf. pre-
and post-condition). This source code is first translated to an Intermediate Representation (IR) by LLVM and pre-processed as explained in Section 4.1. From
the resultant IR, we construct the *TF* formula and the *AS* formula as described
in Section 4.2. Regarding the *error-inducing inputs* (*EIes*), the user has two
choices; he can either use some failing test cases to generate a set *EIes* or he
can let SNIPER compute a single *EI* using BMC, which is repeated to obtain
enough number of *EIes*. Then, using the *TF* formula, the *AS* formula and the
set of *error-inducing inputs EIes* we compute a set of diagnoses (see Section 4.3
for details), and combine them as explained in Section 4.4. The diagnoses, which
are source code lines marked with potential root causes, are output to the user.

5.2   Experimental Setup

In this section we show the capabilities of SNIPER with some experiments made
on the Siemens Test Suite. One of the Siemens Test Suite tasks is the TCAS,
which is an aircraft collision avoidance system. The authors of the suite created
41 versions of the program and in each of these versions one or more faults
were injected. The TCAS task comes with a set of 1578 test cases. However, no
specification is given.

We used the same experimental setup as described in [9]. We first ran the
original program on the test cases in order to get the correct output values
for each test case. These values constitute the test oracles for the program. As
explained in Section 4.4 we use many error-inducing inputs (failing test cases)
in order to deal with multi-fault programs. For the purpose of this experiment
on the TCAS benchmark, we ran all test cases on each faulty version to obtain
the failing test cases, which are the test cases that give an output different from
the correct output.

All the experiments were carried out using an Intel Core 2 Duo 2.4 GHz with
4 GB of RAM on the operating system Mac OS X 10.6 Snow Leopard.

5.3   Results for Single and Multiple Faults

Table 1 reports the results of running SNIPER on each version of the TCAS. The
first column of the table shows the version of the program. The column #Err
shows the number of injected fault in this version. The column #FTC shows the
number of failing test cases included in the TCAS benchmark set. The right part
of Table 1 shows the results of SNIPER and BugAssist. The results of BugAssist
were taken from [9]. Each column shows the number of time the tools were able
to detect at least one of the injected fault locations.

In total, BugAssist pin-pointed 1364 times the injected fault location out of
the 1437 runs (73 misses). SNIPER pin-pointed the injected fault location 1435
times out of the 1437 runs (2 misses). The average ACSR (Average Code Size
Reduction), which is the percentage of code given by the tool on average to locate
the faults, of all the versions is 11.00%. For recall, CSR (Code Size Reduction) is
the ratio of fault locations in a MUS (program slice) to the total number of lines

Table 1. Results of SNIPER and BugAssist on the TCAS. Versions no. 33 and no. 38 are omitted from the table in order to compare the results with BugAssist [9], which does not have entries for them.

Ver	#Err	#FTC	SNIPER	BugAssist	Ver	#Err	#FTC	SNIPER	BugAssist
v1	1	131	131	131	v21	1	16	16	16
v2	1	69	69	69	v22	1	11	11	11
v3	1	23	23	13	v23	1	42	42	41
v4	1	25	24*	25	v24	1	7	7	7
v5	1	10	10	10	v25	1	3	3	3
v6	1	12	12	12	v26	1	11	11	11
v7	1	36	36	36	v27	1	10	10	10
v8	1	1	1	1	v28	1	76	76	58
v9	1	9	9	9	v29	1	18	18	14
v10	2	14	14	14	v30	1	58	58	58
v11	2	14	14	14	v31	2	14	14	14
v12	1	70	70	48	v32	2	2	2	2
v13	1	4	4	4	v34	1	77	77	77
v14	1	50	50	50	v35	1	76	76	58
v15	3	10	10	10	v36	1	126	126	126
v16	1	70	70	70	v37	1	92	92	92
v17	1	35	35	35	v39	1	3	3	3
v18	1	29	29	29	v40	2	126	126	126
v19	1	19	19	19	v41	1	20	19*	20
v20	1	18	18	18					

of code. We obtain a minimum of 2.31% for the version no. 14 and a maximum of 14.01% for the version no. 10. SNIPER was able to identify the exact bug location of all the single fault programs.

Concerning the multi-fault programs, all the faults that can be found with the given test cases were successfully localized. In the version no. 31, the failed test cases only cover one of the two buggy statements. Thereby, the uncovered buggy statement cannot be in the root causes. This shows that the coverage of the test input is an important factor in fault localization.

5.4   Push & Pop Optimization Results

Figure 1 reports the computation times of Algorithm 1 on the TCAS benchmark with and without the *push & pop* optimization, which was explained in Section 4.3. The histograms are separated in two parts for readability. The bars in gray represent the times with the optimization disabled and the bars in black represent the times with the optimization activated.

We can see that the computation time is reduced when using the optimization. The percentage decrease of the average computation time is 49%. The large

---

* A new option of SNIPER that checks the array index overflow/ underflow can detect the missing one.

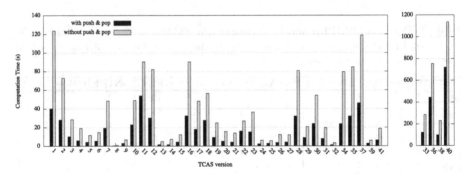

Fig. 1. Results of running SNIPER on the TCAS benchmark with and without push & pop optimization.

difference can be explained by the fact that the same formula is solved many times with only some small modifications between the calls to the solver.

6   Related Work

Program slicing [18] was introduced for localizing faults, and was empirically shown effective [10]. The average code size reduction (CSR) of program slices is around 30% [1]; such amount of program code needs to be inspected to find real root causes. Coverage-based or spectrum-based debugging (cf. [8]) calculates ranking orders between program statements or spectrums to show that a particular fragment of code is more suspicious than the others. The method needs many successful and failing executions to calculate the statistical measures. Generating unbiased input test data set is a major challenge. The formula-based approach is more systematic than the methods that use program slices or the statistical coverages. It has its logical foundation developed in the MBD theory. DiGiuseppe et al [4] empirically studied the coverage-based fault localization on multi-fault programs. They showed that the presence of multiple faults creates interferences, which inhibits the effectiveness of the method. However, it can still localize at least one fault. The qualitative effectiveness of our approach is not disturbed by the number of faults in the program, it only affects the computation time.

BugAssist [9] applied the MaxSAT-based method of Safarpour et al [17] to fault localization of C programs. It uses an iterative localization algorithm to obtain the MCS, from which the CSR is calculated. The CSR is much smaller than the case of program slicing approaches. The algorithm, however, does not guarantee to cover all the root causes. The Trace Formula used in BugAssist encodes a counterexample obtained using the bounded model-checking method. Since this trace formula represents a straight-line program fragment that contains faults, it does not reconstruct information related to the control flow of the original program. To overcome this limitation, flow-sensitive trace formula was proposed [2]. A similar representation was also used in [20]. Furthermore, the approach of BugAssist [9] combines MCSes by taking their union to have a single set. The fault locations in this set are later ordered by a ranking mechanism. As opposed to BugAssist's approach, we generate different sets, each set containing potential root causes for fixing all the faults in the program. The differences in major formula-based tools are summarized in the following table.

	Trace Formula Type	Completeness of MCS Enumeration	MCS Combination Method
BugAssist	Flow-insensitive	NO	union
Wotowa	Flow-sensitive	YES	none
SNIPER	Flow-sensitive	YES	pair-wise union

7 Conclusion

We presented a formula-based method for automatic fault localization, which combined the SAT-based formal verification techniques with the model-based diagnosis theory. It has two core algorithms, computing all the diagnoses and combining them, which enables the localization of root causes of multi-fault programs. SNIPER adapts partial maximum satisfiability to implement the algorithms efficiently, which made use of the *push & pop* mechanism of Yices. Furthermore, the multiple faults in the TCAS benchmark programs could successfully be detected by combining a set of the results obtained from multiple failing program paths.

We have an open question about the generation of adequate test suites for fault localization. It calls for a new test case generation method particularly focusing on exercising paths leading to assertion violations. We need only a set of failing traces, which is different from the coverage-based methods in which unbiased test suits are needed for both successful and failing traces.

Acknowledgement. This research was partially supported by JSPS KAKENHI Grant Number 24300010.

References

1. Binkley, D., Gold, N., Harman, M.: An Empirical Study of Static Program Slice Size. ACM TOSEM 16(2), Article 8 (April 2007)
2. Christ, J., Ermis, E., Schäf, M., Wies, T.: Flow-Sensitive Fault Localization. In: Giacobazzi, R., Berdine, J., Mastroeni, I. (eds.) VMCAI 2013. LNCS, vol. 7737, pp. 189–208. Springer, Heidelberg (2013)
3. Clarke, E., Kroning, D., Lerda, F.: A Tool for Checking ANSI-C Programs. In: Jensen, K., Podelski, A. (eds.) TACAS 2004. LNCS, vol. 2988, pp. 168–176. Springer, Heidelberg (2004)
4. DiGiuseppe, N., Jones, J.A.: On the Influence of Multiple Faults on Coverage-based Fault Localization. In: Proc. ISSTA 2011, pp. 210–220 (2011)
5. Dutertre, B., de Moura, L.: The Yices SMT Solver, http://yices.csl.sri.com
6. Griesmayer, A., Staber, S., Bloem, R.: Fault Localization using a Model Checker. In: STVR, pp. 149–173 (2010)

7. Groce, A., Chaki, S., Kroening, D., Strichman, O.: Error Explanation with Distance Metrics. STTT 8(3), 229–247 (2006)
8. Jones, J.A., Harrold, M.J.: Empirical Evaluation of the Tarantula Automatic Fault-Localization Technique. In: Proc. ASE 2005, pp. 273–282 (2005)
9. Jose, M., Majumdar, R.: Cause Clue Clauses: Error Localization using Maximum Satisfiability. In: Proc. PLDI 2011, pp. 437–446 (2011)
10. Kusumoto, S., Nishimatsu, A., Nishie, K., Inoue, K.: Experimental Evaluation of Program Slicing for Fault Localization. Empirical Software Engineering 7(1), 49–76 (2002)
11. Lattner, C., Adve, V.: LLVM: A Compilation Framework for Lifelong Program Analysis & Transformation. In: Proc. CGO, pp. 78–86 (2004)
12. Liffiton, M.H., Sakallah, K.A.: Algorithms for Computing Minimal Unsatisfiable Subsets of Constraints. Automated Reasoning 40(1), 1–33 (2008)
13. Merz, F., Falke, S., Sinz, C.: LLBMC: Bounded Model Checking of C and C++ Programs Using a Compiler IR. In: Joshi, R., Müller, P., Podelski, A. (eds.) VSTTE 2012. LNCS, vol. 7152, pp. 146–161. Springer, Heidelberg (2012)
14. Morgado, A., Liffiton, M., Marques-Silva, J.: MaxSAT-Based MCS Enumeration. In: Biere, A., Nahir, A., Vos, T. (eds.) HVC. LNCS, vol. 7857, pp. 86–101. Springer, Heidelberg (2013)
15. Prasad, M.R., Biere, A., Gupta, A.: A Survey of Recent Advances in SAT-Based Formal Verification. STTT 7(2), 156–173 (2005)
16. Reiter, R.: A Theory of Diagnosis from First Principles. Artificial Intelligence 32(1), 57–95 (1987)
17. Safarpour, S., Mangassarian, H., Veneris, A., Liffiton, M.H., Sakallah, K.A.: Improved Design Debugging using Maximum Satisfiability. In: Proc. FMCAD 2007, pp. 13–19 (2007)
18. Weiser, M.: Programmers Use Slices When Debugging. Comm. ACM 25(7), 446–452 (1982)
19. Wotawa, F.: On the Relationship between Model-based Debugging and Program Slicing. Artificial Intelligence 135(1), 125–143 (2002)
20. Wotawa, F., Nica, M., Moraru, I.: Automated Debugging based on a Constraint Model of the Program and a Test Case. Logic and Algebraic Programming 81(4), 390–407 (2012)
21. Zeller, A., Hildebrandt, R.: Simplifying and Isolating Failure-Inducing Input. IEEE Trans. Softw. Eng. 28(2), 183–200 (2002)

A Resource-Based Logic for Termination and Non-termination Proofs

Ton Chanh Le[1], Cristian Gherghina[2], Aquinas Hobor[1], and Wei-Ngan Chin[1]

[1] Department of Computer Science, National University of Singapore, Singapore
[2] Singapore University of Technology and Design, Singapore

Abstract. We propose a unified logical framework for specifying and proving *both* termination and non-termination of various programs. Our framework is based on a resource logic which captures both upper *and* lower bounds on resources used by the programs. By an abstraction, we evolve this resource logic for execution length into a temporal logic with three predicates to reason about termination, non-termination or unknown. We introduce a new logical entailment system for temporal constraints and show how Hoare logic can be seamlessly used to prove termination and non-termination in our unified framework. Though this paper's focus is on the formal foundations for a new unified framework, we also report on the usability and practicality of our approach by specifying and verifying both termination and non-termination properties for about 300 programs, collected from a variety of sources. This adds a modest 5-10% verification overhead when compared to underlying partial-correctness verification system.

1 Introduction

Termination proving is an important part of correctness proofs for software systems as "so-called *partial correctness* is inadequate: if a program is intended to terminate, that fact must be part of its specification." – Cliff Jones [26]. Thus, *total correctness* proofs, denoted by the Hoare triple $[P]c[Q]$, require the code fragment c to be shown terminating in addition to meeting the postcondition Q after execution. The termination of a loop or a recursive method is usually proven by a well-founded termination measure given to the specification. However, such a measure is not a component of the logical formulas for pre/post specifications. A reason for this distinction is that specification logic typically describes program states, while the termination proofs are concerned with the existence of well-founded measures to bound the execution length of loops/recursions, as argued by Hehner in [23]. Due to this distinction, we cannot automatically leverage richer logics that have been developed for safety properties to conduct more intricate termination and non-termination reasoning.

For illustration, let us use the Shuffle problem proposed in the Java Bytecode Recursive category of the annual Termination Competition [33]. In this problem, an acyclic linked list is shuffled by the `shuffle` method together with the auxiliary `reverse` method, whose source code is shown in Fig. 1. To prove that `shuffle` terminates, we need to firstly show that `reverse` also terminates. While the termination of `reverse` can be easily proved by current approaches, such as [30,7,11], proving `shuffle` terminates is harder because it requires a functional correctness related fact: the `reverse` method does not change the length of the list. Based on this fact, it is possible to show

S. Merz and J. Pang (Eds.): ICFEM 2014, LNCS 8829, pp. 267–283, 2014.

```
public static List shuffle(List xs) {    public static List reverse(final List l) {
    if (xs == null) return null;              if (l == null || l.next == null)
    else {                                        return l;
        List next = xs.next;                  final List nextItem = l.next;
        return new List(xs.value,             final List reverseRest =
            shuffle(reverse(next)));                       reverse(nextItem);
    }                                         l.next = null;  nextItem.next = l;
}                                             return reverseRest; }
```

Fig. 1. The Shuffle problem from the Termination Competition

that the linked list's length is also decreasing across the recursive method call `shuffle`; as a result, the method always terminates.

Therefore, without an integration of termination specification into logics for functional correctness, such as separation logic [36], the termination of `shuffle` is hardly specified and proved by verification systems based on the traditional Hoare logic for total correctness. Note that automated termination provers, such as APROVE [19] and COSTA [3], are not able to show that `shuffle` terminates, even after applying a numeric abstraction on the size property to `shuffle` [32], due to the lack of information flow between the correctness and the termination arguments. We believe that relatively complex problems, such as Shuffle, highlight the need of a more expressive logic with the ability of integration into various safety logics for termination reasoning.

Moreover, if the termination proof fails, *e.g.*, when the input list of `shuffle` is cyclic, the program will be *implicitly* assumed to be *possibly* non-terminating. That is, *definite* non-termination is neither *explicitly* stated nor proven by Hoare logic. Explicitly proving non-termination has two benefits. First, it allows more comprehensive specifications to be developed for better program understanding. Second, it allows a clearer distinction between expected non-termination (*e.g.*, reactive systems where loops are designed to be infinite) and failure of termination proofs, paving the way for focusing on real non-termination bugs that minimize on false positives.

Some specification languages, such as Dafny [31], ACSL [6] and JML [29], allow the specification of *possible* non-termination but their corresponding verifiers provide limited support for this feature. For example, the verifier of Dafny only allows such specification on loops or tail-recursive methods[1], while Frama-C verifier of ACSL [15] has not implemented it. On the other hand, we can use the `false` postcondition, which indicates that the method's exit is unreachable, to specify *definite* non-termination. However, such postcondition for partial correctness is not preferred as it is logically distinct from termination proofs. This distinction has been designed into Dafny, Frama-C and KeY with JML [2], that makes the tools fail to take into account non-terminating behavior when proving termination. For example, Dafny succeeds in proving the termination of a recursive method[2] though this method contains a call to a non-terminating method.[3] In fact, for termination proofs, these tools simply check that there is a finite number of mutually recursive calls to the analyzed methods, rather than the methods' termination per se.

---

[1] http://www.rise4fun.com/Dafny/PnRX

[2] http://www.rise4fun.com/Dafny/6FuR

[3] The examples in ACSL and JML are at
http://loris-7.ddns.comp.nus.edu.sg/~project/hiptnt/others.zip

Our Proposal. We propose integrating both termination and non-termination requirements directly into the specification logic for functional properties. Our work follows Hoare and He [24] and Hehner [22], in which the termination is reasoned together with partial correctness proof. In [22], the program is instrumented with a time variable t and the termination is proven by a finite bound on the *exact* execution time $t'-t$, where t, t' are the initial, resp. final time. In [24], a special ghost variable ok is used to signify termination. However, these approaches presently do not handle non-termination.

As a formal foundation to unify termination and non-termination reasoning and integrate them into functional correctness proofs, we introduce a new resource logic which captures the concept of resource capacity; tracking both *minimum and maximum* amounts of resources used by some given code. Our logic uses a primitive predicate $\text{RC}\langle l, u \rangle$ with invariant $0 \leq l \leq u$ to capture a semantic notion of resource capacity (l, u) with the lower bound l and the upper bound u. Through this resource logic, we can specify a variety of complexity-related properties, including the notions of termination and non-termination, by tracking the number of calls (and loop iterations) executed by the given code. Termination is denoted by the presence of a *finite* upper bound, while non-termination is denoted an *infinite* lower bound on the execution length.

To support a more effective mechanism, we shall derive a simpler *temporal* logic from the richer resource logic itself. We define three temporal predicates, $\text{Term } M$, Loop and MayLoop, where M is a well-founded termination measure, and associate them with each method in a given program to denote the termination, definite non-termination and possible non-termination of these methods, respectively. In terms of resource reasoning, these predicates represent $\text{RC}\langle 0, \text{embed}(M) \rangle$, $\text{RC}\langle \infty, \infty \rangle$ and $\text{RC}\langle 0, \infty \rangle$, respectively, where $\text{embed}(M)$ is a finite bound obtained through an order-embedding of M into naturals. Using the enriched specification logic, functional correctness, termination and non-termination of methods can be verified under a single modular framework. With this unification, the predicate $\text{Term } M$ denotes exactly definite termination, instead of just denoting the bound on the number of loop iterations or method recursions like the termination measures used in the traditional Hoare logic for total correctness.

Our research contributions can be summarized as follows:

- A new *resource logic* that can capture lower and upper bounds on resource usage via the concept of resource capacity, together with an entailment procedure to support correctness proofs with resource-related properties. (Sec. 3)
- A *temporal logic* that is abstracted from the resource logic to reason about both program termination and non-termination. We introduce three new temporal constraints, its *entailment* and *Hoare rules* lifted from the resource logic. (Sec. 4)
- A successful integration of both resource and temporal logics into a separation logic based verifier [35]. The new temporal logic is expressive enough to specify and successfully verify the (non-)termination behaviors for about 300 benchmark programs collected from a variety of sources, including the SIR/Siemens test suite [17] and problems from the Termination Competition (Sec. 5). The prototype implementation and benchmark are available for online use and download at:

http://loris-7.ddns.comp.nus.edu.sg/~project/hiptnt/

pred isEvenNat(int n) ≡ n≥0 ∧ ∃m · n = 2∗m;
int sumE (int n)
  requires isEvenNat(n) ∧ Term[n] ∨
         ¬isEvenNat(n) ∧ Loop
  ensures true;
{ if (n==0) return 0;
   else return n + sumE(n−2); }
(a)
	while (x>y)
	  requires
	    x≤y ∧ Term[] ∨
	    x>y ∧ x<0 ∧ Loop ∨
	    x>y ∧ x≥0 ∧ MayLoop
	  ensures x′≤y′;
	{ y=x+y; x=x−1; }
	(b)

Fig. 2. Examples on numerical programs

2 From Resource to Temporal Logic

We introduce a general resource predicate $RC\langle l, u \rangle$ where l is a lower bound and u is an upper bound on resource capacity, with invariant $0 \leq l \leq u$. This resource predicate can be specialized to execution capacity to capture a variety of complexity-related properties, via lower and upper bounds on the total number of method calls during the execution of a given piece of code. We shall give an instrumented semantics for this specific resource logic, and also specialize it for reasoning about termination and non-termination. To prove termination, we simply use the predicate $RC\langle 0, u \rangle$ where u is some finite value, namely $u < \infty$. To prove non-termination, we can use the predicate $RC\langle \infty, \infty \rangle$ which signifies an infinite lower bound. Lastly, if we cannot prove either termination or non-termination, we use the predicate $RC\langle 0, \infty \rangle$ which covers all possibilities.

The resource logic we have outlined is quite expressive, and could moreover be specialized for reasoning on just termination and non-termination with the direct handling of infinity ∞ value. In order to design a simpler logic, we introduce a temporal logic with three distinct predicates, as follows: (i) Term M to denote $RC\langle 0, \text{embed}(M) \rangle$, (ii) Loop to denote $RC\langle \infty, \infty \rangle$ and (iii) MayLoop to denote $RC\langle 0, \infty \rangle$. Such a temporal logic is considerably simpler than the more expressive resource logic, since we can omit reasoning with ∞. We can also use a simpler termination measure M, based on depth of recursion rather than number of calls, but relate to the latter using $\text{embed}(M)$. Moreover, these temporal predicates can be made flow-insensitive, and thus need only appear in each method's precondition where they describe execution capacity required for the method's execution. This two-level approach simplifies both the design of a formal semantics, and the development of a verification framework for (non-)termination.

For illustration, let us look at some numerical examples, starting with the method sumE in Fig. 2(a). This method is required to return the sum of all even natural numbers that are less than or equal to the input n. However, the implementation satisfies this requirement only when n is an even natural number, denoted by the predicate isEvenNat(n); otherwise, the method does not terminate[4]. In our approach, these distinct scenarios can be described in a termination-enriched specification by seamlessly integrating the temporal constraints Term[n] and Loop into a logic with disjunctions.

---

[4] The verification system assumes the use of arbitrary precision integers. When finite integers are used, we may give a different temporal specification for those prestates.

JML and ACSL also support the specification of several method behaviors. However, the current ACSL implementation in Frama-C does not allow fine-grained termination related specification of each behavior and ignores conditional termination clauses. As a result, it cannot verify all the (non-)terminating behaviors of sumE together. KeY allows the specification of termination for each individual method behavior but it cannot disprove the termination of sumE when n is an odd positive number, because the variant n is still valid under this precondition.[3] In contrast, our unified termination and non-termination reasoning does not accept the temporal constraint Term[n] in these prestates because the execution starting from them will eventually reach a non-terminating execution when n<0. In terms of resource reasoning, Term[n], denoting a finite resource, is invalid as it cannot satisfy the infinite resource required by the non-termination.

The next example in Fig. 2(b) illustrates a usage of MayLoop constraint. Starting from any prestate satisfying $x>y \land x\geq 0$, the execution of the given loop may reach either the base case (when $x\leq y$, indicated by Term[]) or the non-terminating case (when $x>y \land x<0$, indicated by Loop). We observe that this MayLoop precondition can be strengthened to the *non-linear* constraint $4x^2+4x+8y+9\geq 0$ for non-termination, but this requires stronger arithmetic solvers.

Though our proposal is independent of the underlying logics on functional properties, it can leverage infrastructures of richer logics[5] to conduct termination and non-termination reasoning for more complex domains. For example, our proposed temporal constraints are easily integrated into formulas of separation logic to reason about the termination and non-termination of heap-based programs. We choose a fragment of separation logic with the separating conjunction $*$ and the points-to operator $\mapsto$ to specify the heap assertions. These operators are used to describe several data structures, such as linked list and tree. For example, the inductive predicate $lseg(root, p, n)$ declared in Fig. 3(a) describes a list segment size of n from root to p with an invariant property stated that the list's size is non-negative. This predicate can be used to specify either null-terminating lists (when $p = null$) or circular lists (when $p = root$).

data List { int value; List next; }	List reverse (List l)
	requires $lseg(l, null, n) \land$ Term[n]
pred $lseg(root, p, n) \equiv root=p \land n=0 \lor$	ensures $lseg(res, null, n)$;
$\exists v, q \cdot root\mapsto List(v, q)*lseg(q, p, n-1)$	List shuffle (List xs)
inv $n \geq 0$;	requires $lseg(xs, null, n) \land$ Term[n]
	ensures $lseg(res, null, n)$;
(a)	(b)

Fig. 3. A specification in separation logic to verify the correctness of Shuffle's methods

We then use the predicate lseg for the pre and postconditions of two methods reverse and shuffle in the Shuffle problem. The specification of each method indicates that the method's result res is a linked list with the same size n as the input list. From these safety specifications, the temporal constraint Term[n] integrated into the precondition of each method is able to specify that the depth of recursion is bounded by the size of the input list, thus indicating the method's termination.

---

[5] In comparison with the first-order logic with linear arithmetic for numerical programs.

From the perspective of resource reasoning, a temporal constraint in the precondition of a method defines the bounds of available resource allowed for program executions from prestates satisfying (safety part of) this precondition. This idea is similar to Atkey's logic [5], a type-based amortized resource analysis for imperative programs, which associates a piece of resource with each element of the data structures prior program execution. However, Atkey's approach only tracks the upper bound of resource usage, so that it cannot reason about non-termination. This shortcoming also applies to other type-based approaches for termination reasoning, such as [1,38]. In addition, while the amortized resource analysis accounts for individual time-step (or heap chunk), we use termination measures, which are much simpler, to facilitate termination proofs. For example, to analyze shuffle, Atkey's logic requires the global length property to present the polynomial resource associated with the input list using the technique of Hoffmann and Hofmann [25], which is much harder than locally reasoning about each node of the list as stated in his paper. Finally, this logic is built on top of just separation logic, rather than being generic as our proposal.

3   A Logic for Resource Reasoning

In proving termination and non-termination, our goal is to use resource reasoning based on execution capacity to provide a means for quantitatively assessing the execution length of a program. For this purpose, we introduce a resource logic to formally assess the minimum and a maximum bounds on a program's resource consumption. We first extend the program state model with a mechanism to track resource capacities of the underlying machine. Since the particular consumed resource is countable and possibly infinite, we use the set $\mathbb{N}^\infty$, short for $\mathbb{N} \cup \{\infty\}$, as its domain.

3.1   Resource Capacity

Definition 1 (Program states). *A program state σ is a triple (s, h, r) of stack $s \in S$ (locals), heap $h \in \mathcal{H}$ (memory) and $r \in \mathcal{R}$, resource capacity where r is a pair (r_l, r_u) of bounds in $\mathbb{N}^\infty$, with $0 \leq r_l \leq r_u$, denoting the allowed minimum and maximum resource consumption for executions starting from the current program state.*

Intuitively, a program state's resource capacity (r_l, r_u) ensures that any execution starting from this state must consume *at least* r_l and *at most* r_u of the tracked resource.

Definition 2 (Resource Capacity Ordering). *Let $(\leq_c) \subset \mathbb{N}^\infty \times \mathbb{N}^\infty$ be the resource capacity ordering, such that $(b_l, b_u) \leq_c (a_l, a_u)$ iff $a_l \leq b_l$ and $b_u \leq a_u$.*

The resource capacity (a_l, a_u) is considered larger (or more general) than (b_l, b_u) if $a_l \leq b_l$ and $b_u \leq a_u$. The intuition is that under this condition, any execution which guarantees the capacity (b_l, b_u) also guarantees the capacity (a_l, a_u). Based on this observation, $(0, \infty)$ is the largest resource capacity. In fact, it indicates an unconstrained resource consumption.

In order to properly define an operational semantics in terms of the proposed program state model, we also need to be able to express resource consumption. To this end we define a splitting operation over the resource capacity. We will say that a capacity (a_l, a_u) can be split into capacities (b_l, b_u) and (c_l, c_u), written $(a_l, a_u) \ominus (b_l, b_u) = (c_l, c_u)$, if whenever an execution that guarantees the capacity (b_l, b_u) starts from a state

$$
\begin{array}{lcl}
(s,h,r) \models \Psi_1 \vee \Psi_2 & \equiv & (s,h,r) \models \Psi_1 \text{ or } (s,h,r) \models \Psi_2 \\
(s,h,r) \models \Psi_1 \wedge \Psi_2 & \equiv & (s,h,r) \models \Psi_1 \text{ and } (s,h,r) \models \Psi_2 \\
(s,h,r) \models \exists x_i^* \cdot \Psi & \equiv & \exists \nu_i^* \cdot (s[(x_i \mapsto \nu_i)^*], h, r) \models \Psi \\
(s,h,r) \models \mu & \equiv & (s,h) \models \mu \\
(s,h,r) \models \mathtt{RC}\langle a_l, a_u \rangle & \equiv & (s,h) \models r_l = a_l \wedge r_u = a_u \quad \text{where } r=(r_l, r_u) \\
(s,h,r) \models \rho_1 \blacktriangleright \rho_2 & \equiv & \forall r' \cdot \text{if } (s,h,r') \models \rho_1 \text{ then } (s,h,r \ominus r') \models \rho_2
\end{array}
$$

Fig. 5. Semantics of Assertions in the Resource-Aware Logic

with the capacity (a_l, a_u) then the remaining capacity is (c_l, c_u). In other words, the executions allowed by (a_l, a_u) can be decomposed into executions required by (b_l, b_u) followed by executions required by (c_l, c_u).

Definition 3 (Resource Capacity Splitting). *Given resource capacities* $(a_l, a_u), (b_l, b_u)$ *with* $b_u \leq a_u$ *and* $a_l + b_u \leq a_u + b_l$ *then* $(a_l, a_u) \ominus (b_l, b_u) = (c_l, c_u)$ *where*
$$ c_l = \min\{x_l \in \mathbb{N}^\infty \mid x_l + b_l \geq a_l\} \text{ and } c_u = \max\{x_u \in \mathbb{N}^\infty \mid x_u + b_u \leq a_u\}. $$

From Defn. 3, (c_l, c_u) is the *largest* resource consumption allowed for any execution following executions satisfying (b_l, b_u) such that the overall resource consumption is described by (a_l, a_u). Under this interpretation it follows naturally that when $b_u > a_u$ the splitting operation is undefined as c_u does not exist. In addition, when $a_l + b_u > a_u + b_l$, the splitting operation is also undefined as it would lead to $c_l > c_u$.

3.2 Assertion Language and Semantics for a Resource-Aware Logic

To support resource reasoning, we extend a minimalistic assertion language with two resource assertions, as shown in Fig. 4. We use v and v^* for variables and sequences of variables, $f(v^*)$ for functions from variables to $\mathbb{N}^\infty$, μ and Φ to represent resource-free formulas and ρ for resource assertions.

$$
\begin{array}{l}
\Psi ::= \bigvee (\exists v^* \cdot \mu \wedge \rho)^* \\
\Phi ::= \bigvee (\exists v^* \cdot \mu)^* \\
\rho ::= \mathtt{RC}\langle a_l, a_u \rangle \mid \rho_1 \blacktriangleright \rho_2 \\
a ::= f(v^*)
\end{array}
$$

Fig. 4. The Assertion Language

The resource assertion ρ ranges over (i) *atomic* resource assertions $\mathtt{RC}\langle a_l, a_u \rangle$, where a_l, a_u are functions from variables to $\mathbb{N}^\infty$; and (ii) *splitting* resource assertions $\rho_1 \blacktriangleright \rho_2$, which holds for states that allow executions to be split into two execution fragments, on which ρ_1 and ρ_2 hold respectively.

We concisely list in Fig. 5 the semantic model for the assertion language. We observe that the usual semantics of the logical connectives, *e.g.*, conjunctions and disjunctions, lifts naturally over resource assertions. The semantics of the resource-free assertions is straightforward: a resource-free formula μ holds for all states (s, h, r) such that $(s, h) \models \mu$ with respect to the semantics of the corresponding underlying logic.

We point out that we have chosen to model the $\mathtt{RC}\langle a_l, a_u \rangle$ assertion as a precise predicate. That is, a program state σ satisfies a resource constraint ρ if the resource capacity in σ is equal to the evaluation, in the context of σ, of the upper and lower functions associated with ρ. This modeling relation ensures that the resource assertion ρ is *precise* with regards to the resource capacity, where $(s, h, r) \models \rho$ does not imply

$(s, h, r') \models \rho$ whenever r' is larger than r, i.e., $r' \geq_c r$. Consequently, $\text{RC}\langle a_l, a_u \rangle \vdash \text{RC}\langle b_l, b_u \rangle$ iff $(s, h) \models a_l = b_l \wedge a_u = b_u$. Additionally, $\text{RC}\langle a_l, a_u \rangle \wedge \text{RC}\langle b_l, b_u \rangle \equiv \text{RC}\langle a_l, a_u \rangle$ iff $a_l = b_l \wedge a_u = b_u$; otherwise, $\text{RC}\langle a_l, a_u \rangle \wedge \text{RC}\langle b_l, b_u \rangle \equiv \texttt{false}$.

To provide a precise modular resource reasoning, we lift the semantic split operation into a resource splitting assertion $\rho_1 \blacktriangleright \rho_2$. This enables our proof construction to follow the same style of other resource manipulating logics, such as separation logic. The intuition behind the splitting resource assertions is that $\rho_1 \blacktriangleright \rho_2$ holds for any program state from which it is possible to consume as many resources as ρ_1 requires and end in a state that satisfies ρ_2. Or equivalently, $\rho_1 \blacktriangleright \rho_2$ holds for all states whose resource capacity can be split into two portions, such that the resulting capacities satisfy ρ_1 and ρ_2, respectively. In addition, we can use $\blacktriangleright$ to add a resource capacity ρ_1 into the current available resource capacity ρ, resulting in $\rho \blacktriangleright \rho_1$. The semantics of $\rho_1 \blacktriangleright \rho_2$ is also given in Fig. 5.

3.3 Resource-Enhanced Entailment with Frame Inference

Based on the semantics of resource assertions and the standard definition of the logical entailment relation (i.e., $\Psi_1 \vdash \Psi_2$ iff $\forall \sigma \cdot$ if $\sigma \models \Psi_1$ then $\sigma \models \Psi_2$), it is possible to define an entailment for resource constraints of the form $\rho \vdash \rho_1 \blacktriangleright \rho_2$ as follows:

Lemma 1 (Resource Entailments). *Given resource assertions ρ, ρ_1 and ρ_2, $\rho \vdash \rho_1 \blacktriangleright \rho_2$ iff $\forall s, h, r, r_1 \cdot$ if $(s, h, r) \models \rho$ and $(s, h, r_1) \models \rho_1$ then $(s, h, r \ominus r_1) \models \rho_2$.*

Proof. The proofs of all lemmas in this paper can be found in the technical report [28].

It follows that given $\ominus_f$, a lifting of resource capacity splitting to functions, then:

$$\frac{(\rho_l^2, \rho_u^2) = (\rho_l, \rho_u) \ominus_f (\rho_l^1, \rho_u^1)}{\text{RC}\langle \rho_l, \rho_u \rangle \vdash \text{RC}\langle \rho_l^1, \rho_u^1 \rangle \blacktriangleright \text{RC}\langle \rho_l^2, \rho_u^2 \rangle}$$

Entailments of the form $\rho \vdash \rho_1 \blacktriangleright \rho_2$ are of particular interest in the context of program verification as they naturally encode the restriction imposed at a method call and the remaining restriction after the execution of this method. For the proposed resource logic, we construct a general entailment system with frame inference by merging the entailment of resource constraints presented earlier with the entailment system corresponding to the underlying logic. Let the underlying entailment system be of the general form $\Psi \vdash \Phi \rightsquigarrow \Phi_r$ denoting that Ψ implies Φ with frame Φ_r. In sub-structural logics such as separation logic, the frame captures any residual state that is not required by the entailment. In pure logics where the program states are not changed, the frame is simply the antecedent of the entailment.

To support logics with disjunctions, the entailment system firstly deconstructs disjunctive antecedents (e.g., using the rule [ENT–DISJ–LHS]) and consequents until formulas of the form $\mu \wedge \rho$ with a single resource constraint[6] are encountered in both sides of the sub-entailments. The judgment system then applies the rule [ENT–CONJ] that is slightly changed to handle resource constraints by splitting an entailment into two parts, namely *logical* part and *resource* part. The logical goal is solved by the entailment system $\mu_a \vdash \mu_c \rightsquigarrow \Phi_r$ of the underlying logic. The resource goal is solved by using

---

[6] A conjunction of resource constraints can be simplified to either a single resource constraint or `false` as discussed in Sec. 3.2.

the resource entailment rules presented above. The solving process for the resource part leverages the entailment outcome Φ_r from the underlying logic, which is simply added to the antecedent of the resource entailment, to check the condition stated in Defn. 3 for the resource capacity splitting operation to be defined.

$$\boxed{\text{ENT–DISJ–LHS}}$$
$$\frac{\Psi \;=\; \bigvee \exists v_i^* \cdot (\mu_i \wedge \rho_i) \qquad \forall i \cdot (\mu_i \wedge \rho_i) \vdash \Phi \rightsquigarrow \Psi_r^i}{\Psi \vdash \Phi \rightsquigarrow \bigvee \exists v_i^* \cdot \Psi_r^i}$$

$$\boxed{\text{ENT–CONJ}}$$
$$\frac{\mu_a \vdash \mu_c \rightsquigarrow \Phi_r \qquad \mu_a \wedge \Phi_r \wedge \rho_a \vdash \rho_c \blacktriangleright \rho_r}{\mu_a \wedge \rho_a \vdash \mu_c \wedge \rho_c \rightsquigarrow (\Phi_r \wedge \rho_r)}$$

3.4 Hoare Logic for Resource Verification

Language. We provide a core strict imperative language with usual constructs, such as type declarations, method declarations, method calls, assignments, etc. to facilitate the verification for multiple front-end imperative languages. For simplicity, we choose a core language without while-loop constructs and assume a preprocessing step that applies an automatic translation into tail-recursive methods with reference-type parameters (declared by the keyword `ref`).

The pre and post conditions of a method are specified by the `requires` and `ensures` keywords, followed by logic formulas in the assertion language in Fig. 4. Resource-related assertions always appear in the method preconditions to denote resource requirements imposed on the caller for its execution. In contrast, resource assertions in the postconditions denote unspent/generated fuel returned to the caller, so that these assertions may not appear in the postconditions, depending on the analyzed resource. For example, as execution length (*i.e.*, a temporal resource) can only be consumed, it is safe and convenient to assume that the method consumes all the initially required resource; thus we can avoid the need for execution length related assertions in postconditions.

Hoare Logic. We observe that the resource consumption of each program statement is dependent on the tracked resource. As a result, the resource-aware Hoare logic needs to be adapted accordingly for each resource type. In terms of termination and non-termination reasoning, we are interested in the execution length as the tracked resource capacity. In the next section, we will construct a specific Hoare logic to reason about this resource.

4   (Non-)Termination Proofs via Resource Reasoning

For termination and non-termination reasoning, we have proposed three temporal constraints to capture: guaranteed termination Term X, guaranteed non-termination Loop and possible non-termination MayLoop, where X is a ranking function built from program variables. First, we define these constraints as resource capacity assertions, using the more general RC predicate. Next, we leverage the resource logic in Sec. 3, specialized in execution capacity, to construct a logic for termination and non-termination reasoning. A resource-based definition for the proposed temporal constraints is as follows:

Definition 4 (Temporal Constraints). *Temporal constraints are resource assertions over program execution lengths, such that* Term $X \equiv \text{RC}\langle 0_f, \varpi \rangle$, Loop $\equiv \text{RC}\langle \infty_f, \infty_f \rangle$

and MayLoop $\equiv$ RC$\langle 0_f, \infty_f \rangle$ *where* 0_f *and* ∞_f *denote the constant functions always returning* 0 *respectively* ∞. ϖ *is a function of program variables to naturals, imposing a finite upper bound on the execution length of a terminating program.*

Using the definition of resource entailments in Lemma 1, we formalize the set of valid entailments for temporal constraints below:

$$\begin{array}{ll} \text{MayLoop} \vdash \text{MayLoop} \blacktriangleright \text{MayLoop} & \quad \text{Loop} \vdash \text{Term } X \blacktriangleright \text{Loop} \\ \text{MayLoop} \vdash \text{Term } X \blacktriangleright \text{MayLoop} & \quad \text{Loop} \vdash \text{Loop} \blacktriangleright \text{MayLoop} \\ \text{MayLoop} \vdash \text{Loop} \blacktriangleright \text{MayLoop} & \quad \dfrac{\mu \Longrightarrow Y \leq_d X}{\mu \wedge \text{Term } X \vdash \text{Term } Y \blacktriangleright \text{Term } X -_d Y} \\ \text{Loop} \quad\; \vdash \text{MayLoop} \blacktriangleright \text{Loop} \end{array}$$

where $\leq_d$ and $-_d$ are the ordering and the subtraction operation on the domain of the termination measures X and Y, respectively. All other decomposition attempts, such as Term $X \vdash$ MayLoop $\blacktriangleright\_$ and Term $X \vdash$ Loop $\blacktriangleright\_$, describe unfeasible splits. Thus in those cases, the entailment fails and an error is signaled.

4.1 From Termination Measures to Execution Capacity's Finite Upper Bounds

In Defn. 4, as X denotes a termination measure, a bounded function that decreases across recursive method calls, the resource upper bound ϖ must also follow. Thus, the mapping function from X to ϖ must be an *order-embedding* denoted by embed(X). In our approach, the termination measure X is a list of arithmetic formulas over naturals since this formulation is simpler to write than a single but more complex termination measure and it can be used for a wider range of programs. In general, an order-embedding of lists of unbounded elements requires *ordinals*. However, transfinite ordinals are not suitable to model finite computational resources denoted by Term X.

By a *co-inductive* argument that every execution of a terminating method only computes finitely many different values, it follows that every non-negative element of a lexicographic termination measure applied to states of the corresponding call tree is upper-bounded. We then show that there always exists an order-embedding $\mathcal{L}$ from the codomain of a termination measure (*i.e.*, tuples of bounded naturals) to naturals, such that embed(X) = $\mathcal{L} \circ X$.

Lemma 2. *If the termination of a program can be proven by a given lexicographic termination measure, then for each call tree τ of the program, every element of the termination measure applied to the program states corresponding to the nodes in the call tree τ is bounded.*

If every element x_i, where $0 \leq i \leq n - 1$, of a lexicographic termination measure $[x_n, x_{n-1}, \ldots, x_0]$ corresponding to a given call tree τ is bounded by a constant k, we can use the base $b = k+1$ to construct a possible order-embedding function $\mathcal{D}([x_n, x_{n-1}, \ldots, x_0]) = x_n * b^n + x_{n-1} * b^{n-1} + \ldots + x_0$. The function $\mathcal{D}$ preserves the order of the given measure along every trace of τ, as stated by Lemma 3.

Lemma 3. *For all $x_n, \ldots, x_0, y_n, \ldots, y_0 \in \mathbb{N}$ such that $\forall i \in \{0..n - 1\} \cdot x_i, y_i < b$, $[x_n, \ldots, x_0] >_l [y_n, \ldots, y_0]$ iff $\mathcal{D}([x_n, \ldots, x_0]) > \mathcal{D}([y_n, \ldots, y_0])$, where $>_l$ is the lexicographic ordering.*

$$\frac{\text{CheckMin}(\Psi_1) \quad \text{CheckMin}(\Psi_2)}{\text{CheckMin}(\Psi_1 \vee \Psi_2)} \qquad \frac{\mu \vdash \rho_l = 0}{\text{CheckMin}(\mu \wedge \text{RC}\langle \rho_l, \rho_u \rangle)}$$

$$\frac{[\textbf{FV-CALL}]}{t_0 \; mn((t \; v)^*) \; (\Psi_{\text{Pre}}, \Phi_{\text{Post}}) \; \{code\} \in Prog} \qquad [\textbf{FV-RET}]$$

$$\frac{\Psi \vdash \text{RC}\langle 1, 1 \rangle \rightsquigarrow \Theta \quad \Theta \vdash \Psi_{\text{Pre}} \rightsquigarrow \Phi \quad \Psi_r = \Phi \wedge \Phi_{\text{Post}}}{\vdash \{\Psi\} \; mn(v^*) \; \{\Psi_r\}} \qquad \frac{\text{CheckMin}(\Psi)}{\vdash \{\Psi\} \, \texttt{return} \; v \; \{\Psi \wedge \text{res} = v'\}}$$

Fig. 6. Hoare Verification Rules: Method Call and Return

In general, such a bounded constant k for a call tree τ can be determined by a function $\mathcal{K}$ of initial values of the call tree's variables. Since the execution of a loop has only a single trace, the order-embedding $\mathcal{D}$, constructed from the constant k, would be enough to ensure the sufficiency of execution capacity for the loop. However, in order to give a proper estimate of the execution capacity for more complex recursion patterns, especially when the termination measures are based on the depth of recursion, we propose using a more refined embedding for a call tree, that is $\mathcal{L} = \begin{cases} \mathcal{D} & , \mathcal{N} \leq 1 \\ \mathcal{N}^{\mathcal{D}} & , \mathcal{N} > 1 \end{cases}$, where $\mathcal{N}$ is the maximum number of children for each node of the call tree.

Therefore, given the termination measure X of a terminating program, there always exists an order-embedding $\mathcal{L}$ from the codomain of X to naturals. The function $\mathcal{L}$ can be constructed from initial values of program variables and the call trees corresponding to these initial values. As a result, $\texttt{embed}(X) = \mathcal{L} \circ X$ is a function from program variables to naturals, which describes an upper bound on the number of method calls taken by any execution of the program.

4.2   Termination and Non-termination Verification

Here we elaborate on the construction of both termination and non-termination proofs based on Defn. 4 and the verification framework in Fig. 6 for tracking execution length as resource. Although execution length can be tracked at various levels of granularities, we choose to track it only at method calls (*i.e.*, as the total number of method calls) in order to simplify the verification rules and the operational semantics. In Fig. 6, we only outline the Hoare logic rules for the method call and the return statements, which are especially relevant to the verification of execution lengths as they encode the resource consumption. The Hoare rules for other constructs are standard because they do not interact with the resource of interest.

As a standard preprocessing step, we check that all predicate invariants are satisfied, including the invariants of resource constraints: the resource assertion $\text{RC}\langle \rho_l, \rho_u \rangle$ in precondition Ψ_{Pre} is consistent if $0 \leq \rho_l \leq \rho_u$, that is, for each disjunct $\mu \wedge \text{RC}\langle \rho_l, \rho_u \rangle$ of Ψ_{Pre} it follows that $\mu \vdash \rho_u \geq \rho_l \wedge \rho_l \geq 0$. We observe that the invariant check on $\texttt{Term} \; X$ requires that every element of X be non-negative to ensure a non-negative upper-bound $\mathcal{L} \circ X$, so that the execution capacity satisfies the invariant $0 \leq 0_f \leq \mathcal{L} \circ X$.

In the method call rule $[\textbf{FV-CALL}]$, the available execution capacity is first decreased by one step, denoted by $\text{RC}\langle 1, 1 \rangle$, to account the cost of method call, followed by a check that the callee's requirements are met. This check is translated into an entailment for proving the method precondition. Finally, the poststate after this method call is computed. With the help of the resource-enhanced entailment system introduced in

Sec. 3.3, both logical and resource proving are combined into one entailment, resulting in a standard-looking Hoare rule for method call.

In addition, specifically for temporal constraints, two entailments $\Psi \vdash \mathrm{RC}\langle 1, 1\rangle \rightsquigarrow \Theta$ and $\Theta \vdash \Psi_{\mathrm{Pre}} \rightsquigarrow \Phi$ can be combined into $\Psi \vdash \Psi_{\mathrm{Pre}} \rightsquigarrow \Phi$ by using a new entailment $\vdash_t$ for temporal constraints.

Definition 5 (Unit Reduction Temporal Entailments). *Given temporal constraints θ, θ_1 and θ_2, $\theta \vdash_t \theta_1 \blacktriangleright \theta_2$ iff $\forall s, h, r \cdot$ if $(s, h, r) \models \theta$ then $(s, h, r \ominus (1, 1)) \models \theta_1 \blacktriangleright \theta_2$.*

Therefore, if θ is Loop or MayLoop then $\theta \vdash_t \theta_1 \blacktriangleright \theta_2$ iff $\theta \vdash \theta_1 \blacktriangleright \theta_2$. If θ is Term X then $\mu \wedge$ Term $X \vdash_t$ Term $Y \blacktriangleright$ Term $((X -_d 1_d) -_d Y)$ if $\mu \implies Y <_d X$, where 1_d is the unit of termination measures' domain. Basically, the check $Y <_d X$ is equivalent to the check that termination measures are decreasing across recursive method calls in the traditional termination proof. By introducing the temporal entailment $\vdash_t$, we obtain a resource-based temporal logic which is related to only the temporal constraints and thus the underlying resource reasoning becomes implicit.

In the method return rule $[\text{FV–RET}]$, the CheckMin predicate, which is also defined in Fig. 6, ensures that the specified minimum computation resource has been completely consumed when the method returns. Note that if the method does not terminate, the minimum guaranteed execution length is always satisfied since the actual return point is never reached. For temporal constraints, CheckMin holds for any Term X and MayLoop as the lower bounds in their execution capacities are always 0. In non-termination cases, CheckMin($\mu \wedge$Loop) only holds when μ is unsatisfiable. This check ensures that a return statement cannot be executed/reachable from a state satisfying Loop.

We now state the soundness of this resource-aware Hoare logic as follows:

Theorem 1. *The standard Hoare rules (e.g., assignment, conditional, sequential composition) and the Hoare rules for method call and return are sound.*

Proof. The proof can be found in the technical report [28].

4.3 Flow-Insensitive Temporal Logic

Observe that the current formulation of the temporal logic with temporal constraints is *flow-sensitive* since the entailment $\theta \vdash_t \theta_1 \blacktriangleright \theta_2$ might return a residue θ_2 distinct from θ. However, with the following observations, we can formalize a *flow-insensitive* version of the temporal logic and provide a further abstraction on the resource-based framework presented so far.

First, it is possible to refine the granularity of the termination and non-termination verification by tracking only execution lengths of (mutually) recursive method calls. Second, using König's lemma [27], it is sufficient to inspect individual execution traces in the call tree for deciding just termination or non-termination, instead of tracking the total execution length of all traces in the call tree. That is, a program terminates iff every execution trace is finite; otherwise, the program is non-terminating.

Based on these observations, the tracked resource will be abstracted to capture the execution capacity required for the longest trace in the call tree, instead of the execution capacity required for the remaining program. With this, the resource (for the longest trace allowed) remains unchanged after each splitting operation, which determines the residue resource needed for subsequent method calls. Thus, for every method, we endeavor to provide a single abstract resource that is sufficient for executing a given method call and also its remaining code sequences.

Benchmarks	Programs	Term	Loop	MayLoop	PC(s)	TC(s)	Overhead (%)
Invel	59	137	81	12	14.88	15.96	6.77
AProVE	124	534	120	8	15.73	17.21	8.60
Pasta	44	219	10	3	4.95	5.79	14.51
Others	48	194	32	22	7.35	8.78	16.29
Totals/(%)	275	1084 (79.0%)	243 (17.7%)	45 (3.3%)	42.91	47.74	10.12%

Fig. 7. Termination Verification for Numerical Programs

By using this abstraction, we can obtain a formulation on temporal entailment that ensures $\theta \vdash_t \theta_1 \blacktriangleright \theta$ whereby the temporal constraint in residue is always identical to the one in the antecedent. Hence, the operator $-_d$ can be fully circumvented. Moreover, the finite upper bound ϖ used for the definition of Term X in Defn. 4 can be determined as $\varpi = \mathcal{D} \circ X$, instead of the larger $\mathcal{L} \circ X$. As a result, without any change to the Hoare rules, during a method's verification, the same initial resource capacity is used for the verification of call traces and thus facilitating a simpler verification procedure for temporal constraint. As a direct outcome of this abstraction, the temporal assertions Loop, MayLoop and Term X are now *flow-insensitive*, and therefore closer to the pure logic form, as opposed to the sub-structural form of resource logics. Note that flow-insensitive label applies to only the temporal constraints. In general, program states (*e.g.*, denoted by separation logic as the underlying logic) remain flow-sensitive since they might be changed due to changes on heap state and program variables.

5   Experiments

We have implemented the proposed termination logic into an automated verification system, called *HipTNT*. The integration of the termination logic into an existing system allows us to utilize the infrastructure that has been developed for some richer specification logics, such as separation logic, beyond a simple first-order logic. Consequently, we are able to *specify* and *verify* both termination and non-termination properties, in addition to correctness properties for a much wider class of programs, including heap-manipulating programs. In this system, the final proof obligations are automatically discharged by off-the-shelf provers, such as Z3 [16]. The expressivity of our new integrated logic is shown in the following experimental results, in which the lexicographic order is needed for about 25% of the considered programs in our experiments.

5.1   Numerical Programs

HipTNT was evaluated using a benchmark of over 200 small numerical programs selected from a variety of sources: (i) from the literature, such as [13,11], (ii) from benchmarks used by other systems (that are AProVE [19], Invel [37] and Pasta [18]) and (iii) some realistic programs, such as the Microsoft Zune's clock driver that has a leap-year non-termination bug. Most of the methods in these benchmark programs contain either terminating or non-terminating code fragments, expressed in (mutual) recursive calls or (nested) loops. To construct these benchmarks we added the novel termination specifications to the original examples from the analysis tools for termination and non-termination. We have chosen these benchmarks in order to show the usability and practicality of our approach. A comparison with these tools would be of less relevance as our proposal focuses on verifying the given specifications rather than infer them.

Fig. 7 summarizes the characteristics and the verification times for a benchmark of numerical programs. Columns 3-5 describe the number of preconditions that have been specified and successfully verified as *terminating*, *non-terminating* or *unknown*, respectively. As hoped for, the number of preconditions annotated by MayLoop occupies the smallest fragment (about 3%) of the total number of preconditions. Such MayLoop constraints were only used in some unavoidable scenarios, such as (non-)termination depends on unpredictable user input or non-deterministic assignments to variables. In contrast, the Term constraints (with the given measures) are in the majority because most of the methods are expected to be terminating, except for the Invel benchmark which focuses on mostly non-terminating programs.

Our verification system can perform both correctness and termination proofs. Column 7 (**TC**) gives the total timings (in seconds) needed to perform both termination and correctness proofs for all the programs in each row, while column 6 (**PC**) gives the timings needed for just correctness proofs. The difference in the two timings represents the small overhead needed for termination and non-termination reasoning.

5.2 Heap-Manipulating Programs

We have also conducted termination reasoning on our own benchmark of heap-based programs using various data structures, on problems under Java Bytecode categories of the Termination Competition [33] and on some medium programs taken from the SIR/Siemens test suite [17]. Due to the tight integration with the underlying logics, the task of specifying and verifying the termination properties was easy even though some of the programs use non-trivial data structures (*e.g.*, Red-Black and AVL-trees), or non-linear constraints (*e.g.*, the BigNat program, which implements infinite precision natural numbers (by linked lists) with procedures for some arithmetic operations, in addition to a fast multiplication method based on the Karatsuba algorithm). We report that the termination and expected non-termination of all programs in these benchmarks are verified successfully with a small overhead ($< 5\%$). Due to space limitation, the detailed experimental results and discussion on these benchmarks are put in [28].

6 Related Work and Conclusion

There exists a rich body of related works on automatic analysis for termination [30,8,14], non-termination [21,37,10], and both [19]. However, they consider termination and non-termination reasoning as distinct from functional correctness reasoning. Therefore, these works cannot leverage the result of functional correctness analysis to conduct more intricate (non-)termination reasoning. Recently, Brockschmidt *et al.* [9] propose a cooperation between safety and termination analysis to find sufficient supporting invariants for the construction of termination arguments but not considering non-termination. Chen *et al.* [12] introduce a similar approach for proving only non-termination. Our proposal complements these works since our aim is to construct a logic where termination and non-termination properties are directly integrated into specification logics, and thus utilize the available infrastructure on functional correctness proofs. We have achieved this, and have also successfully evaluated its applicability on a wide range of programs, covering both numerical and heap-based programs.

Related to resource verification, [4] introduces a resource logic for a low-level language. While this logic avoids the need of auxiliary counters, it redefines the semantic model of the underlying logic to track the resource consumption via logical assertions, making the proposal harder to retrofit to other logics. Moreover, this logic only targets partial correctness, so that it does not take into account infinite resource consumption.

There are some works that are based on the well-foundedness of inductive definitions of heap predicates [7,11] or user-defined quantitative functions over data structures [20] to prove termination of heap-manipulating programs. On one hand, they do not require any explicit ranking function. On the other hand, these approaches might have problems with programs like the Karatsuba multiplication method, in which the arguments of the recursive calls are not substructures of the input lists. In addition, the automated tools, such as AProVE and COSTA, cannot prove the termination of this method. In contrast, our approach is more flexible as it allows explicit termination measures, that are possibly non-linear, for proving programs' termination. These termination measures can be constructed from not only the heap structures but also the values of the data structures' elements. For example, we use the actual value of the natural presented by a linked list to bound the execution of the Karatsuba method. Moreover, we also allow non-termination to be specified and verified for these programs. We believe that relatively complex examples, such as the Karatsuba method, highlight the benefits of our approach, which trades a lower level of automation but gains additional power.

The comparison of our approach with the other specification languages, *i.e.*. Dafny [31], JML [29], etc., has been discussed in Sec. 1. Another closely related work to ours is that of Nakata and Uustalu [34]. In this work, a Hoare logic for reasoning about non-termination of simple While programs (without method calls) was introduced. The logic is based on a trace-based semantics, in which the infiniteness of non-terminating traces is defined by coinduction. However, induction is still needed to define the finiteness of traces. In contrast, with resources, we can unify the semantics of the proposed termination and non-termination temporal constraints and allow the Hoare logic for functional correctness to be enhanced for termination and non-termination reasoning with minor changes. Moreover, our logic allows interprocedural verification in a modular fashion.

Conclusion. Termination reasoning has been intensively studied in the past, but it remains a challenge for the technology developed there to keep up with improvements to specification logic infrastructure, and vice versa. We propose an approach that would combine the two areas more closely together, through a tightly coupled union. Our unique contribution is to embed both termination and non-termination reasoning directly into specification logics, and to do so with the help of temporal entailment. We also show how its properties can be captured by a resource logic based on execution capacity, and how it could be abstracted into a flow-insensitive temporal logic. We believe this approach would have benefits. Its expressiveness is immediately enhanced by any improvement to the underlying logics. It can also benefit from infrastructures that have been developed for the underlying logics, including those that are related to program analysis. In particular we believe that a possible future avenue for investigation is to use the safety specifications as a basis for termination specification inference. Last, but not least, it has placed termination and non-termination reasoning as a first-class concept, much like what was originally envisioned by Hoare's logic for total correctness.

Acknowledgement. This work was supported by MoE/NUS research project R-252-000-469-112.

References

1. Abel, A.: Type-based termination of generic programs. SCP 74(8) (2009)
2. Ahrendt, W., Baar, T., Beckert, B., Bubel, R., Giese, M., Hähnle, R., Menzel, W., Mostowski, W., Roth, A., Schlager, S., Schmitt, P.H.: The KeY tool. SSM 4 (2005)
3. Albert, E., Arenas, P., Genaim, S., Puebla, G., Zanardini, D.: COSTA: Design and Implementation of a Cost and Termination Analyzer for Java Bytecode. In: de Boer, F.S., Bonsangue, M.M., Graf, S., de Roever, W.-P. (eds.) FMCO 2007. LNCS, vol. 5382, pp. 113–132. Springer, Heidelberg (2008)
4. Aspinall, D., Beringer, L., Hofmann, M., Loidl, H.-W., Momigliano, A.: A program logic for resources. TCS 389(3) (2007)
5. Atkey, R.: Amortised resource analysis with separation logic. LMCS 7(2) (2011)
6. Baudin, P., Cuoq, P., Filliâtre, J.-C., Marché, C., Monate, B., Moy, Y., Prevosto, V.: ACSL: ANSI/ISO C Specification Language Version 1.8. (2013), http://frama-c.com/acsl.html
7. Berdine, J., Cook, B., Distefano, D., O'Hearn, P.W.: Automatic termination proofs for programs with shape-shifting heaps. In: Ball, T., Jones, R.B. (eds.) CAV 2006. LNCS, vol. 4144, pp. 386–400. Springer, Heidelberg (2006)
8. Bradley, A.R., Manna, Z., Sipma, H.B.: The polyranking principle. In: Caires, L., Italiano, G.F., Monteiro, L., Palamidessi, C., Yung, M. (eds.) ICALP 2005. LNCS, vol. 3580, pp. 1349–1361. Springer, Heidelberg (2005)
9. Brockschmidt, M., Cook, B., Fuhs, C.: Better termination proving through cooperation. In: Sharygina, N., Veith, H. (eds.) CAV 2013. LNCS, vol. 8044, pp. 413–429. Springer, Heidelberg (2013)
10. Brockschmidt, M., Ströder, T., Otto, C., Giesl, J.: Automated detection of non-termination and NullPointerExceptions for java bytecode. In: Beckert, B., Damiani, F., Gurov, D. (eds.) FoVeOOS 2011. LNCS, vol. 7421, pp. 123–141. Springer, Heidelberg (2012)
11. Brotherston, J., Bornat, R., Calcagno, C.: Cyclic proofs of program termination in separation logic. In: POPL (2008)
12. Chen, H.-Y., Cook, B., Fuhs, C., Nimkar, K., O'Hearn, P.: Proving nontermination via safety. In: Ábrahám, E., Havelund, K. (eds.) TACAS 2014 (ETAPS). LNCS, vol. 8413, pp. 156–171. Springer, Heidelberg (2014)
13. Cook, B., Gulwani, S., Lev-Ami, T., Rybalchenko, A., Sagiv, M.: Proving conditional termination. In: Gupta, A., Malik, S. (eds.) CAV 2008. LNCS, vol. 5123, pp. 328–340. Springer, Heidelberg (2008)
14. Cook, B., Podelski, A., Rybalchenko, A.: Termination proofs for systems code. In: PLDI (2006)
15. Cuoq, P., Kirchner, F., Kosmatov, N., Prevosto, V., Signoles, J., Yakobowski, B.: Frama-C. In: Eleftherakis, G., Hinchey, M., Holcombe, M. (eds.) SEFM 2012. LNCS, vol. 7504, pp. 233–247. Springer, Heidelberg (2012)
16. de Moura, L., Bjørner, N.S.: Z3: An Efficient SMT Solver. In: Ramakrishnan, C.R., Rehof, J. (eds.) TACAS 2008. LNCS, vol. 4963, pp. 337–340. Springer, Heidelberg (2008)
17. Do, H., Elbaum, S.G., Rothermel, G.: Supporting Controlled Experimentation with Testing Techniques: An Infrastructure and its Potential Impact. In: ESE, vol. 10 (2005)

18. Falke, S., Kapur, D.: A term rewriting approach to the automated termination analysis of imperative programs. In: Schmidt, R.A. (ed.) CADE-22. LNCS, vol. 5663, pp. 277–293. Springer, Heidelberg (2009)
19. Giesl, J., Schneider-Kamp, P., Thiemann, R.: aProVE 1.2: automatic termination proofs in the dependency pair framework. In: Furbach, U., Shankar, N. (eds.) IJCAR 2006. LNCS (LNAI), vol. 4130, pp. 281–286. Springer, Heidelberg (2006)
20. Gulwani, S., Mehra, K.K., Chilimbi, T.: Speed: Precise and efficient static estimation of program computational complexity. In: POPL (2009)
21. Gupta, A., Henzinger, T.A., Majumdar, R., Rybalchenko, A., Xu, R.-G.: Proving non-termination. In: POPL (2008)
22. Hehner, E.C.R.: Termination is timing. In: van de Snepscheut, J.L.A. (ed.) MPC 1989. LNCS, vol. 375, pp. 36–47. Springer, Heidelberg (1989)
23. Hehner, E.C.R.: Specifications, programs, and total correctness. SCP 34(3) (1999)
24. Hoare, C.A.R., He, J.: Unifying Theories of Programming. Prentice-Hall (1998)
25. Hoffmann, J., Hofmann, M.: Amortized resource analysis with polynomial potential. In: Gordon, A.D. (ed.) ESOP 2010. LNCS, vol. 6012, pp. 287–306. Springer, Heidelberg (2010)
26. Jones, C.B.: Balancing expressiveness in formal approaches to concurrency (2013)
27. Kleene, S.: Mathematical logic. Wiley (1967)
28. Le, T.C., Gherghina, C., Hobor, A., Chin, W.-N.: A Resource-Based Logic for Termination and Non-Termination Proofs, Technical Report (2014),
    http://loris-7.ddns.comp.nus.edu.sg/~project/hiptnt/HipTNT.pdf
29. Leavens, G.T., Baker, A.L., Ruby, C.: Preliminary design of JML: A behavioral interface specification language for Java. SIGSOFT Softw. Eng. Notes 31(3), 1–38 (2006)
30. Lee, C.S., Jones, N.D., Ben-Amram, A.M.: The size-change principle for program termination. In: POPL (2001)
31. Leino, K.R.M.: Dafny: An automatic program verifier for functional correctness. In: Clarke, E.M., Voronkov, A. (eds.) LPAR-16 2010. LNCS, vol. 6355, pp. 348–370. Springer, Heidelberg (2010)
32. Magill, S., Tsai, M.-H., Lee, P., Tsay, Y.-K.: Automatic numeric abstractions for heap-manipulating programs. In: POPL (2010)
33. Marché, C., Zantema, H.: The termination competition. In: Baader, F. (ed.) RTA 2007. LNCS, vol. 4533, pp. 303–313. Springer, Heidelberg (2007)
34. Nakata, K., Uustalu, T.: A hoare logic for the coinductive trace-based big-step semantics of while. In: Gordon, A.D. (ed.) ESOP 2010. LNCS, vol. 6012, pp. 488–506. Springer, Heidelberg (2010)
35. Nguyen, H.H., David, C., Qin, S.C., Chin, W.-N.: Automated Verification of Shape and Size Properties Via Separation Logic. In: Cook, B., Podelski, A. (eds.) VMCAI 2007. LNCS, vol. 4349, pp. 251–266. Springer, Heidelberg (2007)
36. Reynolds, J.: Separation Logic: A Logic for Shared Mutable Data Structures. In: LICS (2002)
37. Velroyen, H., Rümmer, P.: Non-termination checking for imperative programs. In: Beckert, B., Hähnle, R. (eds.) TAP 2008. LNCS, vol. 4966, pp. 154–170. Springer, Heidelberg (2008)
38. Xi, H.: Dependent Types for Program Termination Verification. In: LICS (2001)

Practical Analysis Framework for Software-Based Attestation Scheme

Li Li[1], Hong Hu[1], Jun Sun[2], Yang Liu[3], and Jin Song Dong[1]

[1] National University of Singapore, Singapore
[2] Singapore University of Technology and Design, Singapore
[3] Nanyang Technological University, Singapore

Abstract. An increasing number of "smart" embedded devices are employed in our living environment nowadays. Unlike traditional computer systems, these devices are often physically accessible to the attackers. It is therefore almost impossible to guarantee that they are un-compromised, i.e., that indeed the devices are executing the intended software. In such a context, software-based attestation is deemed as a promising solution to validate their software integrity. It guarantees that the software running on the embedded devices are un-compromised without any hardware support. However, designing software-based attestation protocols are shown to be error-prone. In this work, we develop a framework for design and analysis of software-based attestation protocols. We first propose a generic attestation scheme that captures most existing software-based attestation protocols. After formalizing the security criteria for the generic scheme, we apply our analysis framework to several well-known software-based attestation protocols and report various potential vulnerabilities. To the best of our knowledge, this is the first practical analysis framework for software-based attestation protocols.

1 Introduction

"Smart" sensory embedded devices are getting more and more popular nowadays. They are frequently used for temperature measurement, fire detection, water saving, etc. In the near future, they are expected to be ubiquitous. However, their wide adoption poses threats to our safety and privacy as well. Unlike traditional computer systems, these devices are often physically accessible to the attackers and it is almost impossible to guarantee that they are un-compromised, i.e., that indeed the devices are executing the intended software. Effective techniques for verifying and validating the embedded devices against malicious adversary becomes increasingly important and urgent. Traditional hardware-based attestation [1,2,3,4] is cost-ineffective in such a context. Thus, software-based attestation [5,6,7], which aims to function without any dedicated security hardware, is deemed as a promising solution for verifying the integrity of these massive, inexpensive, and resource constrained devices.

Software-based attestation is based on the challenge-response paradigm between the trusted verifier and the potentially compromised prover (the embedded device). It typically works as follows. The verifier first sends a random challenge to the prover and asks the prover to generate a checksum for its memory state based on the challenge. Since the prover's computing and memory resources are designed to be fully utilized

S. Merz and J. Pang (Eds.): ICFEM 2014, LNCS 8829, pp. 284–299, 2014.

in the attestation, if the memory is tampered by the adversary, the prover needs to take extra time to compute the correct checksum. We further assume that the verifier knows the expected memory state of the prover. He thus can compute the same checksum and compare it with the one received from the prover. By exploiting the fact that the prover is resource constrained, software-based attestation ensures that the prover can return the correct response in time only if it is genuine. On the other hand, whenever the prover fails to reply in time or returns an incorrect checksum, it is highly likely compromised.

The software-based attestation protocol design is challenging and error-prone [8,9]. Hence, in this work, we propose an analysis framework for software-based attestation that can be easily adopted in practice. First, our framework provides a parameterized generic software-based attestation scheme that captures most existing software-based attestation protocols. The adversary modeled in this work can not only compromise the prover before the attestation, but also communicate with the compromised prover during the attestation. We then formalize the security criteria for the generic scheme based on the knowledge of network latency (which is important as timing is essential here) and adversary model. Since the real software-based attestation protocols are instances of the generic scheme, these criteria thus naturally should be hold in the real protocols as well. Hence, we apply our analysis framework to three well-known software-based attestation schemes, i.e., SWATT [5], SCUBA [7] and VIPER [10], and find four potential vulnerabilities that have not been reported before. As far as we know, this is the first framework that can give practical analysis to real software-based attestation protocols.

2   Generic Specification for Software-Based Attestation

We start with defining a generic software-based attestation scheme which captures most existing software-based attestation protocols. The idea is that analysis results based on the generic schema can be extended to concrete protocols readily as we show in later sections. The generic software-based attestation scheme involves three parties, i.e., the trusted verifier V, the prover (the embedded device) P and the adversary A. We denote the genuine prover and the compromised prover as P_g and P_c respectively. In this section, we first present the system model, including the system architecture, the security property and the threat model. Then we propose a generic software-based attestation scheme between the trusted verifier V and the genuine prover P_g based on our system.

2.1   System Overview

Software-based attestation is proposed to verify the resource constrained embedded devices without using any security hardware (e.g., TPMs [11]). Before presenting the details of the generic attestation scheme, we first describe the system model employed in this work. The attestation procedure is conducted between a trusted verifier V and a prover P over the network. We explicitly consider the network round-trip time (RTT).

The architecture of the verifier V and the prover P considered in this work are depicted as follows. P consists of a computing processor, several registers and a memory M. The data memory M_d and the program memory M_p are two different memory space that should be attested in M. Specifically, M_d stores the runtime data (e.g., stack information, data collected from the environment) that are unpredictable to $\mathcal{V}$, hence its content cannot be attested directly in the attestation procedure. M_p stores the program code which is known to $\mathcal{V}$. The attestation routine *verif* on the prover side is pre-installed in M_p before the attestation starts. In general, the size of M_d could be 0 when the attestation for the data memory is not required. Notice that some memory can be excluded from the attestation in some specific attestation protocols [12,7,10], and thus $M_d + M_p$ may not equal to M. Meanwhile, $\mathcal{V}$ is a powerful base station who can simulate the execution of $\mathcal{P}$. When $\mathcal{V}$ has the image of both M_d and M_p in $\mathcal{P}$, $\mathcal{V}$ can compute the memory checksum based on the image.

During the attestation, $\mathcal{P}$'s data memory M_d will be first overwritten into a state that is known to $\mathcal{V}$. The attestation then aims at verifying whether $\mathcal{P}$ has a genuine state for both M_d and M_p as $\mathcal{V}$ expected. Let $State(\mathcal{P})$ be the memory state of $M_d + M_p$ in the prover $\mathcal{P}$. When $State(\mathcal{P})$ is known to $\mathcal{V}$, the attestation can be modeled by a game between the verifier $\mathcal{V}$ and the prover $\mathcal{P}$. In the game, $\mathcal{V}$ first sends a random challenge to $\mathcal{P}$, and then $\mathcal{P}$ picks a checksum reply based on the challenge. The prover $\mathcal{P}$ wins if the used time is less than some threshold and the checksum is correct, otherwise $\mathcal{P}$ loses the game. We denote the percentage of differences between two memory states S and S' as $\lambda(S, S')$ and the winning probability of $\mathcal{P}$ as $\mathbb{P}_w(\mathcal{L}, \mathcal{P})$, where $\mathcal{L}$ denotes the system and its configurations. We define an attestation protocol as *correct* if $\mathbb{P}_w(\mathcal{L}, \mathcal{P}_g) = 1$, which means that the genuine prover $\mathcal{P}_g$ can always win. On the other hand, when μ is the least memory proportion that should be modified in the compromised prover $\mathcal{P}_c$ to perform a meaningful attack, we define an attestation protocol as $\langle \varepsilon, \mu \rangle$-*secure* if $\forall \mathcal{P}_c, \lambda(State(\mathcal{P}_c), State(\mathcal{P}_g)) \geq \mu > 0 \Rightarrow \mathbb{P}_w(\mathcal{L}, \mathcal{P}_c) \leq \varepsilon$, which means that any prover who needs to overwrite at least μ percentage of the attested memory has the winning probability of no more than ε. In the attestation, the adversary wins if and only if he can keep the malicious code in the attested memory after the attestation. However, software-based attestation does not guarantee that the device is unmodified before the attestation.

The adversary $\mathcal{A}$'s capability is specified with two phases. Before the attestation begins, $\mathcal{A}$ can use unlimited resources to reprogram the memory in $\mathcal{P}_c$. However, $\mathcal{A}$ cannot change the physical hardware and the network infrastructure, so $\mathcal{P}_c$'s memory storage, computing power and network latency are fixed. Once the attestation starts, $\mathcal{A}$ cannot modify $\mathcal{P}_c$'s memory content anymore. Nevertheless, $\mathcal{A}$ can communicate with $\mathcal{P}_c$ over the network and compute with unlimited resources.

Notations. The notations used in this paper are listed as follows. We write X, Y, Z to denote sets and x, y, z to denote elements in the sets. $f(x : X, y : Y) \to z : Z$ represents a function f that maps the tuple of two elements x, y to the element z. Let n be a natural number. X^n stands for the concatenation of n elements in X. $X \times Y$ is the Cartesian product of X and Y. Let $\mathbb{D}$ be a probabilistic distribution over set X. $x \hookleftarrow \mathbb{D} \vdash X$ means assigning an element of X to x according to $\mathbb{D}$. $[n \ldots m]$ represents the integers from n to m. $[n, m]$ stands for the real numbers from n to m. $max_{x,y}\{f(x, y)\}$ stands for the maximum value of $f(x, y)$ for any x and y. $Pr[x]$ denotes the probability of x.

Checksum Computation $comp(S_a, g_0, r_0)$
S_a is the memory state of $\mathcal{P}$ under attestation.
g_0 is the address generator seed.
r_0 is the checksum response seed.
for i **in** $[1 \ldots n]$ **do**
$\quad g_i = Gen(g_{i-1});$
$\quad a_i = Addr(g_i);$
$\quad c_i = Read(S_a, a_i);$
$\quad r_i = Chk(r_{i-1}, c_i);$
end
return $r_n;$

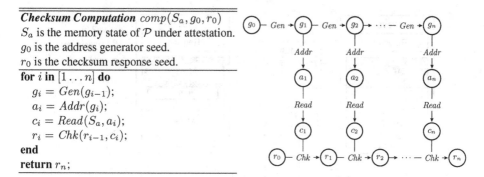

Fig. 1. Checksum Computation

2.2 Generic Attestation Scheme

In this section, we propose a generic specification for software-based attestation scheme that captures most existing software-based attestation protocols. The specification is described in two parts. First, given a memory state $S_a = State(\mathcal{P})$ of both M_d and M_p, we introduce the *checksum computation routine* that compute the memory checksum as shown in Figure 1. Then, we illustrate the *generic software-based attestation scheme* which first securely erases the data memory M_d and then attests the whole memory $M_d + M_p$ with the *checksum computation routine*.

The Checksum Computation Routine $comp(S_a, g_0, r_0)$ aims at computing the unforgeable checksum for memory state S_a based on the initial address generator g_0 and initial memory checksum r_0. It iteratively computes the address generator g_i, the memory address a_i, the memory content c_i and the checksum response r_i for $i \in [1 \ldots n]$ as shown in Figure 1. The four functions used in the generic scheme are illustrated as follows. In the following paper, l_g, l_a, l_c and l_r represent lengths of g_i, a_i, c_i and r_i respectively.

- $Gen(g_{i-1} : \{0,1\}^{l_g}) \rightarrow g_i : \{0,1\}^{l_g}$ computes the generator g_i of the memory addresses in a random manner incrementally.
- $Addr(g_i : \{0,1\}^{l_g}) \rightarrow a_i : \{0,1\}^{l_a}$ converts the random generator g_i to the memory address a_i.
- $Read(S_a : \{0,1\}^{l_a} \times \{0,1\}^{l_c}, a_i : \{0,1\}^{l_a}) \rightarrow c_i : \{0,1\}^{l_c}$ reads the memory content c_i located at the address a_i in S_a.
- $Chk(r_{i-1} : \{0,1\}^{l_r}, c_i : \{0,1\}^{l_c}) \rightarrow r_i\{0,1\}^{l_r}$ updates the last checksum response r_{i-1} with the memory content c_i to the new checksum r_i.

The Generic Software-Based Attestation Scheme is shown in Figure 2. The functions used in the figure are illustrated as follows. $rand(x)$ generates a random bitstring and stores it into x. $fill(M, S)$ fills the memory M with state S. $Gen_0(o, g_0)$ and $Chk_0(o, r_0)$ derive the initial values for the generator and the checksum from the challenge o and store them into g_0 and r_0 respectively. $comp(S_a, g_0, r_0)$ illustrated previously computes the checksum for memory state S_a with the generator seed g_0 and

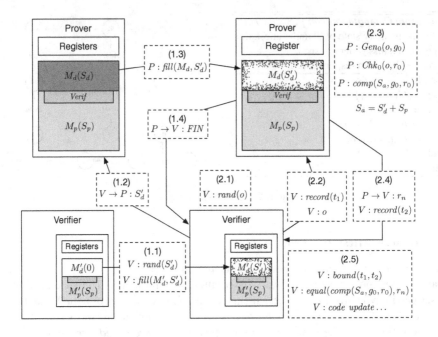

Fig. 2. Generic Software-based Attestation Scheme

the response seed r_0. $record(t)$ records the current time into t. $bound(t_1, t_2)$ checks whether $t_2 - t_1$ is smaller than a time bound. $equal(x, y)$ checks if x and y are equivalent. $I : op$ means that I conducts the operation op. $I_1 \rightarrow I_2 : m$ means that I_1 sends the message m to I_2. The generic software-based attestation scheme proposed in this work is divided into two phases as shown in Figure 2.

Phase 1. Secure Erasure overwrites the data memory M_d with random noise. Initially, $\mathcal{P}$'s data memory image M'_d in $\mathcal{V}$ are filled with 0, while M_d in $\mathcal{P}$ has the memory state S_d consisting of information generated at runtime. At the end of this phase, $\mathcal{P}$ and $\mathcal{P}$'s image in $\mathcal{V}$ have the same memory state S'_d filled with random noise.

1. When $\mathcal{V}$ wants to start the attestation, it first overwrites $\mathcal{P}$'s data memory image M'_d in $\mathcal{V}$ to a random state S'_d, which is generated by the $rand(S'_d)$ function.
2. $\mathcal{V}$ sends S'_d to $\mathcal{P}$ and asks $\mathcal{P}$ to overwrite its M_d with S'_d.
3. $\mathcal{P}$ accepts $\mathcal{V}$'s requests and updates his M_d with S'_d. In fact, the last step (1.2) and this step (1.3) can be streamlined. Whenever $\mathcal{P}$ receives a value from $\mathcal{V}$, he writes it into the corresponding data memory location.
4. When M_d is filled with S'_d, $\mathcal{P}$ sends a FIN signal to start the second phase.

Phase 2. Checksum Computation aims at attesting both M_d and M_p in $\mathcal{P}$ and discovering memory modification with overwhelming probability. When the first phase is finished, $\mathcal{V}$ can run the second phase for multiple times consecutively. Upon the beginning of the second phase, $\mathcal{V}$ knows the memory state $S_a = State(\mathcal{P})$.

1. $\mathcal{V}$ first picks a random challenge o.

2. V sends o to P and asks P to compute the checksum for his memory state $S_a = S_p + S'_d$. V also records the time t_1 when the request is sent.
3. After P derives the initial address generator g_0 and the initial checksum response r_0 from the challenge o, he computes the checksum over the memory state S_a with $comp(S_a, g_0, r_0)$ illustrated in Figure 1.
4. As soon as the checksum computation routine is finished, P sends the checksum r_n back to V. V again records the time t_2 when r_n is received.
5. Once V receives r_n from P, he checks two conditions: (1) whether the checksum is received within the timing threshold $\{bound(t_1, t_2) = true\}$ and (2) whether the checksum is correct $\{equal(comp(S_a, g_0, r_0), r_n) = true\}$. If both of the conditions are satisfied, P is trusted as genuine and V will update P's unattested memory. Otherwise, P is deemed as compromised.

Assumptions. In order to guarantee the correctness of the protocol, we make the following assumptions. First, P either has the attestation procedure *verif* pre-deployed in its program memory M_p or can download it into a pre-allocated memory space in M_p at runtime before the attestation starts. Second, V knows the exact memory image of M_p in P. M_d and M_p share the same address space. Third, the attestation procedure *verif* implemented in P is optimal in terms of execution speed. Fourth, S'_d and o are unpredictable to the prover. Fifth, the cryptographic primitives used in the attestation procedure are perfect. This assumption does not reduce the security offered by our framework to the real applications. We can update the attestation procedure with the state-of-the-art cryptographic implementations that are unbreakable at the moment. For instance, when a hash function is needed in the attestation, we use *SHA-2* or *SHA-3* that are safe for the time being. Sixth, the adversary cannot personate the prover and communicate with the verifier directly, which means that the verifier is connected to the prover via a controllable channel during the attestation, e.g., a *bus* used in [10]. When the adversary can personate the prover, the software-based attestation protocol is trivially broken because the adversary can answer the challenge for the prover.

3   Security Criteria Formalization

In this section, we introduce several attack scenarios. Based on the attacks, we formalize the security criteria for the generic attestation scheme. When the compromised prover P_c computes the checksum by itself, we need to discuss two cases: (1) the checksum is computed with the checksum computation routine at runtime, or (2) the checksum is pre-computed. In the first case, when the memory and the registers are fully utilized as shown in Section 3.1, we measure the winning probability of P_c who trades computation power for memory space (*memory recovering attack*) in Section 3.2. In the second case, we discuss the scenario where P_c stores the pre-computed challenge-response pairs in the its memory (*challenge buffering attack*) in Section 3.3. On the other hand, when P_c does not compute the checksum by itself, it can ask A to compute the checksum (*proxy attack*) as introduced in Section 3.4. When the memory and the registers are fully attested, since the above three attack methods are orthogonal, the winning probability of the compromised prover $\mathbb{P}_w(\mathcal{L}, P_c)$ then can be calculated by the most effective attack among them. Some used notations are summarized in Table 1.

Table 1. Notation Summary

Name	Explanation	Size
$M_d(S_d)$	Data memory M_d filled with memory image state S_d	m_d unit
$M_p(S_p)$	Program memory M_p filled with memory image state S_p	m_p unit
$M(S)$	Overall memory M filled with memory image state S	m unit [a]
o	The challenge sent from $\mathcal{V}$ to $\mathcal{P}$	l_o bit
g_i	Address generators for $i \in [0 \ldots n]$	l_g bit
a_i	Memory addresses for $i \in [0 \ldots n]$	l_a bit
c_i	Memory contents for $i \in [0 \ldots n]$	l_c bit
r_i	Checksum responses for $i \in [0 \ldots n]$	l_r bit
$T_{\mathcal{V}}^{min}, T_{\mathcal{V}}^{max}$	Network RTT between $\mathcal{V}$ and $\mathcal{P}_g$ varies from d_g^{min} to d_g^{max}	-
$T_{\mathcal{A}}^{min}, T_{\mathcal{A}}^{max}$	Network RTT between $\mathcal{A}$ and $\mathcal{P}_c$ varies from d_c^{min} to d_c^{max}	-
$d_{Gen}, d_{Addr}, d_{Read}, d_{Chk}$	Computation time for $Gen, Addr, Read$ and Chk resp.	-
d_g	The time needed by $\mathcal{P}_g$ to compute the memory checksum	-
d_{th}	The timing threshold on the verifier side	-
n	The number of iterations in a single checksum computation	-
k	The number of consecutive checksum computation (Phase 2)	-
u	The number of registers used to store the checksum	-

[a] m may not equal to $m_d + m_p$ when some memory is left unattested.

3.1 Full Utilization of Memory and Registers

In the checksum computation routine, the memory are accessed in a random manner which is unpredictable for the prover before the attestation. Whenever the attested memory is tampered, the malicious prover thus need to take extra time to recover the original memory. In order to prevent the malicious prover from cheating, every memory address should be accessible in the checksum computation. Additionally, the registers should be fully occupied as well. In this section, we formalize several design principles to ensure fully utilization of the memory and registers in the checksum computation routine.

Choosing Random Function. During the checksum computation, Gen is a random function from l_g bits to l_g bits, and $Addr$ converts the l_g bit generators to the l_a bit addresses. Thus, we can take the concatenation of Gen and $Addr$ as a random function from l_g bits to l_a bits. Since all possible addresses should be accessible when the generators are traversed, proper configuration of the random function in the attestation scheme becomes non-trivial. We discuss two kinds of randomization functions in this work, i.e., the *hash oracle* and the *encryption oracle*.

The *hash oracle* receives a bit-string as input and returns a corresponding random bit-string as output. Since every hash output is computed independently, according to the *coupon collector's problem*, the expected number of independent runs to cover all possible output values grows as $\Theta(t \cdot log(t))$ where t is the number of possible output values. In other words, if the addresses (a_i) and the generators (g_i) have the same length, it is very likely that some memory addresses are uncovered. For instance, when the hash function *SHA-2* is used and both of the generator and the memory address have the same length of 32bit, only 64% of the addresses can be covered on average when the generators are traversed in our experiments. By enumerating all possible generators in the preparation phase, the adversary may find sufficient *uncovered* addresses and use them to store the malicious code. As a consequence, when hash oracle is used in the attestation protocols, the number of generators should be much larger than the number of addresses. By applying the tail estimate to the *coupon collector's problem*, we can calculate the probability lower-bound of covering all addresses under attestation as $1 - (m_d + m_p)^{1-2^{l_g}/((m_d+m_p)\cdot log(m_d+m_p))}$.

On the other hand, the *encryption oracle* can be used to generate random numbers as well by revealing the encryption key to the public. Since the encryption oracle is bijective, all of the memory addresses should be covered in the generator traversal when the generator length is not less than the address length. As a result, the *encryption oracle* becomes very suitable for the random number generation in software-based attestation. Two heavily used implementations of the encryption oracle in the software-based attestation protocols are the stream cipher RC4 and the T-function [13]. RC4 is chosen as the PRNG in SWATT [5] because of its extreme efficiency and compact implementation in the embedded devices. Meanwhile, T-function can produce a single cycle, which ensures the traversal of generators. Thus, it is employed in ICE scheme proposed in ICUBA [7]. A widely used T-function is $x \leftarrow x + (x^2 \vee 5)$ where $\vee$ is the bitwise *or* operator.

Full Address Coverage at Runtime. Even though the addresses can be fully covered in the generator traversal, the actual address coverage is also related to the number of addresses generated at the runtime, which is decided by the number n in the checksum computation routine (Figure 2) and the repeat time k of the consecutive checksum computation (Phase 2). According to the *coupon collector's problem*, in order to fully traverse the whole memory space in the attestation procedure, the minimal number of memory access $n \cdot k$ should satisfy

$$Pr[n \cdot k > c \cdot (m_d + m_p) \cdot log(m_d + m_p)] \leq (m_d + m_p)^{1-c}. \qquad (1)$$

Full Register Occupation. According to several existing works [5,7,10], the registers in $\mathcal{P}$ are frequently used to store the checksum results. During every iteration in the checksum computation, one of them gets updated to a new value. When any register is unused in the attestation, the malicious prover can exploit it to conduct attacks. Thus, all the registers should be occupied. Moreover, the registers should be chosen in a random order so the malicious prover cannot predict which one is used next. Let the total number of registers used for storing the checksum be u. According to the *coupon collector's problem*, the probability of covering all registers in the checksum computation is lower-bounded by $1 - u^{1-n/(u\cdot log(u))}$.

3.2 $\mathcal{P}_c$ Follow Checksum Computation Routine: Memory Recovering Attack

Given a genuine prover $\mathcal{P}_g$ with the memory state S_g and a compromised prover $\mathcal{P}_c$ with the memory state S_c, the probability of distinguishing their states with a single memory access depends on two factors. The first factor is the percentage of the differences between S_g and S_c, which could be defined as $\lambda(S_g, S_c) = Pr[Read(S_g, a) \neq Read(S_c, a)|a \in \{0,1\}^{l_a}]$. When $\lambda(S_g, S_c)$ is sufficiently large, we can easily detect the modifications in the memory. The second factor is related to the memory content bias in $\mathcal{P}_g$. For instance, the program in $\mathcal{P}_g$ usually contains a large amount of duplicated assembly code such as *mov, jmp, call, cmp, nop*, etc. These assembly code can be approximated with high probability. As a consequence, the compromised prover can overwrite the biased memory content into malicious code and recover the original content using a recovering algorithm $\mathcal{C}$ with high probability. Assume the overwriting algorithm is $\mathcal{W}$, the minimal overwriting potion is μ, and memory recovering time $d_{\mathcal{C}}$ is no more than $\delta \cdot d_{Read}$ as required, we could calculate the optimal success probability of the memory recovery as

$$\mathbb{P}_m(S, \mu, \delta) = max_{\mathcal{C}, \mathcal{W}}\{Pr[Read(S, a) = \mathcal{C}(\mathcal{W}(S), a)$$
$$| a \in \{0, 1\}^{l_a}]|\ \delta \cdot d_{Read} \geq d_{\mathcal{C}} \wedge \lambda(S, \mathcal{W}(S)) \geq \mu\}$$

for any recovering algorithm $\mathcal{C}$ and overwriting algorithm $\mathcal{W}$. δ is the allowed timing overhead for the recovering algorithm comparing with the *Read* operation. We will discuss more about δ in Section 3.4. When $\delta \geq 1$, we can always implement the recovering algorithm $\mathcal{C}$ for any S as $\mathcal{C}(S, a) = Read(S, a)$, so $\mathbb{P}_m(S, \mu, \delta) \geq 1 - \mu$.

Since $\mathcal{P}_c$ needs to recover the memory content for n times in the checksum computation routine, he can compute the correct checksum if either the memory is recovered successfully for every iteration or the computed checksum collides with the correct one. So overall success probability for $\mathcal{P}_c$ is $\mathbb{P}_m^n(S, \mu, \delta) + (1 - \mathbb{P}_m^n(S, \mu, \delta)) \cdot 2^{-l_r}$. As can be seen from the formula, the success probability is lower-bounded by 2^{-l_r}. So increasing n becomes less significant when n becomes larger. As a consequence, we can define a threshold η for the potential probability increase and then give a lower-bound to the n used in the checksum computation.

$$\mathbb{P}_m^n(S, \mu, \delta) \cdot (1 - 2^{-l_r}) \leq \eta \quad \Longrightarrow \quad n \geq \frac{log(\eta) - log(1 - 2^{-l_r})}{log(\mathbb{P}_m(S, \mu, \delta))} \qquad (2)$$

In this work, we suggest to set $\eta = 2^{-l_r}$ which is the success probability's lower-bound. Additionally, we recommend the attestation protocols to set n as the lower-bound given in formula (2) for efficiency and conduct the checksum computation phase (Phase 2) for multiple times to give better security guarantee.

Full Randomization of Data Memory. In the first phase of the generic attestation scheme, $\mathcal{V}$ asks $\mathcal{P}$ to overwrite its data memory with S_d' filled with noise. The unpredictability of S_d' enforces $\mathcal{P}$ to erase its data memory completely. A similar design is taken in [14], but its S_d' is generated by $\mathcal{P}$ using a PRNG seeded by a challenge sent from $\mathcal{V}$. As we discussed above, the recovering algorithm can use the PRNG to generate the memory state with the received challenge at runtime, so $\mathcal{P}_c$ can trade the computation time for memory space. As a result, $\mathcal{P}_c$ can keep the malicious code in its memory, but still produce a valid checksum. In Section 3.4, we show that the checksum computation can have overhead to a degree, so this attack is practical. We thus emphasize that S_d' should be fully randomized by $\mathcal{V}$.

3.3 $\mathcal{P}_c$ Pre-compute Checksum: Challenge Buffering Attack

The attestation scheme is trivially vulnerable to challenge buffering attack that stores the challenge-response pairs directly in the memory. Upon receiving a particular challenge from $\mathcal{V}$, $\mathcal{P}_c$ looks for the corresponding checksum from its memory without computation. Since S'_d and o are received in the attestation procedure, the challenge-response stored in the memory is the tuple $\langle S'_d, o, r_n \rangle$ which has the length of $m_d \cdot l_c + l_o + l_r$. Thus, the memory can hold $m \cdot l_c / (m_d \cdot l_c + l_o + l_r)$ records at most. Additionally, we have $2^{m_d \cdot l_c + l_o}$ different receivable values. When $\mathcal{P}_c$ cannot find the record, he can choose a random response from $\{0, 1\}^{l_r}$. As a consequence, the probability of computing the correct response with challenge buffering attack method for $\mathcal{P}_c$ can be expressed as follows.

$$\mathbb{P}_b(l_o, l_c, l_r, m_d, m) = b + \frac{1-b}{2^{l_r}} \text{ where } b = \frac{m \cdot l_c}{(m_d \cdot l_c + l_o + l_r) \cdot 2^{m_d \cdot l_c + l_o}} \qquad (3)$$

As can be seen, $\mathbb{P}_b(l_o, l_c, l_r, m_d, m)$ is also lower-bounded by 2^{-l_r}. So we make the similar suggestion for formula (3) as in Section 3.2 that $b \cdot (1 - 2^{-l_r}) \le 2^{-l_r}$.

3.4 $\mathcal{P}_c$ Forward Checksum Computation to $\mathcal{A}$: Proxy Attack

As reported in [10], the software-based attestation is particular vulnerable to the proxy attack, in which the compromised prover $\mathcal{P}_c$ forwards the challenge to the adversary $\mathcal{A}$ (a base station) and asks $\mathcal{A}$ to compute the checksum for it. In order to prevent the proxy attack, the expected checksum computation time should be no larger than a time bound, so that $\mathcal{P}_c$ does not have time to wait for the response from $\mathcal{A}$. However, one assumption should be made that $\mathcal{A}$ cannot personate $\mathcal{P}_c$ and communicate with $\mathcal{V}$ directly. Otherwise, the software-based attestation is trivially broken. The assumption can be hold when $\mathcal{V}$ is connected to $\mathcal{P}_c$ using special channels (e.g., bus, usb) that $\mathcal{A}$ has no direct access to.

Assume the network RTT between $\mathcal{V}$ and $\mathcal{P}_g$ varies from $T_{\mathcal{V}}^{min}$ to $T_{\mathcal{V}}^{max}$ and the honest prover $\mathcal{P}_g$ can finish the checksum computation with time $d_g = n \cdot (d_{Gen} + d_{Addr} + d_{Read} + d_{Chk})$, the timing threshold d_{th} on the verifier side thus should be configured as

$$d_{th} \ge d_g + T_{\mathcal{V}}^{max} \qquad (4)$$

to ensure the correctness of the attestation protocol defined in Section 2.1. Hence, the maximum usable time for $\mathcal{P}_c$ can be defined as $d_c(T) = d_{th} - T$, where $T \in [T_{\mathcal{V}}^{min}, T_{\mathcal{V}}^{max}]$ is the real network latency between $\mathcal{P}_c$ and $\mathcal{V}$.

On one hand, $\mathcal{P}_c$ could use $d_c(T)$ to conduct the proxy attack. If the network RTT between $\mathcal{A}$ and $\mathcal{P}_c$ varies from $T_{\mathcal{A}}^{min}$ and $T_{\mathcal{A}}^{max}$, in order to prevent the proxy attack completely, we need to make sure that $d_c(T_{\mathcal{V}}^{min}) < T_{\mathcal{A}}^{min}$, which means the proxy attack cannot be conducted even under the optimal RTT for $\mathcal{P}_c$. Thus, the attestation time for the genuine prover should be constrained by

$$d_{th} < T_{\mathcal{A}}^{min} + T_{\mathcal{V}}^{min}. \qquad (5)$$

Table 2. Settings of Software-based Attestation Protocols Studied in Section 4

Parameters	SWATT	SCUBA	VIPER
l_o, l_g, l_r (bit)	2048^a, 16, 64	128, 16, 160	-, 32, 832
l_c, l_a (bit)	8, 14	8, 7	8, 13
m_d, m_p, m (unit)	0K, 16K, 17K	0K, 512, 58K	0K, 8K, 4120K
T_A^{min}, T_A^{max}	-	≤ 22ms, 51ms	1152ns(43.34ms)^b, 44.10ms
T_V^{min}, T_V^{max}	-	≤ 22ms, 51ms	1375ns, 1375ns
d_{th}, d_g	-, 1.8s	2.915s, 2.864s	2300ns, 827ns
n, k, u	3.2E+05, 1, 8	4.0E+04, 1, 10	3, 300, 26

^{a} This value is absent in [5] and assigned by us. The justification is made in
  Section 4.1.
^{b} The RTT in the parentheses is the real network latency collected in the exper-
  iments of [10]. The RTT in front is the theoretical lower-bound used in [10].

On the other hand, $\mathcal{P}_c$ could use $d_c(T)$ to conduct the memory recovering attack. So
we calculate the δ specified in the *memory recovery attack* as follows.

$$\frac{d_{Gen} + d_{Addr} + \delta \cdot d_{Read} + d_{Chk}}{d_{Gen} + d_{Addr} + d_{Read} + d_{Chk}} = \frac{d_c(T)}{d_g} = \frac{d_{th} - T}{d_g} \qquad (6)$$

Since, $\delta \propto d_g^{-1} \propto n^{-1}$, in order to keep the δ small, the checksum computation routine
should use the largest n as possible, when formula (4) and (5) are still satisfied.

4 Case Studies

In this section, we analyze three well-known software-based attestation protocols, i.e.,
SWATT [5], SCUBA [7] and VIPER [10]. Since the generic software-based attestation
scheme is configured with the parameters listed in Table 1, we first extract them from
the real protocols as shown in Table 2. As can be seen, our generic attestation scheme
can capture existing software-based attestation protocols readily. Then, we apply the
security criteria described in Section 3 manually to the extracted parameters to find
security flaws. In the following subsections, we briefly introduce the protocols first, and
then give detailed vulnerabilities and justifications grouped by the topics in **bold** font.
We mark the topics with " $\star$ " if they are reported for the first time in the literature.

4.1 SWATT

SWATT [5] randomly traverses the memory to compute the checksum. Its security
is guaranteed by the side channel on time consumed in the checksum computation.
SWATT does not consider network RTT, so we do not discuss time related properties
for SWATT. In addition, SWATT uses RC4 as the PRNG and takes the challenge as the
seed of the RC4. As the length of the challenge chosen in the SWATT is not mentioned
in [5], we assume that the challenge is long enough to fully randomize the initial state
of RC4, which means $l_o = 256 \cdot 8$ bits.

Unattested Data Memory. The micro-controller in SWATT has $16KB$ program memory and $1KB$ data memory. Based on the analysis of the generic attestation scheme, SWATT is insecure because it neither has Secure Erasure Phase to overwrite the data memory nor uses any additional complement to secure the data memory. In fact, the authors of SWATT assumed in [5] that non-executable data memory can do no harm to the security of software-based attestation by mistake. In [9], Castelluccia et al. point out that the data memory should be verified in SWATT, otherwise the protocol is vulnerable to the ROP [15,16] attack. In this work, we suggest to securely erase the data memory in SWATT by following our generic attestation scheme.

*Too Large Iteration Number for Computing One Checksum. The main loop of SWATT has only 16 assembly instructions, which takes 23 machine cycles. Inserting one *if* statement in the loop will cause additional 13% overhead. As a result, we assume that the recovering algorithm $\mathcal{C}$ only has time to read the memory content as *Read* does without doing any extra computation. Hence, the success probability of the memory recovering of SWATT becomes $\mathbb{P}_m(S, \mu, \delta) = 1 - \mu$, where μ is the percentage of the modified memory. According to the formula (2), after setting η as suggested, we have $n \geq -64/log(1 - \mu)$. When $\mu = 0.001$ which left only 16 byte memory for the adversary, we should set n as 44340, which is much smaller than the iteration number 320000 used in SWATT. In order to increase the difficulty of attacking the attestation protocol and traverse the memory address in the platform, more rounds of checksum computation could be conducted. According to formula (1), when $\mu = 0.001$, $n = 44340$ and $c = 2$ (the same setting in SWATT), we have $k \geq 11$. So we should conduct the checksum computation for 11 times. By using this new configuration, the overall memory access time is approximately the same as SWATT while security guarantee becomes dramatically better.

4.2 SCUBA

SCUBA [7] is a software-based attestation protocol that based on Indisputable Code Execution (ICE). Rather than attesting the whole memory, the ICE offers security guarantee by only verifying a small portion of the code. The *Read* and *Chk* implemented in the ICE scheme are different from those given in Section 2.2. However, they can be generalized into our framework. In SCUBA, *Read* not only reads the memory content, but also returns the Program Pointer (PC), the current address, the current generator, the loop counter and other registers. The *Chk* function then computes the checksum based on all of them. In order to compute the correct checksum for the modified attestation routine, the malicious prover has to simulate the execution for all of them, which thus lead to large and detectable overhead on the computation time. If the malicious prover do not change the attested code, the attested code can update the prover's whole memory to a genuine state so the malicious code shall be removed from the prover.

*Proxy Attack is Indefensible. In SCUBA, network RTT is explicitly evaluated in the experiment as summarized in Table 2. The prover in SCUBA communicates with the verifier over wireless network. Even though the adversary is assumed to be physically absent during the attestation in SCUBA, this assumption seems to be too strong to be hold in a wireless network. Thus, we analyze the proxy attack for SCUBA as follows.

According to [7], the maximum network RTT is $51ms$ in SCUBA. By observing the experiment results, the minimum network RTT should be no larger than $22ms$. As the adversary and the verifier share the same wireless network, the network latency for their communication with the prover should be indifferent. So we have $T_{\mathcal{A}}^{min} = T_{\mathcal{V}}^{min} \leq 22ms$ and $T_{\mathcal{A}}^{max} = T_{\mathcal{V}}^{max} = 51ms$. According to formula (4), we have $d_{th} \geq d_g + T_{\mathcal{V}}^{max} \geq 51ms$. On the other hand, according to formula (5), we have $d_{th} < T_{\mathcal{A}}^{min} + T_{\mathcal{V}}^{min} \leq 44ms$. Hence, we cannot find a valid threshold d_{th} from this network configuration. When the adversary presents in the attestation, the proxy attack thus cannot be defended by SCUBA without additional assumptions.

Moreover, if the verifier does not communicate with the prover with a secure channel (e.g., the verifier uses the wireless network to the communicate with the prover in this case), the adversary can personate the prover and send the checksum to the verifier directly. Since the adversary can compromise the prover, he can obtain the secret key stored in the prover as well. So encrypting the wireless channel will not work. We suggest that the verifier should communicate with the prover in an exclusive method, such as the usb connection, which is also inexpensive. More importantly, the adversary cannot use this communication method as it is highly controllable.

Security Claim Justification. Our framework can not only be used to find potential vulnerabilities, but also give justifications to the security claims made in existing works. In SCUBA [7], the malicious prover may exploit the network latency to conduct memory recovering attack without being detected. However, if the timing overhead of the attack is even larger than the largest network latency, the attack then becomes detectable. According to this, the authors of SCUBA claim that the checksum computation time adopted in SCUBA can always detect the memory copy attack, which is the most efficient memory recovering attack method known to the authors, even if the malicious prover can communicate without network delay.

In this work, we can justify their security claim with our framework. When the proxy attack is not considered in SCUBA, increasing the checksum computation time does not introduce vulnerability. According to formula (6), we have $d_c(T)/d_g = (d_{th} - T)/d_g$. The experiment results in [7] show that the memory copy attack is most efficient attack which introduces 3% overhead to the checksum computation. In order to detect the memory copy attack, we should ensure that $\forall T \in [T_{\mathcal{V}}^{min}, T_{\mathcal{V}}^{max}], d_c(T)/d_g < 1.03$. As we assume that the malicious prover can communicate without network delay, we set $T_{\mathcal{V}}^{min}$ as 0. By applying formula (4), we have $d_g > 1700ms$. Since d_g chosen in SCUBA is indeed larger than $1700ms$, the security claim made by the authors is valid.

4.3   VIPER

VIPER [10] is a software-based attestation scheme designed to verify the integrity of peripherals' firmware in a typical x86 computer system. They are proposed to defend all known software-based attacks, including the proxy attack.

*Absence of Random Function.** VIPER uses a similar design as ICE scheme, while its generators are not produced by a PRNG during the checksum computation, which does not comply to our generic attestation scheme. The authors implement the checksum function into 32 code blocks. One register is updated in every code block with the memory content and the program counter (PC). Both of the code block and the memory address are chosen based on the current checksum. Thus, the randomness of the checksum is purely introduced by the PC and the memory content. However, the PC is incremented in a deterministic way inside each code block and the memory content usually is biased as illustrated in Section 3.2. As the randomness could be biased, the adversary can traverse all challenge values and he may find some memory addresses that are unreachable for the checksum computation routine, as we discussed in Section 3.1. Hence, the security provided by VIPER is unclear.

Insufficient Iteration Number. In VIPER, the number of iterations used in the checksum computation routine is only 3, which leads to at least 23 unused registers in the attestation. Vulnerabilities may be introduced as discussed in Section 3.1. Even if the registers are chosen in a fully randomized manner and the adversary cannot predict which register will be used beforehand, the malicious prover still has a high probability to use some registers without being detected. In fact, two or even one register could be enough for conducting an attack in practice.

5   Related Works

A large amount of software-based attestation protocols have been designed and implemented [17,5,18,6,12,7,19,20,21,22,10,23]. Specifically, SWATT [5] is a software-based attestation scheme that uses the response timing of the memory checksum computation to identify the compromised embedded devices. In order to prevent replay attack, the prover's memory is traversed in SWATT in a random manner based on a challenge sent from the verifier. Rather than attesting the whole memory content, SCUBA [7] only checks the protocol implemented in the embedded devices and securely updates the memory content of the embedded devices after the attestation is finished successfully. It is based on the ICE (Indisputable Code Execution) checksum computation scheme, which enables the verifier to obtain an indisputable guarantee that the SCUBA protocol will be executed as untampered in the embedded devices. VIPER [10] is later proposed to defense against the adversary who can communicate with the embedded devices during the attestation. Network latency is consider in VIPER to prevent the proxy attack. Perito et al. [22] develop a software-based secure code update protocol. It first overwrites the target device's whole memory with random noise and then asks the target device to generate a checksum based on its memory state. The target device could generate the correct checksum only if it has erased all its memory content, so the malicious code should also be removed. Besides the attestation protocol designed for resource constrained devices, Seshadri et al. [12] develop the software-based attestation protocol named Pioneer for the Intel Pentium IV Xeon Processor with x86 architecture.

However, the software-based attestation protocol design is challenging and error-prone [8,9]. Hence, it becomes necessary and urgent to develop an analysis framework for the attestation protocol design. Armknecht et al. [24] recently provide a security framework for the analysis and design of software attestation. In their work, they assume the cryptographic primitives such as Pseudo-Random Number Generators (PRNGs) and hash functions might be insecure and give a upper-bound to the advantage of the malicious prover in the attestation scheme. They mainly consider six factors: (1) the memory content could be biased; (2) the memory addresses traversed in the checksum computation may not be fully randomized; (3) the memory addresses could be computed without using the default method; (4) the correct checksum could be computed without finishing the checksum computation routine; (5) the checksum could be generated without using the default checksum computation function; (6) the challenge-response pairs could be pre-computed and stored in the memory. In this work, we do not consider factor (2-5) based on two reasons. First, the attestation routine used in the protocol can be updated at runtime, so we can always update the cryptographic functions to meet the higher security standard and requirement. For instance, since the hash function like *MD5* is insecure nowadays, we can replace it with *SHA-2* or *SHA-3* to reclaim security. More importantly, the upper-bounds of the factor (2-5) are very hard to measure in practice. For example, given a well-known weak hash function like *MD5*, it is hard to measure the *time-bounded pseudo-randomness*, corresponding to factor (2), defined in [24]. Comparing with [24], we additionally consider observable network latency, stronger threat model, unpredictable data memory, several security criteria and various attack schemes. More importantly, our framework has been successfully applied to several existing software-based attestation protocols to find vulnerabilities.

6   Discussions and Future Works

In this work, we present a practical analysis framework for software-based attestation scheme. We explicitly consider the network latency and the data memory in the system. Furthermore, the adversary presented in this work can not only reprogram the compromised provers before the attestation but also communicate with them during the attestation. We successfully apply our framework to three well-known software-based attestation protocols manually. The results show that our framework can practically find security flaws in their protocol design and give justifications to their security claims.

The deployment environment, including device architecture, network environment, efficiency requirement, etc. usually complicates the correctness of the software-based attestation protocols. Specifically, identifying the most effective overwriting and recovering algorithms becomes very hard, which limits the application of our framework. For future works, we believe that fine-grain measurement for the overwriting and recovering algorithms in the practical application context is useful. Another future work is investigating the impact of timing requirement when the attestation efficiency is concerned. In this work, we assume that software-based attestation can take as much time as it needs. Nevertheless, in reality, we may require the attestation protocols to be finished within a timing threshold. Hence, the probability of identifying the compromised prover will be affected, and choosing the right configurations becomes more challenging.

Acknowledgements. This project is partially supported by project IGDSi1305012 from SUTD.

References

1. Arbaugh, W.A., Farber, D.J., Smith, J.M.: A secure and reliable bootstrap architecture. In: S&P, pp. 65–71. IEEE CS (1997)
2. England, P., Lampson, B.W., Manferdelli, J., Peinado, M., Willman, B.: A trusted open platform. IEEE Computer 36(7), 55–62 (2003)

3. Sailer, R., Zhang, X., Jaeger, T., van Doorn, L.: Design and implementation of a tcg-based integrity measurement architecture. In: USENIX Security, pp. 223–238. USENIX (2004)

4. Kil, C., Sezer, E.C., Azab, A.M., Ning, P., Zhang, X.: Remote attestation to dynamic system properties: Towards providing complete system integrity evidence. In: DSN, pp. 115–124. IEEE (2009)

5. Seshadri, A., Perrig, A., van Doorn, L., Khosla, P.K.: Swatt: Software-based attestation for embedded devices. In: S&P, pp. 272–282. IEEE CS (2004)

6. Shaneck, M., Mahadevan, K., Kher, V., Kim, Y.-D.: Remote software-based attestation for wireless sensors. In: Molva, R., Tsudik, G., Westhoff, D. (eds.) ESAS 2005. LNCS, vol. 3813, pp. 27–41. Springer, Heidelberg (2005)

7. Seshadri, A., Luk, M., Perrig, A., van Doorn, L., Khosla, P.K.: Scuba: Secure code update by attestation in sensor networks. In: WiSe, pp. 85–94. ACM (2006)

8. Shankar, U., Chew, M., Tygar, J.D.: Side effects are not sufficient to authenticate software. In: USENIX Security, pp. 89–102. USENIX (2004)

9. Castelluccia, C., Francillon, A., Perito, D., Soriente, C.: On the difficulty of software-based attestation of embedded devices. In: CCS, pp. 400–409. ACM (2009)

10. Li, Y., McCune, J.M., Perrig, A.: Viper: verifying the integrity of peripherals' firmware. In: CCS, pp. 3–16. ACM (2011)

11. "Trusted Platform Module", http://www.trustedcomputinggroup.org/developers/trusted_platform_module

12. Seshadri, A., Luk, M., Shi, E., Perrig, A., van Doorn, L., Khosla, P.K.: Pioneer: verifying code integrity and enforcing untampered code execution on legacy systems. In: SOSP, pp. 1–16. ACM (2005)

13. Klimov, A., Shamir, A.: New cryptographic primitives based on multiword t-functions. In: Roy, B., Meier, W. (eds.) FSE 2004. LNCS, vol. 3017, pp. 1–15. Springer, Heidelberg (2004)

14. Choi, Y.-G., Kang, J., Nyang, D.: Proactive code verification protocol in wireless sensor network. In: Gervasi, O., Gavrilova, M.L. (eds.) ICCSA 2007, Part II. LNCS, vol. 4706, pp. 1085–1096. Springer, Heidelberg (2007)

15. Shacham, H.: The geometry of innocent flesh on the bone: return-into-libc without function calls (on the x86). In: CCS, pp. 552–561. ACM (2007)

16. Buchanan, E., Roemer, R., Shacham, H., Savage, S.: When good instructions go bad: generalizing return-oriented programming to risc. In: CCS, pp. 27–38. ACM (2008)

17. Kennell, R., Jamieson, L.H.: Establishing the genuinity of remote computer systems. In: USENIX Security, p. 21. USENIX (2003)

18. Giffin, J.T., Christodorescu, M., Kruger, L.: Strengthening software self-checksumming via self-modifying code. In: ACSAC, pp. 23–32. IEEE CS (2005)

19. Yang, Y., Wang, X., Zhu, S., Cao, G.: Distributed software-based attestation for node compromise detection in sensor networks. In: SRDS, pp. 219–230. IEEE CS (2007)

20. Gardner, R.W., Garera, S., Rubin, A.D.: Detecting code alteration by creating a temporary memory bottleneck. IEEE Trans. Inf. Forensics Security 4(4) (2009)

21. AbuHmed, T., Nyamaa, N., Nyang, D.: Software-based remote code attestation in wireless sensor network. In: GLOBECOM, pp. 1–8. IEEE (2009)

22. Perito, D., Tsudik, G.: Secure code update for embedded devices via proofs of secure erasure. In: Gritzalis, D., Preneel, B., Theoharidou, M. (eds.) ESORICS 2010. LNCS, vol. 6345, pp. 643–662. Springer, Heidelberg (2010)

23. Kovah, X., Kallenberg, C., Weathers, C., Herzog, A., Albin, M., Butterworth, J.: New results for timing-based attestation. In: S&P, pp. 239–253. IEEE CS (2012)

24. Armknecht, F., Sadeghi, A.-R., Schulz, S., Wachsmann, C.: A security framework for the analysis and design of software attestation. In: CCS, pp. 1–12. ACM (2013)

TAuth: Verifying Timed Security Protocols

Li Li[1], Jun Sun[2], Yang Liu[3], and Jin Song Dong[1]

[1] National University of Singapore, Singapore
[2] Singapore University of Technology and Design, Singapore
[3] Nanyang Technological University, Singapore

Abstract. Quantitative timing is often relevant to the security of systems, like web applications, cyber-physical systems, etc. Verifying timed security protocols is however challenging as both arbitrary attacking behaviors and quantitative timing may lead to undecidability. In this work, we develop a service framework to support intuitive modeling of the timed protocol, as well as automatic verification with an unbounded number of sessions. The partial soundness and completeness of our verification algorithms are formally defined and proved. We implement our method into a tool called TAuth and the experiment results show that our approach is efficient and effective in both finding security flaws and giving proofs.

1 Introduction

Timed security protocols are used extensively nowadays. Many security applications [29,9,4] use time to guarantee the freshness of messages received over the network. In these applications, messages are associated with timing constraints so that they can only be accepted in a predefined time window. As a result, relaying and replaying messages are allowed only in a timely fashion. It is known that security protocols and their manual proofs are error-prone, which has been evidenced by multiple flaws found in existing proved protocols [30,27,17]. It is therefore important to have automatic tools to formally verify these protocols.

However, existing methods and tools for security protocol verification often abstract timestamps away by replacing them with nonces. The main reason is that most of the decidability results are given for untimed protocols [24,28]. Thus, the state-of-the-art security protocol verifiers, e.g., ProVerif [6], Athena [31], Scyther [13] and Tamarin [25], are not designed to specify and verify time sensitive cryptographic protocols. Abstracting time away may lead to several problems. First, since the timestamps are abstracted as nonces, the message freshness checking in the protocol cannot be correctly specified. As a consequence, attacks found in the verification may be false alarms because they could be impractical when the timestamps are checked. Second, omitting the timestamp checking could also result in missing attacks. For instance, the timed authentication property ensures the satisfaction of the timing constraints in addition to the establishment of the event correspondence. Without considering the timing constraints, even though the agreement is verified under the untimed configuration correctly, the protocol may still be vulnerable to timing attacks. Third, with light-weight encryption, which are often employed in cyber-physical systems, it might be possible to decrypt secret messages in a brute-force manner given sufficient time. In applications where long network

S. Merz and J. Pang (Eds.): ICFEM 2014, LNCS 8829, pp. 300–315, 2014.

latency is expected, it is therefore essential to consider timing constraints explicitly and check the feasibility of attacks.

Contributions. In this work, we provide a fully automatic approach to verify timed security protocols with an unbounded number of sessions. Our contributions are fourfold. (1) In order to precisely specify the capabilities of the adversary, we propose a service framework in which the adversary's capabilities are modeled as various services according to the protocol specification and cryptographic primitives. Thus, when the protocol is vulnerable, there should exist an attack trace consisting of the services in a certain sequence. (2) An automatic algorithm is developed in this work to verify the timed authentication properties with an unbounded number of sessions. Since security protocol verification is undecidable in general [11], we cannot guarantee the termination of our algorithm. We thus define partial soundness and completeness in Section 2.3 and prove that our algorithm is partially sound and complete in Section 3. (3) Having time in security protocol verification adds another dimension of complexity. Thus we propose the finite symbolic representation for the timing constraints with approximation. We prove that the protocol is guaranteed to be secure when it is full verified by our algorithm. Additionally, when the protocol specification is in a specific form, we also prove that our algorithm does not introduce false alarms. (4) A verifier named TAuth is developed based on our method. We evaluate TAuth using several timed and untimed security protocols [8,10,26,19,7,29]. The experiment results show that our approach is efficient and effective in both finding security flaws and giving proofs.

Related Works. Evans et al. [16] introduced a semi-automated way to analyze timed security protocols. They modeled the protocols with CSP and checked them with PVS. In [23], Lowe proposed finite state model checking to verify bounded timed authentication. In order to avoid the state space explosion problem, protocol instances and time window are bounded in the verification. Jakubowska et al. [18] and Corin et al. [12] used Timed Automata to specify the protocols and used Uppaal to give bounded verifications. Our method is different from theirs as our verification algorithm is fully automatic and the verification result is given for an unbounded number of sessions.

The work closest to ours was proposed by Delzanno and Ganty [14] which applies $MSR(\mathcal{L})$ to specify unbounded crypto protocols by combining first order multiset rewriting rules and linear constraints. According to [14], the protocol specification is modified by explicitly encoding an additional timestamp, which represents the protocol initialization time, into some messages. Thus the attack could be found by comparing that timestamp with the original timestamps in the messages. However, it is not clearly illustrated in their paper how their approach can be applied to timed security protocol verification in general. On the other hand, our approach could be directly applied to crypto protocols without any manual modification to the protocol specification.

We adopt the horn logic which is similar to the one used in ProVerif [6], a very efficient security protocol verifier designed for untimed cryptographic protocol, and extend it with timestamps and timing constraints. However, the extension for time is nontrivial. In ProVerif, the fresh nonces are merged under the same execution trace, which is one of major reasons for its efficiency. When time is involved in the protocol, the generation time of the nonces in the protocol becomes important for the verification. Thus merging the session nonces under the same execution trace often introduces false

Table 1. Service Syntax Hierarchy

Type	Expression	
Timestamp(t)	t	
Message(m)	$g(m_1, m_2, ..., m_n)$	(function)
	$a[]$	(name)
	$[n]$	(nonce)
	v	(variable)
	t	(timestamp)
Fact(f)	$\langle m, t \rangle$	(timed communication)
	$e(m_1, m_2, ..., m_n)$	(event)
Constraint($\mathcal{B}$)	$\mathcal{C}(t_1, t_2, ..., t_n)$	
Service(S)	$f_1, f_2, ..., f_n \dashv \mathcal{B} \mapsto f$	
Query($\mathcal{Q}$)	$accept(...) \twoheadleftarrow \mathcal{B} \vdash init_1(...), ..., init_n(...)$	

alarms into the verification results. In order to differentiate the nonces generated in the sessions, we encode the session nonces into the events engaged in the protocol and use the events to distinguish them. Additionally, our approach takes care of the infinite expansion of timing constraints, which is discussed in Section 3.1.

2   Protocol Specification Framework

We introduce the proposed protocol specification framework in this section. In the framework, the security protocols and the cryptographic primitives are modeled as various services accessible to the *Adversary* for conducting attacks. Generally, these services receive inputs from the adversary and send the results back to the adversary as output over the network. Timestamps are tagged to the messages to denote when they are known to the adversary. We assume the adversary model presented in this framework is an active attacker who can intercept all communications, compute new messages and send any messages he obtained. For instance, he can use all the publicly available functions including encryptions, decryptions, concatenations, etc. He can also ask legal protocol participants to take part in the protocol when he needs. Thanks to the introduction of time, key expiration and message compromise can also be specified by adding additional services.

2.1   Service Syntax

In our framework, services are represented by a set of horn logic rules guarded by timing constraints. We adopt the syntax shown in Table 1 to define the services. *Messages* could be defined as *functions, names, nonces, variables* or *timestamps*. *Functions* can be applied to a sequence of *messages*; *names* are globally shared constants; *nonces* are freshly generated values in sessions; *variables* are memory spaces for holding *messages*; and *timestamps* are values extracted from the global clock during the protocol execution. A *fact* can be a *message* tagged by a *timestamp* denoted as $\langle m, t \rangle$, which means that the message m is known to the adversary at time t. Otherwise, it is an *event* in the form of $e(m_1, \ldots, m_n)$ where e is the event name and $m_1, \ldots, m_n$ are the event arguments. The events are used for specifying authentication properties and distinguishing different sessions. $\mathcal{B}$ is a set of closed timing constraints assigned on the *timestamp* pairs. Each constraint is in the form of $t - t' \sim d$ where t and t' are *timestamps*, d is an integer constant (∞ is omitted), and $\sim$ denotes either $<$ or $\leq$. We denote the maximum value of d in a timing constraint set $\mathcal{B}$ as $max(\mathcal{B})$. For simplicity, when a timing constraint $t - t' \sim d \in \mathcal{B}$, we write $d(\mathcal{B}, t, t')$ to denote the integer constant d, and $c(\mathcal{B}, t, t')$ to denote the comparator $\sim^1$. A *service* $f_1, f_2, ..., f_n \dashv \mathcal{B} \vdash\!\!\!\rightarrow f$ means that if the *facts* $f_1, f_2, ..., f_n$ and the constraints $\mathcal{B}$ are satisfied, the adversary can invoke this service and obtain f as the result.

2.2 Service Modeling

In the following, we show how to model the timed authentication protocols in our framework. We illustrate the service modeling using a simple example called the Wide Mouthed Frog (WMF) protocol [8] as described below.

$$A \rightarrow S : A, \{t_A, B, k\}_{k_A}$$
$$S \rightarrow B : \{t_S, A, k\}_{k_B}$$

In the protocol, A and B are two users *Alice* and *Bob*, and S is a trust server who shares different secret keys with different users. The goal of this protocol is to share a fresh key k from *Alice* to *Bob*. k_A is the secret key shared between server and *Alice*, and k_B is the corresponding secret key for *Bob*. k is a fresh session key generated by *Alice*, which should be different in different sessions. t_A is a timestamp generated by *Alice*. Similarly, t_S is a timestamp generated by the server. In the protocol, we assume that the clock drift for every participants is negligible, so that the message freshness checking is valid during the execution.

When the server receives the request from *Alice*, it checks its freshness by comparing the t_A with the current clock reading t_S. If t_A and t_S satisfy the pre-defined constraint C_1, the server then sends the second message to *Bob*. Upon receiving the message from the server, *Bob* decrypts it and compares t_S with his clock reading t_B. If the timestamp checking C_2 is passed and the message is properly formed, *Bob* then believes that k is a fresh key shared with *Alice*. In fact, there exists an attack [3] to the protocol which is resulted from the symmetric structure of the exchanged messages.

$$
\begin{aligned}
A \rightarrow S : &\quad A, \{t_A, B, k\}_{k_A} \\
S \rightarrow I(B) : &\quad \{t_S, A, k\}_{k_B} \\
I(B) \rightarrow S : &\quad B, \{t_S, A, k\}_{k_B} \\
S \rightarrow I(A) : &\quad \{t_{S'}, B, k\}_{k_A} \\
I(A) \rightarrow S : &\quad A, \{t_{S'}, B, k\}_{k_A} \\
S \rightarrow B : &\quad \{t_{S''}, A, k\}_{k_B}
\end{aligned}
$$

---

[1] If a timing constraint is not specified exactly in this form, it should be possible to change the constraint into this form. For instance, $t - t' > 3$ can be changed into $t' - t < -3$.

In the attack trace, the adversary I personates *Bob*, hijacks the second message and sends it back to the server within the timing constraint C_1. Then, the server would treat it as a valid request from *Bob* and update the t_S to its current clock reading. By doing this repeatedly, the timestamp in the request can be extended to an arbitrary large value. As a result, when *Bob* receives a message that passes the timestamp checking, the request from *Alice* may not be timely any more. Hereafter, we assume that the server and *Bob* check the freshness of the received messages with following timing constraints: $C_1 = t_S - t_A \leq 2$ and $C_2 = t_B - t_S \leq 2$. Notice that in general, the constraints should be set according to the protocol specification, network latency, etc.

Crypto Services. Cryptographic primitives are usually specified as services without network latency. Generally, we have two types of crypto services, which are constructors and destructors. Constructors are used to generate new messages such as concatenation and encryption, whereas destructors are used to extract messages from the constructed messages. For instance, the constructor and the destructor for symmetric encryption can be modeled as follows.

$$\langle m, t_1 \rangle, \langle k, t_2 \rangle \dashv t_1 \leq t \wedge t_2 \leq t \mapsto \langle enc_s(m, k), t \rangle \tag{1}$$

$$\langle enc_s(m, k), t_1 \rangle, \langle k, t_2 \rangle \dashv t_1 \leq t \wedge t_2 \leq t \mapsto \langle m, t \rangle \tag{2}$$

The service (1) means that if the adversary has a message m and a key k, this service can generate the symmetric encryption for m by k, and the timing t of receiving the encryption should be later than the timing t_1 and t_2 when m and k are known to the adversary. The symmetric decryption service is similarly defined in service 2.

For some cryptographic primitives, additional constraints can be added for special purposes. For instance, RSA encryption may consume non-negligible time to compute. If the encryption time has a lower bound d, we could use the following constructor to model the additional requirement on time.

$$\langle m, t_1 \rangle, \langle pk, t_2 \rangle \dashv t - t_1 > d, t - t_2 > d \mapsto \langle RSA(m, pk), t \rangle$$

Protocol Services. Protocol services are used to specify the execution of the protocol. These services are directly derived from the protocol specification. Specifically, for the WMF protocol, the server S answers queries from all its users. After receiving a request from a user I, S extracts the message content and checks the timestamp. If the timestamp is generated within 2 time units, S sends out the encryption of an updated timestamp t_S, the initiator's name and the session key k under the responder's shared key. The service provided by the server can be specified with

$$\langle enc_s((t_I, R, k), key(I)), t \rangle, \langle I, t' \rangle \dashv 0 \leq t_S - t_I \leq 2 \wedge t \leq t_S \wedge t' \leq t_S \mapsto$$
$$\langle enc_s((t_S, I, k), key(R)), t_S \rangle \tag{3}$$

in which $key(U)$ represents the secret key shared between the server and the user U. Since the keys are only shared with the user and the server, We do not treat the key constructor as a public service. Besides, the names of the two participants should be known to the adversary, so we have services for publishing their names.

$$\dashv \ \mapsto \langle A[], t \rangle \tag{4}$$

$$\dashv \ \mapsto \langle B[], t \rangle \tag{5}$$

Event Services. In order to ensure the authenticity between participants, we introduce two special events *init* and *accept*. The *init* event is explicitly engaged by the adversary when he wants to start a new protocol session, while the *accept* event is engaged by the protocol when the timed authentication is established successfully. According to [22], the timed authentication is correct if and only if every *accept* event is emitted with its corresponding *init* event engaged before, and the timing constraints should always be satisfied. For the WMF protocol, the adversary engages an event *init* when he wants *Alice* to start a session with R.

$$init(A[], R, [k], t_A) \dashv \{ \} \mapsto \langle enc_s((t_A, R, [k]), key(A[])), t_A \rangle \qquad (6)$$

When the user *Bob* gets the message from the server, he decrypts it with his shared key $key(B[])$ and checks its freshness. If the timestamp checking is passed and the initiator is I, he then believes that he has established a timely authenticated connection under session key k with I and engages an *accept* event as follows.

$$\langle enc_s((t_S, I, k), key(B[])), t \rangle \dashv \{ t_B - t_S \leq 2 \} \mapsto accept(I, B[], k, t_B) \qquad (7)$$

Additional Services. Introducing time allows to model systems which are not possible previously. For instance, some applications require that the passwords are used only if they are unexpired. One possible scenario is that the token $token(s, pw, t_k)$ can only be opened within the lifetime $[t_k, t_k + d]$ of the password pw.

$$\langle token(s, pw, t_k), t_1 \rangle, \langle pw, t_2 \rangle \dashv \{ t_k \leq \begin{Bmatrix} t_1 \\ t_2 \end{Bmatrix} \leq \begin{Bmatrix} t_k + d \\ t \end{Bmatrix} \} \mapsto \langle s, t \rangle$$

If the adversary can obtain both of the token and the password within $[t_k, t_k + d]$, the secret s can be extracted from the token. Another possible service that could be accessible to the adversary is the brute force attack on the encrypted messages, which allows the adversary to extract the encrypted data without knowing the key. Suppose the least time of cracking the crypto is d, the attacking behavior can be modeled with

$$\langle Crypto(m, k), t \rangle \dashv \{ t' - t > d \} \mapsto \langle m, t' \rangle.$$

For some ciphers like RC4 which is used by WEP, key compromise on a busy network can be conducted after a short time. Given an application scenario where such attack is possible and the attacking time has a lower bound d, we can model it as follows.

$$\langle RC4(m, k), t \rangle \dashv \{ t' - t > d \} \mapsto \langle k, t' \rangle$$

Remarks. Even though the services specified in our framework can directly extract the message from the encryption without the key and so on, a given protocol can still guarantee correctness as long as proper timing checking is in place, e.g., authentication should be established before the adversary has the time to finish the brute-force attack.

2.3   Security Properties

In this work, we focus on verifying that the authentication between the two participants is timely, which means every *accept* event is preceded by a corresponding *init* event satisfying the timing constraints. Thus we formalize the *timed authentication* property by extending the definition in [22] as follows.

Definition 1. *Timed Authentication.* *In a timed security protocol, timed authentication holds for an* accept *event f with a set of* init *events H agreed on arguments encoded in the events and the timing constraints B, if and only if for every occurrence of f, all of the corresponding* init *events in H should be engaged before, and their timestamps should always satisfy the timing constraints B. We denote the* timed authentication *query as $f \leftarrow\!\!\!\mid B \mid\!- H$. In order to ensure general timed authentication, the arguments encoded in events should only be different variables and timestamps.*

We remark that the *timed authentication* defined above is the non-injective agreement. Since injective agreement is usually implemented by duplication checking, which is unrelated to time, we do not discuss *injective timed authentication* [22] in this work. Because the legitimate run of WMF protocols requires that the authentication should be established within 4 time units, its query is modeled as follows.

$$accept(I, R, k, t) \leftarrow\!\!\!\mid t - t' \leq 4 \mid\!- init(I, R, k, t') \tag{8}$$

In Section 3, we present a verification algorithm to check the authentication. Since the verification for security protocol is generally undecidable [11], our algorithm cannot guarantee termination. Hence, we claim our attack searching algorithm as partial sound and partial complete under the condition of termination (partial correctness).

3   Verification Algorithm

Given the specification formalized in Section 2, our verification algorithm is divided into two phases. The attack searching service basis is constructed in the first phase so that attacks can be found in a straight forward method in the second phase. Specifically, every service consists of several inputs, one output and some timing constraints. When a service's input can be provided by another service's output, we could compose these two services together to form a composite service. In the first phase, our algorithm composes the services repeatedly until a fixed-point is reached. When such a fixed-point exists, we call it the *guided service basis*. However, the above process may not terminate because of two reasons. The first reason is the infinite knowledge deduction. For example, given two services $m \dashrightarrow h(m)$ and $h(m) \dashrightarrow h(h(m))$, we can compose them to obtain a new service $m \dashrightarrow h(h(m))$, which could be composed to the second service again. In this way, infinitely many composite services can be generated. The second reason is the infinite expansion of timing constraints. For instance, assume we have $S_0 = \langle enc(t', k), t_1 \rangle \dashrightarrow\mid t'' - t' \leq 2 \land t_1 \leq t'' \mid\!\!\rightarrow \langle enc(t'', k), t'' \rangle$ and $S_1 = init(t, [k]) \dashrightarrow\mid t' - t \leq 2 \land t \leq t' \mid\!\!\rightarrow \langle enc(t', [k]), t' \rangle$ in the service basis. When we compose S_1 to S_0, their composition $S_2 = init(t, [k]) \dashrightarrow\mid t'' - t \leq 4 \land t \leq t'' \mid\!\!\rightarrow \langle enc(t'', [k]), t'' \rangle$ has a larger range than S_1. Besides, we could compose S_2 to S_0 again to obtain an even larger range, so the service composition never ends. Since verification for untimed security protocol is undecidable, we, same as state-of-the-art tools like ProVerif, cannot handle the first scenario. We thus focus on solving the second scenario by approximating the timing constraints into a finite set. The fixed-point is then called the *approximated service basis*. When the over-approximation is applied, false alarms may be introduced into the verification result so that, generally, only partial completeness is preserved by our attack searching algorithm. Finally, we present our attack searching algorithm in the end of this section.

3.1 Service Basis Construction

In the first phase, our goal is to construct a set of services that allows us to find security attacks in the second phase. In order to construct such a service basis, new services are generated by composing existing services. In this way, the new composite services can also be treated as services directly accessible to the adversary and the algorithm continues until the fixed-point is reached, i.e., no new service can be generated. We use the most general unifier to unify the input and the output.

Definition 2. *Most General Unifier.* *If σ is a substitution for both messages m_1 and m_2 so that $\sigma m_1 = \sigma m_2$, we say m_1 and m_2 are unifiable and σ is an unifier for m_1 and m_2. If m_1 and m_2 are unifiable, the most general unifier for m_1 and m_2 is an unifier σ such that for all unifiers σ' of m_1 and m_2 there exists a substitution σ'' such that $\sigma' = \sigma'' \sigma$.*

Since the adversary in our framework has the capability to generate new names and new timestamps, when a service input is a variable or a timestamp that is unrelated to other facts in a service, the adversary should be able to generate a random fact and use it to fulfill that input. In this way, that input can be removed in the composite service. Hence, we define service composition as follows. For simplicity, we define a *singleton* as a fact of the form $\langle x, t \rangle$ where x is a variable or a timestamp.

Definition 3. *Service Composition.* *Let $S = H \dashv B \mapsto f$ and $S' = H' \dashv B' \mapsto f'$ be two services. Assume there exists $f_0 \in H'$ such that f and f_0 are unifiable, their most general unifier is σ and $\sigma B \cap \sigma B' \neq \phi$. The service composition of S with S' on a fact f_0 is defined as $S \circ_{f_0} S' = clear(\sigma(H \cup (H' - \{f_0\}))) \dashv sim(\sigma B \cap \sigma B') \mapsto \sigma f'$, where the function clear merges duplicated facts from the inputs and removes any singleton $\langle x, t \rangle$ where x does not appear in other facts of the rule, and the function sim removes timestamps that are no longer used in the composite service.*

When new composite services are added into the service basis, redundancies should be eliminated from the service basis. As the timing constraints can be viewed as a set of clock valuations which satisfy the constraints, they thus can be naturally applied with semantic operations of set, e.g., $B \subseteq B'$, $B \cap B'$, etc.

Definition 4. *Service Implication.* *Let $S = H \dashv B \mapsto f$ and $S' = H' \dashv B' \mapsto f'$ be two services. S implies S' denoted as $S \Rightarrow S'$ if and only if $\exists \sigma, \sigma f = f' \land \sigma H \subseteq H' \land B' \subseteq \sigma B$.*

When services are composed in an unlimited way, infinitely many composite services could be generated. For instance, composing the symmetric encryption service (1) to itself on the fact $\langle m, k \rangle$ leads to a new service encrypting the message twice, that is $\langle m, t \rangle, \langle k_1, t_1 \rangle, \langle k_2, t_2 \rangle \dashv \ldots \mapsto \langle enc_s(enc_s(m, k_1), k_2), t' \rangle$, which can be composed to the encryption service again. In order to avoid these service compositions, we adopt a similar strategy proposed in [6] such that the unified fact in the service composition should not be singletons. Moreover, the events in our system cannot be unified[2], thus we define $\mathcal{V}$ as a set of facts that should not be unified, consisting of all events and singletons.

We denote $\beta(\alpha, \mathcal{R}_{init})$ as the fixed-point, where $\mathcal{R}_{init}$ is the initial service set and α is a service approximation function adopted during the construction. In order to compute $\beta(\alpha, \mathcal{R}_{init})$, we first define $\mathcal{R}_v$ based on the following rules, where $inputs(S)$ represents the inputs of service S.

1. $\forall S \in \mathcal{R}_{init}, \exists S' \in \mathcal{R}_v, S' \Rightarrow S$;
2. $\forall S, S' \in \mathcal{R}_v, S \not\approx S'$;
3. $\forall S, S' \in \mathcal{R}_v$, if $\forall f_{in} \in inputs(S), f_{in} \in \mathcal{V}$ and $\exists f \notin \mathcal{V}, S \circ_f S'$ is defined, $\exists S'' \in \mathcal{R}_v, S'' \Rightarrow \alpha(S \circ_f S')$.

The first rule means that every initial service is implied by a service in $\mathcal{R}_v$. The second rule means that no duplicated service exists in $\mathcal{R}_v$. The third rule means that for any two services in $\mathcal{R}_v$, if the first service's inputs are in $\mathcal{V}$ and their composition exists, their approximated composition is also implied by a service in $\mathcal{R}_v$. These three rules means $\mathcal{R}_v$ is the minimal closure of the initial service set $\mathcal{R}_{init}$. Based on $\mathcal{R}_v$, we have

$$\beta(\alpha, \mathcal{R}_{init}) = \{S \mid S \in \mathcal{R}_v \land \forall f_{in} \in inputs(S) : f_{in} \in \mathcal{V}\}.$$

In the latter part of this section, α will be instantiated with no-approximation and over-approximation. (The detailed algorithm is available in the full paper version [1].)

For any service, it is derivable from a service basis $\mathcal{R}$ if and only if there is a derivation tree that represents how the service is composed.

Definition 5. Derivation Tree. *Let $\mathcal{R}$ be a set of closed services and S be a closed service, where a closed service is a service with its output initiated by its inputs. Let S be a service in the form of $f_1, \ldots, f_n \dashv \mathcal{B} \mapsto f$. S can be derived from $\mathcal{R}$ if and only if there exists a finite derivation tree defined as*

1. *edges in the tree are labeled by facts;*
2. *nodes are labeled by the services in $\mathcal{R}$;*
3. *if a node labeled by S has incoming edges of $f_1^s, \ldots, f_n^s$, an outgoing edge of f^s, and the timestamps among these facts satisfy the timing constraints $\mathcal{B}^s$, then $S \Rightarrow f_1^s, \ldots, f_n^s \dashv \mathcal{B}^s \mapsto f^s$;*
4. *the outgoing edge of the root is the fact f;*
5. *the incoming edges of the leaves are $f_1, \ldots, f_n$.*

Additionally, if all the timing constraints in the derivation tree form $\mathcal{B}$, then the timing constraints for S is $sim(\mathcal{B})$, where sim removes timestamps that are no longer used. We name this tree as the derivation tree for S on $\mathcal{R}$.

Guided Service Basis. When no approximation is used in the service basis construction, the fixed-point is called *guided service basis* denoted as $\mathcal{R}_{guided} = \beta(\alpha_{guided}, \mathcal{R}_{init})$ where, for any service S, $\alpha_{guided}(S) = S$. In such a case, we prove that a service can be derived from $\mathcal{R}_{guided}$ whenever it can also be derived from $\mathcal{R}_{init}$, and vice versa.

---

[2] *init* events only appear in the inputs and *accept* events only appear in the output.

Theorem 1. *For any service S in the form of $H \dashv\!\{\, \mathcal{B} \,\}\!\!\mapsto f$ where $\forall f_{in} \in H : f_{in} \in \mathcal{V}$, S is derivable from $\mathcal{R}_{init}$ if and only if S is derivable from $\mathcal{R}_{guided}$.*

Proof Sketch. **Only if.** Given a service, if it is derivable from the initial service set, its derivation tree should exist. We thus compose the directly connected nodes in its derivation tree and show that the new composite node is implied by a service in $\mathcal{R}_v$. When no directly connected nodes can be composed, we then prove that the rest of the nodes are labeled by services in $\mathcal{R}_{guided}$, which implies that this service is also derivable from $\mathcal{R}_{guided}$. **If.** On the other hand, $\mathcal{R}_{guided}$ does not introduce extra services except for services derivable from $\mathcal{R}_{init}$, so the theorem is proved. The detailed proof is available in the full paper version [1].

Approximated Service Basis. New timestamps are often introduced in the service composition. When no longer used timestamps are removed from the composite service, the timing constraints can be deemed as extended for unification. On the other hand, given two services with the same inputs and output but they have different timing constraints, they may be indifferent if all of the different constraints have exceeded a ceiling. For instance, if the password has a fixed lifetime, its usefulness for the adversary remains the same when the password has already expired. Since these services can be deemed as the same, we remove their exceeded timing constraints to generalize their expressiveness. In this work, heuristically, we assume that every service is very likely to be used by the adversary for at least once in the attack trace and the timing constraints in the query also play important role in the reachability checking, so we set the ceiling as $1 + \sum max(\mathcal{B})$ in which $\mathcal{B}$ comes from the initial service set and the query. For instance, in the WMF protocol, the $max(\mathcal{B})$ is 2 for both of the service (3) and (7), 0 for other initial services, and 4 for the query, so we have the ceiling set as 9. We refer to the set of services with the ceiling U as approximated service basis $\mathcal{R}_{approx} = \beta(\alpha^{U}_{approx}, \mathcal{R}_{init})$. The service approximation function α^{U}_{approx} is defined as follows.

Definition 6. *Service approximation. Let $S = H \dashv\!\{\, \mathcal{B} \,\}\!\!\mapsto f$. We define the service approximation with ceiling U as $\alpha^{U}_{approx}(S) = H \dashv\!\{\, \mathcal{B}' \,\}\!\!\mapsto f$. For any two timestamps t, t' in the service S, if $d(\mathcal{B}, t, t') \le U$, then $d(\mathcal{B}', t, t') = d(\mathcal{B}, t, t')$ and $c(\mathcal{B}', t, t') = c(\mathcal{B}, t, t')$; else if $d(\mathcal{B}, t, t') > U$, then $d(\mathcal{B}', t, t')$ is ∞ and $c(\mathcal{B}', t, t')$ is $<$.*

Since the timing constraints are enlarged after the approximation, false alarms may be introduced into verification result. However, according to the experiment results shown in Section 4, the false alarms could be prevented when the ceiling is properly configured. On the other hand, whenever a timed protocol is verified as correct under the approximation, it is guaranteed to be attack-free, which is the same as ProVerif.

Theorem 2. *Let U be the ceiling. For any service S in the form of $H \dashv\!\{\, \mathcal{B} \,\}\!\!\mapsto f$ where $\forall f_{in} \in H : f_{in} \in \mathcal{V}$, if S is derivable from $\mathcal{R}_{init}$, S is also derivable from $\mathcal{R}_{approx}$.*

Proof Sketch. Since the timing constraints are only enlarged in the service basis, according to Theorem 1, it is clear that Theorem 2 also holds. Due to the limitation of the space, the detailed proof is available in the full paper version [1].

3.2   Query Searching

When the query is violated by a service in the service basis, we call it a contradiction to the query. A service is a contradiction to the query if and only if its output event can be unified to the query's output, while it does not require all the predicate events in the query or it has a larger timing range than the query constraints.

Definition 7. Contradiction. *A service* $S = H \dashv\!\!\mid \mathcal{B} \mid\!\!\rightarrow f$ *is a contradiction to the query* $Q = f' \dashv\!\!\mid \mathcal{B}' \vdash H'$ *if and only if* f *and* f' *are unifiable with the most general unifier* σ *and* $\forall \sigma', \sigma'\sigma H' \not\subseteq \sigma H \vee \sigma \mathcal{B} \not\subseteq \sigma'\sigma \mathcal{B}'$.

If we rewrite the query Q into a service of $S_q = H' \dashv\!\!\mid \mathcal{B}' \mid\!\!\rightarrow f'$, S is a contradiction to Q if and only if f' and f are unifiable with the most general unifier σ and we have $\sigma S_q \not\twoheadrightarrow \sigma S$. According to Definition 1, events in the query only contain variables and timestamps that are different. Thus the *accept* event in S_q can be unified with any other *accept* event. The contradiction checking could then be simplified to check whether S outputs an *accept* event and satisfies $S_q \not\twoheadrightarrow S$. Given the service basis $\mathcal{R}$, we thus search the attacks as follows. (The detailed algorithm is available in the full paper version [1].)

$$\mathcal{R}_f = \{S | S \in \mathcal{R}, \text{the output of } S \text{ is an } accept \text{ event} \wedge S_q \not\twoheadrightarrow S\}$$

$\mathcal{R}_f$ consists of the contradiction instances. We prove its partial correctness as follows.

Theorem 3. Partial Soundness. *Assume* $\mathcal{R}$ *is* $\mathcal{R}_{guided}$. *Let* Q *be a query of* $f' \dashv\!\!\mid \mathcal{B}' \vdash H'$ *and* $S_q = H' \dashv\!\!\mid \mathcal{B}' \mid\!\!\rightarrow f'$. *There exists* S *derivable from* $\mathcal{R}_{init}$ *such that* S *is a contradiction to* Q *if there exists* $S' \in \mathcal{R}$ *such that the output of* S' *is an accept event and* $S_q \not\twoheadrightarrow S'$.

Proof Sketch. According to Theorem 1, we have $\forall S' \in \mathcal{R}_{guided}$, S' should be derivable from $\mathcal{R}_{init}$, so any contradiction found in $\mathcal{R}_f$ is valid when $\mathcal{R}$ is $\mathcal{R}_{guided}$.

Theorem 4. Partial Completeness. *Assume* $\mathcal{R}$ *is either* $\mathcal{R}_{guided}$ *or* $\mathcal{R}_{approx}$. *Let* Q *be a query of* $f' \dashv\!\!\mid \mathcal{B}' \vdash H'$ *and* $S_q = H' \dashv\!\!\mid \mathcal{B}' \mid\!\!\rightarrow f'$. *There exists* S *derivable from* $\mathcal{R}_{init}$ *such that* S *is a contradiction to* Q *only if there exists* $S' \in \mathcal{R}$ *such that the output of* S' *is an accept event and* $S_q \not\twoheadrightarrow S'$.

Proof Sketch. We need to prove that we can find the attack whenever it exists. Since for any service there exists a derivation tree labeled by services in $\mathcal{R}_{guided}$ ($\mathcal{R}_{approx}$ resp.) according to Theorem 1 (Theorem 2 resp.), we prove that if the service S is a contradiction to the query, the service S_r labeled to the root of the tree is also a contradiction to the query. The theorem is thus proved. Due to the limitation of the space, the detailed proofs for the above theorems are available in the full paper version [1].

Partial Soundness for Approximated Service Basis under Restriction. The partial soundness is not guaranteed for our verification algorithm when approximated service basis is used. However, when the initial services are specified in some restricted form, even though the approximated service basis is over-approximated, the partial soundness of our query searching algorithm can be proved as well. One possible restriction is that for any two timestamps t and t' in every initial service with $\mathcal{B}$, $d(\mathcal{B}', t, t')$ is required to be no less than 0. If the ceiling is set to be larger than $max(\mathcal{B}_q) + 1$ where $\mathcal{B}_q$ is the timing constraints of the query, we prove the partial soundness of our verification algorithm as follows. First, we prove that, under this restriction, for any service S in the approximated service basis, we have a corresponding service S' in the guided service basis such that $S = \alpha_{approx}^U(S')$. Second, when the contradiction instance set $\mathcal{R}_f$ is not empty for the approximated service basis, we prove the existence of a corresponding attack instance in the guided service basis. According to the Theorem 1, the attack found in the guided service basis is guaranteed to be valid. So the protocol indeed has an attack and the following theorem is thus proved.

Lemma 1. *Given an initial service set $\mathcal{R}_{init}$ and a ceiling U. Every service in $\mathcal{R}_{init}$ satisfies the restriction that for any two timestamps t and t' in the service with $\mathcal{B}$, $d(\mathcal{B}', t, t')$ is no less than 0. We have $\forall S \in \beta(\alpha_{approx}^U, \mathcal{R}_{init})$, $\exists S' \in \beta(\alpha_{guided}, \mathcal{R}_{init})$ such that $S = \alpha_{approx}^U(S')$.*

Theorem 5. *Partial Soundness under Restriction. Assume $\mathcal{R}$ is $\mathcal{R}_{approx}$. Every service in $\mathcal{R}_{init}$ satisfies the restriction that for any two timestamps t and t' in the service with $\mathcal{B}$, $d(\mathcal{B}', t, t')$ is no less than 0. If the ceiling U is set to be larger than $max(\mathcal{B}_q) + 1$ where $\mathcal{B}_q$ is the timing constraints of the query, $\mathcal{R} = \beta(\alpha_{approx}^U, \mathcal{R}_{init})$. Let $\mathcal{Q}$ be a query of $f' \dashleftarrow \{\mathcal{B}' \vdash H'$ and $S_q = H' \dashv \{\mathcal{B}' \} \mapsto f'$. There exists S derivable from $\mathcal{R}_{init}$ such that S is a contradiction to $\mathcal{Q}$ if there exists $S' \in \mathcal{R}$ such that the output of S' is an accept event and $S_q \not\approx S'$.*

Due to the limitation of space, the proofs are available in [1]. We also indicate whether this restriction is applicable to the experiments evaluated in Section 4.

Remarks. Given a protocol with a valid attack, there should exist a derivation tree for that attack. Since we do not bound the number of events presented in a derivation tree (a composite service), we effectively deal with an unbounded number of sessions. The reason why our algorithm could work (i.e., terminate with correct result) is mainly because of two reasons. First, different from the explicit attack searching, we do not actively instantiate the variables in the services. So it becomes possible to represent the infinite adversary behaviors with a finite number of services. Second, we made a reasonable assumption in this work such that different nonces have different values. If the same nonce is generated in two sessions, those two sessions should be the same. Thus we merge them during the verification. As a consequence, even though we do not abstract the nonces used in the protocol as ProVerif does, this assumption could help us to find inconsistency in the service and remove the invalid ones from the service basis.

4   Implementation and Experiments

The flexibility and expressiveness of our service framework make it suitable for specifying and verifying timed security protocols, for instance, timed authentication protocols and distance bound protocols, etc. We have implemented our verifier TAuth in C++ with about 8K LoC. All the experiments shown in this section are conducted under Mac OS X 10.9.1 with 2.3 GHz Intel Core i5 and 16G 1333MHz DDR3. The TAuth verifier and the models shown in this section are available in [1].

Table 2. Verification results for timed authentication protocols

Protocol	$\mathcal{R}_{guided}$			$\mathcal{R}_{approx}$			
	$\sharp\mathcal{R}^a$	Result	Time	$\sharp\mathcal{R}$	Result	Restriction[b]	Time
Wide Mouthed Frog [8]	26	Attack [21]	3ms	26	Attack	SAT	4ms
Wide Mouthed Frog c [14]	19	Secure	3ms	19	Secure	SAT	3ms
Wide Mouthed Frog Lowe [21]	-	-	-	32	Secure	SAT	8ms
CCITT X.509(1) [10]	35	Attack [2]	4ms	35	Attack	SAT	3ms
CCITT X.509(1c) [2]	45	Secure	7ms	45	Secure	SAT	7ms
CCITT X.509(3) [10]	111	Attack [8]	52ms	111	Attack	SAT	51ms
CCITT X.509(3) BAN [8]	106	Secure	74ms	106	Secure	SAT	70ms
NS PK [26]	50	Attack [20]	6ms	50	Attack	SAT	6ms
NS PK Lowe [20]	51	Secure	8ms	51	Secure	SAT	9ms
NS PK Lowe Na Compromise [15]	51	Secure	8ms	51	Secure	SAT	8ms
NS PK Lowe Nb Compromise [15]	42	Attack [15]	3ms	42	Attack	SAT	3ms
NS PK Lowe NC Time [15]	48	Secure	10ms	48	Secure	UNSAT	10ms
SKEME [19]	77	Secure	73m	77	Secure	SAT	74ms
Auth Range [7,9]	17	Secure	2ms	17	Secure	UNSAT	1ms
Ultrasound Dist Bound [29]	35	Attack [30]	2ms	35	Attack	UNSAT	2ms

[a] Overall service number generated in the verification.
[b] Whether the restriction is satisfied for the initial service specification.

We summarize some implementation choices in TAuth below. First, the timing constraints in the service are represented by Difference Bound Matrices (DBMs) [5]. Since timestamps are unified and new timestamps are introduced in the service composition, we use unique identifiers to distinguish the timestamps generated in the system so that different timestamps have different identifiers among services. Second, events in a service are merged when the encoded fresh nonces are evaluated to a same value. The reason is that the value of nonces generated in the session should be random, so different fresh nonces should have different values. For instance, if the session key k is initiated in the *init* event, $init(A[], R_1, [k])$ and $init(I, R_2, [k])$ should be merged and the substitution $\{A[]/I, R_1/R_2\}$ should be applied to the service. If such events cannot be merged, the service is invalid. Third, we check the query contradiction on the fly when new services are composed. Whenever we find a contradiction, we stop the verification process and report the security flaw. This optimization can potentially give the early termination to the verification process when the protocol has security flaws.

Several different types of security protocols are analyzed in our experiments. In the experiments, *all* the protocols are proved or dis-proved in a short time as summarized in Table 2. For some protocols, the restriction mentioned in the Section 3.2 is applicable, so that the attack is guaranteed to be correct whenever it can be found, which is indicated in the table. Notice that, even though some protocols do not satisfy the restriction, all the attacks found in the experiments are valid. First, untimed protocols such as Needham-Schroeder series and SKEME are analyzed with TAuth. We use these protocols to show that TAuth can work with untimed protocols. Additionally, timed protocols like CCITT series are also checked by TAuth. However, the attacks found in these protocols are untimed. Furthermore, timed authentication protocols like the WMF series and the NS PK Lowe NC Time are correctly analyzed as well. We use these protocols to demonstrate that our approach can work with timed protocols and find timed attacks. Specifically, in the NS PK Lowe Nb Compromise version, the nonces generated by the responder in the protocol could be compromised [15], so the adversary could perform attacks to the protocol. Denning and Sacco [15] proposed a way to fix these security flaws by checking the timestamps. In the NS PK Lowe NC Time version, we assume that extra time is needed for the nonce compromise, so that freshness checking for the messages could ensure the authentication is attack-free. Notice that the service approximation only works for WMF Lowe version [21] in our experiment, because it is the only protocol that cannot be early terminated by the on-the-fly algorithm (it is attack-free) and its timing constraints involve infinite expansion.

Moreover, we successfully analyze two distance bounding protocols, that are Auth Range [7,9] and Ultrasound Dist Bound [29]. In the Auth Range protocol, the prover wants to convince the verifier that he is within a pre-agreed distance with the verifier. For instance, in a keyless entry system frequently adopted by cars, the prover is the remote key and verifier is the car. In the Auth Range protocol, it is assumed that the prover is honest and nothing can travel faster than light, so they could securely use the travel time of radio signals to measure the distance. In the Ultrasound Dist Bound protocol which has the same application scenario as the Auth Range protocol, the verifier uses radio signals to send requests while the prover uses ultrasound to return the answers. Since ultrasound travels much slower than radio and other processing time is negligible, the travel time of ultrasound dominates the whole protocol execution time. However, this protocol does not require the prover to be honest, so the prover can send his answer by either radio or ultrasound to others. When the adversary has a cooperator near the verifier, he can send the answer to the cooperator by radio and ask the cooperator to forward the answer by ultrasound to the verifier. As a consequence, the verifier can be convinced that the prover is within the distance even though the prover is not.

Table 3. Comparison with other untimed protocol verifiers

Protocol	Result	TAuth	ProVerif	Scyther
NS PK	Attack	6ms	6ms	200ms
NS PK Lowe	Secure	8ms	5ms	177ms
NS PK Lowe Na Compromise	Secure	8ms	5ms	170ms
NS PK Lowe Nb Compromise	Attack	3ms	5ms	31ms

Finally, we compare our tool TAuth with other successful untimed protocol verifiers, i.e., ProVerif [6] and Scyther [13]. The Needham Schroeder public key authentication protocols except for its timed variant are chosen for the comparison as timestamps are absent in these protocols. The comparison results are summarized in the Table 3. It can be seen that TAuth is almost as fast as ProVerif. TAuth is slightly slower mainly due to overhead on handling timing constraints. Thanks to the on-the-fly algorithm, TAuth is faster than ProVerif in finding the attack for the Lowe Nb Compromise version. Furthermore, TAuth is much faster than Scyther. Notice that Scyther could only verify the Lowe version and Lowe Na Compromise version with a bounded number of sessions while TAuth proves for infinitely many sessions.

5 Conclusions and Discussions

We present a service framework which can automatically verify the timed authentication protocols with an unbounded number of sessions. The partial correctness of our approach have been formally proved in this work. The experiment results for four different types of scenarios show that our framework is efficient and effective to verify a large range of timed security protocols. Even though we only check timed authentication properties for security protocols in this work, our framework could be easily extended to secrecy checking with timing constraints.

For future works, a throughout study on the termination of the algorithm would be very interesting. Since the problem of verifying security protocols is undecidable in general, we cannot guarantee the termination of our algorithm, but identifying the terminable scenario for practical security protocol could help the general adoption of our techniques. Our approach is inspired by the method used in ProVerif [6]. As is discussed in Section 3, TAuth is as terminable as ProVerif when the service approximation is used. However, the over-approximation also introduces false alarms. In order to remove the false alarms, as is discussed in Section 3, we can apply some restriction to the specification so that the found attacks are guaranteed to be valid. However, the restriction mentioned previously is quite restrictive because network latency, brute force attack, etc. cannot be specified under that restriction. Hence, how to restrict the specification in a practical way is another interesting future work direction.

Acknowledgements. The authors are grateful to Jun Pang, Jingyi Wang and the anonymous reviewers for valuable comments on earlier versions of this paper. This project is partially supported by project IGDSi1305012 from SUTD.

References

1. TAuth tool and experiment models,
   http://www.comp.nus.edu.sg/~li-li/r/tauth.html
2. Abadi, M., Needham, R.M.: Prudent engineering practice for cryptographic protocols. IEEE Trans. Software Eng. 22(1), 6–15 (1996)
3. Anderson, R., Needham, R.: Programming satan's computer. In: van Leeuwen, J. (ed.) Computer Science Today. LNCS, vol. 1000, pp. 426–440. Springer, Heidelberg (1995)
4. Basin, D.A., Capkun, S., Schaller, P., Schmidt, B.: Formal reasoning about physical properties of security protocols. ACM Trans. Inf. Syst. Secur. 14(2), 16 (2011)
5. Bellman, R.: Dynamic Programming. Princeton University Press (1957)
6. Blanchet, B.: An efficient cryptographic protocol verifier based on Prolog rules. In: CSFW, pp. 82–96. IEEE CS (2001)
7. Brands, S., Chaum, D.: Distance bounding protocols. In: Helleseth, T. (ed.) EUROCRYPT 1993. LNCS, vol. 765, pp. 344–359. Springer, Heidelberg (1994)
8. Burrows, M., Abadi, M., Needham, R.M.: A logic of authentication. ACM Trans. Comput. Syst. 8(1), 18–36 (1990)

9. Capkun, S., Hubaux, J.-P.: Secure positioning in wireless networks. IEEE Journal on Selected Areas in Communications 24(2), 221–232 (2006)

10. CCITT. The directory authentication framework - Version 7, Draft Recommendation X.509 (1987)

11. Cervesato, I., Durgin, N.A., Lincoln, P., Mitchell, J.C., Scedrov, A.: A meta-notation for protocol analysis. In: CSFW, pp. 55–69. IEEE Computer Society (1999)

12. Corin, R., Etalle, S., Hartel, P.H., Mader, A.: Timed model checking of security protocols. In: FMSE, pp. 23–32. ACM (2004)

13. Cremers, C.J.F.: The scyther tool: Verification, falsification, and analysis of security protocols. In: Gupta, A., Malik, S. (eds.) CAV 2008. LNCS, vol. 5123, pp. 414–418. Springer, Heidelberg (2008)

14. Delzanno, G., Ganty, P.: Automatic verification of time sensitive cryptographic protocols. In: Jensen, K., Podelski, A. (eds.) TACAS 2004. LNCS, vol. 2988, pp. 342–356. Springer, Heidelberg (2004)

15. Denning, D.E., Sacco, G.M.: Timestamps in key distribution protocols. Commun. ACM 24(8), 533–536 (1981)

16. Evans, N., Schneider, S.: Analysing time dependent security properties in csp using pvs. In: Cuppens, F., Deswarte, Y., Gollmann, D., Waidner, M. (eds.) ESORICS 2000. LNCS, vol. 1895, pp. 222–237. Springer, Heidelberg (2000)

17. Francillon, A., Danev, B., Capkun, S.: Relay attacks on passive keyless entry and start systems in modern cars. In: NDSS. The Internet Society (2011)

18. Jakubowska, G., Penczek, W.: Is your security protocol on time? In: Arbab, F., Sirjani, M. (eds.) FSEN 2007. LNCS, vol. 4767, pp. 65–80. Springer, Heidelberg (2007)

19. Krawczyk, H.: Skeme: a versatile secure key exchange mechanism for internet. In: NDSS, pp. 114–127. IEEE Computer Society (1996)

20. Lowe, G.: An attack on the needham-schroeder public-key authentication protocol. Information Processing Letters 56, 131–133 (1995)

21. Lowe, G.: A family of attacks upon authentication protocols. Technical report, Department of Mathematics and Computer Science, University of Leicester (1997)

22. Lowe, G.: A hierarchy of authentication specification. In: CSFW, pp. 31–44. IEEE Computer Society (1997)

23. Lowe, G.: Casper: A compiler for the analysis of security protocols. Journal of Computer Security 6(1-2), 53–84 (1998)

24. Lowe, G.: Towards a completeness result for model checking of security protocols. Journal of Computer Security 7(1), 89–146 (1999)

25. Meier, S., Schmidt, B., Cremers, C., Basin, D.: The TAMARIN prover for the symbolic analysis of security protocols. In: Sharygina, N., Veith, H. (eds.) CAV 2013. LNCS, vol. 8044, pp. 696–701. Springer, Heidelberg (2013)

26. Needham, R.M., Schroeder, M.D.: Using encryption for authentication in large networks of computers. Commun. ACM 21(12), 993–999 (1978)

27. Rasmussen, K.B., Castelluccia, C., Heydt-Benjamin, T.S., Capkun, S.: Proximity-based access control for implantable medical devices. In: CCS, pp. 410–419. ACM (2009)

28. Roscoe, A.W., Broadfoot, P.J.: Proving security protocols with model checkers by data independence techniques. Journal of Computer Security 7(1), 147–190 (1999)

29. Sastry, N., Shankar, U., Wagner, D.: Secure verification of location claims. In: Workshop on Wireless Security, pp. 1–10. ACM (2003)

30. Sedighpour, S., Capkun, S., Ganeriwal, S., Srivastava, M.B.: Implementation of attacks on ultrasonic ranging systems (demo). In: SenSys, p. 312. ACM (2005)

31. Song, D.X., Berezin, S., Perrig, A.: Athena: a novel approach to efficient automatic security protocol analysis. Journal of Computer Security 9(1-2), 47–74 (2001)

On the Formal Analysis of HMM Using Theorem Proving

Liya Liu, Vincent Aravantinos, Osman Hasan, and Sofiène Tahar

Dept. of Electrical & Computer Engineering, Concordia University
1455 de Maisonneuve W., Montreal, Quebec, H3G 1M8, Canada
{liy_liu,vincent,o_hasan,tahar}@ece.concordia.ca

Abstract. Hidden Markov Models (HMMs) have been widely utilized for modeling time series data in various engineering and biological systems. The analyses of these models are usually conducted using computer simulations and paper-and-pencil proof methods and, more recently, using probabilistic model-checking. However, all these methods either do not guarantee accurate analysis or are not scalable (for instance, they can hardly handle the computation when some parameters become very huge). As an alternative, we propose to use higher-order logic theorem proving to reason about properties of discrete HMMs by applying automated verification techniques. This paper presents some foundational formalizations in this regard, namely an extended-real numbers based formalization of finite-state Discrete-Time Markov chains and HMMs along with the verification of some of their fundamental properties. The distinguishing feature of our work is that it facilitates automatic verification of systems involving HMMs. For illustration purposes, we utilize our results for the formal analysis of a DNA sequence.

Keywords: HMMs, HOL4, Theorem Proving, DNA, Probability Theory.

1 Introduction

Hidden Markov Models (HMMs) [16] provide a useful statistical method for analyzing random processes based on their observable output samples. As their name suggests, HMMs assume that the observed samples are generated by a Markov process [3], for which the states are hidden from the observer. Initially HMMs were proposed to solve optimal linear filtering problems as the simplest dynamic Bayesian networks [27]. However, due to their usefulness in effectively analyzing probability distributions over a sequence of observations, HMMs are now extensively used in many applications involving speech recognition, cryptanalysis, molecular biology, data compression, financial market forecasting and artificial intelligence.

Traditionally, simulation has been the most commonly used computer-based analysis technique for HMMs. Based on this technique, HMMs are used to solve three types of problems: 1) evaluating the probability of occurrence of a particular observed sequence; 2) finding the most probable state sequence to generate

S. Merz and J. Pang (Eds.): ICFEM 2014, LNCS 8829, pp. 316–331, 2014.

given observations; and 3) learning parameters in the presumed model. These problems are typically solved by applying complex algorithms, like Forward-Backward, Viterbi, or Baum-Welch algorithms [16], whose implementations are usually not formally verified. This fact, along with the inherent limitations of computer simulation, like usage of computer arithmetic and pseudo random numbers, makes the analysis of HMMs approximate and thus the analysis based on HMMs becomes unreliable. This problem can have severe consequences when it comes to analyzing critical applications like Electrocardiogram Signal Processing [7] or Computational Biology [8], which is mainly used in determining and/or analyzing cancer, tumor and human genome. The analysis results directly affect the treatment of patients and their lifetime.

Formal methods allow to overcome the above mentioned limitations. For instance, probabilistic model checking guarantees precise system analysis by modeling the system behavior, including its random components, in a given logic and reasoning about its probabilistic properties. Some model checking algorithms have been proposed for analyzing HMMs [26]. However, the state-space explosion problem [2] limits the usage of probabilistic model checking to a very small subset of HMM applications. In addition, it cannot verify generic mathematical expressions for probabilistic analysis. Finally, the proposed model checking algorithms for HMMs in [25] are also complex and make use of many optimizations that are difficult to verify, and thus force the user to trust the developer of a given model checker.

The other widely used formal method is theorem proving [10], which provides a conceptually simple formalism with a precise semantics and can express all classical mathematical theories. Due to the highly expressive nature of higher-order logic and the inherent soundness of interactive theorem proving tools, this technique can provide precise analysis of HMMs. Although three chapters of measure theory were formalized in Isabelle/HOL [13] and the formalization of probability theory was simplified in Coq [6][1], to the best of our knowledge, foundational mathematics for HMMs has not been formalized in higher-order logic. Moreover, the interactive nature of higher-order logic theorem proving makes it quite unattractive for engineers and scientists involved in analyzing HMMs. This is one of the main reasons why theorem proving has not been used for the analysis of HMMs despite its ability to provide exact answers.

In this paper, we address both of the concerns mentioned above to facilitate the formal analysis of HMMs using theorem proving. Firstly, we present a higher-order logic formalization of mathematical foundations for HMMs. This includes the formalization of discrete time Markov chains (DTMCs), HMMs and the formal verification of some of their widely used properties. Our formalization of DTMCs is an improved version of the formalization of DTMCs presented in [15] since it is based on a more general probability theory and can handle inhomogeneous DTMCs with generic state spaces, which are the foremost prerequisites for modeling HMMs. Our formalization of HMMs also allows to reduce user intervention in formal modelling and analysis of real-world systems that can be expressed in terms of HMMs. The main challenge of this work is to express the conditional independency of two stochastic processes in higher-order logic. To facilitate this process further, we introduce some automatic simplifiers to make the proposed method a very practical solution for the formal analysis of HMMs. For illustration purposes, we present a case study about DNA sequence analysis.

2   Related Work

Various simulation-based HMM analysis tools, dedicated to a particular system domain, have been reported in the literature. Some prominent examples include *HMMTool* [12] as part of the *NHMMtoolbox* [21] to predict daily rainfall sequence. *ChIP-Seq* [4], MArkov MOdeling Tool (*MAMOT*) [9] and *HMMER* [11] are some of the popular simulation software in biological research. As mentioned in the previous section, due to their approximate nature, all these simulation techniques are not reliable enough for critical applications.

Probabilistic model checking [22] is the state-of-the-art formal Markov chain analysis technique. Numerous model checkers, e.g., *PRISM* [20], *VESTA* [23], *MRMC* [18], *Ymer* [24], etc., are available and have been used to analyze a variety of systems. In [25], the author defined probability spaces for modeling HMMs and presented model checking algorithms using Probabilistic Observation CTL (POCTL) for specifying properties of parameterized HMMs. The complexity of these algorithms depends on the size of the model and the number of variables involved in the property formula. This factor, coupled with the inherent nature of model checking, severely limits the usage of this algorithm for analyzing real-world examples. In addition, no HMM can be analyzed by model checker PRISM.

Higher-order-logic theorem proving overcomes the limitations of model checking and has been used to successfully formalize DTMCs [15]. However this formalization was not general enough to formalize HMMs. This was due to the fact that the underlying probability theory did not allow the definition of two distinct state spaces, which is a requirement in order to model HMMs. Nevertheless, recent developments have yielded a more general probability theory [17], that we use, in the present work, to develop an improved formalization of DTMCs. This allows, in particular, to define both time-homogeneous and time-inhomogeneous DTMCs, and HMMs, which in turn can be used to conduct formal analysis of HMMs within the sound core of a theorem prover.

3   Formalization of Discrete-Time Markov Chains

A *probability space* is a measure space $(\Omega, \Sigma, \mathcal{P}r)$ such that $\mathcal{P}r(\Omega) = 1$ [3]. Σ is a collection of subsets of Ω (these should satisfy some closure axioms that we do not specify here) which are called *measurable sets*. In [17], a higher-order logic probability theory is developed, where given a probability space p, the functions space and subsets return the corresponding Ω and Σ, respectively. Mathematically, a *random variable* is a measurable function between a probability space and a *measurable space*, which refers to a pair $(S, \mathcal{A})$, where S is a set and $\mathcal{A}$

is a σ-algebra, i.e., a collection of subsets of S satisfying some particular properties [3]. In HOL, we write `random_variable X p s` to state that a function X is a random variable on a probability space p and the measurable outcome space s. Meanwhile, the mathematical probability $\mathcal{Pr}$ is denoted as $\mathbb{P}$ in this paper. Building on these foundations, measure theoretic formalizations of probability, Lebesgue integral and information theories are presented in [17]. In this paper, we build upon these results to first formalize DTMCs and then use this to formalize HMMs.

3.1 Definition of Discrete-Time Markov Chains

A *stochastic process* [3] is a function $X : T \to \Omega$ where $T = \mathbb{N}$ (*discrete-time process*) or $T = \mathbb{R}$ (*continuous-time process*) and Ω is a measurable set called the *state space* of X. A *(finite-state) DTMC* is a discrete-time stochastic process that has a finite Ω and satisfies the *Markov property* [5]: for $0 \leq t_0 \leq \cdots \leq t_n$ and $f_0, \cdots, f_{n+1}$ in the state space, then: $\mathcal{Pr}\{X_{t_{n+1}} = f_{n+1} | X_{t_n} = f_n, \ldots, X_{t_0} = f_0\} = \mathcal{Pr}\{X_{t_{n+1}} = f_{n+1} | X_{t_n} = f_n\}$.

This allows to formalize the Markov property as follows:

Definition 1. (Markov Property)

```
⊢ ∀ X p s.
  mc_property X p s =
  (∀ t. random_variable (X t) p s) ∧
  ∀ f t n.
    increasing_seq t ∧ P(⋂ₖ∈ [0,n−1]{x | X tₖ x = f k}) ≠ 0 ⇒
    (P({x | X tₙ₊₁ x = f (n + 1)}|{x | X tₙ x = f n} ∩
                    ⋂ₖ∈ [0,n−1]{x | X tₖ x = f k}) =
    P({x | X tₙ₊₁ x = f (n + 1)}|{x | X tₙ x = f n}))
```

where `increasing_seq t` is defined as $\forall$ `i j. i < j ⇒ t i < t j`, thus formalizing the notion of increasing sequence. The first conjunct indicates that the Markov property is based on a random process $\{X_t : \Omega \to S\}$. The quantified variable X represents a function of the random variables associated with time t which has the type `num`. This ensures the process is a *discrete time* random process. The random variables in this process are the functions built on the probability space p and a measurable space s. The conjunct $\mathbb{P}(\bigcap_{k \in [0,n-1]}\{x \mid$ `X tₖ x = f k`$\}) \neq 0$ ensures that the corresponding conditional probabilities are well-defined, where `f k` returns the kth element of the state sequence.

A DTMC is usually expressed by specifying: an initial distribution p_0 which gives the probability of initial occurrence $\mathcal{Pr}(X_0 = s) = p_0(s)$ for every state; and transition probabilities $p_{ij}(t)$ which give the probability of going from i to j for every pair of states i, j in the state space [19]. For states i, j and a time t, the *transition probability* $p_{ij}(t)$ is defined as $\mathcal{Pr}\{X_{t+1} = j | X_t = i\}$, which can be easily generalized to *n-step transition probability*.

$$p_{ij}^{(n)} = \begin{cases} \begin{cases} 0 & \text{if } i \neq j \\ 1 & \text{if } i = j \end{cases} & n = 0 \\ \mathcal{Pr}\{X_{t+n} = j | X_t = i\} & n > 0 \end{cases}$$

This is formalized in HOL as follows:

Definition 2. (Transition Probability)

```
⊢ ∀ X p s t n i j.
  Trans X p s t n i j =
  if i ∈ space s ∧ j ∈ space s then
    if (n = 0) then
      if (i = j) then 1 else 0
    else ℙ({x | X (t + n) x = j}|{x | X t x = i})
  else 0
```

We will write $p_{ij}^{(n)}(t)$ for the n-step transition probability (note that the notations $p_{ij}(t)$ and $p_{ij}^{(1)}(t)$ are then equivalent).

Based on the concepts of Markov property and transition probability, the notion of a DTMC can be formalized as follows:

Definition 3. (DTMC)

```
⊢ ∀ X p s p₀ pᵢⱼ.
  dtmc X p s p₀ pᵢⱼ =
  mc_property X p s ∧ (∀ i. i ∈ space s ⇒ {i} ∈ subsets s) ∧
  (∀ i. i ∈ space s ⇒ (p₀ i = ℙ{x | X 0 x = i})) ∧
  (∀ t i j. ℙ{x | X t x = i} ≠ 0 ⇒ (pᵢⱼ t i j = Trans X p s t 1 i j))
```

The first conjunct states that a DTMC satisfies Markov property [19]. The second one ensures that every set containing just one state is measurable. The last two conjuncts indicate that p_0 is the initial distribution and p_{ij} are the transition probabilities, respectively. It is important to note that X is polymorphic, i.e., it is not constrained to a particular type, which is a very useful advantage of our definition.

In practice, many applications actually make use of *time-homogenous DTMCs*, i.e., DTMCs with finite state-space and time-independent transition probabilities [2]. This is formalized as follows:

Definition 4. (Time-homogeneous DTMC)

```
⊢ ∀ X p s p₀ pᵢⱼ.
  th_dtmc X p s p₀ pᵢⱼ =
  dtmc X p s p₀ pᵢⱼ ∧ FINITE (space s) ∧
  (∀ t i j. ℙ{x | X t x = i} ≠ 0 ∧ ℙ{x | X (t + 1) x = i} ≠ 0 ⇒
    (Trans X p s (t + 1) 1 i j = Trans X p s t 1 i j))
```

where the assumptions $\mathbb{P}\{x \mid X\ t\ x = i\} \neq 0$ and $\mathbb{P}\{x \mid X\ (t+1)\ x = i\} \neq 0$ ensure that the conditional probabilities involved in the last conjunct are well-defined. For time-homogenous DTMCs, $p_{ij}(t) = p_{ij}(t')$ for any t, t', thus $p_{ij}(t)$ will simply be written p_{ij} in this case.

Using these fundamental definitions, we formally verified most of the classical properties of DTMCs with finite state-space using the HOL theorem prover. Because of space limitations, we present only the formal verification of the most important properties in the following subsections and the remaining ones can be found in our proof script [14].

3.2   Joint Probability

The *joint probability* of a DTMC is the probability of a chain of states to occur. It is very useful, e.g., in analyzing multi-stage experiments. In addition, this concept is the basis for joint probability generating functions, which are frequently used in considerable system analysis problems. Mathematically, the joint probability of $n + 1$ discrete random variables $X_0, \ldots, X_n$ in a DTMC can be expressed as:

$$\mathcal{P}r(X_t = L_0, \cdots, X_{t+n} = L_n) = \prod_{k=0}^{n-1} \mathcal{P}r(X_{t+k+1} = L_{k+1}|X_{t+k} = L_k)\mathcal{P}r(X_t = L_0)$$

We verified this property in HOL as the following theorem:

Theorem 1. (Joint Probability)

```
⊢ ∀ X p s t L p₀ pᵢⱼ.
    dtmc X p s p₀ pᵢⱼ ⇒
    (ℙ(⋂ⁿₖ₌₀{x | X (t + k) x = EL k L}) =
    (∏ⁿ⁻¹ₖ₌₀ℙ({x | X (t + k + 1) x = EL (k + 1) L}|
            {x | X (t + k) x = EL k L}))ℙ{x | X t x = EL 0 L})
```

3.3   Chapman-Kolmogorov Equation

The Chapman-Kolmogorov equation [3] is a widely used property of time-homogeneous Markov chains since it facilitates the use of a matrix theory to analyze large Markov chains. It basically gives the probability of going from state i to j in $m + n$ steps. Assuming the first m steps take the system from state i to some intermediate state k, which is in the state space Ω and the remaining n steps then take the system from state k to j, we can obtain the desired probability by adding the probabilities associated with all the intermediate steps:

$$p_{ij}^{(m+n)} = \sum_{k \in \Omega} p_{kj}^{(n)} p_{ik}^{(m)} \tag{1}$$

Based on Equation (1) and Definition 4, the Chapman-Kolmogorov equation is formally verified as follows:

Theorem 2. (Chapman-Kolmogorov Equation)

```
⊢ ∀ X p s i j t m n p₀ pᵢⱼ.
    th_dtmc X p s p₀ pᵢⱼ ⇒
    (Trans X p s t (m + n) i j =
    ∑ₖ∈space s (Trans X p s t n k j * Trans X p s t m i k))
```

3.4   Absolute Probabilities

The unconditional probabilities associated with a Markov chain are called *absolute probabilities* which are expressed as follows:

$$p_j^{(n)} = \mathcal{P}r(X_n = j) = \sum_{k \in \Omega} \mathcal{P}r(X_0 = k)\mathcal{P}r(X_n = j|X_0 = k) \tag{2}$$

This property is formally verified as the following theorem:

Theorem 3. (Absolute Probability)

⊢ ∀ X p s j n p₀ pᵢⱼ.
  dtmc X p s p₀ pᵢⱼ ⇒
  ($\mathbb{P}\{x \mid X n x = j\}$ =
  $\sum_{k \in \text{space s}}$ ($\mathbb{P}\{x \mid X 0 x = k\}\mathbb{P}(\{x \mid X n x = j\}|\{x \mid X 0 x = k\})))$

The formal proof script for the above mentioned properties and many other useful properties is composed of 1200 lines of HOL code, which is used in the interactive verification process. The usefulness of this development is that it can be built upon to formalize HMMs as will be shown in the next section.

4   Formalization of Hidden Markov Models

An HMM [16] is a pair of two stochastic processes $\{X_k, Y_k\}_{k \geq 0}$, where $\{X_k\}_{k \geq 0}$ is a Markov chain and $\{Y_k\}_{k \geq 0}$ denotes an observable sequence, with the *conditional independency* property [27]. The observer can visualize the output of the random process shown in $\{Y_k\}_{k \geq 0}$ but not the underlying states in $\{X_k\}_{k \geq 0}$. That is the reason why the Markov chain involved in this process is called *hidden Markov chain*.

A HMM is defined as a triple $\lambda = (A, B, \pi(0))$ with the following conditions:

1. A Markov chain $\{X_k\}_{k \geq 0}$ with state space S, the initial distribution $\pi(0) = \{Pr\{X_0 = i\}\}_{i \in S}$ and the transition probabilities $A = \{Pr\{X_{n+1} = j | X_n = i\}\}_{i \in S, j \in S}$.
2. A random process $\{Y_k\}_{k \geq 0}$ with finite state space O. $\{X_k\}_{k \geq 0}$ and $\{Y_k\}_{k \geq 0}$ are associated with the *emission probabilities* B, which is $\{Pr\{Y_n = O_k | X_n = j\}\}_{j \in S, O_k \in O}$.
3. $\{Y_k\}_{k \geq 0}$ is conditional independent of $\{X_k\}_{k \geq 0}$, i.e. Y_k depends only on X_k and not on any X_t, such that $t \neq k$.

In our work, we consider mainly discrete time and finite-state space HMMs, which is the most frequently used case. Now, HMM is formalized as follows:

Definition 5. (HMM)

⊢ ∀ X Y p sₓ sᵧ p₀ pᵢⱼ pₓᵧ.
  hmm X Y p sₓ sᵧ p₀ pᵢⱼ pₓᵧ =
  dtmc X p sₓ p₀ pᵢⱼ ∧ (∀ t. random_variable (Y t) p sᵧ) ∧
  (∀ i. i ∈ space sᵧ ⇒ {i} ∈ subsets sᵧ) ∧
  (∀ t a i. $\mathbb{P}\{x \mid X t x = i\} \neq 0$ ⇒
    ($\mathbb{P}(\{x \mid Y t x = a\}|\{x \mid X t x = i\})$ = pₓᵧ t a i)) ∧
  ∀ t a i t$_{x_0}$ t$_{y_0}$ stsₓ stsᵧ tsₓ tsᵧ.
    $\mathbb{P}(\{x \mid X t x = i\} \cap \bigcap_{k \in \text{tsₓ}} \{x \mid X (t_{x_0} + k) x = \text{EL k stsₓ}\} \cap$
    $\bigcap_{k \in \text{tsᵧ}} \{x \mid Y (t_{y_0} + k) x = \text{EL k stsᵧ}\}) \neq 0$ ⇒
    ($\mathbb{P}(\{x \mid Y t x = a\}|\{x \mid X t x = i\} \cap$
      $\bigcap_{k \in \text{tsₓ}} \{x \mid X (t_{x_0} + k) x = \text{EL k stsₓ}\} \cap$
      $\bigcap_{k \in \text{tsᵧ}} \{x \mid Y (t_{y_0} + k) x = \text{EL k stsᵧ}\})$ =
    $\mathbb{P}(\{x \mid Y t x = a\}|\{x \mid X t x = i\}))$

The variable X denotes the random variable in the underlying DTMC, Y indicates the random observations, and p_{XY} indicates the emission probabilities. The following two conditions define a random process $\{Y_t\}_{t\geq 0}$ with a discrete state space. The fourth condition assigns the emission distributions given by p_{XY}. The last condition ensures the above mentioned conditional independence.

The *time-homogenous HMMs* can also be formalized in a way similar to time-homogenous DTMCs:

Definition 6. (Time-homogeneous HMM)

⊢ ∀ X Y p sₓ sᵧ p₀ pᵢⱼ pₓᵧ .
    thmm X Y p sₓ sᵧ p₀ pᵢⱼ pₓᵧ =
    hmm X Y p sₓ sᵧ p₀ pᵢⱼ pₓᵧ ∧ FINITE (space sₓ) ∧ FINITE (space sᵧ) ∧
    ∀ t a i j. ℙ{x | X t x = i} ≠ 0 ∧ ℙ{x | X (t + 1) x = i} ≠ 0 ⇒
      (Trans X p sₓ (t + 1) 1 i j = Trans X p sₓ t 1 i j) ∧
      (pₓᵧ (t + 1) i j = pₓᵧ t i j)

Next, we verify some classical properties of HMMs, which play a vital role in reducing the user interaction for the formal analysis of systems that can be represented in terms of HMMs.

4.1 Joint Probability of HMMs

The most important property of time homogeneous HMMs is the expression of the joint distribution of a sequence of states and its corresponding observation, which can be expressed using products of its emission probabilities and transition probabilities. This is frequently used to find the best state path or estimate model's parameters. Mathematically, this is expressed as the following equation:

$$Pr(Y_0, \cdots, Y_t, X_0, \cdots, X_t) = Pr(X_0)Pr(Y_0|X_0)\prod_{k=0}^{t-1} Pr(X_{k+1}|X_k)Pr(Y_{k+1}|X_{k+1})$$

and has been formally verified using the HOL theorem prover as follows:

Theorem 4. (Joint Probability of HMM)

⊢ ∀ X Y p t sₓ sᵧ p₀ pᵢⱼ pₓᵧ stsₓ stsᵧ .
    thmm X Y p sₓ sᵧ p₀ pᵢⱼ pₓᵧ ⇒
    (ℙ(⋂ₖ₌₀ᵗ{x | X k x = EL k stsₓ} ∩ ⋂ₖ₌₀ᵗ{x | Y k x = EL k stsᵧ}) =
    ℙ{x | X 0 x = EL 0 stsₓ}
    ℙ({x | Y 0 x = EL 0 stsᵧ}|{x | X 0 x = EL 0 stsₓ})
    (∏ₖ₌₀ᵗ⁻¹ℙ({x | X (k + 1) x = EL (k + 1) stsₓ}|{x | X k x = EL k stsₓ})
      ℙ({x | Y (k + 1) x = EL (k + 1) stsᵧ}|
      {x | X (k + 1) x = EL (k + 1) stsₓ}))

4.2 Joint Probability of an Observable Path

In addition to the above property, researchers are often interested in the probability of a particular observation, independently of any underlying state path.

This can be mathematically expressed as:

$$\mathcal{P}r(Y_0, \cdots, Y_t) = \sum_{\substack{X_0, \cdots, X_t \in \\ space\ s}} \mathcal{P}r(X_0)\mathcal{P}r(Y_0|X_0) \prod_{k=0}^{t-1} \mathcal{P}r(X_{k+1}|X_k)\mathcal{P}r(Y_{k+1}|X_{k+1})$$

Using Theorem 4, we can formally verify this equation as follows.

Theorem 5. (Joint Probability of Observable Path)

```
⊢ ∀ X Y p s n sₓ sʏ p₀ pᵢⱼ pₓʏ stsₓ.
    thmm X Y p sₓ sʏ p₀ pᵢⱼ pₓʏ ⟹
        let 𝓛 = {L | EVERY (λx. x ∈ space sₓ) L ∧ (|L| = n + 1)} in
        (ℙ(⋂ⁿₖ₌₀{x | Y k x = EL k stsʏ}) =
        ∑ₛₜₛₓ∈𝓛(ℙ{x | X 0 x = EL 0 stsₓ}
            ℙ({x | Y 0 x = EL 0 stsʏ}|{x | X 0 x = EL 0 stsₓ})
            (∏ⁿ⁻¹ₖ₌₀ℙ({x | X (k + 1) x = EL (k + 1) stsₓ}|
                {x | X k x = EL k stsₓ})
            ℙ({x | Y (k + 1) x = EL (k + 1) stsʏ}|
                {x | X (k + 1) x = EL (k + 1) stsₓ}))))
```

where |L| returns the length of the list L and **EVERY** p L is a predicate which is true iff the predicate p holds for every element of the list L.

One can note that Theorems 4 and 5 provide ways to *compute* the probabilities that are usually desired while analyzing HMMs. Consequently, if the theorems are instantiated with concrete values for their parameters, then a real number can be obtained for the corresponding probability. Thus, it seems natural to try to *automatize* such computations. Moreover, this is extremely useful since, in practice, one is always interested in applying the theorems to concrete situations. In the next subsection, we describe how to automatically acquire interesting probabilities and find the best state path, for a given HMM, using the results of Theorems 4 and 5. This makes the accuracy of theorem proving available even to users with no knowledge about logic or theorem proving, hence making our technique closer to practical usability.

4.3   Automating the HOL Computations

In order to automate the computation associated with Theorem 4, we define an SML function `hmm_joint_distribution ini_distr trans_distr e_distr sts obs` which takes as input the initial distributions, the transition probabilities, the emission distributions, a list of states and a list of observations: When calling this function, these parameters will be automatically substituted to p_0, p_{ij}, p_{XY}, sts_X and sts_Y, respectively, of Theorem 4. We then take t to be the length of `sts` (which should be the same as `obs`): this seems to be the most common case in practice, but could be easily relaxed if needed by adding a parameter to the function. We can then compute, using HOL4 theorems about lists, real numbers, etc., the right-hand side of the equation in Theorem 4 in an exact way (as a fraction). In the end, the function returns the corresponding instantiation of HOL4 theorem stating the equality between the joint probability and its value. Note that the result is really a HOL4 theorem: even the operations between real numbers like multiplication or addition are obtained by deductive reasoning, thus making every single step of the computation completely reliable and *traceable*. An example of this function will be presented in the next section. The implementation of the function hmm_joint_distribution requires the development of an intermediate lemma and makes heavy but fine-grain use of rewriting techniques in order to have a reasonable efficiency. We do not go into implementation details due to the lack of space.

The computations associated with Theorem 5 can also be automated similarly, but we can actually go further: A problem which arises very often in practice is to find the state path which has the best probability of generating a given observation sequence. To obtain this, we need to compute the set of all possible state paths, compute the probability of each of these paths as hmm_joint_distribution does, and then return the path which has the best probability. Once again, in order to be the most accurate as possible, all these computations shall be done inside HOL4. This can be achieved by an SML function best_path ini_distr trans_distr e_distr st_ty obs where ini_distr, trans_distr, e_distr, and obs denote the same objects as for hmm_joint_distribution and st_ty denotes the type of terms representing states. This type should be a non-recursive enumerated type, i.e., defined as $C_1 \mid C_2 \mid \ldots C_k$, where $C_1, \ldots, C_k$ are constructors without arguments: this ensures that the state-space is finite. The function then takes care of computing the list of all possible paths, then computes the corresponding joint probability as hmm_joint_distribution does, and, in the end, returns the state path which has the best such probability (note that the notion of "best probability" is also defined inside HOL4 by using the axiomatic definition of the order on real numbers). This function is currently very slow (with a 3-state path, it will take around one second to obtain the best path; for a 5-state path, it takes around one minute) due to the computation of the set of all possible state paths, but there is a lot of room for improvement, in particular by filtering paths which have trivially a null transition probability or null emission probability. This is a first step, which is not as fast as other statistical tools, on developing a tool to formally analyze HMMs.

We now show how to apply these theorems and functions in practice, by providing the formal analysis of a HMM of DNA model in the next section.

5   Application: Formal Analysis of DNA Sequence

DNA sequence analysis plays a vital role in constructing gene mapping, discovering new species and investigating disease-manifestations in genetic linkage, parental testing and criminal investigation. Statistical methods are mainly applied for analyzing DNA sequence. In particular, obtaining the probability of a state path underlying the DNA fragment is the most critical step in identifying a particular DNA sequence.

A DNA fragment is a sequence of nucleotides called A (Adenine), T (Thymine), G (Guanine) and C (Cytosine). However, nucleotide composition of DNA is in

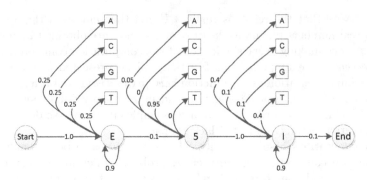

Fig. 1. 5' splice site recognition model

general not uniformly distributed (because every DNA sequence can be synthe-
sised): some regularities can be found among the possible sequences. For instance,
it might be that all four nucleotides can appear with equal probability at the beginning of the sequence, but, after a particular point, only A and G can appear,
and then all four can appear again but with higher probabilities for A and T.
In this application, there are thus three different "states" of the DNA, characterized by the probabilities of occurrence of each base. In this DNA model, the
first state is called *exon* (E), the second one *5' splice site* (5), and the third one
intron (I) [8]. This model is described and studied very naturally using HMMs
[8]: a DTMC over the states E, 5, and I is used in order to know in which state
the nucleotides are, then another random process is defined which characterizes
the emission of A, G, T or C according to the state which the proteins are in.
This is summarized in Fig. 1.

In order to formalize this HMM, we first define types representing the states
and the bases:

Definition 7. (HOL4 Data Types)

⊢ dna = A | G | T | C
⊢ state = START | E | I | FIVE | END

Note that, in order to characterize the sequence, it is a common practice to add
some fake start and end states, which have no connection with the observable
sequence and thus no emission probability is required. Hence START and END are
contained in the definition of state in Definition 7. As examples, we define the
following state and DNA sequences:

Definition 8. (State Path and DNA Sequence)

⊢ state_seq = [START; E; E; E; E; E; E; E; E; E; E; E; E; E; E; E; E; E; FIVE; I; I; I; I; I; I; I; END]
⊢ dna_seq = [C; T; T; C; A; T; G; T; G; A; A; A; G; C; A; G; A; C; G; T; A; A; G; T; C; A]

So as to model the HMM represented in Fig. 1, we need an initial distribution,
the transition probabilities, and the emission probabilities, which we define as
follows:

Definition 9. (DNA Model Parameters)

$\vdash$ ini_distr i = if (i = START) then 1 else 0

$\vdash$ e_distr a i =
case (i, a) of

(E, _)	$\rightarrow$ 0.25
$\|$ (FIVE, A)	$\rightarrow$ 0.05
$\|$ (FIVE, G)	$\rightarrow$ 0.95
$\|$ (I, A)	$\rightarrow$ 0.4
$\|$ (I, T)	$\rightarrow$ 0.4
$\|$ (I, G)	$\rightarrow$ 0.1
$\|$ (I, C)	$\rightarrow$ 0.1
$\|$ -	$\rightarrow$ 0

$\vdash$ trans_distr t i j =
case (i, j) of

(START, E)	$\rightarrow$ 1
$\|$ (E, E)	$\rightarrow$ 0.9
$\|$ (E, FIVE)	$\rightarrow$ 0.1
$\|$ (FIVE, I)	$\rightarrow$ 1
$\|$ (I, I)	$\rightarrow$ 0.9
$\|$ (I, END)	$\rightarrow$ 0.1
$\|$ -	$\rightarrow$ 0

Then, in order to work with random variables X and Y denoting the states and the observations, respectively, on a probability space p, it is sufficient to have the following predicate:

thmm X Y p s_X s_Y ini_distr trans_distr e_distr

$$\wedge \text{ space } s_X = \text{univ}(: \text{state}) \wedge \text{ space } s_Y = \text{univ}(: \text{dna})$$

where univ(:t) is the set of all possible values of type t, e.g., univ(:dna) = {A; G; T; C}.

Now, for instance, we can prove the theorem which gives the probability of obtaining the sequence dna_seq if the underlying state path is state_seq:

Theorem 6. (Joint Probability of a DNA Segment)

$\vdash \forall$ X Y p s_X s_Y.
thmm X Y p s_X s_Y ini_distr trans_distr e_distr $\wedge$
space $s_X = \text{univ}(: \text{state}) \wedge$ space $s_Y = \text{univ}(: \text{dna}) \Rightarrow$

$\mathbb{P}(\bigcap_{k=0}^{|\text{state\_seq}|-1}\{x \mid X \ k \ x = \text{EL} \ k \ \text{state\_seq}\} \cap$
$\bigcap_{k=0}^{|\text{dna\_seq}|-1}\{x \mid Y \ k \ x = \text{EL} \ k \ \text{dna\_seq}\}) = 0.25^{18} * 0.9^{23} * 0.1^4 * 0.95 * 0.4^5$

To verify this theorem, a lemma of Theorem 4 is proved firstly:

Lemma 1.

$\vdash \forall$ X Y p t s_X s_Y p_0 p_{ij} p_{XY} sts_X sts_Y.
thmm X Y p s_X s_Y p_0 p_{ij} p_{XY} $\wedge$ $(|sts_x|=t + 3) \wedge (|sts_y|=t + 1) \Rightarrow$
$(\mathbb{P}(\bigcap_{k=0}^{t+2}\{x \mid X \ k \ x = \text{EL} \ k \ sts_X\} \cap \bigcap_{k=0}^{t}\{x \mid Y \ k \ x = \text{EL} \ k \ sts_Y\})=$
$\mathbb{P}\{x \mid X \ 0 \ x = \text{EL} \ 0 \ sts_X\}$
$\mathbb{P}(\{x \mid X \ (k + 2) \ x = \text{EL} \ (k + 2) \ sts_X\}|$
$\{x \mid X \ (k + 1) \ x = \text{EL} \ (k + 1) \ sts_X\})$
$(\prod_{k=0}^{t}\mathbb{P}(\{x \mid X \ (k + 1) \ x = \text{EL} \ (k + 1) \ sts_X\}|\{x \mid X \ k \ x = \text{EL} \ k \ sts_X\})$
$\mathbb{P}(\{x \mid Y \ (k + 1) \ x = \text{EL} \ k \ sts_Y\}|\{x \mid X \ k \ x = \text{EL} \ (k + 1) \ sts_X\}))$

Actually, a more interesting information than the above number is to find which among all possible state paths has the highest probability to occur given a particular DNA sequence. This state path is called the *best path* in our case. In our particular context, this problem is called *5' splice site recognition*. This is verified as follows:

Theorem 7. (Best State Path)

$\vdash \forall$ X Y p s_X s_Y.
  thmm X Y p s_X s_Y ini_distr trans_distr e_distr $\wedge$
  space $s_X = $ univ(: state) $\wedge$ space $s_Y = $ univ(: dna) $\Rightarrow$
  REAL_MAXIMIZE_SET
    [E; E; E; E; E; E; E; E; E; E; E; E; E; E; E; E; FIVE; I; I; I; I; I; I; I]
    (λsts. $\mathbb{P}(\bigcap_{k=0}^{|\text{sts}|-1}\{x \mid$ X k x $=$ EL k state_seq$\} \bigcap$
      $\bigcap_{k=0}^{|\text{dna\_seq}|-1}\{x \mid$ Y k x $=$ EL k dna_seq$\}))$ $\{$sts $\mid$ $|$sts$| = 26\}$

where REAL_MAXIMIZE_SET m f s is a predicate which is true only if f m is the maximum element of $\{$f x $\mid$ x $\in$ s$\}$ (this is defined as a predicate because there can be several elements of s having this property). Note once again that this theorem is proved in a purely formal way, i.e., even the comparisons between probabilities are proved deductively from the axiomatic definition of real numbers. Consequently, the confidence that we can have in the result is maximal.

While Theorems 6 and 7 have been proved in the classical theorem proving way, i.e., interactively, there are rare chances that a biologist has the required knowledge of higher-order logic and HOL4 so as to conduct such a study. However, we can, by using SML functions that we presented in the previous section, get the same result in a purely automated way. In order to call the functions hmm_joint_distribution and best_path, we need to define their arguments as SML values:

```
> val dna_seq =
"[C;T;T;C;A;T;G;T;G;A;A;A;G;C;A;G;A;C;G;T;A;A;G;T;C;A]";

> val state_seq =
"[START;E;E;E;E;E;E;E;E;E;E;E;E;E;E;E;E;FIVE;I;I;I;I;I;I;I;END]";

> val ini_distr = "λ i. if (i = START) then 1 else 0";

> val trans_distr = "λ t i j. case (i, a) of
    (START, E) → 1 ‖ (E, E) → 0.9 ‖  (E, FIVE) → 0.1 ‖ (FIVE, I) → 1 ‖
    (I, FIVE) → 0.9 ‖ (I, END) → 0.1 ‖ _ → 0"

> val e_distr a i = "λ t a i. case (i, a) of
    (E, _) → 0.25 ‖ (FIVE, A) → 0.05 ‖ (FIVE, G) → 0.95 ‖ (I, A) → 0.4 ‖
    (I, T) → 0.4 ‖ (I, G) → 0.1 ‖ (I, C) →; 0.1 ‖ _ → 0"
```

Note that, contrarily to the previous definitions, dna_seq, state_seq, ini_distr, trans_distr and e_distr are *SML values*, whereas the values with the same names presented in Definitions 8 and 9 are *HOL4 values*. Of course, in practice, these need to be defined only once (in SML if using the automated way, or in HOL4 if using the interactive way). We can then call the SML function hmm_joint_distribution as follows:

> hmm_joint_distribution ini_distr trans_distr e_distr dna_seq state_seq;

which gives the following output:

```
Exact value with the corresponding assumptions (obtained by HOL4):
```

$\forall$ X Y p s_X s_Y.
  thmm X Y p s_X s_Y
    (λ i. if i = START then 1 else 0)
    (λ t i j. case (i,j) of
      (E, _) $\rightarrow$ 0.25 $\|$ (FIVE, A) $\rightarrow$ 0.05 $\|$ (FIVE, G) $\rightarrow$ 0.95 $\|$ (I, A) $\rightarrow$ 0.4 $\|$
      (I, T) $\rightarrow$ 0.4 $\|$ (I, G) $\rightarrow$ 0.1 $\|$ (I, C) $\rightarrow$ 0.1 $\|$ _ $\rightarrow$ 0.1
    (λ t a i. case (i,a) of
      (START, E) $\rightarrow$ 1 $\|$ (E, E) $\rightarrow$ 0.9 $\|$ (E, FIVE) $\rightarrow$ 0.1 $\|$
      (FIVE, I) $\rightarrow$ 1 $\|$ (I, I) $\rightarrow$ 0.9 $\|$ (I, END) $\rightarrow$ 0.1 $\|$ _ $\rightarrow$ 0 $\wedge$
    (space s_X = univ(:state)) $\wedge$ (space s_Y = univ(:dna)) $\Rightarrow$
    $\mathbb{P}(\bigcap_{k=0}^{27}\{x \mid X \; k \; x = $
      EL k [START;E;E;E;E;E;E;E;E;E;E;E;E;E;E;E;E;E;FIVE;I;I;
        I;I;I;I;I;END]\} \cap $
    $\bigcap_{k=0}^{25}\{x \mid Y \; k \; x = $
      EL k [C;T;T;C;A;T;G;T;G;A;A;A;G;C;A;G;A;C;G;T;A;A;G;T;C;A]\}\})
    $= \dfrac{168395824273397520822651}{13421772800000000000000000000000000000000000}$

Thus, as we can see, the SML function is able to return a HOL4 theorem giving the exact value of the desired probability in a purely automated way. For convenience, the approximated value can also be computed by SML from the HOL4 exact value. Similarly, a result corresponding to Theorem 7 can be obtained automatically by using best_path. In [8], the probability of the best path is $e^{-41.22}$ and that of the second best path is $e^{-41.71}$. It is quite likely that the path chosen by numerical algorithm in the simulation tools is not the best one due to the numerical approximations. On the other hand, theorem proving based approach provides the best path with unrivaled accuracy.

This concludes our analysis of the 5' splice site DNA problem. It is, to the best of our knowledge, the first such *formal* analysis. In addition, we demonstrated how useful are our automation functions, since they allow to reduce the interaction with the user to a minimum, especially in reducing interactive guide when computing concrete numerical values in applications. All the proof scripts corresponding to this work are available at [14].

6 Conclusions

HMMs, which are used to model an observable stochastic process with an underlying Markov process, are mainly applied to model and analyze time series data in various engineering and scientific systems. This paper presents a formalization of HMMs based on an enhanced definition of discrete-time Markov chain with finite state-space in a higher-order logic theorem prover. In particular, we present a formal definition of time homogeneous DTMC and formally verify some of their classical properties, such as *joint probabilities*, *Chapman-Kolmogorov Equation* and *absolute probabilities*, using the HOL4 theorem prover. Furthermore, some properties of HMMs are verified in HOL4. This work facilitates the formal analysis of HMMs and provides the foundations for formalizing more advanced concepts of Markov chain theory, like classified DTMCs and useful properties of HMMs. In addition, we automatized some of the most common tasks related to HMMs, thus demonstrating the practical usability of our approach. Due to the inherent soundness of theorem proving, it is guaranteed to provide accurate results, which is a very useful feature while analyzing HMMs associated with safety or mission-critical systems. In order to illustrate the usefulness of the proposed approach, we analyzed an HMM for 5' splice site DNA recognition using our formalization and automation. Our results exactly matched the corresponding paper-and-pencil based analysis [8], which ascertains the precise nature of the proposed approach. Note that our approach is quite general and it can be applied in DNA models, which usually consist of many states.

As the formal analysis of HMMs cannot be achieved in *PRISM*, the presented work opens the door to a new and very promising research direction, i.e., integrating HOL theorem proving in the domain of analyzing HMMs. We are currently working on extending the set of formally verified properties regarding DTMCs and extending our work to time-inhomogeneous discrete-time Markov chains, which will enable us to target a wider set of systems. We also plan to formally verify the *Forward-Backward*, *Viterbi* and *Baum-Welch* algorithms [16], which are widely applied in statistical biology analysis. By improving the efficiency of automation functions and by making their scope broader, we could also consider the development of a purely automated but formal tool to analyse HMMs.

References

1. Affeldt, R., Hagiwara, M.: Formalization of shannon's theorems in sSReflect-coq. In: Beringer, L., Felty, A. (eds.) ITP 2012. LNCS, vol. 7406, pp. 233–249. Springer, Heidelberg (2012)
2. C. Baier and J. Katoen. Principles of Model Checking. MIT Press (2008)
3. Bhattacharya, R.N., Waymire, E.C.: Stochastic Processes with Applications. John Wiley & Sons (1990)
4. ChIP-Seq Tool Set (2012), http://havoc.genomecenter.ucdavis.edu/cgi-bin/chipseq.cgi
5. Chung, K.L.: Markov chains with stationary transition probabilities. Springer, Heidelberg (1960)
6. Coq (2014), http://coq.inria.fr/
7. Daniel, N.: Electrocardiogram Signal Processing using Hidden Markov Models. Ph.D. Thesis, Czech Technical University, Czech Republic (2003)

8. Eddy, S.R.: What is a Hidden Markov Model? Nature Biotechnology 22(10), 1315–1316 (2004)
9. Frédéric, S., Delorenzi, M.: MAMOT: Hidden Markov Modeling Tool. Bioinformatics 24(11), 1399–1400 (2008)
10. Gordon, M.J.C.: Mechanizing Programming Logics in Higher-Order Logic. In: Current Trends in Hardware Verification and Automated Theorem Proving, pp. 387–439. Springer, Heidelberg (1989)
11. HMMER (2013), http://hmmer.janelia.org/
12. HMMTool (2013), http://iri.columbia.edu/climate/forecast/stochastictools/
13. Hölzl, J., Heller, A.: Three Chapters of Measure Theory in Isabelle/HOL. In: van Eekelen, M., Geuvers, H., Schmaltz, J., Wiedijk, F. (eds.) ITP 2011. LNCS, vol. 6898, pp. 135–151. Springer, Heidelberg (2011)
14. L. Liu (2013), http://hvg.ece.concordia.ca/projects/prob-it/dtmc_hmm.html
15. Liu, L., Hasan, O., Tahar, S.: Formalization of finite-state discrete-time markov chains in HOL. In: Bultan, T., Hsiung, P.-A. (eds.) ATVA 2011. LNCS, vol. 6996, pp. 90–104. Springer, Heidelberg (2011)
16. MacDonald, I.L., Zucchini, W.: Hidden Markov and Other Models for Discrete-valued Time Series. Chapman & Hall, London (1997)
17. Mhamdi, T., Hasan, O., Tahar, S.: On the Formalization of the Lebesgue Integration Theory in HOL. In: Kaufmann, M., Paulson, L.C. (eds.) ITP 2010. LNCS, vol. 6172, pp. 387–402. Springer, Heidelberg (2010)
18. MRMC (2013), http://www.mrmc-tool.org/trac/
19. Norris, J.R.: Markov Chains. Cambridge University Press (1999)
20. PRISM (2013), http://www.prismmodelchecker.org
21. Robertson, A.W., Kirshner, S., Smyth, P.: Downscaling of Daily Rainfall Occurrence over Northeast Brazil using a Hidden Markov Model. Journal of Climate 17, 4407–4424 (2004)
22. Rutten, J., Kwaiatkowska, M., Norman, G., Parker, D.: Mathematical Techniques for Analyzing Concurrent and Probabilisitc Systems. CRM Monograph Series, vol. 23. American Mathematical Society (2004)
23. Sen, K., Viswanathan, M., Agha, G.: VESTA: A Statistical Model-Checker and Analyzer for Probabilistic Systems. In: IEEE International Conference on the Quantitative Evaluation of Systems, pp. 251–252 (2005)
24. YMER (2013), http://www.tempastic.org/ymer/
25. Zhang, L., Hermanns, H., Jansen, D.N.: Logic and Model Checking for Hidden Markov Models. In: Wang, F. (ed.) FORTE 2005. LNCS, vol. 3731, pp. 98–112. Springer, Heidelberg (2005)
26. Zhang, L.J.: Logic and Model Checking for Hidden Markov Models. Master Thesis, Universität des Saarlandes, Germany (2004)
27. Zoubin, G.: An Introduction to Hidden Markov Models and Bayesian Networks. International Journal of Pattern Recognition and Artificial Intelligence 15(1), 9–42 (2001)

Formal Modeling and Analysis
of Cassandra in Maude

Si Liu, Muntasir Raihan Rahman, Stephen Skeirik,
Indranil Gupta, and José Meseguer

Department of Computer Science,
University of Illinois at Urbana-Champaign, USA

Abstract. Distributed key-value stores are quickly becoming a key component of cloud computing systems. In order to improve read/write latency, distributed key-value stores offer weak notions of consistency to clients by using many complex design decisions. However, it is challenging to formally analyze consistency behaviors of such systems, both because there are few formal models, and because different consistency level combinations render understanding hard, particularly under communication latency. This paper presents for the first time a formal executable model in Maude of Cassandra, a popular key-value store. We formally models Cassandra's main components and design strategies. We formally specify various *consistency properties* and model check them against our model under various communication latency and consistency combinations.

1 Introduction

Distributed key-value (e.g., Cassandra [2], RIAK [1]) storage systems are increasingly being used to store and query data in today's industrial deployments. Many diverse companies and organizations are moving away from traditional strongly consistent databases and are instead using key-value/NoSQL stores in order to store huge data sets and tackle an increasing number of users. According to DB-Engines Ranking [3] by April 2014, Cassandra advanced into the top 10 most popular database engines among 216 systems, underlining the increasing popularity of key-value database systems.

Distributed key-value stores typically replicate data on multiple servers for greater availability in the presence of failures. Since any of such servers can now respond to client read requests, it becomes costly to always keep all the replicas synchronized. This creates a tension between *consistency* (keeping all replicas synchronized) and *availability* (replying to clients quickly), especially when the network is partitioned [7]. Whereas traditional databases favor consistency over availability, distributed key-value stores risk exposing stale data to clients to remain highly available. This approach was popularized by the Dynamo [20] key-value store architecture from Amazon. Cassandra [2] is an open-source distributed key-value store which closely follows the Dynamo architecture. Many large scale Internet service companies like Netflix, IBM, HP, Facebook, Spotify, and PBS Kids rely heavily on the Cassandra key-value storage system.

S. Merz and J. Pang (Eds.): ICFEM 2014, LNCS 8829, pp. 332–347, 2014.

Weakly consistent key-value stores like Cassandra typically employ many *complex design decisions* that can impact the consistency and availability guarantees offered to the clients. Therefore, there is an urgent need to develop *formal models* for specifying these design decisions and for reasoning about the impact of these design choices on specified consistency (correctness) and availability (performance) guarantees. For distributed key-value stores like Cassandra, at present the only way to understand the inner workings of such a system is to browse the huge code base. For example, the latest version of Apache Cassandra has 342, 519 lines of code. An important part of this work has been to study in detail the Cassandra code for its main components, to incrementally build Maude formal models of such components, and to check that the formal models faithfully capture the Cassandra design decisions. This is one of our main contributions, providing a solid basis for the subsequent formal analysis.

Once we have a formal executable model for Cassandra, we can conveniently model check various important properties about the system. Although we know Cassandra favors eventual consistency, there is no formal treatment that specifies when Cassandra satisfies eventual consistency and when it might actually offer strong consistency. Therefore it is very important to formally specify various consistency properties and check whether the system satisfies those properties under various combinations of message delays and consistency levels.

Currently there are two main approaches for verifying consistency models for distributed key-value stores. First, we can *run a given key-value store under a particular environment*, and *audit* the read/write operation logs to check for consistency violations [17]. Second, we can *analyze the algorithms used by the key-value store to ensure consistency* [15]. However, the former is not guaranteed to find all violations of the consistency model, and the latter is time-consuming and needs to be repeated for every system with different implementations of the underlying algorithms for guaranteeing consistency.

In this paper, we present a formal executable model of Cassandra using Maude [8], a modeling language based on rewriting logic that has proved suitable for modeling and analyzing distributed systems. Our Maude model includes main components of Cassandra such as data partitioning strategies, consistency levels, and timestamp policies for ordering multiple versions of data (the details of these components are given in Section 2.1). We have also specified Cassandra's main consistency properties, *strong consistency* and *eventual consistency*, in *linear temporal logic* (LTL). We have then model checked these properties using Maude's built-in LTL model checker. As a result, we can model check whether the properties hold or not for possibly different delay distributions between clients and servers, and for various combinations of consistency levels used by clients. Our analysis results indicate that eventual consistency is always satisfied by our Cassandra model. However, we discovered violations of the strong consistency property under certain scenarios. Although Cassandra is expected to violate strong consistency under certain conditions, previously there was no formal way of discovering under which conditions such violations could occur. At the software engineering level our formal modeling and analysis compares favorably with previous approaches: our Maude specification is fewer than 1000 lines of code, and consistency verification in our formal approach is faster, more accurate and provides stronger assurance than existing approaches, which require analyzing the extremely large code base.

The two main contributions of this paper are:

- We present, to the best of our knowledge for the first time, a *formal executable model* for the Cassandra key-value store; this has required a large amount of effort due to Cassandra's extremely large code base.
- We formally specify and model check Cassandra' main consistency properties, namely, *strong consistency* and *eventual consistency*, and explicitly show when Cassandra satisfies these properties or not.

Due to lack of space we refer to the techincal report [14] for two more contributions: (i) the formal analysis of Cassandra's *read repair* mechanism, and (ii) the extension of our formal model to easily explore other *design decisions* for key-value stores.

The rest of the paper is organized as follows. Section 2 gives a brief overview of Cassandra and Maude. Next, in Section 3 and Section 4, we present our formal executable model for Cassandra, and the analysis of Cassandra consistency, respectively. Finally, in Section 5 we conclude and discuss related work and future directions.

2   Preliminaries

2.1   Cassandra Overview

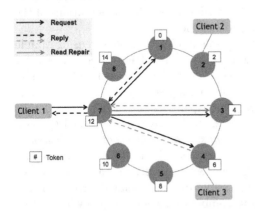

Fig. 1. The architecture of Cassandra deployed in a single data center with an 8 server ring of size 16

Apache Cassandra [2] is a high-performance, extremely scalable, and distributed NoSQL database solution. Cassandra dynamically partitions data across the cluster servers for scalability, so that data can be written to or read from any server in the system. The total amount of data managed by the cluster is represented as a *ring*. The ring is divided into *ranges*, with each server being responsible for one or more ranges of the data. Cassandra allows several *replica* servers to store a particular key-value pair. To place those replicas different strategies can be employed, e.g., the *Simple Strategy* places replicas clockwise in a single data center. For a private cloud, Cassandra is typically deployed in a single data center with a single ring structure shared by all its servers.

When a client issues a read/write request to a data center, a *coordinator* (a server in the cluster) forwards the request to all the replicas that hold copies of the same data. However, based on the specified *consistency level* for a read/write, the coordinator will reply back to the client after receiving responses from some of the replicas. This improves operation latency, since the coordinator does not have to wait for a slow server. Thus, the consistency level is the main dial to trade between consistency and availability. Cassandra supports three main consistency levels, ONE, QUORUM and ALL, for single data center settings, meaning that the coordinator will reply back to the client after hearing from *one* replica, a *majority* of replicas, or *all* replicas. To ensure that all replicas have the *most recent* version of any data item, Cassandra employs a *read repair* mechanism to update the out-of-date replicas.

Fig. 1 shows the architecture of Cassandra deployed in a single data center with an 8 server ring of size 16 (indicated by the tokens), where all servers are placed clockwise with each responsible for the region of the ring between itself (inclusive) and its successor (exclusive). An incoming read/write from client 1 will go to all 3 (the *replication factor* in this case) replicas (indicated by the black solid arrows). If the read/write consistency level specified by the client is ONE, the first node to complete the read/write (node 1 in this example) responds back to the coordinator 7, which then forwards the value or acknowledgement back to the client (indicated by the black dashed arrows). In the case of a read, later replies from the remaining replicas, nodes 3 and 4, may report different versions of the value w.r.t. the key issued by the client (indicated by the grey dashed arrows). If replica 3 holds an out-of-date value, in the background, 7 then issues a write (called a read repair) with the most recent value to 3 (indicated by the red arrow). Note that in a data center different clients may connect to different coordinators, and all servers maintain the same view on the ring structure. Thus, requests from any client on the same key will be always forwarded by the associated coordinator to the same replicas.

2.2 Actors and LTL Model Checking in Maude

Maude [8] is a language and tool that supports the formal specification and analysis of a wide range of concurrent systems. A Maude module specifies a *rewrite theory* $(\Sigma, E \cup A, R)$, where Σ is an algebraic *signature* declaring *sorts, subsorts,* and *function symbols*; $(\Sigma, E \cup A)$ is a *membership equational logic theory* [8], with E a set of possibly conditional equations, and A a set of equational axioms such as associativity, commutativity, and identity; $(\Sigma, E \cup A)$ specifies the system's state space as an algebraic data type; R is a set of *labeled conditional rewrite rules* specifying the system's *local transitions*, each of which has the form $[l] : t \longrightarrow t'$ if $\bigwedge_{j=1}^{m} cond_j$, where each $cond_j$ is either an equality $u_j = v_j$ or a rewrite $t_j \longrightarrow t'_j$, and l is a *label*. Such a rule specifies a transition from an instance of t to the corresponding instance of t', *provided* the condition holds.

The Actor Model in Maude. The *actor model of computation* [4] is a model of concurrent computation based on asynchronous message passing between objects called *actors*. Following the ideas of [16] and [10], the distributed state of an actor system is formalized as a *multiset* of objects and messages, including a scheduler object that keeps track of the *global time*. Multiset union is denoted by an associative and commutative juxtaposition operator, so that rewriting is *multiset rewriting*. An *actor* of the form   < id : class | a1 : v1, a2 : v2, ..., an : vn >   is an object instance of the class class that encapsulates the attributes a1 to an with the current values v1 to vn, respectively, and can be addressed using a unique name id. Actors communicate with each other using asynchronous messages. Upon receiving a message, an actor can change its state and can send messages to other actors. Actors can model a distributed systems such as Cassandra in a natural way. For example, the rewrite rule

```
rl [1] :  m(O,w)   < O : C | a1 : x, a2 : O' >
   =>   < O : C | a1 : x + w, a2 : O' >   m'(O',x) .
```

defines transitions where a message m, with parameters O and w, is read and consumed by an object O of class C, the attribute a1 of object O is changed to x + w, and a new message m'(O',x) is generated.

Formal Analysis. In this paper we use Maude's *linear temporal logic model checker*, which analyzes whether *each* behavior from an initial state satisfies a temporal logic formula. *State propositions* are terms of sort Prop. Their semantics is defined by conditional equations of the form: ceq *statePattern* |= *prop* = b if *cond* ., for b a term of sort Bool, stating that *prop* evaluates to b in states that are instances of *statePattern* when the condition *cond* holds. These equations together define *prop* to hold in all states t where t |= *prop* evaluates to true. A temporal logic *formula* is constructed by state propositions and temporal logic operators such as True, False, ~ (negation), /\, \/, -> (implication), [] ("always"), <> ("eventually"), and U ("until"). The model checking command red modelCheck(t, φ) . checks whether the temporal logic formula φ holds in all behaviors starting from the initial state t.

3   Formalizing Cassandra

This section presents a formal model of Cassandra. Section 3.1 shows how a Cassandra ring structure is specified in Maude, Section 3.2 describes the models of clients and servers, and Section 3.3 shows how we model messages, time and message delays and formalizes Cassandra's dynamic behaviors. The entire executable Maude specification is available at https://sites.google.com/site/siliunobi/icfem-cassandra.

3.1   Modeling the Ring Structure

Cassandra partitions data across a ring of cluster servers and allows several (replication factor) replicas to store a particular key-value pair. For replica placement we specify the *Simple Strategy* [12], which places replicas clockwise in a single data center without considering topology.

We model the Cassandra ring as a ring structure with natural numbers modulo the parametric ring size `RingSize`. Each token on the ring (see Fig. 1) is modeled as a pair of sort `RingPair` of `Position` and `Address`, referring to the position locating the token and the server responsible for it respectively. Each server claims the region of the ring between itself (inclusive) and its successor (exclusive). As an example, a simple 4 server ring of size 16 is specified as `(([0],1),([4],2),([8],3),([12],4))`, where the first server 1 is responsible for the range `[0...3]`, the server 2 for `[4...7]`, the server 3 for `[8...11]` and the server 4 for `[12...15]`.

3.2   Modeling Clients and Servers

Clients. A client in our model generates read or write requests. Our clients also collect responses for analysis purposes, such as checking consistency violations. We can have *one* or *multiple* clients, depending on the analysis we perform (see Section 4.1). We model a client actor with attributes for the address of the coordinator it recognizes, a store used to save the incoming messages, two queues of read/write requests that are ready or pending for sending out, and the corresponding set of locked keys. A key is *locked* if a client issues a read/write on it, and will be unlocked upon the client receiving the associated value/acknowledgement. This ensures that requests from the same client on the same key are ordered, i.e., the client locks the key until the preceding operation completes.

Servers. All servers in Cassandra are peers of each other, and a client's read/write request can reach any server in the cluster. We do not distinguish a coordinator from a replica, since the server receiving the client's request will automatically serve as the coordinator. In addition, a coordinator can also be one of the replicas that store a particular key-value pair. We model a server actor with attributes for a global ring, a table storing data, a buffer (empty if not a coordinator) caching the requests generated for replicas, and a finite set of message delays that are chosen nondeterministically for each outgoing message (see Section 3.3).

As an example, an instance of a client/server can be initialized as:

```
< 100 : Client | coord: 1, store: nil,       < 1 : Server | ring: (([0],1),([4],2),([8],3),
    requestQueue: (r1 r2), lockedKey: empty,      ([12],4)), table: (3 |-> ("tea",10.0),
    pendingQueue: nil >                           8 |-> ("coffee",5.0), 10 |-> ("water", 0.0),
                                                  15 |-> ("coke",2.0)), buffer: empty,
                                                  delays: (1.0,2.0,4.0,8.0) >
```

where client 100 connects to coordinator 1, and intends to send out two requests r1 and r2; server 1 has a view of the ring structure, a set of four possible delays, and a local key-value store modeled using the predefined data module `MAP` in Maude, with each key of sort `Key` mapped to a pair of sort `TableData` consisting of the data of sort `Value` and the timestamp of sort `Float`. For example, key 8 maps to data `("coffee",5.0)`, indicating `"coffee"` is written into Server 1 at global time `5.0s`.

3.3   Formalizing Reads and Writes in Cassandra

Messages and Delays. Regarding its delivery, a message is either *active* (ready for delivery) or *inactive* (scheduled for delivery), depending on whether the associated delay has elapsed, which is determined by the system's *global clock* [10]. An active or inactive message is of the format {T,MSG} or [D,MSG], respectively, where D refers to the delay of message MSG, and T refers to the global time when MSG is ready for delivery. For example, if message [D,MSG] is generated at the current global time GT, T equals to GT + D.

All messages have associated delays. To simplify the model without losing generality, we abstract those delays into two kinds: (i) the delay between a client and a coordinator, and (ii) the delay between a coordinator and a replica. Since we equip a coordinator with a *finite* delay set, as shown in Fig. 2, nondeterministic delays will be added to the messages generated at its side. Fig. 2 shows example delays D4 for a read/write reply from the coordinator to the client, and D2 for a read/write request from the coordinator to the replica, with the other two delays, D1 and D3, set to 0.0s.

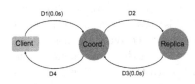

Fig. 2. Message Delays

To appropriately schedule messages, we introduce a *scheduler* object of the form {GT|MS} which maintains a global clock GT indicating the current global time, and provides a deterministic ordering of messages MS [10]. Inactive messages are inserted into the scheduler. When the global time in the scheduler is advanced to the moment when some delay expires, the associated message becomes active and is consumed by the target client/server. Therefore, the scheduler can be also considered as an object that advances the model's global time.

In the context of reads/writes, a message in our model can be defined based on (i) whether it is a read or write; (ii) whether it is a request or a reply; and (iii) which side it is from/to. For example, RReqCS(...) is a client-to-coordinator read request; and WRepSS(...) is a replica-to-coordinator write reply.

Reads and Writes. As mentioned in Section 2.1, communication can be between a client, a coordinator and several replicas. Due to space limitations, we only illustrate the model dynamics: (i) at the client side for generating requests, and (ii) at the coordinator side for routing read requests to the replicas.[1] We refer the reader to our longer report [14] for additional details.

(i) Generating requests by clients. In Cassandra, a client always generates *strictly ordered* requests w.r.t. a certain key. More precisely, when a client wants to issue a read/write (triggered by a bootstrap message to itself), it looks up the associated key in the set of locked keys. If the key is locked, the request will be added to the pending queue; otherwise, the request will be sent out to the

---

[1] We often omit the type declaration for the mathematical variables in the rules, but follow the Maude convention that variables are written in capital letters.

coordinator, and then the key will be locked. To emit all requests that are not restricted by the locked keys, a client will iteratively send itself a `bootstrap` message to trigger the above process until the request queue is empty. Thus, given a key, an associated read/write will block all subsequent operations with the same key until accomplished. The following rewrite rule illustrates the case when a client successfully sends out a request:

```
crl [CLIENT-REQUEST] :
    < A : Client | coord: S, requestQueue: Q, lockedKey: KS, AS > {T, A <- bootstrap}
=> < A : Client | coord: S, requestQueue: tail(Q), lockedKey: add(H,KS), AS >
    [d1, S <- request(H,T)] [ds, A <- bootstrap]
    if H := head(Q) /\ Q =/= nil /\ not pending(H,KS) .
```

where the global time T is put into the outgoing request H by function `request`, meaning that the *timestamp* in a client's request should be the moment when it is generated [12]. `d1` (corresponding to D1 in Fig. 2) and `ds` refer to the *delays* for a client-to-coordinator request and a self-triggered message respectively. Function `pending` determines whether a key is locked. Note that requests generated by different clients are *independent* of each other, i.e., it is not the case that a read/write will block all subsequent operations from other clients on the same key until accomplished.

(ii) Forwarding reads by the coordinator. As shown below, upon receiving the request on key K with consistency level L from client A, coordinator S updates the local buffer with the received information for each request ID, and generates the appropriate number of read requests for the replicas according to replication factor `fa`. Function `rpl` returns a set of replica addresses:

```
crl [COORD-FORWARD-READ-REQUEST] :
    < S : Server | ring: R, buffer: B, delays: DS, AS > {T, S <- RReqCS(ID,K,L,A)}
=> < S : Server | ring: R, buffer: insert(ID,fa,L,K,B), delays: DS,AS > C
    if generate(ID,K,DS,rpl(K,R,fa),S,A) => C .
```

The coordinator nondeterministically selects a message delay D for each outgoing request. The following rewrite rule together with the above one show how the coordinator will send each replica a read request with a nondeterministically chosen delay:

```
rl [GENERATE-READ-REQUEST] : generate(ID,K,(D,DS),(A',AD'),S,A)
=> [D, A' <- RReqSS(ID,K,S,A)] generate(ID,K,(D,DS),AD',S,A) .
```

where the replica address A' is iteratively selected from the address set returned by `rpl`, and the message delay D (corresponding to D2 in Fig. 2) is nondeterministically selected from the delay set.

4 Formal Analysis of Consistency in the Cassandra Model

In this section we formally analyze the Cassandra model built in Section 3, and check for *consistency violations* under various latency and consistency level combinations. Section 4.1 presents the main consistency properties we want to check. Sections 4.2 and 4.3 describe the formal analysis of those properties with one or multiple clients, where the property formalizations, experimental scenarios and model checking results are shown, respectively.

4.1   Consistency Properties

Strong Consistency. A key-value system satisfies strong consistency if each read returns the value of the latest write that occurred before that read. More precisely, let $Tr = o_1, o_2, ..., o_n$ denote a trace of n read/write operations issued by *one* or *more* clients in a key-value system S, where any operation o_i can be expressed as $o_i = (k, v, t)$, where t denotes the *global* time when o_i was issued, and v is the value returned from key k if it is a read, or the value written to key k if it is a write. S satisfies *strong consistency* if for any read $o_i = (k, v_i, t_i)$, provided there exists a write $o_j = (k, v_j, t_j)$ with $t_j < t_i$, and without any other write $o_h = (k, v_h, t_h)$ such that $t_j < t_h < t_i$, we have $v_i = v_j$.

Eventual Consistency. If no new updates are made to a key, a key-value system is *eventually consistent*, if eventually all reads to that key will return the last updated value. More precisely, we again consider a trace $Tr = o_1, o_2, ..., o_n$ of n read/write operations in a key-value system S. Let $o_i = (k, v_i, t_i)$ be a write, and there is no other write $o_j = (k, v_j, t_j)$ such that $t_i < t_j$. S satisfies *eventual consistency* if there exists some $t > t_i$, and for all reads $o_h = (k, v_h, t_h)$ such that $t_h > t$, $v_i = v_h$.

To model check the above properties, we consider strong/eventual consistency experiment scenarios with *one* or *multiple* clients, because:

- from a single client's perspective, consecutive requests on the same key are always *strictly ordered*, i.e., subsequent operations will be pending until a preceding read/write finishes (see Section 3.3);
- for multiple clients, requests generated by different clients are *independent* of each other, i.e., it is not the case that a read/write will block all subsequent operations from other clients on the same key until accomplished.

The purpose of our experiments is to answer the following questions w.r.t. whether strong/eventual consistency is satisfied: does strong/eventual consistency depend on:

- with one client, the combination of consistency levels of consecutive requests?
- with multiple clients, additionally the latency between consecutive requests being issued?

Although a read repair mechanism is not generally used by other key-value systems, it is essential in Cassandra to guarantee consistency. The definition, experimental scenarios and model checking results w.r.t. the eventual consistency properties of the read repair mechanism can be found in our longer report [14].

4.2 Formal Analysis of Consistency with One Client

Scenarios. We define the following setting for our experimental scenarios with *one* client:

(a) We consider a data center with four servers, and a replication factor of 3.
(b) The ring size is 16, and the servers are responsible for the equal range clockwise, with the first server responsible for range [0...3].
(c) The read/write consistency levels can be ONE, QUORUM or ALL.
(d) For strong/eventual consistency, the client issues two consecutive requests on the same key.
(e) The delay set is (1.0,2.0,4.0,8.0).

Moreover, we consider the following scenarios, where, depending on the property and consistency level, we name each subcase Scenario (1-S/E-O/Q/A O/Q/A), e.g., Scenario (1-S-QA) refers to the case checking strong consistency with one client, where two consecutive requests have the consistency levels QUORUM and ALL respectively; Scenario (1-E-AO) refers to the case checking eventual consistency with one client, where two consecutive requests have the consistency levels ALL and ONE, respectively.

In Scenarios (1-S-**) the client issues a write on a key followed by a read on the same key. The initial state of this scenario is specified as follows:

```
eq c1 = one .    eq c2 = one .    --- consistency level: one, quorum or all
eq k = 10 .      eq v = "juice" .
eq initState = { 0.0 | nil } [0.0, 100 <- bootstrap]
    < 100 : Client | coord: 3, requestQueue: (WriteRequestCS(0,k,v,c1,100)
                        ReadRequestCS(1,k,c2,100)), ... >
    < 1 : Server | table: (3 |-> ("tea",0.0),  8 |-> ("coffee",0.0),
                        10 |-> ("water", 0.0), 15 |-> ("coke",0.0)), ...>
    < 2 : Server | ... > < 4 : Server | ... >
    < 3 : Server | ring: (([0],1),([4],2),([8],3),([12],4)), delays: (1.0,2.0,4.0,8.0), ... > .
```

where client 100 connects to server (coordinator) 3, and servers 1, 2 and 4 serve as the replicas. {0.0 | nil} refers to the initial state of the scheduler with the global time 0.0 and the schedule list nil.

In Scenarios (1-E-**) the client issues two consecutive writes on the same key. The initial state of this scenario is like that of Scenarios (1-S-**), except that the second operation is a write request.

Formalizing Consistency Properties. Regarding *strong consistency*, for Scenarios (1-S-**) we define a parameterized atomic proposition strong(A,K,V) that holds if we can match the value V returned by the subsequent read on key K in client A's local store with that in the preceding write.

```
op strong : Address Value -> Prop .
eq < A : Client | store: (ID,K,V), ... > REST |= strong(A,K,V) = true .
```

Since two requests will eventually be consumed with the client receiving the returned value, the strong consistency property can in this case be formalized as the LTL formula <> strong(...). Given an initial state initConfig, the following command returns true if the property eventually holds; otherwise, a trace showing a counterexample is provided.

```
red modelCheck(initConfig, <> strong(client,key,value)) .
```

Regarding *eventual consistency*, we only need to check if eventually all replicas will be consistent with the last updated value. Obviously, if all replicas agree on the last updated value, a sufficiently later read (e.g., after all replicas finish the update with the writes) will return such a value, regardless of the consistency level (we can also check this using the experiment for the read repair property [14]). Thus, we check at each replica's side by defining a parameterized atomic proposition eventual(R1,R2,R3,K, V) to hold if we can match the value V on key K in the subsequent (or the last) write with those in the local tables of all replicas R1, R2 and R3.

```
op eventual : Address Address Address Key Value -> Prop .
eq < R1 : Server | table: (K |-> (V,T1), ...), ... >
   < R2 : Server | table: (K |-> (V,T2), ...), ... >
   < R3 : Server | table: (K |-> (V,T3), ...), ... > REST |= eventual(R1,R2,R3,K,V) = true .
```

The eventual consistency property can then be formalized as the LTL formula <>[] eventual(...). Given an initial state initConfig, the following command returns true if the property eventually always holds; otherwise, a trace showing a counterexample is provided.

```
red modelCheck(initConfig, <>[] eventual(r1,r2,r3,key,value)) .
```

Analysis Results. The model checking results show that strong consistency holds in Scenarios (1-S-OA), (1-S-QQ), (1-S-QA), (1-S-AO), (1-S-AQ) and (1-S-AA), but not in Scenario (1-S-OO), (1-S-OQ) or (1-S-QO), and that eventual consistency holds in all its scenarios.

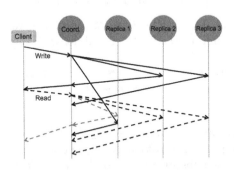

Fig. 3. Sequence chart for a strong consistency violation regarding a ONE write followed by a ONE read issued by one client

For strong consistency, we show the experimental results in Table 1, with a cross (×) marking a violation. Note that three out of nine combinations of consistency levels violate strong consistency, where at least one of the read and the write has a consistency level weaker than QUORUM. Fig. 3 illustrates how a strong consistency violation happens w.r.t. a ONE write *strictly* followed by a ONE read, where the red dashed arrow identifies the violation.

The reason why a strong consistency violation occurs is that some read forwarded by the coordinator reaches a certain replica before a write request does. Thus, it seems fair to say that unless a client uses consistency level at least QUORUM, strong consistency may not be guaranteed.

Table 1 also shows the results of model checking eventual consistency, where no violation occurs, regardless of the consistency level combinations. The reason why eventual consistency holds is that a replica updates its table only if the incoming request has a higher timestamp, and therefore, even if the first request reaches the replica later due to message delay, it will be simply discarded. As a result, the replica will eventually store the value in the last generated request.

Table 1. Results on Checking Strong (indicated by the left table) and Eventual Consistency (indicated by the right table) with One Client

Read$_2$ / Write$_1$	ONE	QUORUM	ALL
ONE	×	×	✓
QUORUM	×	✓	✓
ALL	✓	✓	✓

Write$_2$ / Write$_1$	ONE	QUORUM	ALL
ONE	✓	✓	✓
QUORUM	✓	✓	✓
ALL	✓	✓	✓

4.3 Formal Analysis of Consistency with Multiple Clients

When dealing with multiple clients, requests generated by different clients are *independent of each other*, i.e., it is not the case that a read/write will block all subsequent operations from other clients with the same key until accomplished. Whenever a request is issued by a client, it will be immediately sent out. Thus it will make no difference which consistency level a preceding request uses. For example, if client 2 intends to issue a request R' L seconds after client 1 sends out its request R at global time T, R' will be exactly sent out at global time $T + L$, despite of the arrival of R at client 1. However, as mentioned in Section 3, a single client's consecutive requests are always strictly ordered.

Scenarios. We consider scenarios with two clients, where client 1 first issues its request, and after some time (the latency between two requests) client 2 issues its own. Regarding consistency levels, we fix it as QUORUM for the first request, but parameterize it for the second request. We still use three replicas to store a particular key-value pair. For each replica we have two possibilities about the second request's arrival, either before or after the first request. Therefore, there are eight possible cases (for simplicity we do not consider the case where two requests arrive at the same time). Thus, we need a delay set with at least two different delays. Concretely, we define the following setting for our experimental scenarios with multiple clients:

- (a), (b) and (c) in the Section 4.2 setting for one-client scenarios.
- We consider two clients, each one issuing one request on the same key. Clients 1 and 2 connect to coordinators 1 and 2 respectively.
- The delay set is (2.0,8.0) for coordinator 1, and (0.0) for coordinator 2.
- The latency between two requests can be 1.0s, 5.0s or 10.0s.

Note that, given coordinator 1's delay set, coordinator 2's delay set combined with three different latencies *fully* covers all possible orders of arrivals of two requests.

For example, the initial state of model checking strong consistency with two clients is specified as:

```
...
eq l = 1.0 .    --- latency: 1.0, 5.0 or 10.0
eq initState = ... [1, 200 <- bootstrap]
  < 100 : Client | coord: 3, requestQueue: (WriteRequestCS(0,k,v,c1,100), ... >
  < 200 : Client | coord: 1, requestQueue: (ReadRequestCS(1,k,c2,200)), ... >
  < 1 : Server | delays: (0.0), ... > < 3 : Server | delays: (2.0,8.0), ... > .
```

Table 2. Results on Checking Strong Consistency (indicated by the top table) and Eventual Consistency (indicated by the bottom table) with Two Clients (The delay set is {D1,D2} with D1<D2.)

	Consistency Lv. / Latency	ONE	QUORUM	ALL
Strong	L1 (L1<D1)	×	×	×
	L2 (D1<L2<D2)	×	×	×
	L3 (D2<L3)	✓	✓	✓

	Consistency Lv. / Latency	ONE	QUORUM	ALL
Eventual	L1 (L1<D1)	✓	✓	✓
	L2 (D1<L2<D2)	✓	✓	✓
	L3 (D2<L3)	✓	✓	✓

Table 3. Detailed Results for Latency L2 on Checking Strong Consistency with Two Clients (R1, R2 and R3 refer to the replicas. "1/2" means that client 1/2's request reaches the corresponding replica first. The delay set is {D1,D2} with D1<D2.)

Latency	First Arrival			Consistency Level		
	R1	R2	R3	ONE	QUORUM	ALL
	1	1	1	✓	✓	✓
	1	1	2	×	✓	✓
	1	2	1	×	✓	✓
L2	1	2	2	×	×	✓
(D1<L2<D2)	2	1	1	×	✓	✓
	2	1	2	×	×	✓
	2	2	1	×	×	✓
	2	2	2	×	×	×

Analysis Results. For model checking strong/eventual consistency with two clients, we use the same formalization of each property as mentioned in Section 4.2. The results of model checking *strong consistency* with two clients is shown in Table 2. We observe that whether strong consistency is satisfied or not *depends on the latency* between requests: if it is so high that all preceding requests have reached the replicas, strong consistency holds (case L3); otherwise, strong consistency does not hold, because there is at least one subcase where the later requests reach the replicas before the preceding requests do. Although both cases L1 and L2 fail to satisfy strong consistency as shown by the model checking, we can however find some particular execution sequences in case L2 (not in case L1, because its latency is extremely low), where client 2's read returns the (most recent) value in client 1's write.[2] In Table 3 we list all possbile subcases for case L2, where we mark "1" if client 1's request reaches the corresponding replica first, otherwise "2", and a case of the form "1/2   1/2   1/2" describes which requests reach the three replicas R1, R2 and R3 first respectively. For case L2, except the two extreme subcases "1 1 1" and "2 2 2", strong consistency holds, on the one hand, if the subsequent read uses consistency level ALL; on the other hand, if a majority of replicas receive client 1's request first. For example, in subcase "2 1 1", even if one forwarded request by client 2 reaches R1 first, by using consistency level at least QUORUM in client 2's read, strong consistency holds. In subcase "2 2 1", since two later requests reach the replicas first, strong consistency holds only if client 2 uses consistency level ALL. Thus with two clients (we also believe with more than two clients), it is fair to say that: (i) strong consistency depends on the latency between requests; and (ii) except extreme latencies (almost simultaneous or extremely high), to maximize strong consistency we ought to use consistency level ALL for subsequent requests.

Instead, as mentioned in Section 4.2, strong consistency with one client depends on the combination of consistency levels.

For *eventual consistency*, Table 2 shows the experimental results, where no violation occurs, regardless of the consistency level and latency between requests. Eventual consistency holds for two clients for the same reason why it holds for one client, i.e., a replica updates its table only if the incoming request has a higher timestamp. That is, eventual consistency is always guaranteed by our Cassandra model, regardless of whether we have one or multiple clients.

5   Related Work and Concluding Remarks

Models in Key-value/NoSQL Stores. Amazon's Dynamo [20] was the first system that adopted the eventual consistency model [21]. Recent work on consistency benchmarking includes delta consistency metrics [17], which mine logs to find consistency violations. PBS [5] proposes probabilistic notions of consistency. Compared to this, our model checking based approach can exhaustively search for all possible consistency violations. Compared to eventual-consistency based model, a slightly stronger model is causal+ consistency [15], which maintains causality of reads across writes which are causally related. Red-blue consistency [13] modifies transaction operations into blue operations which are commutatable at datacenters, and red ones, which are serialized across all datacenters. Commutative replicated data types (CRDTs) are distributed data structures insensitive to the order of operations on a key [18], which is being incorporated by RIAK [1].

---

[2] Using Maude's *search* command we can explore the reachable state space for a particular pattern, where the value received by client 2 matches that in client 1's write. See the Maude specification available at
https://sites.google.com/site/siliunobi/icfem-cassandra.

Model Checking Key-value/NoSQL Stores. Despite the importance of such stores, we are not aware of other work formalizing and verifying them with formal verification tools. There is however some recent related work on formal analysis of *cloud computing* systems, including, e.g., [6], which addresses eventual consistency verification by reducing it to reachability and model checking problems; [19], which formally models and analyzes availability properties of a ZooKeeper-based group key management service; [9], which proposes and analyzes DoS resilience mechanisms for cloud-based systems; [22], which gives formal semantics to the KLAIM language and uses it to specify and analyze cloud-based architectures; and [11], which presents a formal model of Megastore —not really a key-value store, but a hybrid between a NoSQL store and a relational database— in Real-Time Maude which has been simulated for QoS estimation and model checked for functional correctness.

Our main focus in this work has been twofold: (i) to obtain for the first time a *formal model* of Cassandra; and (ii) to formally analyze its *correctness* properties, focusing on the crucial issue of Cassandra's *consistency* properties. This work presents for the first time a detailed formal analysis of the conditions under which Cassandra can achieve strong or eventual consistency.

The other side of the coin is *availability*: weaker consistency is the price paid to achieve greater availability. Therefore, as future work we plan to *explore the various design choices* in the consistency-availability spectrum for key-value stores. Formal modeling with *probabilistic rewrite rules* and formal analysis by *statistical model checking*, like done, e.g., in [9,10,22], seems a natural next step for studying *availability and other QoS properties*. Following those ideas, our current Cassandra model can be naturally extended for further statistical model checking (though Real-Time Maude already has a notion of time, there is no systematic support for probabilistic real-time rewrite theories, which is one reason we did not build our model in Real-Time Maude). More broadly, our long-term goal is not Cassandra per se, but developing a library of *formally specified executable components* embodying the key functionalities of key-value stores. We plan to use such components and the formal analysis of their correctness and QoS properties to facilitate the exploration of the design space for such systems.

Acknowledgments. We thank the anonymous reviewers for helpful comments on a previous version of this paper. This work has been partially supported by AFOSR Contract FA8750-11-2-0084, NSF Grant CNS 13-19109, NSF CNS 13-19527 and NSF CCF 09-64471.

References

1. Basho Riak, http://basho.com/riak/
2. Cassandra, http://cassandra.apache.org/
3. DB-Engines, http://db-engines.com/en/ranking
4. Agha, G.: Actors: A Model of Concurrent Computation in Distributed Systems. MIT Press, Cambridge (1986)

5. Bailis, P., Venkataraman, S., Franklin, M.J., Hellerstein, J.M., Stoica, I.: Probabilistically bounded staleness for practical partial quorums. Proc. VLDB Endow. 5(8), 776–787
6. Bouajjani, A., Enea, C., Hamza, J.: Verifying eventual consistency of optimistic replication systems. In: POPL, pp. 285–296 (2014)
7. Brewer, E.A.: Towards robust distributed systems (abstract). In: PODC, p. 7 (2000)
8. Clavel, M., Durán, F., Eker, S., Lincoln, P., Martí-Oliet, N., Meseguer, J., Talcott, C.: All About Maude - A High-Performance Logical Framework. LNCS, vol. 4350. Springer, Heidelberg (2007)
9. Eckhardt, J., Mühlbauer, T., AlTurki, M., Meseguer, J., Wirsing, M.: Stable availability under denial of service attacks through formal patterns. In: de Lara, J., Zisman, A. (eds.) Fundamental Approaches to Software Engineering. LNCS, vol. 7212, pp. 78–93. Springer, Heidelberg (2012)
10. Eckhardt, J., Mühlbauer, T., Meseguer, J., Wirsing, M.: Statistical model checking for composite actor systems. In: Martí-Oliet, N., Palomino, M. (eds.) WADT 2012. LNCS, vol. 7841, pp. 143–160. Springer, Heidelberg (2013)
11. Grov, J., Ölveczky, P.C.: Formal Modeling and Analysis of Google's Megastore in Real-Time Maude. In: Iida, S., Meseguer, J., Ogata, K. (eds.) Specification, Algebra, and Software. LNCS, vol. 8373, pp. 494–519. Springer, Heidelberg (2014)
12. Hewitt, E.: Cassandra: The Definitive Guide. O'Reilly Media, Sebastopol (2010)
13. Li, C., Porto, D., Clement, A., Gehrke, J., Preguiça, N., Rodrigues, R.: Making geo-replicated systems fast as possible, consistent when necessary. In: Proc. USENIX Conference on Operating Systems Design and Implementation (OSDI), pp. 265–278 (2012)
14. Liu, S., Rahman, M., Skeirik, S., Gupta, I., Meseguer, J.: Formal modeling and analysis of Cassandra in Maude (2014), https://sites.google.com/site/siliunobi/icfem-cassandra
15. Lloyd, W., Freedman, M.J., Kaminsky, M., Andersen, D.G.: Don't settle for eventual: Scalable causal consistency for wide-area storage with cops. In: Proc. ACM Symposium on Operating Systems Principles (SOSP), pp. 401–416 (2011)
16. Meseguer, J., Talcott, C.: Semantic models for distributed object reflection. In: Magnusson, B. (ed.) ECOOP 2002. LNCS, vol. 2374, pp. 1–36. Springer, Heidelberg (2002)
17. Rahman, M.R., Golab, W., AuYoung, A., Keeton, K., Wylie, J.J.: Toward a principled framework for benchmarking consistency. In: Proc. USENIX Workshop on Hot Topics in System Dependability, HotDep (2012)
18. Shapiro, M., Preguiça, N.M., Baquero, C., Zawirski, M.: Convergent and commutative replicated data types. Bulletin of the EATCS 104, 67–88 (2011)
19. Skeirik, S., Bobba, R.B., Meseguer, J.: Formal analysis of fault-tolerant group key management using ZooKeeper. In: Proc. Symposium on Cluster, Cloud, and Grid Computing (CCGRID), pp. 636–641 (2013)
20. Vogels, W.: Amazon's dynamo. All Things Distributed (October 2007), http://www.allthingsdistributed.com/2007/10/amazons_dynamo.html
21. Vogels, W.: Eventually consistent. ACM Queue 6(6), 14–19 (2008)
22. Wirsing, M., Eckhardt, J., Mühlbauer, T., Meseguer, J.: Design and analysis of cloud-based architectures with KLAIM and maude. In: Durán, F. (ed.) WRLA 2012. LNCS, vol. 7571, pp. 54–82. Springer, Heidelberg (2012)

Bounded Model Checking High Level Petri Nets in PIPE+Verifier

Su Liu, Reng Zeng, Zhuo Sun, and Xudong He

Florida International University, Miami, Florida 33199, USA
{sliu002,rzeng001,zsun003,hex}@cis.fiu.edu

Abstract. High level Petri nets (HLPNs) have been widely applied to model concurrent and distributed systems in computer science and many other engineering disciplines. However, due to the expressive power of HLPNs, they are more difficult to analyze. Exhaustive analysis methods such as traditional model checking based on fixed point calculation of state space may not work for HLPNs due to the state explosion problem. Bounded model checking (BMC) using satisfiability solvers is a promising analysis method that can handle a much larger state space than traditional model checking method. In this paper, we present an analysis method for HLPNs by leveraging the BMC technique with a state-of-the-art satisfiability modulo theories (SMT) solver Z3. A HLPN model and some safety properties are translated into a first order logic formula that is checked by Z3. This analysis method has been implemented in a tool called PIPE+Verifier and is completely automatic. We show our results of applying PIPE+Verifier to several models from the Model Checking Contest @ Petri Nets and a few other sources.

Keywords: Formal Methods, Petri Nets, Model Checking, Bounded Model Checking.

1 Introduction

Petri nets are a graphical formal language to model concurrent and distributed systems. Low level Petri nets are suitable to model control flows but cannot effectively model data and functionality in complex systems. High level Petri nets (HLPNs) [2] are a more expressive formalism developed to handle data and functionality in addition to control flows.

HLPNs are executable. Tools like CPN Tools [25] and PIPE+ [30] support the modeling and execution of different forms of HLPNs. However, analysis by simulation can only explore a finite number of executions and thus cannot assure safety properties to be satisfied in all possible executions. Traditional model checking [26] is an automatic and exhaustive analysis method to explore all possible executions of a model, but suffers from the state explosion problem. Bounded model checking (BMC) with satisfiability solving [9,13] was proposed as an alternative approach to address the state explosion problem in the traditional model checking approach. In BMC, a feasible symbolic execution of a transition

S. Merz and J. Pang (Eds.): ICFEM 2014, LNCS 8829, pp. 348–363, 2014.

system and the negation of some safety property are translated into a logic formula, which is checked by a satisfiability solver. If the formula is satisfiable, a counter example is found and thus the safety property does not hold. On the other hand, if the formula is not satisfiable up to a pre-defined upper bound k, the safety property holds up to k. Although this approach is not a complete technique for safety property analysis, it has been shown to be very effective in detecting the violation of safety properties in many real-world applications.

Encoding a low level Petri net model into a propositional logic formula is straightforward, but encoding a HLPN model is not since HLPNs use structured data and algebraic expressions to define functionality. In recent years, great progress has been made on satisfiability modulo theories (SMT) [16,32] solvers that can check the satisfiability of a subset of first-order logic formulas with a variety of underlying theories including linear arithmetic, difference arithmetic and arrays. These SMT solvers are expressive enough to represent the data and algebraic expressions in HLPNs naturally. Furthermore, SMT solvers are becoming more efficient according to the annual competitions results from SMT [7], and have been successfully integrated into verification tools such as CBMC [3], SLAM2 [5], and VS3 [33].

In this paper, we present a method for using SMT solvers to perform bounded model checking on HLPNs. We leverage the theory of sets [29] that has been integrated to some SMT solvers to represent HLPNs, where a place can have zero or more tokens. Similar to BMC, our method specifies a k value before checking, which defines the upper bound of transition firing actions (state changes). For each safety property violated within k steps, a transition firing sequence leading to an error state is generated. However, this method is incomplete because the upper bound k is often not given in real applications. Reference [15] discussed the complexity of finding a complete threshold.

We have implemented a prototype tool called PIPE+Verifier, which integrates the state of the art SMT solver Z3 [17]. We have applied PIPE+Verifier to analyze several models from Model Checking Contest @ Petri Net [27], a Mondex model [43] (an electronic purse system proposed as the first pilot project in the worldwide formal verification grand challenge) and a model given in [38,37]. We have provided a comparison of our tool with related Petri nets tools and symbolic model checking tools.

2   High Level Petri Nets

A HLPN graph [2] comprises: a net graph, place types, place markings, arc annotations, transition conditions, and declarations. The net graph is a structure consisting of a finite set of places (drawn as circles), a finite set of transitions (drawn as bars), and a finite set of directed arcs between places and transitions (drawn as arrows). A place type is a power set of tokens. A token type can be a tuple of primitive data types such as integer and string. A place marking is a collection of tokens (data items) associated with the place. Arc annotations are inscribed with expressions that may comprise constants, variables, and function images. Transition conditions are Boolean expressions. Declarations comprise definitions of place types, variable types, and functions.

A HLPN is executable. A transition is enabled if its input places have the right tokens in the current marking that satisfy the transition condition. An enabled transition can fire and result in a new marking by subtracting the tokens from the input places and adding new tokens to the output places according to the corresponding arc annotations. Multiple enabled non-conflict transitions may fire simultaneously. An execution of a HLPN is a sequence of transition firings from the given initial marking. The behavior of a HLPN is the set of all possible executions.

Figure 1 illustrates a dining philosopher problem modeled in HLPN. The net consists of three places $P_{Phil\_Thinking}$, $P_{Chopsticks}$, P_{Phil_Eating} and two transitions T_{Pickup} and $T_{Release}$. All the places' token type is $\langle int \rangle$. $P_{Phil\_Thinking}$ and $P_{Chopsticks}$ are both initiated with markings that have five tokens $\{\langle 0 \rangle, \langle 1 \rangle, \langle 2 \rangle, \langle 3 \rangle, \langle 4 \rangle\}$. T_{Pickup}'s transition condition is $p = c_1 \wedge (p+1)\%5 = c_2 \wedge e = p$. $T_{Release}$'s transition condition is $p = r \wedge c_1 = r \wedge c_2 = (r+1)\%5$.

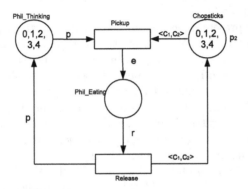

Fig. 1. 5-Dining Philosophers Problem in High Level Petri Net

3   Satisfiability Modulo Theories Solvers

Satisfiability modulo theories (SMT) [16] support a combination of theories such as bit-vectors, rational and integer linear arithmetic, arrays, and uninterpreted functions. SMT solvers are the extensions of satisfiability (SAT) solvers and directly applicable to the decision problems expressed in first order logic formulas with respect to the multiple background theories.

For example, an SMT solver can decide whether a formula in the theory of linear arithmetic is satisfiable:

$$(x + y \leq 0) \wedge (\neg b \vee a \wedge (y = 0)) \wedge (x \leq 0)$$

where x, y are integer variables and a, b are Boolean variables. If the formula is satisfiable, the SMT solver returns a variable assignment satisfying the formula.

3.1 Important Theories

Some important high level theories supported by SMT solvers are listed below as the foundation of our method.

Arrays. The theory of arrays [35,4] in SMT solvers is different from the ones in standard programming languages. In SMT, an array's size can be infinite. There are two built in functions: $select : ARRAY \times INDEX \rightarrow ELEM$ and $store : ARRAY \times INDEX \times ELEM \rightarrow ARRAY$ where $ARRAY$, $INDEX$, $ELEM$ are the sorts of the array, the index of the array and the elements in the array.

Tuples. The theory of tuples [29] supports a data structure with a list of components and access to individual components by projection.

Sets. A set is a collection of objects. Reference [29] has defined a set theory, which has been implemented in several SMT solvers [8]. The theory of sets in SMT solvers supports a list of set operations including set member $\in$, set subset $\subseteq$, set union $\cup$, set intersect $\cap$ and set difference $\backslash$.

3.2 Z3

In recent years, the efficiency of SMT solvers has been greatly improved. An annual SMT competition is held every year [8] and the participants include CVC4 [6], Z3 [17], MathSAT [12], Opensmt [10], and Yices [19]. Among them, Z3 [17], developed by Microsoft Research Institution, is reported to have the largest number of users and supports almost all the popular SMT background theories such as rational and integer arithmetic, bit-vectors, array theory, and set theory. In addition, Z3 has been adopted as the backend verification engine for a variety of tools, such as VS3 [33], SLAM2 [5] and CBMC [3]. Z3's developing team provides api and documentation for different programming languages (C, C++, .NET, Python). Therefore, we have selected and integrated Z3 into our tool as the backend satisfiability solving engine.

4 Bounded Model Checking High Level Petri Nets

Given a finite transition system M, a LTL formula f and an integer k, existential bounded model checking (BMC) [9] tries to determine whether there exists a computation path in M of at most length k (denoted as M_k) that satisfies f. To realize BMC, a logic formula ϕ_k from M, f and k is constructed and checked using a constraint solver. ϕ_k is satisfiable if and only if there is a path p of length at most k in M_k that satisfies f. The satisfying assignment for ϕ_k is called a witness for path p. However, BMC is in general not able to determine the satisfiability of a formula f since k's upper bound is unknown in many real-world applications. [15] shows that finding the upper bound for k is as complex as traditional model checking. To check the validity of a safety property up to k steps using existential BMC, we use f to represent the negated safety property. Thus the safety property holds as long as f is not satisfiable. [9] shows BMC can check all formulas in ACTL* [20].

In the following sections, we present a translation schema of applying bounded model checking to HLPNs.

4.1   General Idea of BMC using SMT Solver

In BMC, a logic formula ϕ_k is constructed from a given M_k, including the initial state I and unrolled transition relations T, and some negated safety properties f. Since T in ϕ_k is unrolled k times, the length of ϕ_k is dependent on k. The logic formula ϕ_k is represented in Equation 1:

$$\phi_k \doteq I(s_0) \wedge \bigwedge_{i=0}^{k-1} T(s_i, s_{i+1}) \wedge \bigvee_{i=0}^{k} f(s_i) \tag{1}$$

where $I(s_0)$ is the characteristic function of the initial state, $T(s_i, s_{i+1})$ is the characteristic function of the transition relation, and $f(s_i)$ represents the negated safety property in unrolled state s_i ($0 \leq i \leq k$). If ϕ_k is satisfiable, there is a firing sequence or a state transition path from the initial state $I(s_0)$ to a state s_i ($0 \leq i \leq k$) that satisfies f, thus violates the safety property. Otherwise, the safety property holds in M within k transition firings.

The general SMT logic context for BMC is shown in Figure 2:

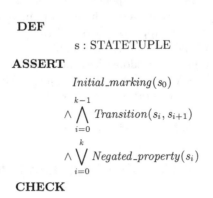

Fig. 2. SMT context for bounded model checking

4.2   Represent HLPNs in SMT Context

Our goal is to translate a given HLPN model to a logic formula shown in Figure 2, and then use an SMT solver to check its satisfiability.

Define States in SMT Context. In HLPNs, a state s_i is defined by a marking that is a distribution of tokens in places. Each place can contain 0 or more tokens (the number may be bounded or unbounded) and tokens can be structured data. To define a state in SMT context, a hierarchical layered data structure is constructed.

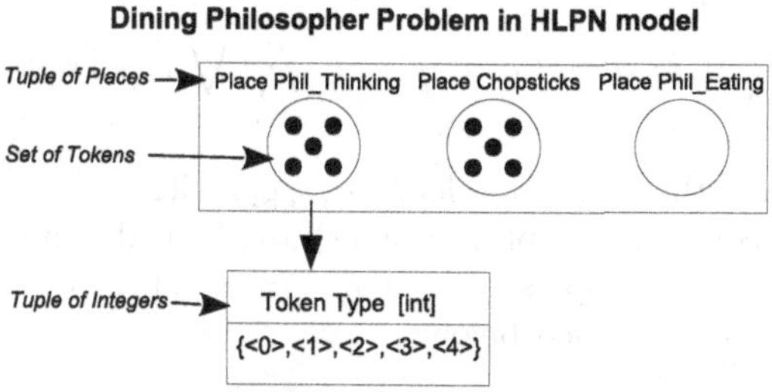

Dining Philosopher Problem in HLPN model

Fig. 3. An inner view of dining philosophers problem in HLPN model

A state s_i is defined by a tuple whose elements are places: $s_i \doteq \langle p_0, p_1, \ldots, p_n \rangle$. Each place p_j $(0 \leq j \leq n)$ is defined by a set containing $m \geq 0$ tokens: $p_j \doteq \{tok_0, tok_1, \ldots, tok_m\}$. Each token tok_k $(0 \leq k \leq m)$ is defined by a tuple of primitive data elements: $tok_k \doteq \langle e_0, e_1, \ldots, e_l \rangle$. Figure 3 shows an inner view of a HLPN model. In Figure 3, the tuple of places is $\langle P_{Phil\_Thinking}, P_{Chopsticks}, P_{Phil\_Eating} \rangle$, in which place $P_{Phil\_Thinking}$ has 5 tokens $\{\langle 0 \rangle, \langle 1 \rangle, \langle 2 \rangle, \langle 3 \rangle, \langle 4 \rangle\}$ and each token tok_k has only one field $\langle ID \rangle$ whose type is Integer.

In the SMT context, a state is defined by type STATETUPLE. The hierarchical data structure that constitutes STATETUPLE is shown in Table 1.

Table 1. High level Petri net elements mapped to SMT theory

HLPN Elements	SMT Theory	In PIPE+Verifier
HLPN Model	Tuple (Places)	STATETUPLE
Place Type	Set (Tokens)	SETiSORT
Token Type	Tuple (Integer or String Values)	DTiSORT
Primitive Data	Integer or String	INTSORT

Define the Initial State. The *Inital_marking* (s_0) in Figure 2 is defined from the initial marking M_0 of a HLPN model. The state s_0 contains tokens of all the places marked in M_0.

Define Transitions in SMT Context. *Transition*(s_i, s_{i+1}) in Figure 2 is a binary relation between the current state s_i and the next state s_{i+1}. In BMC, the upper bound of the transition firing sequence is k, thus the state transition of ϕ_k is unrolled k times, denoted as $\bigwedge_{i=0}^{k-1} Transition(s_i, s_{i+1})$. A HLPN model consists of $n \geq 0$ transitions $t_0, t_1, \ldots, t_n$, and any one of them may fire if enabled, thus $Transition(s_i, s_{i+1})$ is represented by a disjunction of the transitions in the HLPN model $\bigvee_{j=0}^{n} t_j(s_i, s_{i+1})$. Transitions in ϕ_k are defined as the formula shown in Equation 2:

$$\bigwedge_{i=0}^{k-1} (Transition(s_i, s_{i+1})) = \bigwedge_{i=0}^{k-1} (\bigvee_{j=0}^{n} t_j(s_i, s_{i+1})) \tag{2}$$

Each transition in the HLPN model $t_j(s_i, s_{i+1})$ with a precondition (captured by c_0) and a post-condition (captured by c_1) are defined in an if-then-else structure $if\ c_0\ then\ c_1\ else\ c_2$, representing $(c_0 \implies c_1) \wedge (\neg c_0 \implies c_2)$. The translation schema is described below:

- If condition c_0:
  - Use set membership operation to check if each input place in s_i has at least one token;
  - In state s_i, each transition condition clause corresponds to a constraint;
- Case True c_1:
  - Tokens are removed from t_j's input places of state s_i using set difference operation;
  - New tokens are added to t_j's output places of state s_{i+1};
  - Tokens in unrelated places in state s_i remain the same in those places in s_{i+1};
- Case False c_2: tokens in all places in the next state s_{i+1} are the same as in the current state s_i.

Define Properties in SMT Context. To check a safety property, we define $Negated\_property(s_i)$ as the negation of the safety property. If there exists a state s_i satisfies $Negated\_property(s_i)$, the safety property is violated at s_i. Thus, a disjunction of $Negated\_property(s_i)$ $0 \leq i \leq k$ is asserted in ϕ_k.

A Translation Example – Dining Philosophers Problem. From the dining philosophers HLPN given in Figure 1, we obtain the following translation:

1. State Definition: As shown in Figure 4, a state, consists of three places, are defined as three sets in STATETUPLE. All of the sets have the same set type $DTSORT$, and their element types are $INSORT$.
2. Initial state: place $P_{Phil\_Thinking}$ set contains five philosophers whose IDs are $\{\langle 0 \rangle, \langle 1 \rangle, \langle 2 \rangle, \langle 3 \rangle, \langle 4 \rangle\}$ and place $P_{Chopsticks}$ has five chopsticks whose IDs are $\{\langle 0 \rangle, \langle 1 \rangle, \langle 2 \rangle, \langle 3 \rangle, \langle 4 \rangle\}$. Therefore, as shown in Figure 5, both places at state s_0 contain five tokens.

DEF.

$$STATETUPLE \equiv \langle P_{Phil\_Thinking} : SETSORT,$$
$$P_{Chopsticks} : SETSORT,$$
$$P_{Phil\_Eating} : SETSORT \rangle$$
$$SETSORT \equiv \{set : DTSORT\}$$
$$DTSORT \equiv \{int : INTSORT\}$$
$$State \equiv \{s_0 : STATETUPLE$$
$$s_1 : STATETUPLE$$
$$...$$
$$s_k : STATETUPLE \}$$

Fig. 4. State definitions of 5-dining philosophers in SMT logic

$$Initial\_marking(s_0) \equiv P_{Phil\_Thinking}(s_0) = \{\langle 0 \rangle, \langle 1 \rangle, \langle 2 \rangle, \langle 3 \rangle, \langle 4 \rangle\}$$
$$\wedge P_{Chopsticks}(s_0) = \{\langle 0 \rangle, \langle 1 \rangle, \langle 2 \rangle, \langle 3 \rangle, \langle 4 \rangle\}$$
$$\wedge P_{Phil\_Eating}(s_0) = \emptyset$$

Fig. 5. Initial State of 5-Dining Philosopher in SMT Logic

$$\bigwedge_{i=0}^{k-1} Transition(s_i, s_{i+1}) \equiv (T_{Pickup}(s_0, s_1) \vee T_{Release}(s_0, s_1))$$
$$\wedge (T_{Pickup}(s_1, s_2) \vee T_{Release}(s_1, s_2))$$
$$...$$
$$\wedge (T_{Pickup}(s_{k-1}, s_k) \vee T_{Release}(s_{k-1}, s_k))$$

$T_{Pickup}(s, s') \equiv$

  IF $p \in P_{Phil\_Thinking}$

  $\wedge\, l \in P_{Chopsticks}$

  $\wedge\, r \in P_{Chopsticks}$

  $\wedge\, p = l \wedge (p + 1)\%5 = r$

  THEN

$P'_{Phil\_Thinking} = P_{Phil\_Thinking} - \{p\}$

$\wedge\, P'_{Chopsticks} = P_{Chopsticks} - \{l\} - \{r\}$

$\wedge\, P'_{Phil\_Eating} = P_{Phil\_Eating} \cup \{p\}$

ELSE

$P'_{Phil\_Thinking} = P_{Phil\_Thinking}$

$\wedge\, P'_{Chopsticks} = P_{Chopsticks}$

$\wedge\, P'_{Ehil\_Eating} = P_{Phil\_Eating}$

$T_{Release}(s, s') \equiv$

  IF $p \in P_{Phil\_Eating}$

  THEN

$P'_{Phil\_Thinking} = P_{Phil\_Thinking} + \{p\}$

$\wedge\, P'_{Chopsticks} = P_{Chopsticks} \cup \{p\}$

        $\cup \{(p + 1)\%5\}$

ELSE

$P'_{Phil\_Thinking} = P_{Phil\_Thinking}$

$\wedge\, P'_{Chopsticks} = P_{Chopsticks}$

$\wedge\, P'_{Phil\_Eating} = P_{Phil\_Eating}$

Fig. 6. State Transition of 5-Dining Philosophers in SMT Logic

$$\bigvee_{i=0}^{k} Negated\_property(s_i) \equiv (f(s_0) \vee f(s_1) \vee ... \vee f(s_k))$$

$$f \equiv P_{Phil\_Eating} = \{\langle 0 \rangle, \langle 1 \rangle\}$$

Fig. 7. Property Definition of 5-Dining Philosophers in SMT Logic

3. State transition: *Transition* is defined as $k-1$ transition steps that constrain pairs of consecutive states. Each transition step is an if-then-else structure that captures the pre-condition and post-condition of every local transition in HLPN. In Figure 6, s indicates the current state and s' indicates the next state.

4. Property definition: negated property $f(s_i)$ is state based, we need to define k disjunctions of error states. If one of $f(s_i)$ evaluates true, the whole formula is satisfiable and an error state s_i is reached. Figure 7 defines a simple negated safety property that the neighboring philosophers with ID $\{\langle 0 \rangle, \langle 1 \rangle\}$ can eat at the same time.

5   Evaluation

We have implemented an automated prototype tool called PIPE+Verifier to support our method and applied it to check relevant safety (reachability) properties in several benchmark problems modeled in HLPN. All experiments were conducted on a 32-bit Intel Core Duo CPU @3.0GHz box, with 4GB of RAM, running 32-bit Ubuntu.

5.1   Selected Benchmark Problems from Model Checking Contest @ Petri Nets

Model Checking Contest @ Petri nets (MCC) [27,28] is held annually to assess Petri nets based formal verification tools and techniques. Petri net verification tools are compared with regard to the scaling abilities, efficiency, and property checking capabilities on selected benchmark problems. The benchmark problems are modeled in low level Petri nets and Colored Petri nets. However, none of the participating tools produced any promising results on checking colored Petri net models. We have translated several Colored Petri net models into PIPE+Verifier and analyzed their safety (reachability) properties. We have examined the scalability of our tool by changing parameters in the model and varying bound k. The running results are presented below.

Dining Philosophers Model. In the previous section, we presented the 5-dining philosophers model. We have selected the following two negated safety properties to check in PIPE+Verifier.

$$\Box\neg\,(marking\,(Phil\_Eating) = 4 \wedge marking\,(Phil\_Eating) = 3) \qquad (3)$$
$$\Box\neg(marking\,(Phil\_Eating) \neq 4 \wedge marking(Phil\_Eating) = 1$$
$$\wedge marking\,(Chopsticks) \neq 4) \qquad (4)$$

The scaling parameter is the number (up to 20) of philosophers. The experiment results are shown in Table 2. For property 3, the PIPE+Verifier did not return a result when bound k reached 15 due to the exponential growth of the search space of Z3.

Table 2. Verifying Dining Philosophers Model

Philosophers	Formula	Step Bound	Verdict	Property Hold	Time (seconds)	Heap Size (Mb)
5	(3)	5	unsat	yes	0.41	1.72
5	(3)	10	unsat	yes	79.93	9.97
5	(3)	15	N/A	N/A	N/A	N/A
5	(4)	2	sat	no	0.25	1.25
10	(4)	2	sat	no	0.76	1.62
20	(4)	2	sat	no	3.23	2.63

Shared Memory Model. In [11], a shared memory model involving P processors was given. These processors can access their local memories as well as compete for shared global memory using a shared bus. We have built a HLPN model based on the above shared memory model and checked the following two negated safety properties:

$$\Box\neg(marking\,(Ext\_Mem\_Acc) = \langle 1,5\rangle \wedge marking\,(Ext\_Bus) = 1) \qquad (5)$$
$$\Box\neg(marking\,(Ext\_Mem\_Acc) = \langle 1,5\rangle \wedge marking\,(Memory) \neq 4) \qquad (6)$$

The scaling parameter is the number (up to 20) of processors P. The results are shown in Table 3.

Token Ring. A token ring [18] model shows a system with a set of M machines connected in a ring topology. Each machine can determine if it has the privilege (the right) to perform an operation based on its state and its left neighbor.

We have modeled a token ring using HLPN and selected the following two negated safety properties to check:

$$\Box\neg(marking\,(State) = \langle 3,0\rangle \wedge marking\,(State) = \langle 2,4\rangle) \qquad (7)$$
$$\Box\neg(marking\,(State) = \langle 3,0\rangle \vee marking\,(State) = \langle 2,4\rangle) \qquad (8)$$

The scaling parameter is the number of machines M, which is up to 20. The results are shown in Table 4.

Table 3. Verifying Shared Memory Model

Processors	Formula	Step Bound	Verdict	Property Hold	Time (seconds)	Heap Size (Mb)
5	(5)	5	unsat	yes	0.07	0.86
5	(5)	10	unsat	yes	0.3	1.54
5	(5)	15	unsat	yes	1.49	2.53
5	(6)	3	sat	no	0.75	1.80
10	(6)	3	sat	no	1.3	2.09
20	(6)	3	sat	no	13.05	4.35

Table 4. Verifying Token Ring Model

Machines	Formula	Step Bound	Verdict	Property Hold	Time (seconds)	Heap Size (Mb)
5	(7)	5	unsat	yes	0.32	1.34
5	(7)	10	unsat	yes	24.12	5.56
5	(7)	15	N/A	N/A	N/A	N/A
5	(8)	3	sat	no	0.09	1.01
10	(8)	3	sat	no	0.21	1.34
20	(8)	3	sat	no	0.86	2.03

5.2 Mondex

Mondex [43] smart card system is an electronic purse payment system, which involves a number of electronic purses with values and can exchange the values through a communication device. Mondex was the first pilot project of the International Grand Challenge on Verified Software [40], and was awarded the highest assurance level of secure systems, ITSEC Level E6 [41].

Mondex was first formally specified and proved using Z language [34]. Our previous work [43,42] formalized Mondex abstract and concrete models using HLPN. The concrete model depicts a transaction through nine operations {startFrom, startTo, readExceptionLog, req, ask, val, exceptionLogResult, exceptionLog-Clear, forged} and four status {idle, epr, epv, epa}. In this work, we have modeled the Mondex using PIPE+ [30] and verified a property "No Value Created" [42,41].

The HLPN model is initialized with two purses and one transaction proposal message. The safety property specifies that the sum of all the purses' balances does not increase: $\Box$ $purse1.balance + purse2.balance \leq balance\_sum$. Since nine transitions may be involved in this transaction process, we set $k = 9$. Our model-checking result shows this transaction process is preserved since the negation of the safety property defined by f is not reachable in $k = 9$ transition firing steps. The time and memory consumed for this checking process are 27.85s and 11.42 Mbytes respectively.

5.3   Abstract State Machine Model

In [38], a method for checking symbolic bounded reachability of abstract state machines was presented. An abstract state machine written in AsmL was translated into a logic formula checked by an SMT solver with rich background theories including set comprehensions. The running times of the prototype tool in [38] and our tool PIPE+ Verifier on property $Count(n)$ are shown in Table 5.

Table 5. Running time of checking Count model

Model program	Step bound	Verdict	Time of M.Veanes's Tool	Time of PIPE+Verifier
Count(5)	10	Sat	0.14s	1.43s
Count(5)	9	Unsat	1.5s	0.24s
Count(8)	16	Sat	2.2s	86.1s
Count(8)	15	Unsat	152s	15.26s

6   Related Work

6.1   Petri Nets Tools

Model checking Petri nets continues to be an active research topic. Various tools for modeling and verifying various forms of Petri nets have been built. Some of them are no longer maintained due to the evolution of new techniques. A Petri net model checking contest is held annually for the evaluation of some active tools. Table 6 lists the most recent participating tools (except for the last two). In this table, ALPiNA [23], Neco [21], CPN Tools [25] and SAMAT [31] support different types of high level Petri nets.

Colored Petri Nets Tool. Colored Petri Nets (CPNs) [25] are a kind of high level Petri nets that use tokens with typed values and functional programming language Standard ML [36] to define the guards of transitions. CPN Tools [1] is an industrial strength tool that is widely used to analyze modeled systems through simulation and model checking. CPN Tools integrates a model checking engine that explicitly searches the whole state space of a model.

ALPiNA. ALPiNA [23] is a model checker for algebraic Petri nets (APNs), which use algebraic abstract structured data type (AADTs) to define data and term equations to define transition guards and arc expressions. To symbolically model checking APNs, ALPiNA uses extended binary decision diagrams (BDDs) to represent the state space.

Table 6. Analysis Tools for Petri Nets

Name	Petri Net Type	Model Checking Technique
ALPiNA	Algebraic Petri Nets	Decision Diagrams
Cunf	Contextual Net	Net Unfolding, Satisfiability Solving
GreatSPN	Stochastic Petri Nets	Decision Diagrams
ITS-Tools	(Time) Petri Nets, ETF, DVE, GAL	Decision Diagrams, Structural Reductions
LoLA	Place/Transition Nets	Explicit Model Checking, State Compression, Stubborn Sets
Marcie	Stochastic Petri Nets	Decision Diagrams
Neco	High Level Petri Nets	Explicit Model Checking
PNXDD	Place/Transition Nets	Net Unfolding, Decision Diagrams, Topological
Sara	Place/Transition Nets	Satisfiability Solving, Stubborn Sets, Topological
CPN Tools	Colored Petri Nets	Explicit Model Checking
SAMAT	High Level Petri Nets	Explicit Model Checking

Neco. Neco [21] is a Unix toolkit that checks the reachability and other properties of high level Petri nets. Neco supports high level Petri nets annotated with Python objects and Python expressions. For model checking, Neco explicitly builds the state space.

SAMAT. SAMAT [31] is a tool for modeling and analyzing software architecture descriptions where component behavior models are expressed in predicate transition nets. SAMAT leverages an existing on-the-fly model checker SPIN [22] to check the satisfiability of properties expressed in linear time temporal logic in predicate transition net models.

6.2   Symbolic Model Checking Tools

Alloy. Alloy analyzer [24] is a software tool for analyzing a system defined in the Alloy specification language. The analysis in Alloy is based on reducing a model to a propositional formula and leveraging a SAT solver to solve the formula.

Java Path Finder. JPF [39] is a verification and testing environment for Java that integrates techniques such as model checking, program analysis and testing. Despite its state compression technique, JPF still cannot avoid the state explosion problem especially in terms of memory and time in checking high level data structures such as array.

CBMC and SMT-CBMC. C Bounded Model Checker (CBMC) [14] is an SAT based bounded model checker on C programs. SMT-CBMC [3] is an SMT based model checker that has significant improvement over the traditional SAT based model checkers. SMT-CBMC encodes sequential C programs into more compact first-order logic formulas that can be solved by SMT solvers.

7 Conclusion

In this paper, we have presented a method to analyze safety properties of HLPNs. Our method translates a HLPN model along with the negation of safety properties into a first order logic formula and uses the state of the art SMT solver Z3 to solve this formula. Our method is sound but incomplete since it requires a k value as an upper-bound to limit the length of firing sequences. By leveraging the theory of set in SMT solvers, our method supports HLPNs with unlimited number of tokens. However, checking a model with a large number of tokens may lead to an explosion of checking time. We have implemented this analysis method into a prototype, PIPE+Verifier, and embedded it into PIPE+, a graphical HLPNs modeling and simulation tool [30]. PIPE+Verifier is capable of analyzing a system defined in HLPNs automatically. We have applied our tool to analyze the safety properties of HLPN models of various problems from Model Checking Contest @ Petri Nets, the Mondex system, and the counter model. PIPE+Verifier is an open source tool and is available for sharing and continuous enhancements from worldwide research community.

Acknowledgments. This work was partially supported by NSF grants HRD-0833093 and IIP-1237818.

References

1. CPN Tools, http://cpntools.org
2. High-level Petri Nets - Concepts, Definitions and Graphical Notation (2000)
3. Armando, A., Mantovani, J., Platania, L.: Bounded model checking of software using smt solvers instead of sat solvers. Int. J. Softw. Tools Technol. Transf. 11(1), 69–83 (2009)
4. Armando, A., Ranise, S., Rusinowitch, M.: A rewriting approach to satisfiability procedures. Information and Computation 183(2), 140–164 (2003); 12th International Conference on Rewriting Techniques and Applications (RTA 2001)
5. Ball, T., Bounimova, E., Kumar, R., Levin, V.: Slam2: static driver verification with under 4. In: Proceedings of the 2010 Conference on Formal Methods in Computer-Aided Design, FMCAD 2010, Austin, TX, pp. 35–42. FMCAD Inc. (2010)
6. Barrett, C., Conway, C.L., Deters, M., Hadarean, L., Jovanović, D., King, T., Reynolds, A., Tinelli, C.: CVC4. In: Gopalakrishnan, G., Qadeer, S. (eds.) CAV 2011. LNCS, vol. 6806, pp. 171–177. Springer, Heidelberg (2011)
7. Barrett, C., De Moura, L., Stump, A.: Design and results of the 1st satisfiability modulo theories competition (smt-comp.). Journal of Automated Reasoning 35, 2005 (2005)
8. Barrett, C., Stump, A., Tinelli, C.: The Satisfiability Modulo Theories Library, SMT-LIB (2010), http://www.SMT-LIB.org

9. Biere, A., Cimatti, A., Clarke, E., Zhu, Y.: Symbolic Model Checking without BDDs. In: Cleaveland, W.R. (ed.) TACAS 1999. LNCS, vol. 1579, pp. 193–207. Springer, Heidelberg (1999)

10. Bruttomesso, R., Pek, E., Sharygina, N., Tsitovich, A.: The OpenSMT Solver. In: Esparza, J., Majumdar, R. (eds.) TACAS 2010. LNCS, vol. 6015, pp. 150–153. Springer, Heidelberg (2010)

11. Chiola, G., Franceschinis, G.: Colored gspn models and automatic symmetry detection. In: PNPM, pp. 50–60 (1989)

12. Cimatti, A., Griggio, A., Schaafsma, B.J., Sebastiani, R.: The MathSAT5 SMT Solver. In: Piterman, N., Smolka, S.A. (eds.) TACAS 2013 (ETAPS 2013). LNCS, vol. 7795, pp. 93–107. Springer, Heidelberg (2013)

13. Clarke, E., Biere, A., Raimi, R., Zhu, Y.: Bounded model checking using satisfiability solving. In: Formal Methods in System Design, p. 2001. Kluwer Academic Publishers (2001)

14. Clarke, E., Kroning, D., Lerda, F.: A Tool for Checking ANSI-C Programs. In: Jensen, K., Podelski, A. (eds.) TACAS 2004. LNCS, vol. 2988, pp. 168–176. Springer, Heidelberg (2004)

15. Clarke, E., Kroning, D., Ouaknine, J., Strichman, O.: Completeness and complexity of bounded model checking. In: Steffen, B., Levi, G. (eds.) VMCAI 2004. LNCS, vol. 2937, pp. 85–96. Springer, Heidelberg (2004)

16. De Moura, L., Bjørner, N.: Satisfiability modulo theories: introduction and applications. Commun. ACM 54(9), 69–77 (2011)

17. De Moura, L., Bjørner, N.S.: Z3: An efficient SMT solver. In: Ramakrishnan, C.R., Rehof, J. (eds.) TACAS 2008. LNCS, vol. 4963, pp. 337–340. Springer, Heidelberg (2008)

18. Dijkstra, E.W.: Self-stabilizing systems in spite of distributed control. Commun. ACM 17(11), 643–644 (1974)

19. Dutertre, B., De Moura, L.: The yices smt solver 2, 2 (2006), Tool paper, http://yices.csl.sri.com/tool-paper.pdf

20. Allen Emerson, E., Lei, C.-L.: Modalities for model checking: branching time logic strikes back. Sci. Comput. Program. 8(3), 275–306 (1987)

21. Fronc, Ł., Duret-Lutz, A.: LTL model checking with neco. In: Van Hung, D., Ogawa, M. (eds.) ATVA 2013. LNCS, vol. 8172, pp. 451–454. Springer, Heidelberg (2013)

22. Holzmann, G.: Spin model checker, the: primer and reference manual, 1st edn. Addison-Wesley Professional (2003)

23. Hostettler, S., Marechal, A., Linard, A., Risoldi, M., Buchs, D.: High-level petri net model checking with alpina. Fundam. Inf. 113(3-4), 229–264 (2011)

24. Jackson, D.: Software Abstractions: Logic, Language, and Analysis. The MIT Press (2006)

25. Jensen, K., Kristensen, L.M., Wells, L.: Coloured petri nets and cpn tools for modelling and validation of concurrent systems. Int. J. Softw. Tools Technol. Transf. 9(3), 213–254 (2007)

26. Clarke Jr., E.M., Grumberg, O., Peled, D.A.: Model Checking. The MIT Press (1999)

27. Kordon, F., Linard, A., Becutti, M., Buchs, D., Fronc, Ł., Hulin-Hubard, F., Legond-Aubry, F., Lohmann, N., Marechal, A., Paviot-Adet, E., Pommereau, F., Rodrígues, C., Rohr, C., Thierry-Mieg, Y., Wimmel, H., Wolf, K.: Web report on the model checking contest @ petri net 2013 (June 2013), http://mcc.lip6.fr

28. Kordon, F., Linard, A., Beccuti, M., Buchs, D., Fronc, L., Hillah, L.-M., Hulin-Hubard, F., Legond-Aubry, F., Lohmann, N., Marechal, A., Paviot-Adet, E., Pommereau, F., Rodríguez, C., Rohr, C., Thierry-Mieg, Y., Wimmel, H., Wolf, K.: Model checking contest @ petri nets, report on the 2013 edition. CoRR, abs/1309.2485 (2013)
29. Kröning, D., Rümmer, P., Weissenbacher, G.: A proposal for a theory of finite sets, lists, and maps for the smt-lib standard. In: Informal proceedings, 7th International Workshop on Satisfiability Modulo Theories at CADE 22 (2009)
30. Liu, S., Zeng, R., He, X.: Pipe+ - a modeling tool for high level petri nets. In: SEKE, pp. 115–121 (2011)
31. Liu, S., Zeng, R., Sun, Z., He, X.: Samat - a tool for software architecture modeling and analysis. In: SEKE, pp. 352–358 (2012)
32. de Moura, L., Bjørner, N.: Satisfiability Modulo Theories: An Appetizer. In: Oliveira, M.V.M., Woodcock, J. (eds.) SBMF 2009. LNCS, vol. 5902, pp. 23–36. Springer, Heidelberg (2009)
33. Srivastava, S., Gulwani, S., Foster, J.S.: VS^3: SMT Solvers for Program Verification. In: Bouajjani, A., Maler, O. (eds.) CAV 2009. LNCS, vol. 5643, pp. 702–708. Springer, Heidelberg (2009)
34. Stepney, S.: An Electronic Purse: Specification, Refinement, and Proof. Technical monograph. Oxford University Computing Laboratory, Programming Research Group (2000)
35. Stump, A., Barrett, C.W., Dill, D.L.: A decision procedure for an extensional theory of arrays. In: 16th IEEE Symposium on Logic in Computer Science, pp. 29–37. IEEE Computer Society (2001)
36. Ullman, J.D.: Elements of ML programming (ML97 ed.). Prentice-Hall, Inc., Upper Saddle River (1998)
37. Veanes, M., Bjørner, N., Gurevich, Y., Schulte, W.: Symbolic bounded model checking of abstract state machines. Int. J. Software and Informatics 3(2-3), 149–170 (2009)
38. Veanes, M., Bjørner, N.S., Raschke, A.: An SMT approach to bounded reachability analysis of model programs. In: Suzuki, K., Higashino, T., Yasumoto, K., El-Fakih, K. (eds.) FORTE 2008. LNCS, vol. 5048, pp. 53–68. Springer, Heidelberg (2008)
39. Visser, W., Havelund, K., Brat, G., Park, S., Lerda, F.: Model checking programs. Automated Software Engg. 10(2), 203–232 (2003)
40. Woodcock, J.: First steps in the verified software grand challenge. Computer 39(10), 57–64 (2006)
41. Woodcock, J., Stepney, S., Cooper, D., Clark, J.A., Jacob, J.: The certification of the mondex electronic purse to itsec level e6. Formal Asp. Comput. 20(1), 5–19 (2008)
42. Zeng, R., He, X.: Analyzing a formal specification of mondex using model checking. In: Cavalcanti, A., Deharbe, D., Gaudel, M.-C., Woodcock, J. (eds.) ICTAC 2010. LNCS, vol. 6255, pp. 214–229. Springer, Heidelberg (2010)
43. Zeng, R., Liu, J., He, X.: A formal specification of mondex using sam. In: IEEE International Symposium on Service-Oriented System Engineering, SOSE 2008, pp. 97–102 (December 2008)

Fast Translation from LTL to Büchi Automata via Non-transition-based Automata

Shohei Mochizuki, Masaya Shimakawa, Shigeki Hagihara, and Naoki Yonezaki

Department of Computer Science,
Graduate School of Information Science and Engineering,
Tokyo Institute of Technology.
2-12-1-W8-67 Ookayama, Meguro-ku, Tokyo 152-8552, Japan

Abstract. In model checking, properties are typically defined in linear temporal logic (LTL) and are translated into non-deterministic Büchi automata (NBA). In this paper, we propose a new, efficient translation method that is different from those used in LTL2BA, Spot and LTL3BA. Our method produces non-transition-based generalised Büchi automata (GBA) as an intermediate object, whereas LTL2BA, Spot, and LTL3BA use transition-based generalised Büchi automata (TGBA). Our method enables fast conversion because the data structure representing the object is simpler than that used in conversions via TGBA. Furthermore, we have developed techniques to reduce the number of states, similar to techniques that have heretofore only been available for conversions via TGBA. We also propose a technique to suppress the increase in the number of states that normally occurs while GBA is converted into NBA, using characteristics of strongly connected components of the GBA. We implemented our method with these techniques and experimentally compared our method with LTL2BA, Spot, and LTL3BA, which are the fastest translators to date. Our conversion method was much faster than LTL2BA and Spot, and was competitive with LTL3BA. In addition, the number of states in the NBA resulting from our method was comparable to that produced by LTL2BA, Spot, and LTL3BA.

1 Introduction

Recently, formal methods have become essential tools for developing safety critical systems, where behavioural correctness of the systems is the main concern. For instance, model checking [11] is a method for checking whether models of systems satisfy specifications. Satisfiability checking [14] is a method for checking whether specifications are free of contradictions. Realisability checking [13,1] is a method for checking whether a program that satisfies specifications exists and includes synthesis of the program if it does [7,12]. Of these methods, linear temporal logic (LTL) is often used for describing the specifications of systems. In this case, algorithms for converting specifications written in LTL into non-deterministic Büchi automata (NBA) are commonly used. The time complexity for conversion of LTL formulae into NBA is $2^{O(n)}$, where n is the number of

S. Merz and J. Pang (Eds.): ICFEM 2014, LNCS 8829, pp. 364–379, 2014.

formulae. Especially for realisability checking, because a specification includes all the constraints of behaviour of an intended system, the size of the specification can become very large. Therefore, efficient algorithms for converting LTL formulae into NBA are strongly desirable to expand the applicable range of these checking methods.

Many translation tools for converting LTL formulae into NBA have been proposed, such as the tool implemented in the model checker SPIN [9] and several more efficient tools, including LTL2BA [8], Spot [6,5], and LTL3BA[4]. Translation methods are roughly divided into two kinds: methods for conversion via generalised Büchi automata (GBA) as an intermediate object, and methods for conversion via transition-based generalised Büchi automata (TGBA). The methods via GBA were originally the most popular. However, since 2002, the methods via TGBA have become more popular and have outpaced the methods via GBA. The efficient tools LTL2BA, Spot and LTL3BA are classified as methods of conversion via TGBA. Because TGBA can express a given accepting language by a fewer number of states than GBA, TGBA are generally smaller than GBA. This is because an acceptance condition in GBA is defined by the set of final states that are passed infinitely, while an acceptance condition in TGBA is defined by the set of transitions that are passed infinitely. On the other hand, the data structure representing GBA is simpler than that representing TGBA because the number of states is much less than the number of transitions. From this observation, it follows that if techniques for the reduction of states used for conversion via TGBA can be implemented for conversion via GBA, the methods using GBA would be expected to be extremely efficient. In this paper, we adopted the GBA conversion, imported the reduction techniques into it, implemented it and evaluated its efficiency.

Unfortunately, the techniques for reducing the number of states in TGBA, as adopted in Spot and LTL2BA, are not directly applicable to a method of conversion via GBA. Therefore, we developed comparable reduction techniques that can be applied to the conversion of GBA to NBA. This enables us to produce NBA with a comparable number of states as that resulting from TGBA conversion using reduction techniques.

For converting LTL formulae into GBA, we adopted the algorithm proposed by Aoshima et al. [2], with some modification. In its original form, this algorithm intentionally does not execute full LTL formulae, but rather executes LTL formulae without the next operator. This is to prevent introducing unintentional synchronisation by two or more different occurrences of the next operator. However, because our aim was to make it possible to convert general LTL formulae, we extended the algorithm to enable its application to LTL formulae with the next operator. In addition to the reduction techniques mentioned above for converting GBA into NBA, we also developed a technique to suppress the increase in number of states as GBA is converted into NBA, using characteristics of strongly connected components of GBA. We implemented our method using these techniques and experimentally compared our method to LTL2BA, Spot and LTL3BA, which are currently the fastest translators. Our conversion method is faster than Spot and LTL2BA, and is competitive with LTL3BA. In addition, the number of states in the NBA from our method is comparable to that from the other methods.

The remainder of this paper is organised as follows. In Sect. 2, we give definitions of LTL and Büchi automata. In Sect. 3, we propose a new method (an extension of our previous method) to convert LTL formulae into GBA. In Sect. 4, we explain how to convert GBA into NBA. In Sect. 5, we describe our techniques for reducing the number of states in the resulting NBA. In Sect. 6, we discuss the advantages of our method over other approaches. In Sect. 7, we describe the implementation of our method and compare it to LTL2BA, Spot and LTL3BA. Finally, we present our conclusions in Sect. 8.

2   Preliminary

In this section, we introduce the syntax and semantics of LTL, NBA and GBA.

2.1   LTL

Let *Prop* be a finite set of propositions.

Definition 1 (LTL formulae). *Formulae f in LTL are inductively defined as follows:*

$$f ::= p \mid \neg f \mid f \vee f \mid f \wedge f \mid Xf \mid fUf \mid fRf,$$

where $p \in Prop$.

The notation Xf states 'f holds at the next time', while fUg represents 'f always holds until g holds'. fRg is the dual connective of fUg and represents $\neg(\neg fU\neg g)$. The notation $f \to g$, $f \leftrightarrow g$, $\top$, $\bot$, Ff and Gf are abbreviations for $\neg f \vee g$, $(\neg f \vee g) \wedge (\neg g \vee f)$, $p \vee \neg p$, $\neg\top$, $\top Uf$, and $\neg F\neg f$, respectively.

Definition 2 (Semantics). *Let Σ be 2^{Prop}, and let $u = u_0u_1, \ldots$ be an infinite sequence over Σ. Let f be an LTL formula. When a formula f holds on u, we write $u \models f$, and inductively define this relation as follows.*

- $u \models p$ *iff* $p \in u_0$
- $u \models \neg f_1$ *iff* $u \not\models f_1$
- $u \models f_1 \wedge f_2$ *iff* $u \models f_1$ *and* $u \models f_2$
- $u \models f_1 \vee f_2$ *iff* $u \models f_1$ *or* $u \models f_2$
- $u \models Xf_1$ *iff* $u_1u_2\ldots \models f_1$
- $u \models f_1Uf_2$ *iff* $\exists k \geq 0((u_ku_{k+1}\ldots \models f_2)$ *and* $\forall i(0 \leq i < k.\ u_iu_{i+1}\ldots \models f_1))$
- $u \models f_1Rf_2$ *iff* $\forall k \geq 0((u_ku_{k+1}\ldots \models f_2)$ *or* $\exists i(0 \leq i < k.\ u_iu_{i+1}\ldots \models f_1))$

A formula is in negation normal form (nnf) if the negation symbol ($\neg$) occurs only immediately above elementary propositions. Every formula can be transformed to an equivalent formula in nnf. We call a formula f a temporal formula if f is of the form Xf_1, f_1Uf_2, or f_1Rf_2.

2.2 Automata

In this section, we introduce NBA and GBA. NBA is an automaton that accepts ω-words if there exists a corresponding run passing a final state infinitely often, which is defined as follows.

Definition 3 (Büchi automata). *Let Prop be a set of propositions. A nondeterministic Büchi automaton on an alphabet 2^{Prop} is defined by $\mathcal{A} = \langle Q, \Sigma, \delta, I, F \rangle$, where Q is a finite set of states, $\Sigma = 2^{Prop}$, $\delta \subseteq Q \times B(Prop) \times Q$ is a transition relation, $I \subseteq Q$ is a set of initial states, and $F \subseteq Q$ is a set of final states. $B(Prop)$ is a set of Boolean formulae which consist of propositions in Prop and connectives $\neg$, $\vee$, and $\wedge$. A run r of $\mathcal{A}$ on an ω-word $u = u_0 u_1 \ldots$ is an infinite sequence $q_0 q_1 \ldots$ of states, where $q_0 \in I$, $(q_i, b_i, q_{i+1}) \in \delta$, and $u_i \models b_i$ for some b_i for all $i \geq 0$. If $Inf(r) \cap F \neq \emptyset$ holds, a run r is said to be successful, where $Inf(r)$ is a set of states that occur infinitely often in r. If there is a successful run of $\mathcal{A}$ on u, we say that $\mathcal{A}$ accepts u.*

On the other hand, GBA is an automaton with multiple sets of final states (a set of sets of final states). A run is successful if, for each set of final states, it passes infinitely often some state from the set.

Definition 4 (Generalised Büchi Automata). *Let Prop be a set of propositions. A Generalised non-deterministic Büchi automaton on an alphabet 2^{Prop} is defined by $\mathcal{A} = \langle Q, \Sigma, \delta, I, \mathcal{F} \rangle$, where Q, Σ, δ and I are defined as above for NBA. $\mathcal{F} = \{F_1, \ldots, F_n\}$ is a set of sets of final states, and satisfies $F_i \subseteq Q$ for all $1 \leq i \leq n$. A run r is said to be successful if $\forall F_i (Inf(r) \cap F_i \neq \emptyset)$ holds. If there is a successful run of $\mathcal{A}$ on u, we say that $\mathcal{A}$ accepts u.*

A set of ω-words that are accepted by NBA (or GBA) $\mathcal{A}$ is called the language accepted by $\mathcal{A}$, which is represented by $L(\mathcal{A})$.

3 Converting LTL Formulae into GBA

In this section, we propose an algorithm for constructing GBA $\mathcal{A}_\varphi$ from an LTL formula φ, which satisfies $L(\mathcal{A}_\varphi) = \{u \in (2^{Prop})^\omega \mid u \models \varphi\}$. This algorithm is an extended version of a previous algorithm proposed by Aoshima et al. [2], modified to work with LTL with the next operator. Below, we explain the algorithm, and for simplicity of explanation, assume that the input LTL formulae are in nnf.

Let φ be an input LTL formula. A state of GBA consists of a subset of $cl(\varphi) \cup \{(fUg)^{unsat} \mid fUg \in cl(\varphi)\}$, which represents the constraints of the state. Here, $cl(\varphi)$ is the set of subformulae of φ. First, an initial state consists of a singleton $\{\varphi\}$ of an input formula. Next, we decompose the formulae in a state and obtain the set of successive states. We take notice if the state involves the 'until' formula fUg because its meaning has eventuality. If g holds in the state, we accept transition to the state involving no constraints on the 'until' formula. If f holds in the state, we accept transition to the state involving $(fUg)^{unsat}$. The label *unsat* represents 'eventuality (g in this case) is not satisfied'. By setting the transition relation as stated above, if a state does not involve the labelled formula $(fUg)^{unsat}$, we can capture that g holds, (i.e., fUg holds.) If r is a run on an ω-word, such that fUg does not hold and f always holds, then the run r will stay only in states involving $(fUg)^{unsat}$. We judge the run to be successful only if the run infinitely often visits a state that does not involve $(fUg)^{unsat}$.

The procedure *Next*, used to obtain the set of transitions, is defined as follows.

Procedure 1 (*Next*) *Procedure Next takes a state $q = \{\varphi_1, \ldots, \varphi_n\}$ as input and outputs the set of transitions from q. Each transition is of the form (q, b, q'), which indicates that q' is a successive state of q by valuation satisfying b.*

1. $\Sigma := \{q\}$
2. *Repeat the following operations until Σ does not change. For every $S_i \in \Sigma$, apply one of the following, according to $f_{ij} \in S_i$.*
   (a) *if f_{ij} is of the form $f_1 \wedge f_2$, replace S_i with $(S_i - \{f_{ij}\}) \cup \{f_1, f_2\}$.*
   (b) *if f_{ij} is of the form $f_1 \vee f_2$, replace S_i with $(S_i - \{f_{ij}\}) \cup \{f_1\}$, $(S_i - \{f_{ij}\}) \cup \{f_2\}$.*
   (c) *if f_{ij} is of the form $f_1 U f_2$ or $(f_1 U f_2)^{unsat}$, replace S_i with $(S_i - \{f_{ij}\}) \cup \{f_2\}$, $(S_i - \{f_{ij}\}) \cup \{f_1, X(f_1 U f_2)^{unsat}\}$.*
   (d) *if f_{ij} is of the form $f_1 R f_2$, replace S_i with $(S_i - \{f_{ij}\}) \cup \{f_1, f_2\}$, $(S_i - \{f_{ij}\}) \cup \{f_2, X(f_1 R f_2)\}$.*
3. *Output the following δ_q.*

$$\delta_q = \{(q, \bigwedge_{l \in P(m)} l, \{f \mid Xf \in m\}) \mid m \in \Sigma\},$$

where $P(m) = \{p \mid p \in m \wedge p \in Prop\} \cup \{\neg p \mid \neg p \in m \wedge p \in Prop\}$.

In step 2, we obtain multiple sets of formulae by decomposing a formula in a set of formulae according to the semantics of LTL. For instance, because $f_1 U f_2$ indicates that f_2 holds eventually and f_1 always holds until f_2 holds, $\{f_1 U f_2\}$ is separated into two cases $\{f_2\}$ and $\{f_1, X(f_1 U f_2)^{unsat}\}$. These cases mean "$f_2$ currently holds" and "f_1 currently holds and $f_1 U f_2$ holds at the next time", respectively. In brief, if a set of formulae is obtained by step 2, the set represents one of satisfaction of $\varphi_1 \wedge \ldots \wedge \varphi_n$ involved by q. Therefore, in step 3, atomic propositions and their negation in a set of formulae are considered a label of the transition (i.e., a condition of the transition), and a set of formulae obtained by eliminating the next operator X is considered a successive state of q.

Example 1. Let φ be $G(r \to Fs)$. We apply procedure *Next* to φ. The result of step 2 is as follows.

$$\{\{\neg r, X\varphi\}, \{s, X\varphi\}, \{X(Fs)^{unsat}, X\varphi\}\}$$

The result of step 3 is the following transitions.

$$\{(\{\varphi\}, \neg r, \{\varphi\}), (\{\varphi\}, s, \{\varphi\}), (\{\varphi\}, \top, \{(Fs)^{unsat}, \varphi\})\}$$

These transitions are depicted in Fig.1.

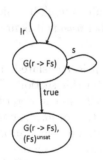

Fig. 1. Transitions generated by *Next* applied to $G(r \to Fs)$

By procedure *Next*, we can obtain the set of successive states of a state. Hence, by setting the initial state as a singleton $\{\varphi\}$ of an input formula and applying procedure *Next* iteratively, we can obtain a transition system that is part of $\mathcal{A}_\varphi$. This procedure is defined as follows.

Procedure 2 (*Construct*) Input: φ*: formula*
Output: Q, δ
Procedure: *Construct*
1: $Q = \{\{\varphi\}\}$
2: $S = \{\{\varphi\}\}$
3: $\delta = \{\}$
4: **while** $S \neq \emptyset$ **do**
5:    *Pick* q *from* S *and* $S = S - \{q\}$
6:    $\delta_q = Next(q)$
7:    $\delta = \delta \cup \delta_q$
8:    **for all** $(curstate, b, nextstate) \in \delta_q$ **do**
9:       **if** $nextstate \notin Q$ **then**
10:          $Q = Q \cup \{nextstate\}$
11:          $S = S \cup \{nextstate\}$
12:       **end if**
13:    **end for**
14: **end while**

Next, we define a set of sets of final states as follows. Let $\varphi_1, \ldots, \varphi_n$ be 'until' formulae, which are subformulae of an input formula φ. The set of sets of final states is $\mathcal{F} = \{F_1, \ldots, F_n\}$, where F_i is the set of states that does not include φ_i^{unsat}.

This method is an extension of our previous method [2], modified to adopt the label *unsat* for setting acceptance conditions correctly. Any successive states of a state involving $X(fUg)$ have fUg. On the other hand, any successive states of a state involving fUg have a labelled formula $(fUg)^{unsat}$ only if g does not hold in the state. With the label *unsat*, we can manage successive states of a state q involving both $X(fUg)$ and fUg. Even if fUg is contained in a successive state

q' of q, if $(fUg)^{unsat}$ is not contained in q', it indicates that fUg is satisfied in q. Without introduction of the label *unsat*, it is impossible to judge whether fUg is satisfied in q for such a case.

Example 2. The formula $GXFp$ is translated into GBA, as shown in Fig. 2 (left), by the method proposed in this section. The set of sets of final states is $\{\{q_1, q_2\}\}$. Due to the label *unsat*, we can determine the final states $\{\{q_1, q_2\}\}$ appropriately. Without introduction of *unsat*, only the transition system shown in Fig. 2 (right) can be obtained, and the appropriate set of sets of final states cannot be determined. This illustrates why it is essential to introduce the label *unsat* to know the acceptance conditions of GBA.

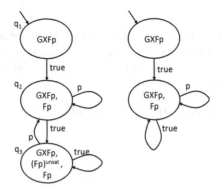

Fig. 2. GBA for $GXFp$, obtained by procedure *Construct*(left), and an incorrect transition system (right)

In the previous method proposed by Aoshima et al. in [2], binary decision diagrams (BDDs) were used to represent transitions from a state, and a BDD-based version of procedure *Next* was also used. In this current work, we have extended the previous method to permit LTL with the next operator, and we adopted the BDD-based procedure *Next*.

4   Converting GBA into NBA

An algorithm that converts TGBA into NBA was proposed for the tool LTL2BA [8]. We modified this algorithm as follows to convert GBA into NBA.

Definition 5 (Translation from GBA to NBA). *Let* $\mathcal{A} = (Q, \Sigma, \delta, I, \mathcal{F} = \{F_1, \ldots, F_k\})$ *be a GBA. The following NBA* $\mathcal{B} = (Q', \Sigma, \delta', I', F')$ *satisfies* $L(\mathcal{A}) = L(\mathcal{B})$.

 – $Q' = Q \times \{1, \ldots, k+1\}$, $I' = I \times \{1\}$, $F' = Q \times \{k+1\}$

$$- ((s, j), a, (t, i)) \in \delta' \text{ iff}$$
$$(s, a, t) \in \delta \wedge \begin{cases} i = next(j, t) & \text{if } j \neq k + 1 \\ i = next(1, t) & \text{if } j = k + 1 \end{cases},$$
$$\text{where } next(i, q) = \begin{cases} min\{j \mid i \leq j \wedge q \notin F_j\} & \text{if } \exists j \geq i \ (q \notin F_j) \\ k + 1 & \text{otherwise} \end{cases}.$$

States of the resulting NBA $\mathcal{B}$ are pairs of a state in GBA $\mathcal{A}$ and an integer between 1 and $k + 1$ (called a counter). This counter is important to translate GBA into NBA. Assume that there is transition (s, a, t) in $\mathcal{A}$. Let us consider the transition from (s, i) of $\mathcal{B}$. If $i \neq k + 1$, $\mathcal{B}$ has transition $((s, i), a, (t, i + 3))$ for the case of $t \in F_i \cap F_{i+1} \cap F_{i+2}$ and $t \notin F_{i+3}$. If $i = k + 1$, $\mathcal{B}$ has transition $((s, k + 1), a, (t, 3))$ for the case of $t \in F_1 \cap F_2$ and $t \notin F_3$. The set of final states of $\mathcal{B}$ is the set of states in which the counter equals $k + 1$. By this definition of final states of NBA, a run infinitely often passes a final state of $\mathcal{B}$ if and only if for every set of final states of $\mathcal{A}$, there is a final state such that the corresponding run infinitely often passes it.

5 Reducing States of Automata

For checking verification properties, such as satisfiability and realisability of specifications written in LTL formulae, automata manipulations such as emptiness checking, determinisation, and complementation are required. To do these kinds of manipulations of NBA efficiently, it is important to reduce the number of states of NBA, without changing the accepting languages. In our work, we adopted the formulae rewriting technique proposed in [15]. Furthermore, in this section, we propose two kinds of reduction techniques. In Sect. 5.1, we propose a technique for reducing states of NBA based on strongly connected components of GBA. In Sect. 5.2, we propose another technique for reducing states of NBA based on equivalence of states in the GBA. Generally, many reduction techniques based on simulation were proposed. This kind of techniques can be applied after the entire autotmata were constructed. The techniques we propose in Sect.5.1 and 5.2 are lightweight and can be applied in the middle of construction of the automata. This reduces time and space required for construction of automata.

5.1 Reduction of NBA Based on SCC of GBA

In the translation method proposed in Sect. 4, $k + 1$ states will be copied from a state in the GBA, where k is the number of sets of final states in the GBA. However, if a state q is not included in any strongly connected components that include final states of the GBA, then it is not necessary to copy q because it is not necessary to check the acceptance condition by q.

Formally, let $\mathcal{F}$ be a set of sets of final states in GBA, and let S be a strongly connected component in GBA. We say that S is acceptable if it satisfies the following condition.

$$(|S| > 1 \wedge \forall F \in \mathcal{F} \exists q \in S(q \in F))$$
$$\vee (|S| = 1 \wedge \exists q \in S(\exists a(q, a, q) \in \delta \wedge \forall F \in \mathcal{F}(q \in F)))$$

If a state q is included in a maximal strongly connected component that is not acceptable, then we do not copy q when we convert GBA to NBA, and we do not include q in the set of final states of NBA.

5.2   Reduction of NBA Based on Equivalence of States in the GBA

In GBA, it is possible to identify multiple equivalent states, and to reduce the number of states in the GBA by combining these equivalent states into one state.

Formally, let $\mathcal{F}$ and δ be a set of sets of final states and a transition relation in the GBA, respectively. We say that states q_1 and q_2 are equivalent if the following two conditions hold.

$$\forall b \in B(Prop) \forall q \in Q((q_1, b, q) \in \delta \Longleftrightarrow (q_2, b, q) \in \delta) \tag{1}$$

$$\forall F \in \mathcal{F}(q_1 \in F \Longleftrightarrow q_2 \in F) \tag{2}$$

If q_1 and q_2 in the GBA satisfy both conditions (1) and (2), we can combine q_1 and q_2 into one state.

Furthermore, even if states q_1 and q_2 in the GBA satisfy condition (1) only, states (q_1, i) and (q_2, i) in the NBA converted according to Def. 5 in Sect. 4 satisfies both conditions (1) and (2) by the following theorem.

Theorem 1. *Let q_1 and q_2 be states in GBA $\mathcal{A}$, and (q_1, i) and (q_2, i) be states in NBA $\mathcal{B}$, which is obtained according to Def. 5. Then, if q_1 and q_2 satisfy condition (1), (q_1, i) and (q_2, i) satisfy condition (1) and the following (2'):*

$$(q_1, i) \in F \Longleftrightarrow (q_2, i) \in F \tag{2'}$$

where F is the set of final states in NBA $\mathcal{B}$.

Proof. It is trivial that (q_1, i) and (q_2, i) satisfy condition (2'), due to the definition of final states of $\mathcal{B}$ in Def. 5. We show that (q_1, i) and (q_2, i) satisfy condition (1). Assume that there is transition $((q_1, i), a, (s, j))$ in $\mathcal{B}$. Then, there is transition (q_1, a, s) in $\mathcal{A}$. Since q_1 and q_2 satisfy condition (1), there is transition (q_2, a, s) in $\mathcal{A}$. According to Def. 5, there exists transition $((q_2, i), a, (s, j'))$ in $\mathcal{B}$. Now, if $i \neq k + 1$ holds, then $j' = next(i, s) = j$ holds, and if $i = k + 1$ holds, then $j' = next(1, s) = j$ holds, where k is the number of sets of final states in $\mathcal{A}$. Hence, $j' = j$ holds. Therefore if there is a transition $((q_1, i), a, (s, j))$ in $\mathcal{B}$, there is also a transition $((q_2, i), a, (s, j))$ in $\mathcal{B}$. This means (q_1, i) and (q_2, i) satisfy condition (1). □

According to Theorem 1, we can obtain reduced NBA directly, without calculating large-scale NBA, by producing the reduced NBA while checking whether states in the GBA satisfy condition (1).

Example 3. We show a GBA converted from the LTL formula $GFp_1 \wedge GFp_2$ in Fig. 3 (left). The initial state is q_1, and a set of sets of final states is $\{\{q_1, q_3\}, \{q_1, q_2\}\}$. The initial state q_1 has four successive states q_1, q_2, q_3, q_4. Any two different states $q_i, q_j \in \{q_1, q_2, q_3, q_4\}$ do not satisfy condition (2), but they always satisfy condition (1). Unfortunately, because conditions (1) and (2) are not both satisfied, we cannot reduce the GBA itself directly. However, due to the fact that condition (1) is satisfied, we can apply our reduction technique to the conversion of the GBA to an NBA, and all of the states $(q_1, i), \dots, (q_4, i)$ in the resulting NBA can be reduced into one state (called i). The resulting NBA is shown in Fig. 3 (right).

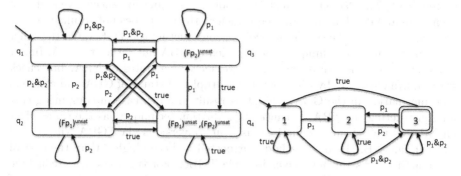

Fig. 3. GBA converted from $GFp_1 \wedge GFp_2$ (left) and a reduced NBA converted from the GBA (right)

6 Advantages of Our Method Over a TGBA-Based Approach

6.1 Features of Our Method

Translation methods are roughly divided into two kinds: those for conversion via GBA as an intermediate object, and those for conversion via TGBA. Originally, conversion via GBA was the most widely adopted method. However, since 2002, most methods are based on conversion via TGBA, (e.g., [10]). This is due to the development of efficient tools such as LTL2BA, Spot and LTL3BA (presented in 2012), all of which are based on conversion via TGBA. One advantage of the TGBA method is that TGBA is smaller than GBA for any given accepting language.

On the other hand, our method is based on conversion via GBA. Unfortunately, techniques that reduce the number of states of TGBA cannot be applied to GBA, as GBA itself cannot be reduced. Hence, we introduced a technique (Sect. 5.2) that has the same effect on the resulting NBA converted from GBA as reduction techniques have on TGBA. This technique can be applied while converting GBA into NBA, which means that GBA can be converted directly into reduced NBA. With this technique, although the number of states of GBA is larger than the number of states of TGBA, the number of states in the resulting NBA from GBA is comparable to the number in the NBA converted from TGBA. As illustrated in Example 3, even in case of $GFp_1 \wedge \ldots \wedge GFp_n,$[1] the number of states in the resulting NBA are the same. Detailed results are presented in Sect. 7.

6.2   Our Method vs. the TGBA-Based Approach

About reduction of states As stated above, during conversion via TGBA, 'strong' reduction techniques can be applied while constructing TGBA as an intermediate object. This 'strong' reduction is done by calculating successive states of each state and checking for state equivalence. Hence, it does not result in a substantial decrease in the computing cost of constructing the TGBA. On the other hand, our reduction technique is not applied to GBA but rather to NBA. In our reduction technique, we do not calculate successive states of NBA, but check state equivalence only by the labels ((q, i): tuples of states of GBA and counter) and information in the GBA. This does result in a decrease in computing cost for constructing the NBA. Because our reduction technique has the same effect on NBA as the 'strong' reductions used in conversions via TGBA, the cost of constructing NBA by our method is expected to be no higher than the cost of constructing NBA during conversions via TGBA. For this reason, we conclude that conversion via TGBA is not always advantageous from the point of view of reduction, compared to conversion via GBA.

About acceptance conditions We have observed that in TGBA converted from LTL formulae, before the application of any reduction, there is only two cases: all the transitions into the same state are included in an acceptance condition, or no transitions into the state is included in the acceptance condition.[2] For instance, in the translation algorithm proposed in [8], if a formula Xf, where f represents eventuality (e.g. $X(fUg)$), does not occur in the input formula, then there is only two cases: all the transitions into the same state are included in an acceptance condition, or no transitions into the state is included in the acceptance condition. Therefore, with respect to efficiency of memory use, the acceptance condition should be defined by a set of states, not by a set of transitions. Hence, in our method, we treat formulae of the form $X(fUg)$ as exceptions by using the special label *unsat*, as stated in Sect. 3. This has the disadvantage of increasing the number of states. However, there are few occurrences of formulae of the form $X(fUg)$ in practical specifications. Therefore, we expect that the advantage of being able to omit redundant space in the acceptance conditions is greater than any disadvantage arising from an increase in the number of states.

Necessity of NBA It is evident that TGBA is preferable to GBA for use in model-checking directly, because the number of states of TGBA is less than the number of states of GBA or NBA. On the other hand, there are many cases in

---

[1] In the conversion of $GFp_1 \wedge \ldots \wedge GFp_n$, the conversion via TGBA works very well.

[2] This observation is satisfied only for TGBA before the application of any reduction techniques including ones based on equivalence of successor states.

which NBA is needed, such as for SPIN or realisability checking. In such cases, the number of states of TGBA or GBA as intermediate objects is unimportant. Therefore, we conclude that our method is valuable.

7 Evaluation

We implemented our method in C++. Our implementation is available at http://www.yonezaki.cs.titech.ac.jp/tools/. In this section, we compare our implementation to other tools. The comparison environment was OS:Ubuntu 12.04 64bit, CPU: Corei7-3820 3.60GHz, 32GB memory.

7.1 Comparison with Other Works

Although there are many tools for converting LTL into NBA, we compared our implementation to LTL2BA (version 1.1, without options), Spot (version 1.1.4, with the option -r1)[3] and LTL3BA (version 1.0.2, without options), because Rozier et al. in [14] showed that LTL2BA [8] and Spot [6] were the most efficient tools at that time, and LTL3BA, presented in 2012, is also known as one of the most efficient tools. These tools are based on conversion via TGBA.

We measured the times for conversion of several LTL formulae. If the tools could not output the results within 300 s, we aborted the execution; this is denoted in the results by na. For our implementation, we measured the conversion times with and without the reduction techniques proposed in Sect. 5.

First, we generated 100 random formulae of equal size (50 characters), following the method of [14], and measured the sum of the conversion times to NBA, as well as the sum of the number of states in the resulting NBA. These results are shown in Table 1.

Table 1. The sum of the number of states and the sum of conversion times (s) for 100 random formulae

Our implementation				Spot		LTL2BA		LTL3BA	
with reduction		without reduction		# of		# of		# of	
# of states	time	# of states	time	states	time	states	time	states	time
37652	2.58	83492	3.10	29308	14.00	65903	64.15	46303	24.00

Next, we measured the conversion times and number of states for the specification of n-floor elevator systems [3]. This is a large-scale specification, with $3n + 6$ propositions and $6n - 1$ temporal operators. The size of the specification is $O(n^3)$. These results are shown in Table 2.

Finally, we measured the conversion times and the number of states for the following four kinds of LTL formulae, which were used as benchmarks in [5].

- $E_1(n) : \bigwedge_{1 \leq i \leq n} F p_i$

---

[3] In Spot, the option -r1 means that formula reduction using basic rewriting is allowed.

Table 2. The number of states and conversion times (s) for specifications of n-floor elevator systems

	Our implementation				Spot		LTL2BA		LTL3BA	
	with reduction		without reduction		# of		# of		# of	
n	# of states	time	# of states	time	states	time	states	time	states	time
2	24	0.01	24	0.01	23	0.05	23	0.04	23	0.01
3	182	0.02	182	0.02	170	0.15	224	5.95	182	0.06
4	1438	0.16	1757	0.17	1333	2.44	na	na	1385	1.83
5	10403	2.46	16660	3.01	9585	53.96	na	na	9524	118.33
6	69685	43.23	145786	90.62	na	na	na	na	na	na

- $E_2(n) : F(p_1 \wedge F(p_2 \wedge \dots F(p_{n-1} \wedge Fp_n) \dots)) \wedge F(q_1 \wedge F(q_2 \wedge \dots F(q_{n-1} \wedge Fq_n) \dots))$
- $U(n) : (\dots (((p_1 U p_2) U p_3) U p_4) \dots) U p_n$
- $C(n) : \bigwedge_{1 \leq i \leq n} GF p_i$

These results are shown in Table 3.[4] The formulae $C(n)$ are known to be efficiently converted by translation methods via TGBA, such as LTL2BA, Spot and LTL3BA. The number of states of the smallest NBA for the formulae $E_1(n)$, $E_2(n)$ and $C(n)$ are 2^n, $(n+1)^2$ and $n+1$, respectively.

7.2   Discussion

With respect to execution time, our implementation with reduction techniques was much more efficient than LTL2BA and Spot for all of the benchmarks. The execution time of our method was about a tenth that of Spot. For all benchmarks except E_2 and C, our implementation was more efficient than LTL3BA. Furthermore, with respect to the size of the resulting NBA, our implementation with reduction techniques was about as efficient as the other tools. For the benchmarks $E_1(n)$, $E_2(n)$ and $C(n)$, the sizes of the NBAs produced by our implementation were 2^n, $(n+1)^2$ and $n+1$, respectively, which are the smallest sizes that can be expected and are the same sizes that Spot produces. Taken together, these results indicate that with our method one can check the satisfiability of LTL formulae 10 times faster than with Spot, and the NBA obtained by our implementation is suitable for manipulations such as determinisation, complementation, and so forth.

A comparison of our implementations with and without reduction techniques confirmed that the reduction techniques effectively reduced conversion times. From the results of $E_1(n)$, $E_2(n)$ and $U(n)$, it is apparent that the number of states of NBA in our implementation is almost the same with and without the reduction techniques. Furthermore, the conversion times for our implementations with and without reduction techniques were approximately equal. These results indicate that the overhead of our reduction techniques is negligible.

---

[4] In this benchmark, we did not use the technique introduced in Sect.5.1, since automata from $C(n)$ have too many transitions to be decomposed into SCCs effectively.

Table 3. The number of states and conversion times (s) for E_1, E_2, C and U

n	Our implementation with reduction # of states	time	without reduction # of states	time	Spot # of states	time	LTL2BA # of states	time	LTL3BA # of states	time
$E_1(5)$	32	0.00	33	0.00	32	0.02	32	0.00	32	0.00
$E_1(8)$	256	0.01	257	0.01	256	0.15	256	0.03	256	0.02
$E_1(11)$	2048	0.13	2049	0.13	2048	6.75	2048	6.34	2048	1.47
$E_1(14)$	16384	3.49	16385	3.57	na	na	na	na	16384	131.86
$E_1(17)$	131072	113.78	131073	106.47	na	na	na	na	na	na
$E_2(11)$	144	0.08	145	0.08	144	0.36	345	0.17	144	0.05
$E_2(18)$	361	1.19	362	1.24	361	4.33	940	3.53	361	0.47
$E_2(25)$	676	9.00	677	9.34	676	27.75	1829	40.66	676	2.86
$E_2(32)$	1089	43.30	1090	45.15	1089	116.46	3012	223.90	1089	10.69
$E_2(39)$	1600	299.31	na	na	na	na	na	na	1600	30.72
$U(4)$	8	0.01	9	0.01	8	0.06	15	0.00	13	0.01
$U(6)$	32	0.01	33	0.01	32	0.05	89	0.01	87	0.02
$U(8)$	128	0.03	129	0.02	128	0.13	481	0.25	479	0.22
$U(10)$	512	0.20	513	0.21	512	1.27	2433	54.27	2431	49.35
$U(12)$	2048	3.33	2049	3.33	2048	23.61	na	na	na	na
$U(14)$	8192	60.41	8193	59.37	na	na	na	na	na	na
$C(3)$	4	0.00	17	0.00	4	0.02	4	0.00	4	0.00
$C(7)$	8	0.00	513	0.04	8	0.17	8	0.27	8	0.01
$C(11)$	12	0.03	12289	17.58	12	0.07	na	na	12	0.02
$C(15)$	16	0.47	na	na	16	0.89	na	na	16	0.17
$C(19)$	20	11.38	na	na	20	29.19	na	na	20	4.78
$C(23)$	na	na	na	na	na	na	na	na	24	180.70

Finally, we discuss the reason why our implementation is more efficient than the implementation of Spot [5], even though our implementation and Spot both utilise BDD for representing transitions. Spot converts LTL formulae into NBA via TGBA, and indicates by BDD whether each transition is included in the acceptance conditions (a set of sets of final transitions). In contrast, our method converts LTL formulae into NBA via GBA, and it is not necessary to represent the acceptance conditions (a set of sets of final states) by BDD. Because the number of transitions is much larger than the number of states, the size of the BDD tends to be larger in Spot than in our method. This difference is the reason why our implementation is more efficient than Spot. LTL3BA also uses BDD for representing transitions from a state. However, from [4], it is not clear if LTL3BA indicates by BDD whether each transition is included in the acceptance conditions.

8   Conclusion

In this paper, we proposed an efficient method for translating LTL formulae into NBA. We also compared our method to LTL2BA, Spot and LTL3BA, which are currently the most efficient tools available. We determined that our method executes much faster than LTL2BA and Spot and is competitive with LTL3BA. Furthermore, the size of the resulting NBA generated by our method is comparable to that generated by the others. These results show that our method of translation via GBA is competitive with the most efficient currently available tools.

Our method does not implement several reduction techniques that are implemented in Spot or LTL3BA. Future work will integrate these reduction techniques into our method and will also evaluate the method by applying it to actual verification processes, such as model-checking, realisability checking, and so forth.

Methods for converting specifications written in LTL into NBA are commonly used in verification processes. We believe that our method will be of practical use for the verification of safety critical systems.

Acknowledgment. This work was supported by JSPS KAKENHI Grant Number 24500032. We would like to thank the reviewers for their valuable comments and suggestions to improve the quality of the paper.

References

1. Abadi, M., Lamport, L., Wolper, P.: Realizable and unrealizable specifications of reactive systems. In: Ronchi Della Rocca, S., Ausiello, G., Dezani-Ciancaglini, M. (eds.) ICALP 1989. LNCS, vol. 372, pp. 1–17. Springer, Heidelberg (1989)
2. Aoshima, T., Sakuma, K., Yonezaki, N.: An efficient verification procedure supporting evolution of reactive system specifications. In: Proc. of the 4th International Workshop on Principles of Software Evolution, pp. 182–185. ACM (2001)
3. Aoshima, T., Yonezaki, N.: Verification of reactive system specification with outer event conditional formula. In: International Symposium on Principles of Software Evolution (ISPSE2000), pp. 195–199 (2000)
4. Babiak, T., Křetínský, M., Řehák, V., Strejček, J.: LTL to büchi automata translation: Fast and more deterministic. In: Flanagan, C., König, B. (eds.) TACAS 2012. LNCS, vol. 7214, pp. 95–109. Springer, Heidelberg (2012)
5. Duret-Lutz, A.: LTL translation improvements in Spot. In: Proc. of the Fifth international conference on Verification and Evaluation of Computer and Communication Systems, VECoS 2011, pp. 72–83. British Computer Society (2011)
6. Duret-Lutz, A., Poitrenaud, D.: Spot: An extensible model checking library using transition-based generalized Büchi automata. In: Proc. of MASCOTS 2004, pp. 76–83. IEEE Computer Society (2004)
7. Filiot, E., Jin, N., Raskin, J.F.: An antichain algorithm for LTL realizability. In: Bouajjani, A., Maler, O. (eds.) CAV 2009. LNCS, vol. 5643, pp. 263–277. Springer, Heidelberg (2009)
8. Gastin, P., Oddoux, D.: Fast LTL to büchi automata translation. In: Berry, G., Comon, H., Finkel, A. (eds.) CAV 2001. LNCS, vol. 2102, pp. 53–65. Springer, Heidelberg (2001)
9. Gerth, R., Peled, D., Vardi, M.Y., Wolper, P.: Simple on-the-fly automatic verification of linear temporal logic. In: Protocol Specification Testing and Verification, pp. 3–18. Chapman & Hall (1995)

10. Giannakopoulou, D., Lerda, F.: From states to transitions: Improving translation of LTL formulae to Büchi automata. In: Peled, D.A., Vardi, M.Y. (eds.) FORTE 2002. LNCS, vol. 2529, pp. 308–326. Springer, Heidelberg (2002)
11. Holzmann, G.J.: The model checker SPIN. IEEE Trans. Softw. Eng. 23(5), 279–295 (1997), http://dx.doi.org/10.1109/32.588521
12. Jobstmann, B., Bloem, R.: Optimizations for LTL synthesis. In: Formal Methods in Computer Aided Design, FMCAD 2006, pp. 117–124 (2006)
13. Pnueli, A., Rosner, R.: On the synthesis of a reactive module. In: POPL 1989, pp. 179–190 (1989)
14. Rozier, K.Y., Vardi, M.Y.: LTL satisfiability checking. In: Bošnački, D., Edelkamp, S. (eds.) SPIN 2007. LNCS, vol. 4595, pp. 149–167. Springer, Heidelberg (2007)
15. Somenzi, F., Bloem, R.: Efficient Büchi automata from LTL formulae. In: Emerson, E.A., Sistla, A.P. (eds.) CAV 2000. LNCS, vol. 1855, pp. 248–263. Springer, Heidelberg (2000)

Complete Model-Based Equivalence Class Testing for the ETCS Ceiling Speed Monitor

Cécile Braunstein[1,*], Anne E. Haxthausen[3,†], Wen-ling Huang[12,***], Felix Hübner[1,**], Jan Peleska[1,***], Uwe Schulze[1,***], and Linh Vu Hong[3,†]

[1] Department of Mathematics and Computer Science,
University of Bremen, Germany
[2] Department of Mathematics,
University of Hamburg, Germany
[3] DTU Compute,
Technical University of Denmark

Abstract. In this paper we present a new test model written in SysML and an associated blackbox test suite for the Ceiling Speed Monitor (CSM) of the European Train Control System (ETCS). The model is publicly available and intended to serve as a novel benchmark for investigating new testing theories and comparing the capabilities of model-based test automation tools. The CSM application inputs velocity values from a domain which could not be completely enumerated for test purposes with reasonable effort. We therefore apply a novel method for equivalence class testing that – despite the conceptually infinite cardinality of the input domains – is capable to produce finite test suites that are complete (i.e. sound and exhaustive) for a given fault model. In this paper, an overview of the model and the equivalence class testing strategy is given, and tool-based evaluation results are presented. For the technical details we refer to the published model and a technical report that is also available on the same website.

Keywords: Model-based testing, Equivalence class partition testing, SysML, European Train Control System ETCS, Ceiling Speed Monitoring.

1 Introduction

In 2011 the *model-based testing benchmarks website* www.mbt-benchmarks.org has been created. Its objective is to publish test models that may serve as chal-

* The author's research is funded by ITEA2 project openETCS under grant agreement 11025.
** The author's research is funded by Siemens AG in the context of the SyDE Graduate School on System Design, http://www.informatik.uni-bremen.de/syde/index.php?home-en
*** The authors' research is funded by the EU FP7 COMPASS project under grant agreement no.287829.
† The authors' research is funded by the RobustRailS project funded by the Danish Council for Strategic Research.

S. Merz and J. Pang (Eds.): ICFEM 2014, LNCS 8829, pp. 380–395, 2014.
© Springer International Publishing Switzerland 2014

lenges or benchmarks for validating testing theories and for comparing the capabilities of model-based testing (MBT) tools [12]. In the present paper a novel
contribution to this website is presented, a SysML model of the Ceiling Speed
Monitor (CSM) which is part of the European Vital Computer (EVC), the on-
board controller of trains conforming to the European Train Control System
(ETCS) standard [4]. In the first part of this paper (Section 2) we give an introduction into the CSM model.

The CSM represents a specific test-related challenge: its behaviour depends
on actual and allowed speed, and these have conceptually real-valued data domains, so that – even when discretising the input space – it would be infeasible
to exercise all possible combinations of inputs on the system under test (SUT).
Therefore test strategies identifying finitely many representatives from the input
domains have to be applied when testing the CSM, and in this paper we focus on
equivalence class partition (ECP) testing. While ECP testing is well-adopted in
a heuristic manner in today's industrial test campaigns, practical application of
equivalence class testing still lacks formal justification of the equivalence classes
selected and the sequences of class representatives selected as test cases: standard text books used in industry, for example [14], only explain the generation
of input equivalence class tests for systems, where the SUT reaction to an input
class representative is independent on the internal state. Moreover, the systematic calculation of classes from models, as well as their formal justification with
respect to test strength and coverage achieved, is not yet part of today's best
practices in industry.

In contrast to this, formal approaches to equivalence class testing have been
studied in the formal methods communities; references to these results are given
in Section 5. In the second part of this paper (Section 3) we therefore describe a
recent formal technique for equivalence class testing and its application to testing
the CSM. The theoretical foundations of this strategy have been published by two
of the authors in [7]. The present paper illustrates its practical application and
presents first evaluation details using a prototype implementation in an existing
MBT tool (Section 4). This ECP strategy introduces test suites depending on
fault models. This well adopted notion has first been introduced in the field of
finite state machine (FSM) testing [13], but is also applicable to other formal
modelling techniques. A fault model consists of a reference model, a conformance
relation and a fault domain. The fault domain is a collection of models whose
behaviour may or may not be consistent with the reference model in the sense
of the conformance relation. The test suites generated by the ECP strategy
described here are *complete* with respect to the given fault model: each system
of the fault domain which conforms to the reference model will pass all the
generated tests (this means that the test suite is *sound*), and each system in the
fault domain that violates the conformity to the reference model will at least fail
once when tested according to the test suite (the test suite is *exhaustive*).

We use state transition systems (STS) for encoding the operational semantics of concrete modelling formalisms like SysML. STS are widely known from
the field of model checking [3], because their extension into Kripke Structures

allows for effective data abstraction techniques. The latter are also applied for equivalence class testing. Since state transition systems are a means for semantic representation, testing theories elaborated for STS are applicable for all concrete formalisms whose behavioural semantics can be expressed by STS. In [8] it is shown how the semantics of general SysML models and models of a process algebra are encoded as STS. In this paper we illustrate how this is achieved for the concrete case of the CSM SysML model.

2   CSM Model Description

Functional Objectives. The European Train Control System ETCS relies on the existence of an onboard controller in train engines, the *European Vital Computer EVC.* Its functionality and basic architectural features are described in the public ETCS system specification [4]. One functional category of the EVC covers aspects of speed and distance monitoring, to accomplish the *"... supervision of the speed of the train versus its position, in order to assure that the train remains within the given speed and distance limits."* [15, 3.13.1.1]. While displaying actual and allowed speed to the train engine driver, the monitoring functions automatically trigger the brakes in case of speed limit violations. Speed and distance monitoring is decomposed into three sub-functions [15, 3.13.10.1.2], where only one out of these three is active at a point in time: (1) *Ceiling speed monitoring (CSM)* supervises the observance of the maximal speed allowed according to the current most restrictive speed profile (MRSP)[1]. CSM is active while the train does not approach a target (train station, level crossing, or any other point that must be reached with predefined speed). (2) *Target speed monitoring (TSM)* enforces speed restrictions applicable while the train brakes to a target, for example, a track section where a significantly lower maximal speed has to be observed. (3) *Release speed monitoring (RSM)* applies when the special target "end of movement authority (EOA)" is approached, where the train must come to a stop. RSM supervises the observance of the distance-depending so-called release speed, when the train approaches the EOA and is allowed to drive at a reduced speed.

The model presented here captures the CSM functionality.

Test Model Semantics. SysML test models are structured using blocks. At the top-level, the model is decomposed into a block representing the SUT and another one representing the test environment (TE); Fig. 1 shows this decomposition for the CSM. Depending on the complexity of the model, blocks can be further decomposed into lower-level block diagrams, until leaf blocks are reached that are associated with behaviour. In our test models this behaviour is specified by sequential hierarchic SysML state machines. Blocks execute concurrently and in a synchronous way, so that transitions of concurrent state machines that are enabled in the same model state execute simultaneously.

---

[1] In some situations, more than one speed restriction may apply, and then the most restrictive one has to be enforced.

The whole model executes according to the *run-to-completion* semantics defined for state machines. The model is in a *quiescent* (or stable) state, if no transition can be executed without an input change.

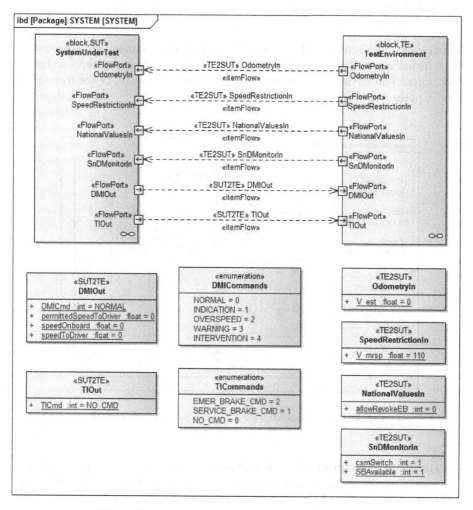

Fig. 1. System interface of the ceiling speed monitor

In a quiescent model state, inputs may be changed. If these changes enable a transition, the latter is executed. Since our SUT model is deterministic – this is typical for sequential safety-critical applications – there is no necessity to handle situations where several transitions are simultaneously enabled. The executed transition, however, may lead to a *transient* state, that is, to a state where another transition is enabled. In the run-to-completion semantics this new transition is also executed, and so forth until a quiescent state is reached.

Conceptually, the consecutive execution of model transitions is executed in zero time, so that input changes cannot happen until the next quiescent state has been reached. Moreover, models admitting unbounded sequences of transitions between transient states are considered as illegal, and this situation is called a *livelock* failure.

Interfaces. The interfaces between SUT and its environment are specified in the internal block diagram displayed in Fig. 1. All interfaces are represented as flow ports. The environment writes to SUT input ports and reads from SUT output ports.

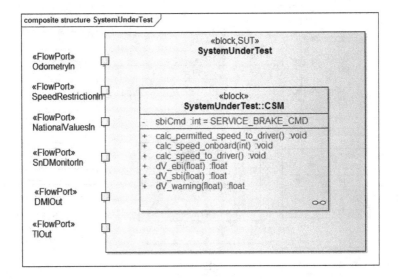

Fig. 2. Block diagram with CSM (sequential behaviour)

Ceiling speed monitoring is activated and de-activated by the speed and distance monitoring (SnD) coordination function that controls CSM, TSM, and RSM: on input interface SnDMonitorIn, variable csmSwitch specifies whether ceiling speed monitoring should be active (csmSwitch = 1) or passive, since target or release speed monitoring is being performed (csmSwitch = 0). Furthermore, this interface carries variable SBAvailable which has value 1, if the train is equipped with a service brake. This brake is then used for slowing down the train if it has exceeded the maximal speed allowed, but not yet reached the threshold for an emergency brake intervention. If SBAvailable = 0, the emergency brake shall be used for slowing down the train in this situation. Input SBAvailable is to be considered as a configuration parameter of the train, since it depends on the availability of the service brake hardware. Therefore this value can be freely selected at start-of-test, but must remain constant during test execution.

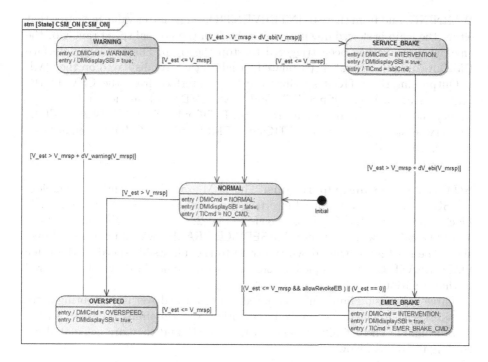

Fig. 3. Ceiling speed monitoring state machine

Input interface OdometryIn provides the current speed value estimated by the odometer equipment in variable V_{est}. Input interface SpeedRestrictionIn provides the current maximal velocity defined by the most restrictive speed profile in variable V_{MRSP}. Input interface NationalValuesIn provides a control flag for the ceiling speed monitor: variable allowRevokeEB is 1, if after an emergency brake intervention the brake may be automatically released as soon as the estimated velocity of the train is again less or equal to the maximal speed allowed. Otherwise (allowRevokeEB = 0) the emergency brakes must only be released after the train has come to a standstill ($V_{est} = 0$). This input parameter is called a "national value", because it may change when a train crosses the boundaries between European countries, due to their local regulations.

Output interface DMIOut sends data from the SUT to the driver machine interface (DMI). It carries five variables. DMICmd is used to display the supervision status to the train engine driver: Value INDICATION may be initially present when CSM is activated, but will be immediately overridden by one of the values NORMAL, OVERSPEED, WARNING, or INTERVENTION, as soon as ceiling speed monitoring becomes active. Value NORMAL is written by the SUT to this variable as long as the ceiling speed is not violated by the current estimated speed. Value OVERSPEED has to be set by the CSM as soon as condition $V_{MRSP} < V_{est}$ becomes true. If the speed increases further (the detailed conditions are described below), the indication changes from OVERSPEED to

WARNING, and from there to INTERVENTION. The latter value indicates that either the train is slowed down until it is back in the normal speed range, or the emergency brake has been triggered to stop the train. Furthermore, interface DMIOut contains several speed-related variables that are displayed on the DMI.

Output interface TIOut specifies the train interface from the CSM to the brakes, using variable TICmd. If TICmd = NO_CMD, both service brakes (if existent) and emergency brakes are released. If TICmd = SERVICE_BRAKE_CMD, the service brake is activated. If TICmd = EMER_BRAKE_CMD, the emergency brake is triggered.

SUT Attributes and Operations. The CSM executes sequentially; therefore the SUT block on the top-level interface diagram (Fig. 1) is refined to a single block representing the CSM, as shown in Fig. 2. There, the SUT uses a local attribute sbiCmd which carries value SERVICE_BRAKE_CMD, if the service brake should be used for slowing down the train to the admissible speed. If the value EMER_BRAKE_CMD is assigned to sbiCmd, the emergency brake will be triggered in this situation.

Three supervision limits are computed to assist the driver in preventing automated service or emergency brake intervention by maintaining the speed within certain limits. These limits depend on the MRSP, and they are calculated according to [15] as follows.

$$
\mathsf{dV_{warning}}(V_{MRSP}) = \begin{cases} \min\{\frac{1}{3} + \frac{1}{30} \cdot V_{MRSP}, 5\} & \text{if } V_{MRSP} > 110 \\ 4 & \text{if } V_{MRSP} \leq 110 \end{cases} \tag{1}
$$

$$
\mathsf{dV_{sbi}}(V_{MRSP}) = \begin{cases} \min\{0.55 + 0.045 \cdot V_{MRSP}, 10\} & \text{if } V_{MRSP} > 110 \\ 5.5 & \text{if } V_{MRSP} \leq 110 \end{cases} \tag{2}
$$

$$
\mathsf{dV_{ebi}}(V_{MRSP}) = \begin{cases} \min\{-0.75 + 0.075 \cdot V_{MRSP}, 15\} & \text{if } V_{MRSP} > 110 \\ 7.5 & \text{if } V_{MRSP} \leq 110 \end{cases} \tag{3}
$$

CSM Behavioural Specification. The behaviour of the ceiling speed monitor is modelled by a hierarchic state machine that is associated with the SUT block of Fig. 2. The top-level machine specifies the activation and de-activation of the CSM during the interplay between CSM, TSM, and RSM. Due to the usual space limitations, we consider here only the lower-level state machine CSM_ON modelling the behaviour of the active CSM, as displayed in Fig. 3.

Its execution starts in basic state NORMAL, where the 'NORMAL' indication is displayed on the DMI and brakes are released (TICmd = NO_CMD). When the speed increases above the maximal speed allowed ($V_{est} > V_{MRSP}$), the state machine transits to basic state OVERSPEED, where the 'OVERSPEED' indication is displayed to the train engine driver. If the train continues overspeeding until the warning threshold $V_{MRSP} + \mathsf{dV_{warning}}(V_{MRSP})$ is exceeded, a transition into the WARNING state is performed, accompanied by an indication change on the DMI. Accelerating further until $V_{est} > V_{MRSP} + dV_{sbi}(V_{MRSP})$ leads to a transition into basic state SERVICE_BRAKE, where either the service brake or the emergency brake is triggered, depending on the value stored before in variable sbiCmd. The DMI display changes to 'INTERVENTION'.

The intervention status is realised by two basic state machine states, SERVICE_BRAKE and EMER_BRAKE. From SERVICE_BRAKE it is still possible to return to NORMAL, as soon as the speed has been decreased below the over-speeding threshold. When the train, however, continues its acceleration until the emergency braking threshold has been exceeded ($V_{est} > V_{MRSP} + dV_{ebi}(V_{MRSP})$), basic state EMER_BRAKE is entered. From there, a state machine transition to NORMAL is only possible if the train comes to a standstill, or if the national regulations (variable allowRevokeEB) allow to release the brakes as soon as over-speeding has stopped.

Observe that the run-to-completion semantics of state machines also allows for zero-time transitions from, for example, NORMAL to EMER_BRAKE. If, while in basic state NORMAL, the inputs change such that $V_{est} > V_{MRSP} + dV_{ebi}(V_{MRSP})$ becomes true[2], the state machine transition from NORMAL to OVERSPEED leads to a transient model state, because guard condition $V_{est} > V_{MRSP} + dV_{warning}(V_{MRSP})$ is already fulfilled, and the state machine transits to WARNING. Similarly, guards $V_{est} > V_{MRSP} + dV_{sbi}(V_{MRSP})$ and $V_{est} > V_{MRSP} + dV_{ebi}(V_{MRSP})$ also evaluate to true, so that the next quiescent state is reached in basic state EMER_BRAKE.

Full Model Description and Requirements Tracing. The complete SysML model of the CSM function is publicly available[3]. A comprehensive description can be found in the technical report [1] which is also available on this website. The SysML modelling formalism supports the specification of relationships between requirements and model elements contributing to their realisation. This allows for requirements-driven testing: test cases supporting the verification of a given requirement have to cover the model elements contributing to the requirement. In [1] the CSM requirements and the tracing from requirements to model elements, as well as an extended model description are presented.

3   Equivalence Class Partition Testing Strategy

The theoretical foundations of the equivalence class partition testing method applied in this paper have been described in [7]. In this section we summarise the results obtained there and show how they are applied for testing the CSM.

---

[2] This would be an exceptional behaviour situation, caused, for example, by temporary unavailability of odometry data, so that a "sudden jump" of V_{est} would be observed by the CSM.

[3] http://www.mbt-benchmarks.org

System Domain. We consider models and SUT whose true behaviour can be represented by state transition systems STS (S, s_0, R) with state space S, initial state $s_0 \in S$ and transition relation $R \subseteq S \times S$. States $s \in S$ are valuation functions $s : V \to D$, where V is a set of variable symbols and $D = \bigcup_{v \in V} D_v$, where D_v is the domain of variable v, and $s(v) \in D_v$ holds for every $v \in V$ and $s \in S$. The variable space V is finite and can be partitioned into disjoint sets $V = I \cup M \cup O$ called input variables, (internal) model variables, and output variables, respectively. The domains of input variables can be infinite, but those of model variables and output variables must be finite. The transition relation $R \subseteq S \times S$ may be infinite, since we allow for infinite input data domains. Admissible STS allow for partitioning of state spaces into quiescent and transient states, $S = S_Q \cup S_T, S_Q \cap S_T = \varnothing$. In a quiescent state $s_1 \in S_Q$ only input changes can occur, leading either to another quiescent, or to a transient post-state s_2. The inputs can then change in an arbitrary way, but the internal and output variables remain unchanged. Transient states $s_1 \in S_T$ have uniquely defined quiescent post-states $s_2 \in S_Q$, and during the transition from s_1 to s_2 only internal variable states and outputs change. The initial state s_0 must be an element of S_Q.

We use initial STS state s_0 to model the quiescent state when "the system is switched off". From there, some input change will drive the STS into the state s the system assumes after initialisation. This state may depend on the new input valuation, so our STS can very well model situations where the initial behaviour depends on the input that is present on system initialisation.

In the exposition below, variable symbols x, m, y are used with the convention that $x \in I, m \in M, y \in O$, and the symbols can be enumerated as $I = \{x_1, \ldots, x_k\}$, $M = \{m_1, \ldots, m_p\}$, $O = \{y_1, \ldots, y_q\}$. We use notation $\boldsymbol{x} = (x_1, \ldots, x_k), s(\boldsymbol{x}) = (s(x_1), \ldots, s(x_k)), D_I = D_{x_1} \times \cdots \times D_{x_k}$ denotes the cartesian product of the input variable domains. Tuples $\boldsymbol{m}, \boldsymbol{y}$ and D_M and D_O are defined over model variables and outputs in an analogous way. By $s \oplus \{\boldsymbol{x} \mapsto \boldsymbol{c}\}, \boldsymbol{c} \in D_I$ we denote the state s' which coincides with s on all variables from $M \cup O$, but returns values $s'(x_i) = c_i, i = 1, \ldots, k$ for the input symbols.

I/O-Equivalence. Applying a trace $\iota = \boldsymbol{c}_1 \ldots \boldsymbol{c}_n$ of input vectors $\boldsymbol{c}_i \in D_I$ to a STS (S, s_0, R) residing in some quiescent state $s \in S$, this stimulates a sequence of state transitions with associated output changes as triggered by the inputs. Restricting this sequence to quiescent states, this results in a trace of states $\tau = s_1 . s_2 \ldots s_n$ such that $s_i(\boldsymbol{x}) = \boldsymbol{c}_i, i = 1, \ldots, n$, and $s_i(\boldsymbol{y})$ is the last STS output resulting from application of $\boldsymbol{c}_1 \ldots \boldsymbol{c}_i$ to state s. This trace τ is generally denoted by s/ι. The restriction of s/ι to output variables is denoted by $(s/\iota)|_O$. Since transient states have unique quiescent post-states, the restriction to quiescent states does not result in a loss of information, if the input trace ι is known: the omitted transient states are some elements of $s \oplus \{\boldsymbol{x} \mapsto \boldsymbol{c}_1\}, \ldots, s_{n-1} \oplus \{\boldsymbol{x} \mapsto \boldsymbol{c}_n\}$, and these states satisfy $R(s \oplus \{\boldsymbol{x} \mapsto \boldsymbol{c}_1\}, s_1), \ldots, R(s_{n-1} \oplus \{\boldsymbol{x} \mapsto \boldsymbol{c}_n\}, s_n)$.

Two states s, s' are *I/O-equivalent*, written $s \sim s'$, if every non-empty input trace ι, when applied to s and s', results in the same outputs, that is, $(s/\iota)|_O = (s'/\iota)|_O$. Two STS $\mathcal{S}, \mathcal{S}'$ are I/O-equivalent, if their initial states are I/O-equivalent. Note that for technical reasons, $s \sim s'$ still admits that $s|_O \neq s'|_O$.

Input Equivalence Class Partitions. Since I/O-equivalence is an equivalence relation, we can factorise STS state spaces by $\sim$, and the resulting equivalence classes $A \in S/_\sim$ have the property that all $s, s' \in A$ yield the same output traces $(s/\iota)|_O = (s'/\iota)|_O$ for arbitrary non-empty input traces ι. For systems like the CSM, the number of classes A is finite, so we can enumerate $S/_\sim = \{A_1, \ldots, A_r\}$. For every $s \in A_i$, applying an input $c \in D_I$ will lead to a quiescent target state denoted by $(s/\!/c)$ in the unique target class A_j. Index j only depends on (i, c), since for $s, s' \in A_i$ all corresponding states s_k, s'_k in $s/\iota = s_1.s_2 \ldots .s_n, s'/\iota = s'_1.s'_2 \ldots .s'_n$ are I/O-equivalent for any $\iota = c_1 \ldots c_n$, $k = 1, \ldots, n$. Therefore $(s/\!/c) \in A_j$ if and only if $(s'/\!/c) \in A_j$. One class A_j, however, may contain elements $s \sim s'$ with different outputs, since I/O-equivalence only states that all future outputs will be identical, when applying the same non-empty input trace to s, s'. Since $D_O = \{d_1, \ldots, d_{|D_O|}\}$ is finite, we can associate the value index $h \in \{1, \ldots, |D_O|\}$ with the target class A_j, if $(s/\!/c)|_O = d_h$. Again, h only depends on (i, c), but not on the choice of $s \in A_i$.

Applying c to elements from all classes $A_1, \ldots, A_r$, results in (not necessarily distinct) index pairs $j(c, i), h(c, i)$, $i = 1, \ldots, r$. This induces a factorisation of the input domain D_I: define $X(c) \subseteq D_I$ as the maximal set containing c, such that $j(c', i) = j(c, i) \wedge h(c', i) = h(c, i)$, $i = 1, \ldots, r$, holds for all $c' \in X(c)$.

Then the *Input Equivalence Class Partitioning (IECP)* $\mathcal{I} = \{X(c) \mid c \in D_I\}$ has the following properties: (1) The elements of $\mathcal{I}$ are pairwise disjoint, (2) The union of all $X \in \mathcal{I}$ equals D_I, (3) $\mathcal{I}$ is finite, and (4) for all $s \in A_i$, $c \in X$, target states $(s/\!/c)$ are contained in the same target class $A_{j(i,c)}$ and have the unique output value $d_{h(i,c)}$. Furthermore, each pair of input traces $\iota = c_1 \ldots c_n$, $\iota' = c'_1 \ldots c'_n$, when applied to the same state s, lead to the same output traces $(s/\iota)|_O = (s/\iota')|_O$, if $c'_i \in X(c_i)$ for each $i = 1, \ldots, n$.

A given IECP $\mathcal{I}$ can be *refined* by selecting input sets $\mathcal{I}_2 = \{X_1, X_2, \ldots\}$ such that $\mathcal{I}_2$ also fulfils the above properties (1), (2), (3), and such that every X_i is a subset of some $X \in \mathcal{I}$. If these conditions hold, $\mathcal{I}_2$ inherits property (4). Refinement is obviously reflexive, transitive and anti-symmetric.

Fault Model. As reference models we use the STS representations $\mathcal{S}$ of models elaborated in concrete formalisms – like the CSM model presented in this paper – such that the expected behaviour of the SUT is specified by $\mathcal{S}$ up to I/O-equivalence. We use I/O-equivalence as conformance relation. The fault domain $\mathcal{D}$ specifies the set of potential systems under test, whose true behaviour can be represented by an STS $\mathcal{S}' \in \mathcal{D}$. For the equivalence class testing strategy, the fault domain depends on the reference model $\mathcal{S}$ and two additional parameters $m \in \mathbb{N}$ and a refinement $\mathcal{I}_2$ of $\mathcal{I}$, the IECP associated with $\mathcal{S}$. $\mathcal{D}(\mathcal{S}, m, \mathcal{I}_2)$ contains all $\mathcal{S}'$ satisfying

1. The states of $\mathcal{S}'$ are defined over the same variable space $V = I \cup M \cup O$ as defined for the model $\mathcal{S}$.
2. Initial state s_0' of $\mathcal{S}'$ coincides with initial state s_0 of $\mathcal{S}$ on $I \cup O$.
3. $\mathcal{S}'$ generates only finitely many different output values and internal state values.
4. The number of I/O-equivalence classes of $\mathcal{S}'$ is less or equal m.
5. Let $\mathcal{I}'$ be the IECP of $\mathcal{S}'$ as defined above. Then

$$\forall X \in \mathcal{I}, X' \in \mathcal{I}' : \left(X \cap X' \neq \varnothing \Rightarrow \exists X_2 \in \mathcal{I}_2 : X_2 \subseteq X \cap X' \right)$$

6. $\mathcal{S}'$ has a well-defined reset operation allowing to re-start the system, in order to perform another test from its initial state.

Requirement 2 is reasonable, since initial states correspond to the system's switched-off state. Therefore we can assume that the implementation produces the same outputs as the reference model as long as it is switched off – otherwise we would not start testing, because $\mathcal{S}$ and $\mathcal{S}'$ differed already in the off-state.

The intuition behind requirement 5 is as follows: for every $X \in \mathcal{I}$ the model $\mathcal{S}$ exhibits equivalent behaviour for every input from X. Non-conforming members $\mathcal{S}'$ of the fault domain may have a different partitioning $\mathcal{I}' \neq \mathcal{I}$. Then there will be some non-empty intersections $X \cap X' \neq \varnothing, X' \in \mathcal{I}'$ that contain inputs for which $\mathcal{S}$ and $\mathcal{S}'$ exhibit different behaviour. It is ensured by requirement 5 that our refined partitioning $\mathcal{I}_2$ has a member X_2 contained in this intersection. This guarantees that an input from $X \cap X'$ will be applied in the test suite introduced below.

The fault domain $\mathcal{D}(\mathcal{S}, m, \mathcal{I}_2)$ is obviously increased by increasing $m \in \mathbb{N}$, and/or further refining $\mathcal{I}_2$: $m' \geq m \wedge \mathcal{I}_3$ refines $\mathcal{I}_2 \Rightarrow \mathcal{D}(\mathcal{S}, m, \mathcal{I}_2) \subseteq \mathcal{D}(\mathcal{S}, m', \mathcal{I}_3)$.

Complete Test Strategy. The main result of the paper [7] states that, given reference model $\mathcal{S}$ and fixing $(m, \mathcal{I}_2)$, it is possible to generate a finite test suite from $\mathcal{S}$, such that (a) this suite accepts every member of $\mathcal{D}(\mathcal{S}, m, \mathcal{I}_2)$ which is I/O-equivalent to $\mathcal{S}$, and (b) at least one test of this suite fails for every non-conforming member of $\mathcal{D}(\mathcal{S}, m, \mathcal{I}_2)$ which violates the I/O-equivalence condition. Test suites satisfying (a) are called *sound*, and those satisfying (b) are called *exhaustive*. Soundness and exhaustiveness together is called *complete*. The test suite is generated as follows.

1. Select one representative input vector $c_X \in X$ from each $X \in \mathcal{I}_2$.
2. Abstract $\mathcal{S}$ to a finite deterministic state machine $\mathcal{M}$ with I/O-equivalence classes $A_1, \ldots, A_r$ as states, input alphabet $\{c_X \mid X \in \mathcal{I}_2\}$ and output alphabet D_O (recall that D_O is finite). This DFSM is well-defined due to the properties of the $A \in \mathcal{S}/\sim$ and the $X \in \mathcal{I}_2$.

3. Since $\mathcal{M}$ is a DFSM, the well known W-Method [16,2] can be used to create a test suite that is complete with respect to reference model $\mathcal{M}$, conformance relation DFSM-equivalence, and the set of all DFSM over the same input/output alphabets as fault domain, whose numbers of states do not exceed m.
4. A STS $\mathcal{S}'$ is I/O-equivalent to $\mathcal{S}$ if and only if its DFSM $\mathcal{M}'$ passes these tests, so that $\mathcal{M}'$ is DFSM-equivalent to $\mathcal{M}$.

4   Evaluation

The coarsest IECP $\mathcal{I}$ for the CSM model has 6 IECs $X_1, \ldots, X_6$; their defining conditions over the input variables are displayed in Table 1. This table also shows the input alphabet, consisting of one input vector selected from each class. It can be easily checked that in a given CSM model state, all inputs from a given X_i lead to the same outputs and into I/O-equivalent quiescent target states.

Table 1. Input Alphabet $\mathcal{A}_I$

c_i	V_{est}	V_{MRSP}	allowRevokeEB	X_i	specified by
c_1	60	90	0	X_1	$0 < V_{est} \leq V_{MRSP} \wedge$ allowRevokeEB $= 0$
c_2	60	90	1	X_2	$V_{est} = 0 \vee (V_{est} \leq V_{MRSP} \wedge$ allowRevokeEB $= 1)$
c_3	152	150	0	X_3	$V_{MRSP} < V_{est} \leq V_{MRSP} + \mathsf{dV}_{\mathsf{warning}}(V_{MRSP})$
c_4	125	120	1	X_4	$V_{MRSP} + \mathsf{dV}_{\mathsf{warning}}(V_{MRSP}) < V_{est} \leq V_{MRSP} + \mathsf{dV}_{\mathsf{sbi}}(V_{MRSP})$
c_5	66	60	0	X_5	$V_{MRSP} + \mathsf{dV}_{\mathsf{sbi}}(V_{MRSP}) < V_{est} \leq V_{MRSP} + \mathsf{dV}_{\mathsf{ebi}}(V_{MRSP})$
c_6	260	230	0	X_6	$V_{MRSP} + \mathsf{dV}_{\mathsf{ebi}}(V_{MRSP}) < V_{est}$

The DFSM used for test suite generation according to the W-method is shown in Fig. 4. The complete test suites for the fault domain $\mathcal{D}(\mathcal{S}, m = 6, \mathcal{I}_2 = \mathcal{I})$ derived by application of the W-method are shown in Table 2. The specification of $m = 6$ implies that the domain contains all models whose minimised DFSM representation contains at most two more states than that of the reference model, as shown in Fig. 4.

The tool-based evaluation has been performed with RT-Tester, an industrial strength MBT tool [11] which has been enhanced by a prototype extension supporting IECP test generation as described above. This tool encodes test objectives as propositional formulas, and an SMT solver calculates solutions from which the concrete test data, i.e., the input vectors to the SUT, can be extracted. RT-Tester has been used to generate various test suites from the CSM model, following different coverage criteria: (1) basic state coverage, (2) transition coverage, (3) MC/DC coverage, (4) hierarchic transition coverage for an extended CSM model version including the activation and deactivation of the CSM, (5) requirements-driven test cases, constructed from the links from ETCS

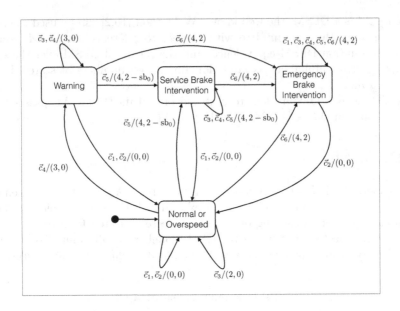

Fig. 4. DFSM abstraction of the CSM. Output assignment actions (DMICmd, TICmd) $= (\alpha, \beta)$ are written as (α, β). The DMICmd are written as 0 for no indication, 2 for overspeed indication, 3 for warning, and 4 for intervention indication. The TICmd are written as 0 for brakes released, 1 for service brake triggered, and 2 for emergency brake triggered.

requirements to model elements, (6) the IECP test suites shown in Table 2, and (7) a more detailed IECP test suite based on a refinement $\mathcal{I}_2$ of $\mathcal{I}$ with 69 input equivalence classes, leading to 273 test cases: Usage of the coarsest IECP $\mathcal{I}_2 = \mathcal{I}$ specified in Table 1 is adequate if a fault domain is applicable, where all representatives use the same guard conditions as the reference model. Then conformity violations can only occur in output calculations, but never in control decisions. Refined IECPs are necessary, as soon as potential errors in guard conditions have to be taken into account.

Test strategies (1) — (5) uncover at most 2 out of three mutants by "accidentally" using input data revealing the deviations from the reference models: the nature of the mutants was such that none of these strategies can guarantee to find the mutations used. None of these strategies are able to uncover the third mutation, not even the test suite (5) which yields 100% requirements coverage (see [1, Table 17] for a more detailed specification of the mutants). As expected, test suites (6) and (7) kill all three mutants. For all test suites (1) — (7) the automated test suite generation time is below 60 seconds. These results are summarised in Table 3.

Table 2. Complete test suite for $\mathcal{D}(\mathcal{S}, m = 6, \mathcal{I}_2 = \mathcal{I})$. TEST_SUITE$_{sb_0=1}$ applies to the case where trains are equipped with a separate service brake. TEST_SUITE$_{sb_0=0}$ applies to train configurations where no separate service brake is available, so that only the emergency brake is used.

$$\text{TEST\_SUITE}_{sb_0=1} = \{c_i.c_j.c_k.c_3 \mid i, j, k = 1, \dots, 6\} \cup$$
$$\{c_j.c_i.c_k.c_h.c_3 \mid h, i, k = 1, \dots, 6, \quad j = 4, \dots, 6\}$$
$$\text{TEST\_SUITE}_{sb_0=0} = \{c_i.c_j.c_h.c_g \mid h, i, j = 1, \dots, 6, \ g = 1, 3\} \cup$$
$$\{c_j.c_i.c_k.c_h.c_g \mid h, i, k = 1, \dots, 6, \quad j = 4, \dots, 6, \ g = 1, 3\}$$

Table 3. Experimental results (see www.mbt-benchmarks.org for more details)

Test-Procedure	Mutant 1	Mutant 2	Mutant 3	Generation Time [s]
Strategy (1)	not detected	not detected	not detected	≤ 60
Strategy (2)	KILLED	KILLED	not detected	≤ 60
Strategy (3)	not detected	not detected	not detected	≤ 60
Strategy (4)	KILLED	KILLED	not detected	≤ 60
Strategy (5)	KILLED	KILLED	not detected	≤ 60
IECP Strategy (6)	KILLED	KILLED	KILLED	≤ 60
IECP Strategy (7)	KILLED	KILLED	KILLED	≤ 60

5   Related Work

The test method described and illustrated in this paper is a specific instance of *partition testing* approaches, where the input domains of the SUT are divided into subsets, and small numbers of candidates are chosen from each of these sets [9]. The formalisation of equivalence classes is typically based on a *uniformity hypothesis* as introduced in [5]. The idea to use data abstraction for the purpose of equivalence class definition has been originally introduced in [6], where the classes are denoted as *hyperstates*, and the concept is applied to testing against abstract state machine models. Complete test suites have been suggested there for grey box scenarios, while our approach considers black-box tests.

Applications of model-based testing in the railway domain are currently investigated by numerous research groups and enterprises. In [1, Section 12] several references are given, and also alternative approaches to tool support are discussed.

The detailed formal behavioural semantics of general SysML test models has been described in [8, pp. 88]. This semantics is consistent with the standard [10], but fixes certain semantic variation points in ways that are admissible according to the standards. In [1, Section 4], the formal semantics of the CSM is presented by specifying the model's transition relation in propositional form. Furthermore, additional details are presented for the IECP $\mathcal{I}$ introduced above [1, Section 5], and IECP refinement alternatives $\mathcal{I}_2$ are discussed [1, Section 6, 10].

6   Conclusion and Ongoing Work

In this paper, a SysML model for the Ceiling Speed Monitor of the ETCS on-board controller has been presented and made publicly available on the website www.mbt-benchmarks.org, for the purpose of testing theory evaluation and MBT tool comparisons. A novel equivalence class testing strategy has been applied to derive tests from the CSM model in an automated way. This strategy allows test suite creation depending on a given fault model and guarantees completeness of the generated suites for all members of the associated fault domain. The evaluation shows that for certain types of mutants, the equivalence class testing strategy is significantly stronger than that of other test strategies, such as model transition coverage or MC/DC coverage.

The usage of SysML was motivated by the fact that this modelling language is very well accepted in industrial applications. It is therefore one of the main modelling formalisms used in the ITEA2 project openETCS[4] and the FP7 project COMPASS[5].

The mutations used for the evaluation in this paper were mainly constructed for illustration purposes. Currently, we are evaluating the test strength of IECP test suites in comparison with other model coverage criteria with large numbers of mutants created by a random generator that mutates models and creates executable "SUT" code from each mutation. These results will also be published on www.mbt-benchmarks.org.

References

1. Braunstein, C., Huang, W.-L., Peleska, J., Schulze, U., Hübner, F., Haxthausen, A.E., vu Hong, L.: A SysML test model and test suite for the ETCS ceiling speed monitor. Technical report, Embedded Systems Testing Benchmarks Site (April 30, 2014), http://www.mbt-benchmarks.org
2. Chow, T.S.: Testing software design modeled by finite-state machines. IEEE Transactions on Software Engineering SE-4(3), 178–186 (1978)
3. Clarke, E.M., Grumberg, O., Peled, D.A.: Model Checking. The MIT Press, Cambridge (1999)
4. European Railway Agency. ERTMS – System Requirements Specification – UNISIG SUBSET-026 (February 2012), http://www.era.europa.eu/Document-Register/Pages/Set-2-System-Requirements-Specification.aspx
5. Gaudel, M.-C.: Testing can be formal, too. In: Mosses, P.D., Nielsen, M. (eds.) CAAP 1995, FASE 1995, and TAPSOFT 1995. LNCS, vol. 915, pp. 82–96. Springer, Heidelberg (1995)
6. Grieskamp, W., Gurevich, Y., Schulte, W., Veanes, M.: Generating finite state machines from abstract state machines. ACM SIGSOFT Software Engineering Notes 27(4), 112–122 (2002)
7. Huang, W.-l., Peleska, J.: Exhaustive model-based equivalence class testing. In: Yenigün, H., Yilmaz, C., Ulrich, A. (eds.) ICTSS 2013. LNCS, vol. 8254, pp. 49–64. Springer, Heidelberg (2013)

---

[4] http://openetcs.org

[5] http://www.compass-research.eu

8. W.-l. Huang, J., Peleska, U.: Schulze. Test automation support. Technical Report D34.1, COMPASS Comprehensive Modelling for Advanced Systems of Systems (2013), http://www.compass-research.eu/deliverables.html

9. De Nicola, G., di Tommaso, P., Rosaria, E., Francesco, F., Pietro, M., Antonio, O.: A Grey-Box Approach to the Functional Testing of Complex Automatic Train Protection Systems. In: Dal Cin, M., Kaâniche, M., Pataricza, A. (eds.) EDCC 2005. LNCS, vol. 3463, pp. 305–317. Springer, Heidelberg (2005)

10. Object Management Group. OMG Systems Modeling Language (OMG SysML^{TM}). Technical report, Object Management Group, OMG Document Number: formal/2010-06-02 (2010)

11. Peleska, J.: Industrial-strength model-based testing - state of the art and current challenges. In: Petrenko, A.K., Schlingloff, H. (eds.) Proceedings Eighth Workshop on Model-Based Testing, Rome, Italy, March 17. Electronic Proceedings in Theoretical Computer Science, vol. 111, pp. 3–28. Open Publishing Association (2013)

12. Peleska, J., Honisch, A., Lapschies, F., Löding, H., Schmid, H., Smuda, P., Vorobev, E., Zahlten, C.: A real-world benchmark model for testing concurrent real-time systems in the automotive domain. In: Wolff, B., Zaïdi, F. (eds.) ICTSS 2011. LNCS, vol. 7019, pp. 146–161. Springer, Heidelberg (2011)

13. Petrenko, A., Yevtushenko, N., van Bochmann, G.: Fault Models for Testing in Context, pp. 163–177. Chapman & Hall (1996)

14. Spillner, A., Linz, T., Schaefer, H.: Software Testing Foundations. dpunkt.verlag, Heidelberg (2006)

15. U.N.I.S.I.G.: ERTMS/ETCS SystemRequirements Specification, Chapter 3, Principles, volume Subset-026-3, Issue 3.3.0 (2012)

16. Vasilevskii, M.P.: Failure diagnosis of automata. Kibernetika (Transl.) 4, 98–108 (1973)

Contract-Based Verification of MATLAB and Simulink Matrix-Manipulating Code[*]

Jonatan Wiik and Pontus Boström

Dept. of Information Technologies, Åbo Akademi University, Finland
{jonatan.wiik,pontus.bostrom}@abo.fi

Abstract. This paper presents an approach to automatic, modular, contract-based verification of programs written in a subset of the MATLAB programming language, with focus on efficiently handling the provided matrix manipulation functions. We statically infer types and shapes for matrices in the language and use this information in the verification. We consider two approaches for verification: direct axiomatisation of the built-in matrix functions and expansion of the functions. We evaluate our approaches on a number of examples and discuss challenges for automatic verification in this setting.

1 Introduction

MATLAB/Simulink[1] has become a widely popular toolset for development of control systems. Simulink has even become de facto standard for model-based design in many domains. MATLAB includes toolboxes for generating embedded C/C++ code for different platforms directly from Simulink models or from code written in a subset of the MATLAB programming language, which we refer to as Embedded MATLAB (EML). MATLAB and Simulink are languages aimed at numerical computing, with matrix computations as a core feature. The languages inherently supports such computations through convenient built-in functions.

In this paper we present a modular approach to automatic contract-based verification of MATLAB style programs. Contracts here refer to functional specifications, given as pre- and postconditions, of functions. We use standard contract-based reasoning as found in many other verifiers [2,3,7], extended with efficient handling of matrix computations. Verification conditions are generated from the programs and contracts, which are then discharged by an automatic SMT solver. The work described in this paper also acts as an extension to an approach for contract-based verification of Simulink models [4,5], by adding support for matrix computations. There Simulink models are automatically verified with respect to contracts by first generating sequential code.

MATLAB is an implicitly and dynamically typed imperative language. However, in EML and Simulink the type and shape of all matrices are determined

---

[*] Work done in the EFFIMA program coordinated by Fimecc and the EDiHy project funded by the Academy of Finland.

[1] http://www.mathworks.com/products/simulink/

S. Merz and J. Pang (Eds.): ICFEM 2014, LNCS 8829, pp. 396–412, 2014.

statically at compile-time, which enables generation of efficient code for embedded software. We focus on EML, since static types and shapes significantly aid verification, while the language is still flexible and convenient to use. Furthermore, embedded systems, which is the target of EML, often have high reliability requirements, justifying the use of rigorous verification methods. We build on existing work on MATLAB type inference [1,16] to obtain matrix types and shapes, but our system is more strict in order to aid verification. We present and evaluate two approaches to encoding verification conditions for matrix-manipulating programs in an SMT solver. In the first approach, matrix functions are viewed as a library and given pre- and postconditions, as in traditional program verification. In the second approach, the inferred information about matrix shapes is used to automatically expand the matrix functions. As we will show, expansion can be very effective when matrix sizes are relatively small, which is common in many embedded applications.

The challenges addressed in this paper relate to efficient handling of built-in matrix functions in MATLAB, as well as inference of information that is not given explicitly, but needed for efficient verification. The main contributions of this paper are: 1) Definition of an expressive language similar to EML that can be effectively encoded into verifiers. 2) A type inference and two automated verification approaches for the language. 3) Evaluation of the approaches on examples, as well as discussion on advantages and drawbacks of the approaches. We have also implemented the verification approaches in the prototype verification tool VerSÅA[2].

The paper begins with a description of the MATLAB programming language and the contract format in section 2. In section 3 we define the grammar of the language. Section 4 describes the type system and the type inference framework. In section 5 we describe the verification approaches and evaluate them on a few examples in section 6. Section 7 discusses related work and section 8 concludes.

2   MATLAB and Contract-Based Verification

The programming language targeted in this paper is EML. EML is essentially a subset of the complete MATLAB language suitable for code generation. It is an implicitly typed imperative programming language. Contrary to the complete MATLAB language, EML is statically typed. All data in the language is ultimately a matrix[3]. A MATLAB matrix type consists of an intrinsic type, such as **double**, **int32**, **boolean** etc., and a shape. We use $\langle m, n \rangle$ to denote a matrix shape with m rows and n columns. We use the term column vector for matrices of shape $\langle m, 1 \rangle$ and row vector for matrices of shape $\langle 1, n \rangle$. In MATLAB also scalars are considered matrices, we thus use the term scalar to mean a matrix of shape $\langle 1, 1 \rangle$. In this work we restrict ourselves to two-dimensional matrix shapes, although the MATLAB language in general supports an arbitrary number of dimensions. There should, however, not be any fundamental problem in extending

---

[2] http://users.abo.fi/pbostrom/slverificationtool/

[3] MATLAB supports other types too, but we do not consider them here.

the approach to support more dimensions. We also require that matrices are non-empty, i.e. that the size along both dimensions is ≥ 1.

The MATLAB language has a large library of built-in functions that directly manipulate matrices. There are both functions and operators (infix functions) and we treat these uniformly in this paper and usually refer to them as functions. As an example, consider the matrices a and b of shape $\langle 2, 2 \rangle$:

$$a = \begin{bmatrix} a_{11} & a_{12} \\ a_{21} & a_{22} \end{bmatrix} \quad b = \begin{bmatrix} b_{11} & b_{12} \\ b_{21} & b_{22} \end{bmatrix}$$

Then we have the following results for $max(a, b)$ and $2 + a$:

$$max(a, b) = \begin{bmatrix} max(a_{11}, b_{11}) & max(a_{12}, b_{12}) \\ max(a_{21}, b_{21}) & max(a_{22}, b_{22}) \end{bmatrix} \quad 2 + a = \begin{bmatrix} 2 + a_{11} & 2 + a_{12} \\ 2 + a_{21} & 2 + a_{22} \end{bmatrix}$$

Both the function max and the operator $+$ thus work *element-wise* on matrices. An element-wise MATLAB function $f(a, b)$ is defined if a and b have the same intrinsic type and $m_1 = n_1$ and $m_2 = n_2$ or either a or b is scalar, i.e. $m_1 = m_2 = 1$ or $n_1 = n_2 = 1$. The resulting matrix will then have the same shape as a and b, or the larger shape if either a or b is scalar. We will later see that many of the built-in MATLAB functions are element-wise. MATLAB also has, e.g., functions that collapse matrices. Consider, for instance, the sum function:

$$sum(a) = \begin{bmatrix} a_{11} + a_{21} & a_{12} + a_{22} \end{bmatrix} \quad sum(sum(a)) = (a_{11} + a_{21}) + (a_{12} + a_{22})$$

Collapsing functions collapse (row and column) vectors to scalars and other matrices to row vectors. Hence, the behaviour of the function depends on the input shape.

MATLAB functions are typically polymorphic, which is also the case for the built-in functions max and sum above. They accept arguments of any intrinsic type t and any shape $\langle m, n \rangle$ and return a matrix of the same intrinsic type and a shape determined as a function of the input shapes.

A MATLAB program consists of a set of functions, of which one is the entry-point for the program. The aim of this paper is to enable automatic contract-based verification of such programs. We use a standard modular verification technique, checking every function with respect to its contract in isolation. For each function body analysed, we check that the postcondition holds if the precondition is satisfied. The contracts are written inside special comments, as in e.g. JML [7]. An example function that computes the maximum element of a column vector is given in Fig. 1[4]. This functionality is also implemented by the built-in function max with one argument, however, the goal here is to demonstrate language features. The specification of the function, i.e. its contract, is written in comments starting with "%@". In addition to traditional preconditions and postconditions, we also annotate functions with types for the inputs and the output.

We first consider the type annotations. Types for all inputs and the output are given in the *types* field. The syntax matrix(t, n, m) denotes a matrix with

---

[4] For clarity we use := for assignment in this paper, although = is used in MATLAB.

```
 1   function m = max_f(a)
 2   %@ typeparameters: t<:numtype, n
 3   %@ types: m:t, a:matrix(t,n,1)
 4   %@ ensures: all(a <= m)
 5   %@ ensures: any(a == m)
 6      m := a(1);
 7      i := int32(2);
 8      while (i <= length(a))
 9      %@ invariant: 1 <= i && i <= n+1
10      %@ invariant: \forall j:int32 . (1 <= j && j < i ==> m >= a(j))
11      %@ invariant: \exists j:int32 . (1 <= j && j < i && m == a(j))
12         if (m < a(i))
13            m := a(i);
14         end
15         i := i+1;
16      end
17   end
```

Fig. 1. A MATLAB function for finding the index of the minimum element in a column vector, annotated with contracts

intrinsic type t and shape $\langle n, m \rangle$. The short-hand form t is used to denote a scalar of intrinsic type t, i.e. matrix$(t, 1, 1)$. The *typeparameters* field declares universally quantified type parameters over which the types declared in the *types* field can be parametrised. A type parameter can parametrise over either intrinsic type or shape. For instance, the *max_f* function in Fig. 1 is parametrised to take as input a matrix of any numeric intrinsic type t and a shape $\langle n, 1 \rangle$ and outputs a scalar of the same intrinsic type t. The type annotations are actually not needed here for type inference, but they are important from a specification point-of-view. Without the type annotations there would exist incorrect implementations satisfying the postconditions of the *max_f* function, e.g. the implementation $m := a$. The type annotations thus provide a form of pre- and postconditions constraining the inputs and outputs on the level of types (and shapes).

We use the standard annotations *requires* and *ensures* for function preconditions and postconditions, as well as *invariant* annotations for loops. For the *max_f* function we have the postcondition $all(a \leq m)$, stating that the output m should be greater than or equal to each element in a. We also have the postcondition $any(a = m)$, stating that there exists an element in a that is equal to m. Note that *all* and *any* are built-in MATLAB functions. They correspond to universal and existential quantifiers over matrices and provide a compact and intuitive way to write contracts for matrix code. The invariants used for the while-loop in *max_f* are needed to prove that the loop establishes the postcondition of the function. Note also that the *all* and *any* functions are not used in the invariants on lines 10-11. In MATLAB these conditions could be written using *all* and *any*, e.g. $all(a(1:i) \leq m)$. However, we want to infer matrix shapes statically. This is not possible for this expression as i is not constant, which means that the shape of $a(1:i)$ is not static.

3   Language Definition

In this section we define the subset of MATLAB considered throughout this paper. In addition to the MATLAB constructs supported, the language is also extended with some specification-oriented constructs not part of pure MATLAB. These constructs can, however, be written inside special comments.

The MATLAB programming language is an imperative language where matrices are immutable objects presumably implemented via copy-on-write. Every function or matrix update can thus be considered to return a new matrix. A MATLAB program consists of a set of function declarations. The grammar of our programs is given in (1).

$$
\begin{aligned}
FuncDecl \quad &::= \textbf{function } Id = f(Id^*) \\
&\quad TypeParams^? \ Types \ Spec^* \ Stmt^? \\
&\quad \textbf{end} \\
TypeParams &::= \textbf{typeparameters } (Id \ (\sqsubseteq_t t)^?)^* \\
Types \quad &::= \textbf{types } (Id:t)^* \\
Spec \quad &::= \textbf{requires } Exp \mid \textbf{ensures } Exp
\end{aligned}
\tag{1}
$$

In this grammar, x^* and $x^?$ denote zero or more and zero or one occurrences of an element x, respectively. We thus extend MATLAB's function declarations with type annotations for the input and output parameters, as well as pre- and postcondition annotations.

The expression language (2) essentially constitutes a subset of the MATLAB expression language. Additionally, it also includes constructs, such as universal and existential quantifiers and conditional expressions, which are not part of the MATLAB language, but often are convenient when writing specifications. The same expression language is used both in statements and in contracts.

$$
\begin{aligned}
Exp ::= & \\
&Exp_1 \oplus Exp_2 \mid & \text{Binary expression} \\
&(\forall \mid \exists) \ (x:t)^* \ \cdot \ Exp \mid & \text{Quantified expression} \\
&\neg Exp \mid -Exp \mid & \text{Unary operators} \\
&Exp_1 \ ? \ Exp_2 : Exp_3 \mid & \text{Conditional expression} \\
&Exp_1 \ (Exp_2 \mid :) \ (Exp_3 \mid :)^? \mid & \text{Matrix accessor} \\
&Id \ Exp_1, \ldots, Exp_n \mid & \text{Function call} \\
&[Exp_{11}, \ldots, Exp_{1n}; \ldots; Exp_{m1}, \ldots, Exp_{mn}] \mid & \text{Matrix literal} \\
&CExp_1 : CExp_2 \mid CExp_1 : CExp_2 : CExp_3 \mid & \text{Range} \\
&Id \mid & \text{Identifier} \\
&Num \mid \textbf{true} \mid \textbf{false} & \text{Number/boolean literal}
\end{aligned}
\tag{2}
$$

In (2) we have $\oplus \in \{+, -, *, /, .*, ./, \wedge, \vee, \Longrightarrow, \Longleftrightarrow, =, \neq, <, >, \geq, \leq\}$. As in MATLAB, we do not separate expressions from predicates, as this is done later in the type checking. Note also that matrix accessors and function calls partially share the same syntax. This is also consistent with MATLAB, and we solve this by requiring that variables do not have the same name as any built-in function or function declared by the user. See [16] for a discussion on the complete mechanism used in MATLAB.

In MATLAB there are also expressions with data-dependent shape, e.g. the Range expression in (2). The shape of a range expression $a{:}b$, where a and b are integers, is $\langle 1, b - a + 1 \rangle$. For these cases we define a separate language, *CExp* (3), for constant expressions. This language is a subset of (2), which can be evaluated by the type checker and hence used in expressions with data-dependent shape. Thus, the type checker does not need to support the complete expression language in order to support static shape inference of such expressions.

$$CExp ::= Id \mid Num \mid int32(CExp) \mid int16(CExp) \mid int8(CExp) \mid \\ uint32(CExp) \mid uint16(CExp) \mid uint8(CExp) \mid length(Exp) \tag{3}$$

Since the expressions in *CExp* are only used for shape information, only numeric scalars are included in the language. Support for a limited set of functions is also included. The supported functions are typecast functions for supported integer types and the *length* function. The typecast functions are used to declare constants of different types. The *length* function is convenient to support in the type checker since it enables obtaining new matrices using size information from another matrix, for instance using $zeros(length(x), 1)$ to create a column vector of zeros with the same length as x. Note that the argument to *length* can be any expression in *Exp*, since only the shape of the argument is used and not its value. While *CExp* is currently very limited, it is straightforward to extend it to support more complex data-dependent expressions.

In the MATLAB language, it is possible to assign variables (complete matrices) or elements in matrices. To reflect this, we define a separate language for the left-hand side of assignments (4). The special colon operator here denotes assignment to an entire row or column. The complete grammar of the statement language, in which function implementations are written, is given in (5).

$$Asgn ::= Id \; (Exp_1 \mid :) \; (Exp_2 \mid :)^? \mid Id \tag{4}$$

$$\begin{array}{lll} Stmt ::= & Asgn := Exp \mid & \text{Assigment} \\ & \textbf{constant } Id := CExp \mid & \text{Constant declaration} \\ & \textbf{if } Exp \; Stmt_1 \; \textbf{else } Stmt_2 \; \textbf{end} \mid & \text{If-statement} \quad\quad (5) \\ & Stmt_1 ; Stmt_2 \mid & \text{Sequential composition} \\ & \textbf{while } Exp \; Inv^* \; Stmt \; \textbf{end} \mid & \text{While loop} \end{array}$$

The language allows declaration of constants, which are not needed in pure MATLAB. Constants are assigned using the constant expression language *CExp* defined in (3), and they can thus be evaluated by the type checker and used as shape information in the type inference. To maintain MATLAB compatibility, the **constant** keyword of constant declarations is written in a comment on the line above the assignment. EML does not have explicit constants, but for clarity we have opted to use explicit declaration of constants here. Although the subset of MATLAB considered here is fairly small, it can be easily extended to handle more features.

4   Type System

Our aim is to have statically determined types and shapes for functions written in the language described in the previous section. This information can be used in the verification and thus the verifier does not need to quantify over types and shapes, which significantly simplifies the verification task. Since the language is implicitly typed, we determine types and shapes of local variables and expressions through inference, to avoid extra annotations.

The approach to type and shape inference we use is inspired by the work of Almási, Padua and de Rose in the context of the MaJIC [1] and FALCON [16] MATLAB compilers. We have, however, made several modifications to their type system, to enable efficient encoding of the programs in a verifier. The type inference we use is also more strict compared to MATLAB's type inference, in order to aid verification. For instance, we do not allow implicit typecasts as is commonly done in MATLAB. In MATLAB it is, for instance, legal to add an integer with a double, since the double will automatically be cast to an integer. Since we do not allow typecasts like these, we also require that matrix indices are integers. We also have a stricter separation between booleans and numeric types, in order to obtain efficient verification conditions. MATLAB does, for instance, accept numeric types as operands to logical operators and also allows booleans to be used in arithmetic expressions, which we do not allow.

In our language all data is of matrix type. Since we only consider matrices with up to two dimensions, a matrix type consists of an intrinsic type t and a shape $\langle n, m \rangle$, where n and m denotes the number of rows and columns, respectively. The intrinsic type is an element in a finite lattice L_t, formed by the elements $\mathcal{I} = \{\textbf{boolean}, \textbf{int8}, \textbf{int16}, \textbf{int32}, \textbf{uint8}, \textbf{uint16}, \textbf{uint32}, \textbf{double}, \textbf{numtype}, \textbf{toptype}\}$ and the comparison operator:

$$L_t = \{\mathcal{I}, \sqsubseteq_t\}, \text{ where:}$$
$$\textbf{boolean} \sqsubseteq_t \textbf{toptype},$$
$$\textbf{int8} \sqsubseteq_t \textbf{int16} \sqsubseteq_t \textbf{int32} \sqsubseteq_t \textbf{numtype},$$
$$\textbf{uint8} \sqsubseteq_t \textbf{uint16} \sqsubseteq_t \textbf{uint32} \sqsubseteq_t \textbf{numtype}, \qquad (6)$$
$$\textbf{double} \sqsubseteq_t \textbf{numtype},$$
$$\textbf{numtype} \sqsubseteq_t \textbf{toptype}$$

As in MATLAB, we have several different sizes of integers. A matrix shape consists of two dimensions $n_1, n_2 \in \mathcal{D}$, where $\mathcal{D}$ is the set of dimensions: $\mathcal{D} = \mathbb{Z}^+ \cup \{\infty\}$. Matrix shapes can then be defined as a lattice L_s, which consists of pairs of dimensions, one for the number of rows and one for the number of columns:

$$L_s = \{\mathcal{D} \times \mathcal{D}, \sqsubseteq_s\} \text{ where:}$$
$$s_1 \sqsubseteq_s s_2 \hat{=} (s_1 = s_2 \vee s_2 = \langle *, \infty \rangle \vee s_2 = \langle \infty, * \rangle) \qquad (7)$$

where $*$ denotes any dimension $d \in \mathcal{D}$. Here ∞ denotes an invalid dimension, which indicates an inference error. Programs can only be verified if every node in the abstract syntax tree has been assigned a valid (finite) shape.

In [1,16] an unknown shape only means fallback to dynamic memory allocation. Also EML has an option for generation of code with variable-size data. Here we require that exact types and shapes are determined statically. Variable-size data should anyway be avoided in safety-critical embedded code.

The type system for our language is given by the Cartesian product of the intrinsic type lattice and the shape lattice: $\mathcal{T} = L_t \times L_s$. We here use matrix$(t, \langle n, m \rangle)$

to denote a type $(t, \langle n, m \rangle) \in \mathcal{T}$ in the language. We can then define the language of types as follows:

$$
\begin{aligned}
t &::= x \mid \textbf{boolean} \mid \textbf{int8} \mid \dots \\
d &::= x \mid n \\
\delta &::= \langle d_1, d_2 \rangle \mid \max_s(\langle d_1, d_2 \rangle, \langle d_3, d_4 \rangle) \mid \text{mul}_s(\langle d_1, d_2 \rangle, \langle d_3, d_4 \rangle) \mid \text{col}_s(\langle d_1, d_2 \rangle) \\
\tau &::= \text{matrix}(t, \delta) \mid d \\
\alpha &::= \tau \mid \alpha_1 \times \alpha_2 \mid \alpha \to \tau \\
\theta &::= \alpha \mid \forall\, \overline{x \sqsubseteq_t t} \cdot \theta \mid \Pi\, \overline{x} \cdot \theta \mid \textbf{unit}
\end{aligned}
\tag{8}
$$

Here x denotes a type parameter identifier and $\overline{x}$ denotes a list of such identifiers. We use n to denote a positive integer. As explained in section 2, we have universally quantified polymorphic functions, which can be quantified over both intrinsic type and shape. We use $\forall$ to denote quantification over intrinsic type and Π to denote quantification over shape.

Functions are typed based on given type signatures. As an example, consider the type signature for an element-wise function such as addition:

$$
\begin{aligned}
&\forall\, t \sqsubseteq_t \textbf{numtype} \cdot \Pi\, m_1, m_2, n_1, n_2 \cdot \\
&\quad \text{matrix}(t, \langle m_1, m_2 \rangle) \times \text{matrix}(t, \langle n_1, n_2 \rangle) \to \text{matrix}(t, \max_s(\langle m_1, m_2 \rangle, \langle n_1, n_2 \rangle))
\end{aligned}
$$

The quantification over intrinsic type is bounded, denoted by $t \sqsubseteq_t u$, meaning that t is a subtype of u. Bounds for quantification over shape is currently not supported, but we have not come across any built-in MATLAB function of interest for embedded applications, where such a declaration would be useful. The kind of polymorphism supported is similar to Let-polymorphism found in ML and related languages, i.e. type parameters cannot be instantiated with polymorphic types. A consequence is that all valid types can be written in a form in which quantifiers only appear in the outermost position of types [15].

The shape function $\max_s$ used in the type signature above is defined in the following way:

$$
\max_s(\langle m_1, m_2 \rangle, \langle n_1, n_2 \rangle) = \begin{cases} \langle m_1, m_2 \rangle & \text{if } m_1 = n_1 \text{ and } m_2 = n_2 \\ \langle m_1, m_2 \rangle & \text{if } n_1 = n_2 = 1 \\ \langle n_1, n_2 \rangle & \text{if } m_1 = m_2 = 1 \\ \langle \infty, \infty \rangle & \text{otherwise} \end{cases}
\tag{9}
$$

The output shape for all binary element-wise functions are defined in the same way. Not all MATLAB functions are, however, element-wise. The type signature for matrix multiplication, for instance, is the following:

$$
\begin{aligned}
&\forall\, t \sqsubseteq_t \textbf{numtype} \cdot \Pi\, m_1, m_2, n_1, n_2 \cdot \\
&\quad \text{matrix}(t, \langle m_1, m_2 \rangle) \times \text{matrix}(t, \langle n_1, n_2 \rangle) \to \text{matrix}(t, \text{mul}_s(\langle m_1, m_2 \rangle, \langle n_1, n_2 \rangle))
\end{aligned}
$$

where the shape function mul_s is defined in the following way:

$$
\text{mul}_s(\langle m_1, m_2 \rangle, \langle n_1, n_2 \rangle) = \begin{cases} \langle m_1, n_2 \rangle & \text{if } m_2 = n_1 \\ \langle m_1, m_2 \rangle & \text{if } n_1 = n_2 = 1 \\ \langle n_1, n_2 \rangle & \text{if } m_1 = m_2 = 1 \\ \langle \infty, \infty \rangle & \text{otherwise} \end{cases}
\tag{10}
$$

$$\frac{f : \forall\; \overline{x \sqsubseteq_t y} \cdot \varPi\; \overline{s} \cdot \overline{\tau_i} \to \tau_o \quad dom(\sigma_t) = \{\overline{x}\} \quad dom(\sigma_s) = \{\overline{s}\}}{\mathcal{V}, \mathcal{C} \vdash E : \tau_i[\sigma_t, \sigma_s]\; \text{forall}\; (E, \tau_i) \in (\overline{E}, \overline{\tau_i})}$$
$$\frac{}{\mathcal{V}, \mathcal{C} \vdash f(\overline{E}) : \tau_o[\sigma_t, \sigma_s]} \quad \textbf{(fun-call)}$$

$$\frac{\mathcal{V}, \mathcal{C} \vdash E : \textbf{boolean} \quad \AE \in \{\forall, \exists\}}{\mathcal{V}, \mathcal{C} \vdash \AE\; \overline{x : \tau} \cdot E : \textbf{boolean}} \quad \textbf{(quant-exp)}$$

$$\frac{\mathcal{V}, \mathcal{C} \vdash E_1 : t, \ldots E_m : t}{\mathcal{V}, \mathcal{C} \vdash [E_1, \ldots, E_m] : \mathrm{matrix}(t, \langle 1, m \rangle)} \quad \textbf{(mat-cons-row)}$$

$$\frac{\mathcal{V}, \mathcal{C} \vdash E_1 : \mathrm{matrix}(t, \langle 1, m \rangle), \ldots E_n : \mathrm{matrix}(t, \langle 1, m \rangle)}{\mathcal{V}, \mathcal{C} \vdash [E_1; \ldots; E_n] : \mathrm{matrix}(t, \langle n, m \rangle)} \quad \textbf{(mat-cons-col)}$$

$$\frac{\mathcal{V}, \mathcal{C} \vdash C : t \quad t \sqsubseteq_t \textbf{int32} \quad C > 0}{\mathcal{V}, \mathcal{C} \vdash \#C \in \mathcal{D}} \quad \textbf{(shp-1)} \qquad \frac{\mathcal{V}, \mathcal{C} \vdash C : t \quad t \sqsubseteq_t \textbf{uint32} \quad C > 0}{\mathcal{V}, \mathcal{C} \vdash \#C \in \mathcal{D}} \quad \textbf{(shp-2)}$$

Fig. 2. Typing rules for expressions

Additionally, there are collapsing functions, such as *all*, *any* and *sum*, which collapses matrices. Consider, for instance, the type signature of the *sum* function:

$$\forall\; t \sqsubseteq_t \textbf{numtype} \cdot \varPi\; n_1, n_2 \cdot \mathrm{matrix}(t, \langle n_1, n_2 \rangle) \to \mathrm{matrix}(t, \mathrm{col_s}(\langle n_1, n_2 \rangle))$$

where $\mathrm{col_s}$ is given by:

$$\mathrm{col_s}(\langle n_1, n_2 \rangle) = \begin{cases} \langle 1, n_2 \rangle & \text{if } n_1 > 1 \text{ and } n_2 > 1 \\ \langle 1, 1 \rangle & \text{if } n_1 = 1 \text{ or } n_2 = 1 \end{cases} \qquad (11)$$

Note that for MATLAB compatibility, numeric constants can also be type parameterised. E.g. 0 can be a scalar of any type, including boolean, $0 : \forall\; t \cdot \mathrm{matrix}(t, \langle 1, 1 \rangle)$.

There are also built-in functions with data-dependent output shape. Examples of such functions are $zeros(a, b)$ and $ones(a, b)$, which return a matrix of shape $\langle a, b \rangle$ in which each element is 0 and 1, respectively. These functions are typically used to initialise matrices in EML and supporting them is thus essential. However, the shape of the output of these functions cannot, in general, be determined at compile-time. We have opted to solve this issue by introducing constants in our language and restricting these functions to only accept constant expressions as input. Constant expressions can be evaluated during type inference and coerced to shape information, which can be used in the inference. As an example, consider the type signature for the functions $zeros$ and $ones$:

$$\#a \times \#b \to \mathrm{matrix}(\textbf{double}, \langle \#a, \#b \rangle)$$

where $\#a$ denotes coercion of the constant value a to shape information. The coercion is only defined for constant integer expressions, defined in (3). The arguments a and b are thus also integer scalars.

Inference rules for typing expressions are listed in Fig. 2. Here $\mathcal{V}$ maps variables to types and $\mathcal{C}$ maps constants to types. Typing of statements is straightforward and only presented in our technical report [17]. The typing rules describes typing of both intrinsic type and shape. As operators and function calls are treated uniformly, there is only one typing rule, **(fun-call)**, for function applications. Even matrix accesses are treated as function calls. The function calls are typed based on the type signature of the function: Let σ_t be a mapping from type parameters to intrinsic types and let σ_s be a mapping from type parameters to shapes. The notation $\tau[\sigma_t, \sigma_s]$ then denotes the type τ instantiated with the mappings σ_t and σ_s. Thus, if the types of all inputs are instantiations of the inputs $\overline{\tau_i}$ of the function type signature under the type parameter mappings σ_t and σ_s, the output type of the function call will be τ_o instantiated with σ_t and σ_s. Other noteworthy rules are **(shp-1)** and **(shp-2)**, which are used for coercion of constant expressions to shape information. The coerced expression must be an integer constant.

The type inference for expressions is done using a traditional unification algorithm [13] where the constraints are derived directly from the typing rules, while statements are handled using forward propagation of the type information. This is similar to the approach in [1,16], where a combination of forward and backward propagation of shape and type information is used. Intrinsic type and shape are orthogonal aspects, meaning that inference can be done independently for intrinsic type and shape. Inference of intrinsic type is standard. For shape inference we use the shape functions (9), (10) and (11) to build constraints. The inference is successful if all nodes in the AST are assigned an intrinsic type and a valid (positive and finite) shape.

5 Verification

Our verification approach is based on standard modular assume-guarantee reasoning. The preconditions of the function are turned into assumptions and the postconditions into assertions when verifying function bodies, while the preconditions are asserted and postconditions are assumed in function calls. In the type inference, we have inferred exact intrinsic type and shape (i.e. instantiation of type parameters) for each function call. All invoked user-implemented functions are verified independently for each type instantiation occurring in the program. Thus, we do not verify that a function satisfies its contract for every valid instantiation of type parameters, but only for the instantiations actually used. Hence, the inference of types and shapes is non-modular, while function bodies are verified modularly based on the inferred type and shape information. This eliminates the need to quantify over intrinsic types and shapes in the verification of functions.

The statement language, given in (5), has standard weakest precondition semantics. Loops are verified based on the classical Hoare logic in the same way as e.g. Spec# [3] and Boogie [2]. In addition to verifying conformance to contracts, the verifier checks the absence of runtime errors in the function implementations. The runtime errors checked for are bounds on matrix accesses, integer overflow and preconditions of functions, e.g., absence of division by zero. The verifier only checks partial correctness, as termination is not checked for neither iteration nor recursion. Termination checks could be added analogously to how it has been done in other verifiers [8]. However, we have chosen to focus on verification of properties regarding matrix computations.

To verify MATLAB code that involves matrices and vectors, matrix functions need to be efficiently encoded in a verifier. We have used the SMT solver Z3 [9] by Microsoft Research as a verification backend. Z3 includes a theory for arrays [14], which we use to represent our matrices. We encode matrices as arrays of arrays. Each subarray is thus a matrix row. In the representation of a row vector there is only one subarray. For column vectors all subarrays are of size 1. Scalars, i.e. matrices of shape $\langle 1, 1 \rangle$, are not encoded as arrays.

In the first approach, which we call axiomatisation, we view the functions as a library and provide pre- and postconditions, as in traditional program verification. It is thus possible to axiomatise the functions directly. In the second approach we use the information about matrix shapes to expand the matrix functions. The approaches are evaluated on a number of examples in section 6.

5.1 Axiomatisation

In the axiomatisation approach, matrix functions are axiomatised to have their desired meanings. We list axioms for a number of common functions. In these formulas we have the matrices $a : \mathrm{matrix}(t, \langle n_1, n_2 \rangle)$ and $b : \mathrm{matrix}(t, \langle n_1, n_2 \rangle)$. Note also that all the axioms are actually quantified over the function inputs, which we have left out here for brevity. The complete axiom for a function $f(a, b)$ is thus $\forall\, a : \tau_1, b : \tau_2 \cdot A$, where A is an axiom in the format presented below.

$$
\begin{aligned}
f(a,b) \quad &: \forall\, i_1 : \mathbf{int32}, i_2 : \mathbf{int32} \cdot 1 \leq i_1 \leq n_1 \wedge 1 \leq i_2 \leq n_2 \\
&\implies f(a,b)(i_1, i_2) = f_s(a(i_1, i_2), b(i_1, i_2)) \\
a * b \quad &: \forall\, i_1 : \mathbf{int32}, i_2 : \mathbf{int32} \cdot 1 \leq i_1 \leq n_1 \wedge 1 \leq i_2 \leq n_2 \\
&\implies (a * b)(i_1, i_2) = \sum_{k=1}^{k=n_2}(a(i_1, :) \,.* \, b(:, i_2))(k) \\
length(a) \quad &: length(a) = max(n_1, n_2)
\end{aligned}
\tag{12}
$$

Here f_s denotes the corresponding scalar function for an element-wise function f. The meaning of a function can depend on the input types and shapes. Element-wise functions such as f, for instance, have two additional cases for when either of the inputs is scalar. Since types and shapes are determined statically, the correct axioms can be chosen. The axioms are separated by renaming functions based on input types and shapes. We also handle polymorphism by generating separate axioms for each type instantiation occurring in the program. Note also that the operator $.*$ used in (12) denotes element-wise multiplication.

In (13) we show the axiomatisations of the collapsing functions sum and all. Here we have a matrix $a : \mathrm{matrix}(t, \langle n_1, n_2 \rangle)$ and a row vector $b : \mathrm{matrix}(t, \langle 1, n_2 \rangle)$, where the transpose b^T is the corresponding column vector:

$$
\begin{aligned}
sum(a) \quad &: \forall\, i_2 : \mathbf{int32} \cdot 1 \leq i_2 \leq n_2 \implies sum(a)(1, i_2) = \sum_{k=1}^{k=n_1} a(k, i_2) \\
sum(b) \quad &: sum(b) = \sum_{k=1}^{k=n_2} b(1, k) \\
sum(b^T) \quad &: sum(b^T) = sum(b) \\
all(a) \quad &: \forall\, i_2 : \mathbf{int32} \cdot 1 \leq i_2 \leq n_2 \\
&\implies all(a)(1, i_2) = \forall\, k : \mathbf{int32} \cdot 1 \leq k \leq n_1 \cdot a(k, i_2) \\
all(b) \quad &: all(b) = \forall\, k : \mathbf{int32} \cdot 1 \leq k \leq n_2 \implies b(1, k)
\end{aligned}
\tag{13}
$$

Collapsing functions such as Σ here, must be defined recursively in SMT solvers. The functions *all* and *any* are, however, exceptions, as these functions can be directly encoded using universal and existential quantifiers.

The axioms for element-wise functions, such as f in (12), can be directly and efficiently encoded in SMT solvers. Efficient encoding of collapsing functions and other recursively defined functions, on the other hand, is hard [12]. The reason is that proofs of properties regarding these functions are typically done by induction, which typically cannot be done automatically by an SMT solver. The needed specifications for induction proofs for these functions would thus have to be provided manually, which is not feasible in practice.

5.2 Expansion

We now present another approach to encoding the verification conditions. Here we utilise the inferred shapes of matrices to expand the matrix functions. We will see that this approach is very efficient for matrices of relatively small size.

We have the matrices a : matrix$(t, \langle n_1, n_2 \rangle)$, b : matrix$(t, \langle n_1, n_2 \rangle)$ and c : matrix$(t, \langle 1, n_2 \rangle)$. Then $[\![a]\!]$ denotes the syntactically expanded matrix:

$$[\![a]\!] = \begin{bmatrix} [\![a(1,1)]\!] & \cdots & [\![a(1,n_2)]\!] \\ \vdots & \ddots & \vdots \\ [\![a(n_1,1)]\!] & \cdots & [\![a(n_1,n_2)]\!] \end{bmatrix} \tag{14}$$

where matrix accesses are also expanded, $[\![a(i_1, i_2)]\!] = [\![a]\!](i_1, i_2)$. If a is an expanded matrix and the indices are constant, the correct element can be directly chosen. However, we still need to use arrays in the SMT encoding as indices in matrix accesses are not always constant. If a is an identifier then the expansion $[\![a]\!]$ does nothing. This is actually important in order to handle many cases efficiently. This means that we can use quantified expressions to write down expressions that are effectively scalar and hence not expanded. This is particularly useful for verification of loops, such as in Fig. 1, where no matrix functions other than matrix accessors are used in the invariants.

The expanded definition of an element-wise function f applied to the expanded matrices $[\![a]\!]$ and $[\![b]\!]$ is given as follows:

$$[\![f(a,b)]\!] = \begin{bmatrix} f_s([\![a(1,1)]\!], [\![b(1,1)]\!]) & \cdots & f_s([\![a(1,n_2)]\!], [\![b(1,n_2)]\!]) \\ \vdots & \ddots & \vdots \\ f_s([\![a(n_1,1)]\!], [\![b(n_1,1)]\!]) & \cdots & f_s([\![a(n_1,n_2)]\!], [\![b(n_1,n_2)]\!]) \end{bmatrix} \tag{15}$$

Again, the function f_s here denotes the corresponding scalar version of the function f. The expansions of all other element-wise functions follow the same pattern. Collapsing functions, such as *sum*, *all* and *any* are also expanded. The expansions for *sum* are given in (16).

$$\begin{aligned} [\![sum(c)]\!] &= [\![c(1)]\!] + \ldots + [\![c(n_1)]\!] \quad [\![sum(c^T)]\!] = [\![c(1)]\!] + \ldots + [\![c(n_1)]\!] \\ [\![sum(a)]\!] &= [\![a(1,1)]\!] + \ldots + [\![a(n_1,1)]\!] \ldots [\![a(1,n_2)]\!] + \ldots + [\![a(n_1,n_2)]\!] \end{aligned} \tag{16}$$

Table 1. Verification benchmarks for different sizes of matrices

Addition					Multiplication				
$\langle n, n \rangle$	50	100	200	400	$\langle n, n \rangle$	3	4	10	20
Ax (s)	1.1	1.1	1.1	1.1	Ax (s)	1.1	n/a	n/a	n/a
Exp (s)	3.7	10.2	35.3	151.0	Exp (s)	1.2	1.3	6.2	81.0

max_f				$fibonacci$				$gauss$			
n	1000	2000	3000	n	250	500	1000	n	2	3	4
Ax (s)	n/a	n/a	n/a	Ax (s)	1.3	1.3	1.3	Ax (s)	n/a	n/a	n/a
Exp (s)	4.5	16.5	61.3	Exp (s)	4.5	13.7	50.5	Exp (s)	3.3	10.3	n/a

There is also a special case for expansion of matrix multiplication. Here we have the matrices $a : matrix(t, \langle n_1, n_2 \rangle)$ and $b : matrix(t, \langle n_2, n_3 \rangle)$:

$$[\![a * b]\!] = \begin{bmatrix} [\![sum(a(1,:).*b(:,1))]\!] & \cdots & [\![sum(a(1,:).*b(:,n_3))]\!] \\ \vdots & \ddots & \vdots \\ [\![sum(a(n_1,:).*b(:,1))]\!] & \cdots & [\![sum(a(n_1,:).*b(:,n_3))]\!] \end{bmatrix} \quad (17)$$

All other functions are encoded in a similar way as the functions presented above.

6   Benchmarks

We have evaluated the two approaches to encoding verification conditions, described in the previous section, on a number of small examples. We have used Z3 version 4.3.0 on a modern laptop in the evaluation.

We start with proving associativity of matrix addition and associativity of matrix multiplication using our encoding in the SMT solver. The execution times for different sizes of matrices are listed in Table 1. For the element-wise matrix addition, the axiom encoding is very efficient and the execution time is invariant with respect to the size of the matrix. For the matrix multiplication, whose definition involves recursive functions, axiomatisation is not a feasible approach, since inductive proofs regarding the properties of the function would be needed. The SMT solver is only able to unfold the definition for matrices up to the size $\langle 3, 3 \rangle$. Expansion, on the other hand, is an efficient approach as long as the matrices are kept fairly small.

We would like to point out that the most interesting part of these benchmarks is the growth rate of the execution times rather than the actual execution time. This is because the current implementation of the expansion in the tool generates a new AST from the unexpanded AST. Copying of subtrees in this step currently amounts to the vast majority of the execution time. This step could be optimised by doing the expansion and SMT encoding in one step.

Verification benchmarks for three example programs are given in Table 1. The programs are the max_f function listed in Fig. 1, a program returning a vector containing the n first Fibonacci numbers and an implementation of the Gaussian elimination method for solving systems of linear equations. Source code for these programs, along with more examples, are available in our technical report [17]. The benchmarks list execution times for verification of the programs with different input sizes. Again, expansion works well for matrices of relatively small size. The axiomatisation approach is only efficient for the *fibonacci* example. The reason is that that all contract conditions are expressed directly using universal and existential quantifiers and no recursively defined functions are used. In the *max_f* case, the postcondition on line 4, which uses the *all* collapsing function, is proved by the verifier. The verifier is, however, not able to prove the postcondition on line 5, which uses the *any* function. The problem seems to be the combination of universal and existential quantifiers used in the axiom for the *any* function: $\forall\, a : \mathrm{matrix}(\textbf{boolean}, \langle n, 1\rangle) \cdot (any(a) = \exists\, j : \textbf{int32} \cdot 1 \leq j \leq n \wedge a(j))$. It seems that the SMT solver is not able to instantiate these quantifiers successfully. In general, we noted that the SMT solver seems to quickly run into problems with the axioms for the *all* and *any* functions. For the Gaussian elimination example, Z3 is only successful on inputs up to size 3, even when expansion is used, possibly due to complex expressions in the invariants with many array updates in the encoding, caused by a combination of matrix multiplication and row update.

The results indicate that expansion can be a robust and efficient approach, while the performance of axiomatisation heavily depends on how well the verifier does quantifier instantiation in a given situation. We have here only evaluated the axiomatisation and expansion approaches separately. The results, however, suggests that a hybrid approach, where only functions that are problematic to axiomatise effectively are expanded, could be efficient. We have here used Z3 with the default settings. It might be possible to tune it for better performance for these kind of problems.

7 Related Work

Contract-based static verification has been implemented for many different programming languages e.g., Java [7], C# [3] and .NET [10]. (Multi-dimensional) arrays are supported in all these verifiers. It would be possible to implement the matrix functions as a library in any of these frameworks. However, there are three challenges: 1) The languages are statically and explicitly typed and matrix shapes are not part of the type systems. 2) Only axiomatisation is directly supported. 3) Arrays are there mutable objects.

In [12] they discuss axiomatisations of comprehension functions, which are similar to our recursive functions, suitable for use in SMT solvers. Their focus is on verification of loops that computes results involving these comprehensions, not programs that use functions specified by them. This means that the recursive definitions typically have to be unfolded only a few times. Their work focuses on bounding the unfolding.

Simulink Design Verifier[5] (SLDV) can handle a large subset of the built-in functions in EML. How matrix calculations are handled cannot be found in the

---

[5] http://www.mathworks.com/products/sldesignverifier/

documentation. The performance is not always good, e.g. proving associativity of matrix multiplication fails (in MATLAB 2014a, SLDV 2.6), since non-linear arithmetic is not supported for rational numbers. Loops are unfolded, which means static bounds on loops are needed.

Type and shape inference for MATLAB programs have been studied before in the context of program optimisation [16,1,11], with the goal of pre-allocating matrices and avoid bounds checks at runtime. There, an unknown type or shape means fallback to dynamic allocation. Here we need exact shapes. We require that matrices do not change their shape, which is handled in their frameworks. This is not a necessary restriction in our case either. However, we can only handle matrix shapes that depend on constants, i.e., data-dependent shapes in loops and recursion is not allowed. In [16,1] they use a combination of forward propagation and backward propagation of type information. This is very similar to our constraint-based type inference. In [11] they use algebraic properties regarding shapes of the matrix functions in MATLAB to perform shape analysis. They allow matrices with arbitrary many dimensions. They can also infer other relationships between data than concrete values obtained by forward and backward propagation in [16,1]. MATLAB also performs static type and shape analysis for data in EML. It appears that forward propagation of matrix shapes is performed. Use of variable-sized data can be enabled through an option. As function parameters can be declared to be constants, we can use these parameters in matrix shapes, which cannot be done for fixed-sized data in EML. However, currently they can use more complex expressions in matrix creation expressions. These limitations can be remedied in our tool also, by increasing the subset of the language handled by the type checker.

Languages that are designed to be aware of the shape of the data exist. The language FiSH [6] allows type annotations involving matrix and vector shapes. Also an inference algorithm is discussed. However, they do not allow converting values to matrix shapes, as we do e.g. for the function *zeros*. A dependent type system in ML [18] has also been studied. One goal with this type system is analysis of array bounds. The index language used for array shapes can be arbitrarily complex only limited by the choice of constraint solver. This approach is potentially more general than ours, but it is aimed at a functional language.

8   Conclusions

In this paper we have described an approach to automatically verify that programs written in Embedded MATLAB satisfy specifications given as contracts. The most important goal is efficient handling of the built-in functions for matrix manipulation. This is achieved by using inference of shapes and types of matrices to make the verification process efficient. We evaluate two approaches: direct axiomatisation of matrix functions and expansion of all matrix functions. We found expansion to be efficient for relatively small matrices commonly found in embedded control and signal processing applications. This allows complete automation with relatively small annotation overhead. In the axiomatisation approach we need to either manually provide the needed specifications for recursively defined functions or have the verifier unfold the function definition, neither of which are desirable. We demonstrated the usefulness of our approach on a number of examples.

There are many directions for future work. Matrix accesses are now limited to one element or a complete row or column. EML allows more flexibility and allows choosing any sub-matrix. This should not present any fundamental problem for our approach. Complete support for the control flow constructs in EML should also be provided. Currently, only if-statements and while-loops are supported. The verifier only checks partial correctness. The plan is to implement checks for termination of both iteration and recursion. Techniques based on abstract interpretation, e.g. [10], could perhaps also be used to infer the needed properties of recursively defined functions, which would allow for more automation when axiomatisation of functions are used. However, we believe that our approach is a good start towards fully automated efficient verification of EML programs.

References

1. Almási, G., Padua, D.: MaJIC: Compiling MATLAB for speed and responsiveness. SIGPLAN Not. 37(5) (2002)
2. Barnett, M., Chang, B.-Y.E., DeLine, R., Jacobs, B., Leino, K.R. M.: Boogie: A modular reusable verifier for object-oriented programs. In: de Boer, F.S., Bonsangue, M.M., Graf, S., de Roever, W.-P. (eds.) FMCO 2005. LNCS, vol. 4111, pp. 364–387. Springer, Heidelberg (2006)
3. Barnett, M., Fähndrich, M., Leino, K.R.M., Müller, P., Schulte, W., Venter, H.: Specification and verification: The Spec# experience. Commun. ACM 54(6) (2011)
4. Boström, P.: Contract-based verification of simulink models. In: Qin, S., Qiu, Z. (eds.) ICFEM 2011. LNCS, vol. 6991, pp. 291–306. Springer, Heidelberg (2011)
5. Boström, P., Morel, L., Waldén, M.: Stepwise development of simulink models using the refinement calculus framework. In: Jones, C.B., Liu, Z., Woodcock, J. (eds.) ICTAC 2007. LNCS, vol. 4711, pp. 79–93. Springer, Heidelberg (2007)
6. Jay, C.B., Steckler, P.A.: The functional imperative: Shape! In: Hankin, C. (ed.) ESOP 1998. LNCS, vol. 1381, p. 139. Springer, Heidelberg (1998)
7. Chalin, P., Kiniry, J.R., Leavens, G.T., Poll, E.: Beyond assertions: Advanced specification and verification with JML and ESC/Java2. In: de Boer, F.S., Bonsangue, M.M., Graf, S., de Roever, W.-P. (eds.) FMCO 2005. LNCS, vol. 4111, pp. 342–363. Springer, Heidelberg (2006)
8. Cook, B., Podelski, A., Rybalchenko, A.: Proving program termination. Commun. ACM 54 (2011)
9. de Moura, L., Bjørner, N.S.: Z3: An efficient SMT solver. In: Ramakrishnan, C.R., Rehof, J. (eds.) TACAS 2008. LNCS, vol. 4963, pp. 337–340. Springer, Heidelberg (2008)
10. Fähndrich, M., Logozzo, F.: Static contract checking with abstract interpretation. In: Beckert, B., Marché, C. (eds.) FoVeOOS 2010. LNCS, vol. 6528, pp. 10–30. Springer, Heidelberg (2011)
11. Joisha, P.G., Banerjee, P.: An algebraic array shape inference system for MATLAB. ACM TOPLAS 28(5) (2006)

12. Leino, K.R.M., Monahan, R.: Reasoning about comprehensions with first-order SMT-solvers. In: SAC 2009. ACM (2009)
13. Milner, R.: A theory of type polymorphism in programming. J. Comput. System Sci. 17 (1978)
14. de Moura, L., Bjorner, N.: Generalized, efficient array decision procedures. In: FMCAD 2009. IEEE (2009)
15. Pierce, B.C.: Types and Programming Languages. MIT Press, Cambridge (2002)
16. de Rose, L., Padua, D.: Techniques for the translation of MATLAB programs into Fortran 90. ACM TOPLAS 21(2) (1999)
17. Wiik, J., Boström, P.: Contract-based verification of MATLAB and Simulink matrix-manipulating code. Tech. Rep. 1107, TUCS (2014)
18. Xi, H.: Dependent ML: An approach to practical programming with dependent types. J. Funct. Programming 17(2) (2007)

GPU Accelerated Counterexample Generation in LTL Model Checking

Zhimin Wu[1], Yang Liu[1], Yun Liang[2], and Jun Sun[3]

[1] Nanyang Technological University, Singapore
[2] Peking University, China
[3] Singapore University of Technology and Design, Singapore

Abstract. Strongly Connected Component (SCC) based searching is one of the most popular LTL model checking algorithms. When the SCCs are huge, the counterexample generation process can be time-consuming, especially when dealing with fairness assumptions. In this work, we propose a GPU accelerated counterexample generation algorithm, which improves the performance by parallelizing the Breadth First Search (BFS) used in the counterexample generation. BFS work is irregular, which means it is hard to allocate resources and may suffer from imbalanced load. We make use of the features of latest CUDA Compute Architecture-*NVIDIA Kepler GK110* to achieve the dynamic parallelism and memory hierarchy so as to handle the irregular searching pattern in BFS. We build dynamic queue management, task scheduler and path recording such that the counterexample generation process can be completely finished by GPU without involving CPU. We have implemented the proposed approach in PAT model checker. Our experiments show that our approach is effective and scalable.

1 Introduction

The LTL model checking problem is known as the emptiness checking of the product between M and $A_{\neg\varphi}$, where M represents the model and $A_{\neg\varphi}$ represents the Büchi automaton that expresses the negation of an LTL property φ. The emptiness checking is to detect if there exists an execution path in the product that can be accepted by the Büchi automaton. There are two main streams of LTL model checking approaches: nested Depth First Search (NDFS) and Strongly Connected Component (SCC) search, where the latter one is more suitable to handle fairness assumptions.

SCC based verification algorithms aim to find an SCC with at least one accepting state. If such SCC exists, it means that there is a run that can be accepted by the $A_{\neg\varphi}$, i.e., the violation of the LTL property φ. To generate a counterexample in such case is to produce an infinite path $\pi = \rho_1 \rho_2 \rho_3$, which consists of three parts: a path ρ_1 from the initial state to a state s in the SCC, a path ρ_2 from the s to an accepting state a in the SCC and a loop ρ_3 that starts and ends at a. To generate such a path, currently, some algorithms [12,6] work on DFS-related solution with high complexity. Some work on BFS-related solution, such as in [5], which focus on building the minimal size counterexample to deal with the memory constraint.

In this paper, we propose an approach that has the potential to accelerate the counterexample generation process using GPU. The problem here is equivalent to building a

S. Merz and J. Pang (Eds.): ICFEM 2014, LNCS 8829, pp. 413–429, 2014.

solution to improve the performance of BFS with path recording. Compared with multi-core CPU architecture, GPU typically has a lot more cores and high memory bandwidth, which potentially provides high parallelism. Because the number of nodes in each layer of BFS is changing, it makes the resource allocation and the load balancing a challenging task in in GPU-based BFS searching. In the CUDA programming model, CPU will launch the kernel in GPU with static grid and block structures, which result in the lack or waste of compute resources. In previous research such as CUDA IIIT-BFS [7], it is necessary to launch the kernel each time when the BFS starts a new layer. It is costly and even slower than CPU-BFS in some cases. To deal with this problem, CUDA UIUC-BFS [9] has been proposed based on a hierarchical memory management solution. It builds a three-level queue for BFS to avoid consequent kernel launching, which offers certain speedup. But it is still a static method that cannot adjust according to the task size. Furthermore, there is no load balance approach in it.

In this work, we propose an almost CPU-free BFS based path generation process by leveraging on the new dynamic parallelism feature of CUDA. The key problem addressed is the number of tasks during BFS based path generation is dynamically changing. In this paper we propose four contributions. (1) Compared to related works of parallelizing BFS for model checking problems, our approach is totally CPU-Free. Existing related works allocate GPU resources in a static way. The resources can be re-allocated only by CPU when the execution of a kernel ends and launches a new kernel. For irregular graphs, it is costly and not flexible. Our approach presents a runtime resource adjustment approach for BFS and can be tailored for model checking problems. (2) We propose an approach to build dynamic parent-child relationship and a dynamic hierarchical task scheduler for dynamic load balancing. (3) We develop a three-level queue management to fit the dynamic parallelism and dynamic BFS layer expanding. Based on it, we propose a dynamic path recording approach, which helps duplicate elimination in BFS at the same time. Hierarchical memory structure of GPU is fully utilized for data accessing. (4) We implement our approach in PAT model checker and evaluate them to show the effectiveness of our approach.

Related Works. In the area of model checking, as the verification problem can be transformed to a graph search problem, there have been many works on accelerating model checking algorithms with CUDA. [3] focuses on the duplicate detection in external memory model checking. It utilizes GPU to accelerate sorting process in duplicate detection in BFS and builds a delayed duplicated detection on GPU. In [1], the authors propose a design of maximal accepting predecessors algorithm for accelerating LTL model checking in GPU. [4] accelerates the state space exploration for explicit-state model checking by utilizing GPU to do the breadth-first layered construction. [2] shows how the LTL model checking algorithms can be redesigned to fit on many-core GPU platforms so as to accelerate LTL model checking. [13] focuses on the on-the-fly state space exploration in GPU and proposes several options to implement this. All these research has proved CUDA compute architecture can be well utilized in solving model checking problems. In this paper, different from previous research in which most are based on a static way to allocate computing resource in advance and involve CPU frequently, we build an approach for counterexample generation which can completely put

Algorithm 1. Counterexample Generation Algorithm

Input: $init, SCC, \rightarrow$
Output: π_{ce}
1 $\pi_{ce} \leftarrow Init2SCCBFS(init, SCC, \rightarrow)$;
2 $\pi_{ce} \leftarrow \pi_{ce} \; ^\frown \; Path2AccBFS(\pi_{ce}, SCC, \rightarrow)$;
3 $\pi_{ce} \leftarrow \pi_{ce} \; ^\frown \; SelfLoopBFS(\pi_{ce}, SCC, \rightarrow)$;

---

the work to execute in GPU and dynamically fit the feature of BFS. Then the dynamic parallelism and memory hierarchy from latest CUDA Architecture-*Kepler GK110* and its corresponding GPU device serve as the basis of our design.

2 Background

LTL Model Checking and Counterexample Generation. LTL model checking is to verify that a model satisfies a property expressed in LTL, which has been shown to be equivalent to checking the non-emptiness of the product between a Büchi automaton (which is the negation of the LTL property) and a system model. A Büchi automaton can be defined as a tuple $\mathcal{A} = (B, \mathcal{T}, b_i, \mathcal{F})$ where B represents a finite set of states; $\mathcal{T} \subseteq B \times B$ represents the set of transition between states; $b_i \in B$ represents the initial state, and $\mathcal{F} \subset B$ is a set of accept states. An infinite input sequence can be accepted by a Büchi Automaton if there exists an execution path that will visit an accept state infinitely often. Let AP be a set of atomic propositions. The system model can be represented with a Kripke Structure $\mathcal{M} = (S, \mathcal{I}, \mathcal{R}, \mathcal{L})$ where S is a finite set of states; $\mathcal{I} \subset S$ is the set of initial states, $\mathcal{R} \subseteq S \times S$ is the transition set and L is a labeling function: $L : S \rightarrow 2^{AP}$. Given a Büchi automaton $\mathcal{A}$ and a Kripke Structure $\mathcal{M}$, their product is defined as $\mathcal{P} = (B \times S, \rightarrow, \{b_i\} \times \mathcal{I})$, where $\rightarrow \subseteq (B \times S) \times (B \times S)$ is the product of $\mathcal{T}$ and $\mathcal{R}$.

Based on the definitions above, the non-emptiness checking is to search whether there exists an infinite run π such that π reaches a state (b, s) infinitely often and $b \in \mathcal{F}$. This is equivalent to detecting if a run contains a loop and (b, s) is included in the loop. For SCC based LTL model checking, the process is to detect an SCC containing an accepting state. When such an SCC is detected, it can be concluded that the model violates the LTL property. Counterexample generation process then start to produce a trace to reflect the errors in the model.

There are many counterexample generation algorithms [12,6,5], mostly using BFS searching to find the shortest counterexamples. Therefore, a way to accelerate BFS, combined with counterexample generation requirement, will work for these solutions. In this paper, we choose the counterexample generation algorithm (Algorithm 1) as the basis for our design. There are three inputs, *init* is an initial state in $\mathcal{P}$; *SCC* is a list that contains all nodes belong to the SCC; $\rightarrow$ is the outgoing transition relation of each node in $\mathcal{P}$. Strictly speaking, this transition relation is made up of the current explored transitions during the SCC searching process. Algorithm 1 contains three steps. (1) *Init2SCCBFS* is to find the path from *init* to any state in the *SCC* using BFS. (2) *Path2AccBFS* is to find the path from the SCC state found with *Init2SCCBFS* to the nearest accepting state. (3) *SelfLoopBFS* is to find a loop that starts from the accepting

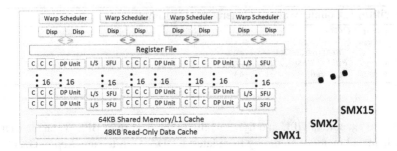

Fig. 1. Kepler-CUDA Hardware Model

state. π_{ce} is the returned counterexample run, which is the concatenation of the three path during the process. All these three steps are BFS based. In this paper, we will deal with accelerating these three steps in GPU with CUDA and merging them into one algorithm.

GPU and CUDA Architecture-Kepler. With its high parallel computational capability and wide memory bandwidth, GPU can speedup large scale data processing. CUDA is a parallel computing platform and programming model [11] designed for NVIDIA GPUs. As shown in Fig. 1, *NVIDIA Kepler GK110* is the new GPU Computing Architecture.

On the hardware level, a GPU consists of tens of streamed multiprocessors (SMX), each of which contains a lot of streamed processors (CUDA cores, marked as C in Fig. 1), instruction units and hierarchical memory. Streamed processor is the most basic processing unit in GPU. The hierarchical memory design is common in CUDA architecture, which contains Global Memory (GM), Constant Memory (CM), Texture Memory (TM), Shared Memory (SM) and Local Memory (LM) (i.e., registers). The access rates of these memories are in the descending order: GM<CM/TM<SM<LM. SM can be used to exchange data within an SMX, and GM is used to exchange data among SMXs. For the use of the other memories, readers can refer to [11]. The hierarchical memory is critical for GPU programming as it determines the data access cost.

On the software level, applications developed with CUDA are launched by CPU and running on GPU. The running application is called *kernel*. Each kernel runs the same program in many independent data-parallel light weight threads [10]. In CUDA runtime environment, threads are organized into three levels: *warp, block and grid*. Warp is the most basic execution and scheduling unit in CUDA. A warp usually contains 32 threads. A streamed processor only handles one warp at a time. A block contains several warps, which must be executed in the same SMX. Grid is the combination of blocks. The block size and the grid size are configured when launching the grid from CPU.

Compared with previous versions, *Kepler GK110* comes with four significant updates. (1) The new multiprocessor architecture. *Kepler GK110* owns 15 SMX units in general. Each SMX contains 192 CUDA cores. The number of warp schedulers increases to 4, which means 4 warp threads can be started together. (2) The Hyper-Q, which is to enable multiple parallel CPU tasks to launch work in a single GPU simultaneously. Hyper-Q can dramatically increase GPU utilization and reduce CPU idle

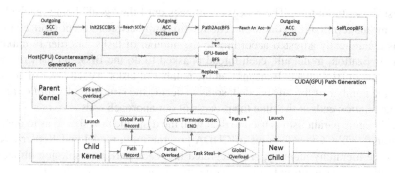

Fig. 2. Overall Design

time [10]. (3) Dynamic parallelism, which is the key feature we utilize in this paper, enables the kernel running in GPU to launch a new kernel to finish other works without involving CPU. Its presentation can be referred to *page 143* in [11]. The kernel launched from CPU is called *parent kernel*. One thread in parent grid can launch a *Child Kernel*. When the execution of the child kernel completes, it will stop and return to its parent. With this feature, the application running on GPU can make full use of the resource by dynamically launching new kernels. It can help developers to put the whole application to GPU for execution, which is efficient and cost effective. (4) The updated memory hierarchy. It introduces a 48KB cache for data known to be read-only during the execution.

3   CUDA Accelerated Counterexample Generation

The overall design of our approach is presented in Fig. 2. *Host (CPU) counterexample generation* represents the process in Algorithm 1. We build a general path generation approach to reach the target of function *Init2SCCBFS*, *Path2AccBFS* and *SelfLoopBFS* in Algorithm 1 based on different input. Our approach for handling the BFS based path generation is presented as *CUDA (GPU) Path Generation*. The complete counterexample generation process in Algorithm 1 can be replaced by executing GPU-based BFS for three times.

Our approach consists of two parts: *Parent Kernel* and *Child Kernel*. The overall process is described as follows. CPU launches the *Parent Grid* to execute *Parent Kernel*. *Parent Kernel* starts the BFS based path generation to generate one or more new layers of tasks. When the task size exceeds the thread number in *Parent Grid*, it launches *Child Grid* to execute *Child Kernel*. *Child Kernel* starts to do path generation and records path data. After generating a layer, the task scheduler will check whether any warp or block being overload. We define **overload** as the number of tasks exceeds the thread number in the GPU or no more tasks can be added to the BFS queue. Tasks rescheduling will start to do load balancing within the *Child Kernel*. If the whole *Child Grid* is **overloaded**, it will return to *Parent*. *Child Kernel* stops running. Resources of *Child Grid* are released. *Parent Kernel* reallocates tasks, launches a new *Child Grid* to execute *Child Kernel* and distributes tasks to it. The process continues until the "goal" being reached. The "goal" means terminating condition. The relationship between *Parent Grid* and *Child Grid* is dynamically adjusted according to the number of tasks. In order to maximize the parallelization, in default, each thread is asked to do the BFS and path recording for one state in BFS queue. It means that the number of tasks in each layer of BFS will decide the number of threads needed, so as to decide the structure of *Child Grid*. This dynamic relation ends at the time the process of our approach ends.

The dynamic parallelism is used to deal with the dynamic task size so as to make the execution flexible. Other features of CUDA programming model and *Kepler GK110*, such as the hierarchy memory, are integrated into each part. Our solution utilizes the latest GPU features to provide a novel counterexample generation solution.

3.1   Detailed Approach

We present Algorithm 2 and Algorithm 3 in this section for *Parent Kernel* and *Child Kernel* based on the process in Fig. 2. They follow the CUDA dynamic parallelism programming model presented in *pages 141 to 159* in [11]. Note that in CUDA, there are build-in objects *blockIdx* and *threadIdx* to record the ID of block and the ID of

---

Algorithm 2. CudaParentCounterexampleGeneration Algorithm

Input: $init, TerminatingCondition, \rightarrow$
1 $inblocktid = threadIdx.x; inwarptid = inblocktid\%32;$
2 Define: $WarpQueue, WarpPathQueue$ in SM;
3 **if** $inblocktid = 0$ **then**
4 $\quad\lfloor\;\; WarpQueue[0].enqueue(init); WarpPathQueue[0].enqueue((-1, init));$

5 CUDA-API:$\_\_synthreads();$
6 **while** $TRUE$ **do**
7 $\quad$**if** $WarpQueue[inwarptid] \neq \emptyset$ **then**
8 $\quad\quad S \leftarrow WarpQueue[inwarptid].Dequeue();$
9 $\quad\quad\lfloor$ **Shared Code** with $MemoryOption = SM$

10 $\quad$**if** $inwarptid = 0$ **then**
11 $\quad\quad$**if** $|WarpQueue| > WARPQUEUE\_SIZE$ **then**
12 $\quad\quad\quad\lfloor$ Intra_Warp_task_transfer;

13 $\quad$**if** $inblocktid = 0$ **then**
14 $\quad\quad$**if** $|TasksInBlock| > InitialT$ **then**
15 $\quad\quad\quad\lfloor$ break;

16 $\quad\quad$**else**
17 $\quad\quad\quad\lfloor$ Inter_Warps_task_transfer;

18 CUDA-API:$\_\_synthreads();$
19 **if** $\neg TerminatingCondition(anyState)$ **then**
20 $\quad$**if** $inblocktid = 0$ **then**
21 $\quad\quad ChildSizeCalculation(EXPAND\_LEVEL);$
22 $\quad\quad$write $WarpPathQueue$ to GM;
23 $\quad\quad\lfloor$ write $WarpQueue$ to GM with Duplicate Elimination;

24 $\quad$**while** $\neg TerminatingCondition(anyState)$ **do**
25 $\quad\quad$**if** $inblocktid = 0$ **then**
26 $\quad\quad\quad$ Generate Tasks Distribution Offset;
27 $\quad\quad\quad$ Launch ChildKernel, Transfer tasks in GM to Child Grid;
28 $\quad\quad\quad\lfloor$ CUDA-API:$cudaDeviceSynchronize():$ //If Child returns to Parent;

29 CUDA-API:$\_\_synthreads();$

---

thread in each block. But there is no object to represent the ID of threads in warp. It can be calculated directly as the warp is built in sequence, means that threads with index $0 \sim 31$ will be warp 1.

To simplify the presentations of the two algorithms, we abstract the common part in both of two algorithms in List. 1.1. It corresponds to lines 9 in Algorithm 2 and lines 8. The details will be introduced together with the algorithms.

Algorithm 2 corresponds to the *Parent Kernel* executed in *Parent Grid*, named by *CudaParentCounterexampleGeneration*. It focuses on the task schedule and parent-child relation management. In Algorithm 2, the input variable *init* means the initial state. *TerminatingCondition* is a Boolean function which decides whether the algorithm should terminate at the current state. The condition in our approach means that the path generation process reaches any target state in the target states set, which can be be an SCC or an accept state list based on the input of each process in Algorithm 1. Line 1 presents two types of thread ID mentioned above. Line 2 presents the two types of queues used in the algorithm. *WarpQueue* is an array of queues that represents the task queue for each thread. *WarpPathQueue* has the same structure, which is to record the path to the target state. They are all allocated dynamically in SM. The details structure and operation rules can be referred to Sec. 3.2 and 3.4. Lines 3 and 4 are the first step of path generation. The initial state and initial path record are added to the queue of the first thread in the block. Here the path record is a tuple with two components: $(Predecessor, StateID)$. The function shown in lines 5, 18 and 29 is CUDA build-in API for intra-block synchronization [11]. The loop from line 6 to line 17 is the major path generation process in *Parent Kernel*. The condition to break the loop is that *Parent Grid* being overloaded. Line 7 means that the thread works when its queue is not empty. In line 8, the thread will get task S from its queue, then line 9 mentions the *Shared Code*, which is the abstraction of the BFS and counterexample generation related work. The *Shared Code* is presented in List. 1.1.

Listing 1.1. Shared Code

```
1    if (TerminatingCondition(anyState)) {
2        write WarpPathQueue[inwarptid] to GM;
3        broadcast to other threads through MemoryOption;
4        Iterativebacktracking → FullPath;
5        break;
6    }
7    S_new = NewLayerTaskGeneration(S);
8    if (|WarpPathQueue[inwarptid]| = WARPPATHQUEUE_SIZE) {
9        write WarpPathQueue to GM;
10       WarpPathQueue[inwarptid].enqueue({S, S_new});
11   }
12   WarpQueue[inwarptid].enqueue(S_new);
13   if (inwarptid = 0) {
14       Transfer tasks among queues in WarpQueue;
15   }
```

In List. 1.1, line 1 is the target state detection. When the path generation of any thread reaches any state in the target states set, path records stored in *WarpPathQueue* in SM will be copied back to GM (using atomic operation *atomicAdd*) in line 2 and this information will be broadcasted through *MemoryOption* in line 3. For Algorithm 2, *MemoryOption* is set to *SM*. Then other threads will stop running and the thread which detects the terminating condition will deal with backtracking to generate the full path in line 4. Successors generation in line 7 is based on S and $\rightarrow$. In line 12, new successors S_{new} will be added to the queue of corresponding thread in $WarpQueue$. Lines 8 to 10 are to record path information. Path records will be stored in $WarpPathQueue$ in SM firstly, when the element number in the queue exceeds the constant *WARPPATHQUEUE_SIZE*, it will be copied back to GM (using atomic operation *atomicAdd*). The record in GM can also work as the preparation for future duplicate elimination, which will be detailed in Sec. 3.4. At the beginning, only thread 0 has tasks in its queue. So lines 13 and 14 are to involve other threads in the same warp by transferring tasks to threads with empty queue, which is done in central mode by the first thread in a warp.

Back to Algorithm 2, lines 10 to 12 perform load balancing within a warp. The constant *WARPQUEUE_SIZE* means the configured size of each queue in the array $WarpQueue$. Lines 13 to 17 are the inter-warps load balancing and the checking of *Parent Grid* being overload. The constant *INITIAL_T* means the thread number in *Parent Grid*. Lines 20 to 23 work on the calculation of *Child Grid* size and transfer data from SM to GM so as to transfer data from *Parent Kernel* to *Child Kernel*. Note that line 23 shows that a duplicate elimination approach takes action when copying back the content in task queue from SM to GM, which utilizes the path record information in GM. Details are also shown in Sec. 3.4. Line 26 shows that *Parent Kernel* needs to calculate the task distribution offset, which records the tasks storage index in GM for each block in *Child Grid*. Constant *EXPAND_LEVEL* means the times of *INITIAL_T* threads for *Child Grid*. Finally, lines 27 and 28 are the process to launch *Child Grid*. The loop from lines 24 to 28 is the loop in which *Parent Kernel* working as a scheduler to reallocate *Child Grid* to execute *Child Kernel* iteratively. This loop breaks only when the path generation detects any target state.

Algorithm 3 corresponds to the *Child Kernel* executed in *Child Grid* in Fig. 2. Functionally, it works on the path generation and the task schedule approach is also implemented in it. In Algorithm 3, variables or functions with the same name as in Algorithm 2 have the same meaning. The tasks in GM and the $Distribution offset$ generated in Algorithm 2 are the inputs. In line 1, $globaltid$ represents the first thread among all blocks. Line 2 defines two variables in GM for communication among threads in different blocks. A loop from lines 3 to 32 is the major executing process. The break conditions of the loop are that path generation detects any terminal states or the whole *Child Grid* being overloaded. Lines 4 and 5 are for each warp to get its own tasks and push to the queue of each thread in balance. This is based on the $Distribution offset$. Lines 6 to 8 are shared code with $MemoryOption$ being $SM+GM$. The full path generated will be "returned" to *Parent Kernel* through GM. Lines 10 to 22 are the intra warp and inter-warps load balancing. Lines 23 to 32 are the process to check if the whole *Child Grid* being overloaded and whether inter-blocks load balancing is needed. These three load balancing approaches make up the complete hierarchical task scheduling. And they can be regarded as three levels schedule: Warp level, means task adjustment among threads in a warp; Block level, means task adjustment among blocks of *Child Grid*; Grid level means returning the control to parent. Block level and Grid level need to copy the content in task queue to GM with the duplicate elimination approach. It decides at which level task scheduling will be taken dynamically. Lines 24 and 32

Algorithm 3. CudaChildCounterexampleGeneration Algorithm

Input: $Tasks, DistributionOffset, TerminatingCondition, \rightarrow$
1 $globaltid = blockDim.x * blockIdx.x + threadIdx.x$;
2 Define $WarpQueue, WarpPathQueue$ in SM $Child\_return2Parent, ChildSynNeed$ in GM;
3 **while** $\neg TerminatingCondition(anyState)$ **or** $Child\_return2Parent$ **do**
4   **if** $inwarptid = 0$ **and** $interblockstaskschedulehappens$ **then**
5        $WarpQueue[0...31].enqueue(GetTasks(Tasks, DistributionOffset))$;

6   **while** $WarpQueue[inwarptid] \neq \emptyset$ **do**
7        $S = WarpQueue[inwarptid].dequeue()$;
8   **Shared Code with** $MemoryOption = SM + GM$

9   CUDA-API:$\_\_synthreads()$;
10   **if** $inwarptid = 0$ **then**
11   **if** $|WarpQueue[0...31]| > WarpQueueSize$ **then**
12           $InWarpadjustment = true$;

13   **if** $TasksInWarp > 32$ **then**
14           $InBlockadjustment = true$;
15           $Ats = AvailableTaskSize$;

16   **if** $inblocktid = 0$ **then**
17   **if** $TasksInBlock > ThreadNumInBlock$ **then**
18           $ChildSynNeed = TRUE$;

19   **else if** $TasksInBlock \leq ThreadNumInBlock$ **and** $InWarpadjustment = true$ **then**
20   Intra_Warp_task_transfer;

21   **else**
22   Inter_Warps_task_transfer$\Leftarrow Ats$;

23     $CudaInterBlocksSyn()$;
24   **if** $ChildSynNeed = TRUE$ **then**
25   **if** $globaltid = 0$ **then**
26   **if** $TasksInChild > ThreadNumInChild$ **then**
27              $Child\_return2Parent = TRUE$;
28   write $WarpQueue$ to GM;

29   **else**
30   write $WarpQueue$ to GM;
31   Inter Blocks Task Scheduler;

32     $CudaInterblocksSyn()$;

---

represent the invocation of the inter blocks synchronization interface. It is not CUDA built-in API. This will be described in following parts.

Specifically, Algorithm 2 is designed to be executed among threads in a block, while Algorithm 3 is to be executed among threads in multi blocks. This is because *Parent Kernel* focuses on task rescheduling while *Child Kernel* focuses on the path generation.

Some other functions are cited for Algorithm 2 and 3: function *CudaQuicksort* utilizes the dynamic parallelism feature of CUDA [11] to do quick sort for preprocessing the target states set. *CudaInterBlocksSyn* refers to the algorithm mentioned in [14]. It is for inter-blocks synchronization as CUDA does not supply API for this.

Synchronization and Atomic Operation. In our algorithm, synchronization happens in each layer expanding by default as the algorithm need to do load balancing. After any task scheduling, synchronization is needed to make sure that each thread gets its own tasks correctly. In previous algorithms, the atomic operation can be used to work as the

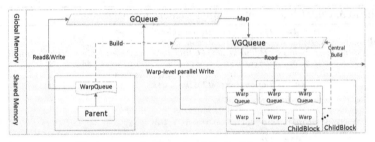

Fig. 3. Dynamic Three-level Queue Management

a *lock*. When some threads want to write the same memory address at the same time, only the first one which calls the lock will get the access right and others will discard their write operations and continue their executing.

3.2 Dynamic Three-Level Queue Management

As discussed in Sec. 2, GM can be read or written by all blocks running in different SMX, and SM is just available to blocks running in the same SMX. Read or write operations in SM cost much less than operations in GM. But the size of SM is much smaller than GM. Since our algorithm refers to huge data size, we cannot avoid accessing GM. However, as our tasks are distributed to the parallel threads, we can utilize SM to accelerate local data accessing. Considering that our algorithm is building dynamic Parent-Child relationship, we need a dynamic task distribution. We build a dynamic hierarchical queue to utilize the hierarchical memory. In order to fit our dynamic parallelism design, we build a three-level queue management approach, shown in Fig. 3. The first level queue is stored in SM, i.e., $WarpQueue$ in Algorithm 2 and 3. The second level queue is stored in GM, denoted as $GQueue$. The third level queue is also stored in GM, named Virtual Global Queue, denoted as $VGQueue$. For simplicity, we denote GQueue and VGQueue as GM in Algorithm 2 and 3.

Here, as there are many threads working together, the problem of read-write conflict when parallel threads write or read at the same time is necessary to be considered in the queue structure and the design of task schedule approach. One potential solution is to use lock or atomic operation to prevent conflict, which will lead to a huge cost with frequently write requests at the same time. Another potential solution is to use lock-free structure is preferred. We take two types of lock-free structures into consideration: first, as mentioned, the Kepler GK110 contains four warp schedulers in a single SMX, i.e., 4 warps can run in parallel. We build a lock-free queue with 4 sub-queues so as to avoid the conflict. However, it is hardly feasible because the warp scheduling in GPU is not visible to us. Therefore we adopt the design as showed in Fig. 3. In each block, no matter in *Parent Grid* or *Child Grid*, we make the first-level queue in SM a dynamic sub-queue set based on the warp number in one block. As shown in Fig. 4 part A, each $WarpQueue$ consists of 32 queues, which is due to the size of warp so as to make it lock-free. As we want to guarantee one thread holds only one expanding task, if the task size in a block exceeds the number of threads, the tasks will be re-scheduled and transferred to $GQueue$ in GM.

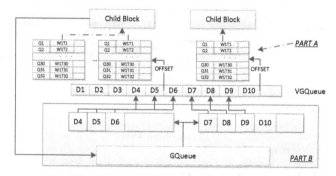

Fig. 4. Structure of WarpQueue, GQueue and VGQueue

In Fig. 3, *GQueue* is built at the first time when *Parent Grid* launches a *Child Grid*, it is also a group of array shown in Fig. 4, part *B*. As the *Parent Grid* communicates with *Child Grid* via GM, which is also the way blocks communicate with each other, it is used to transfer tasks to *Child Grid* and used by *Child Kernel* to execute. In following execution, *GQueue* stores the tasks when blocks being overloaded or the task reschedule among the blocks in *Child Grid* is needed. As in the global view, the tasks stored in the *GQueue* is not continuous, *VGQueue*, shown in Fig. 4, is dynamically built as the third level and it is used for sequential accessing tasks data. This three-level queue follows the rules of dynamic parallelism, aiming at building a flexible way of data accessing and improving the performance. It works for the task schedule and can completely match the *Parent-Child* structure.

3.3 Dynamic Hierarchical Task Schedule

As the task size during the execution dynamically changes, unbalanced load or overload will happen frequently, especially for an irregular graph. Launching kernel is an expensive work. So we cannot rearrange the structure of *Child Grid* at each time that the unbalanced load happens. Flexible task scheduling methods are necessary. Combined with our path generation problem, there are several conditions that the program needs to do task scheduling in hierarchical level. Algorithm 2 lines 10 to 17 and Algorithm 3 lines 10 to 32 are related to these:

- The first time to launch *Child Grid* from *Parent Grid*. When *Parent Kernel* finishes some layers of BFS-related path generation and makes that *Parent Grid* cannot hold more tasks, the *Parent Grid* needs to launch *Child Grid* and schedules initial tasks to *Child Grid* and used by *Child Kernel*.
- The inside warp task transfer to make each thread has tasks in its queue. When each warp begins the execution after getting tasks, it needs to guarantee that each thread is involved in the path generation procedure.
- When the whole tasks in a warp make a warp overload, it needs to do inter warps task transfer. This is similar to the inside warp data transfer.
- When the tasks in a block make it overload, inter blocks task rescheduling will occur.

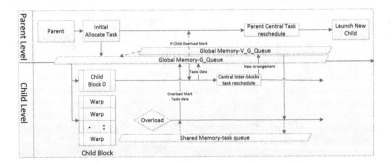

Fig. 5. Dynamic Hierarchical Task Schedule-block and grid level

– When the whole tasks in the *Child Grid* make it overloaded, *Child Kernel* will stop executing and the control will return to *Parent Grid* to rearrange the *Child grid* so as to reschedule the tasks. This and the inter blocks one are shown in Fig. 5. Both the inter blocks schedule and the *Parent Grid* schedule utilize *GQueue* and *VGQueue* GM to redistribute tasks. While inter warps or inside warp schedule is based on SM.

These make up a hierarchical fine-grained task scheduling. As many steps are in SM, it can make full use of the fast access feature. And only *Child Grid* being overloaded will cause the structure of *Child Grid* to be rearranged. In common, we will arrange the grid size of child bigger than needed at the beginning, to set the constant *EXPAND_LEVEL* so as to make the size of grid and block bigger than required, i.e., *INITIAL_T* × *EXPAND_LEVEL* in Algorithm 3. The *EXPAND_LEVEL* will based on the restriction of GPU architecture, which will be mentioned in Sec. 4. It is to make a compromise between resource cost and rescheduling cost. As the decision to do which level task rescheduling is due to the runtime task size, our design is a Dynamic Hierarchical Task Schedule method.

Note that after each layer of path generation, the overload detection will occur. This, together with the terminating condition detection, are in a central mode. This is to get rid of frequent communication among threads. When the whole block is overloaded and needs to copy tasks in each *WarpQueue* back to *GQueue*, each warp will do its own transfer, makes it a parallel data transfer. Here, the targets of task scheduling are to balance workload in each warp/block and to allocate enough resources for future execution.

3.4 Dynamic Duplicate Eliminated Path Recording

Our algorithm is to deal with the counterexample generation, where path recording is necessary. Path recording should also be parallelized. As our approach performs BFS, the counterexample path is updated in each layer. Note that our path recording is to record the visited state ID and its first *Predecessor*. The "first Predecessor" means the firstly recorded predecessor. In fact, our algorithm is to find a path to reach the target set, So one predecessor for one state is enough to generate a complete path. Take Fig. 6

as example, record $(2, 4)$ and record $(3, 4)$ will not be recorded together, just $(3, 4)$ is recorded as it is reached earlier.

Combined with our previous design, the path recording is happening in two levels: (1) warp level in SM, each warp owns a $WarpPathQueue$, which is mentioned in Sec. 3.1. (2) block level in GM, path recording will be taken under three conditions: When the number of records in $WarpPathQueue$ exceeds the configured WARPPATHQUEUE_SIZE, it is executed independently in each warp and mentioned in line 9 in List. 1.1. Another two conditions are that path recording is taken before the task being copied back to GM or after the terminating condition being detected, mentioned in lines 22 in Algorithm 2 and line 9 in List. 1.1. The structure for path recording in this level is two arrays. One is the $path\_recording\_array$, the index of array represents the ID of state and the value represents the predecessor. The other is the $predecessor\_visited\_array$, different from the first array, its value represents if the corresponding state is visited. The example of this procedure can be shown in Fig. 6. When the record $(1, 2)$ is copied back to GM, it will be recorded as $path\_recording\_array[2] = 1$ then $predecessor\_visited\_array[1] = true$. And for record $(n, 3)$, as $predecessor\_visited\_array[3] = true$, this record will be discarded. But $predecessor\_visited\_array[n]$ will be marked $true$. Atomic operations are used for writing these two arrays.

We call this approach $Dynamic$ $Duplicate$ $Eliminated$ $Path$ $Recording$. The duplicate elimination here does not mean duplicate path record elimination. It is for duplicate BFS tasks elimination. When the tasks being copied back to $GQueue$, it should first detect if the corresponding value of task state in $predecessor\_visited\_array$ is true. If so, this state will not be copied back to GM for following task reschedule. So it reaches the duplicate elimination target to some extent. It is mentioned in Algorithm 2 and 3 when the algorithms proceed to $write$ $WarpQueue$ to GM.

When the terminal states being detected, we need to generate the full path, which is mentioned in line 4 in List. 1.1. The process start from the target state reached by path generation process, marked as s. The iteration is started to find predecessor of s by getting value $prec(s) = predecessor\_visited\_array[s]$. This terminates when $predecessor\_visited\_array[s] = Init$. We generate the full path by recording each $prec(s)$ during the iteration. Atomic operation is also needed in getting the full path as we only need one path. Overall, our path recording also fits the idea of dynamic parallelism.

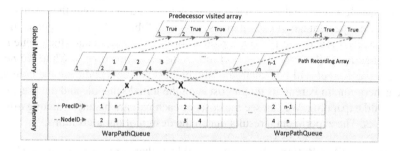

Fig. 6. Block-level Path Recording

Table 1. Parameters in the Algorithms

Parameter	Meaning	Default Value
INITIAL_T	The thread number of parent	32
WARPQUEUE_SIZE	The length of queue in WarpQueue	32
WARPPATHQUEUE_SIZE	The length of queue in WarpPathQueue	32
EXPAND_LEVEL	The times of thread number to expand compared to statistic requirement	2

4   Experiments and Evaluation

We evaluate our algorithms in two aspects. Firstly, we test the performance of our dynamic CUDA counterexample generation with models in different size and structures. Secondly, we analyze the effects of GPU parameters to our algorithms and discuss the limitation of the algorithms. We also propose two optimization options. The basic implementation of our algorithm uses C++. The system model is from PAT model checker [8]. Our experiments are conducted using a PC with Intel(R) Xeon(R) CPU E5-2620 @ 2.00GHz and a Tesla $K20c$ GPU @ 2.6 GHz with 5GB global memory, 13 SMXs and totally 2496 CUDA cores.

Performance Analysis. To analyze the performance, we choose the classic dinning philosophers problem (DP) as the input model. We use different process number to get different SCC size. The four GPU parameters used in the algorithms and their default value are shown in Table 1. The value of the parameters should be controlled in a fixed range based on hardware specifications. Their influence on our task schedule and their restrictions will be discussed in next section.

Based on the default configuration, our algorithms succeed in generating the counterexample for the verification of DP model in sizes from 5 to 8. We record the execution time for each process in *Parent Kernel* (Algorithm. 2), as well as the execution time of *Child Kernel* (Algorithm. 3). Firstly, Fig. 7 shows the distribution of the execution time for each BFS work in Algorithm. 1. *Init2SCCBFS*, *Path2AccBFS* and *SelfLoopBFS* are the three steps mentioned in Sec. 2. We can see that the first path generation costs more than the other two. This is because the $\rightarrow$ (outgoing transition table) for the first path generation is bigger as it contains all transitions generated during the model verification. So schedule, dynamic expanding and data transfer cost more. When doing $scc \rightarrow acc \rightarrow accloop$, the $\rightarrow$ is much smaller as we are preprocessing to eliminate non-SCC states in the $\rightarrow$.

We choose the data from the *Parent Kernel* execution of *Init2SCCBFS* path generation, as well as the total cost of *Child Kernel* execution. We get the results of the execution time percentage of each part, as shown in Table 2: *Schedule* means the task schedule; *Search* means the BFS with path recording; *Prepare* means the queue build-up for launching *Child Grid*; And *Child* means the execution time of *Child Kernel*. we can see *Child Kernel* will take charge of the highest percentage during the counterexample generation. In Parent, its major cost is on the initial schedule and the preparation for the child expanding. We can see the costs of each part are balanced among different size of tasks. The experimental results match the design of our algorithms.

Evaluation and Limitation. As shown in Table 1, there are four constants which affect the performance. We mentioned their meaning in Sec. 3.1. Firstly, The value of

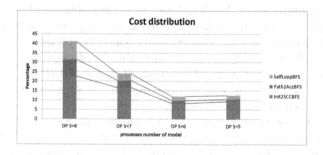

Fig. 7. Distribute of cost in three path generation

Table 2. Performance Analysis

Processes	TotalSize	SCCSize	AccSize	Schedule	Search	Prepare	Child	DataTrans	Total
5	348	120	36	20.7%	20.6%	20.5%	34.8%	0.57	9.3
6	1013	508	112	21.9%	22%	23.3%	30.8%	0.6	8.3
7	3420	2047	365	20.7%	20.6%	22.6%	35.5%	0.64	16.2
8	12339	7980	1195	24.4%	24.2%	25.4%	26.8%	1.01	19.7

INITIAL_T is due to the structure of the state space of the model. If the model's width is always short, setting a large INITIAL_T can reduce the chance to launch Child Grid. Too large value will waste a lot of resources when the Child is working on the major process. Secondly, based on our algorithm design, the hierarchical task scheduler is based on the grid size, means the number of threads. However, as the task size of each layer during the path generation of an irregular graph is unknown, if the size of one layer is larger than the remaining space of the WarpQueue, the task reschedule may occur, which is costly. So for the models with irregular state space, WARPQUEUE_SIZE will affect the performance. Thirdly, as the path records in warp level need to be copied back to GM when the $|WarpPathQueue|$ exceeds the WARPPATHQUEUE_SIZE. So set a large value to WARPPATHQUEUE_SIZE will definitely reduce the cost. At last, EXPAND_LEVEL, as we mentioned, if we just set the exact size of Child Grid according to the realistic requirement, it may cause the Child being overloaded soon and the Parent do rescheduling again. EXPAND_LEVEL is to make the compromise. It decides how much more resources to be allocated to the Child.

However, the size of the queue needs to be bounded. All above are restricted by the size of SM in each SMX. As described in Sec. 2, the size of chip memory in each SMX is 64KB. According to max SM per multiprocessor, only 48KB are available for SM. Before we launch the kernel, we need to decide how many SMs a block can use. In our algorithms, each item in the queue is an int. We represent the total shared memory cost as $MemC$, as defined below:

$$MemC = sizeof(int) \times (|WarpQueue| + |WarpPathQueue|) \times PG(INITIAL\_T) \times EXPAND\_LEVEL \qquad (1)$$

It requires $MemC < 48$KB. $PG(INITIAL\_T)$ denotes the statistic required size of resources (thread number), which starts from INITIAL_T. This is a dynamic variable so we combine the $(PG(INITIAL\_T) \times EXPAND\_LEVEL)$ to be $MaxWarpsize$. We can learn from equation (1) that these parameters are conditioned by each other.

Considering the restriction of CUDA architecture, the available size of SM is set before launching the kernel. If queue size described above is too large, the number of threads in one block will be restricted. During the execution, data in *WarpQueue* is flushed in each layer as old data being visited, and the size of data in *WarpPathQueue* is increasing all the time. so the constants *WARPPATHQUEUE_SIZE* and *WARPQUEUE_SIZE* will decide the extra GM accessing times. In fact, the value of all these parameters should be decided based on the structure of model.

The values of these parameters are also related to the grid level task schedule (*Parent Grid launch Child Grid*) in our design. We take the default setting in Table. 1 as an example. Suppose the total task size currently is T_{total}. The structure of *Child Grid*, means blocks number in grid, is marked as B_c. In default, we guarantee each block in *Child Grid* starts with tasks $T_s = 32$, equals to the thread number in a warp. Then $B_c = T_{total} \div T_s(+1)$. With the setting, each block will owns $ExpandLevel \times T_s = 64$ threads, means 2 warps. With these, total shared memory cost in a block TC_B will be: $TC_B = 64 \times (WarpQueueSize + WarpPathQueueSize) \times sizeof(int) = 16384 bytes$. Compared with $MemC$, it means two more warps can be added in a single block. and $B_c \leq 13(SMX\ number)$. So the max threads number available under this setting will be 1664, means if any layer in a graph contains more than 1664 states, the schedule cannot work.

In summary, due to the restriction of SM size in CUDA, our approach does not work well for graph with large branching nodes. A solution to this problem can be using more global memory, or building united memory space with host memory, which has been proposed in the new CUDA 6.0.

Optimization Options. The experiments show that our approach is scalable in dealing with the counterexample generation problem. In our CUDA Dynamic Path Generation algorithm, the task schedule, as well as the queue building, take a substantial on the total cost. Based on this, we present two optimization options as follows. (1) According to [4], GPU works fast on short data. So building a compact graph representation to represent the model can improve the performance significantly. (2) Reduce the times of scheduling and global memory accessing. These can be done by applying latency task schedule, making each thread hold more tasks and performing the load balance after several layer expanding. The low cost intra block and warp level task schedule should take majority parts, means to increase the threshold to do inter-blocks or parent level schedule. These potential optimizations are important in the improvement of our algorithm and can be easily supported based on current design.

5 Conclusion

In this work, we proposed a CUDA Dynamic Counterexample Generation approach for SCC-based LTL model checking. We designed the dynamic queue management, hierarchical task scheduler and the dynamic parent-relation, path recording scheme by adopting the new features of dynamic parallelism of CUDA. The experiments show that our algorithm can be scalable in solving the counterexample generation problem.

In future work, we plan to optimize this algorithm to build a space-efficient encoding for the task data and path record data in order to save resources.

Acknowledgement. This work is supported by "Formal Verification on Cloud" project under Grant No: M4081155.020 and "Verification of Security Protocol Implementations" project under Grant No: M4080996.020.

References

1. Barnat, J., Brim, L., Ceska, M., Lamr, T.: CUDA Accelerated LTL Model Checking. In: ICPADS, pp. 34–41. IEEE (2009)
2. Barnat, J., Bauch, P., Brim, L., Češka, M.: Designing Fast LTL Model Checking Algorithms for Many-core GPUs. In: JPDC, pp. 1083–1097 (2012)
3. Edelkamp, S., Sulewski, D. Model Checking via Delayed Duplicatedetection on The GPU. In Technical Report 821. Dekanat Informatik, Univ. (2008)
4. Edelkamp, S., Sulewski, D.: Efficient Explicit-State Model Checking on General Purpose Graphics Processors. In: van de Pol, J., Weber, M. (eds.) Model Checking Software. LNCS, vol. 6349, pp. 106–123. Springer, Heidelberg (2010)
5. Gastin, P., Moro, P.: Minimal Counterexample Generation for SPIN. In: Bošnački, D., Edelkamp, S. (eds.) SPIN 2007. LNCS, vol. 4595, pp. 24–38. Springer, Heidelberg (2007)
6. Gastin, P., Moro, P., Zeitoun, M.: Minimization of Counterexamples in SPIN. In: Graf, S., Mounier, L. (eds.) SPIN 2004. LNCS, vol. 2989, pp. 92–108. Springer, Heidelberg (2004)
7. Harish, P., Narayanan, P.J.: Accelerating Large Graph Algorithms on the GPU Using CUDA. In: Aluru, S., Parashar, M., Badrinath, R., Prasanna, V.K. (eds.) HiPC 2007. LNCS, vol. 4873, pp. 197–208. Springer, Heidelberg (2007)
8. Sun, J., Liu, Y., Dong, J.S., Pang, J.: PAT: Towards flexible verification under fairness. In: Bouajjani, A., Maler, O. (eds.) CAV 2009. LNCS, vol. 5643, pp. 709–714. Springer, Heidelberg (2009)
9. Luo, L., Wong, M., Hwu, W.-M.: An Effective GPU Implementation of Breadth-first Search. In: DAC, pp. 52–55. ACM (2010)
10. Nvidia Corporation. Whitepaper: NVIDIA's Next Generation CUDA Compute Architecture: Kepler GK110 (2012)
11. Nvidia Corporation. Nvidia CUDA C Programming Guide 5.5 (2013)
12. Schwoon, S., Esparza, J.: A Note on On-the-Fly Verification Algorithms. In: Halbwachs, N., Zuck, L.D. (eds.) TACAS 2005. LNCS, vol. 3440, pp. 174–190. Springer, Heidelberg (2005)
13. Wijs, A., Bošnački, D.: GPUexplore: Many-core on-the-fly state space exploration using gPUs. In: Ábrahám, E., Havelund, K. (eds.) TACAS 2014 (ETAPS). LNCS, vol. 8413, pp. 233–247. Springer, Heidelberg (2014)
14. Xiao, S., Feng, W. Inter-block GPU Communication via Fast Barrier Synchronization. In: IPDPS, pp. 1–12. IEEE (2010)

Formal Throughput and Response Time Analysis of MARTE Models*

Gaogao Yan, Xue-Yang Zhu, Rongjie Yan, and Guangyuan Li

State Key Laboratory of Computer Science,
Institute of Software, Chinese Academy of Sciences, China
{yangg,zxy,yrj,ligy}@ios.ac.cn

Abstract. UML Profile for MARTE is an extension of UML in the domain of real-time and embedded systems. In this paper, we present a method to evaluate throughput and response time of systems described in MARTE models. A MARTE model we consider includes a use case diagram, a deployment diagram and a set of activity diagrams. We transform a MARTE model into a network of timed automata in UPPAAL and use UPPAAL to find the possible best throughput and response time of a system, and the best solution in the worst cases for both of them. The two case studies demonstrate our support of decision makings for designers in analyzing models with different parameters, such as the number of concurrent activities and the number of resources. In the first case study, we analyze the throughput of a system deploying on multiprocessor platforms. The second analyzes the response time of an order processing system.

Keywords: MARTE Models, Timed Automata in UPPAAL, Throughput, Response Time.

1 Introduction

Real-time and embedded systems are usually associated with limited resources and strict real-time requirements. They are widely used in aerospace, communications and industrial control. In this paper, we focus on the model-based timing analysis of such systems.

MARTE (Modeling and Analysis of Real Time and Embedded systems) [1] is a UML (Unified Modeling Language) profile for modeling real-time and embedded systems. It can be used to model not only system behaviors but also other concepts such as time and resource constraints. Intuitively, MARTE models encapsulate required information for performance analysis of a given system. However, the lack of precise semantics makes it difficult to analyze exact system behaviors. Fortunately, formal methods can be applied to make up for the shortage.

---

* This work is partially supported by National Key Basic Research Program of China (973 program) (No. 2014CB340701), the Open Project of Shanghai Key Laboratory of Trustworthy Computing (No. 07dz22304201302), and the National Natural Science Foundation of China (No. 61361136002 and No. 61100074).

S. Merz and J. Pang (Eds.): ICFEM 2014, LNCS 8829, pp. 430–445, 2014.

Many works have been done for analyzing UML models using formal methods. Bernardi et al. analyze the correctness and performance of UML sequence diagrams and state machine diagrams using Petri net based techniques [2]. Holzmann et al. use model checking tool SPIN [3] to analyze UML activity diagrams [4]. In [5], Piel et al. convert the platform-independent MPSoC model in MARTE into a SystemC code and then validate the SystemC code via simulation. Merseguer et al. propose a method to transform UML state machines with MARTE profile into Deterministic and Stochastic Petri nets and to formalize the dependability analysis [6]. Suryadevara et al. propose a technique to transform MARTE/CCSL mode behaviors described in state machines into timed automata [7], and verify logical and chronometric properties [8].

In this paper, we use real-time model checking tool UPPAAL [9] to analyze throughput and response time of MARTE models. UPPAAL is a model checker based on the theory of timed automata, which is a well-established formal model for modeling behaviors of real-time systems. It can be used to verify various timing properties, and has been successfully applied to many industrial case studies [10,11].

A MARTE model we consider includes a use case diagram, a deployment diagram and a set of activity diagrams. We transform a MARTE model into a network of timed automata in UPPAAL and formalize the throughput and response time properties as temporal logic formulae. The network of timed automata and the formulae are then used as the input of UPPAAL. Based on the results returned by the tool, we can find the possible best throughput and response time of a MARTE model, and the best solution in the worst cases for both of them. For the best of our knowledge, this is the first work on throughput analysis and response time analysis of such MARTE models.

Our methods can analyze models with different parameters, such as the number of concurrent activities allowed and the number of resources. We can derive important influence factors for system performance from the obtained results, which can assist decision making for designers during system development. We present two case studies to demonstrate the effectiveness of our methods. In the first one, we analyze the throughput of a system deploying on multiprocessor platforms. The second analyzes the response time of an order processing system.

The remainder of this paper is organized as follows. In Section 2, we introduce the concepts on MARTE models and timed automata in UPPAAL. Section 3 provides the mapping rules from the subset of concerned MARTE models and Section 4 explains the timing properties in UPPAAL on throughput and response time and how they are analyzed. Implementation and case studies are presented in Section 5. Section 6 concludes the paper and discusses the future work.

2   MARTE Models and Timed Automata in UPPAAL

2.1   MARTE Models

MARTE extends UML by means of stereotypes, which allow designers to extend the vocabulary of UML in order to create new model elements that have specific properties that are suitable for a particular domain, and tagged values of stereotypes. We present a running example in MARTE model in Fig. 1, describing the starting procedure of a pulse oximeter. Fig. 1 (a) is the use case diagram, which contains an actor named "user", a use case named "startOximeter" and an association between them. Fig. 1 (b) is the deployment diagram, which declares a kind of resource named "microprocessor". The activity diagram describing the behavior of use case "startOximeter" is given in Fig. 1 (c). The tagged values in annotations in the figures are the constraints added according to the MARTE stereotype. For example, in Fig. 1 (c), action node "SetLEDInfra" is stereotyped <<PaStep>>, which has two tags, "host" and "hostDemand". The tagged value "host=microprocessor" means that action "SetLEDinfra" will be executed on resource "microprocessor", and "hostDemand=[(1469,max),(1411,min)]" defines the execution time of "SetLEDinfra" within [1411, 1469].

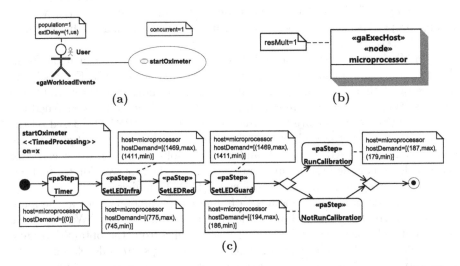

Fig. 1. A MARTE model for the starting procedure of a pulse oximeter. (a) The use case diagram; (b) the deployment diagram; (c) the activity diagram of use case "startOximeter".

2.2 Timed Automata in UPPAAL

UPPAAL is a tool for modeling, validation and verification of real-time systems modeled with *networks of timed automata*. A timed automaton (TA) is a finite state automaton equipped with a finite set of real-valued clock variables, called *clocks*. The timed automata in UPPAAL is an extension of the standard syntax of timed automata. We first review the definition of timed automata [7].

Definition 1 (Syntax of Timed Automata). *A timed automaton is a tuple* $A =< L, \Sigma, X, E, l_0, Inv >$ *where L is a finite set of locations, Σ is a finite set* *of actions, X is a finite set of clocks, $E \subseteq L \times C(X) \times \Sigma \times 2^X \times L$ is a transition relation, $l_0 \in L$ is an initial location and $Inv : L \rightarrow C(X)$ is an invariant-assignment function. $C(X)$ denotes the set of clock constraints over X, where a clock constraint over X is in the form of:*

$$g ::= true \mid x < c \mid x \leq c \mid x > c \mid x \geq c \mid g \wedge g,$$

where $c \in \mathbb{N}$, $\mathbb{N}$ is the set of non-negative integers, and $x \in X$.

The paths in TA are discrete representations of continuous-time "behavior" of TA. A path consists of a set of transitions. Fig. 2 shows the timed automaton for a simple light switch example. At location *off*, the light may be turned on at any time by executing the action *switch_on*, and at the same time clock x is reset to 0 to record the delay since the last time the light has been switched on. The user may switch off (by executing the action *switch_off*) the light at least one time unit (required by the guard $x \geq 1$) later after the latest *switch_on* action. The light can not be on for more than two time units, which is constrained by the invariant $x \leq 2$ of location *on*.

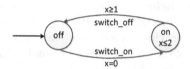

Fig. 2. The timed automaton of a simple light switch

The components in the network of timed automata (NTA) in UPPAAL and their relation are shown in Fig. 3. An NTA consists of three parts: ntadeclaration, automata templates and system definition. The *ntadeclaration* is global and may contain declarations of clocks, channels and other variables. The *automata template* defines a set of templates in the form of the extended TA, and a template includes a local declaration, parameters and a set of locations and edges. A *location* has four attributes: *name*, the mark for an initial location (*isInitial*), the mark for an urgent location (*isUrgent*), and *invariant*. An *edge* may

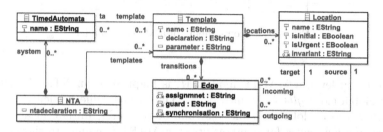

Fig. 3. The main components of NTA in UPPAAL

be annotated with *assignment expressions, guard expressions* and *synchronisation expressions*. The concurrent processes of a system are described in *system definition*. A path in an NTA is similar with that in TA except that the state in the path of the NTA is defined by the locations of all TAs in the NTA.

Compared with the standard timed automata, the TA in UPPAAL have some additional features such as *urgent channels* and *urgent locations* to facilitate the modeling and validation process (please refer to [12] for more details). In UPPAAL, the types of synchronization include rendezvous and broadcast. Additional to the regular channels to define the types of synchronization, there are two kinds of special channels, i.e., urgent and commit channels, to restrict the trigger condition of the corresponding synchronization. The pairs of synchronization are labeled on edges, where the sender is in the form of *e!*, the receiver is in the form of *e?*, and *e* is the name of the channel. Moreover, *urgent locations* are supported in UPPAAL to forbid time delay in such kind of locations.

3   Model Transformation

In this section, we illustrate the transformation rules from MARTE models to NTAs in UPPAAL for throughput analysis. The rules for response time analysis, a slight variant of that of throughput analysis, is introduced in Section 4.2.

MARTE specification provides rich elements for system modeling and analysis. We use only a subset of the specification. The main components of a MARTE model we consider, as shown in Fig. 4, include a use case diagram (UCD), a deployment diagram (DD) and a set of activity diagrams (AD). A MARTE model is stereotyped <<GaAnalysisContext>>, in which tagged value "concurrent=N" specifies that the maximum concurrent activities allowed in the system is N. The behavior of each use case of a UCD is described by an AD, which we denote as the AD of the use case.

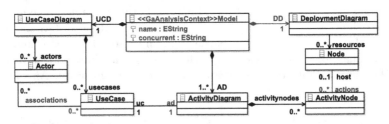

Fig. 4. The components of a MARTE model

At the top level, a MARTE model, M, is mapped to an NTA of UPPAAL with a global clock $glbClk$, named M_{nta}. The tagged value "concurrent=N" is translated into a global variable sys_conc of the NTA, initialized as N. The detailed mapping rules for components of a MARTE model are shown in the following sections.

3.1   Use Case Diagrams to TAs

A *use case diagram* contains a set of actors, use cases and associations between them. A *use case* specifies a required function of the system, whose behavior is modeled by an activity diagram, which we denote as *the AD of the use case*. An *actor* is an external entity interacting with the system. An *instance* of an actor represents a *request* for the system, activating the AD of a use case connected to the actor by an *association*. When there are n requests being processed, there are n concurrent active ADs, where n is limited by tagged value "concurrent=N". An actor is stereotyped <<GaWorkloadEvent>>, which has two tags, "population", specifying the number of the instances of the actor, and "extDelay", specifying the interval between the arriving time of each instance of the actor.

A UCD with n actors and m use cases is transformed to $m + n$ global variables, m channels and n TA templates in M_{nta}. In M_{nta}, there is an integer variable A_num initialized as p for each actor A to model its tagged value "population=p"; there is an integer variable U_num and a channel $trigger\_U$ for each use case U, the former for counting the number of the requests for U and the latter modeling the activation of the AD of U. For actor A with k associated use cases, U_1, ..., and U_k, there is a TA template, A_{ta}, with a local clock x, a location and $2k + 1$ edges. For each A_{ta}, there is a process in M_{nta}. In A_{ta}, there is a unique edge to keep the TA deadlock-free, denoted by $liveE$. For each U_i, there are two edges, one for receiving a request from actor A, denoted by $recE\_U_i$, and another for triggering a TA process of the AD of U_i, denoted by $triE\_U_i$. Tagged value "extDelay=d" of A is mapped to an invariant $x \leq d$ on the location and clock guards $x \geq d$ on edges.

The transformation from the UCD in Fig. 1(a) is shown in Fig. 5. Edges $liveE$, $recE\_startOximeter$ and $triE\_startOximeter$ are upper, below left and below right edges, respectively.

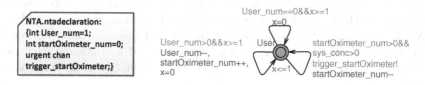

Fig. 5. The TA template transformed from the UCD in Fig. 1(a)

3.2   Deployment Diagrams to TAs

A *deployment diagram* includes a set of nodes, representing different resources. A *node* is stereotyped <<GaExecHost>> with tagged value "resMult=n" indicating that the available number of instances of the resource is n.

A DD with m nodes is transformed to $3m$ global variables and m TA templates in M_{nta}. For node R with "resMult=n", there are a global integer variable

R_num initialized as n to count the remained number of available instances of R, a pair of channels get_R and rel_R to model the request and the release of an instance of R respectively, and a TA template, named R_{ta}, with one location and two edges. For each R_{ta}, there is a process in M_{nta}. The transformation from the DD in Fig. 1(b) is shown in Fig. 6.

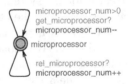

NTA.ntadeclaration:
{int microprocessor_num=1;
urgent chan get_microprocessor;
chan rel_microprocessor;}

microprocessor_num>0
get_microprocessor?
microprocessor_num--

microprocessor

rel_microprocessor?
microprocessor_num++

Fig. 6. The TA template transformed from the DD in Fig. 1(b)

3.3 Activity Diagrams to TAs

Each use case in the UCD employs an activity diagram to describe its behavior. An *activity diagram* consists of a set of activity nodes and control flows. The activity nodes we consider includes: initial node, action node, decision node, merge node, fork node, join node, and final node. An AD is stereotyped <<TimedProcessing>>. An action node is stereotyped <<PaStep>> with two tagged values, "host=R", indicating the resource it requires is R in the DD, and "hostDemand", recording the execution time of the action on R.

The AD of use case U in the UCD is mapped to a TA template, U_{ta}, with a local clock x. Let $A.p$ be the population of actor A and $\mathcal{A}$ be the set of actors associated with U. Then there are $\sum_{A \in \mathcal{A}} A.p$ processes of U_{ta} in M_{nta}. Fig. 7 presents the transformation rules. The *initial node* is the start point of the AD. The node and its outgoing control flow are translated into the initial location and an outgoing edge of U_{ta}, as shown in Fig. 7(a). Channel $trigger\_U$ is used to synchronize with A_{ta}s which are transformed by the actors associated with U.

As the *final node* defines the end of an AD and takes no time, we map it to an urgent location, as shown in Fig. 7(b). We add an outgoing edge from the location to the initial location, to model the termination of an execution of the AD.

The *decision node* and *merge node* are used in pairs. A pair of decision and merge nodes are mapped to a pair of urgent locations, as shown in Fig. 7(c). The guards on the outgoing edges of decision node are abstracted as non-determination.

An *action node* requiring resource R keeps waiting until the number of remained R is larger than one. The action node and its outgoing edge are mapped to two locations to express the waiting and executing states, respectively, as shown in Fig. 7(d). The execution time of the action on R, represented as tagged value "hostDemand=[a,b]" is mapped to an invariant of the location for executing the action and a guard on its outgoing edge. Channels get_R and rel_R are used to synchronize with R_{ta}.

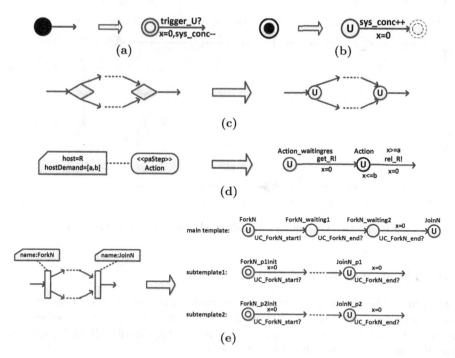

Fig. 7. The transformation rules from AD to TA. (a) The initial node; (b) the final node; (c) the decision and merge nodes; (d) the action node; (e) the fork and join nodes.

The *fork node* and *join node* are also used in pairs. A pair of fork and join nodes with n concurrent subprocesses are mapped to $n + 2$ locations and n TA templates, as shown in Fig. 7(e). The broadcast channel UC_ForkN_start and the regular channel UC_ForkN_end are used to synchronize between the original TA and the new TAs for subprocesses.

The TA template transformed from the AD in Fig. 1 (c) is shown in Fig. 8. The number of concurrently active processes of U_{ta}s in M_{nta} is limited by the value of tag "concurrent" in M. Here, an active process of U_{ta} means that the process currently is not at the initial location.

4   Model Analysis

Throughput and response time are two important timing properties of real-time systems. The throughput defines the number of requests that the system can process per time unit. The response time is the time the system responds to a user's request. In this section, we describe how to formalize them as the properties of UPPAAL.

Given a MARTE model M, in this section, we explain how to use UPPAAL, which deals with M_{nta}, to analyze throughput and response time of M.

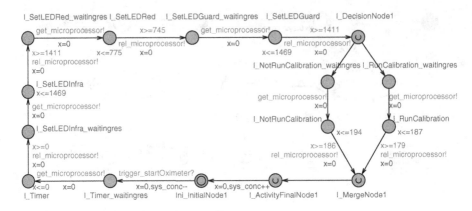

Fig. 8. The TA template transformed from the AD in Fig. 1(c)

4.1 Throughput Analysis

Let $\mathcal{A}$ and $\mathcal{U}$ be the sets of actors and use cases of the UCD in M, respectively. Let $A.p$ represents the value of "population" of actor A. The number of service requests is $k = \sum_{A \in \mathcal{A}} A.p$. Assume T is the processing time for all the k requests, the *throughput* of M is defined as $TP = k/T$.

Recall that sys_conc of M_{nta} is initialized as N, the value of "concurrent". It records the remained number of allowed concurrently active TA processes. $sys\_conc = N$ means no process is running in the system, that is to say, there is no active processes. For an actor A in M, global variable A_num in M_{nta} represents the number of remained requests of A, initialized as $A.p$. It is decreased by 1 when an instance of A arrives. $A\_num = 0$ means that all the requests from A have arrived. For a use case U in M, U_num in M_{nta} is used for counting the number of the requests of U. U_num is increased by 1 when an instance of actor associated with U arrives and is decreased by 1 when it triggers its AD once. $U\_num = 0$ means that there is no request from actors. Then the fact that, at some time points, all the requests of M have been processed, can be formulated as f using variables in M_{nta}.

$$f \equiv_{def} sys\_conc = N \wedge \forall A \in \mathcal{A} : A\_num = 0 \wedge \forall U \in \mathcal{U} : U\_num = 0$$

CTL (Computation Tree Logic) formula **AF**f is true when f is eventually true on all the paths of M_{nta}, denoted by $M_{nta} \models \mathbf{AF}f$. Then the question whether all the requests of M have been processed in time t, no matter how to schedule M to run, can be formulated as:

$$f_\forall(t) \equiv_{def} \mathbf{AF}(f \wedge glbClk \leq t),$$

where $glbClk$ is a global clock of M_{nta}.

Similarly, CTL formula $\mathbf{EF}f$ is true when f is eventually true on some path of M_{nta}. Then the question whether there are schedules of M to make sure that all the requests have been processed in time t, can be formulated as:

$$f_\exists(t) \equiv_{def} \mathbf{EF}(f \wedge glbClk \leq t)$$

Two lower bounds of the processing times of M can be formulated as follows.

$$T_\forall = \min\{t \mid t \in \mathbb{N} \text{ and } M_{nta} \models f_\forall(t)\}$$

$$T_\exists = \min\{t \mid t \in \mathbb{N} \text{ and } M_{nta} \models f_\exists(t)\}$$

A throughput larger than $\frac{k}{T_\exists}$ can never be reached and the throughput no larger than $\frac{k}{T_\forall}$ can always be achieved. Therefore, the possible maximal throughput of M is $\frac{k}{T_\exists}$, denoted by TP_{max}. In the worst case, M can at least achieve the throughput $\frac{k}{T_\forall}$, denoted by TP_{min}.

Using M_{nta} and $f_\forall(t)$ (or $f_\exists(t)$) as the input of UPPAAL, we can get TP_{min} (or TP_{max}).

The procedure to find TP_{min} is as follows: estimate the upper bound of t, T_1, as the execution time when only one resource is available; perform a binary search on $[1, T_1]$, and assuming t is the time considered, use UPPAAL to check whether $M_{nta} \models f_\forall(t)$ is satisfied.

To find TP_{max}, we can use the similar procedure as that of TP_{min}. A better, we can ask UPPAAL to return the *fastest* trace, and $T_\exists$ is the value of $glbClk$ in the last state of the trace.

4.2   Response Time Analysis

Response time is a criterion about how fast a use case reacts to a request of an actor. Denote the actor and the use case under analysis as A and U, respectively. The set of instances of A is denoted by $\{A_1, ..., A_P\}$, where P is the value of "population" of A. Tag "extDelay" defines the arriving interval of each instance.

The time when A_i arrives is denoted by $A_i.T_a$ and the time when A_i gets the required return is denoted by $A_i.T_f$. The *response time* of A_i is defined as $A_i.rt = A_i.T_f - A_i.T_a$.

Suppose the required response time of A is D, i.e., $\forall i \in [1, P] : A_i.rt \leq D$. Next, we explain the way to answer whether the requirement is satisfied.

In Section 3, We have illustrated the transformation from MARTE models to NTAs mainly for the throughput analysis. A slight variant is necessary for the response time analysis. The difference is introduced below and shown in Fig. 9. In M, one more stereotype <<SaStep>> is added to A, with a tagged value "deadline=D", specifying the required response time of A.

Suppose the TA templates of A and the AD of U are A_{ta} and U_{ta}, respectively. We add a global channel *arrive* to M_{nta}. A constant integer variable dl with the value of "deadline", a boolean variable *finished* and a local clock y are added to U_{ta}. Channel *arrive* is used to synchronize between A_{ta} and U_{ta}. A sender *arrive*!

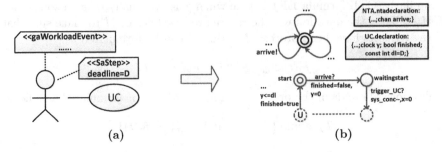

Fig. 9. The difference of models and transformation for response time analysis. (a) The difference in actor A of M; (b) the difference in TA templates A_{ta} and U_{ta} in M_{nta}.

is added to the edge $recE\_U$ of A_{ta}. To facilitate the analysis process, an edge and a location are inserted between the initial location and its original successor, and a guard $y \leq dl$ and an update of $finished$ are added to the incoming edge of the initial location. Each actor instance A_i will trigger a process of U_{ta}, named U_{ta_i}. Local clock y of U_{ta_i} is used to measure the response time of A_i. The guard $y \leq dl$ is used to model constraint $A_i.rt \leq D$. Only when the guard is true, can $finished$ become true. Then whether all the requests from A can be responded in time D, no matter how to schedule M to run, is formulated as formula $r_\forall$.

$$r_\forall(dl) \equiv_{def} \mathbf{AF}(\forall i \in [1, P] : U_{ta\_i}.finished = true)$$

The question whether there are schedules of M to make sure that all the requests from A can be responded in time D is formulated as formula $r_\exists$.

$$r_\exists(dl) \equiv_{def} \mathbf{EF}(\forall i \in [1, P] : U_{ta\_i}.finished = true)$$

With M_{nta} and $r_\forall(dl)$ (or $r_\exists(dl)$) as the input of UPPAAL, we can answer above-mentioned questions.

A possible minimal response time RT_{min} can be found by a procedure similar to that of TP_{max}, using $r_\exists$. In the worst case, the response time is at most RT_{max}, which can be computed by a procedure like that of TP_{min}, using $r_\forall$.

5   Case Studies

We implement our approaches in the toolkit FMPAer (Formal Models based Performance Analyzer) [13]. Modeling tool Papyrus [14] is used for creating a MARTE model. The transformation rules from MARTE models to NTAs in UPPAAL are written by model transformation language ATL (Atlas Transformation Language) [15]. The CTL formulae are generated according to the formulae introduced in Section 4 by searching the NTAs. The generated NTA and formulae are then checked by UPPAAL.

In this section, we present two case studies to demonstrate the effectiveness of our methods. In the first case study, we analyze the throughput of a system deploying on a platform with heterogeneous processors. The second case study analyzes the response time of an order processing system.

5.1 Throughput of a System Mapping on Multiprocessor

Consider a multiprocessor mapping problem from [1], as shown in Fig. 10. There are two different kinds of processors, $P1$ and $P2$. The task includes 5 subtasks, which may be mapped on $P1$ or $P2$. Subtasks $inpC$ and $oper2$ can use either one; $oper1$ and $outW$ can use only $P1$ and $outZ$ only $P2$. $oper1$ and $outW$ can run in parallel with $oper2$ and $outZ$, as shown in Fig. 10(a). The time consumptions when they are assigned to different processors are shown in Fig. 10(b). Since the execution time may be different when a subtask is assigned to different processors, different assignment will affect the throughput of the system. It is interesting to ask what is the maximal reachable throughput and what a throughput we can get even in the worst situation. That is, what are the values of TP_{max} and TP_{min} of the system. We answer these questions below.

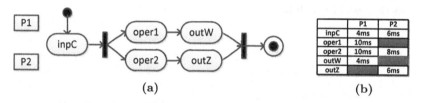

	P1	P2
inpC	4ms	6ms
oper1	10ms	
oper2	10ms	8ms
outW	4ms	
outZ		6ms

(a)   (b)

Fig. 10. A System Mapping on Multiprocessor. (a) The task and processors; (b) the execution time of each action on different processors.

Suppose there are two processors, one of $P1$ and one of $P2$. Totally there are 5 users arriving one by one in an interval of 1 millisecond, and 2 concurrent active tasks are allowed. The MARTE model of this system is shown in Fig. 11. The number of processors are represented by the tagged value "resMult=1" in DD, shown in Fig. 11 (b); the number of users and their arrival pattern are represented by the tagged values "population=5" and "extDelay=(1,ms)" in UCD, shown in Fig. 11 (a); and the number of allowed concurrent active tasks is represented by the tagged value "concurrent=2" of the model. In the AD shown in Fig. 11 (c), the parallel subtasks are modeled by fork and join nodes; and an alternative assignment of a subtask is modeled by decision and merge nodes.

The NTA transformed from Fig. 11 is shown in Fig. 12. By checking the NTA and formulae $f_\forall(t)$ and $f_\exists(t)$ using UPPAAL, we get $TP_{max} = 5/69 = 0.0549$ and $TP_{min} = 5/141 = 0.0355$.

Furthermore, with the change of the parameters of a MARTE model, e.g., the number of processors, the throughput of a system may be different. In Fig. 13, we show the impacts of the number of processors and the number of allowed

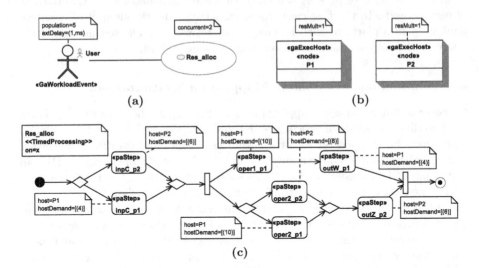

Fig. 11. The MARTE model for deploying different operations on multiprocessor issue. (a) The use case diagram; (b) the deployment diagram; (c) the activity diagram that describes the task in Fig. 10(a).

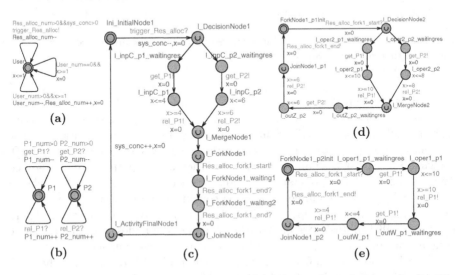

Fig. 12. The NTA transformed from Fig. 11. (a) TA template of the actor; (b) TA template of the resource; (c) TA template of the activity; (d) and (e) the forked TA templates of (c).

concurrent activities on throughput. In Fig. 13 (a), the throughput improves when the number of $P1$ is increased to 2, and then it keeps the same when further increasing the number of $P1$. The case for $P2$ is similar. These attempts show that when 5 users and 2 concurrent activities are allowed, 2 $P1$s and 2 $P2$s are sufficient for the best throughput performance. We show the impact of concurrent numbers in Fig. 13 (b), which has more distinct effect on TP_{max} than on TP_{min}.

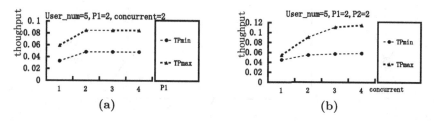

Fig. 13. The impact of different parameters on throughput. (a) The impact of the number of processors; (b) the impact of the number of allowed concurrent activities.

5.2   Response Time of an Order Processing System

In an order processing system [16], when a request of a user arrives, the system first sets up an order for the user, then carries out different operations according to whether the user is a VIP or not and sends a message to the user after the whole procedure is finished. We present the AD of the MARTE model describing this system in Fig. 14. It is interesting to know whether the user's request can be processed in time.

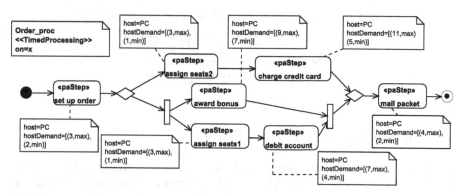

Fig. 14. The activity diagram of an order processing system

The transformed NTA of this system is shown in Fig. 15. Let the response time requirements be Ds. The transformed NTAs for different Ds are different only

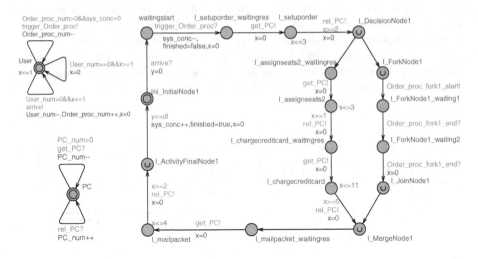

Fig. 15. The NTA of the order processing system

on values of constant variable $dl = D$ according to the requirements. Suppose the number of users is 3, the number of resource "PC" is 2 and the number of allowed concurrent activities is 3. The values of D are 13s, 14s, 20s, 45s and 46s, respectively. The results returned by checking the NTAs and formulae $r_\forall(dl)$ and $r_\exists(dl)$ using UPPAAL are shown in Table 1, from which we can conclude that all the 3 requests can be responded in 46s, no matter how to schedule the system to run. There are no schedulers of the system to make all the 3 requests being responded in 13s. Table 1 also reveals that $RT_{min} = 14$ and $RT_{max} = 46$.

Table 1. Response time analysis of the order processing system

dl	13	14	20	45	46
$r_\forall$	false	false	false	false	true
$r_\exists$	false	true	true	true	true

6   Conclusions and Future Work

In this paper, we have presented methods to analyze the throughput and response time of systems described in MARTE models, which include a use case diagram, a deployment diagram and a set of activity diagrams. We transform a MARTE model into an NTA and compile the concerned properties into CTL formulae, then use UPPAAL to check whether the NTA satisfies the formulae. According to the results returned by UPPAAL, we find the possible best throughput and response time of MARTE models, and the best solution in the worst cases for

both of them. Two case studies we have conducted to demonstrate our support
of decision makings for designers in analyzing models with different parameters,
such as the number of concurrent activities and the number of resources.

The MARTE models we use in this paper only involve a small subset of
elements of the MARTE specification. As the future work, we will consider more
elements, such as sequence diagrams and state machines, to make our models
more expressive. We will also integrate more valuable and verifiable properties
into our method.

References

1. OMG. UML Profile for MARTE, Beta 2,
   http://www.omg.org/cgi-bin/doc?ptc/2008-06-08
2. Bernardi, S., Donatelli, S., Merseguer, J.: From UML sequence diagrams and statecharts to analysable petri net models. In: WOSP 2002, pp. 35–45 (2002)
3. Holzmann, G.J.: The model checker SPIN. J. TSE 23(5), 279–295 (1997)
4. Guelfi, N., Mammar, A.: A formal semantics of timed activity diagrams and its
   PROMELA translation. In: APSEC 2005, pp. 283–290 (2005)
5. Piel, E., Atitallah, R.B., Marquet, P., et al.: Gaspard2: from MARTE to SystemC
   simulation. In: DATE 2008, pp. 23–28 (2008)
6. Merseguer, J., Bernardi, S.: Dependability analysis of DES based on MARTE and
   UML state machines models. J. DEDS 22(2), 163–178 (2012)
7. Alur, R., Dill, D.L.: A theory of timed automata. J. TCS 126(2), 183–235 (1994)
8. Suryadevara, J., Seceleanu, C., Mallet, F., Pettersson, P.: Verifying MARTE/CCSL
   mode behaviors using UPPAAL. In: Hierons, R.M., Merayo, M.G., Bravetti, M.
   (eds.) SEFM 2013. LNCS, vol. 8137, pp. 1–15. Springer, Heidelberg (2013)
9. Bengtsson, J., Larsen, K., Larsson, F., et al.: UPPAAL-a tool suite for automatic
   verification of real-time systems. J. Hybrid Systems III. 1066, 232–243 (1996)
10. Ravn, A.P., Srba, J., Vighio, S.: A formal analysis of the web services atomic
    transaction protocol with UPPAAL. In: Margaria, T., Steffen, B. (eds.) ISoLA
    2010, Part I. LNCS, vol. 6415, pp. 579–593. Springer, Heidelberg (2010)
11. Ravn, A.P., Srba, J., Vighio, S.: Modelling and verification of web services business
    activity protocol. In: Abdulla, P.A., Leino, K.R.M. (eds.) TACAS 2011. LNCS,
    vol. 6605, pp. 357–371. Springer, Heidelberg (2011)
12. Larsen, K.G., Pettersson, P., Wang, Y.: UPPAAL in a nutshell. J. STTT 1(1),
    134–152 (1997)
13. FMPAer, http://lcs.ios.ac.cn/~zxy/tools/fmpaer.htm
14. Papyrus, http://www.papyrusuml.org
15. Jouault, F., Allilaire, F., Bzivin, J., et al.: ATL: A model transformation tool. J.
    SCP 72(1), 31–39 (2008)
16. Xuandong, L., Meng, C., Yu, P., Jianhua, Z., Guoliang, Z.: Timing analysis of UML
    activity diagrams. In: Gogolla, M., Kobryn, C. (eds.) UML 2001. LNCS, vol. 2185,
    p. 62. Springer, Heidelberg (2001)

Extending MSVL with Function Calls*

Nan Zhang, Zhenhua Duan**, and Cong Tian

Institute of Computing Theory and Technology,
and ISN Laboratory Xidian University, Xi'an 710071, China
zhhduan@mail.xidian.edu.cn, nanzhang@xidian.edu.cn

Abstract. Modeling, Simulation and Verification Language (MSVL) is a useful formalism for specification and verification of concurrent systems. To make it more practical and easier to use, we extend MSVL with function calls in this paper. To do so, an approach for function calls similar as in imperative programming languages is presented. Further, the semantics of expressions is redefined and the semantics of new added function call statements is formalized. Moreover, an example is given to illustrate how to use function calls in practice with MSVL.

Keywords: Temporal Logic Programming, Projection, Function Call, Modeling, Simulation, Verification.

1 Introduction

Modeling, Simulation and Verification Language (MSVL) [1] is a useful formalism for specification and verification of concurrent and real time systems [2,4,6,7,11]. It contains common statements used in most of imperative programming languages (e.g. C, Java) such as assignment, sequential ($\varphi_1; \varphi_2$), branch (if b then φ_1 else φ_2) and iteration (while b do φ) statements but also parallel and concurrent statements such as conjunct (φ_1 and φ_2), parallel ($\varphi_1 \| \varphi_2$) and projection (($\varphi_1, \ldots, \varphi_m$) prj φ) statements. The projection construct enables us to model a system in two time scales: with the fine-grained time interval, $\varphi_1, \ldots, \varphi_m$ are sequentially executed whereas with the coarse-grained interval called projected interval consisting of the executing end points of each program φ_i, φ is paralleled executed to monitor or control all or some of φ_i. This construct is particularly useful for modeling and simulating scheduling and real time systems [3,9,11]. Further, a Cylinder Computation Model (CCM) is proposed and included into MSVL [10,11], which can be used to describe and reason about multi-core parallel programs. Moreover, asynchronous communication mechanism has also been implemented in MSVL [5] which can be employed to model and verify distributed systems. To make MSVL more practical and useful, multi-types such as integer, float, char, string, pointer and struct etc. [8] have been recently formalized and implemented. Therefore, multi-typed values, functions and predicates concerning the extended data domain can be defined. However, functions calls as a kind of useful building

---

* The research is supported by the National Program on Key Basic Research Project of China (973 Program) Grant No.2010CB328102, National Natural Science Foundation of China under Grant No. 61133001, 61202038, 61272117, 61272118, 61322202 and 91218301.
** Corresponding author.

S. Merz and J. Pang (Eds.): ICFEM 2014, LNCS 8829, pp. 446–458, 2014.
© Springer International Publishing Switzerland 2014

block have not been formalized and implemented in MSVL yet so far. So, we are motivated to formalize a scheme to realize function calls based on multi-types.

The contributions of the paper are twofold: (1) Function definitions are formalized. With our scheme, a programmer is allowed not only to define new functions themselves but also to directly employ C library functions. Function definitions can be classified into four categories in terms of arguments and return value: with arguments and return value, with arguments but no return value, without arguments but with return value, with no arguments or return value. (2) Two kinds of function calls, black-box calling (short for b-call or ext-call) and white-box calling (short for w-call), are formalized. If we concern only the return value of a function but do not care about the interval over which the function is executed, a function ext-call should be employed. Most of function ext-calls are used in expressions. On the other hand, if we concern both the return value and the executed interval of a function, a function w-call should be used.

The rest of the paper is organized as follows: PTL and MSVL are briefly reviewed in the next section. Then, functions calls scheme is introduced in section 3, including the formalization of function definitions and function calls. In section 4, an example is given to illustrate how to program and call functions in MSVL. Finally, conclusions are drawn in section 5.

2   Preliminaries

2.1   PTL

In this section, the syntax and semantics of the underlying logic, Projection Temporal Logic (PTL), are briefly introduced. For more detail, please refer to paper [1].

SYNTAX Let $\mathbb{P}$ be a countable set of propositions, and $\mathbb{V}$ a countable set of typed variables consisting of static and dynamic variables. It is assumed that the value of a static variable remains the same over an interval (defined later) whereas a dynamic variable can have different values at different states. $\mathbb{B}$ represents the boolean domain $\{tt, ff\}$, $\mathbb{D}$ denotes all data needed by us including integers, lists, sets etc. $\mathbb{Z}$ denotes all integers, $\mathbb{N}_0$ stands for non-negative integers and $\mathbb{N}$ denotes positive integers. Terms e and formulas ϕ are inductively defined as follows:

$$e ::= u \mid \bigcirc e \mid \ominus e \mid f(e_1, \ldots, e_n)$$
$$\phi ::= q \mid e_1 = e_2 \mid P(e_1, \ldots, e_n) \mid \neg\phi \mid \phi_1 \wedge \phi_2 \mid \exists x : \phi \mid \bigcirc \phi \mid (\phi_1, \ldots, \phi_m) \, \mathsf{prj} \, \phi$$

where u, $x \in \mathbb{V}$ and $q \in \mathbb{P}$. A formula (term) is called a state formula (term) if it contains no temporal operators, i.e. $\bigcirc$, $\ominus$, prj, otherwise it is a temporal formula (term).

SEMANTICS A state s over $\mathbb{V} \cup \mathbb{P}$ is defined to be a pair (I_v, I_p) of state interpretations I_v and I_p. I_v assigns each variable $u \in \mathbb{V}$ a value in $\mathbb{D}$ or nil (undefined) and the total domain is denoted by $\mathbb{D}' = \mathbb{D} \cup \{nil\}$, whereas I_p assigns each proposition $q \in \mathbb{P}$ a truth value in $\mathbb{B}$. $s[u]$ denotes the value of u at state s.

An interval σ is a non-empty sequence of states, which can be finite or infinite. The length, $|\sigma|$, of σ is ω if σ is infinite, and the number of states minus 1 if σ is finite. We extend the set $\mathbb{N}_0$ of non-negative integers to include ω, denoted by $\mathbb{N}_\omega = \mathbb{N}_0 \cup \{\omega\}$ and extend the comparison operators, $=, <, \leq$, to $\mathbb{N}_\omega$ by considering $\omega = \omega$, and for all $i \in \mathbb{N}_0$, $i < \omega$. Furthermore, we define $\preceq$ as $\leq -\{(\omega,\omega)\}$. For conciseness of presentation, $\langle s_0, \ldots, s_{|\sigma|} \rangle$ is denoted by σ, where $s_{|\sigma|}$ is undefined if σ is infinite. The concatenation of a finite σ with another interval (or empty string) σ' is denoted by $\sigma \cdot \sigma'$ (not sharing any states). Let $\sigma = \langle s_0, s_1, \ldots, s_{|\sigma|} \rangle$ be an interval and $r_1, \ldots, r_h$ be integers ($h \geq 1$) such that $0 \leq r_1 \leq r_2 \leq \ldots \leq r_h \preceq |\sigma|$. The projection of σ onto $r_1, \ldots, r_h$ is the interval (called projected interval) $\sigma \downarrow (r_1, \ldots, r_h) = \langle s_{t_1}, s_{t_2}, \ldots, s_{t_l} \rangle$ where $t_1, \ldots, t_l$ are obtained from $r_1, \ldots, r_h$ by deleting all duplicates. That is, $t_1, \ldots, t_l$ is the longest strictly increasing subsequence of $r_1, \ldots, r_h$. For instance, $\langle s_0, s_1, s_2, s_3, s_4 \rangle \downarrow (0, 0, 2, 2, 2, 3) = \langle s_0, s_2, s_3 \rangle$. We also need to generalize the notation of $\sigma \downarrow (r_1, \ldots, r_h)$ to allow r_i to be ω. For an interval $\sigma = \langle s_0, s_1, \ldots, s_{|\sigma|} \rangle$ and $0 \leq r_1 \leq r_2 \leq \ldots \leq r_h \leq |\sigma|$ ($r_i \in \mathbb{N}_\omega$), we define $\sigma \downarrow (r_1, \ldots, r_h, \omega) = \sigma \downarrow (r_1, \ldots, r_h)$. To evaluate the existential quantification, an equivalence relation is required and given below. We use I_v^k and I_p^k to denote the state interpretations at state s_k.

Definition 1 (x- equivalence) Two intervals, σ and σ', are x-equivalent, denoted by $\sigma' \overset{x}{=} \sigma$, if $|\sigma| = |\sigma'|$, $I_v^h[y] = I_v'^h[y]$ for all $y \in \mathbb{V} - \{x\}$, and $I_p^h[q] = I_p'^h[q]$ for all $q \in \mathbb{P}$ ($0 \leq h \preceq |\sigma|$).

An interpretation is a quadruple $\mathcal{I} = (\sigma, i, k, j)$, where σ is an interval, $i, k \in \mathbb{N}_0$, and $j \in \mathbb{N}_\omega$ such that $0 \leq i \leq k \preceq j \leq |\sigma|$. We use the notation (σ, i, k, j) to indicate that some formula ϕ or term e is interpreted over the subinterval $\langle s_i, \ldots, s_j \rangle$ of σ with the current state being s_k. For every term e, the evaluation of e relative to interpretation $\mathcal{I} = (\sigma, i, k, j)$, denoted by $\mathcal{I}[e]$, is defined by induction on terms as follows:

---

1. $\mathcal{I}[u] \quad = \begin{cases} s_k[u] = I_v^k[u] = I_v^i[u] & \text{if } u \text{ is a static variable.} \\ s_k[u] = I_v^k[u] & \text{if } u \text{ is a dynamic variable.} \end{cases}$

2. $\mathcal{I}[\bigcirc e] \quad = \begin{cases} (\sigma, i, k+1, j)[e] & \text{if } k < j \\ nil & \text{otherwise} \end{cases}$

3. $\mathcal{I}[\ominus e] \quad = \begin{cases} (\sigma, i, k-1, j)[e] & \text{if } i < k \\ nil & \text{otherwise} \end{cases}$

4. $\mathcal{I}[f(e_1, \ldots, e_n)] = \begin{cases} nil & \text{if } \mathcal{I}[e_h] = nil, \text{ for some } h \in \{1, \ldots, n\} \\ \mathcal{I}[f](\mathcal{I}[e_1], \ldots, \mathcal{I}[e_n]) & \text{otherwise} \end{cases}$

The meaning of formulas is given by the satisfaction relation, $\models$, which is inductively defined as follows:

---

1. $\mathcal{I} \models q$ iff $I_p^k[q] = tt$, for any given proposition q.

2. $\mathcal{I} \models P(e_1, \ldots, e_n)$ iff P is a primitive predicate other than $=$ and, for all h, $1 \leq h \leq n$, $\mathcal{I}[e_h] \neq nil$ and $P(\mathcal{I}[e_1], \ldots, \mathcal{I}[e_n]) = tt$.

3. $\mathcal{I} \models e_1 = e_2$ iff e_1 and e_2 are terms and $\mathcal{I}[e_1] = \mathcal{I}[e_2]$.

4. $\mathcal{I} \models \neg\phi$ iff $\mathcal{I} \not\models \phi$.
5. $\mathcal{I} \models \bigcirc\phi$ iff $k < j$ and $(\sigma, i, k+1, j) \models \phi$.
6. $\mathcal{I} \models \phi_1 \wedge \phi_2$ iff $\mathcal{I} \models \phi_1$ and $\mathcal{I} \models \phi_2$.
7. $\mathcal{I} \models \exists x : \phi$ iff there exists an interval σ' such that $\sigma'_{(i..j)} \overset{x}{=} \sigma_{(i..j)}$ and $(\sigma', i, k, j) \models \phi$.
8. $\mathcal{I} \models (\phi_1, \ldots, \phi_m)$ prj ϕ iff there exist integers $k = r_0 \leq \cdots \leq r_{m-1} \preceq r_m \leq j$ such that for all $1 \leq l \leq m$, $(\sigma, i, r_{l-1}, r_l) \models \phi_l$, and $(\sigma', 0, 0, |\sigma'|) \models \phi$ for one of the following σ' :
    (a) $r_m < j$ and $\sigma' = \sigma \downarrow (r_0, \ldots, r_m) \cdot \sigma_{(r_m+1..j)}$, or
    (b) $r_m = j$ and $\sigma' = \sigma \downarrow (r_0, \ldots, r_h)$ for some $0 \leq h \leq m$.

ABBREVIATION The abbreviations *true*, *false*, $\wedge$, $\rightarrow$ and $\leftrightarrow$ are defined as usual. In particular, $true \overset{def}{=} \phi \vee \neg\phi$ and $false \overset{def}{=} \phi \wedge \neg\phi$ for any formula ϕ. The derived formulas are given as follows, where $n \in \mathbb{N}_0$.

A1	$more \overset{def}{=} \bigcirc true$		A2	$\varepsilon \overset{def}{=} \neg\bigcirc true$	
A3	$\bigcirc^0\phi \overset{def}{=} \phi$		A4	$\bigcirc^{n+1}\phi \overset{def}{=} \bigcirc(\bigcirc^n\phi)$	
A5	$\phi_1; \phi_2 \overset{def}{=} (\phi_1, \phi_2)\,prj\,\varepsilon$		A6	$\Diamond\phi \overset{def}{=} true; \phi$	
A7	$\Box\phi \overset{def}{=} \neg\Diamond\neg\phi$		A8	$\odot\phi \overset{def}{=} \varepsilon \vee \bigcirc\phi$	
A9	$\phi^0 \overset{def}{=} \varepsilon$		A10	$\phi^{n+1} \overset{def}{=} \phi^n; \phi$	
A11	$len(n) \overset{def}{=} \bigcirc^n\varepsilon$		A12	$skip \overset{def}{=} len(1)$	
A13	$fin(p) \overset{def}{=} \Box(\varepsilon \rightarrow p)$		A14	$inf \overset{def}{=} \neg\Diamond\varepsilon$	
A15	$keep(p) \overset{def}{=} \Box(more \rightarrow p)$		A16	$halt(p) \overset{def}{=} \Box(\varepsilon \leftrightarrow p)$	

2.2 MSVL

Modeling, Simulation and Verification Language (MSVL) is an executable subset of PTL. The following is a snapshot of the simple kernel of MSVL. For more detail, please refer to paper [1]. With MSVL, expressions can be treated as terms and statements can be treated as formulas in PTL. The arithmetic and boolean expressions of MSVL can be inductively defined as follows:

$$e ::= n \mid x \mid \bigcirc x \mid \odot x \mid e_0 + e_1 \mid e_0 - e_1 \mid e_0 * e_1 \mid e_0 \% e_1$$
$$b ::= tt \mid f\!f \mid \neg b \mid b_0 \wedge b_1 \mid e_0 = e_1 \mid e_0 < e_1$$

where n is an integer and x is a static or dynamic variable. One may refer to the value of a variable at the previous state or the next state. The statements of MSVL can be inductively defined in the following table:

	Name	Symbol φ	PTL Definition $\mathcal{F}(\varphi)$
1	Termination	$empty$	ε
2	Assignment	$x := e$	$\bigcirc x = e \wedge \bigcirc p_x \wedge skip$
3	Positive Immediate Assignment	$x \mathrel{<}== e$	$x = e \wedge p_x$
4	State Frame	$lbf(x)$	$\neg af(x) \rightarrow \exists b : (\odot x = b \wedge x = b)$

5	Interval Frame	frame(x)	$\Box(more \rightarrow \bigcirc\mathcal{F}(\mathsf{lbf}(x)))$
6	Next	next φ	$\bigcirc\mathcal{F}(\varphi)$
7	Always	always φ	$\Box\mathcal{F}(\varphi)$
8	Conditional	if b then φ_0 else φ_1	$(b \rightarrow \mathcal{F}(\varphi_0)) \wedge (\neg b \rightarrow \mathcal{F}(\varphi_1))$
9	Existential Quantification	exist $x : \varphi$	$\exists x : \mathcal{F}(\varphi)$
10	Sequential	$\varphi_0 ; \varphi_1$	$\mathcal{F}(\varphi_0) ; \mathcal{F}(\varphi_1)$
11	Conjunction	φ_0 and φ_1	$\mathcal{F}(\varphi_0) \wedge \mathcal{F}(\varphi_1)$
12	While	while b do φ	$(b \wedge \mathcal{F}(\varphi))^* \wedge \Box(\varepsilon \rightarrow \neg b)$
13	Selection	φ_0 or φ_1	$\mathcal{F}(\varphi_0) \vee \mathcal{F}(\varphi_1)$
14	Parallel	$\varphi_0 \| \varphi_1$	$\mathcal{F}(\varphi_0) \wedge (\mathcal{F}(\varphi_1) ; tt) \vee (\mathcal{F}(\varphi_0) ; tt) \wedge \mathcal{F}(\varphi_1)$
15	Projection	$(\varphi_1, \ldots, \varphi_m)$ prj φ	$(\mathcal{F}(\varphi_1), \ldots, \mathcal{F}(\varphi_m))$ prj $\mathcal{F}(\varphi)$
16	Interval Length	len(n)	$\bigcirc^n \varepsilon$
17	Synchronous Communication	await(c)	$\mathcal{F}(\text{frame}(x_1, \ldots, x_n)) \wedge \Box(\varepsilon \leftrightarrow c)$

MSVL supports structured programming and covers some basic control flow statements such as sequential statement, conditional statement, while-loop statement and so
on. Further, MSVL also supports non-determinism and concurrent programming by including selection, conjunction and parallel statements. Moreover, a framing technique
is introduced to improve the efficiency of programs and synchronize communication
for parallel processes. In addition, MSVL has been extended in a variety of ways. For
instance, multi-types have been recently formalized and implemented [8]. Hence, typed
variables, typed functions and predicates over the extended data domain can be defined.

3   Introducing Function Calls into MSVL

We extend MSVL in this section by introducing and formalizing function definitions
and calls, including the syntax and semantics. Since we permit the appearance of function calls with return values in expressions, the form and interpretation of MSVL expressions also need to be reconsidered.

3.1   Data Types

Like C programming language, MSVL provides a variety of data types. The fundamental types are unsigned characters (char), unsigned integers (int) and floating point
numbers (float). In addition, there is a hierarchy of derived data types built with
strings (string), lists (list), pointers (pointer), arrays (array), structures (struct)
and unions (union). For more detail, please refer to paper [8].

3.2   Function Calls

There are two kinds of functions in MSVL: one is external functions, written in other
programming languages such as C and Java and the other is user-defined functions
written in MSVL.

General Principles. MSVL can only define functions and predicates. The so called functions in C are mixed cases of functions and predicates. Generally speaking, the following statements can be used to define state functions and predicates:

$$\textbf{define type } f(\text{type}_1 \ x_1, ..., \text{type}_n \ x_n) \overset{\text{def}}{=} e$$
$$\textbf{define } P(\text{type}_1 \ x_1, ..., \text{type}_n \ x_n) \overset{\text{def}}{=} \varphi$$

where $x_1, ..., x_n$ are typed state variables and e a typed expression while φ is a statement. Thus, f is defined as a typed n arity function while P is defined as an n arity predicate. A state function can be called by substituting arguments $e_1, ..., e_n$ for parameters $x_1, ..., x_n$ respectively within an expression while a predicate can be invocated in a similar way but as a statement. For example,

$$\textbf{define float } max(\text{float } x, \text{float } y) \overset{\text{def}}{=} \text{if } (x > y) \text{ then } x \text{ else } y$$

defines a state function max which can be used in an expression such as $9.5 + max(7.5, 8.5)$.

$$
\begin{aligned}
&\textbf{define } max(\text{int } a[\,], \text{int } lim, \text{int } x) \\
&\overset{\text{def}}{=} \text{frame}(temp, i) \text{ and } (\\
&\quad \text{int } temp := a[0]; \\
&\quad \text{int } i := 1; \\
&\quad \text{while } (i \leq lim - 1) \text{ do} \\
&\quad \{(\text{if } a[i] > temp \text{ then } temp := a[i]); i := i + 1\}; \\
&\quad x := temp; \\
&)
\end{aligned}
$$

The above defines a predicate max which chooses a maximum element from an array with length lim. To call it, we only need to replace all parameters by arguments and make a statement: $max(x[9, 8, 7, 1, 9, 2, 3, 6, 5], 9, y)$, which chooses the maximum from the array x and stores the result into the variable y.

(1) External function calls

If we permit an MSVL program to call an external functions written in C or Java such as C standard library functions, the situation turns to be complicated since we do not know the interval of the execution of an external function. Nevertheless if we do not care about the executed interval of an external function but concern only with its return value and output results, we could simplify the calling process. In fact, a standard definition of C functions is of the following form:

$$\textbf{return\_type } g(\textbf{in\_type}_1 \ x_1, ..., \textbf{in\_type}_n \ x_n, \textbf{out\_type}_1 \ y_1, ..., \textbf{out\_type}_m \ y_m)$$

where g is a function with $x_1, ..., x_n$ as its typed input parameters while $y_1, ..., y_m$ as its typed output parameters and return_type as the type of its return value. For example,

$$\text{int } getline(\text{int } lim, \text{char } s[\,])$$

is a C function which reads a character line into array $s[\,]$ with length limited by input parameter lim and returns the actual length of the string. In some circumstances, input or output parameters or return value or all of them can be omitted (denoted by void). In order to call this type of functions as a statement in an MSVL program, the C functions need to be slightly modified in C as shown below:

$$\texttt{void } g(\textbf{in\_type}_1\ x_1, ..., \textbf{in\_type}_n\ x_n, \textbf{out\_type}_1\ y_1, ..., \textbf{out\_type}_m\ y_m, \textbf{return\_type}\ RV[\,])$$

where we add an extra typed return parameter to the function. Note that the last "**return** val" statement in a C function now needs to be replaced by an assignment "$RV[0] = val$" statement in the function without changing other statements.

To call this kind of functions as a statement in an MSVL program without concerning the interval on which the function is executed, we make a new statement below:

$$\texttt{ext } g(\ e_1, ..., e_n,\ z_1, ..., z_m,\ R)$$

For example, *getline* function written in C can be re-written as follows:

$$\texttt{void } getline(\texttt{int } lim, \texttt{char } s[\,], \texttt{int } rv[\,])$$

This new function can be directly called in an MSVL program as a statement:

$$\texttt{ext } getline(10, x, l);$$

Of course, a C function without a return value can be directly called using the above form.

If an external function without output parameters but with a return value, since we only concern the return value of an external function, it can directly be called in an expression. For example, C function $\texttt{int } strlen(\texttt{char } s[\,])$, returning the length of a string s, can be employed in an expression in MSVL program:

$$\texttt{ext } strlen(\text{"hello world!"}) + \texttt{ext } strlen(\text{"Good morning!"}) \geq 10$$

(2) User-defined function calls

If an external function modifies memory units or program variables, it is required to redefine in MSVL and cannot be directly called from an MSVL program. For example, $\texttt{void} * memcpy(s, ct, n)$ is a standard C function which copies n characters from ct to s and returns s. When this function is used, a pointer pointing memory address could be returned. Therefore, it is not permitted to be called in an MSVL program. To use this kind of external functions, the only way is to redefine them in MSVL. User defined functions can be classified into four categories: (a) functions with arguments and return value; (b) functions with return value but without arguments; (c) functions with arguments but without return value; (d) functions with no arguments or return value. Generally, a user defined function is of the following form in MSVL:

$$\texttt{define } g(\textbf{in\_type}_1\ x_1, ..., \textbf{in\_type}_n\ x_n, \textbf{out\_type}_1\ y_1, ..., \textbf{out\_type}_m\ y_m, \textbf{return\_type}\ RV[\,])$$

where we add an extra typed return parameter to the function as output parameter. Note that the last "**return** val" statement in a C function now needs to be replaced by an assignment "$RV[0] := val$" statement in an MSVL function if we try to redefine the C function. In fact, it is really a predicate with two kinds of parameters: input and output parameters. To call this kind of functions in an MSVL program, it is simply to write the following statement with input arguments $e_1, ..., e_n$ and output arguments $z_1, ..., z_m$ and R:

$$g(e_1, ..., e_n, z_1, ..., z_m, R);$$

For example, *getline* function written in C can be re-written as follows:

$$getline(\text{int } lim, \text{char } s[\,], \text{int } rv[\,]) \stackrel{\text{def}}{=} Q$$

where Q is defined in the MSVL program below:

```
/* getline: get line into s, store length into rv */
define getline(int lim, char s[ ], int rv[ ])
{
        frame(s[ ], lim, c, RValue)
        and int RValue <== 0
        and char c <== ext getchar( )
        and (
            while (lim − 1 > 0 and c! = EOF and c! = '\n')
            {
                s[RValue] <== c  and
                RValue := RValue + 1  and
                lim := lim − 1  and
                c := ext  getchar( )
            };
            if (c = '\n') then s[RValue] <== c and RValue := RValue + 1;
            s[RValue] <== '\0';
            rv[0] := RValue
        )
}
```

Now *getline* function can now be called as follows:

$$\text{ext } getline(10, x, l);$$

3.3   Interpretation of Function Calls

There are two kinds of function calls in MSVL: (1) Black-box call or external call (short for b-calls or ext-calls): the interval over which the called function is executed is ignored. If a function neither changes any memory units nor uses any external variables whose scopes are not limited to the function, it can be called using black-box manner by the calling function. Such kind of function calls often appears in expressions. In other words, all the function calls appearing in expressions are external calls. (2) White-box call: the interval over which the called function is executed is inserted and concatenated with the main interval over which the calling function is executed. If a function uses some external variables, it should be called using white-box manner by the calling function.

(1) Interpretation of function calls in expressions

With expressions, function calls with black-box manner are only allowed. Since more data types have been included into MSVL, expressions should also be extended to cover more types. Thus expressions are inductively redefined as follows:

- Individual typed constants are basic expressions: a, b, c, ... $\in \mathbb{D}$ possibly with subscripts.
- Individual typed variables (static or dynamic) are basic expressions: u, v, x, y, z, ... $\in \mathbb{V}$ possibly with subscripts.
- Temporal operators: if e is an expression, then $\bigcirc e$ and $\ominus e$ are expressions.
- Non-temporal operators: if op is an operator of arity n $(n > 0)$ in MSVL and $e_1, \ldots, e_n$ are expressions of types compatible with types of parameters of op, then $\mathrm{op}(e_1, \ldots, e_n)$ is an expression. The operators allowed in MSVL are given in the following list.

Multiplicative operators:	$*, /, \%$
Unary additive operators:	$+, -$
Binary additive operators:	$+, -$
Relational operators:	$=, !=, <, <=, >, >=$
Bitwise operators:	$\&, |, \hat{\ }, <<, >>$
Logical operators:	$\neg, \wedge, \vee$

- if h is a user defined state function of arity n $(n > 0)$ and $e_1, \ldots, e_n$ are expressions of types compatible with types of parameters of h, then $h(e_1, \ldots, e_n)$ is an expression;
- if f is a user defined function of arity n $(n > 0)$ and $e_1, \ldots, e_n$ are expressions of types compatible with types of parameters of f, then ext $f(e_1, \ldots, e_n)$ is an expression;
- if g is an external function of arity n $(n > 0)$ and $e_1, \ldots, e_n$ are expressions of types compatible with types of parameters of g, then ext $g(e_1, \ldots, e_n)$ is an expression;

For each expression e, the evaluation of e related to interpretation $\mathcal{I} = (\sigma, i, k, j)$, denoted by $\mathcal{I}[e]$, is redefined based on the semantics of PTL.

---

1. $\mathcal{I}[a] = a$ for each typed constant $a \in \mathbb{D}$.

2. $\mathcal{I}[u] = \begin{cases} s_k[u] = I_v^k[u] = I_v^i[u] & \text{if } u \text{ is a static variable.} \\ s_k[u] = I_v^k[u] & \text{if } u \text{ is a dynamic variable.} \end{cases}$

3. $\mathcal{I}[\bigcirc e] = \begin{cases} (\sigma, i, k+1, j)[e] & \text{if } k < j. \\ nil & \text{otherwise.} \end{cases}$

4. $\mathcal{I}[\ominus e] = \begin{cases} (\sigma, i, k-1, j)[e] & \text{if } i < k. \\ nil & \text{otherwise.} \end{cases}$

5. $\mathcal{I}[\mathsf{op}(e_1, \ldots, e_n)] = \begin{cases} nil & \text{if } \mathcal{I}[e_i] = nil \text{ for some } i \in \{1, \ldots, n\}. \\ \mathcal{I}[\mathsf{op}](\mathcal{I}[e_1], \ldots, \mathcal{I}[e_n]) & \text{otherwise.} \end{cases}$

op is an operator.

6. $\mathcal{I}[h(e_1, \ldots, e_n)] = \begin{cases} nil & \text{if } \mathcal{I}[e_i] = nil \text{ for some } i \in \{1, \ldots, n\}. \\ \mathcal{I}[h](\mathcal{I}[e_1], \ldots, \mathcal{I}[e_n]) & \text{otherwise.} \end{cases}$

h is a state function.

7. $\mathcal{I}[\mathsf{ext}\, f(e_1, \ldots, e_n)] = \begin{cases} nil & \text{if } \mathcal{I}[e_i] = nil \text{ for some } i \in \{1, \ldots, n\}. \\ \mathcal{I}[f](\mathcal{I}[e_1], \ldots, \mathcal{I}[e_n]) & \text{otherwise.} \end{cases}$

f is a non-state function.

8. $\mathcal{I}[\mathsf{ext}\, g(e_1, \ldots, e_n)] = \begin{cases} nil & \text{if } \mathcal{I}[e_i] = nil \text{ for some } i \in \{1, \ldots, n\}. \\ \mathcal{I}[g](\mathcal{I}[e_1], \ldots, \mathcal{I}[e_n]) & \text{otherwise.} \end{cases}$

g is an external function.

---

(2) Interpretation of function calls in statements

For the new statement $\mathsf{ext}\, g(e_1, ..., e_n, z_1, ..., z_m, R)$, its interpretation is given as follows: Let $\sigma = < s_0, ..., s_k, ..., s_{|\sigma|} >$ be an interval, and $\mathcal{I} = (\sigma, i, k, j)$ be the interpretation, $Q \overset{\text{def}}{=} (g(e_1, ..., e_n, z_1, ..., z_m, R) \wedge \exists b_1 \cdots \exists b_n \exists r : \bigwedge_{i=1}^{m} fin(z_i = b_i) \wedge fin(R = r))$ prj $(z_i := b_i \wedge R := r)$. Thus,

---

$\mathcal{I} \models \mathsf{ext}\, g(e_1, ..., e_n, z_1, ..., z_m, R)$ iff $j = k + 1$ and there exists an interval $\sigma'' = < s_k, s_1'', ..., s_{k+1} >$ such that $\sigma' = \sigma_{(0..k)} \cdot \sigma''$ and $(\sigma', i, k, |\sigma'|) \models Q$.

The model of Q is illustrated in Fig.1.

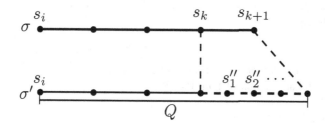

Fig. 1. Interpretation of external function calls

4   Example

In this section, we write a MSVL program to print each line of its input that contains a particular "pattern" of characters. For example, searching for the pattern of letters "ould" in the set of lines

> Ah Love! could you and I with Fate conspire
> To grasp this sorry Scheme of Things entire,
> Would not we shatter it to bits – and then
> Re-mould it nearer to the Heart's Desire!

will produce the output

> Ah Love! could you and I with Fate conspire
> Would not we shatter it to bits – and then
> Re-mould it nearer to the Heart's Desire!

The MSVL program calls two functions: *getline* and *strindex*, which are defined in C before the main program. The *getline* function fetches the next line of input, stores it into s and stores the length of the line into RV. The *strindex* function records the position or index in the string s where the string t begins, or -1 if s doesn't contain t, and stores the result into RV.

C Program
___

```
/* getline: get line into s, store length into RV*/
void getline(int lim, char s[ ], int RV[ ])
{
      int c, i;
      i=0;
      while(− −lim>0 && (c=getchar( ))!=EOF && c!=’\n’)
             s[i++]=c;
      if(c==’\n’)
             s[i++]=c;
      s[i]=’\0’;
      RV[0]=i;

}

/* strindex: store index of t in s into RV, -1 if none */
void strindex(char s[ ], char t[ ], int RV[ ])
{
      int i, j, k, r=0;
      for (i=0; s[i]!=’\0’&& r=0;i++) {
             for (j=i, k=0; t[k]!=’\0’ && s[j]==t[k]; j++, k++)
                    ;
```

```
        if (k>0 && t[k]=='\0')
            { r=1; RV[0]=i};
    }
    RV=-1;
}
```

MSVL Program

```
/* main program: find all lines matching pattern */
```
frame($MAX, pattern[\,], line[MAX], l[\,], in[\,], found, length, index$)
and int $MAX <== 1000$ and char $pattern[\,] <==$ "ould"
and int $found <== 0$ and int $length$ and int $index$
and (
  ext $getline(MAX, line, l)$;
  $length := l[0]$;
  while ($length > 0$)
   {
   ext $strindex(line, pattern, in)$;
   $index := in[0]$;
   if ($index >= 0$) then ($printf("\%s", line); found := found + 1$);
   ext $getline(MAX, line, l)$;
   $length := l[0]$;
   }
)

---

5   Conclusion

In this paper, MSVL is extended by means of formalizing function definitions and function calls. Functions with return value and no external variables are used to extend expressions. The function calls appear in expressions are called black-box (or external) calls. Functions with external variables can be called with the white-box manner as individual statement. With black-box calling, the intermediate execution detail of functions is ignored and only the return value is concerned. In white-box calling, the interval over which the function is interpreted makes up a part of the interval over which the whole program is interpreted. The function calls approach presented in this paper has been implemented in the interpreter of MSVL. In the future, we will apply MSVL to model, simulate and verify more practical applications.

References

1. Duan, Z.: Temporal logic and temporal logic programming. Science Press, Beijing (2005)
2. Han, M., Duan, Z., Wang, X.: Time constraints with temporal logic programming. In: Aoki, T., Taguchi, K. (eds.) ICFEM 2012. LNCS, vol. 7635, pp. 266–282. Springer, Heidelberg (2012)
3. Liu, C., Layland, J.: Scheduling algorithm for multiprogramming in a hard real-time environment. Journal of the ACM 20(1), 46–61 (1973)
4. Manna, Z., Pnueli, A.: The temporal logic of reactive and concurrent system. Springer, New York (1992)
5. Mo, D., Wang, X., Duan, Z.: Asynchronous communication in MSVL. In: Qin, S., Qiu, Z. (eds.) ICFEM 2011. LNCS, vol. 6991, pp. 82–97. Springer, Heidelberg (2011)
6. Pnueli, A.: The temporal logic of programs. In: Proceedings of the 18th Annual Symposium on the Foundations of Computer Science, pp. 46–57. IEEE Computer Society, Providence (1977)
7. Queille, J., Sifakis, J.: Specification and verification of concurrent systems in cesar. In: Dezani-Ciancaglini, M., Montanari, U. (eds.) Proceedings of the 5th Colloquium on International Symposium in Programming. LNCS, vol. 137, pp. 337–351. Springer, Springer (1982)
8. Wang, X., Duan, Z., Zhao, L.: Formalizing and implementing types in msvl, pp. 62–75 (2013)
9. Zhan, N.: An intuitive formal proof for deadline driven scheduler. Journal of Computer Science and Technology 16(2), 146–158 (2001)
10. Zhang, N., Duan, Z., Tian, C.: A cylinder computation model for many-core parallel computing. Theoretical Computer Science 497, 68–83 (2013)
11. Zhang, N., Duan, Z., Tian, C., Du, D.: A formal proof of the deadline driven scheduler in pptl axiomatic system. Theoretical Computer Science (2014)

Author Index